Drawing Nature

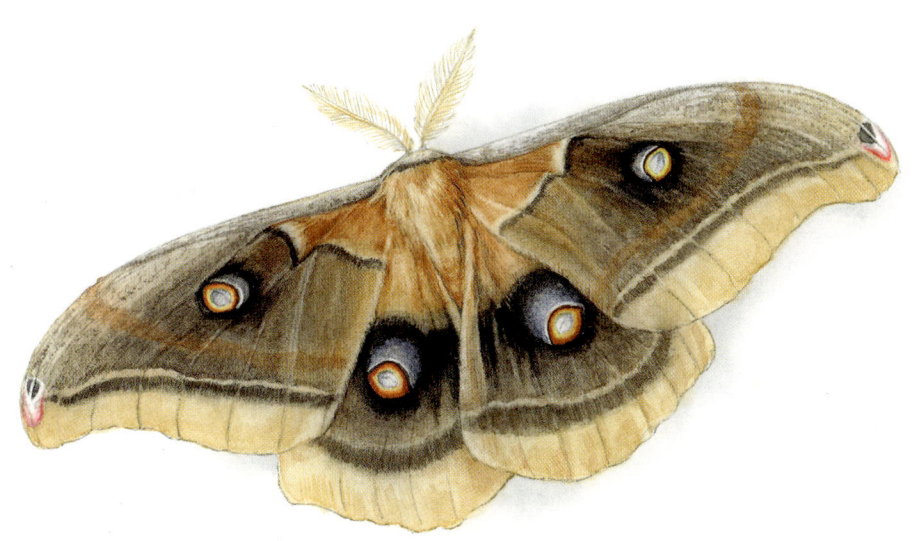

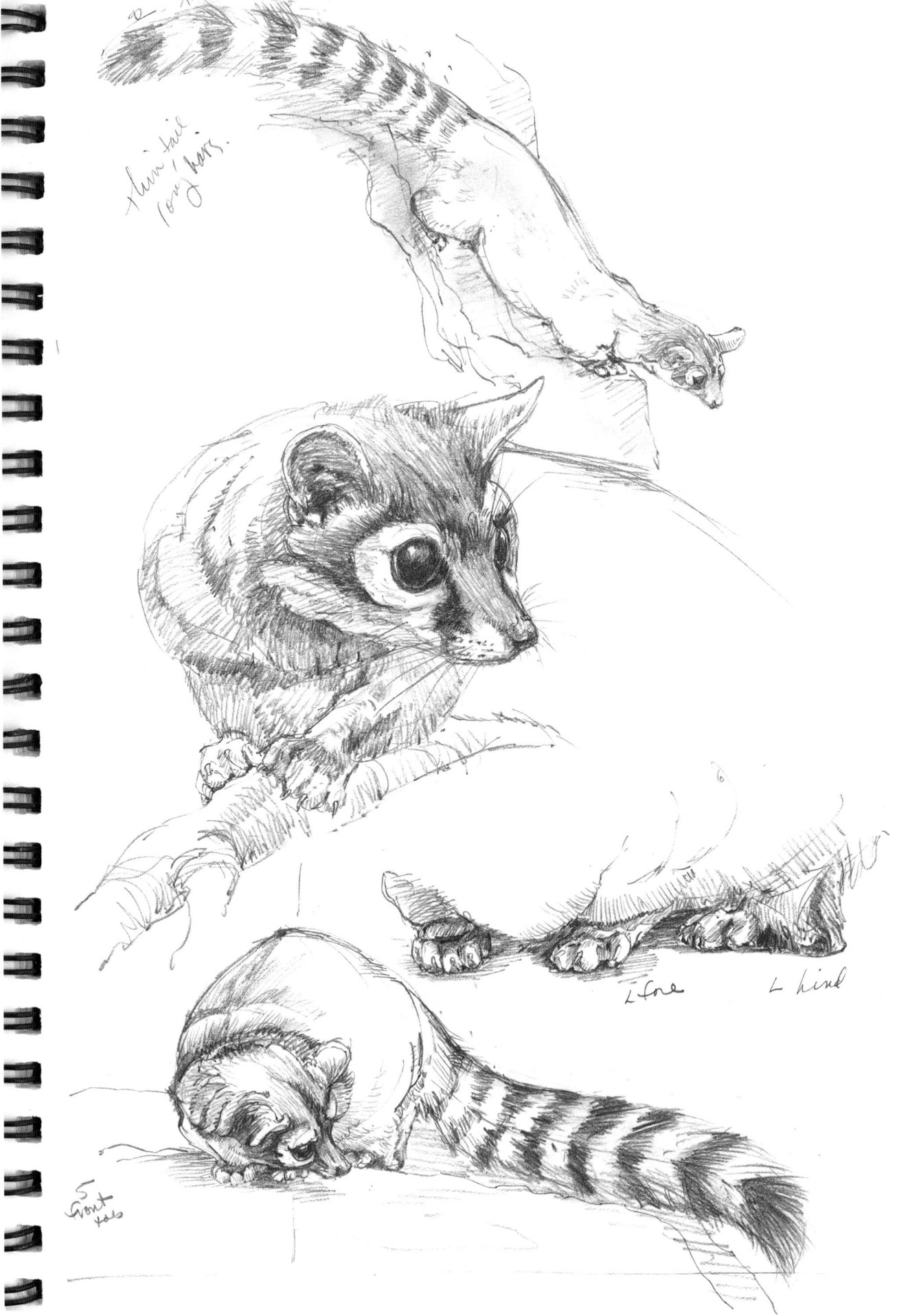

thin tail
long hairs.

L fore   L hind

S
Grout
hairs

Drawing Nature

The Creative Process of an Artist, Illustrator, and Naturalist

Linda Miller Feltner

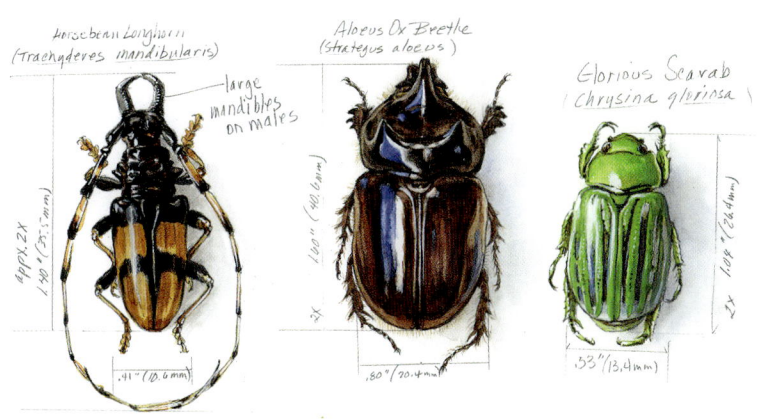

Princeton University Press
Princeton and Oxford

Published by Princeton University Press
41 William Street, Princeton, New Jersey 08540
99 Banbury Road, Oxford OX2 6JX

press.princeton.edu

ISBN 9780691255385
ISBN (e-book) 9780691255453

Library of Congress Control Number: 2024931231

British Library Cataloging-in-Publication Data is available

Editorial: Robert Kirk and Megan Mendonça
Production Editorial: Karen Carter
Text Design: Linda Miller Feltner
Typesetter: D & N Publishing, Wiltshire, UK
Jacket/Cover Design: Linda Miller Feltner and Wanda España
Production: Steven Sears
Publicity: Caitlyn Robson and Matthew Taylor
Copyeditor: Lachlan Brooks

This book has been composed in Acumin (main text), Konditorei (headings), and Lmfeltner Hand V6 (author's custom hand-written font for captions and labels)

Printed in Italy

10 9 8 7 6 5 4 3 2 1

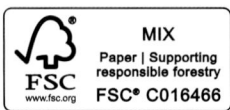

MIX
Paper | Supporting responsible forestry
FSC® C016466

To my husband, Trevor Ben, the Blue Jay. The Legend.

Thank you for being my witty and perspicacious companion on many adventures and for your steadfast dedication to nature.

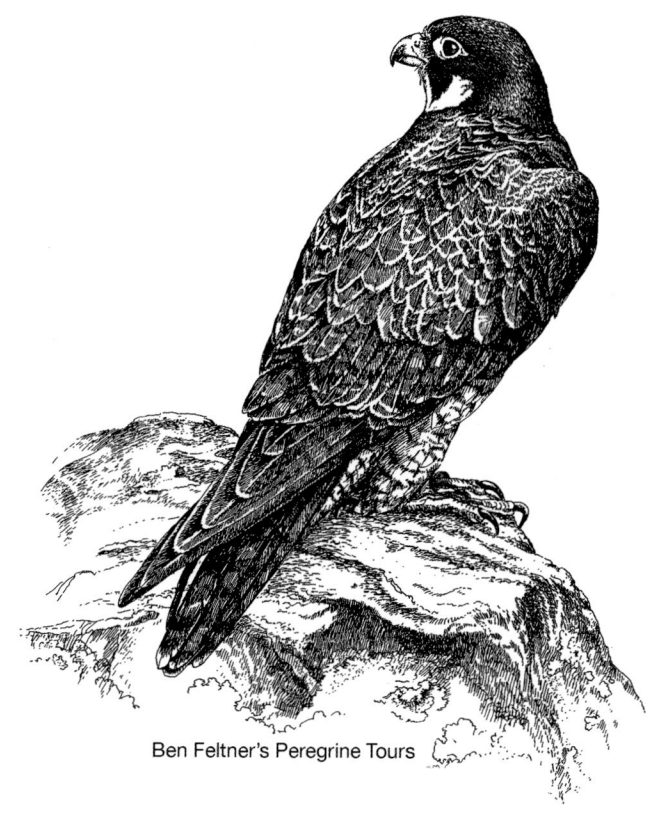

Ben Feltner's Peregrine Tours

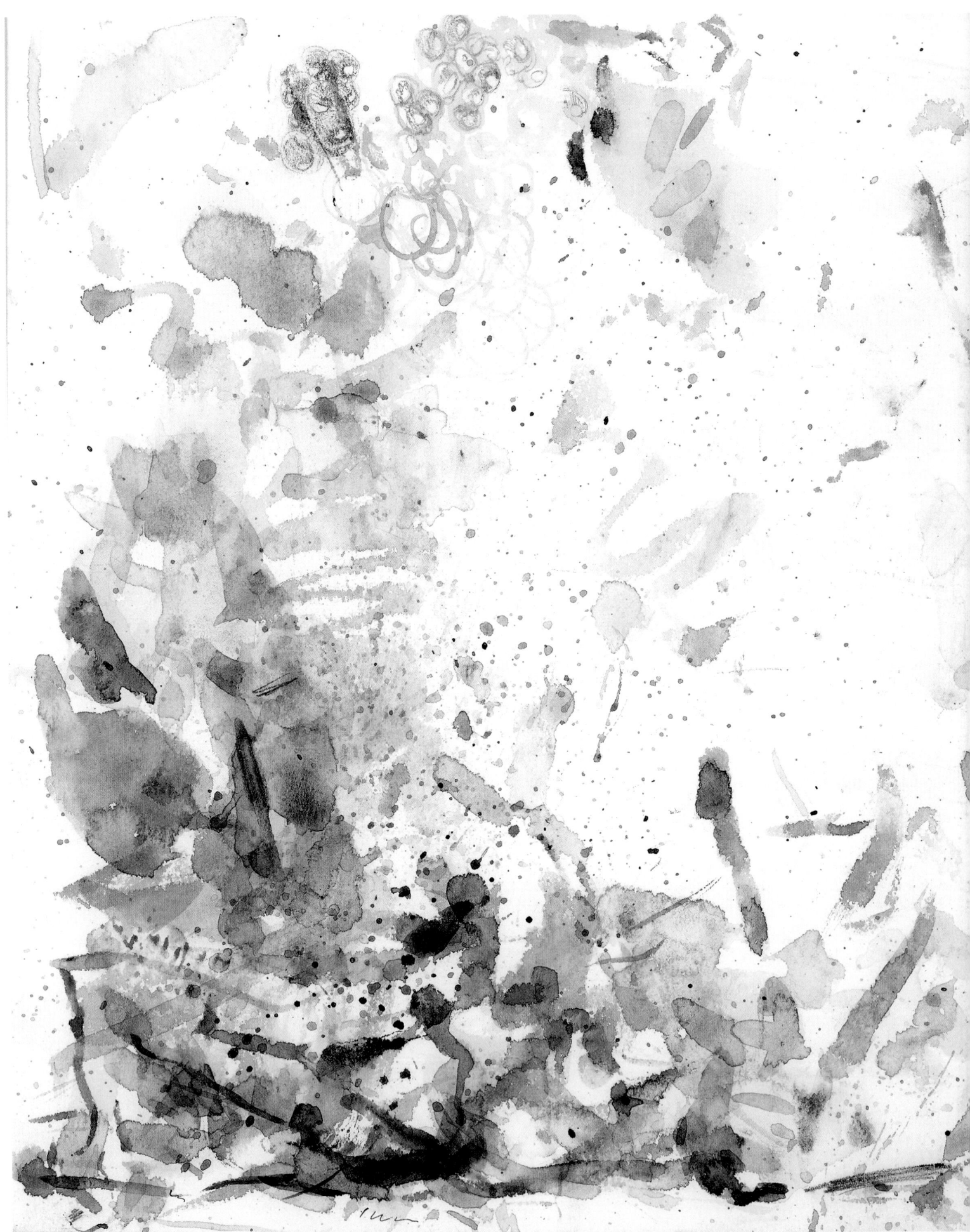

Contents

Acknowledgments

First, I want to thank my husband, Trevor Ben Feltner. From our earliest birding adventures, you could not have imagined how I absorbed, sponge-like, your unaffected remarks about flowers, plants, bugs, snakes, and assorted critters. The scope of your knowledge enabled me and countless others to discover the connections within and complexity of nature.

I am grateful to Robert Kirk and Megan Mendonça of Princeton University Press for your steadfast enthusiasm for this combination of art and science. You have bolstered my efforts from the beginning. I'm also grateful to the production editor, Karen Carter, the copyeditor, Lachlan Brooks, and the graphic designer, David Price-Goodfellow, for their superb attention to detail.

I want to express my unending gratitude equally to Carolyn Z. Shelton and Wendy C. Walker for graciously giving their time to review the drafts and offer critiques and suggestions from the beginning.

I am thankful for the inspiration and cherished friendship of Jo Ann Woodley, a talented botanical artist and birder, with whom I have shared many fantastic times. And to her husband, Joseph Woodley, who has shared our birding adventures with quick wit, expertise, and laughter. I would not have been as aware of Huachuca Mountain's ecology without the expertise and passion of Virginia C. Bealer, who shares the same fascination for all things, big or small, that we encounter on our Monday Morning Moseys. I am deeply grateful.

This book would not have been possible without the kindness, strength, and encouragement of Joan H. Lee, Nancy R. Halliday, Patricia L. Savage, Lynette R. Cook, Ikumi Kayama, Karen Johnson, Marlene Donnelly, Gale Sherman, Susan Shirley, Pamela Blotner, and Linda Tabor. You've been with me throughout, providing comfort, advice, a great deal of humor, and naturally, chocolate.

I am very grateful to those who provided me with encouragement, advice, and technical expertise for the content of my work. A special thank you goes to Dennis R. Paulson, a remarkable scientist and communicator. He is a good friend of many years who unreservedly offered museum specimens or photographs from his vast collection when I needed a reference for almost anything. Additionally, I extend my gratitude to Steven W. Lingafelter, Norman E. Woodley, Charles W. Melton, William R. Radke, Andy L. Fisher, Britt Griswold, William B. Westwood, and William Hamilton, who graciously shared their expertise, collection specimens, or inspirational insights. Their support for my work has enriched my efforts for authenticity and accuracy, and I sincerely appreciate it.

I hold great respect for the Guild of Natural Science Illustrators, a group dedicated to creating art that supports science. Here, I found like-minded colleagues with prodigious skills and scientific knowledge to accurately represent all things seen and unseen on Earth and beyond.

I also want to thank the Arizona-Sonora Desert Museum Art Institute and Priscilla Baldwin for hiring me those many years ago and introducing me to the educational partners, staff, and amazing students and colleagues. Your support has been invaluable.

Finally, I wish to acknowledge and thank the countless colleagues, students, and friends who have continuously encouraged me to create this book and kept me curious. There will never be enough space to thank them all.

Introduction

I invite the viewer to look through my artist's eyes and observe how I create my art, from spark to finish. This book is a personal journey that delights in revealing the developing process. The many iterations of a work demonstrate how I build an image. The book celebrates curiosity and illustrates by example how sketching, painting, and the importance of accuracy are crucial from my perspective.

Like a trail through the forest, the spark of curiosity can take me down a path with many side trails to entice my interest in other subjects. All diversions eventually merge back together to form the single pathway that becomes the story I depict. There is no straight route to the finished painting. I may get distracted by a bug or plant, but it might be the key to revealing an exciting story.

As an artist, illustrator, educator, and naturalist, a combination of skills enhances my career path, which has been varied and immensely fulfilling. I am a curious wanderer in nature as well as a keen birder. My fine art background blends with my love of nature to make me a scientific illustrator. It is the very best of both worlds, and I enjoy it immensely.

This book should be inspiring and thought-provoking for both beginning and advanced artists. It encourages those who have never laid a pencil to paper to draw or write. It reassures hesitant sketchers that they do not have to create perfect drawings the first time without erasing them. Seasoned artists are interested in methods of problem-solving for challenging subjects. I work to solve those issues, along with planning and composition, long before painting begins.

I applaud the many guides on how to draw and paint and highly recommend them. The popularity of nature journaling is growing, encouraging enthusiasm for nature and investigation, and engaging people who have never thought about being creative through art or writing. This trend focuses on the same curiosity and observational skills I encourage in my readers. The published work of renowned artists enchants me with inspirational sketches and spontaneous color studies. Whether their art is similar to what I do or entirely different, other artists provide immense inspiration.

Bring your curiosity, wander with a chance to pause, engage all the senses, and let the restorative power of nature fill your imagination.

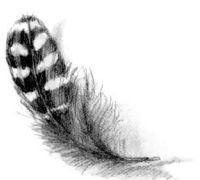

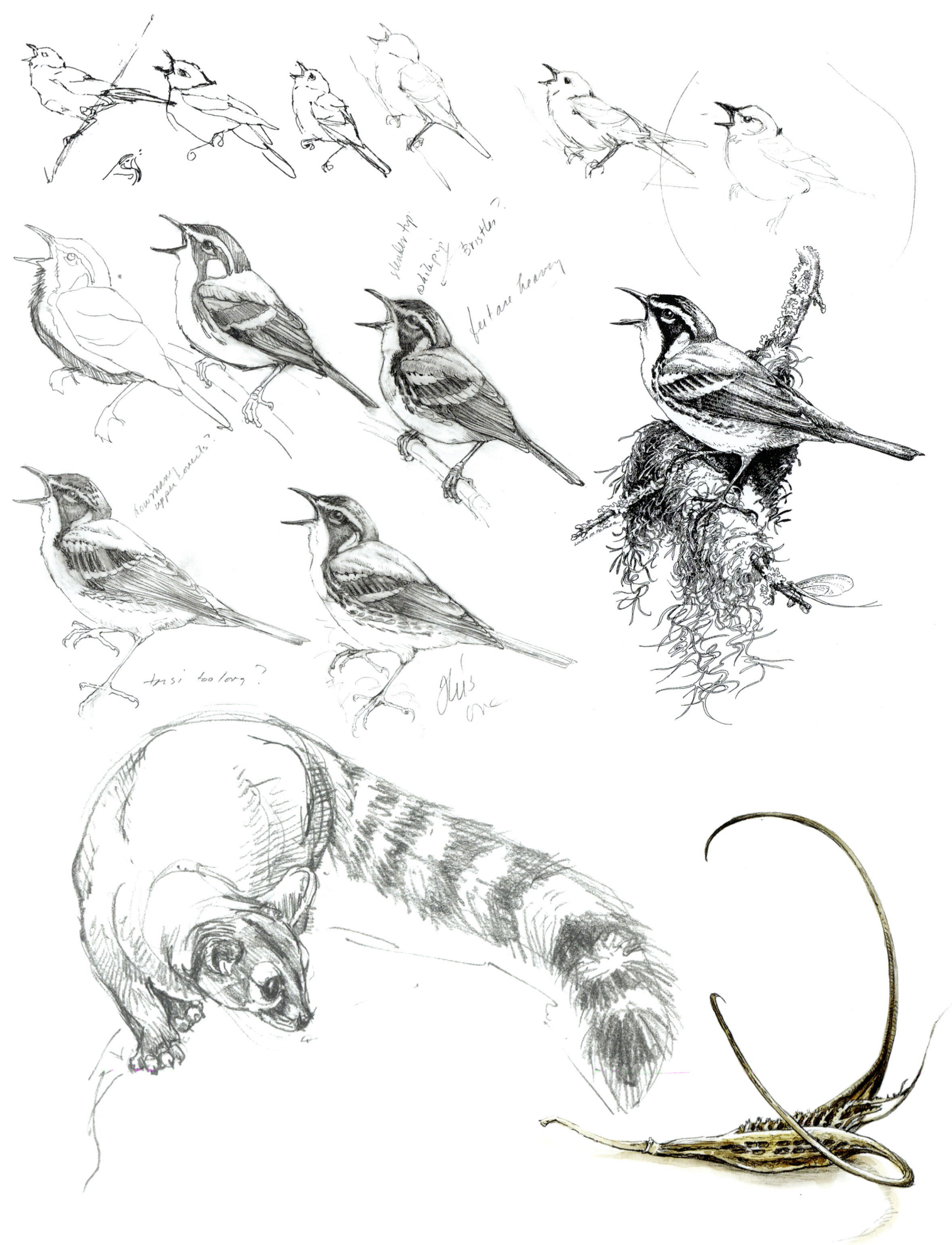

shorter?
whispy bristles?

feel are heavy

how many upper coverts?

tarsi too long?

this one

CHAPTER 1

A Spark of Curiosity

It all starts with a spark of curiosity, something eye-catching or fascinating.

Open my sketchbooks and you will find scribbles, gestures, and detailed drawings. They record my briefest glances as well as detailed observations. I experiment freely with loose gestures, poses, and concepts. Some may turn into finished paintings and others may not. As records of my observations, they are invaluable to my process.

Whether on a walk, trail, or city street, observing leads to questions: What is that critter? Where did that object come from? How weird is that? I enjoy solving the mysteries and finding the connections as I read my notations, relive discoveries, and research further.

This book introduces my artistic process from field notebooks to final art. It includes artwork for zoos, parks, galleries, and many personal favorites. Examples come from my early love of nature, developed in Texas, intensified in Washington, and expanded in Arizona. The chapters illustrate the progression from sketches and gestures to firm drawings and polished final art.

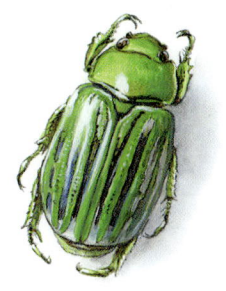

Welcome to my
celebration of curiosity!

First Impressions

There are times when a quick look is all I get. Observing first and then drawing is a great way to train the memory to retain details. Gesture drawing can help the process.

My first drawing classes introduced gesture drawing as a valuable tool for drawing moving figures. I find it natural to begin with deliberate strokes to express the form's line. Lines turn into a gesture, and an image builds. Someone once taught me (in the Pleistocene of my art education) that the worst scribbling mark is better than not doing it at all. That has remained a fundamental lesson for my artistic journey. Sometimes we do not need to achieve perfection and should draw the moment.

Show no fear! Each sketch does not have to be precious. However, the experience of drawing *is*. The process of eye-to-brain-to-hand coordination grows with greater accuracy when sketching. Creative activities such as drawing, painting, and sculpture engage the brain. They enable a stronger focus and enhance the memory.

How often are we working on one thing, and new insights occur?

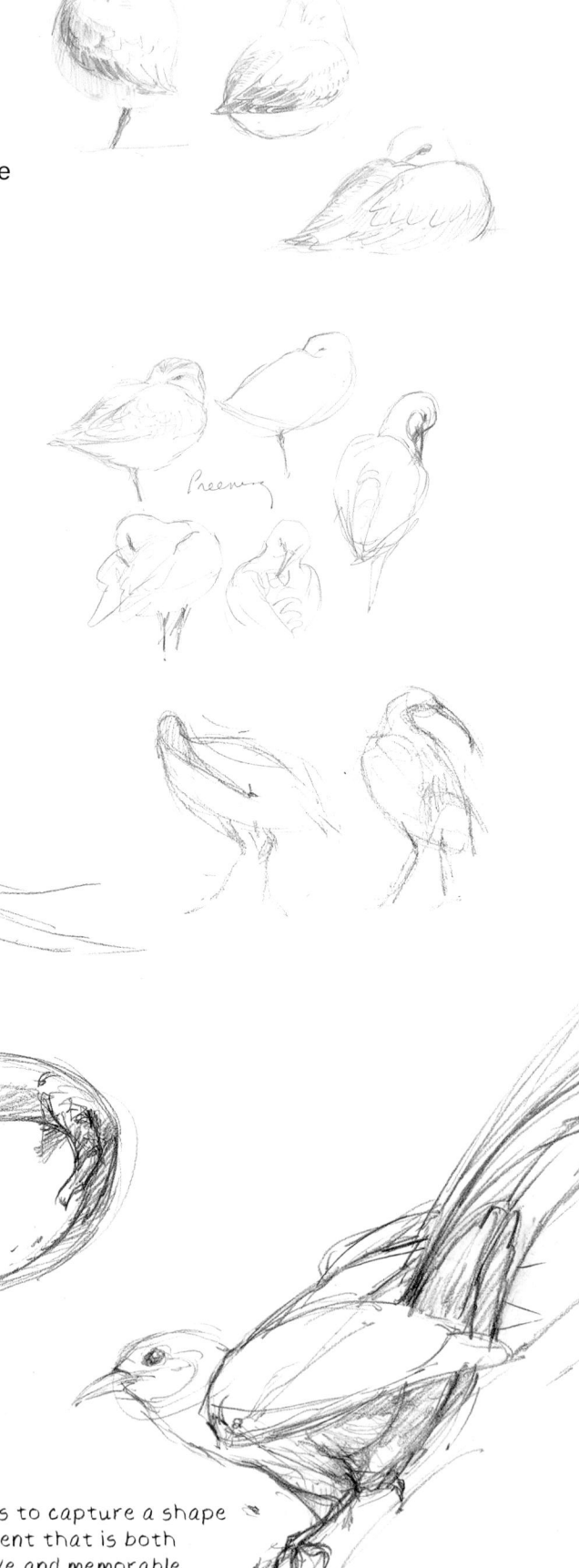

The goal is to capture a shape or movement that is both descriptive and memorable.

4

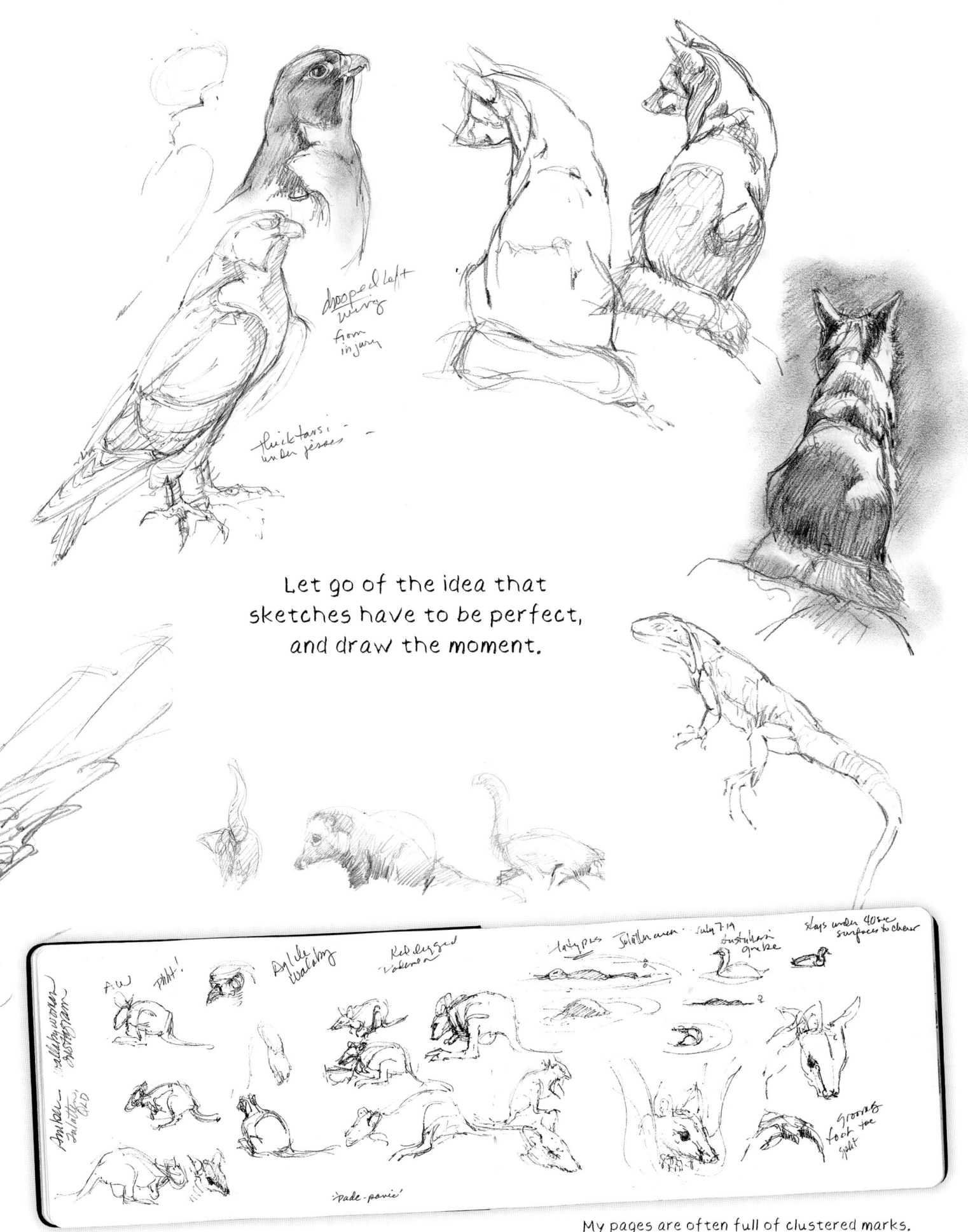

Let go of the idea that
sketches have to be perfect,
and draw the moment.

My pages are often full of clustered marks.

5

First Impressions: Making the Mark

The terms sketching and drawing are often interchangeable. Sketching may suggest a quick, dynamic image, whereas a drawing implies either a fresh, rapid mark or a deliberate execution of a subject. My sketchbooks contain the entire range from quick scribbles to precise, measured drawings. I am not bothered if they are unfinished ink outlines, or smeared thumbnails. I may only have ten minutes in one spot or hours of pleasant contemplation.

Make the most of the time available. Sketch, then build with value studies and thumbnail sketches. It does not matter whether drawings are in a sketchbook, notebook, nature journal, hand-crafted book, on a brown paper bag, or chalk on a sidewalk. I encourage any creative experience.

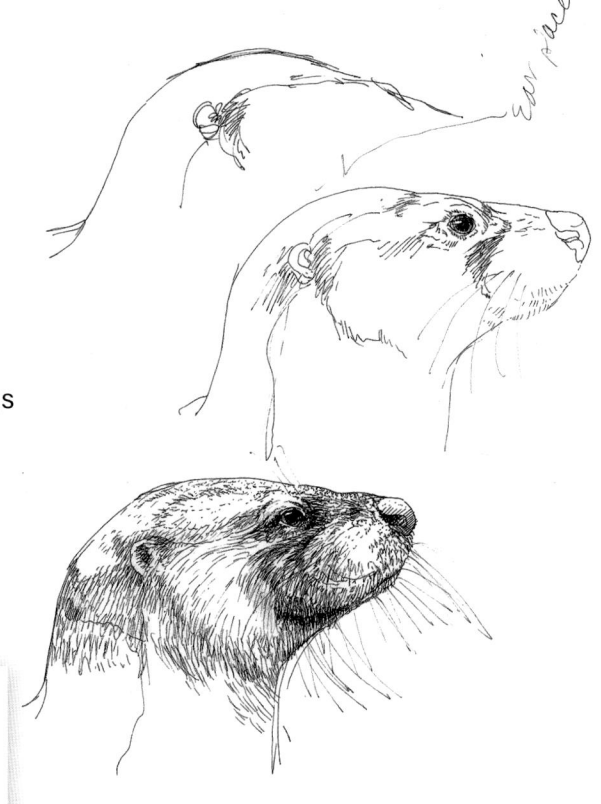

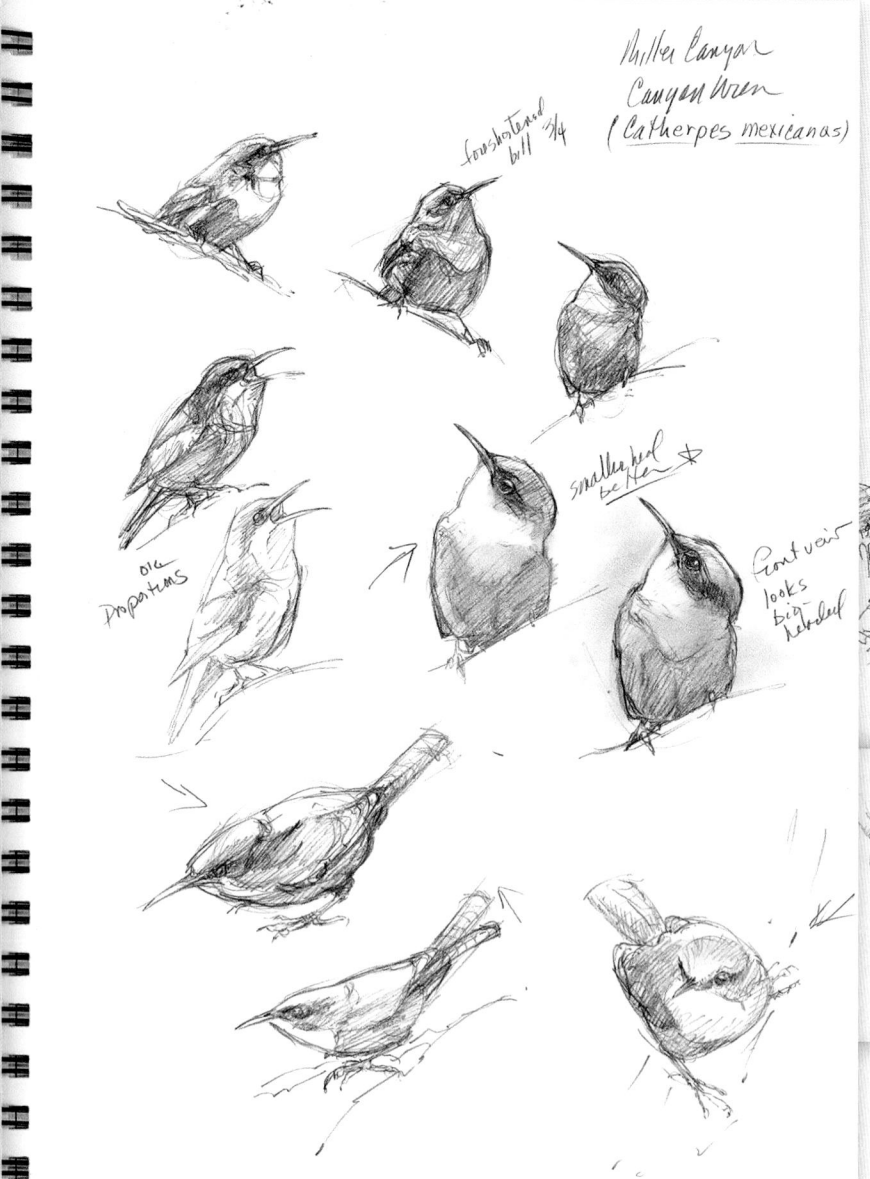

The crucial element is to make the mark.

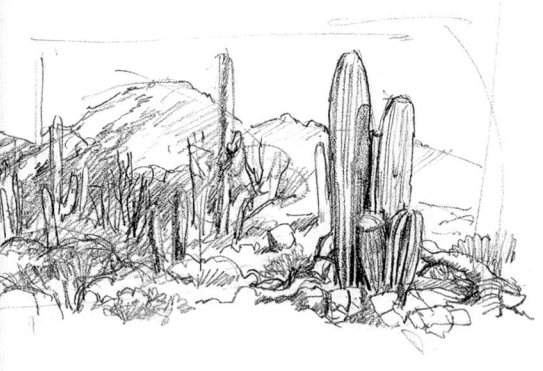

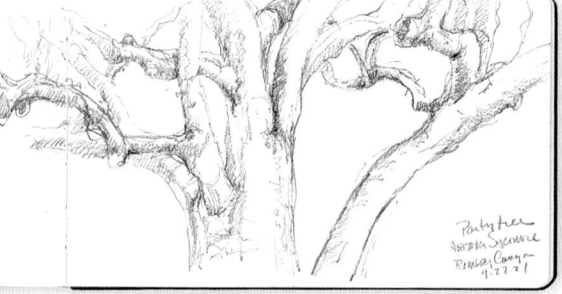

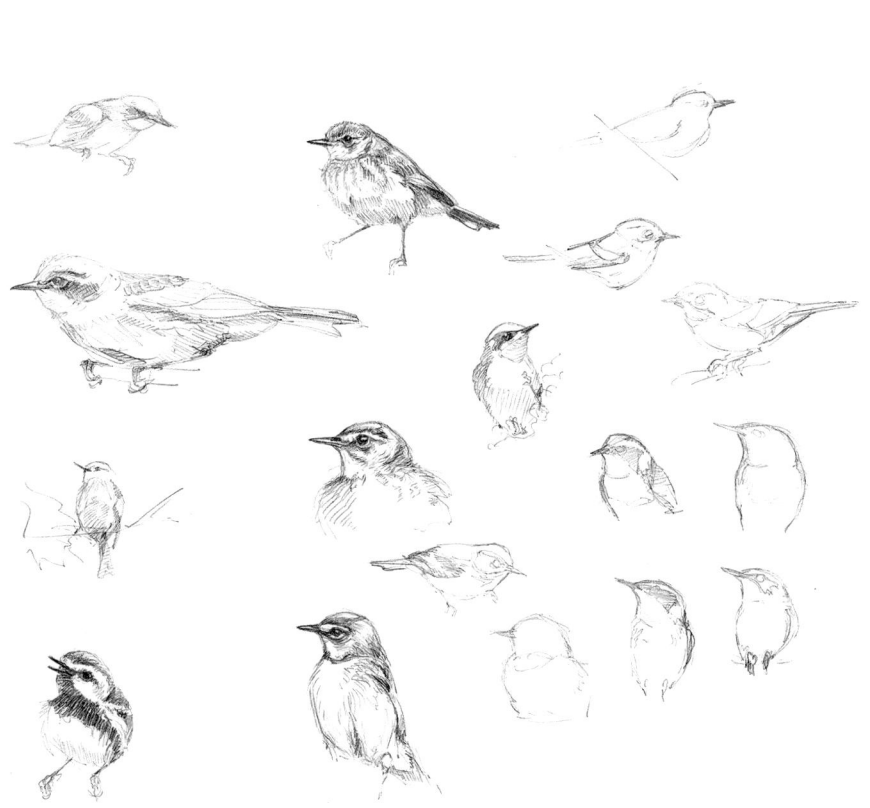

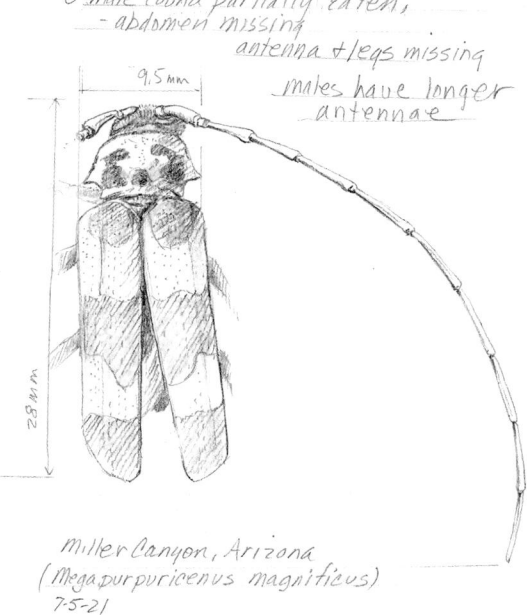

♂ male found partially eaten,
– abdomen missing
antenna + legs missing
males have longer
antennae

9.5mm

2.9mm

Miller Canyon, Arizona
(Megapurpuricenus magnificus)
7-5-21

Detailed drawings, observed and measured
in the studio, are not hurried but drawn for
the record of information seen at that time.
The date and place of finding your object are
crucial to a measured drawing. Dates provide
insight into migration patterns and depict a
molt cycle during the year or when a plant
starts blooming.

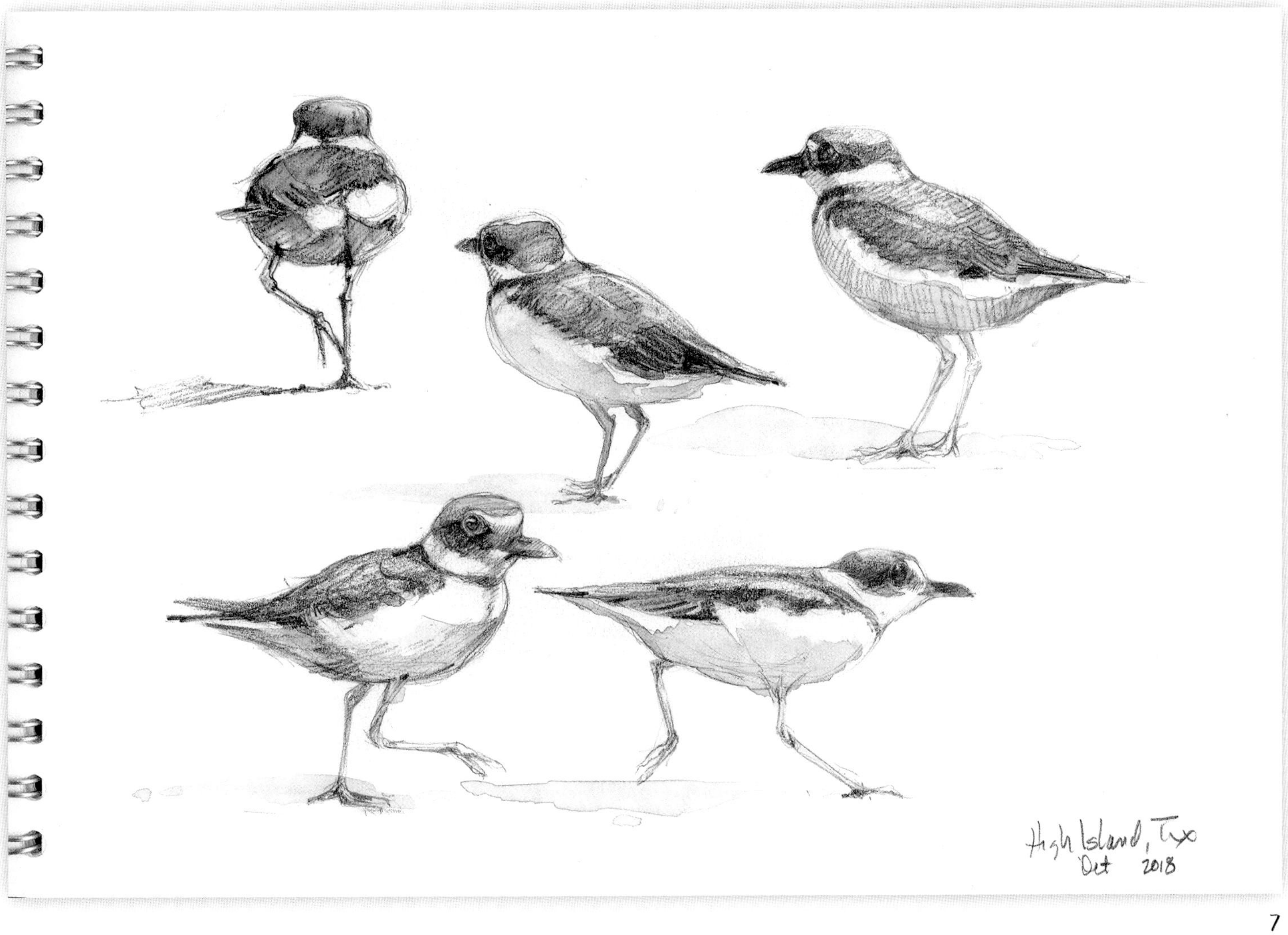

High Island, Tex
Oct 2018

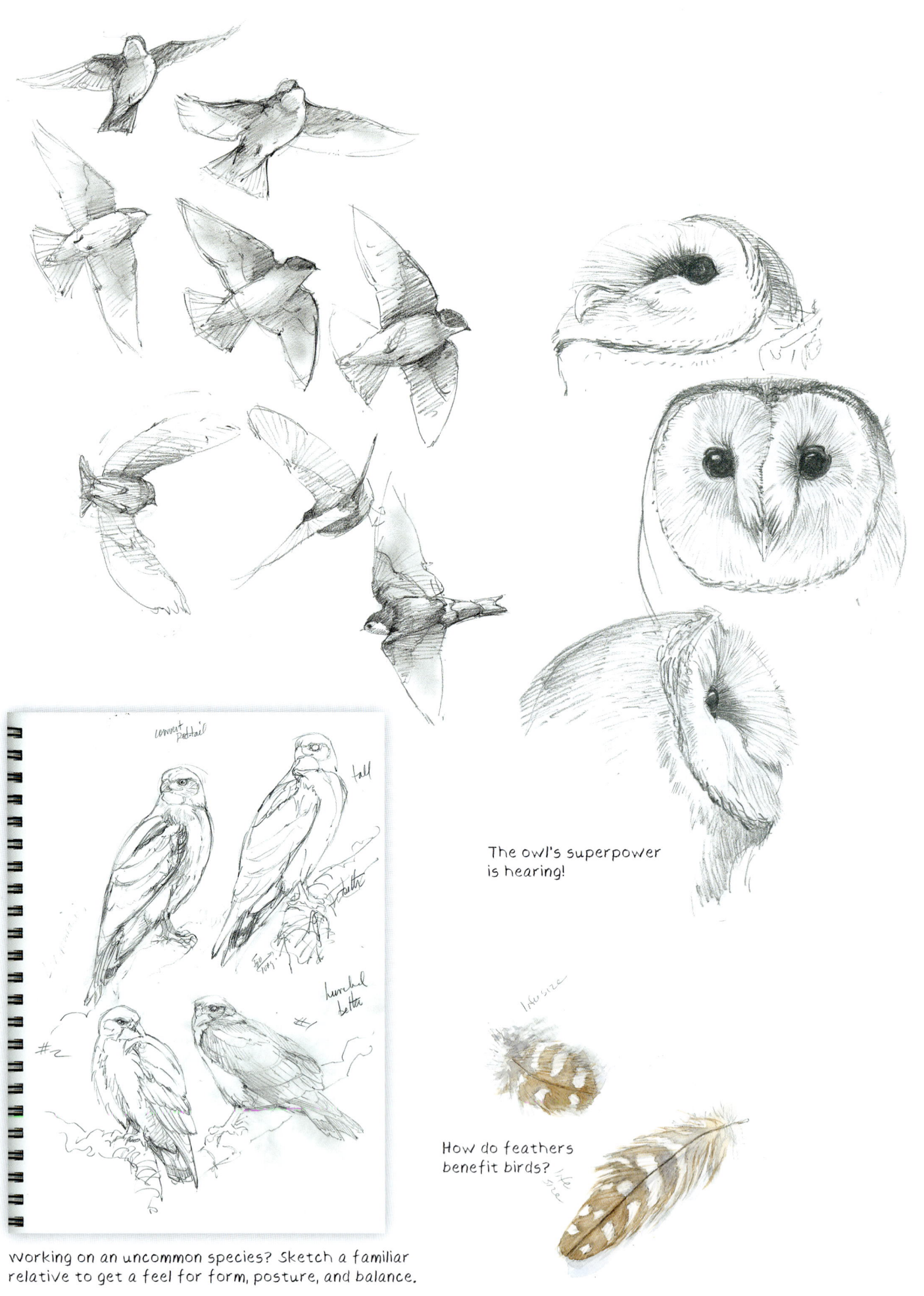

The owl's superpower is hearing!

How do feathers benefit birds?

working on an uncommon species? Sketch a familiar relative to get a feel for form, posture, and balance.

CHAPTER 2

The Nature of Drawing Birds

My spark began while sketching large wintering hawks on telephone poles in Texas. While most mammals have knees and elbows that poke out, what goes on beneath the hawk's cloak of feathers? My interest ignited while sitting a few feet away from a Great Horned Owl and a Red-tailed Hawk that were being nurtured by a local rehabilitator.

Birds lead fascinating lives, from a songbird that hunts underwater, to a hunting owl that keeps focused on a meal half a mile away, to a bird that dives greater than 1,500 feet (457 meters). Whether you find birds in a city park, hike the thickest jungle trail to spot them, or observe them from a window, you catch a glimpse into their avian world. Today, my bird classes bring live birds into the classroom to encourage that spark in others.

The following pages are my way of approaching drawing and painting birds. The chapter demonstrates the awkward as well as the successful, in the hopes of helping the reader to become comfortable drawing birds or to have fun trying.

Extreme detail isn't the key to successful bird painting. An exquisitely rendered work can be spoiled by bad drawing, structure, and composition. It doesn't take much research to make better decisions. For all that, an impressionist style can be exhilarating if it holds true to the bird and excels in composition.

There is no single way to go about drawing and painting birds. Find your path to a fun and rewarding experience. Show no fear and sketch away!

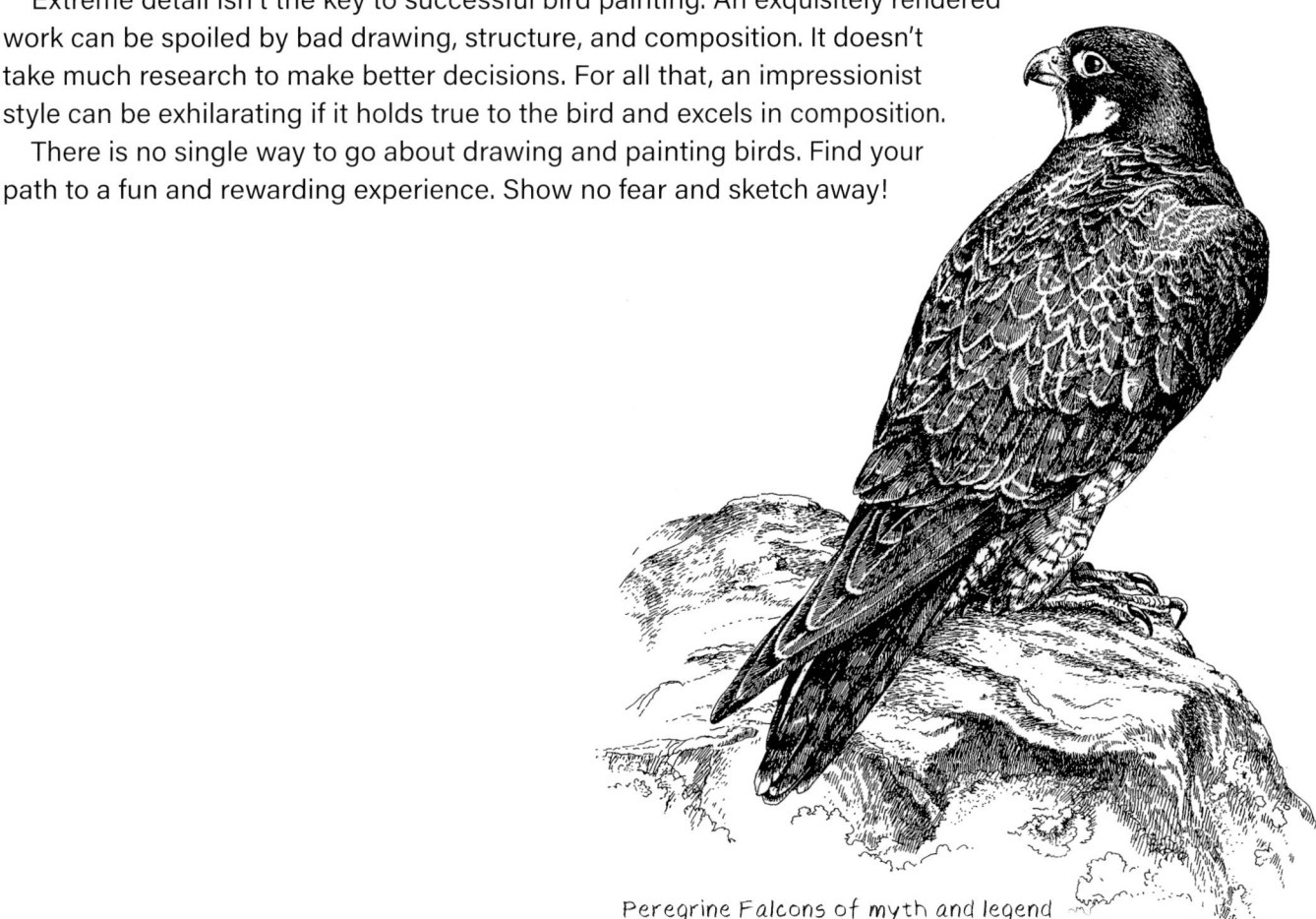

Peregrine Falcons of myth and legend epitomize a noble attitude, even today.

I Found a Feather ...

A chance discovery along a trail—a single feather—reveals a story.
Curiosity encourages us to ask how it got there, who lost it, and
what was the lifestyle of the bird?

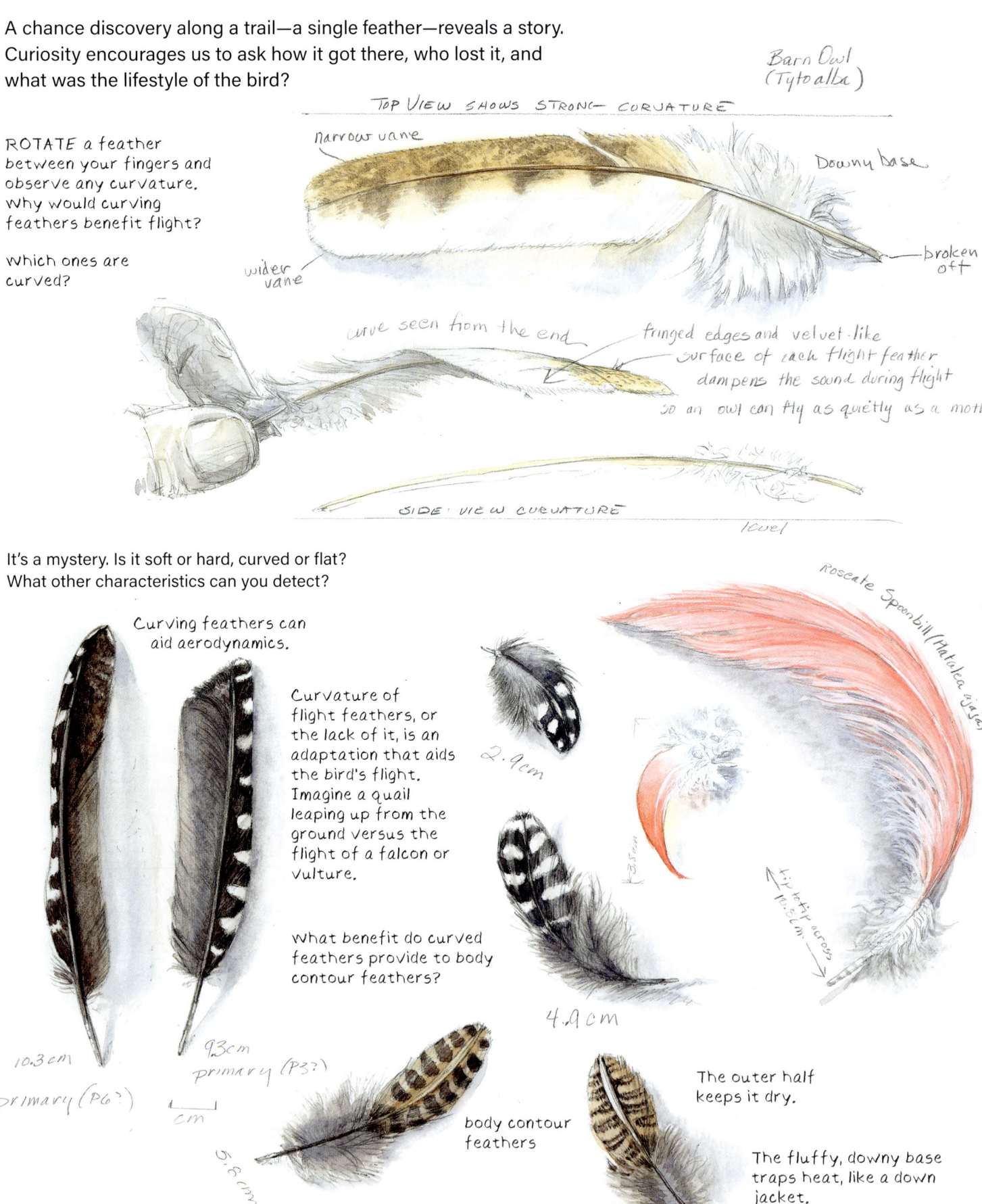

ROTATE a feather
between your fingers and
observe any curvature.
Why would curving
feathers benefit flight?

which ones are
curved?

Barn Owl
(Tyto alba)

TOP VIEW SHOWS STRONG CURVATURE

narrow vane

Downy base

broken
off

wider vane

curve seen from the end

fringed edges and velvet-like
surface of each flight feather
dampens the sound during flight
so an owl can fly as quietly as a moth.

SIDE VIEW CURVATURE

level

It's a mystery. Is it soft or hard, curved or flat?
What other characteristics can you detect?

Curving feathers can
aid aerodynamics.

Curvature of
flight feathers, or
the lack of it, is an
adaptation that aids
the bird's flight.
Imagine a quail
leaping up from the
ground versus the
flight of a falcon or
vulture.

what benefit do curved
feathers provide to body
contour feathers?

Roseate Spoonbill (Platalea ajaja)

2.9 cm

4.9 cm

10.3 cm

primary (P6?)

9.3 cm

primary (P3?)

cm

5.6 cm

body contour
feathers

The outer half
keeps it dry.

The fluffy, downy base
traps heat, like a down
jacket.

Montezuma Quail (Cyrtonyx montezumae)

4.1 cm

10

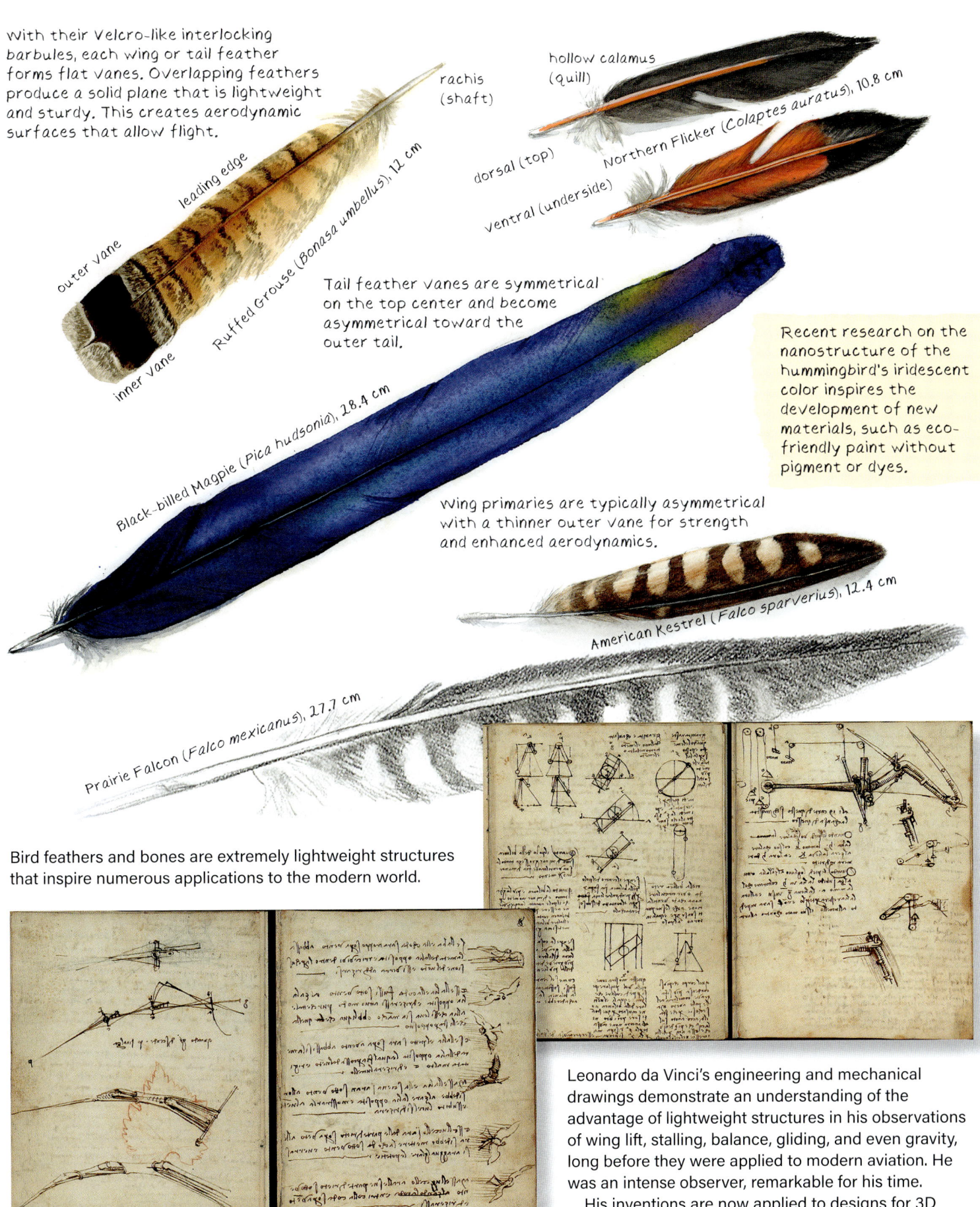

With their Velcro-like interlocking barbules, each wing or tail feather forms flat vanes. Overlapping feathers produce a solid plane that is lightweight and sturdy. This creates aerodynamic surfaces that allow flight.

rachis (shaft)

leading edge

outer vane

inner vane

Ruffed Grouse (*Bonasa umbellus*), 12 cm

hollow calamus (quill)

dorsal (top)

ventral (underside)

Northern Flicker (*Colaptes auratus*), 10.8 cm

Tail feather vanes are symmetrical on the top center and become asymmetrical toward the outer tail.

Black-billed Magpie (*Pica hudsonia*), 28.4 cm

Recent research on the nanostructure of the hummingbird's iridescent color inspires the development of new materials, such as eco-friendly paint without pigment or dyes.

Wing primaries are typically asymmetrical with a thinner outer vane for strength and enhanced aerodynamics.

American Kestrel (*Falco sparverius*), 12.4 cm

Prairie Falcon (*Falco mexicanus*), 27.7 cm

Bird feathers and bones are extremely lightweight structures that inspire numerous applications to the modern world.

Codex on the Flight of Birds, Leonardo da Vinci, 1505–1506, World Digital Library.

Leonardo da Vinci's engineering and mechanical drawings demonstrate an understanding of the advantage of lightweight structures in his observations of wing lift, stalling, balance, gliding, and even gravity, long before they were applied to modern aviation. He was an intense observer, remarkable for his time.

His inventions are now applied to designs for 3D printing and also support columns for earthquake-resistant buildings. What other applications are possible for a strong lightweight structure?

When Counting Feathers Counts

There is a specific number of flight feathers in a wing or tail. This number is consistent within the bird's taxonomic family.

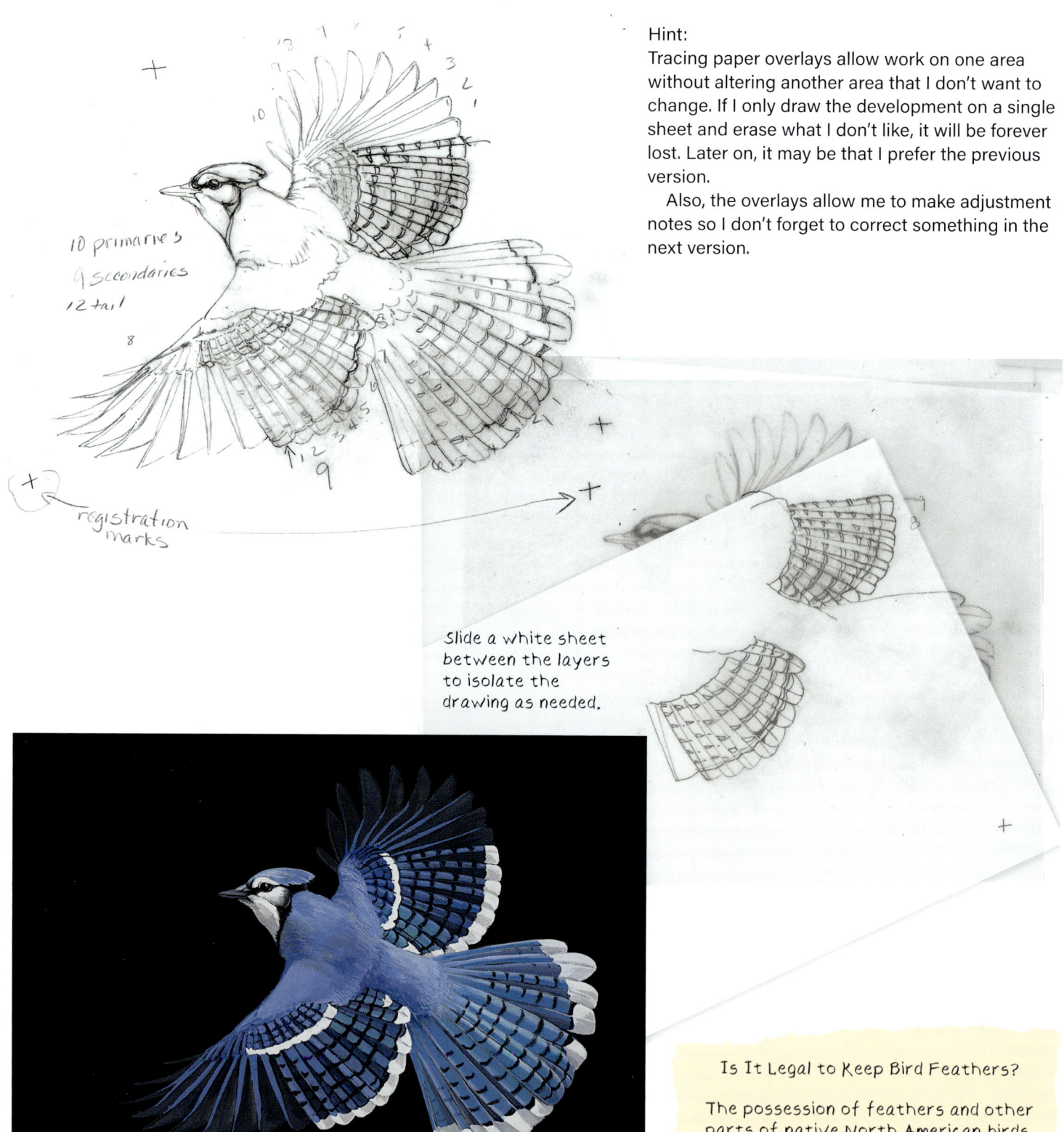

10 primaries
9 secondaries
12 tail
8

registration marks

Slide a white sheet between the layers to isolate the drawing as needed.

Hint:
Tracing paper overlays allow work on one area without altering another area that I don't want to change. If I only draw the development on a single sheet and erase what I don't like, it will be forever lost. Later on, it may be that I prefer the previous version.

Also, the overlays allow me to make adjustment notes so I don't forget to correct something in the next version.

Blue Jay (*Cyanocitta cristata*), 5 × 7 in (12.7 × 17.78 cm), gouache.

Is It Legal to Keep Bird Feathers?

The possession of feathers and other parts of native North American birds without a permit is prohibited by the Migratory Bird Treaty Act. There are exceptions; please look up advice. However, appreciating feathers is perfectly legal.

A Feather Mystery

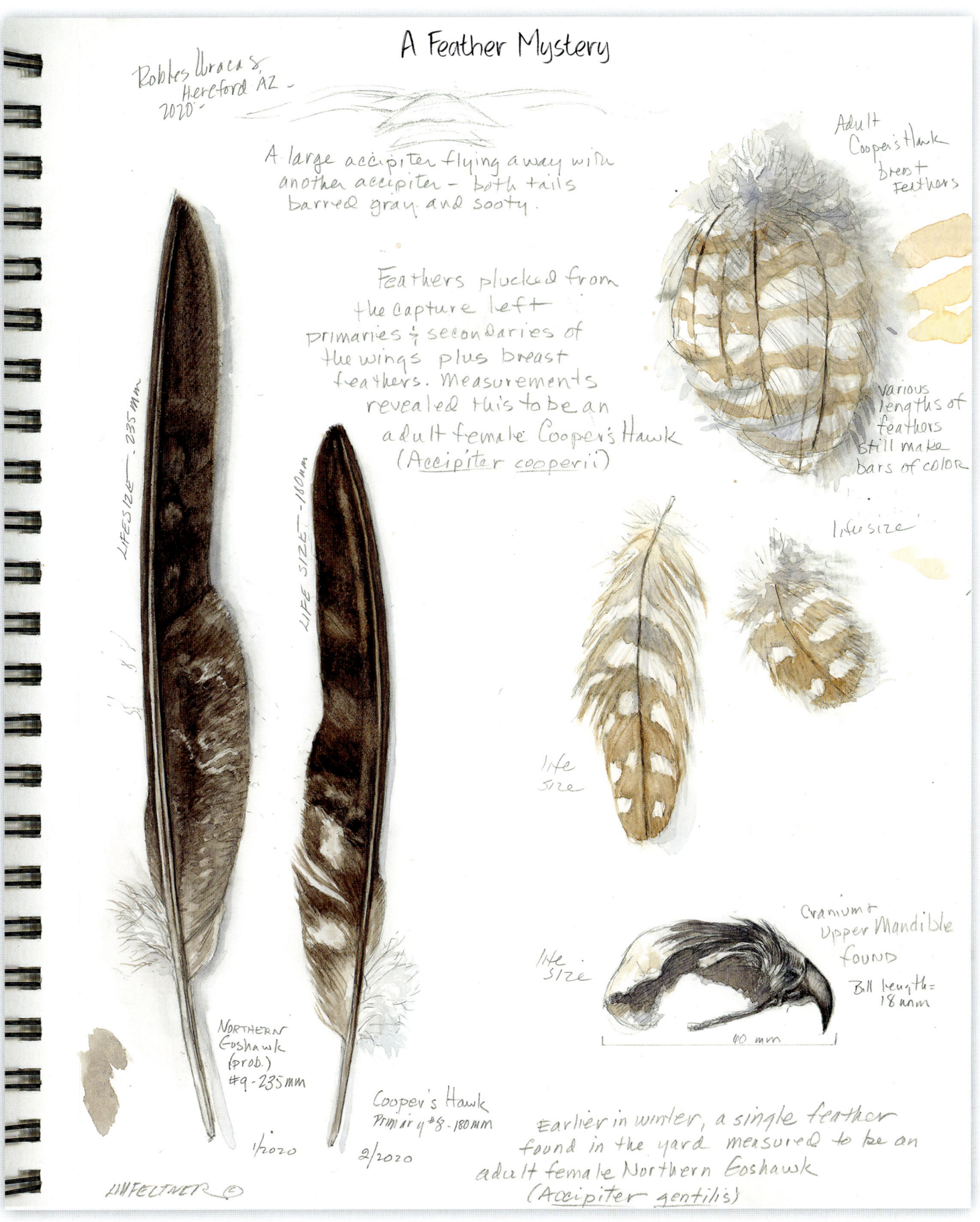

Robles Unacas,
Hereford AZ -
2020 -

A large accipiter flying away with
another accipiter - both tails
barred gray and sooty.

Feathers plucked from
the capture left
primaries & secondaries of
the wings plus breast
feathers. Measurements
revealed this to be an
adult female Cooper's Hawk
(Accipiter cooperii)

Adult
Cooper's Hawk
breast
feathers

Various
lengths of
feathers
still make
bars of color

Life size

life
size

LIFE SIZE - 235 mm

LIFE SIZE - 180 mm

life
size

Cranium &
Upper Mandible
found

Bill length=
18 mm

60 mm

NORTHERN
Goshawk
(prob.)
#9 - 235 mm

1/2020

Cooper's Hawk
Primary #8 - 180 mm

2/2020

LINFELTNER ©

Earlier in winter, a single feather
found in the yard measured to be an
adult female Northern Goshawk
(Accipiter gentilis)

Curious Beaks—Impressive Survival Tools

The bill's outer keratin layer covers the bone and provides a durable survival tool. Like your fingernails, keratin continues to grow and wears down from use. Birds thrive without teeth, an adaptation for a lightweight lifestyle.

Some aquatic birds like ducks have hard, saw-toothed edges for grasping fish. Flamingos have comb-like sieves that filter water and capture tiny shrimp.

Inside the mouth, sensory receptors distinguish a yummy bite of food from a bitter bug that needs spitting out. They help a duck judge a food item versus a rock in murky pond water.

Hummingbirds and woodpeckers can extend their tongues way beyond the tip of the bill. They are the only birds that enjoy my hummingbird feeders, where others cannot reach the sweet liquid.

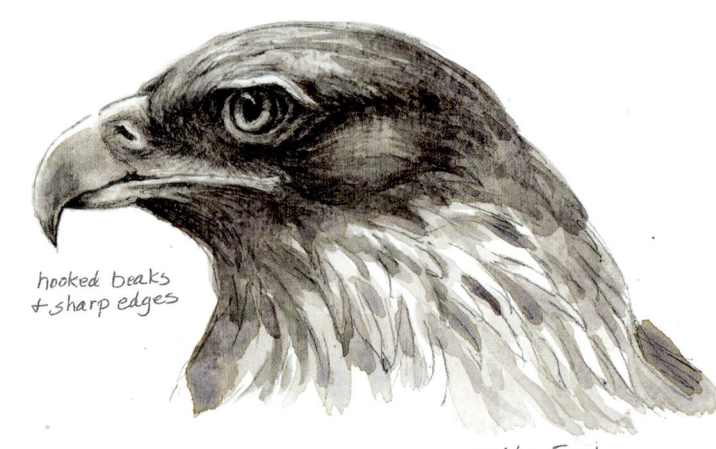

hooked beaks + sharp edges

Golden Eagle
(Aquila chrysaetos)

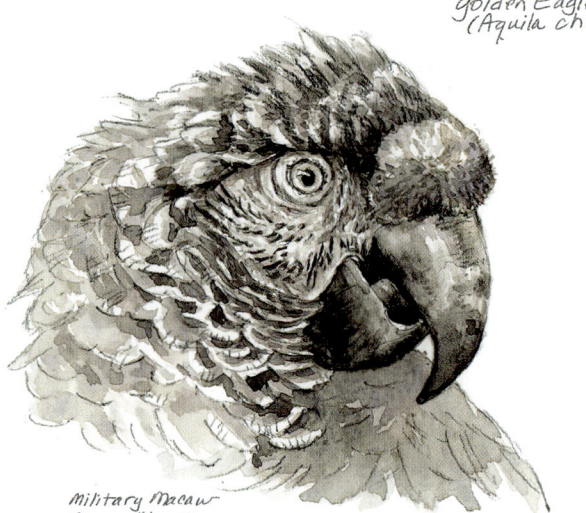

Military Macaw
(Ara militaris)
cracks hard nuts

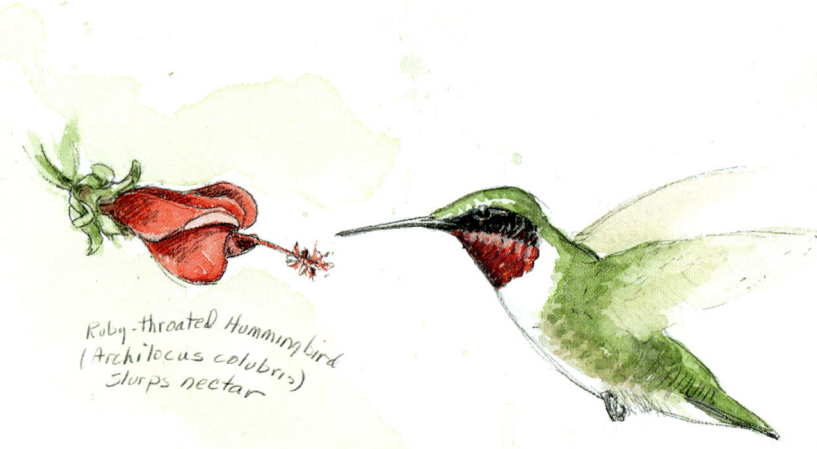

Ruby-throated Hummingbird
(Archilocus colubris)
slurps nectar

One bill size does not fit all warblers.

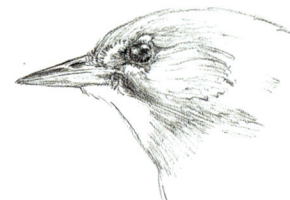

Northern Parula
(Setophaga americana)
tiny bills glean small caterpillars

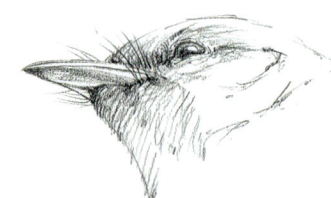

American Redstart
(Setophaga ruticilla)
broader bills with bristles aid flycatching

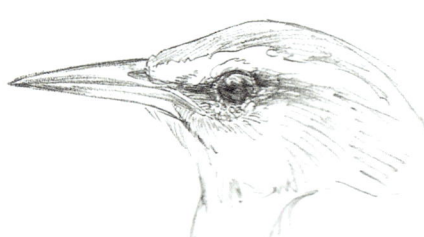

Swainson's Warbler
(Limnothlypis swainsonii)
strong bills flip over dead leaves

The Right Tool for the Job

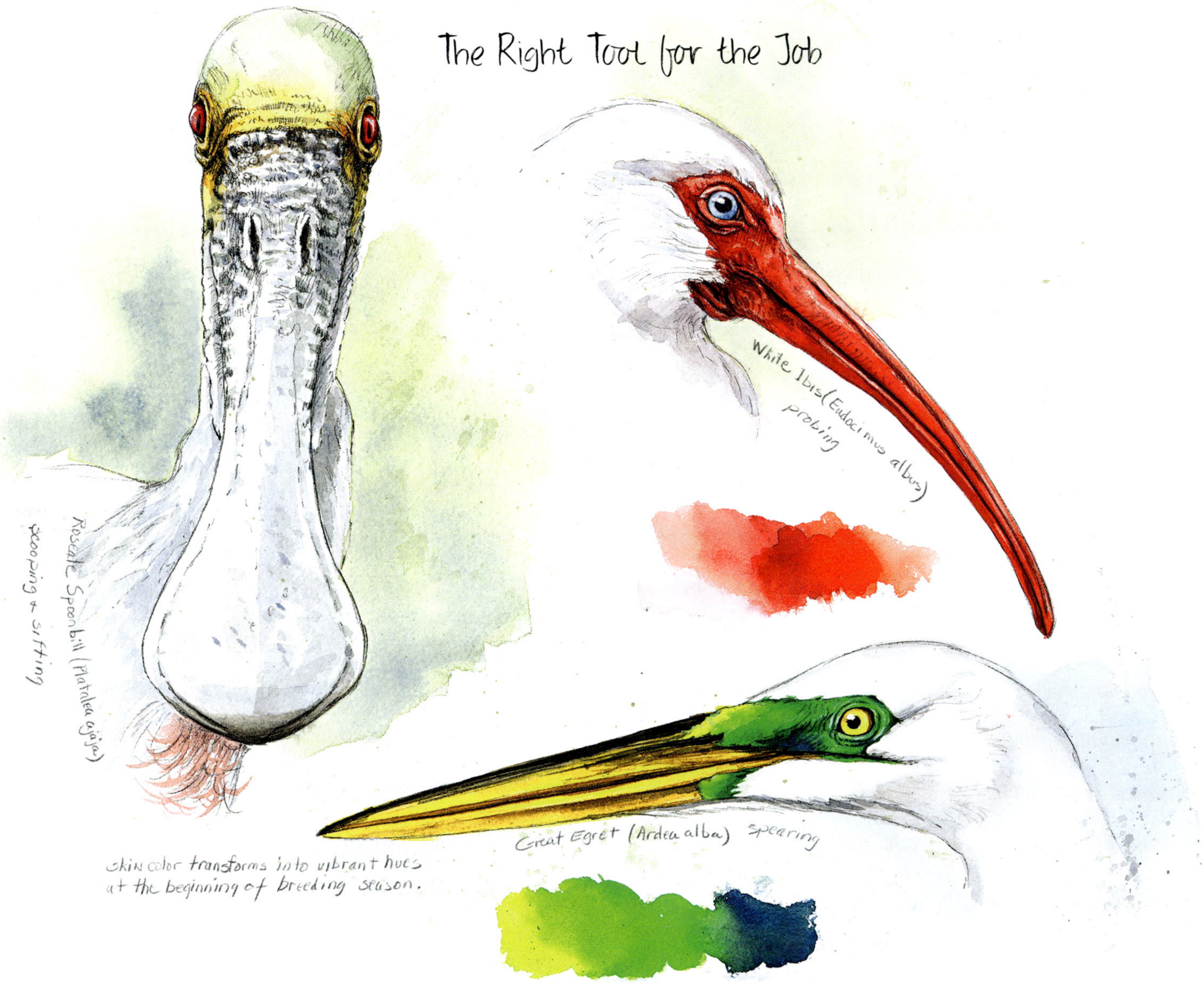

Roseate Spoonbill (Platalea ajaja)
scooping + sifting

White Ibis (Eudocimus albus)
probing

skin color transforms into vibrant hues
at the beginning of breeding season.

Great Egret (Ardea alba) spearing

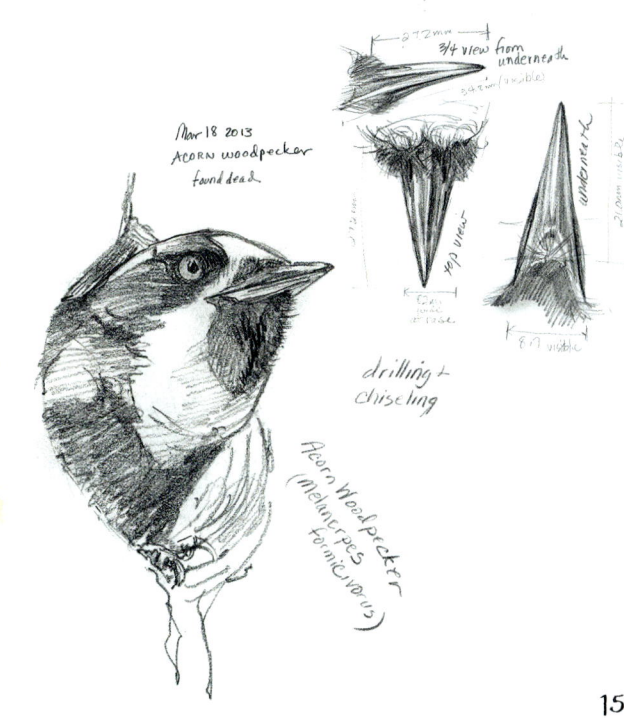

Mar 18 2013
ACORN Woodpecker
found dead

3/4 view from underneath

drilling +
chiseling

Acorn Woodpecker
(Melanerpes formicivorus)

"We have hands to build a house, catch a ball, grab a bite to eat, feed our kids, and comb our hair. But with the modification of those long-ago dinosaur forelimbs for flight, birds lost those abilities. So their bills have adapted to do exactly the same things. Watch a bird preening, building a nest, capturing an insect out of the air or feeding its young, and marvel at these adaptations. Birds have also evolved relatively long necks with special vertebrae, presumably to facilitate the many uses of the bill."

—Dennis R. Paulson, PhD, Director Emeritus, Puget Sound Museum of Natural History, University of Puget Sound

Curious Beaks for "Darwin's Shorebirds"

Note the shape and size of a beak. It is an important clue as to how it makes a living. Even within a closely related group, bill size and shape vary among species. Small, straight-billed birds pick invertebrates off the surface of the mud and shallows. Longer bills, often straight or downcurved, probe the soft mud or forest floor using sensitive sensors at the bill's tip to detect an unseen morsel. The American Avocet sweeps its upcurved bill from side to side in the water to glean what's near the surface.

OK

Wilson's Snipe
(Gallinago delicata)

semipalmated Plover
(Charadrius semipalmatus)

Solitary Sandpiper
(Tringa solitaria)

OK

American Avocet (Recurvirostra americana)

Because bills have real significance, they require special attention to detail. Tracing paper overlays allowed me to make subtle adjustments. Each species started with the loosest drawings and each layer shows the adjustments.

Long-billed Curlew (Numenius americanus)

OK

16

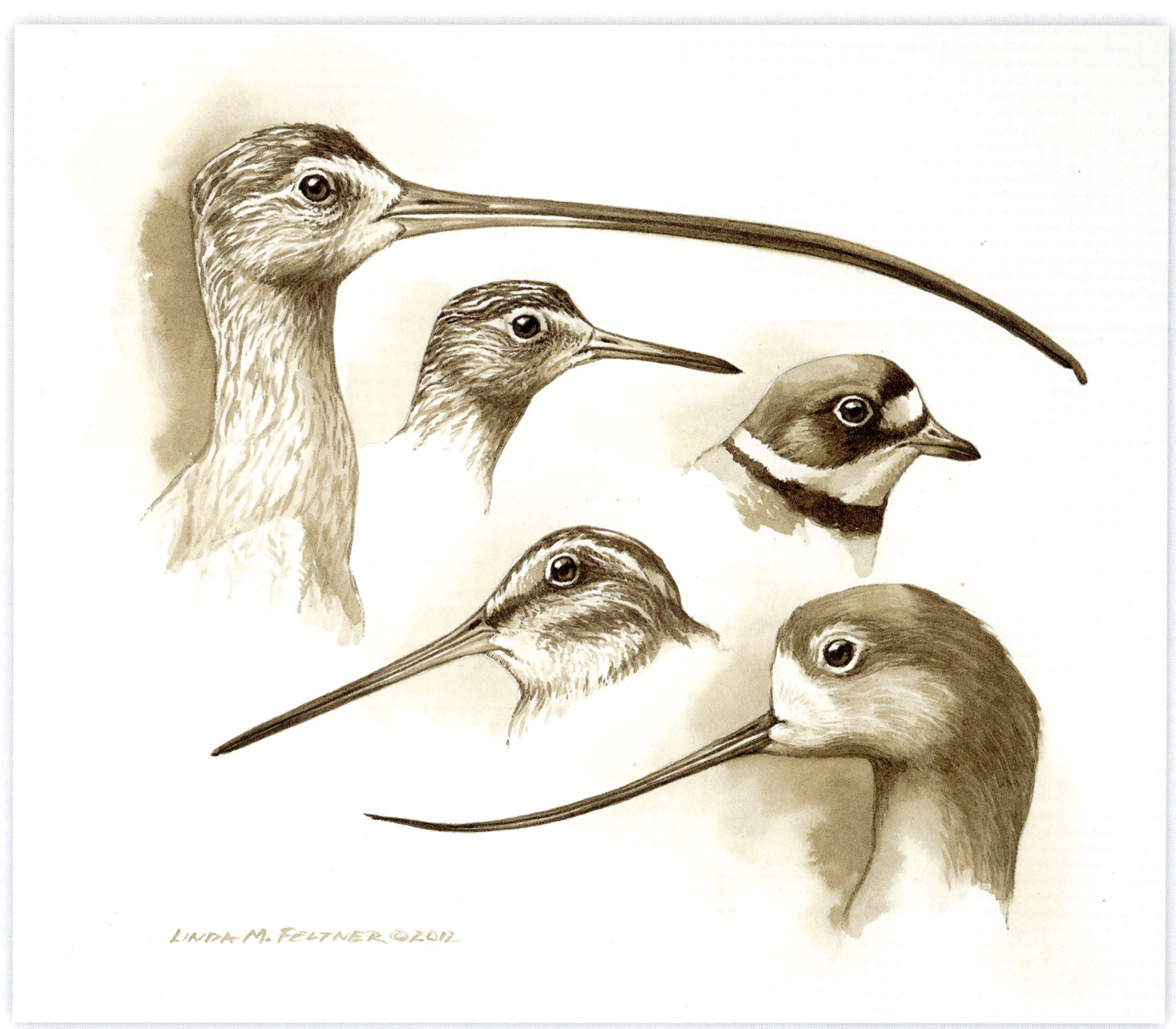

"Darwin's Shorebirds"

Not all of us can study Darwin's finches in their native Galapagos Islands, but we can observe evolutionary adaptations in local birds. Shorebirds developed extraordinary diversity in their bills, enabling them to take advantage of separate ecological niches. Coastal estuaries, inland ponds, grasslands, deserts, and even forests are home to shorebirds because of their varied adaptations for finding food. The survival of migratory shorebirds depends on the conservation of these rich habitats.

Long-billed Curlew (*Numenius americanus*)
Solitary Sandpiper (*Tringa solitaria*)
Semipalmated Plover (*Charadrius semipalmatus*)
Wilson's Snipe (*Gallinago delicata*)
American Avocet (*Recurvirostra americana*)

Darwin's Shorebirds, 9 × 8 in (22.86 × 20.32 cm), Walnut ink.

Under the Feathered Cloak

Discovering what goes on underneath the feathers provides clues to how birds walk, eat, fly, and survive.

Have you seen an owl pouncing on a meal hidden in deep grass? How does it locate dinner in the dark of winter under the snow?

The owl's superpower is hearing. It is often more important to their lifestyle than sight because most species locate their food by sound. Their super soft feathers permit a silent flight while they can hear—but not be heard.

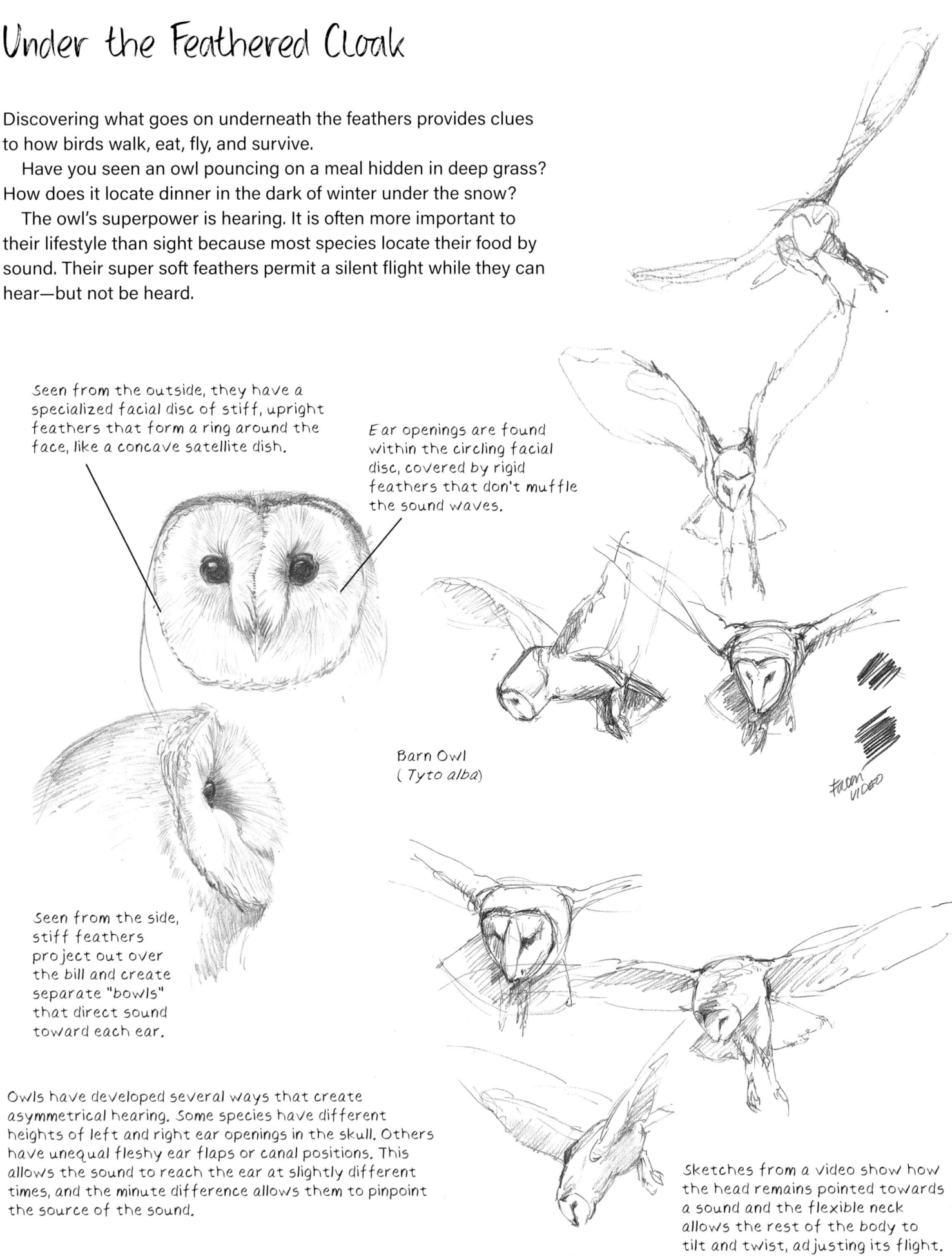

Seen from the outside, they have a specialized facial disc of stiff, upright feathers that form a ring around the face, like a concave satellite dish.

Ear openings are found within the circling facial disc, covered by rigid feathers that don't muffle the sound waves.

Barn Owl
(Tyto alba)

Seen from the side, stiff feathers project out over the bill and create separate "bowls" that direct sound toward each ear.

Owls have developed several ways that create asymmetrical hearing. Some species have different heights of left and right ear openings in the skull. Others have unequal fleshy ear flaps or canal positions. This allows the sound to reach the ear at slightly different times, and the minute difference allows them to pinpoint the source of the sound.

Sketches from a video show how the head remains pointed towards a sound and the flexible neck allows the rest of the body to tilt and twist, adjusting its flight.

The ability to fly requires a different anatomical structure from their reptilian ancestors. The Great Horned Owl (*Bubo virginianus*) is an excellent model in my classes for its large size, compact body, and distinctive markings. Females are typically larger than males, as is indicated by the size and weight range. Length: 18-25 in (46-63 cm), weight 32-88 oz (910-2500 g), wingspan: 40-57 in (101-145 cm).

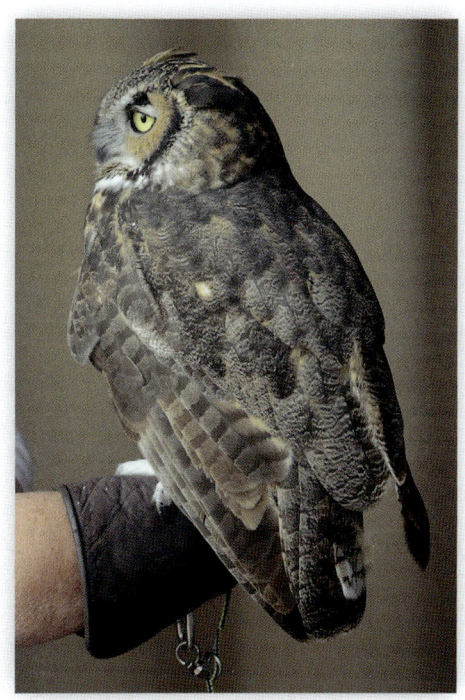

Although this owl's neck looks short, in reality, it is long and curved with 14 vertebrae (we have 7). It's very flexible and can rotate the head up to 270 degrees.

Feathers might hide most of the bill. The jaw hinge lies below and behind the eye and allows the bill to open wide.

The hand and finger bones are reduced and fused for strength to the outer wing.

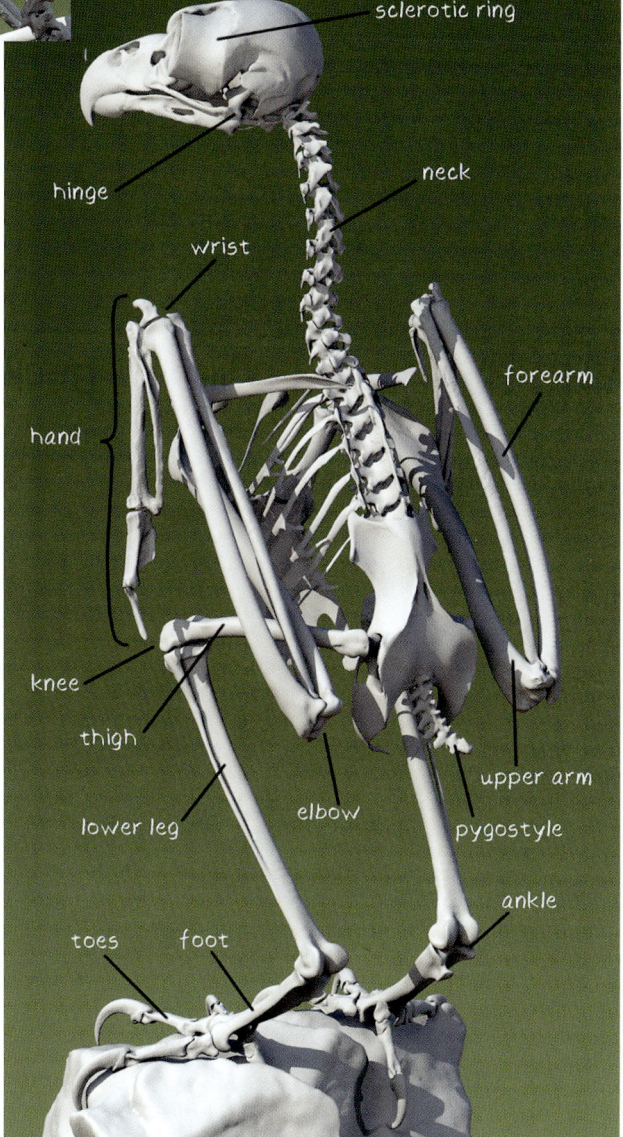

sclerotic ring

hinge

neck

wrist

forearm

hand

knee

thigh

lower leg

elbow

upper arm

pygostyle

ankle

toes   foot

Single frame from the Idaho Virtual Museum,
3-D model IMNH R-1183—*Bubo virginianus*.
Courtesy of the Idaho Museum of Natural History.

Myth busting! Some confuse the ankle with the knee and assume the knee bends backward. A bird's arm and leg joints, such as the elbow, knee, ankle, and foot, bend in the same direction as ours. Different species have bone adaptations to suit their lifestyle, but the joints bend the same.

The organs within the ribcage are a stable center of gravity above the toes, aiding balance. Some of the bones in the vertebral column and pelvic area are fused, providing light weight and strength.

From the outside, the owl's legs look short, but the skeleton shows its long legs and knees hidden beneath skin and feathers.

The bone that supports the most flamboyant tail feathers is only a small stub called the pygostyle.

Practicing with a Living Bird

Owls in my classroom demonstrate that the living bird provides numerous gestures and poses for the artist.

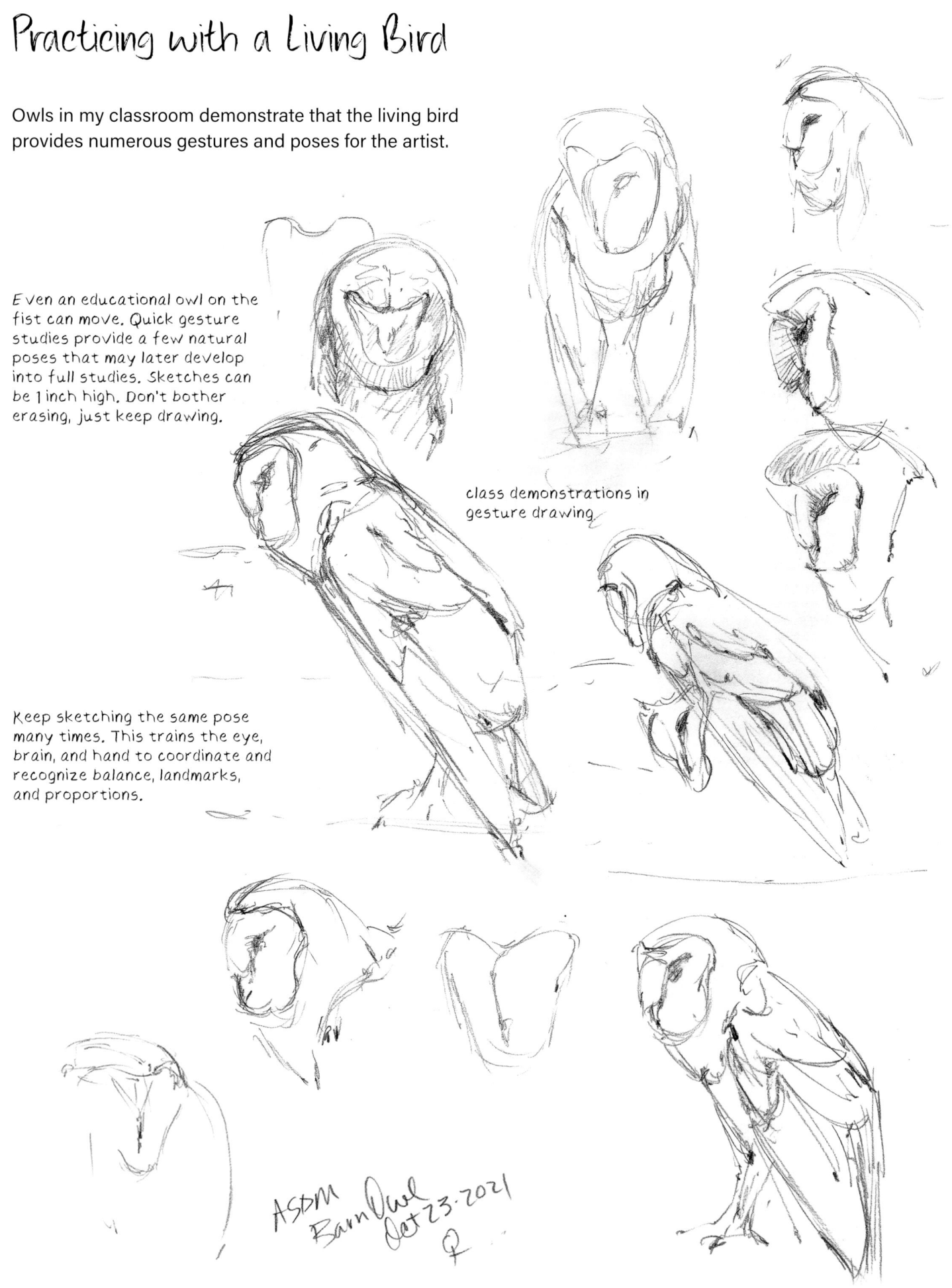

Even an educational owl on the fist can move. Quick gesture studies provide a few natural poses that may later develop into full studies. Sketches can be 1 inch high. Don't bother erasing, just keep drawing.

class demonstrations in gesture drawing

Keep sketching the same pose many times. This trains the eye, brain, and hand to coordinate and recognize balance, landmarks, and proportions.

ASDM
BarnOwl
Oct 23·2021

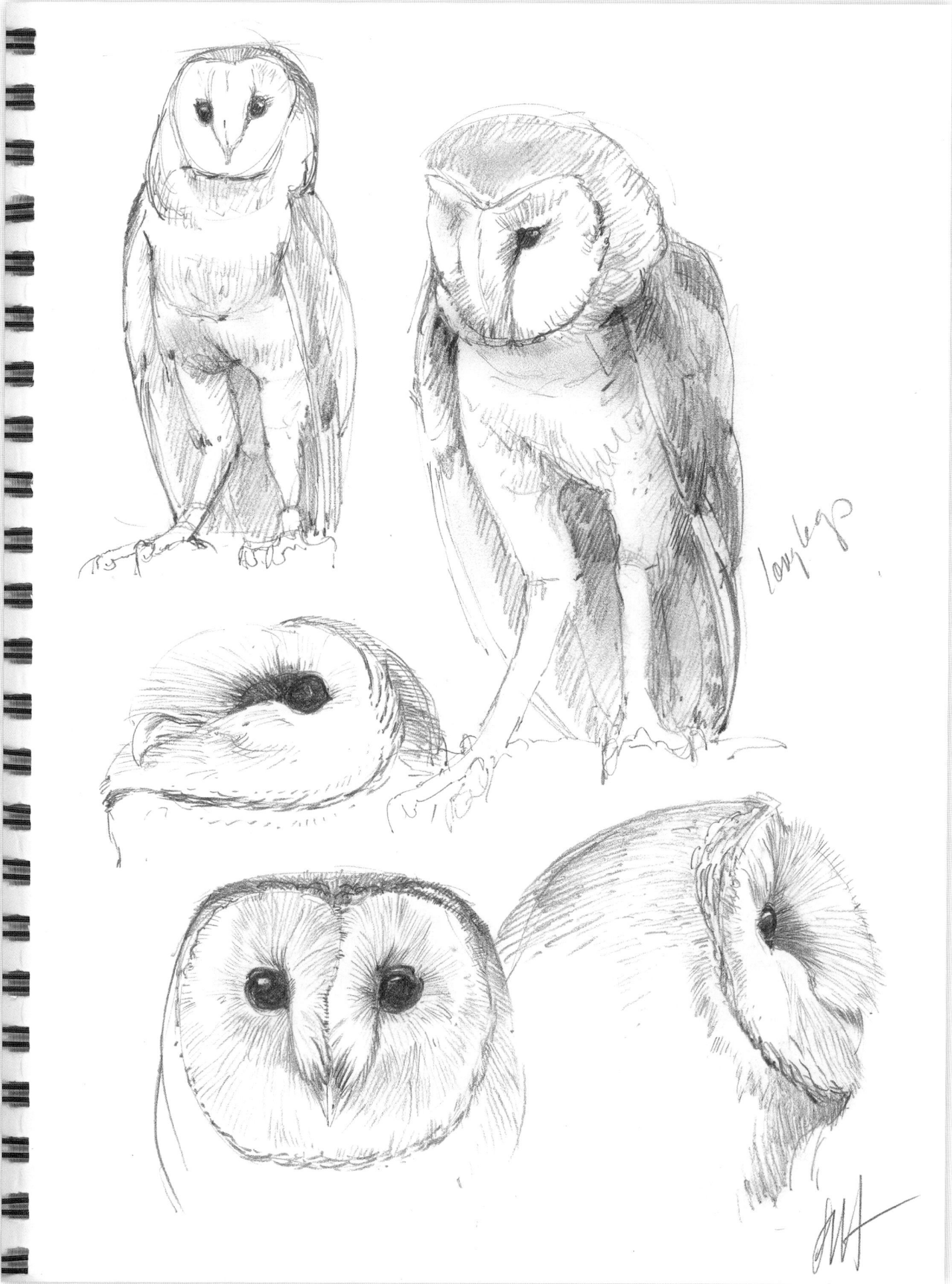

long legs

Practicing with a Patient Bird

Warming up with gesture sketches allows focus on proportion and observation. Longer study reveals the bird's attitude. Observe the body posture, whether nervous or unsettled with feathers tight against a rigid body, or with a relaxed demeanor. Draw what you see.

Sketch whatever angle is available, even if it's the backside. Constantly reinforce the training of eye-brain-hand coordination.

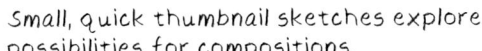

Small, quick thumbnail sketches explore possibilities for compositions.

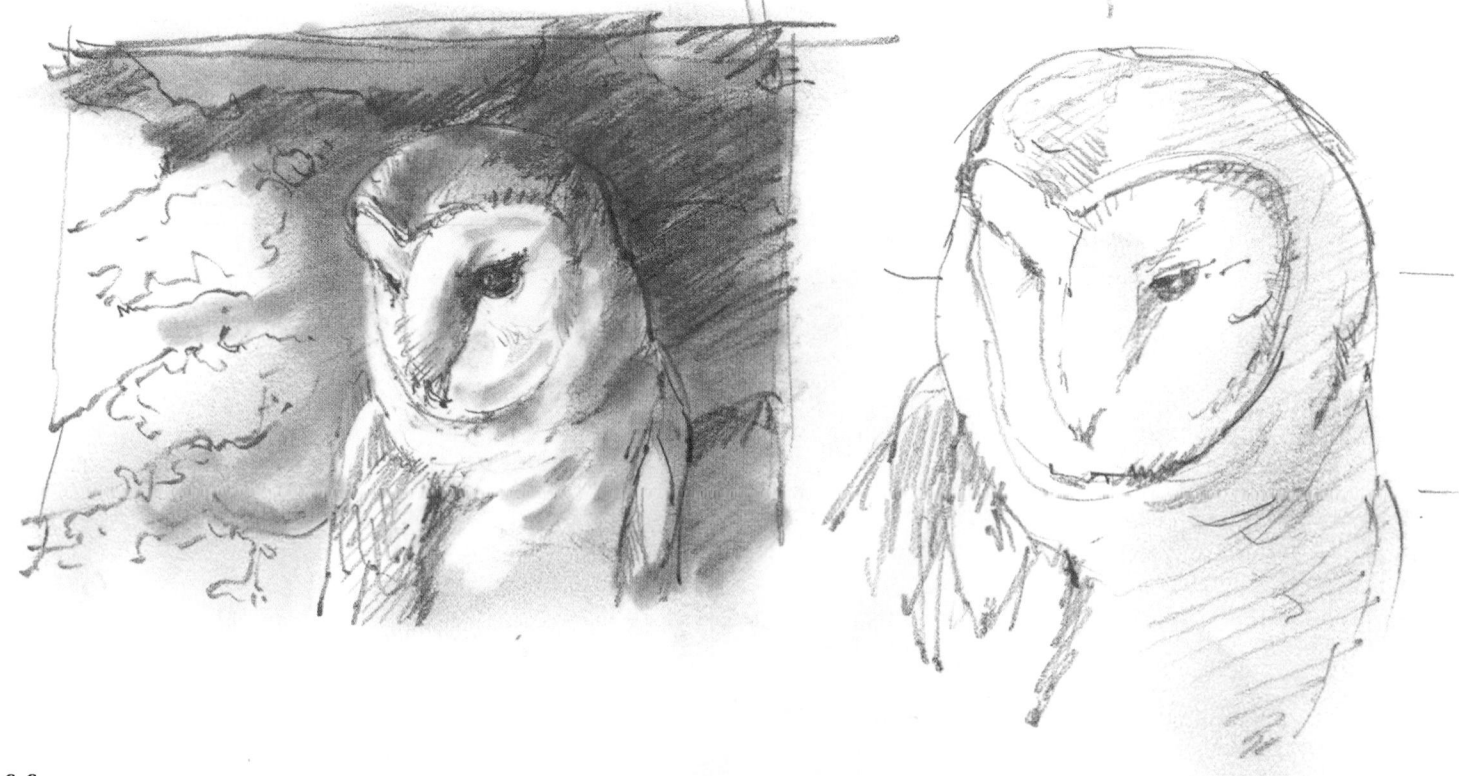

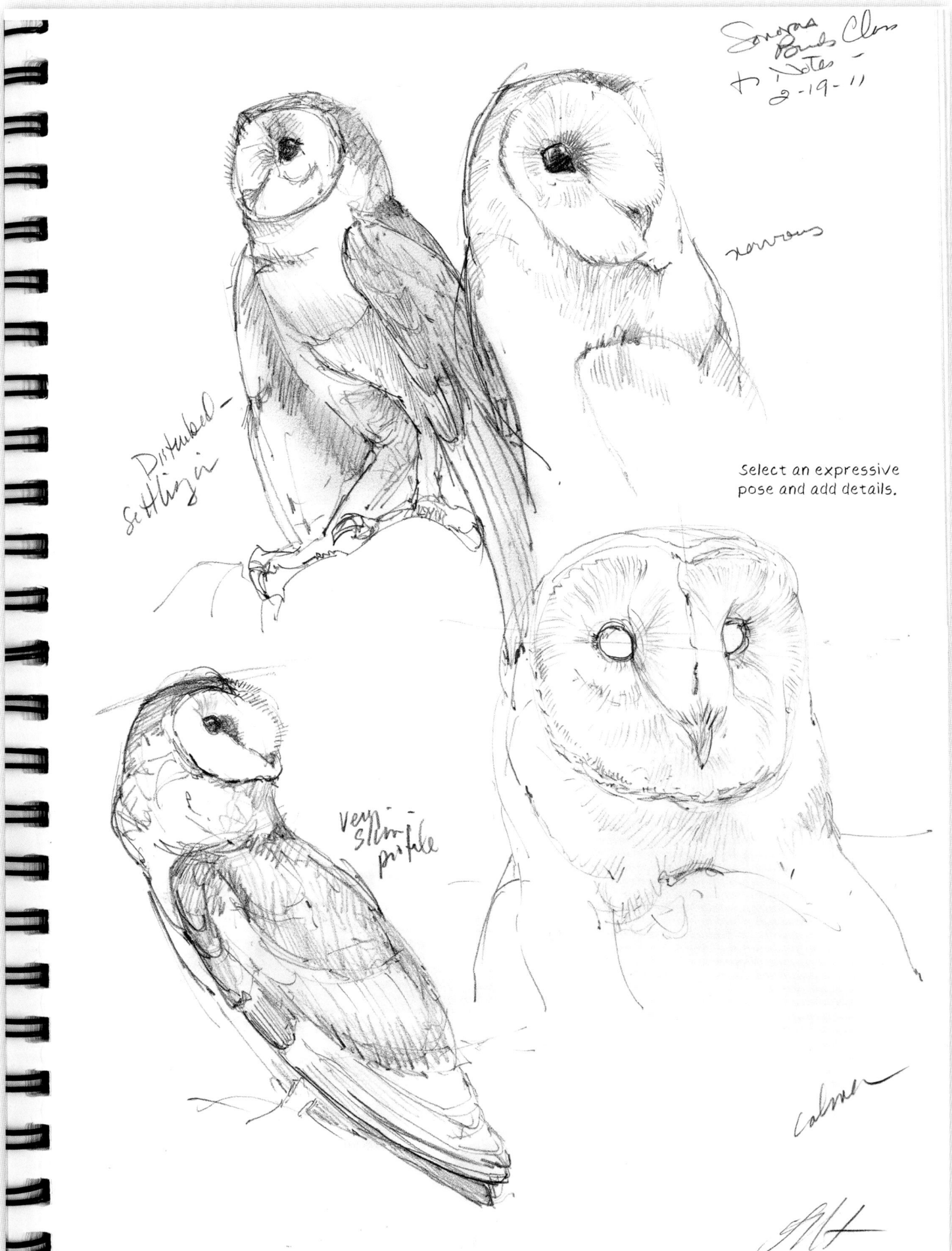

Select an expressive
pose and add details.

Observing Proportions

Have you ever started sketching a bird's mesmerizing eyes, only to realize later that the rest of the bird drawing won't fit on the page?

A large and impressive Great Horned Owl is an excellent model for practicing proportions. Eagerness to begin with the head sometimes gives it greater prominence and it ends up being drawn too large. First draw the proportion of the whole bird to create the foundation.

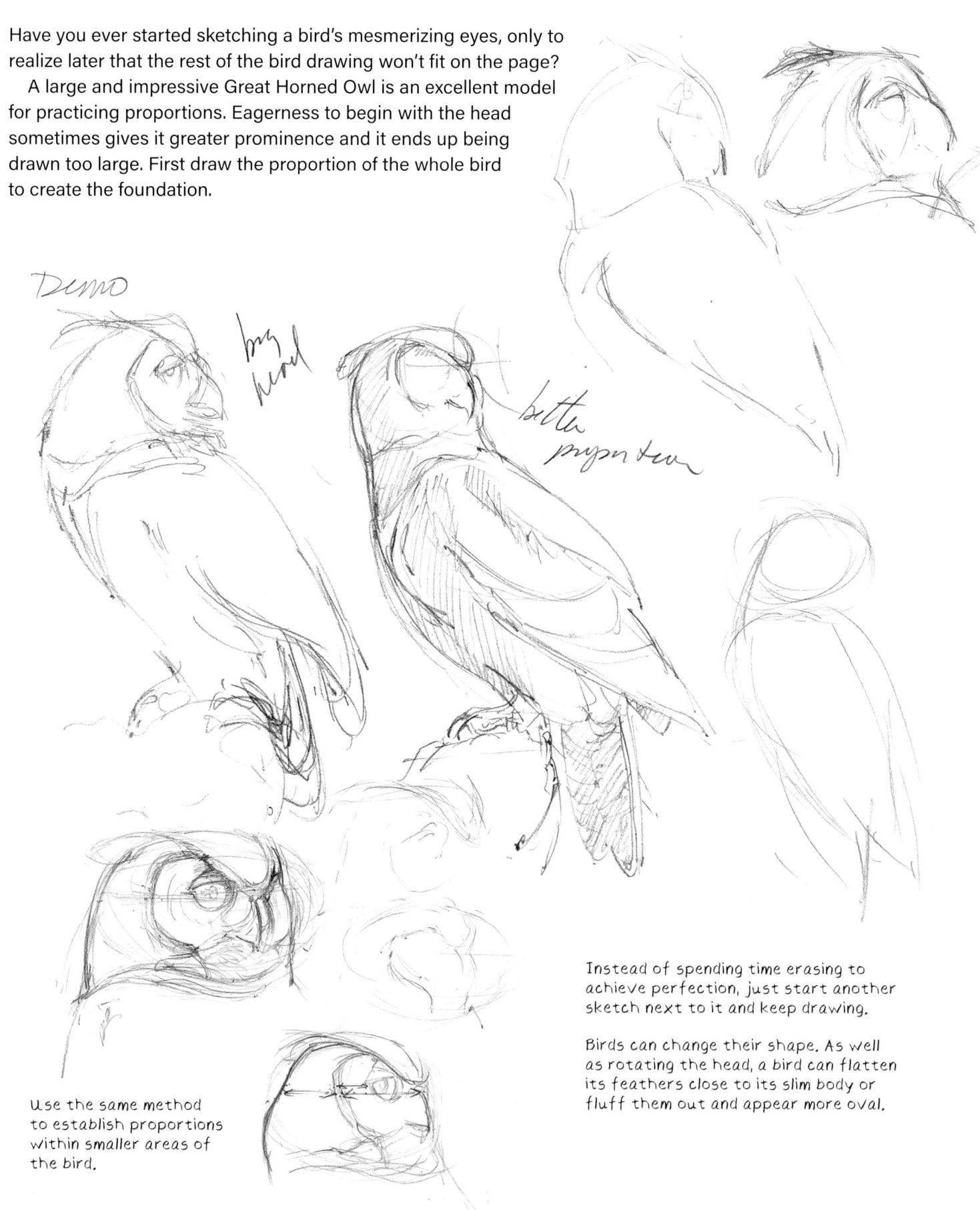

Demo

big head

better proportion

Instead of spending time erasing to achieve perfection, just start another sketch next to it and keep drawing.

Birds can change their shape. As well as rotating the head, a bird can flatten its feathers close to its slim body or fluff them out and appear more oval.

Use the same method to establish proportions within smaller areas of the bird.

How Many Heads High?

A traditional figure drawing technique is an easy method to estimate the whole bird. Use a pencil as a tool to visually measure the bird for its height and width. Stand back and away from the bird. With your arm outstretched and elbow locked, hold the pencil vertically and look through the pencil on to the bird. Close one eye. Visually align the pencil tip with one end of a "fixed area" (like the top of the head). Hold that position and slide your thumb down the pencil to mark the visual distance for the bottom of another "fixed area" (like the bill tip in this example). That unit is "one head high." While keeping your thumb positioned on the pencil and elbow locked, move your arm down to count how many "heads high" the whole bird is. Turn your wrist sideways to determine how many "heads high" the width is. These are rough, general guides.

If the head doesn't work as a fixed area, find a landmark that will not likely change shape, perhaps the tarsi on a hawk or the bill of a heron.

This method will position the drawing on the page first. Then you can add the details over the initial proportion.

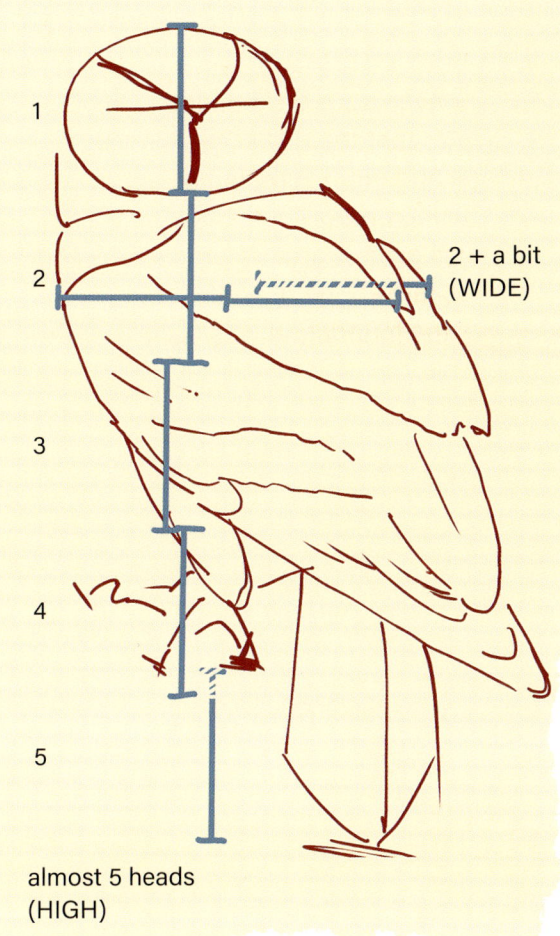

2 + a bit
(WIDE)

almost 5 heads
(HIGH)

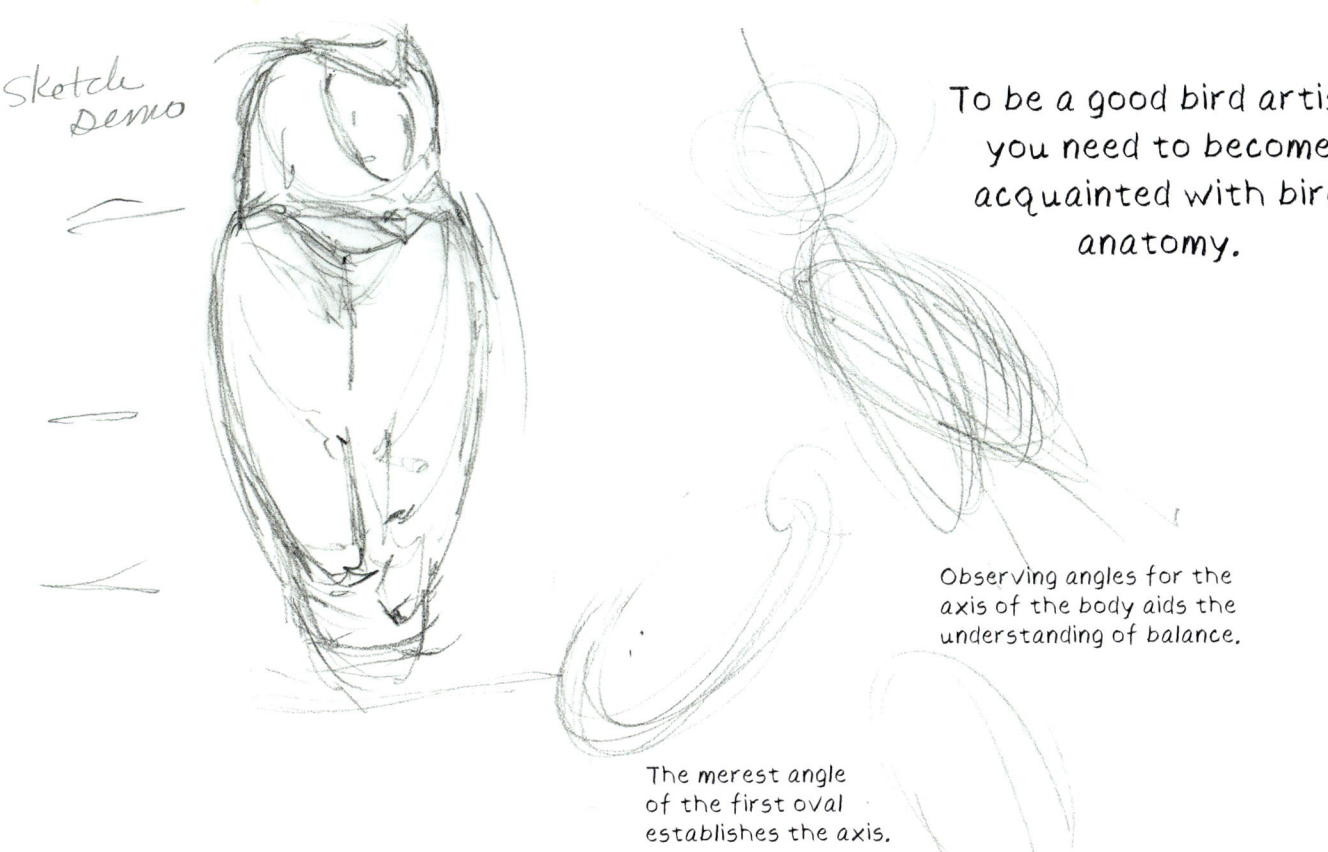

Sketch Demo

To be a good bird artist, you need to become acquainted with bird anatomy.

Observing angles for the axis of the body aids the understanding of balance.

The merest angle of the first oval establishes the axis.

25

Adjustments on Overlays

Class demonstrations often use projected photographs. These four Great Horned Owl heads present various angles with special attention on the facial discs, eyebrows, eyes, and beaks. Landmarks emerge as distinct ovals, triangles, and odd shapes that fit together and aid perspective.

  For the first sketches, concentrate on proportions. Use tracing paper as an overlay to adjust and tweak the features. Make adjustments on the tracing paper because it's quicker than erasing. This way, the original gesture drawing remains preserved. If the first sketch is altered or erased, its spontaneous lines cannot be recovered.

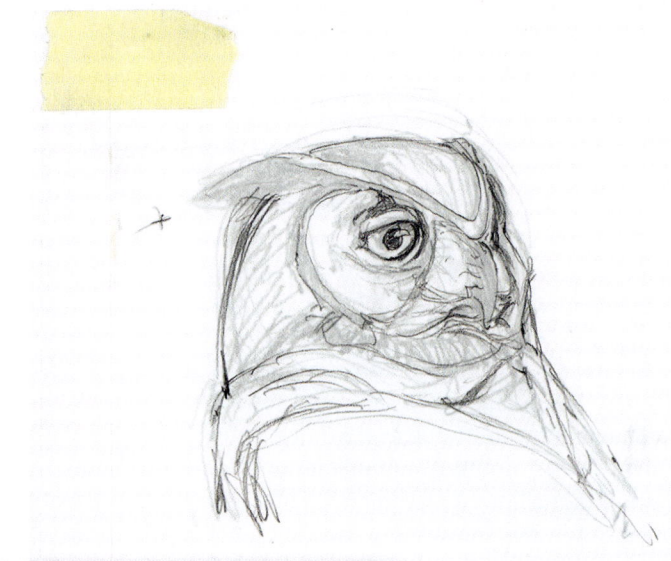

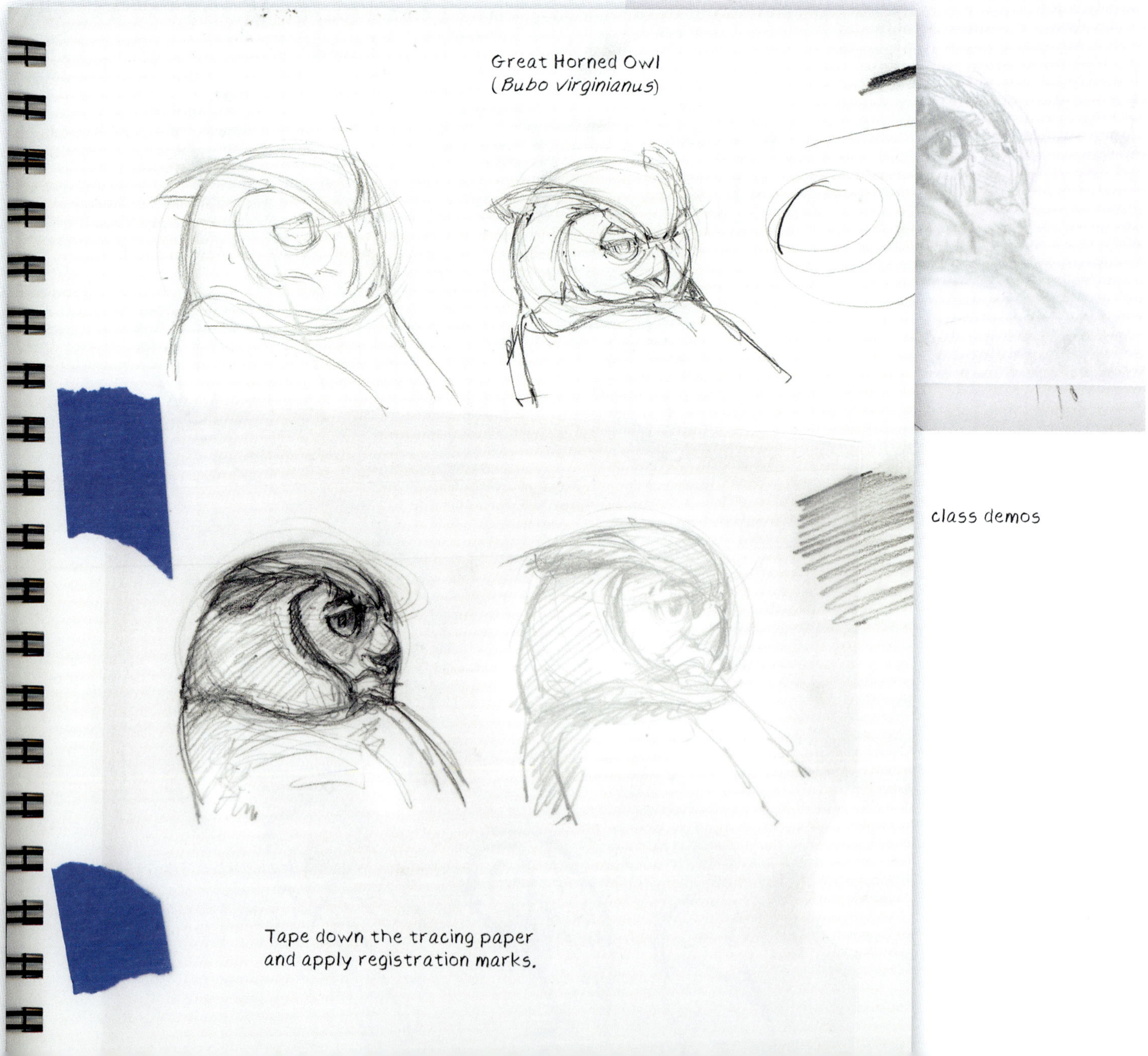

Great Horned Owl
(*Bubo virginianus*)

class demos

Tape down the tracing paper
and apply registration marks.

Overlays are valuable to building an image while preserving the original, spontaneous sketch.

I experiment with value studies in a sketchbook, refining the drawings to a higher level of detail, light direction, and composition in preparation for painting. I keep them in the sketchbook for future inspiration.

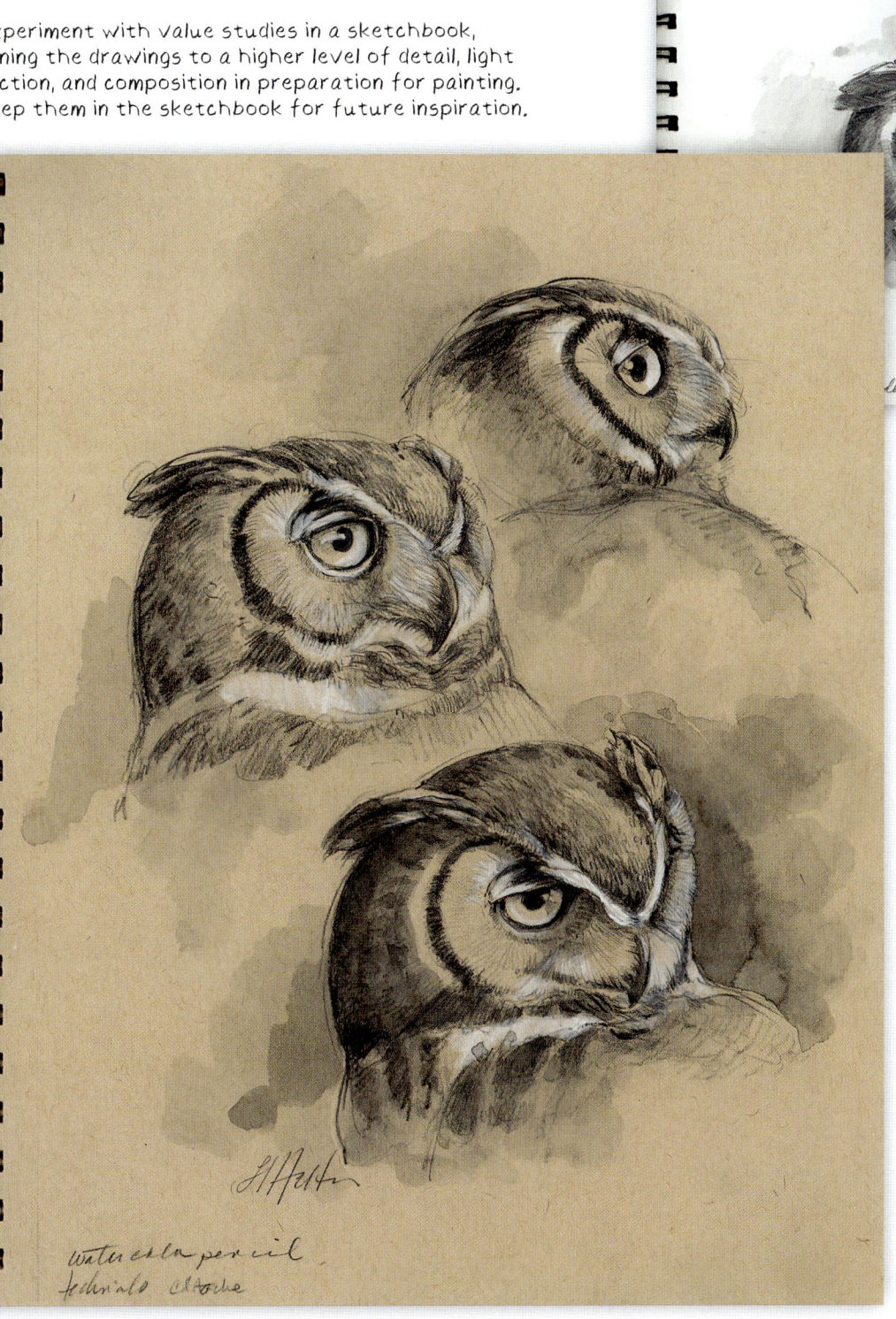

Caran d'Ache Technalo water soluble graphite pencil on bond sketchbook paper

Caran d'Ache Technalo water soluble graphite pencil and white gouache on Strathmore toned tan sketch paper

Explore, Experiment, and Have Fun!

From the mass of scribbles, one or two poses hold potential.

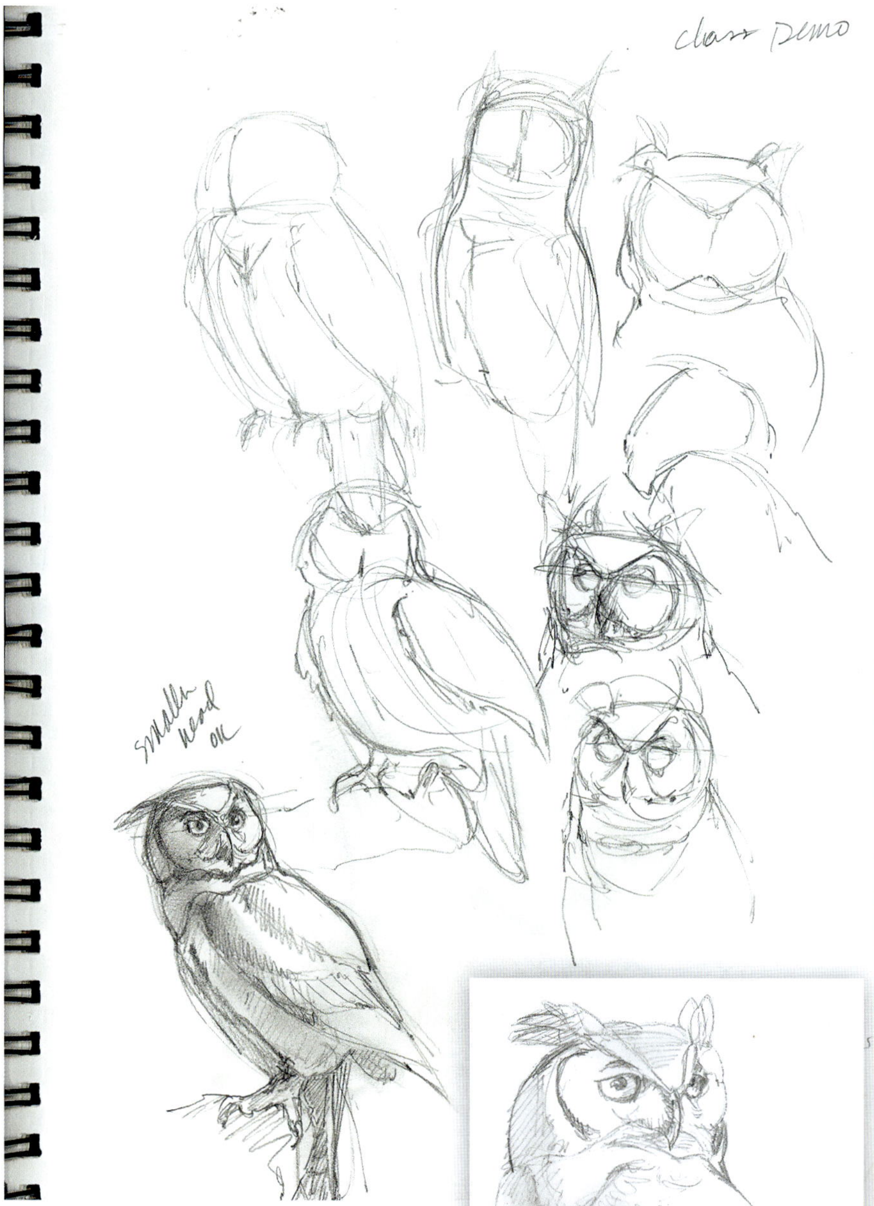

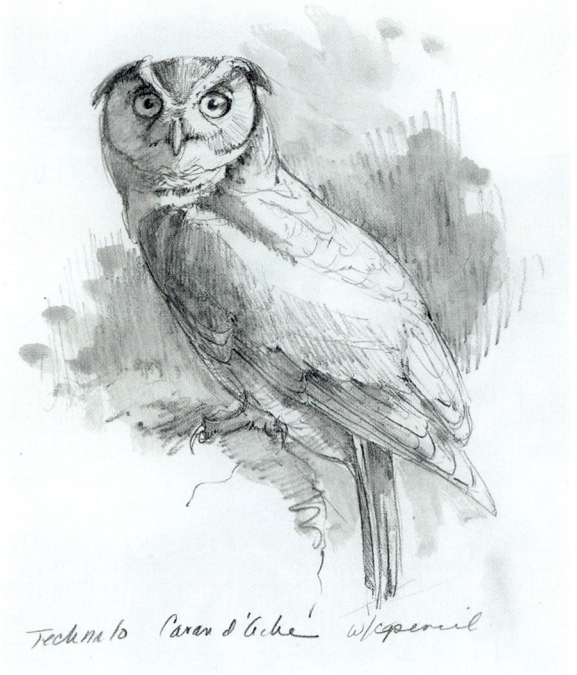

Caran d'Ache Technalo water soluble graphite pencil on bond sketch book paper

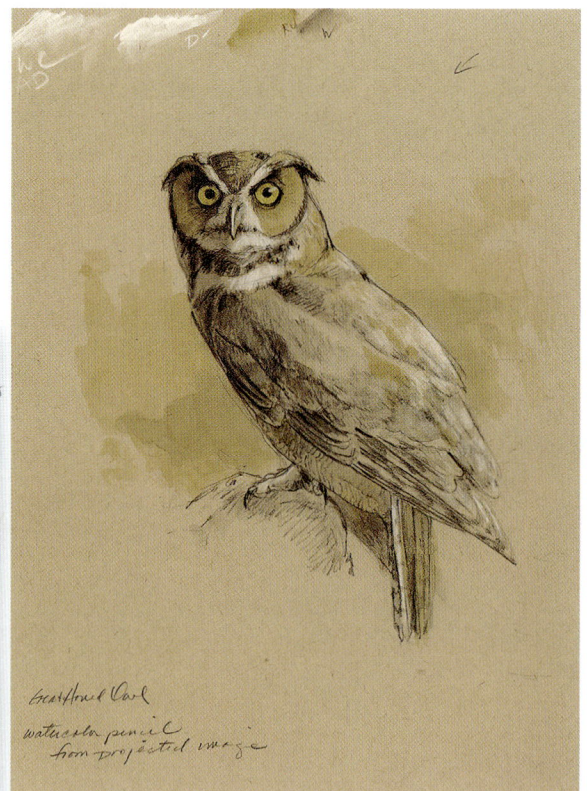

Graphite and Faber-Castell Albrecht Dürer watercolor pencils on Strathmore toned tan sketch paper

Select a pose and develop a fuller sketch with detailed landmarks and shadows.

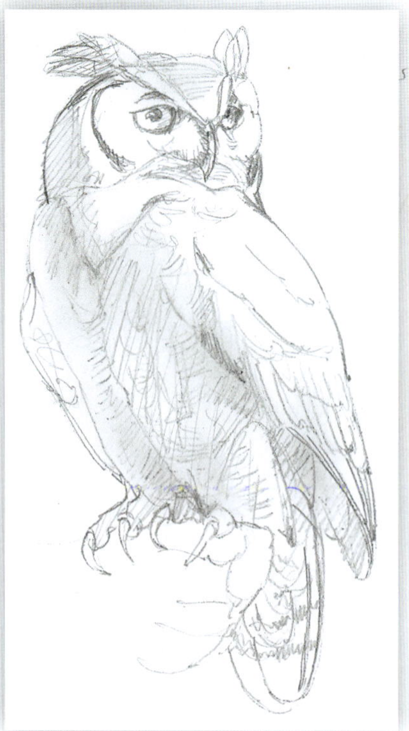

Graphite on bond paper

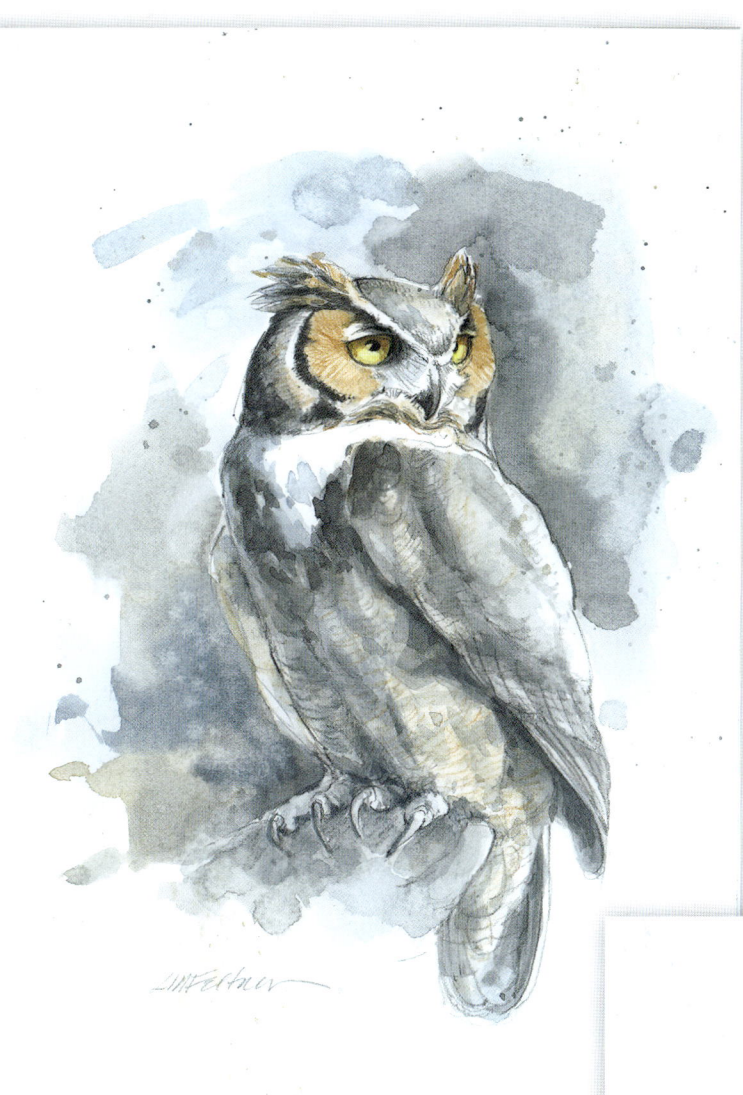

transparent watercolor on
Strathmore Bristol vellum

Select one sketch and transfer it to various
papers. Repeating the same sketch eliminates
the time spent creating a new pose and leaves
more time to experiment. Try manufacturer's
sample papers or trimmings from larger sheets.

With the freedom to try something new,
loosen up and try old familiar colors on new
papers, or dive into those new vivid colors just
purchased.

Derwent Inktense watercolor
pencil and PigmaMicron pen on
Multimedia Board

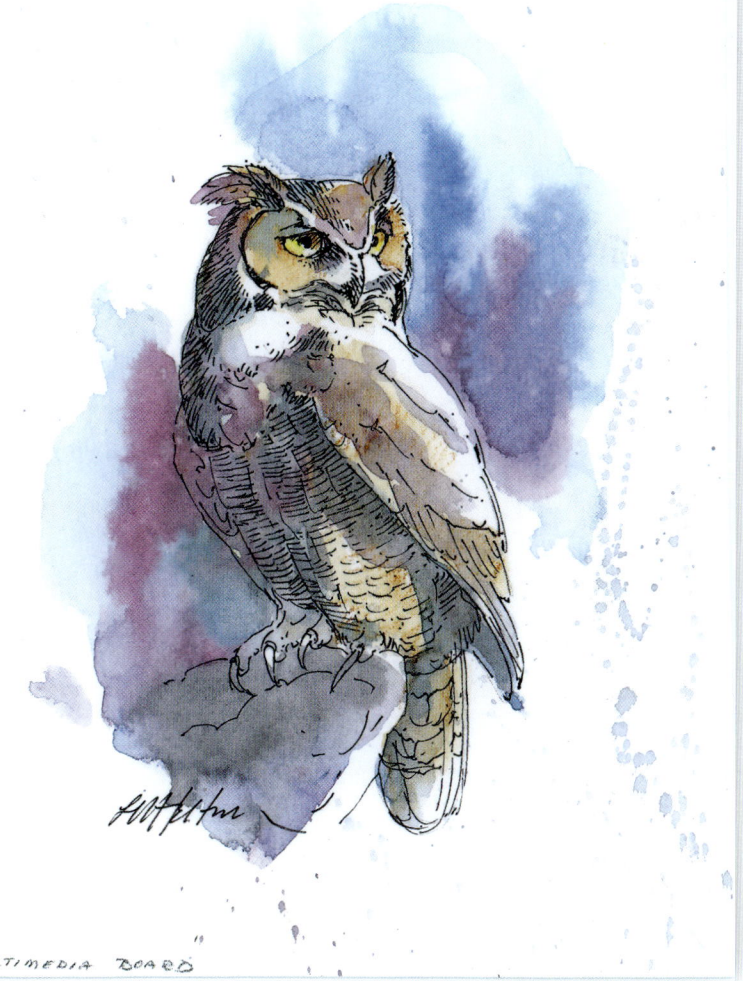

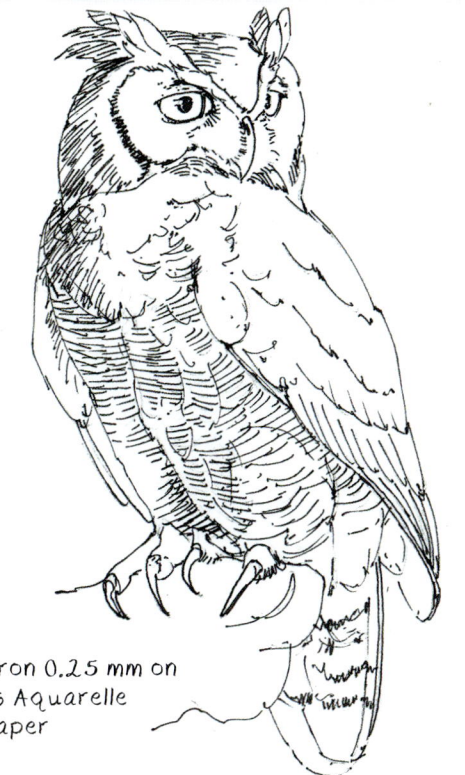

PigmaMicron 0.25 mm on
hot press Aquarelle
Arches paper

An Elegant Pair

Typically found in the tropics around the world, some species of trogons reach northward into Arizona. One species, Elegant Trogons, range from Guatemala to southern Arizona's sky islands. Here they are found in forested riparian canyons of oaks, pines, and sycamores, ranging from mid- to high-level elevations (2,000–6,000 ft or 610–1,829 m). They are one of the most sought-after species for birders in the United States.

Perched upright and motionless on a mid-canopy branch, they are often easily overlooked. Quietly observing their surroundings, their heads rotate slowly with almost reptilian deliberation. After spotting a tasty morsel, they leap into the air to snatch a flying insect or pluck a berry from a hanging cluster.

My goal was to portray a breeding pair. Research led me to find an active nest hole in Arizona Sycamores. I wanted to depict a nest hole that the birds had selected, and not one I had chosen for artistic license.

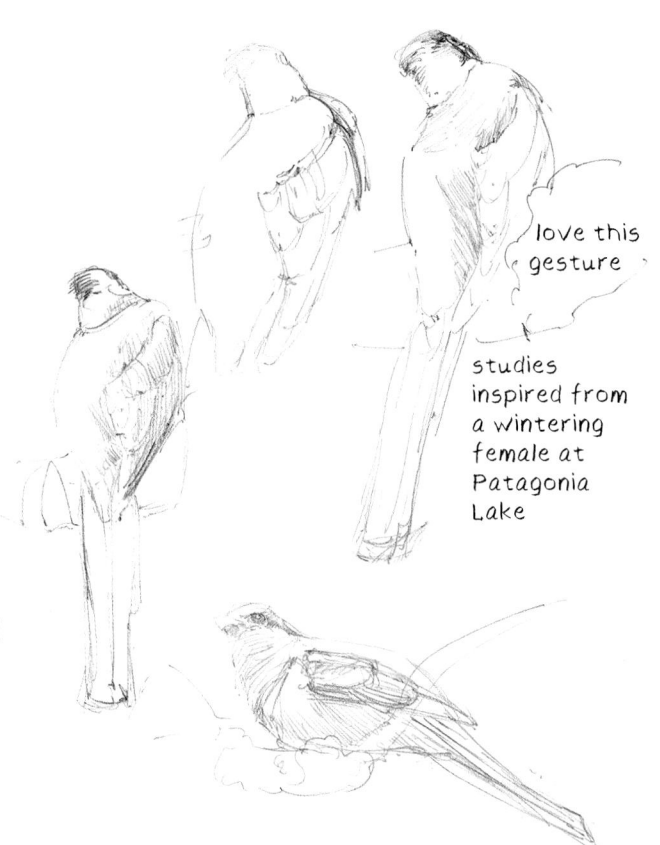

love this gesture

studies inspired from a wintering female at Patagonia Lake

First establish proportions, gesture, and balance. Details come later.

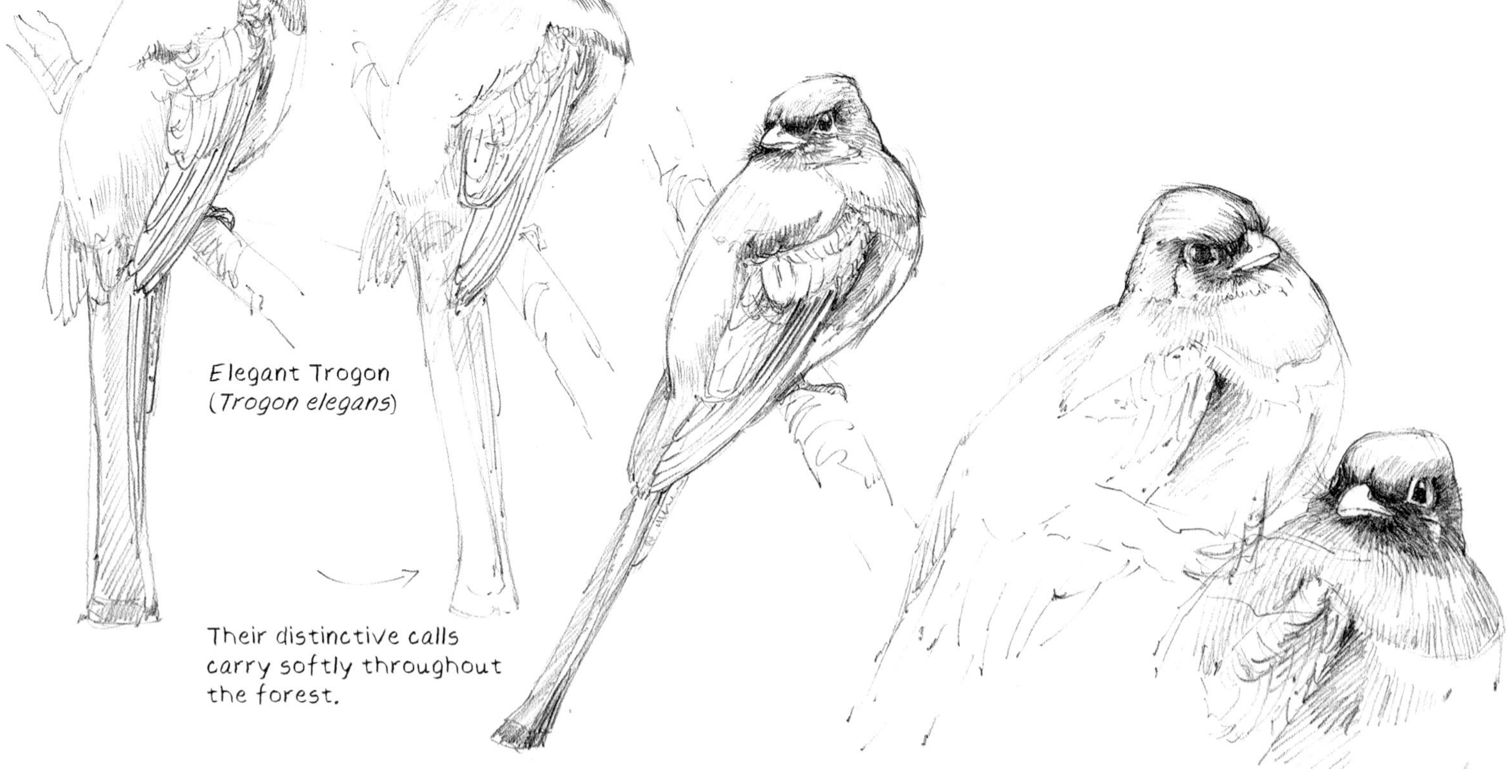

Elegant Trogon
(*Trogon elegans*)

Their distinctive calls carry softly throughout the forest.

Stout hooked bills capture large insects like katydids, cicadas, and caterpillars, and nutritious berries like chokecherry, grape, and hackberry.

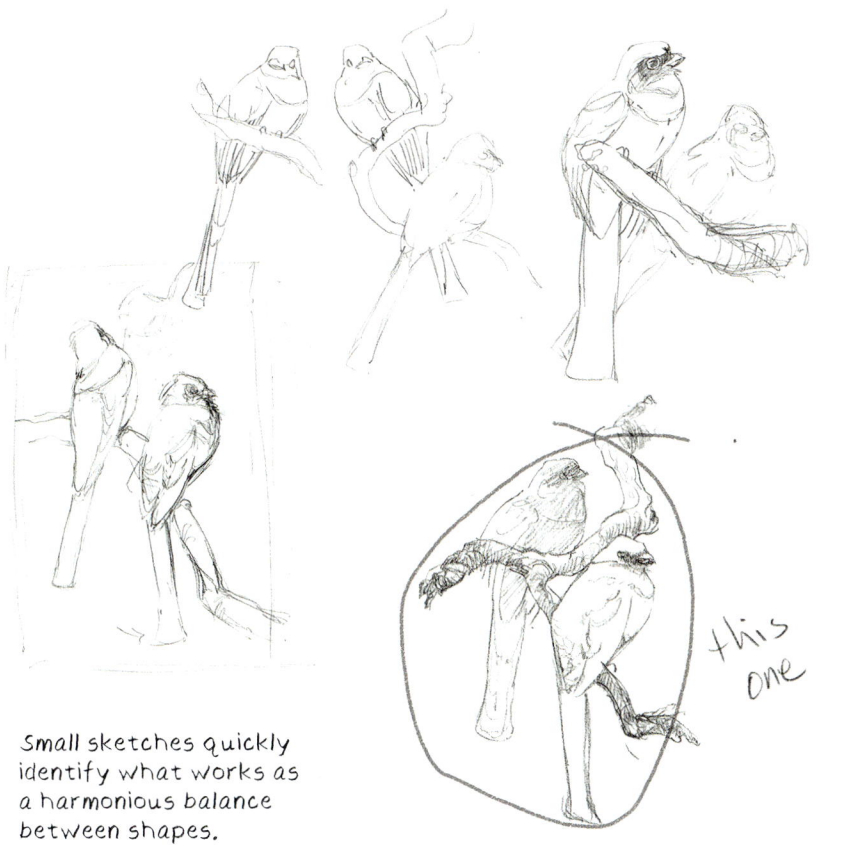

Small sketches quickly identify what works as a harmonious balance between shapes.

this one

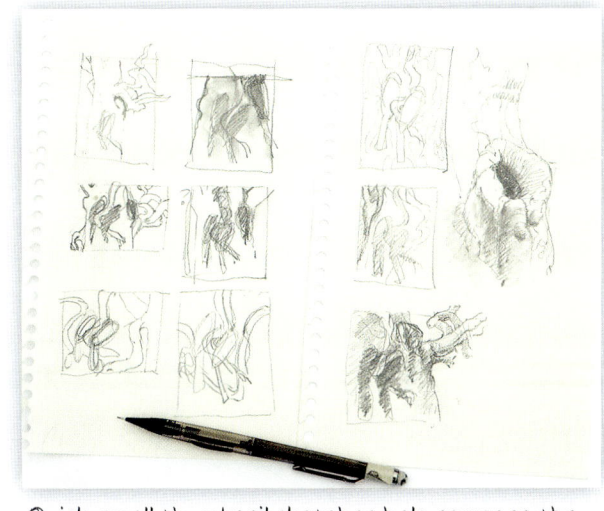

Quick, small thumbnail sketches help compose the pair and nest hole together as a unit.

Elegant Trogon, UWBM 82854a, male, May

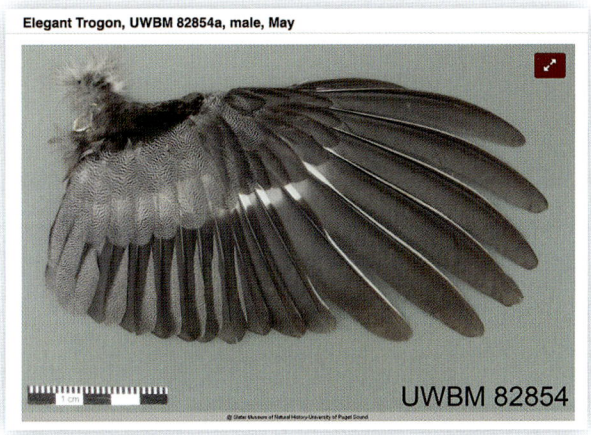

UWBM 82854

Count the number of primary and secondary wing feathers.

The Puget Sound Museum of Natural History has an online Wing & Tail Image Collection that is a great resource for scientists and artists alike. The zoom feature is superb! Reproduced with permission.

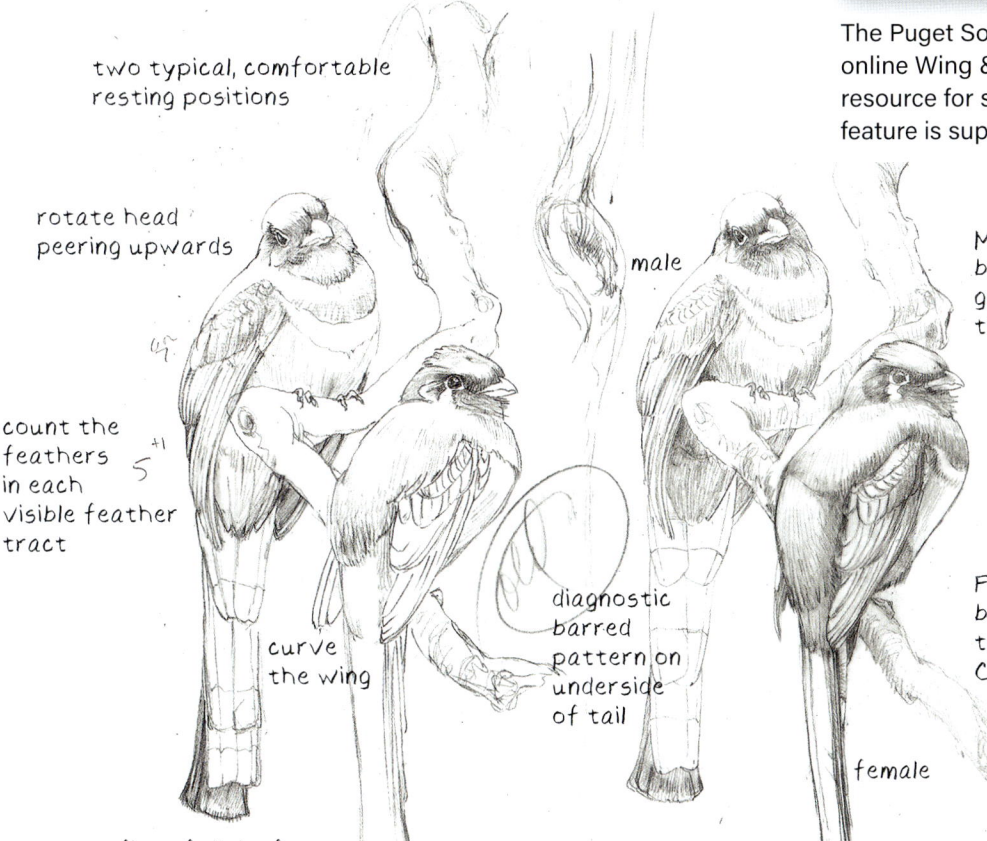

two typical, comfortable resting positions

rotate head peering upwards

count the feathers in each visible feather tract

curve the wing

first full draft

diagnostic barred pattern on underside of tail

male

female

final drawing

Male: Frontal view shows bright tropical reds and greens and fine barring on the underside of the tail.

Female: Subdued shades of beige and copper. Top side of tail describes its old name of Coppery-tailed Trogon.

Balancing Content Supports the Story

Composing the mated pair alongside their nest hole creates a triad of shapes. Adding sinuous curving branches provides reference to how the tree develops these curious holes.

Bizarre holes develop after branches break off and heal with sculpted shapes. Woodpeckers also excavate cavities, and many birds and mammals use them. I wondered if the strange nest hole would be recognizable to those unfamiliar with this tree. The decision to add a graceful curving branch helped describe the tree's character.

nest hole
Overlay 2

Drawing major elements on separate tracing paper overlays allows positioning of elements until satisfied with the alignment.

find an interesting branch
Overlay 1

typical branch
Overlay 3

Sliding the overlays shows options for the strongest composition.

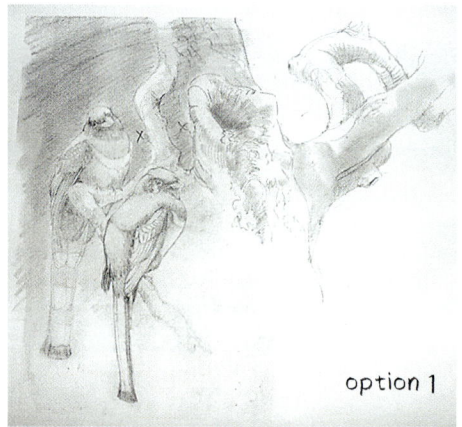

option 1

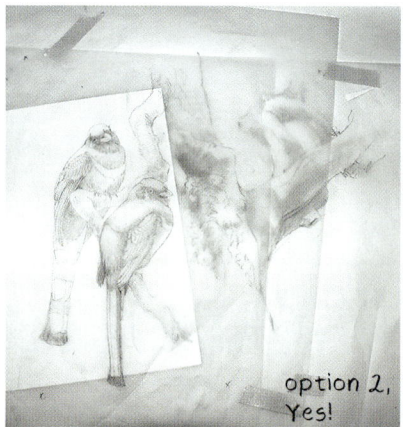

option 2,
Yes!

Positioning the birds closer to the nest hole reinforces the triad.

When the strongest composition is determined, the overlays are taped together and scanned.

The scanned pencil compositions are printed on thin 8 × 10 inch watercolor paper. Copies are a speedy way to avoid drawing it several times when used only for color testing.

Color mixing experiments aid in color selection, creating vibrant or pale areas, and color harmony. Gauging the humidity of the day is helpful if painting in watercolor.

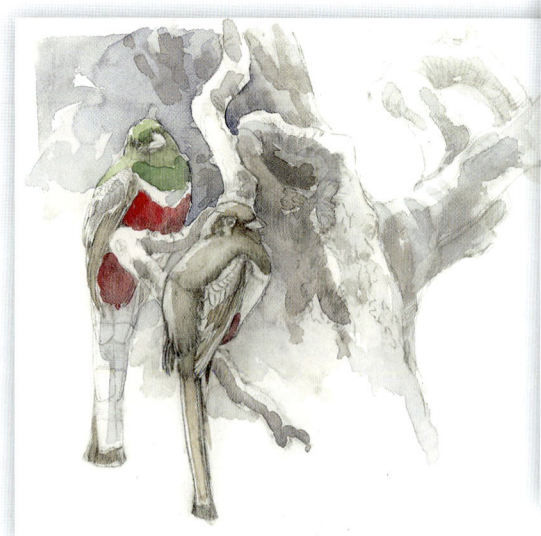

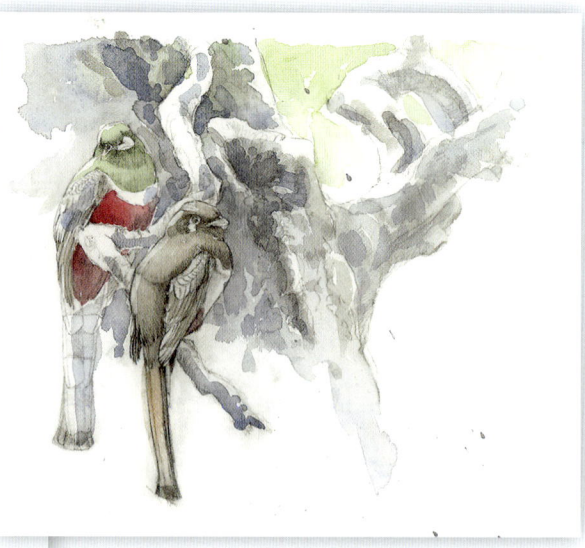

Details That Matter

Arizona Sycamore (*Platanus wrightii*)

Large, velvety leaves. How many lobes? Does one side feel different than the other?

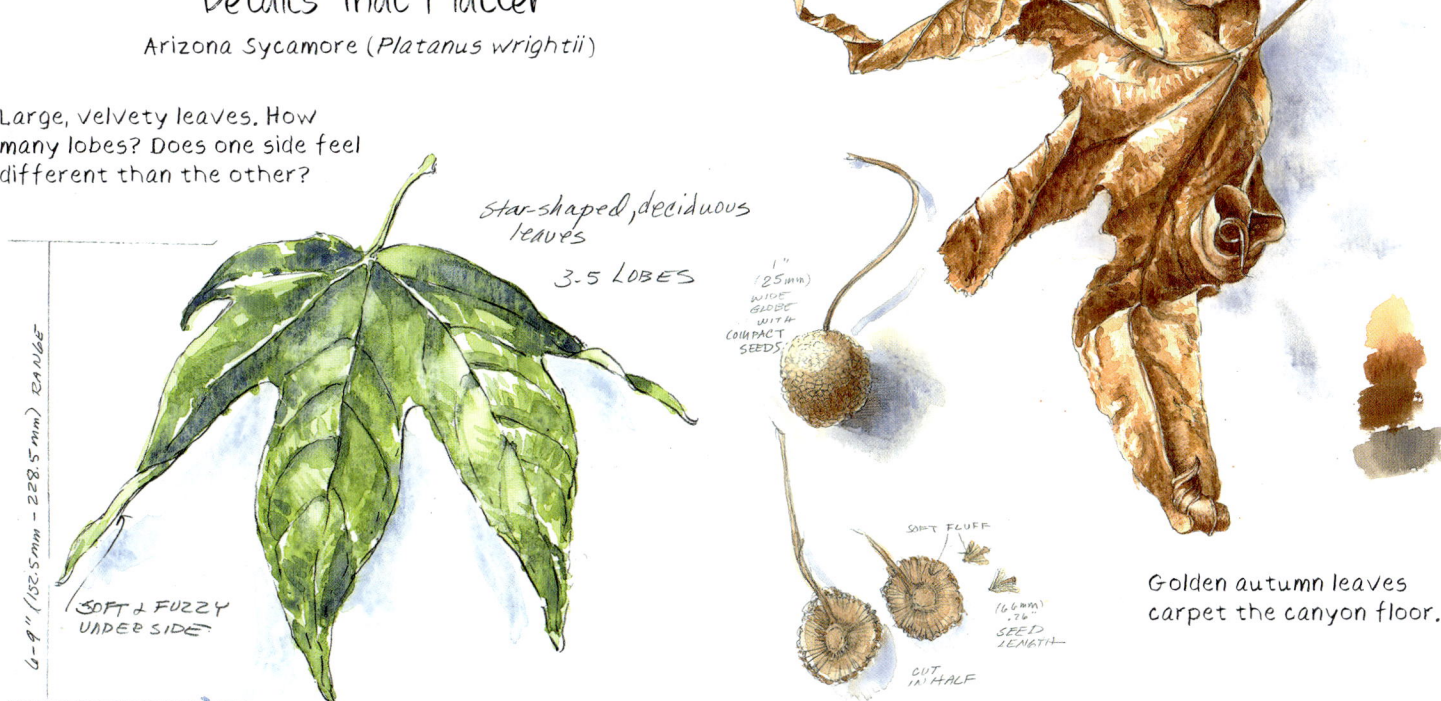

Star-shaped, deciduous leaves

3-5 LOBES

SOFT & FUZZY UNDER SIDE

6-9" (152.5mm - 228.5 mm) RANGE

1" (25mm) WIDE GLOBE WITH COMPACT SEEDS

SOFT FLUFF

(1.6 mm) .06" SEED LENGTH

CUT IN HALF

Golden autumn leaves carpet the canyon floor.

You could write a whole book on the animals that benefit from the sycamores.

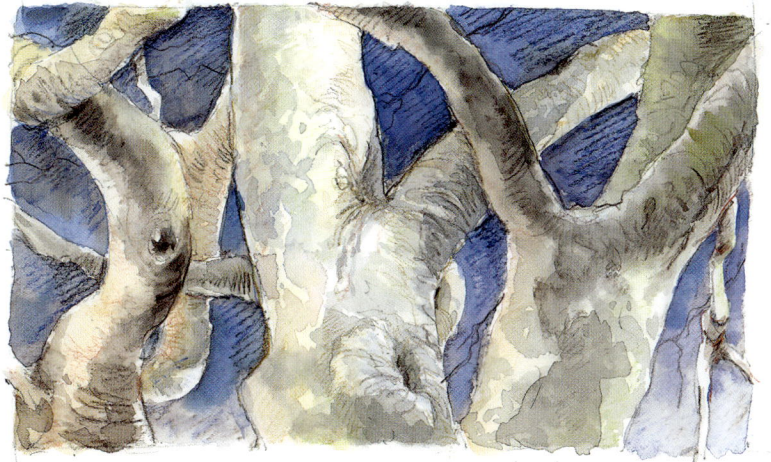

watercolor pencil study

Majestic to 80 ft (24.4 m) high, it is a striking tree with a huge trunk and spreading, sculptural limbs. The outer gray bark flakes off to reveal a jigsaw pattern of gray, tan, ochre, pink, and white.

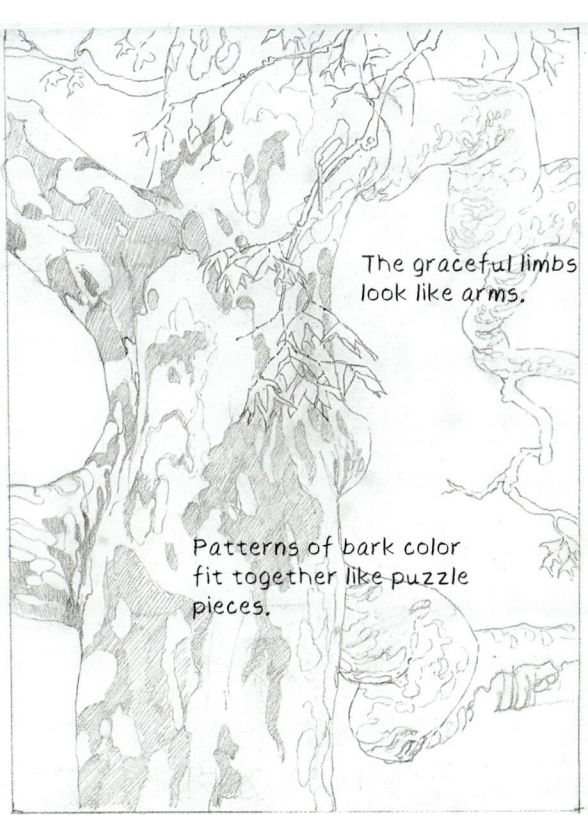

The graceful limbs look like arms.

Patterns of bark color fit together like puzzle pieces.

Final pencil sketch on tracing paper, 22 × 30 in (55.88 × 76.2 cm). Ready to transfer to watercolor paper at 100 percent size using graphite transfer paper.

There are several ways I transfer images onto the final paper. Draft sizes vary, and it is quick to scan, scale to size, and print them on bond paper. If enlarged, I splice the letter-sized sheets together. For paintings on heavy watercolor paper, a sheet of Saral graphite paper is sandwiched between the laser print above and the final paper below. My stylus is a metal, fine-point pen that leaves crisp lines and little graphite. A thinner, final paper is taped to a window and is traced directly from the bond print below. I abandoned projecting from a computer because it may slightly keystone the image, and the tiniest fraction will distort my accurate proportions.

Swatches of bark colors. Do colors change after a rain?

"Elegant Pair"

After moving to southeast Arizona, I began to paint the plants and animals that flourish here in the Huachuca Mountains. In spring, Elegant Trogons arrive in the riparian canyons. I portrayed them in the strikingly beautiful Arizona Sycamore where they frequently find nesting holes. Trogons calmly settle on a branch and slowly rotate their heads to look for a cluster of berries. The subtle coloration of the female and the rich plumage of the male are perfect for watercolor. The sycamore's pale blended colors and smooth texture and the sculptural shapes of its limbs make it one of my favorite trees to paint. I located the pair next to a nest hole and included a sinuous branch that illustrates the properties of growth that produce such unusual nesting cavities.

Elegant Trogons (*Trogon elegans*) and Arizona Sycamore (*Platanus wrightii*)

Elegant Pair, 16.5 × 15 in (41.91 × 38.1 cm), transparent watercolor, Sonoran Experience Collection, courtesy of the Arizona-Sonora Desert Museum Art Institute.

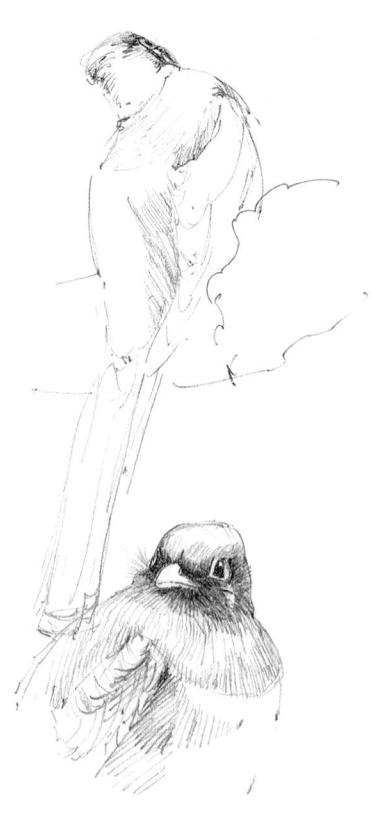

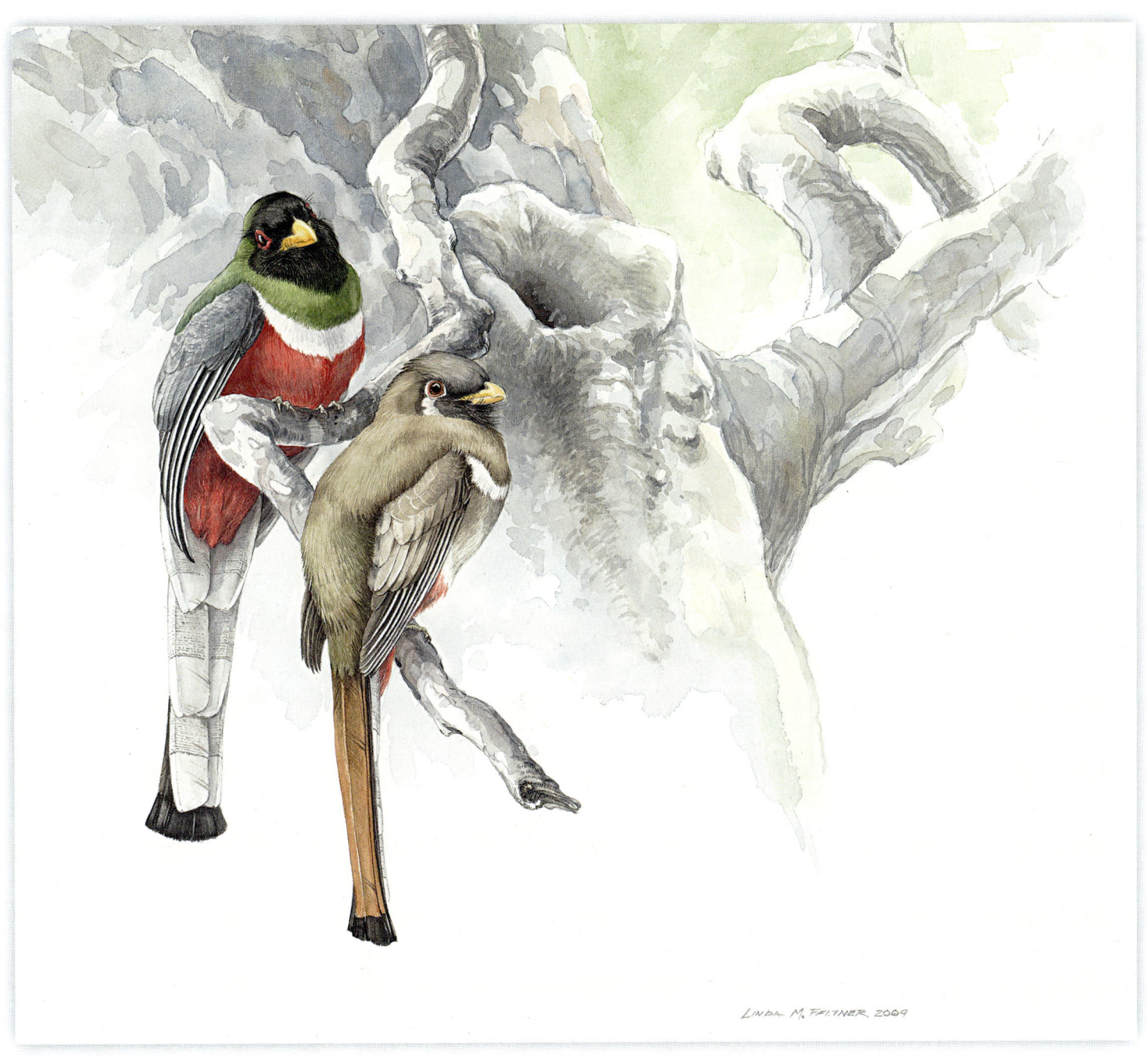

Linda M. Feltner 2009

"Sycamore Sentinel"

Arizona Sycamores are majestic sentinels in the forested canyons of southeast Arizona's sky islands. Preferring canyons with permanent streams, mature trees can reach eighty feet tall with enormous girths. The constantly shedding bark reveals a smooth surface with myriad subtle colors. Strikingly beautiful, with sinuous limbs and curious bumps and shapes, it is one of my favorite trees to paint.

To emphasize its prodigious size, a male Elegant Trogon, about a foot in length, sits high in the branches.

Arizona Sycamores (*Platanus wrightii*) and
Elegant Trogon (*Trogon elegans*)

Sycamore Sentinel, 22 × 30 in (55.88 × 76.2 cm),
transparent watercolor.

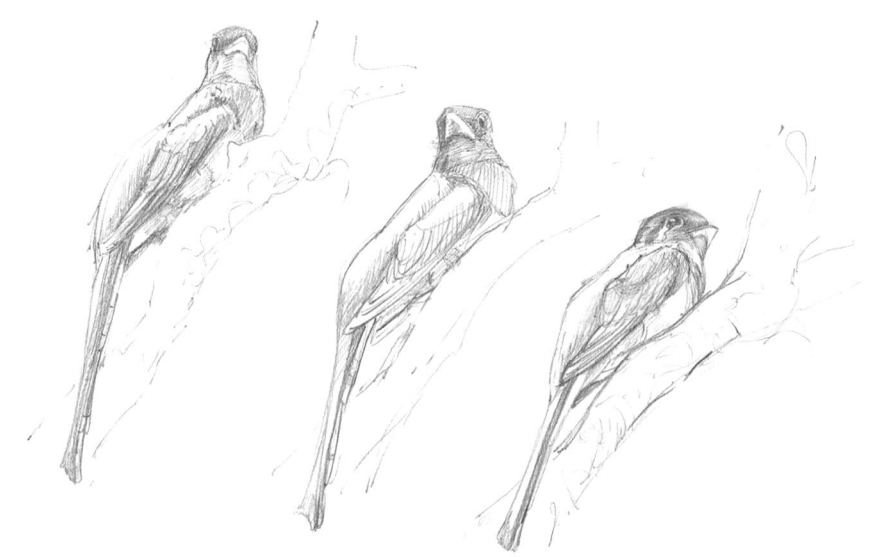

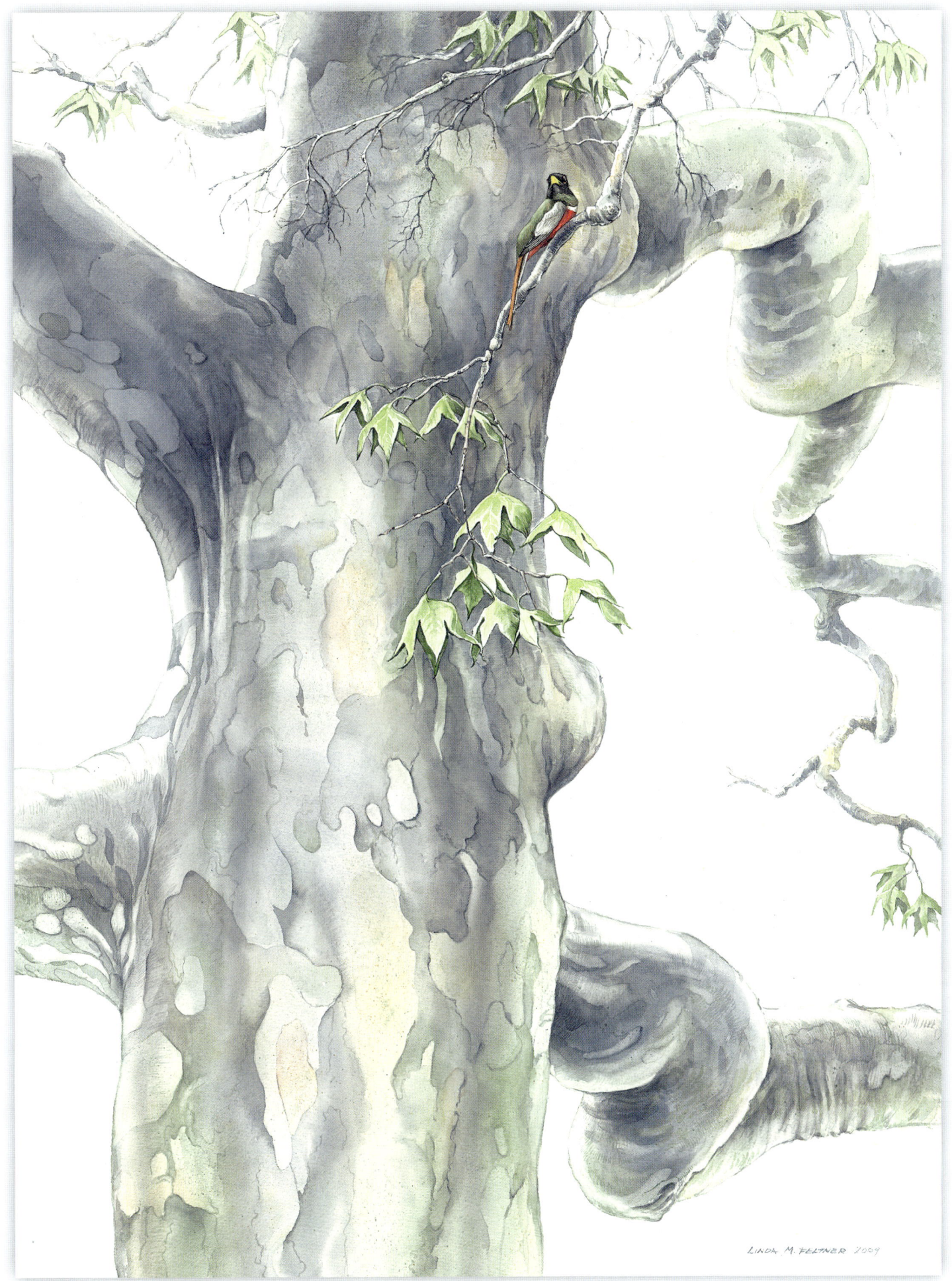

LINDA M. FELTNER 2004

The Curious Quail

It's an exciting event when Montezuma Quail visit the yard. A dripping water feature is perfect for ground-loving birds, as well as lizards, foxes, and deer. These small quail secretively weave through tall grasses to cautiously appear at the water's edge.

Observed from inside the studio, they relax under overhanging sage bushes. After some slight wriggling, they create a shallow depression where they rest concealed in dappled shadows. A chance to study them like this would be impossible for me in the field. Although the face pattern is bold, their intricate camouflage hides them perfectly in the grassy pine-oak woodlands.

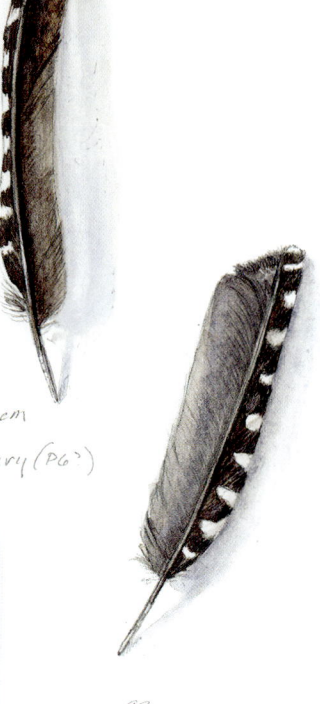

10.3 cm
primary (P6?)

9.3 cm
primary (P3?)

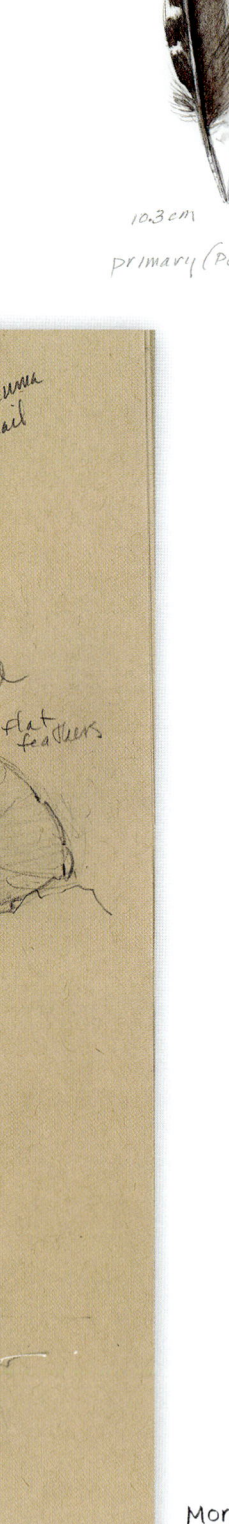

Montezuma Quail

larger head

flat feathers

feathers flattened on head

Montezuma Quail (*Cyrtonyx montezumae*), graphite and white gouache, Strathmore toned tan sketchbook.

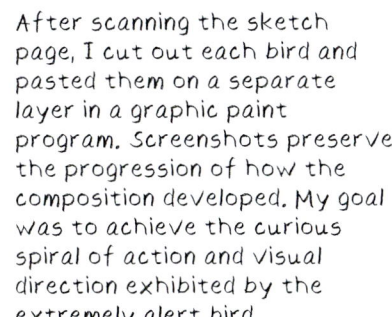

They do not leap up when first alerted to a predator but crouch to avoid detection.

One male was feeding in the open when alerted to my dog, who was casually returning to the studio. First, the bird stretched up for a good look. Instead of bolting for the bushes, it slowly rotated position following the circular approach of the dog and spiraled into the lowest profile possible while the dog passed the quail within fifteen feet. Reaching the studio, the dog never knew it was there. As the bird faced me, I was captivated by the famous facial pattern and found the spark behind the story.

After scanning the sketch page, I cut out each bird and pasted them on a separate layer in a graphic paint program. Screenshots preserve the progression of how the composition developed. My goal was to achieve the curious spiral of action and visual direction exhibited by the extremely alert bird.

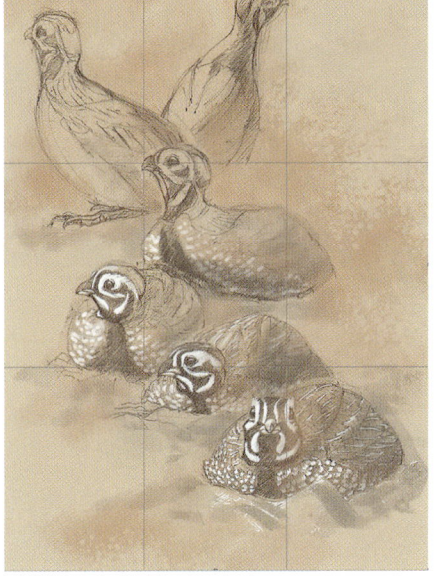

As infrequent visitors to the studio, they bring a wide smile to my face each time I turn my head and see them at the drip. I never thought I'd fall in love with a chicken.

"The Full Monte": Work in Progress

Ink or graphite with white highlights brings an earthy, organic feel to sketches on toned paper. To maintain that style, I considered staining watercolor paper with tea or coffee. Not knowing if this was archival, the use of a burnt umber wash with variations of salt and paint spatter appealed as an easy solution. I painted several sheets and selected one for this painting, saving the others for future use.

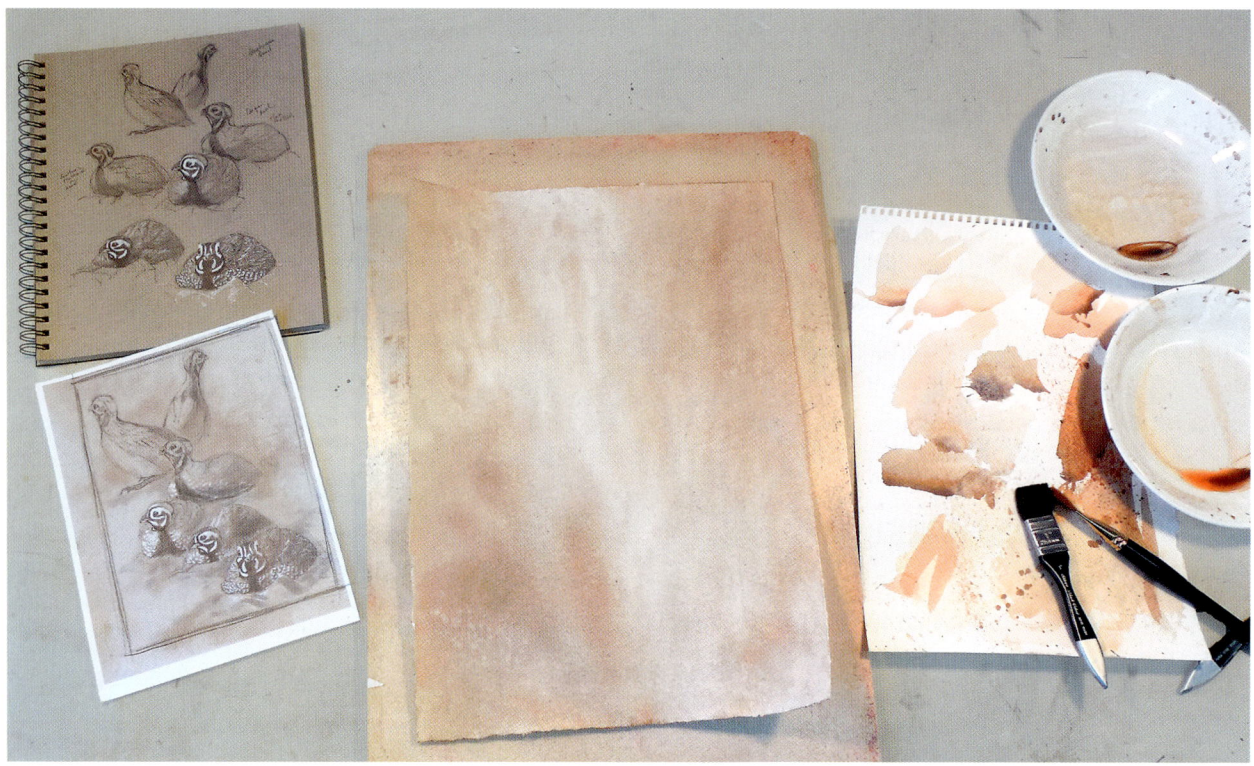

A half-sheet of Fabriano Artistico watercolor paper was thoroughly soaked with plain water. A 2-inch brush was used to float watery pigment onto wet paper and tilted so the paint would run. Small white bowls are handy for mixing large amounts of various colors that will softly mingle on moist paper. Smaller brushes, 1 inch flat and #8 round, were used to spatter.

15 x 22 in (38.1 x 55.88 cm), 140 lb (300 gsm) cold press Fabriano Artistico paper.

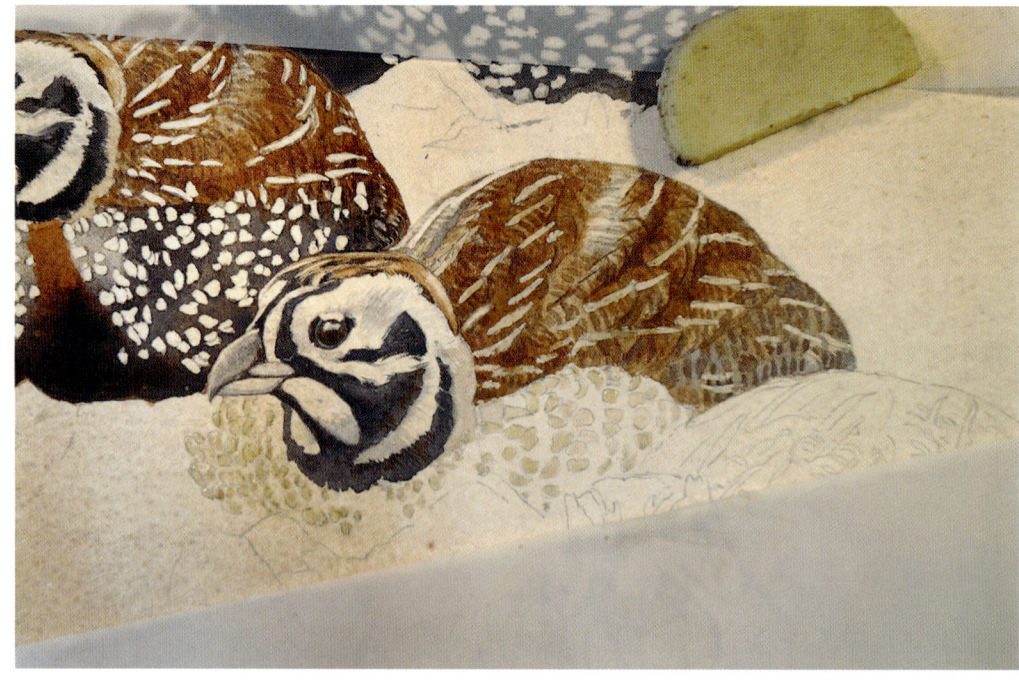

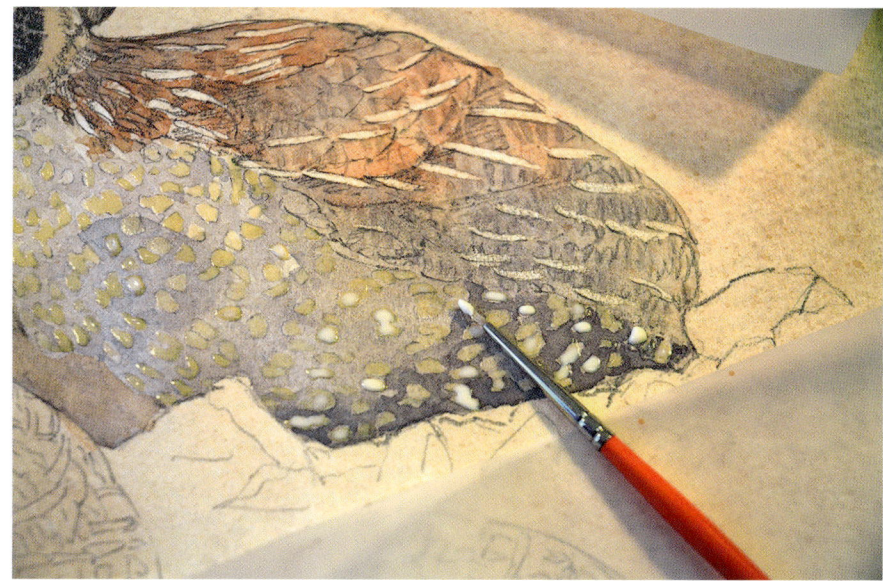

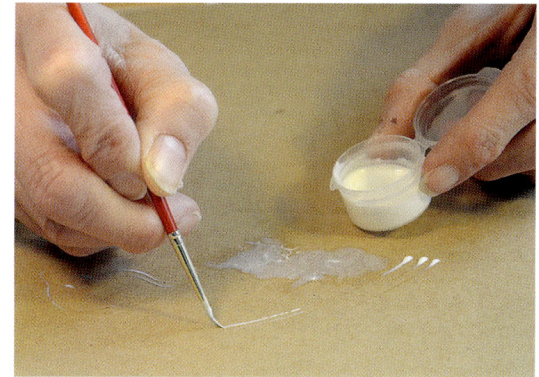

Masking fluid applied to the feather pattern preserves areas that should remain the lightest. A size 3x0 synthetic brush gives precise control for the individual shapes of spots and dashes. A small air-tight container is convenient for frequent dipping. It allows the larger container it came in to stay fresh. Once the latex meets air, it immediately dries. Keep a cup of soapy water handy to frequently clean the brush, as it easily clogs.

I applied the masking fluid to one bird at a time, covering the rest with protective tracing paper. After the fluid dried thoroughly, darker washes allowed enough contrast to remove the masked areas. The latex did not remain on the paper for more than twenty-four hours and was removed with a rubber cement pick-up eraser. To reclaim the white on the face, I gently lifted the background pigment off with a thirsty brush.

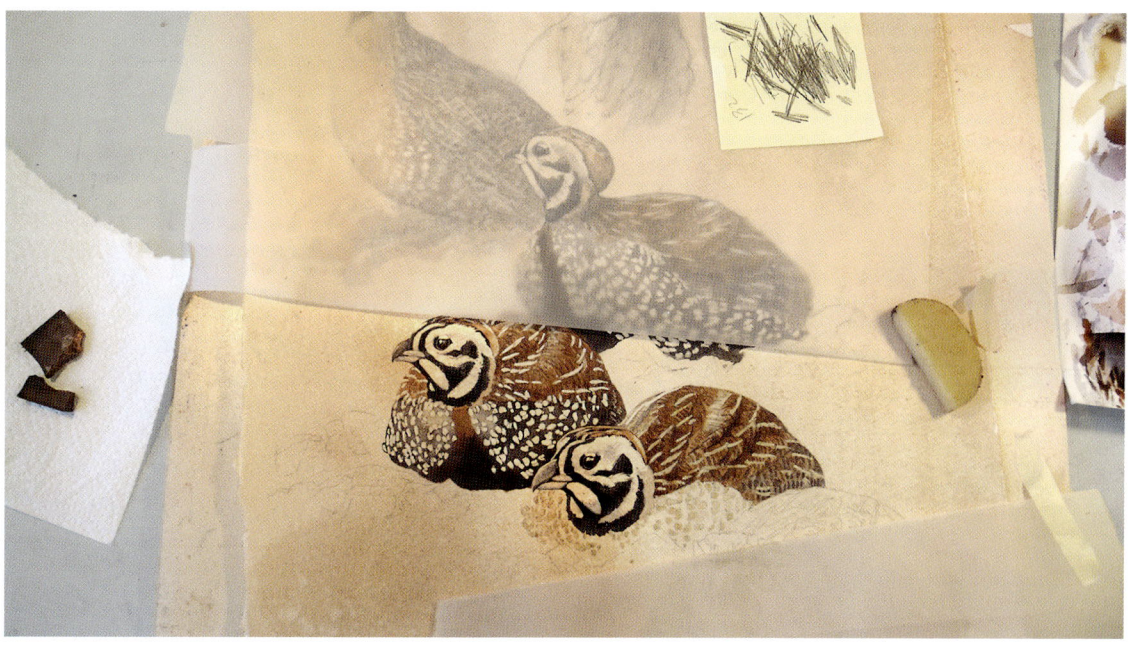

Dark chocolate seems to appear in several of my work-in-progress photos, so it must be an essential part of my process.

"The Full Monte"

A striking denizen of open, grassy woodlands in the mountains of southeastern Arizona, the Montezuma Quail is extremely secretive and expertly camouflaged. Three pairs came to the studio water drip saucer. The male wears the harlequin pattern, and I could not distinguish the individuals. However, I could tell the females apart by subtle differences in their coloration: a paler face, broader and brighter eyebrow line, or darker cheek patch. The bird was once known as "Fool's Quail," for its habit of crouching when alarmed. The male shown here exhibits its ability to crouch and freeze while following the circling movement of a potential predator until viewed fully from the front.

Montezuma Quail (*Cyrtonyx montezumae*) and
Ground Spider (Gnaphosidae)

The Full Monte, 13 × 18.5 in (33.02 × 46.99 cm),
graphite and transparent watercolor, Sonoran
Experience Collection, courtesy of the Arizona-Sonora
Desert Museum Art Institute.

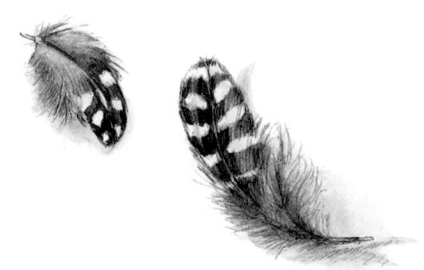

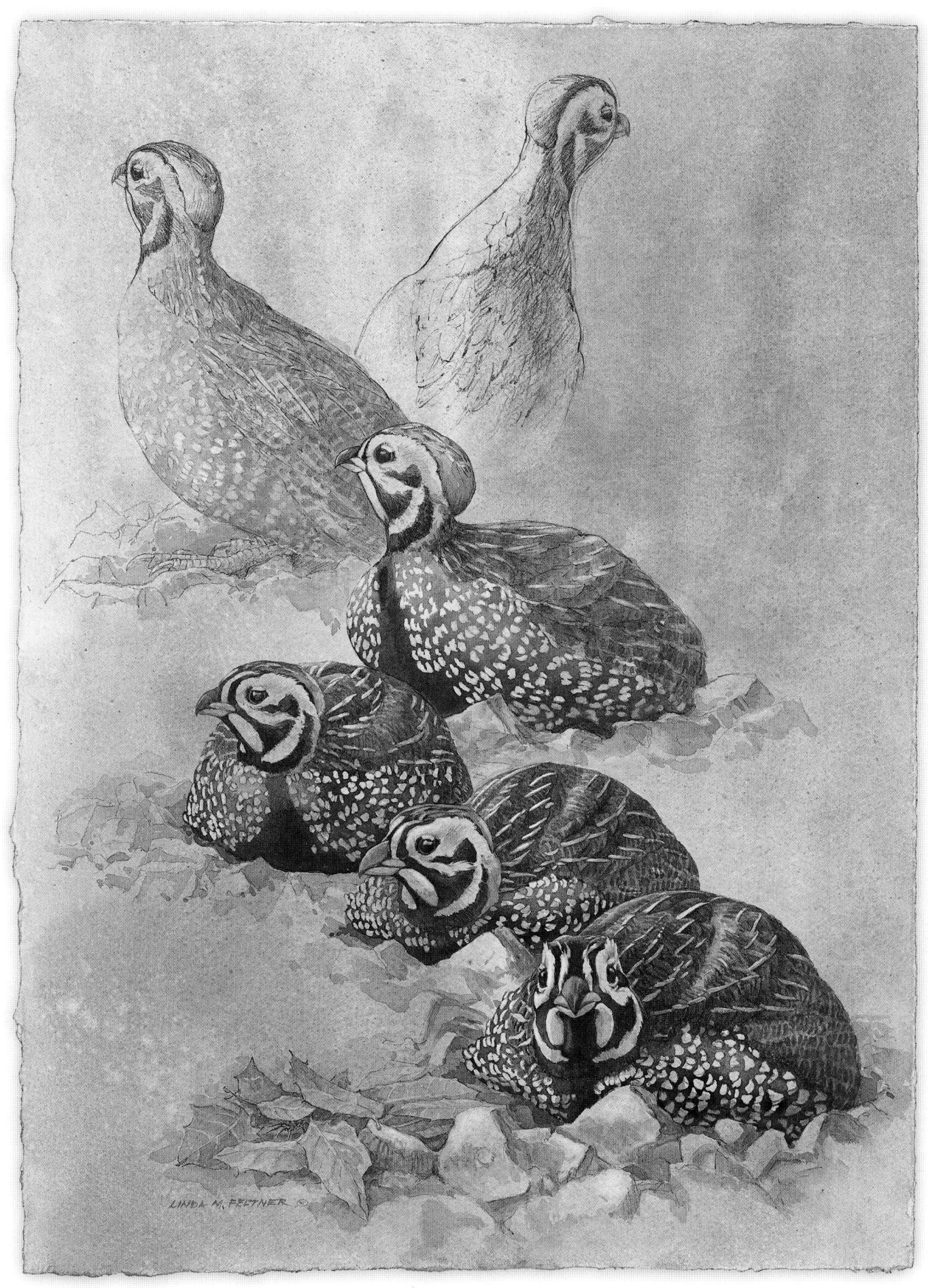

LINDA M. FELTNER ©

"Ladies First"

The courting call of the Montezuma Quail is as elusive as the bird itself. Descending whistles emanate from within grassy woodlands, announcing that spring has come to the mountain foothills. It's not easy to catch a glimpse of them. The intricate markings of both sexes provide exquisite camouflage, creating the male's harlequin pattern and the female's delicate cloak of buff and umber. They do not readily flush when disturbed but quickly slip away into the cover or crouch immobile until the danger has passed. At dawn, the male stands sentry as his lady sips from a pool.

Montezuma Quail (*Cyrtonyx montezumae*) and
Harvester Ant (*Pogonomyrmex maricopa*)

Ladies First, 14.5 × 21 in (36.83 × 53.34 cm), transparent watercolor, Sonoran Experience Collection, courtesy of the Arizona-Sonora Desert Museum Art Institute.

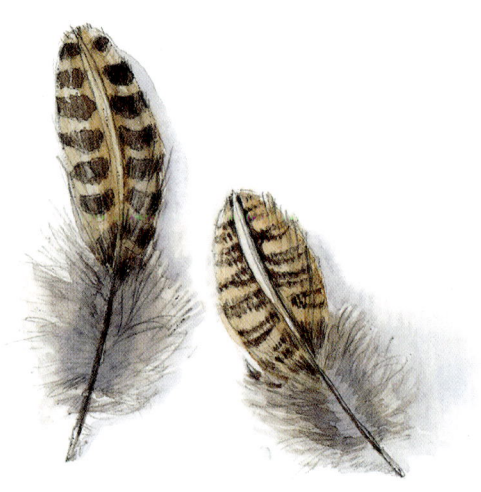

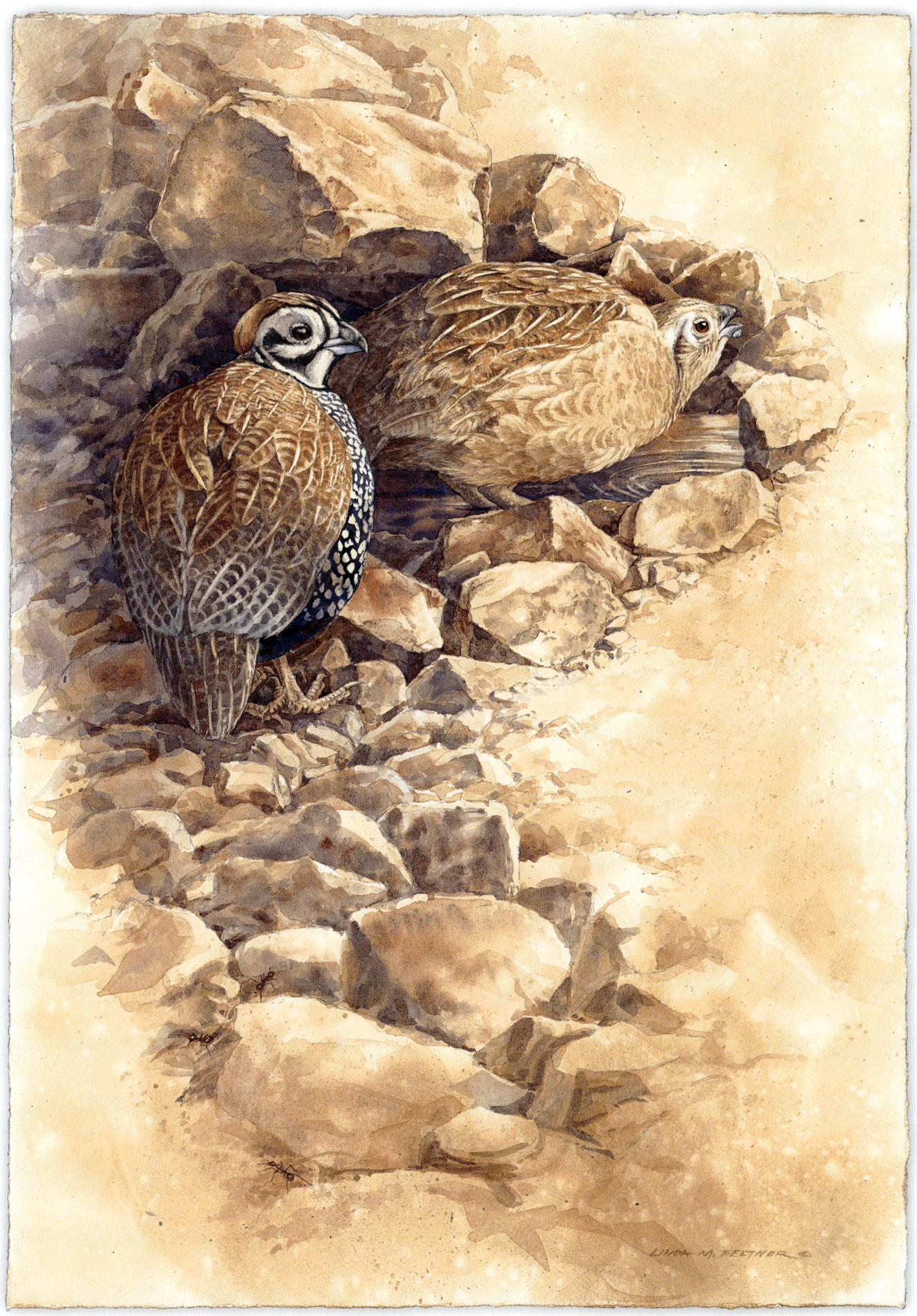

"Manzanita Afternoon—Gambel's Quail": Work in Progress

The Gambel's Quail is the most common quail to visit our wooded yard. A compact ground-dwelling bird, it sports a forward-facing feathered topknot that nods when it parades upright on its short legs. Strong feet scratch the soil to uncover seeds and berries.

Famous for bolting into the air when predators approach too closely, the bird's startle factor gets my heart pumping! Their rounded wings provide a rocket-like take-off, but they do not fly far.

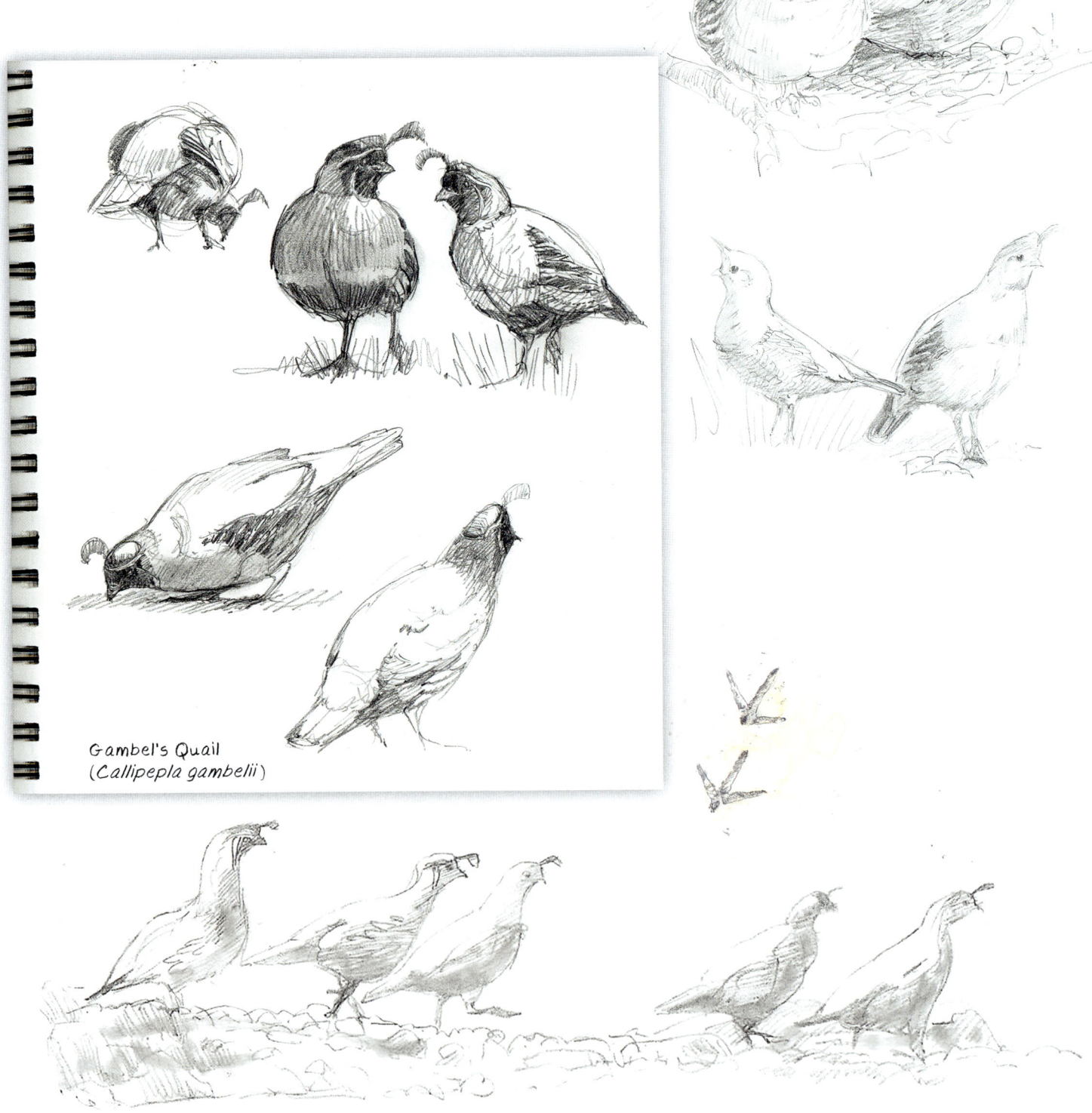

Gambel's Quail
(*Callipepla gambelii*)

Gregarious coveys scurry through the grasses, pausing to feed and rest beneath the leafy manzanita bushes. Pointleaf Manzanitas are among my favorite shrubs with their maroon and gray bark. Lithe and supple, the smooth limbs are a richly colored accent to the green leaves and red berries.

This manzanita grows between the studio and house where the quail often gather. Four o'clock in the afternoon was perfect for the light and shadows to lead the eye through the painting.

sketches with morning light
and shadows

Pointleaf Manzanita
(*Arctostaphylos pungens*)

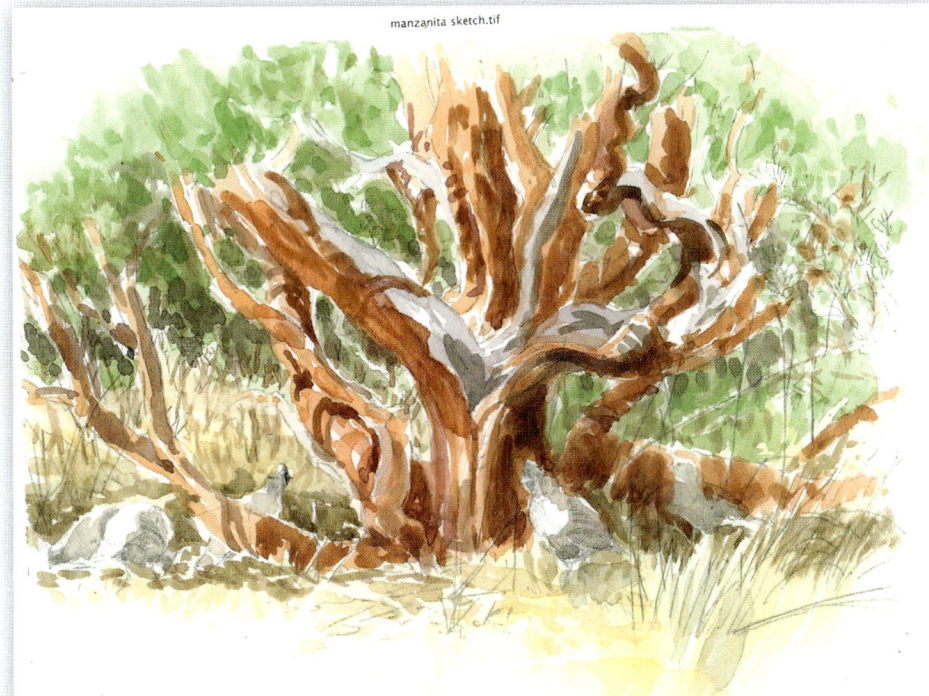

manzanita sketch.tif

The final composition is scanned and printed onto student-grade, lightweight watercolor paper. This is a quick way to create preparatory color studies without drawing them multiple times. It simply saves time, especially when outside with rapidly changing light. These color studies allow me to experiment with color mixing within the actual design. They also allow me to determine humidity and how juicy the washes should be for the desired watercolor technique.

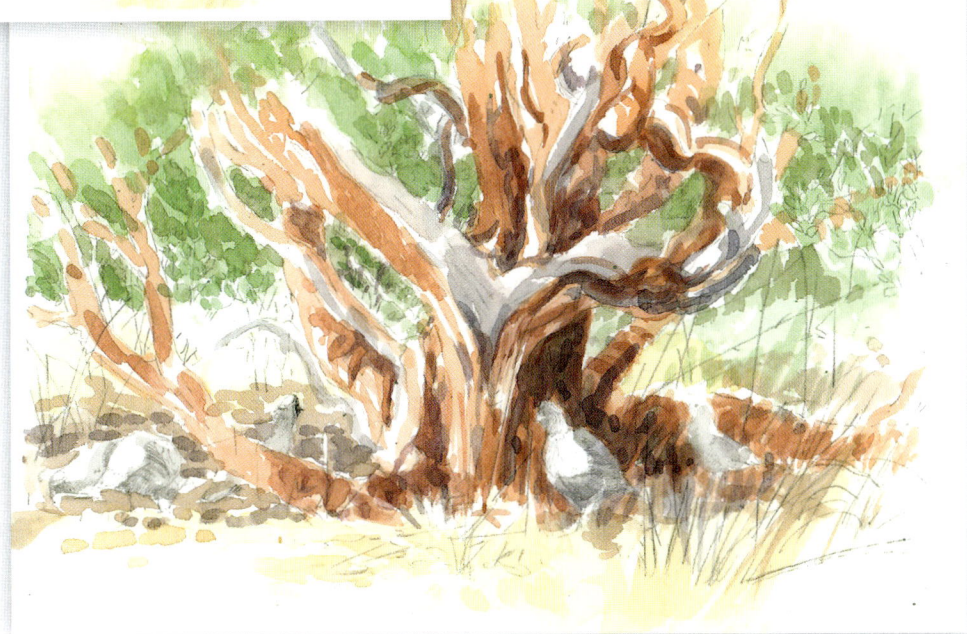

nita sketch.tif

8 x 10 in (20.32 x 25.40 cm), Strathmore #400 watercolor paper.

"Manzanita Afternoon–Gambel's Quail"

A flock of Gambel's Quail rushes across the open grass to gather in the shade of this old Pointleaf Manzanita that grows between the house and studio. The smooth, curved limbs with their curious stripes of gray and maroon make this a striking subject to paint in watercolor. The sun-dappled and spontaneous nature of the quail moving beneath their shelter sparked the story. While they peck and scratch, a Tarantula Hawk wasp also searches among the plant duff. The quail soon leave this camouflage and scurry across the grass toward other safe covers.

Pointleaf Manzanita (*Arctostaphylos pungens*), Gambel's Quail (*Callipepla gambelii*), and Tarantula Hawk (*Hemipepsis* sp.)

Manzanita Afternoon–Gambel's Quail, 22 × 30 in (55.88 × 76.20 cm), transparent watercolor.

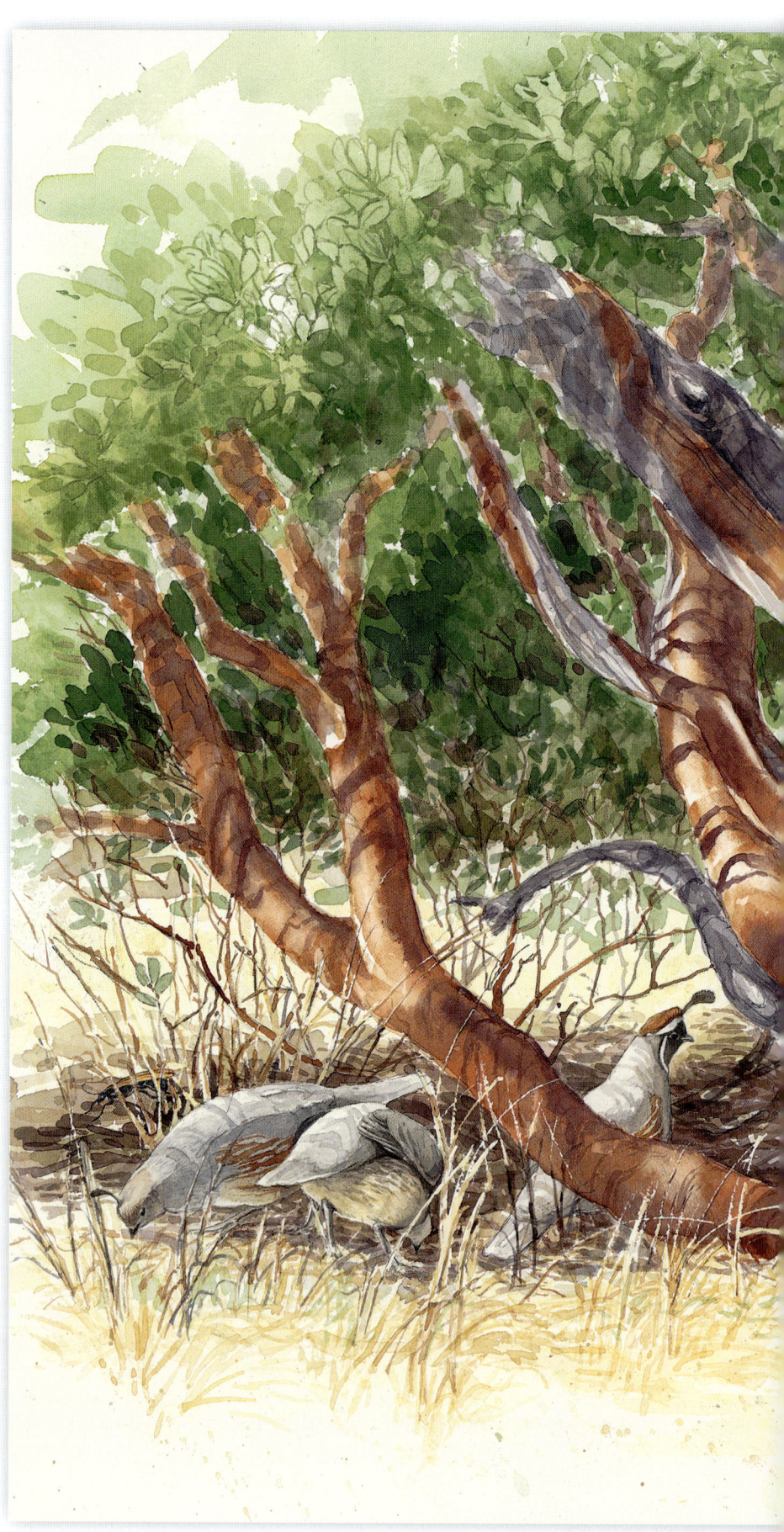

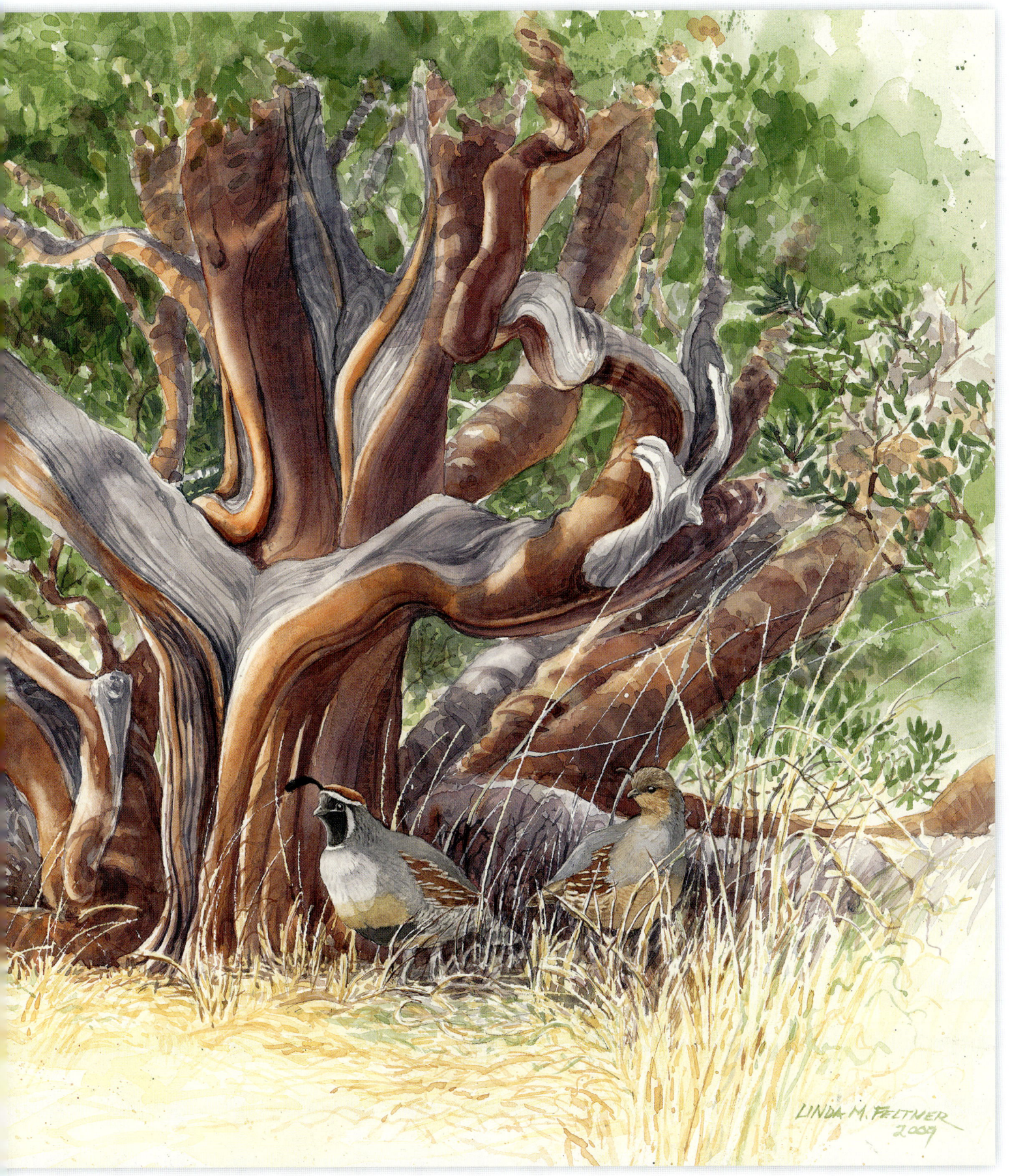

LINDA M. FELTNER
2009

49

"Saguaro Sentinel": At First Glance

On a late evening walk in the Sonoran Desert, I came upon a desiccated Saguaro cactus, a perfect subject for a painting. All it needed was a tiny roosting owl and a camouflaged insect. Imagine the owl's sleepy eyes awakening from a daytime rest and waiting for night to begin its hunt for moths.

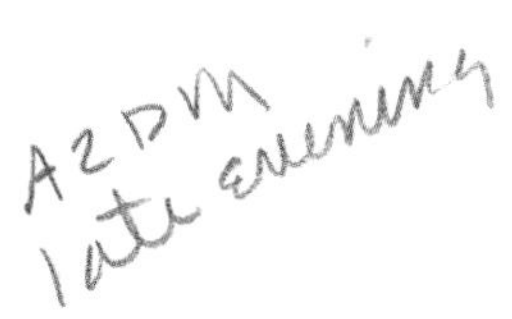

A2DM
late evening

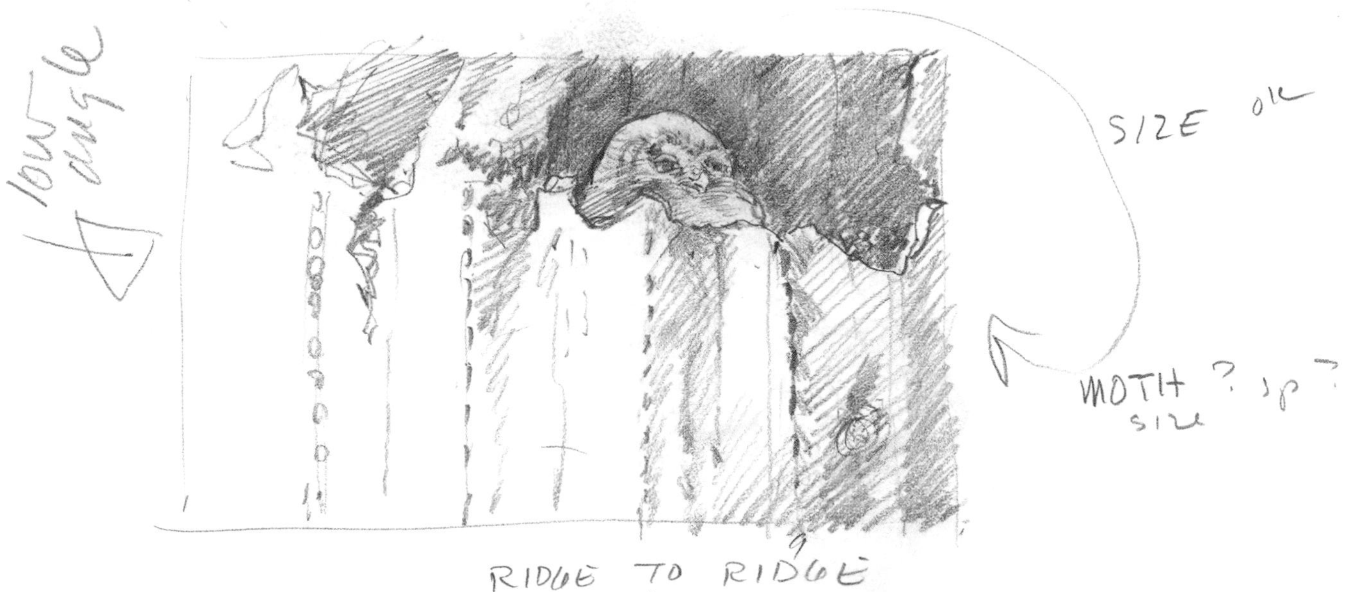

low angle

SIZE ok

MOTH ? sp?
size

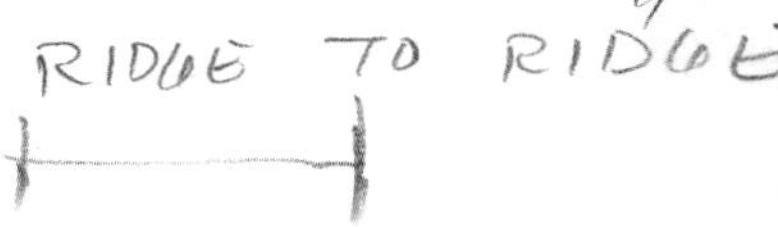

RIDGE TO RIDGE

The ridges on the surface, curving into the distance, reminded me of a mountain range seen from an airplane.

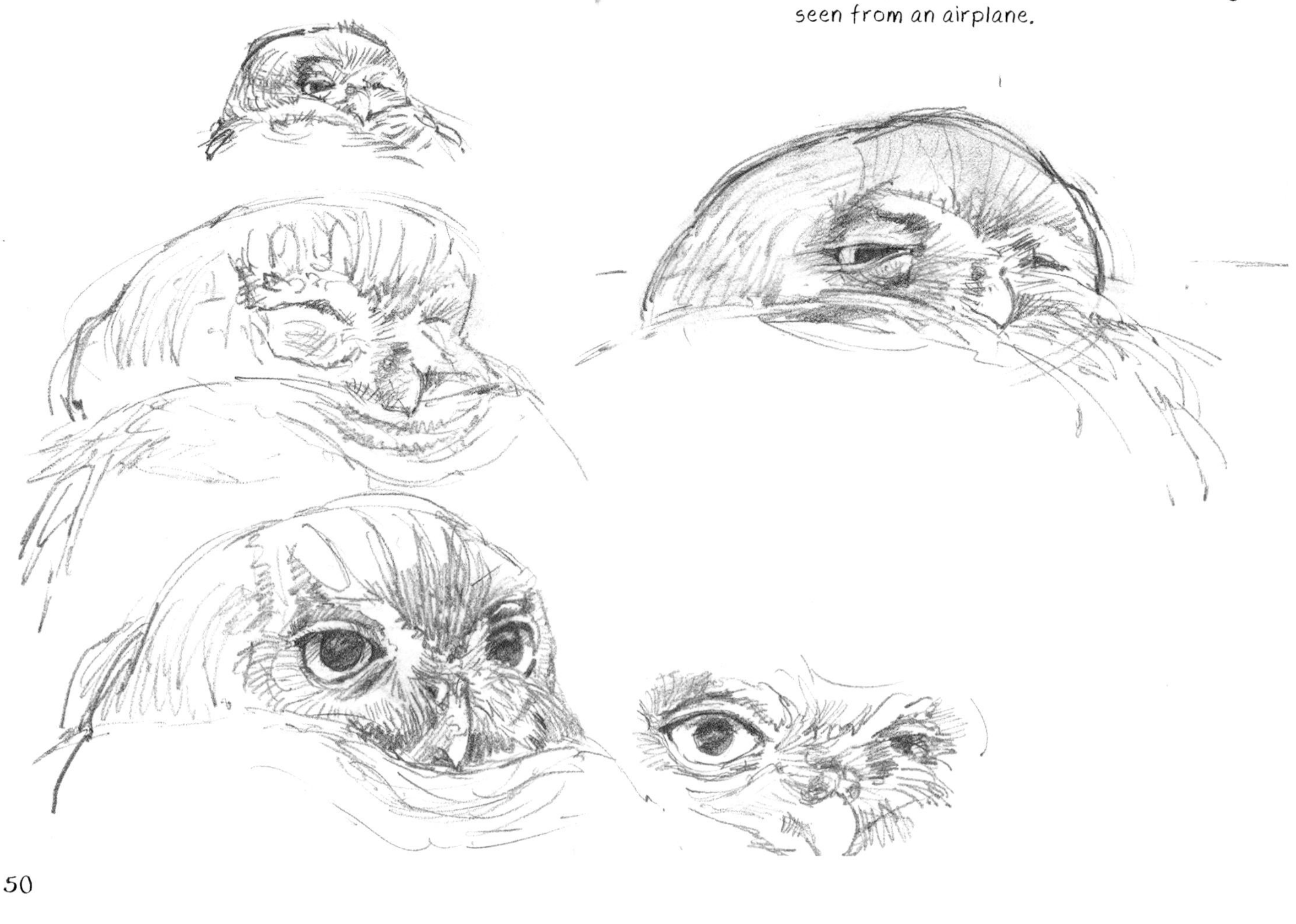

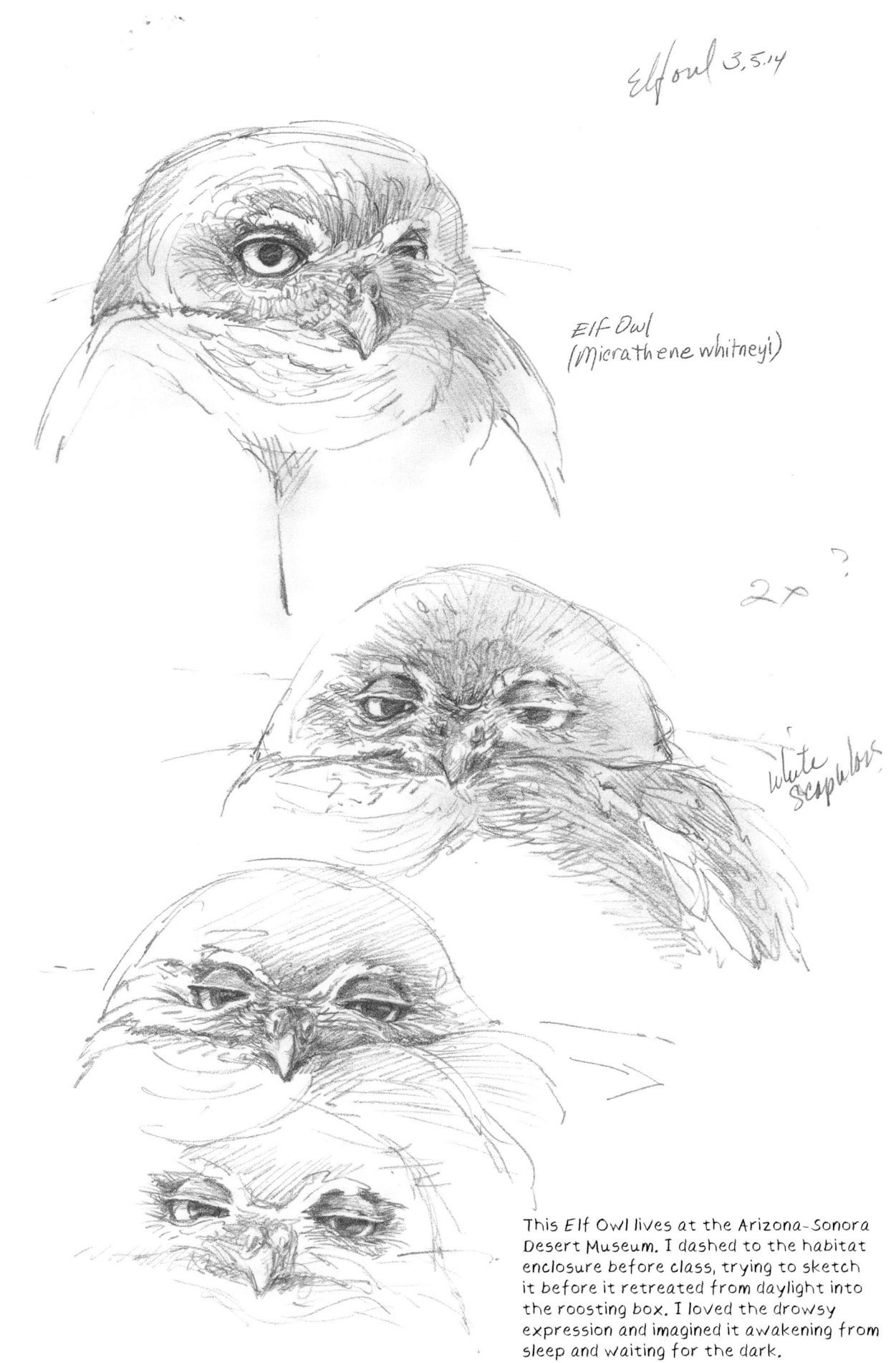

Elf owl 3.5.14

Elf Owl
(*Micrathene whitneyi*)

2x ?

White
Scapulars

This *Elf Owl* lives at the Arizona-Sonora
Desert Museum. I dashed to the habitat
enclosure before class, trying to sketch
it before it retreated from daylight into
the roosting box. I loved the drowsy
expression and imagined it awakening from
sleep and waiting for the dark.

51

"Saguaro Sentinel": Work in Progress

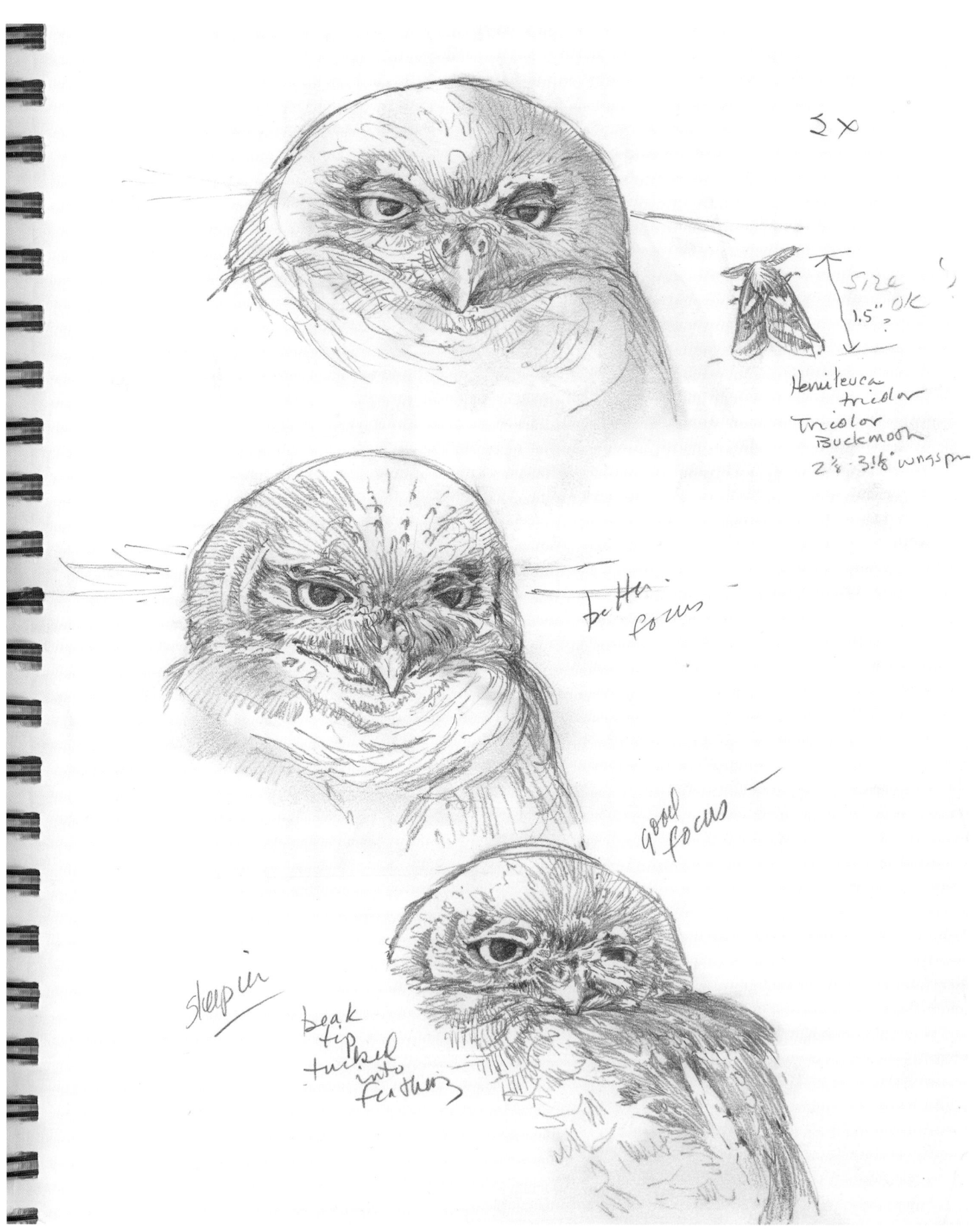

5x

size?
1.5" OK

Hemileuca
    tricolor
Tricolor
Buckmoth
2⅜ - 3⅛" wngspn

better
focus

good
focus

sleepin

beak
tip
tucked
into
feathers

Preliminary color test, 9 x 12 in (22.86 x 30.48 cm), on 140 lb (300 gsm) cold press Fabriano Artistico paper.

Mixing colors in a traditional wet-in-wet technique with large-grain salt for organic effects.

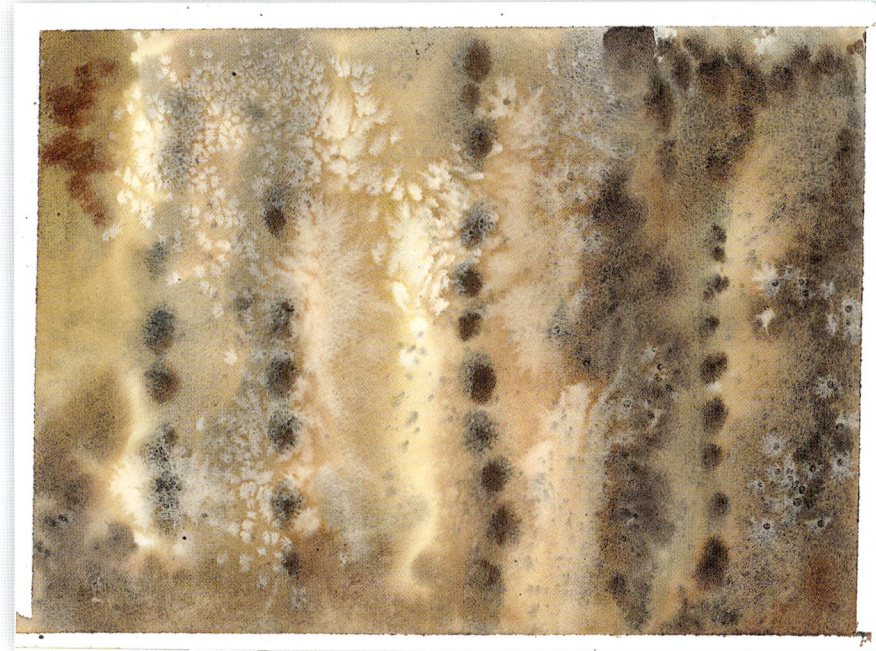

The day after the color test, I began the full-sized painting. But the humidity was drier, the pigment and salt acted differently. Liquid masking fluid protected the bird and the highlighted edge from paint. The first and second washes were applied, letting the paper dry thoroughly between washes. I wasn't happy with the first sheet and painted a second to achieve the desired texture. The lighter version was preferred and used to paint the finished piece.

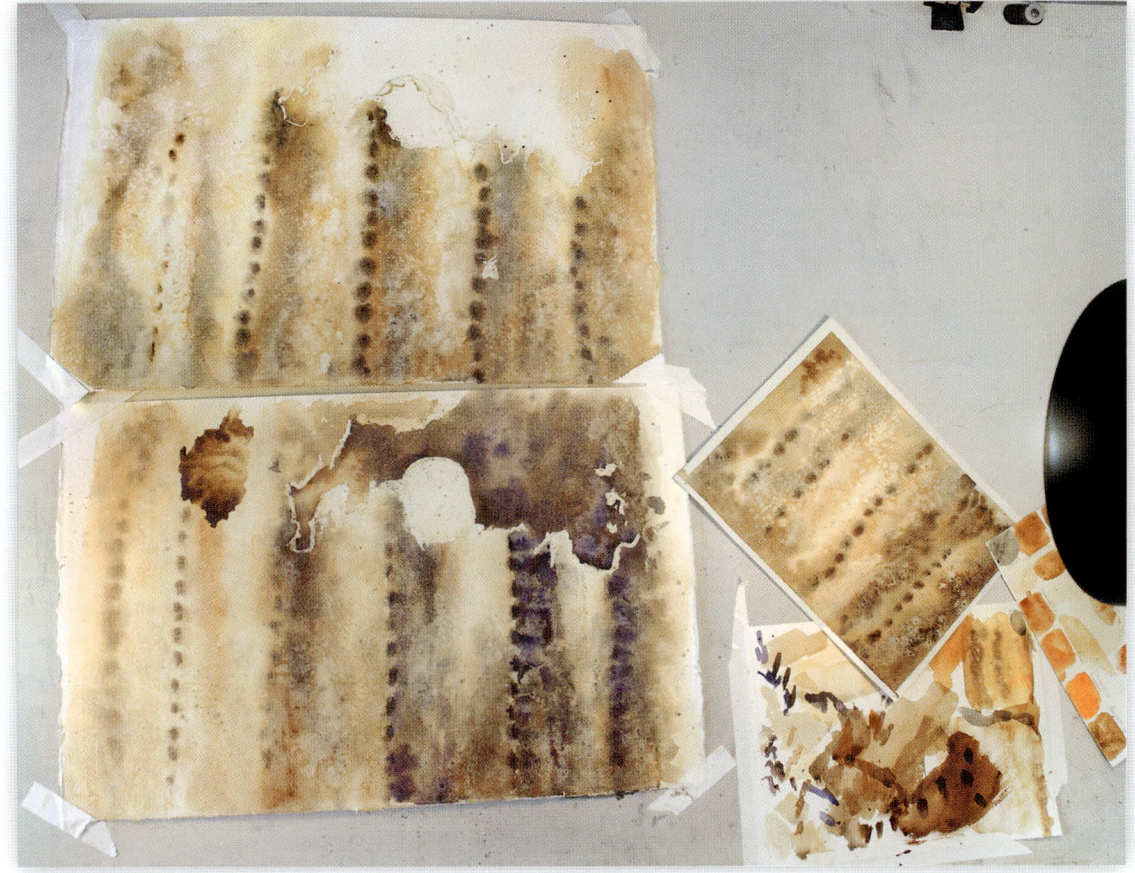

First washes, 19 x 13 in (48.26 x 33.02 cm), on 300 lb (640 gsm) cold press Fabriano Artisico paper.

"Saguaro Sentinel"

In a protected roost well above the desert floor, a diminutive Elf Owl waits for the evening to begin its nighttime hunt. Soft feathers mute the sound of the owl's flight as it pursues moths, beetles, and scorpions. By day the desert may seem devoid of life, but after dark, the evening concert begins with chuckling owls, buzzing insects, and barking mammals. Crevices and cracks in old saguaros provide quiet places for desert dwellers to hide from their predators and the day's heat as they wait to emerge in the cool of the evening.

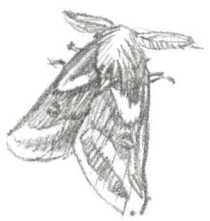

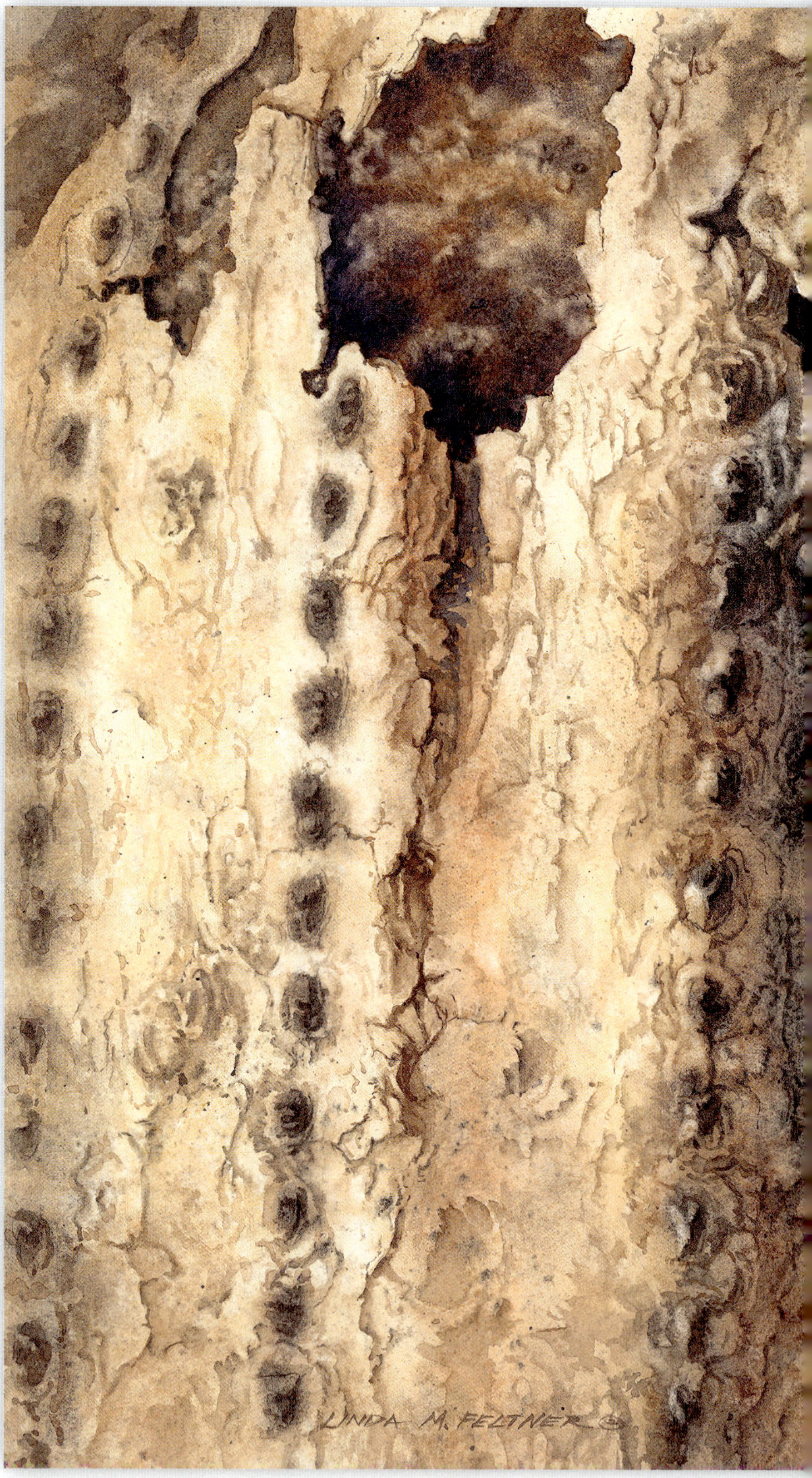

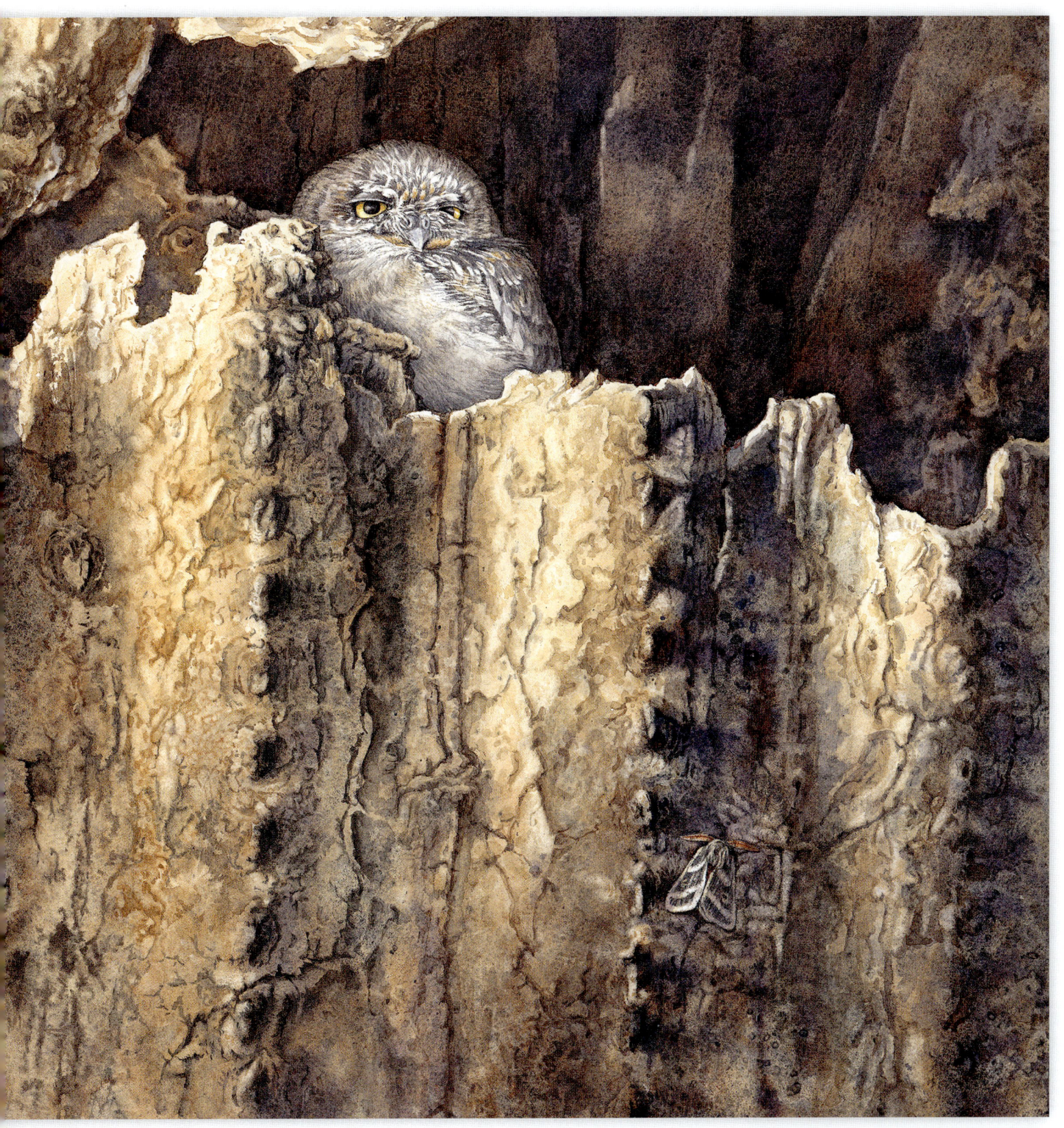

Elf Owl (*Micrathene whitneyi*) and Tricolor Buckmoth
(*Hemileuca tricolor*), Saguaro (*Carnegiea gigantea*)

Saguaro Sentinel, 13 × 19 in (33.02 × 48.26 cm), transparent
watercolor, Sonoran Experience Collection, courtesy of the
Arizona-Sonora Desert Museum Art Institute.

"Pygmy Huntress": Work in Progress

A sideways glance out the window revealed an unusual lump in the gravel pathway. A soft, tan-colored Northern Pygmy-Owl had captured a House Sparrow and landed on the ground, an unusual occurrence for a secretive bird during the day—and a perfect study for a painting.

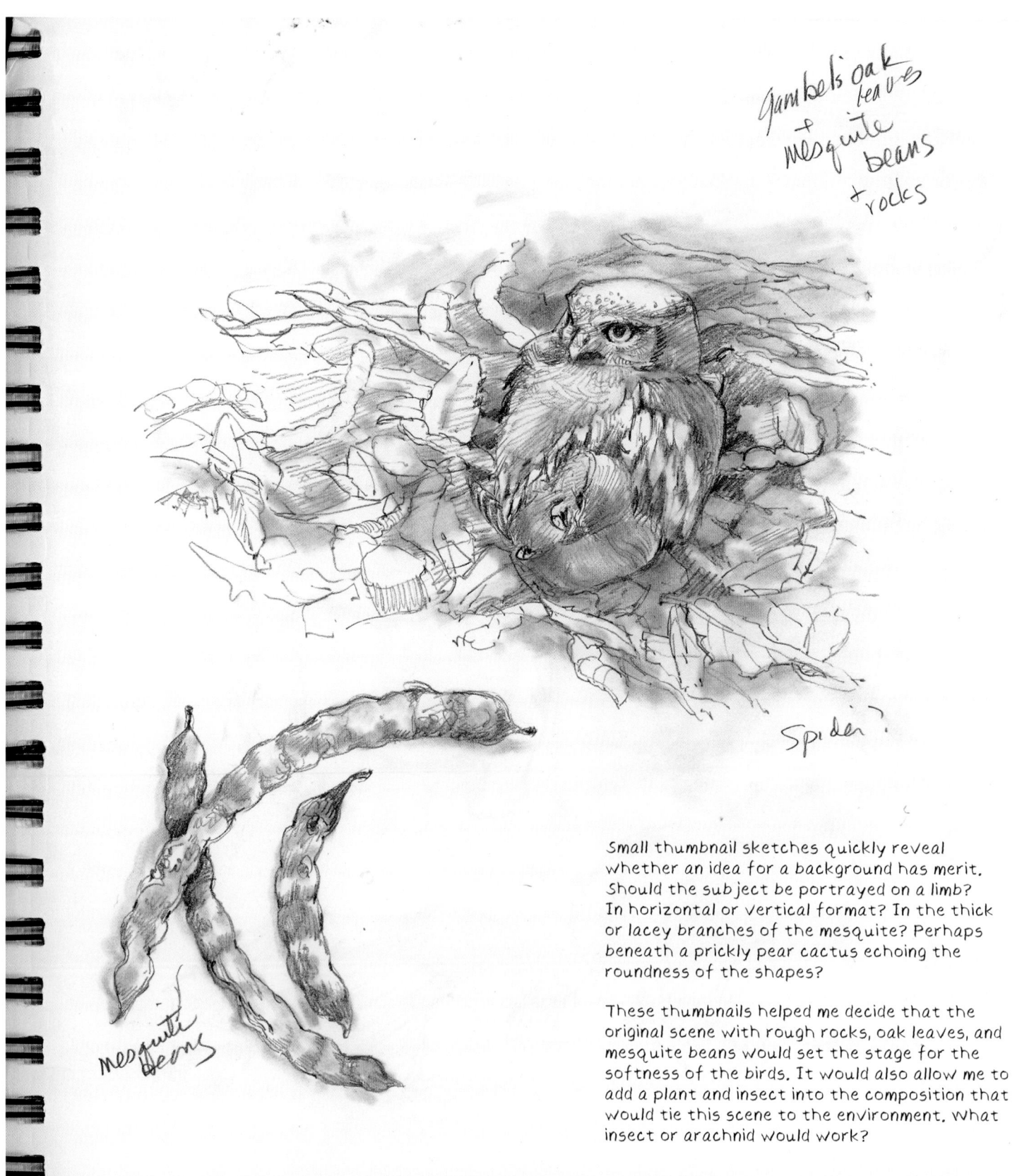

Gambel's oak leaves + mesquite beans + rocks

Spider.

mesquite beans

Small thumbnail sketches quickly reveal whether an idea for a background has merit. Should the subject be portrayed on a limb? In horizontal or vertical format? In the thick or lacey branches of the mesquite? Perhaps beneath a prickly pear cactus echoing the roundness of the shapes?

These thumbnails helped me decide that the original scene with rough rocks, oak leaves, and mesquite beans would set the stage for the softness of the birds. It would also allow me to add a plant and insect into the composition that would tie this scene to the environment. What insect or arachnid would work?

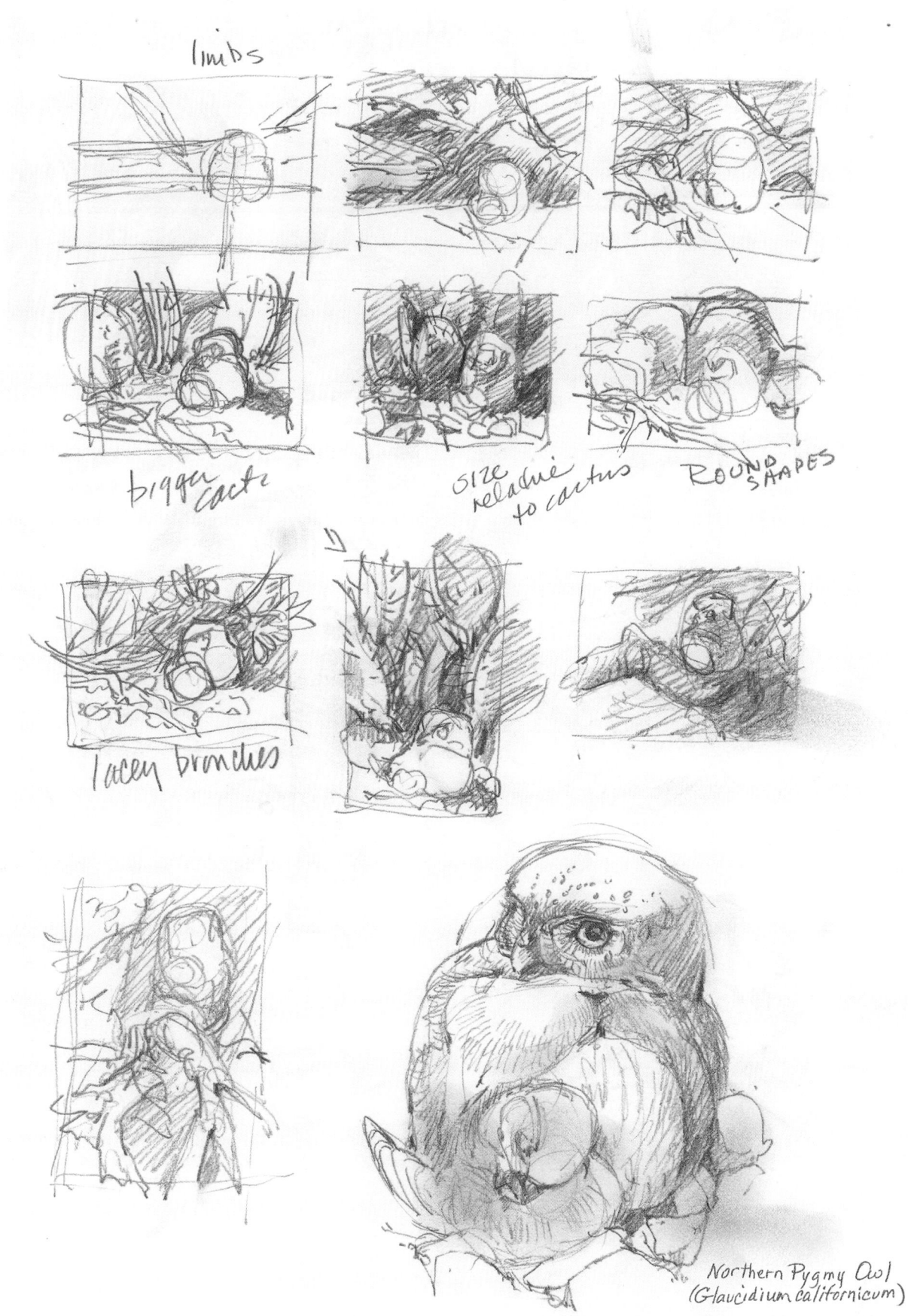

limbs

bigger cacti

size relative to cactus

ROUND SHAPES

lacey branches

Northern Pygmy Owl
(Glaucidium californicum)

"Pygmy Huntress"

The Northern Pygmy-Owl is not much larger than a House Sparrow. It is capable of capturing prey up to and including its own size. Populations in western North America frequently hunt during the day. Their repetitive tooting call heard in the mountains and canyons of the West may attract small birds like warblers, wrens, and chickadees who will mob around the owl and scold furiously while keeping an eye on the skilled huntress.

Northern Pygmy-Owl (*Glaucidium californicum*),
House Sparrow (*Passer domesticus*), and Harvester Ant
(*Pogonomyrmex* sp.)

Pygmy Huntress, 9 × 12.5 in (22.86 × 31.75 cm),
transparent watercolor on handmade Twinrocker paper.

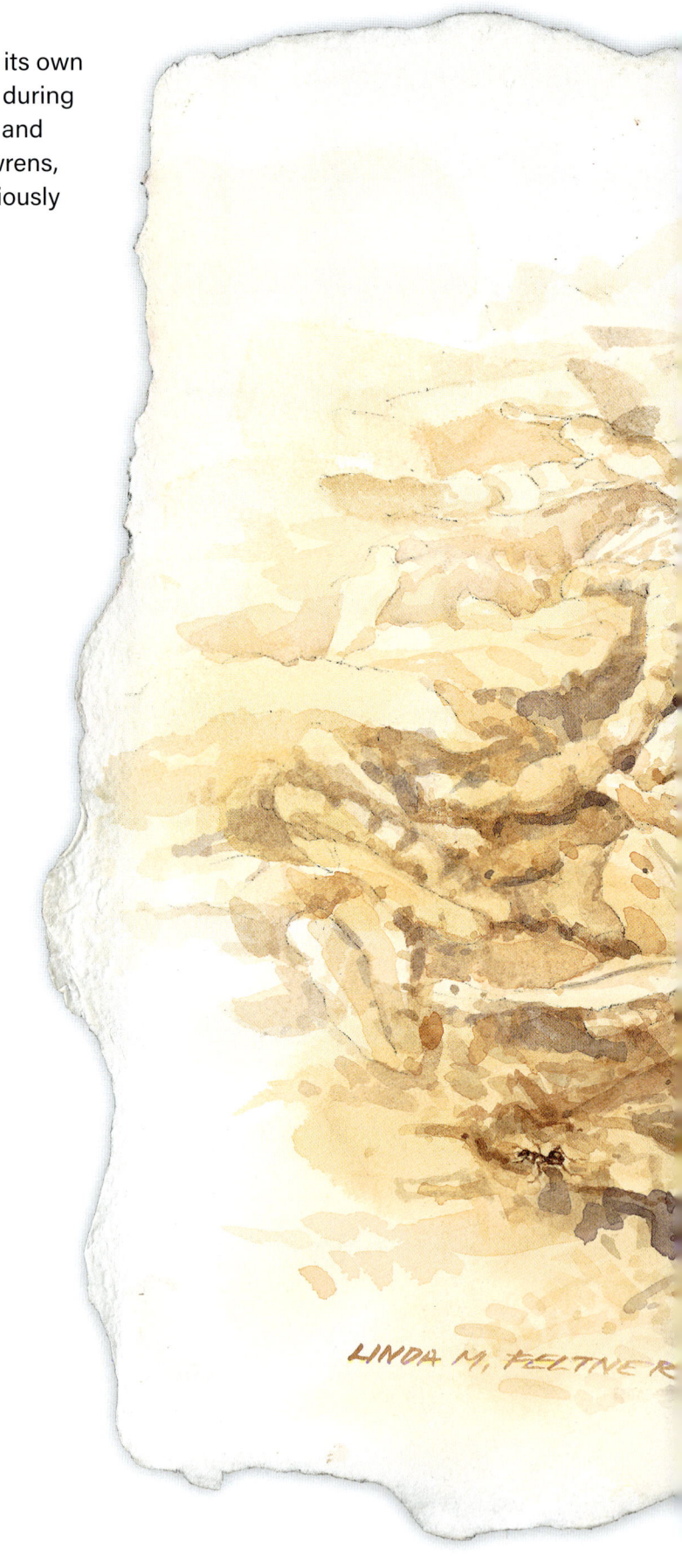

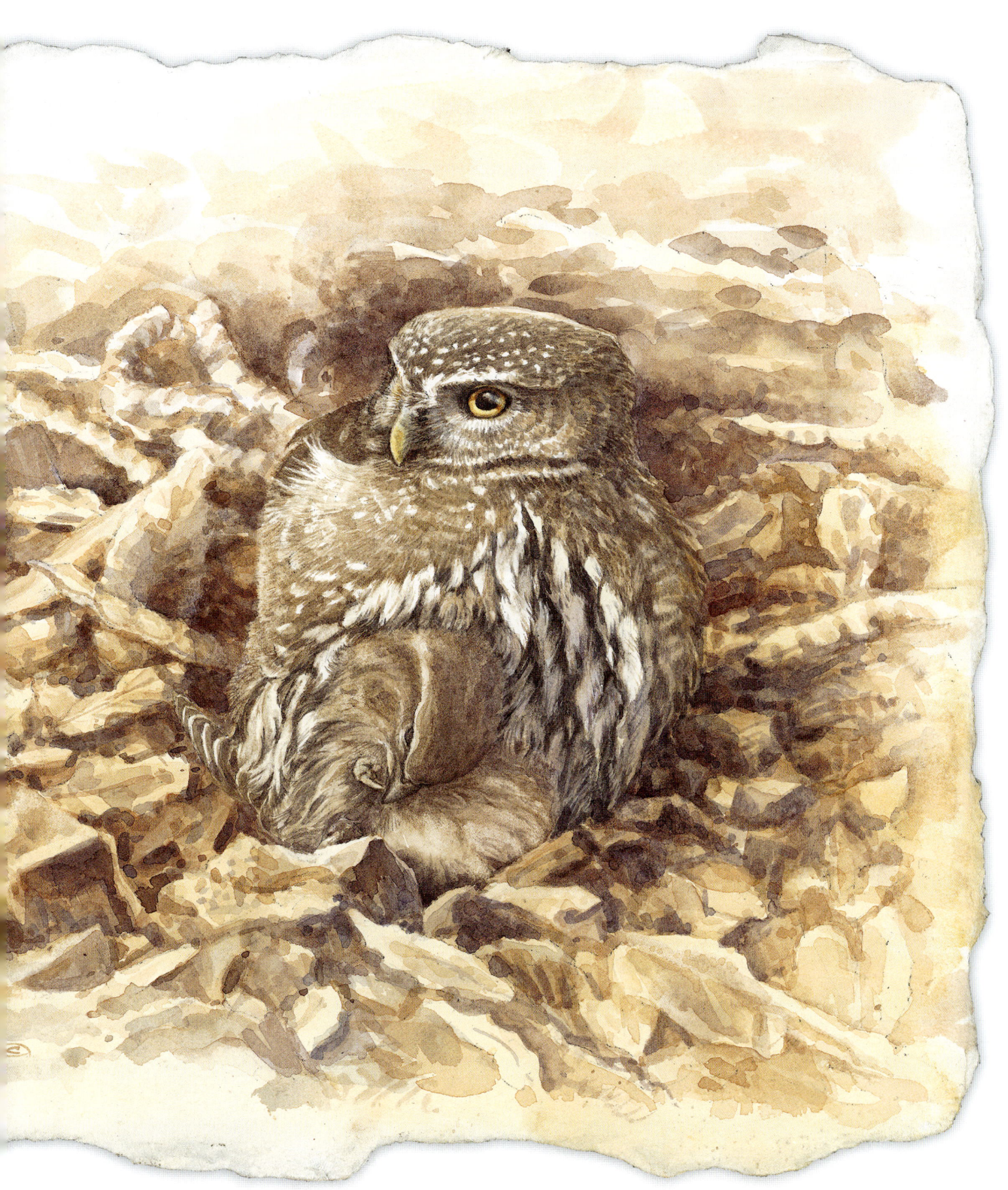

A Passion for Corvids

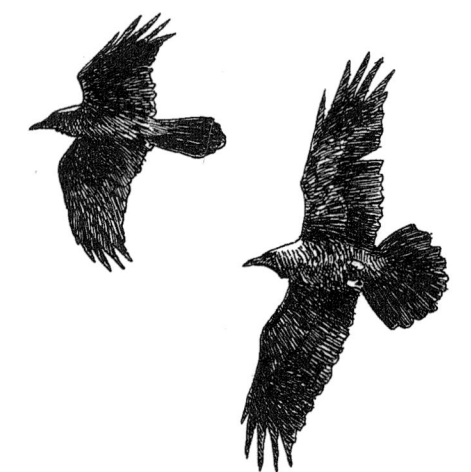

Corvids are members of a family of birds (Corvidae) that includes jays, ravens, crows, magpies, nutcrackers, and around 125 more species around the globe. They can be elegantly flashy with vivid blues and greens or cloaked in soft gray tones or shiny, iridescent blacks. Highly intelligent and social, they have inspired stories and myths throughout human history.

Their exceptional group behavior and reasoning have generated many studies demonstrating how remarkable they are.

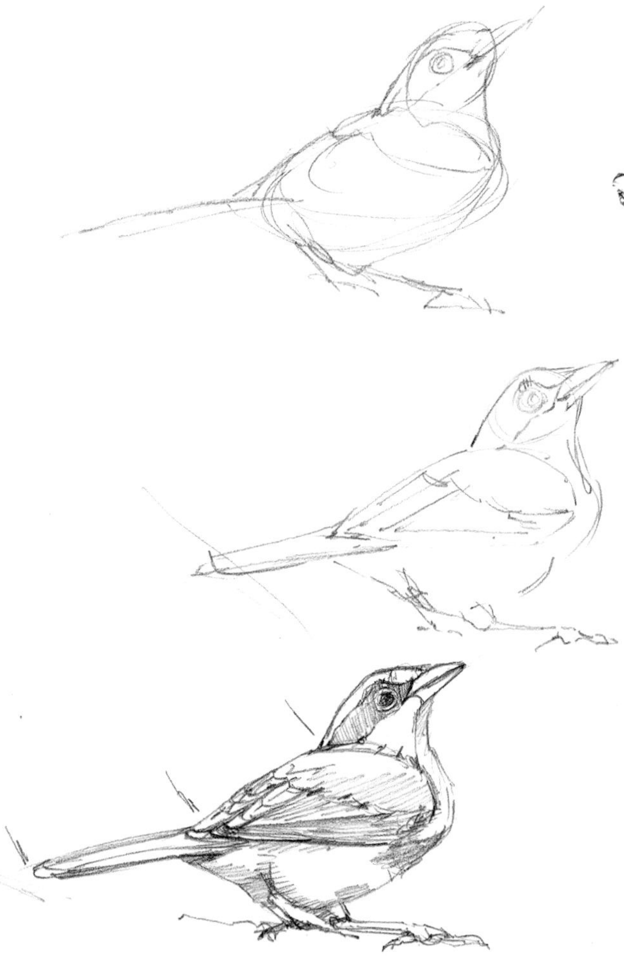

gray eyes

leucistic wing

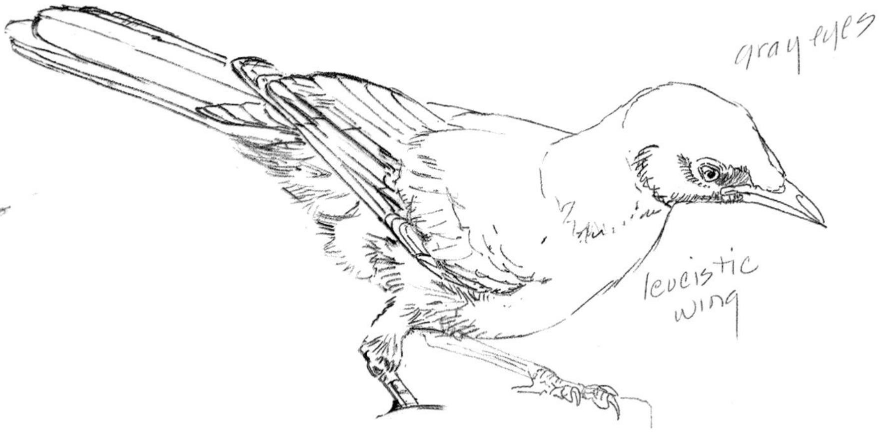

young Mexican Jay
(*Aphelocoma wollweberi*)

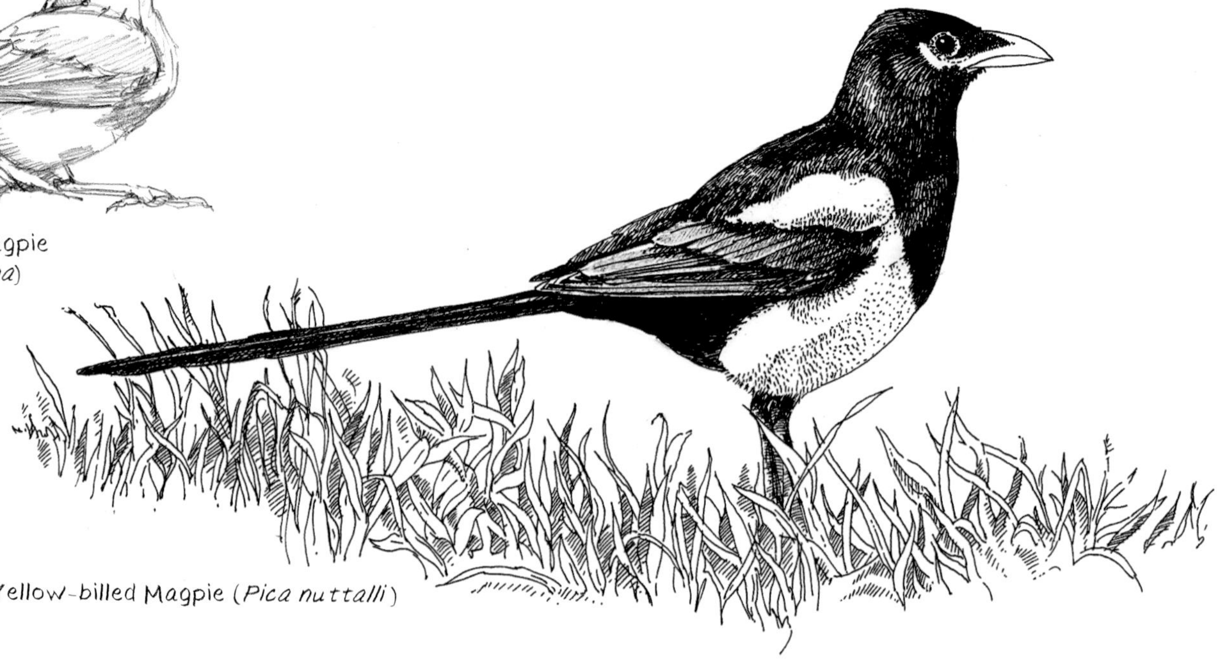

Javan Green Magpie
(*Cissa thalassina*)

Yellow-billed Magpie (*Pica nuttalli*)

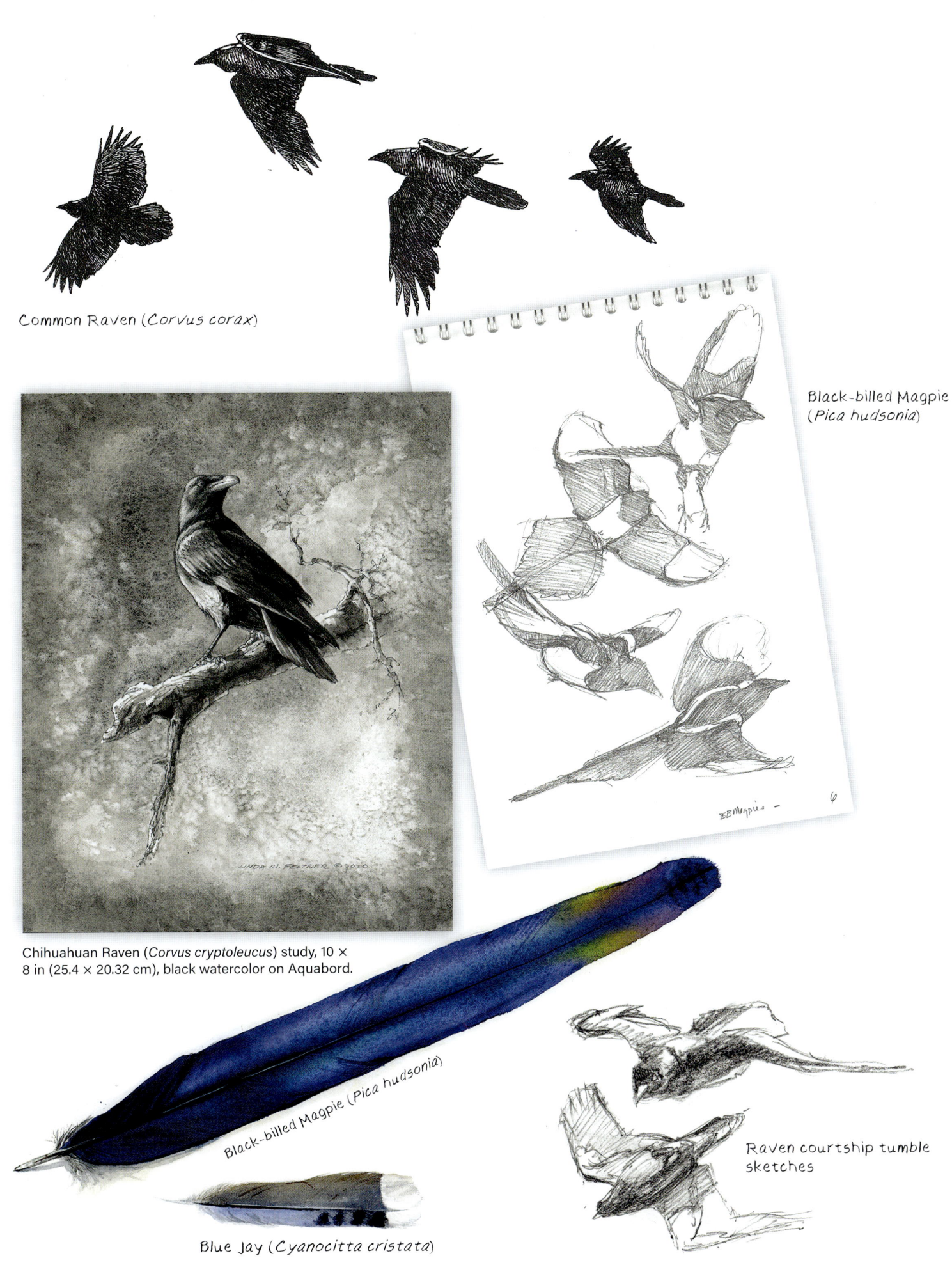

Common Raven (*Corvus corax*)

Black-billed Magpie
(*Pica hudsonia*)

Chihuahuan Raven (*Corvus cryptoleucus*) study, 10 × 8 in (25.4 × 20.32 cm), black watercolor on Aquabord.

Black-billed Magpie (*Pica hudsonia*)

Raven courtship tumble sketches

Blue Jay (*Cyanocitta cristata*)

"A Mischief of Jays": Inspiration and Development

The Mexican Jay is one of the few species that stay together in family groups. We watch the family dynamics from year to year in the yard. The one-year-old young stay around to help collect nesting material and food for the next generation of chicks. The fledged babies spend the following year watching their family group members. Critical life skills include learning when an acorn is ripe as well as which insect to eat and which ones squirt a foul defensive spray.

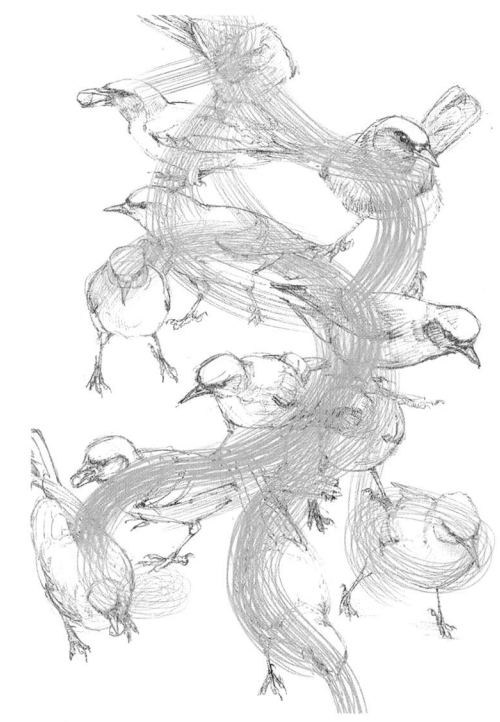

The final composition emphasizes the flow of a story. The eye moves through the group, ending up with a yearling bird contemplating an insect.

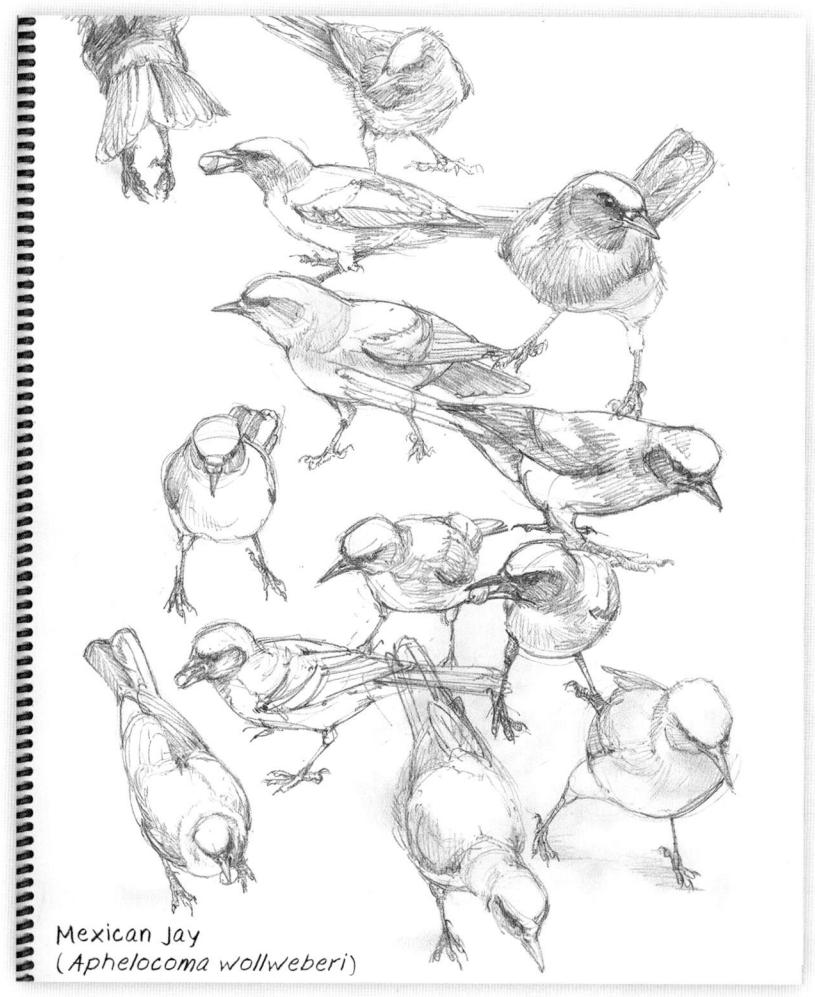

Mexican Jay
(*Aphelocoma wollweberi*)

For the initial sketch while observing jays out the window (above), the intent was an abstract composition using several birds. I was not paying attention to individual size or fine-tuning anatomical details. The sketch was inspirational.

Once there were enough poses to work with, I scanned the page. Clipped and placed into a graphics program with layers, individual birds were repositioned, enlarged, or reduced to create an aesthetic flow. Particular attention was given to negative spaces where feet or heads did not rest awkwardly against the next shape.

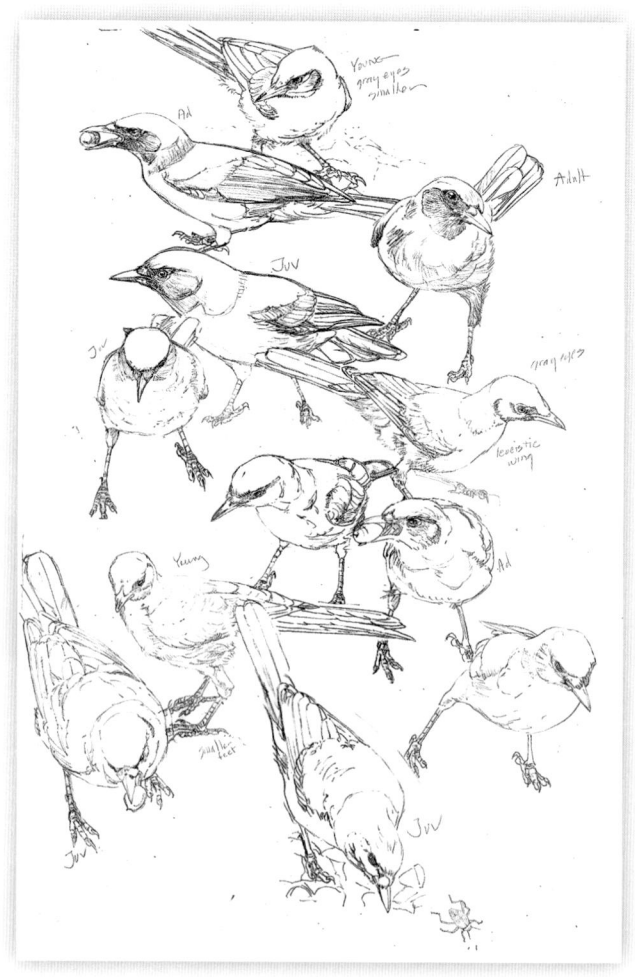

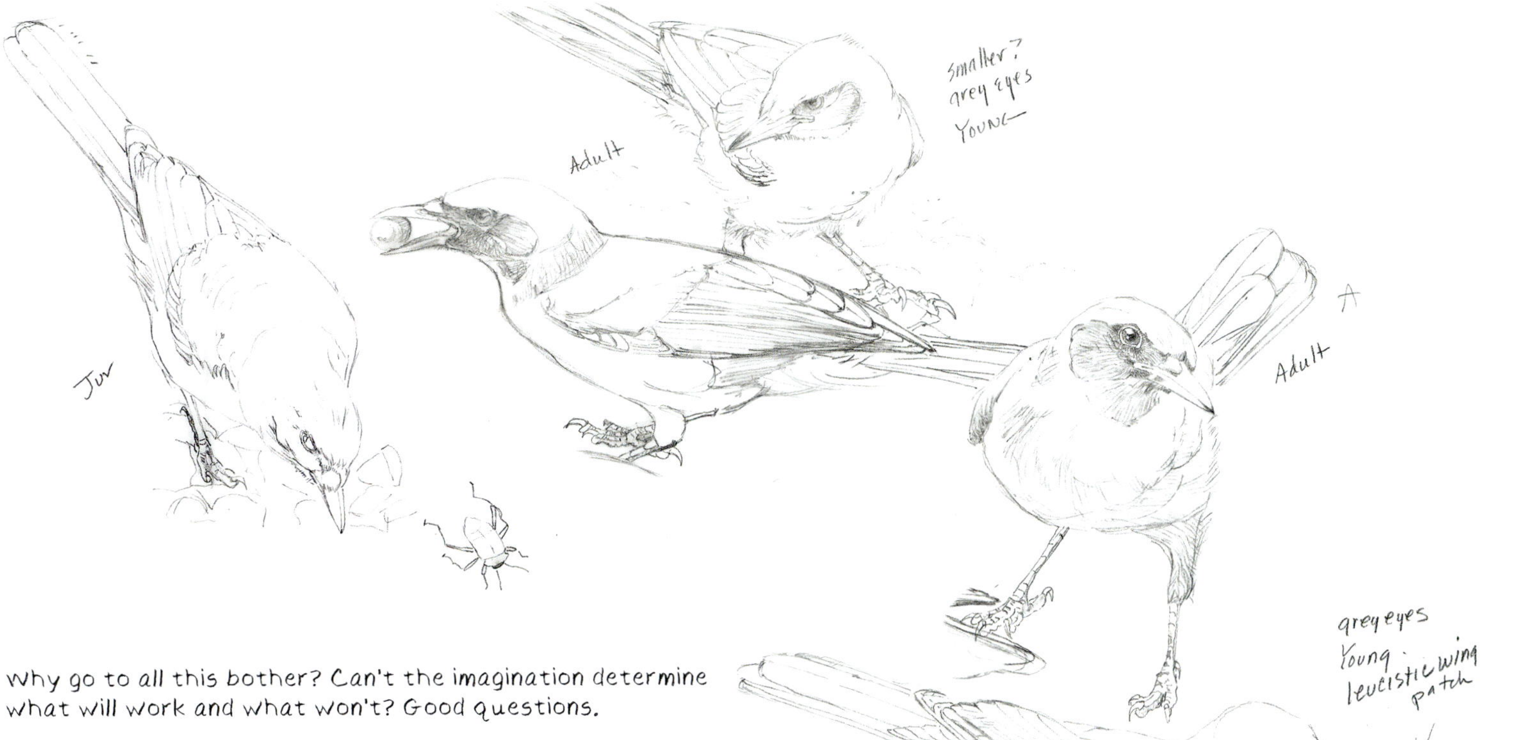

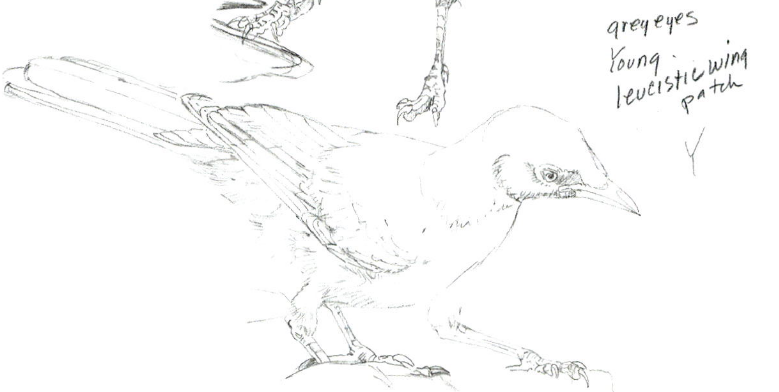

Jur

Adult

smaller?
grey eyes
YOUNG—

Adult

grey eyes
Young,
leucistic wing
patch

Why go to all this bother? Can't the imagination determine what will work and what won't? Good questions.

Quick studies help you focus on the essentials. Seeing it on the page as a whole helps rapid analysis. Abandon the bad ones—don't erase them, just let them go. Continue creating color swatches or thumbnails until you find the right aesthetic balance. Occasionally, you need to see it to evaluate it.

Painting on layers in a graphics program provides a quick way to experiment with background colors.

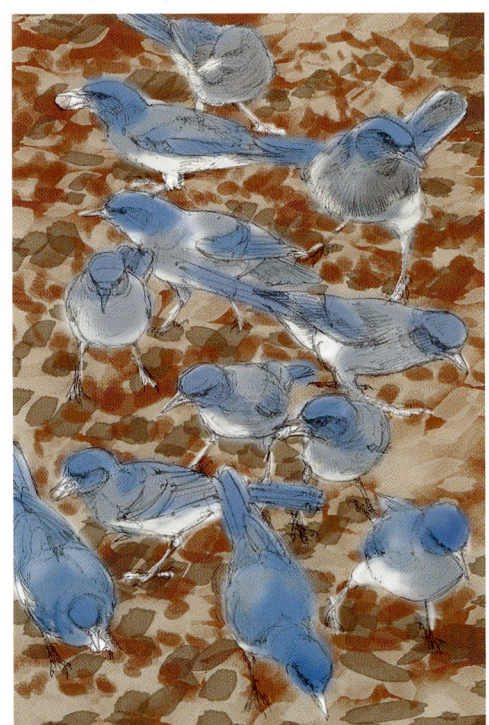

(a) Burnt sienna complements cerulean. At first try, it was obvious that the brown background entirely destroyed the abstract compositional flow.

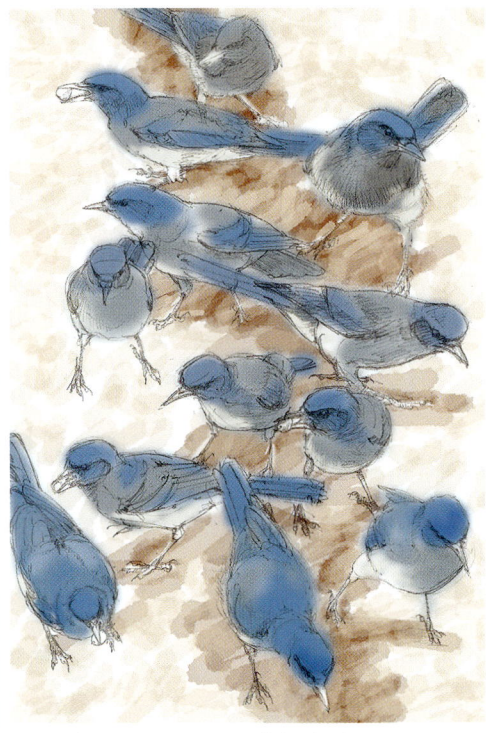

(b) A lighter brown with darker areas in the center was also rejected.

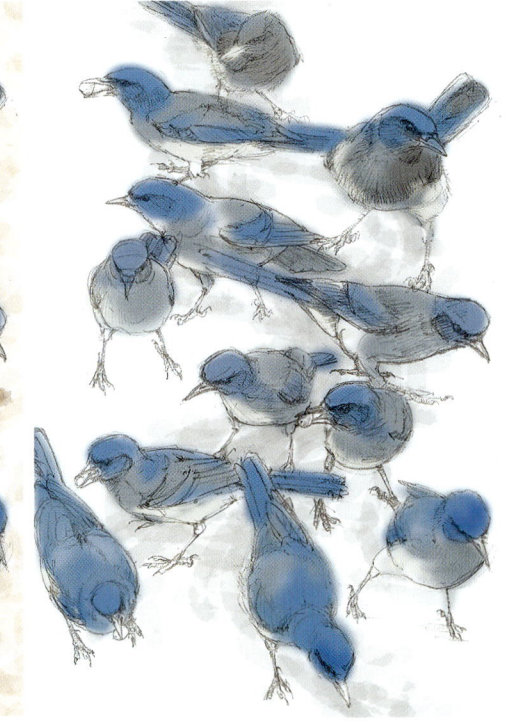

(c) Hiding the brown layers revealed that the strongest background was the most subtle gray.

"A Mischief of Jays"

Coursing through the oaks with rowdy cries and whooshing wings, Mexican Jays are a resident family group. They form a social group of family members whose nonbreeding juveniles from previous years act as helpers in raising a new brood. The youngest has a pale pink bill with a dark tip. Yearlings develop bills that are half black with a pink base, and as an adult, the bill becomes entirely black. These vocal, curious, and intelligent corvids are both lively and captivating. Gawky young intently watch the older birds and learn the ways of their intricate world. Can you follow their story?

Mexican Jay (*Aphelocoma wollweberi*), Arizona Darkling (*Eleodes obscura*), and Emory Oak (*Quercus emoryi*)

A Mischief of Jays, 14 × 21.5 in (35.56 × 54.61 cm), pastel. Society of Animal Artists' "Ethology Award for the Best Depiction of Natural Behavior in Any Medium" and Western Art Collector Magazine "Editor's Choice Award."

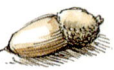

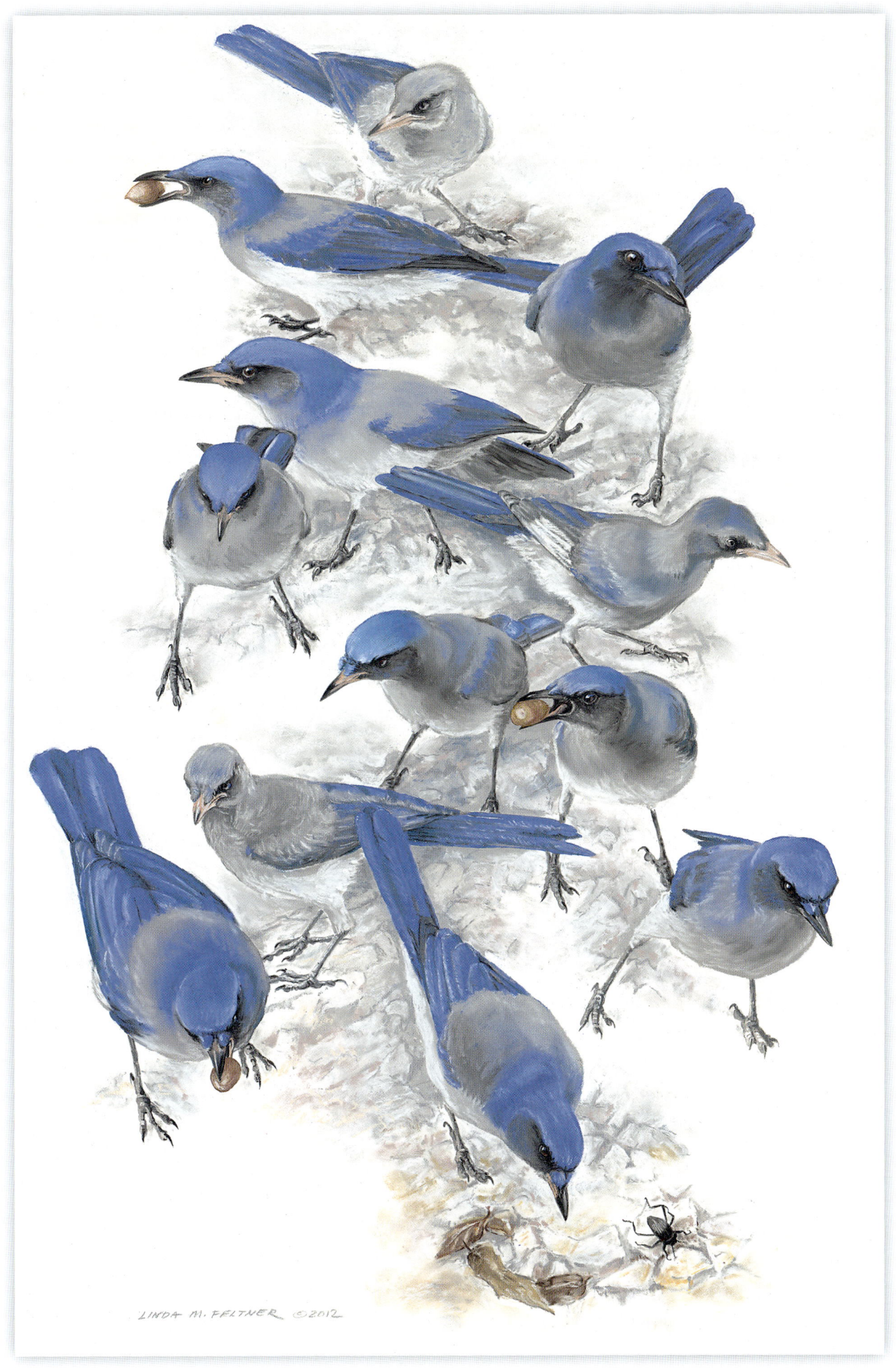

LINDA M. FELTNER ©2012

65

Celebrating Ravens

Four young ravens fledged in the canyon, displaying their exuberant enjoyment of life with swooping, calling in baby voices, and cavorting as ravens do. Sadly, a power pole claimed two of their lives. Reverently bringing them into the studio, I gathered the courage to draw them with objectivity and honor.

I had not examined a raven this close, even in a museum. The first sketches were for measurements and observation, followed by color notes and reminders for the future. The birds are now part of a museum collection, where they can inspire and inform others.

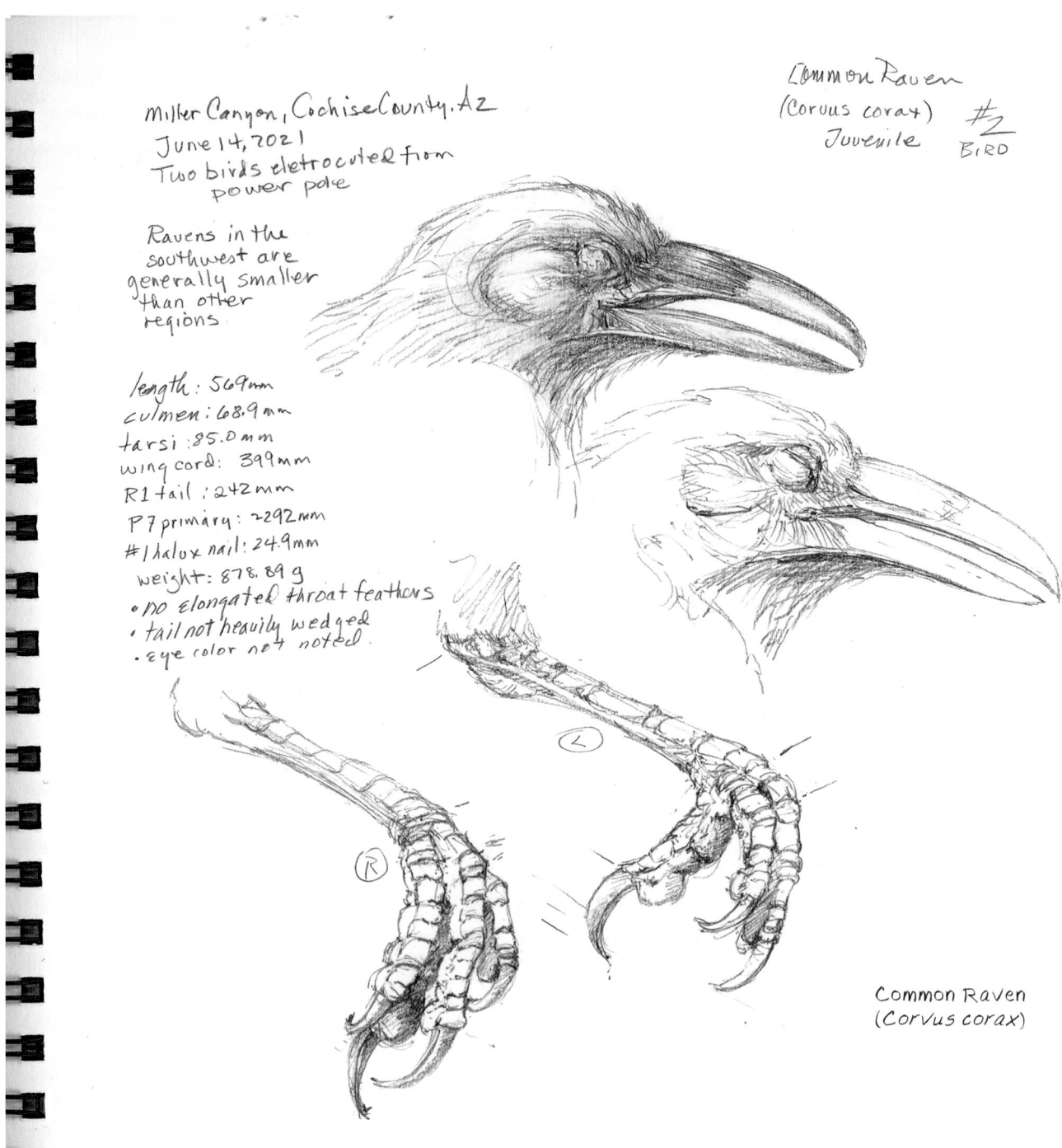

Miller Canyon, Cochise County, AZ
June 14, 2021
Two birds electrocuted from power pole

Ravens in the southwest are generally smaller than other regions.

length: 569mm
culmen: 68.9mm
tarsi: 85.0mm
wing cord: 399mm
R1 tail: 242mm
P7 primary: 2292mm
#1 halux nail: 24.9mm
weight: 878.89 g
• no elongated throat feathers
• tail not heavily wedged
• eye color not noted.

Common Raven
(Corvus corax)
Juvenile   #2 Bird

Ⓛ

Ⓡ

Common Raven
(Corvus corax)

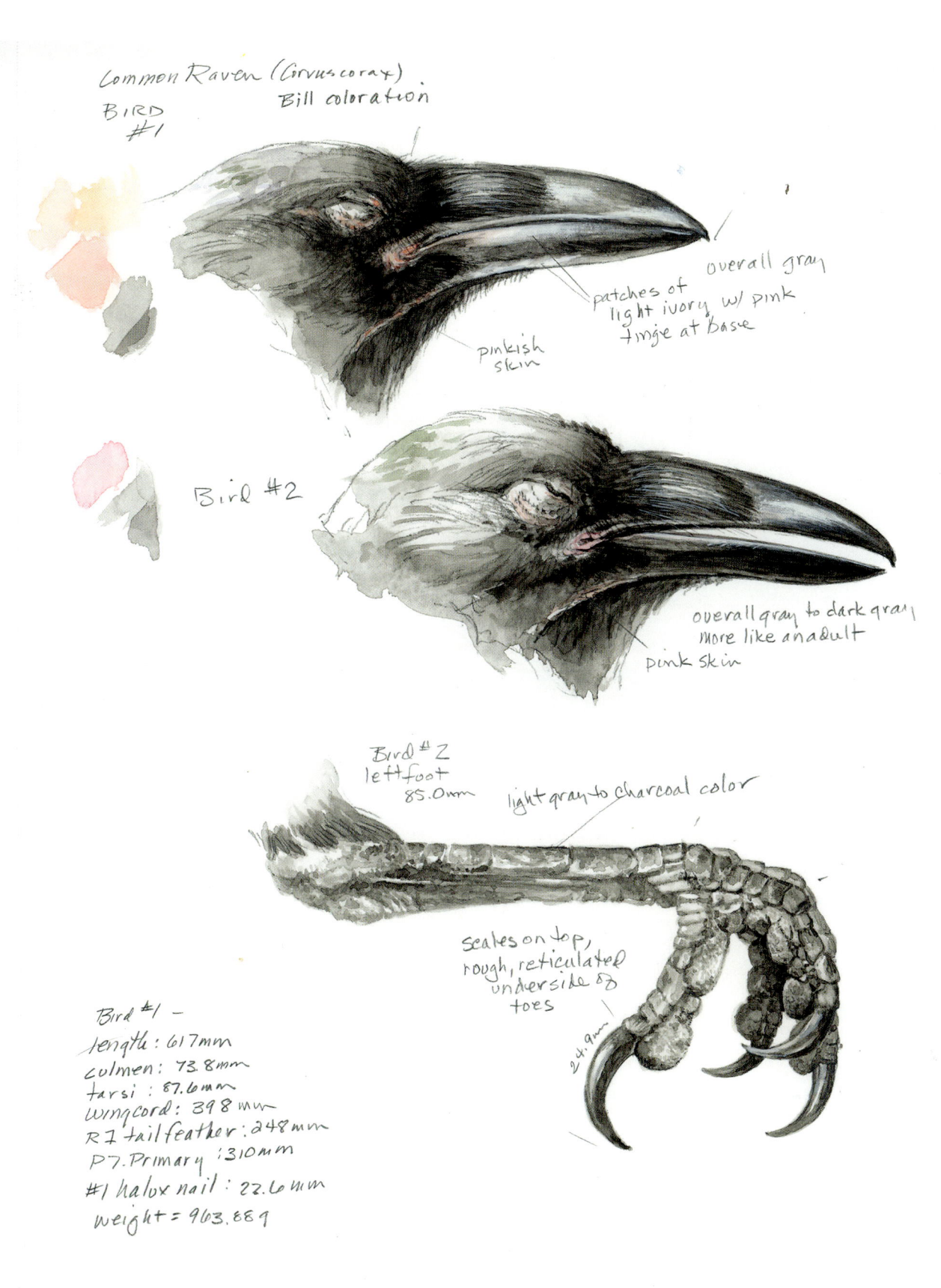

Common Raven (Corvus corax)
Bill coloration

BIRD
#1

overall gray

patches of
light ivory w/ pink
tinge at base

pinkish
skin

Bird #2

overall gray to dark gray
more like an adult

pink skin

Bird #2
left foot
85.0mm

light gray to charcoal color

scales on top,
rough, reticulated
underside of
toes

24.9mm

Bird #1 –
length: 617mm
culmen: 73.8mm
tarsi: 87.6mm
wingcord: 398mm
R7 tail feather: 248mm
P7 Primary: 310mm
#1 halux nail: 22.6mm
weight = 963.88g

LINDA M. FEETNER

Celebrating Ravens, Continued

Although the color of the raven appears shiny black, a closer inspection reveals a color sheen on specific feather groups. In outdoor light, at a certain angle, the feathers reflect cerulean blue, a purplish ultramarine, or olive-green among the black. The open-wing study is not a painting of local color but is a color map noting parts of the bird that reflect a particular color.

the color map

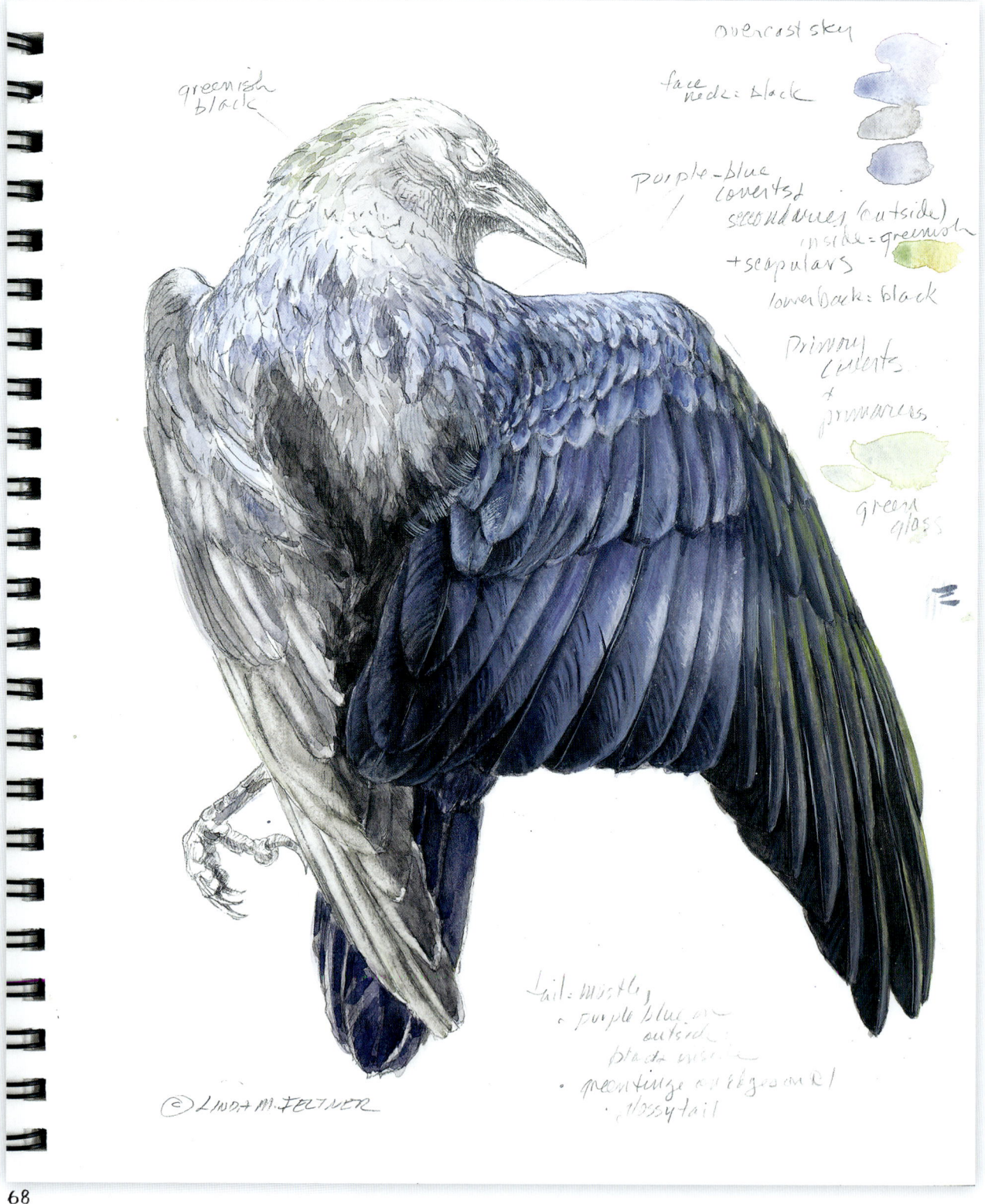

greenish black

overcast sky

face neck: black

purple-blue coverts, secondaries (outside) inside = greenish + scapulars

lower back: black

Primary coverts + primaries

green gloss

tail: mostly
• purple blue on outside
  black inside
• greentinge on edges on R
• glossy tail

© LINDA M. FELTNER

Flying with Ravens

I wanted to celebrate the unique joie de vivre of living ravens. Flight and courtship were the inspiration.

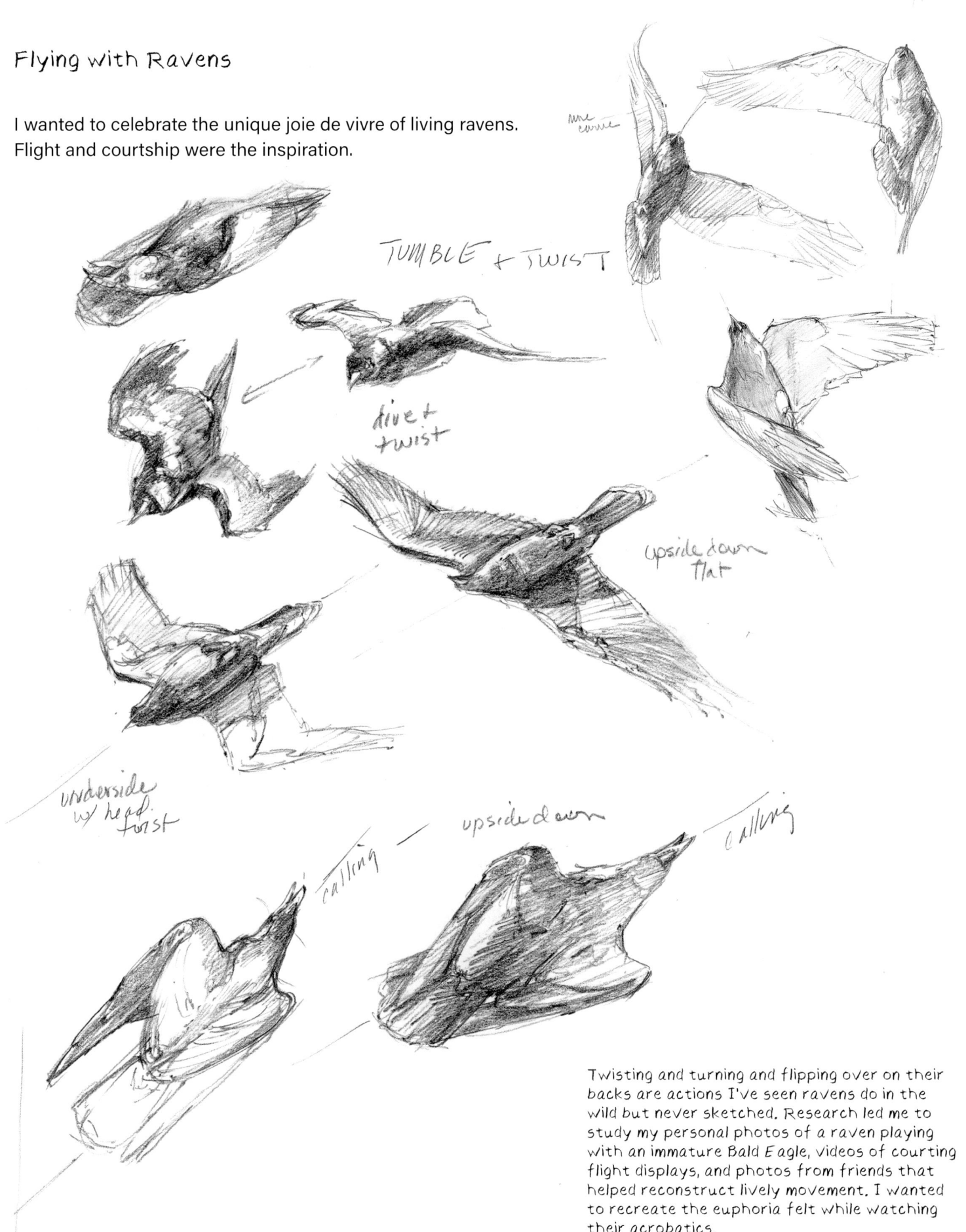

TUMBLE + TWIST

dive + twist

upside down flat

underside w/ head twist

calling — upside down — calling

Twisting and turning and flipping over on their backs are actions I've seen ravens do in the wild but never sketched. Research led me to study my personal photos of a raven playing with an immature Bald Eagle, videos of courting flight displays, and photos from friends that helped reconstruct lively movement. I wanted to recreate the euphoria felt while watching their acrobatics.

Flight Composure

Courting ravens synchronize their movements in a display that coordinates gliding, spilling, rolling, and tumbling. The measured distances between the aerial dancers make their movements appear choreographed.

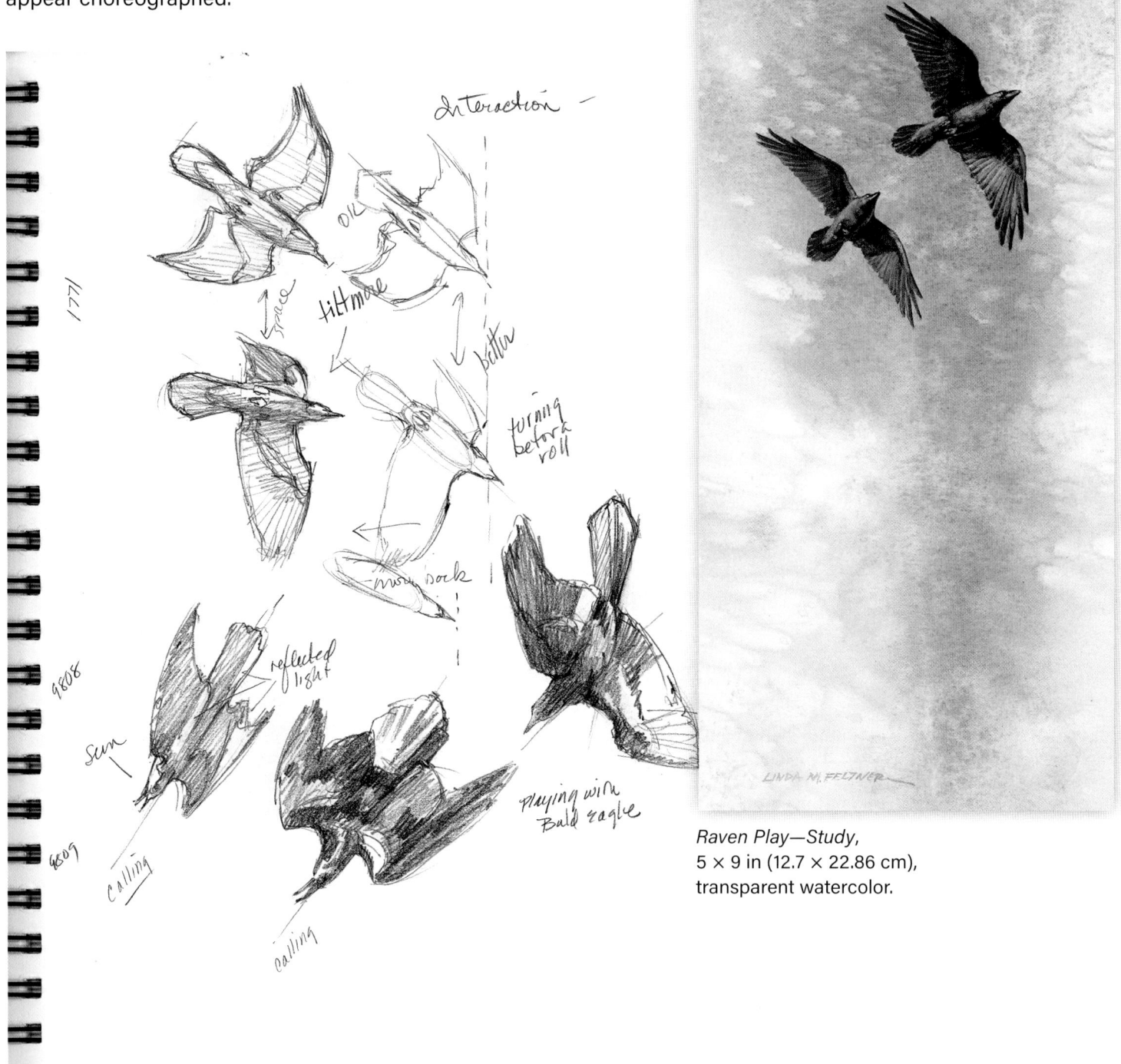

Interaction

space

titmouse

OIL

better

turning before a roll

reflected light

sun

mush back

playing with Bald eagle

9808

4807

1771

calling

calling

Raven Play—Study,
5 × 9 in (12.7 × 22.86 cm),
transparent watercolor.

LINDA M. FELTNER

One will often call while flipped
over on its back.

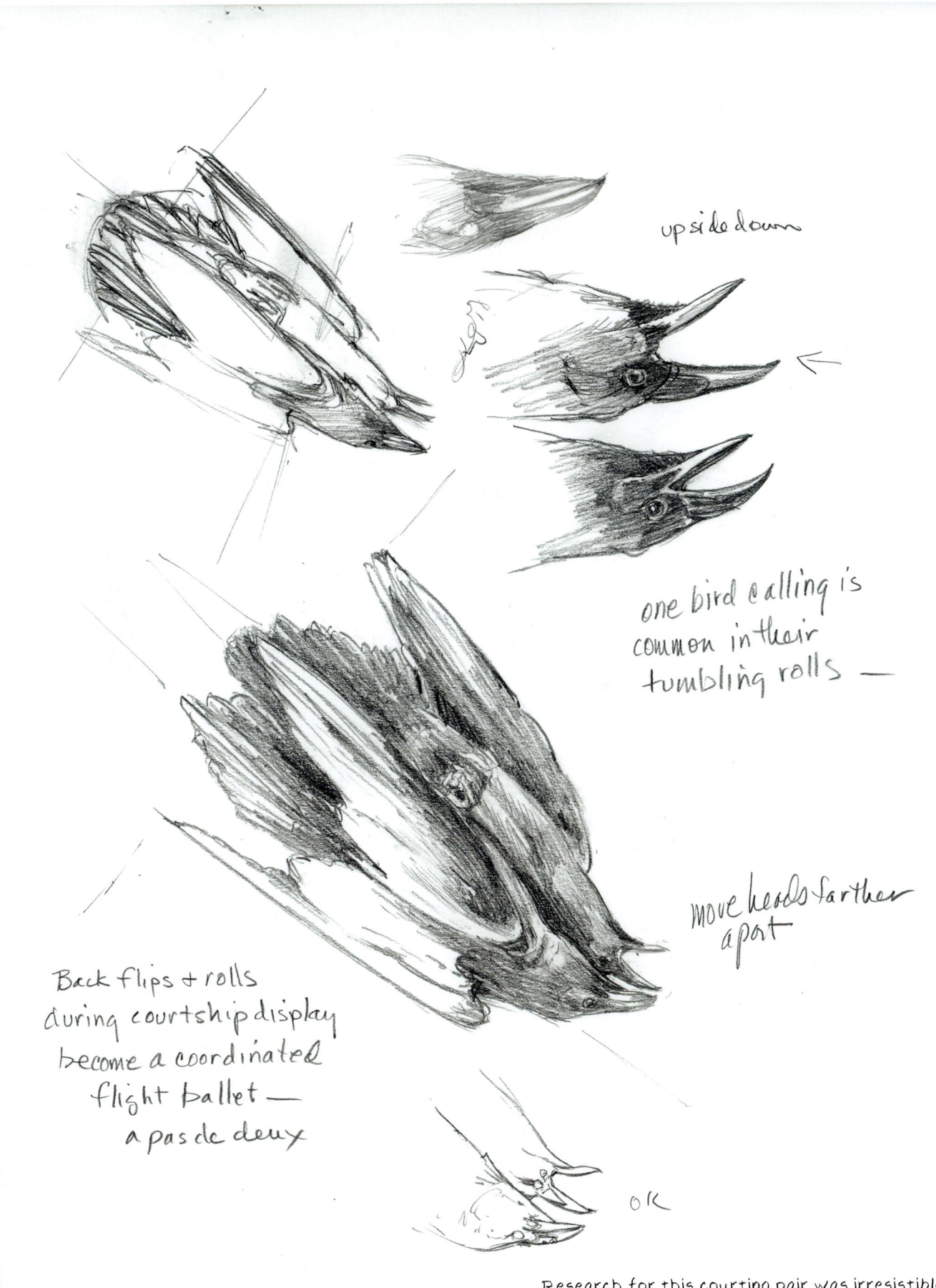

upside down

one bird calling is
common in their
tumbling rolls —

move heads farther
apart

Back flips + rolls
during courtship display
become a coordinated
flight ballet —
a pas de deux

OK

Research for this courting pair was irresistible,
as I worked on the brief moment when both have
flipped onto their backs while dropping from a
height in what seems the pure joy of flight.

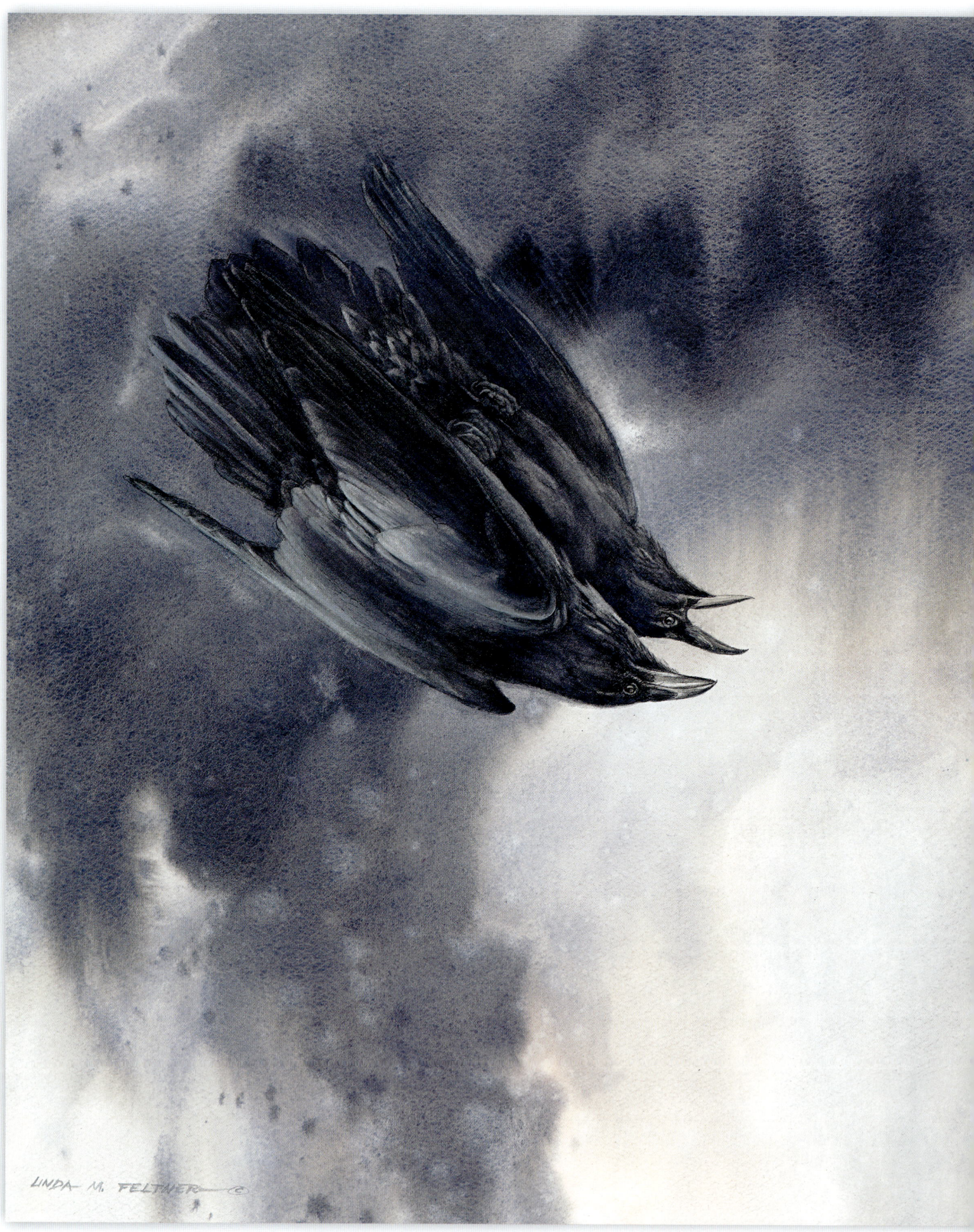

LINDA M. FELTNER ©

"Love at First Flight"

Ravens epitomize both mystery and nobility. Admired for their intelligence and curiosity, they inspire artists, writers, and philosophers to portray and consider their character. Their level of social behavior, as well as their learning abilities, problem-solving, and arithmetic skills have ranked them among the smartest of animals. Watching ravens in flight, their soaring, diving, and rolling appears to be an enjoyable play. Observe a courtship performance to see concerted acrobatics, dramatic dives, choreographed flips, and tight turns.

A thrilling moment comes when the pair flips onto their backs, one calling out, and they harmoniously plunge with absolute precision of movement.

Common Raven (*Corvus corax*)

Love at First Flight, 17 × 17 in (43.18 × 43.18 cm), transparent watercolor.

A Tiding of Magpies

Magpies exemplify the endless possibilities for drawing birds. Their lively personalities, bold attitudes, and flouncy tails provide myriad poses that evoke the bird's lifestyle. I first study shape, form, and anatomy to build my confidence before creating action poses that illustrate how exciting the birds are.

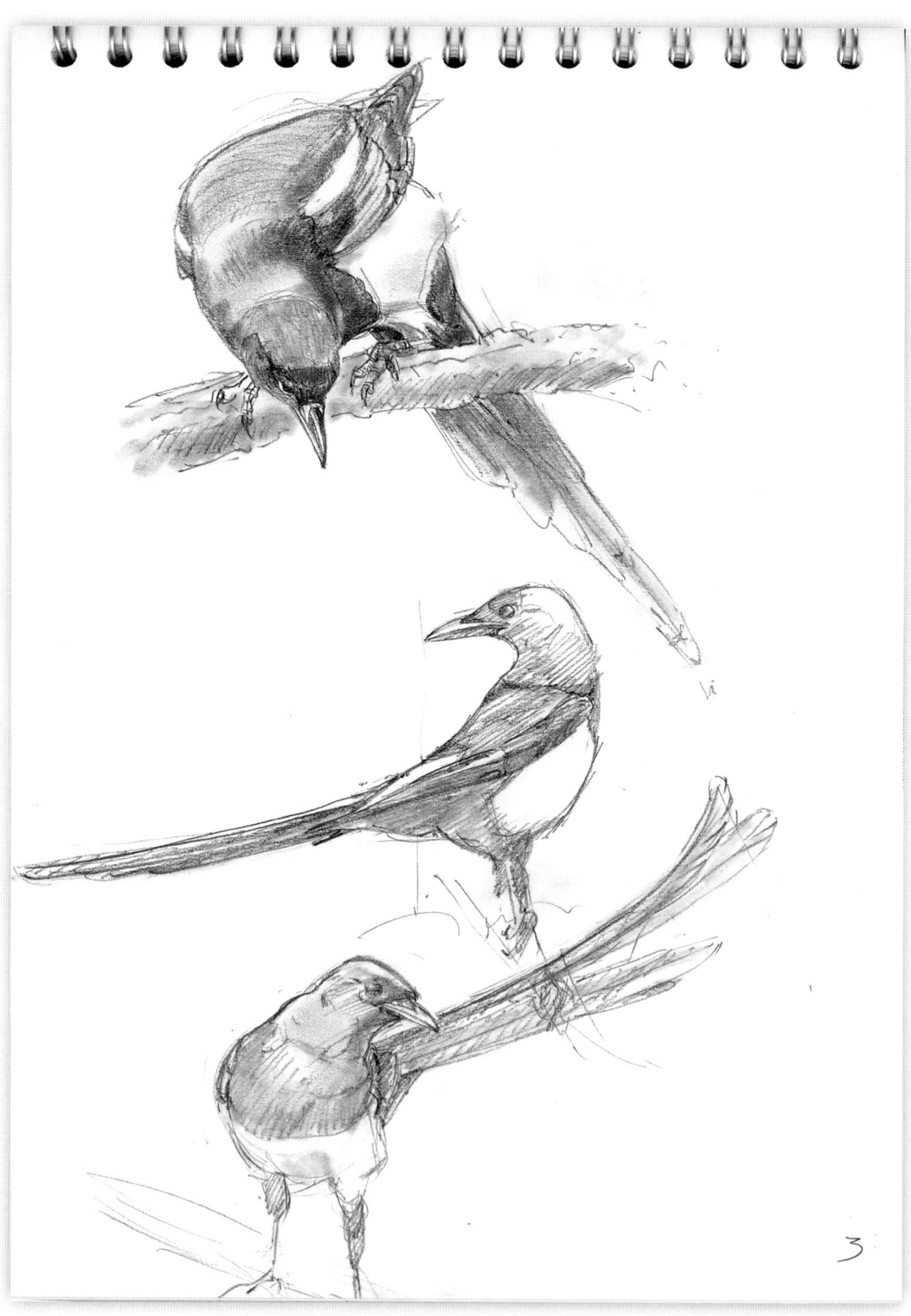

Go ahead, let the pencil
swing to the rhythm of
the magpie's tail.

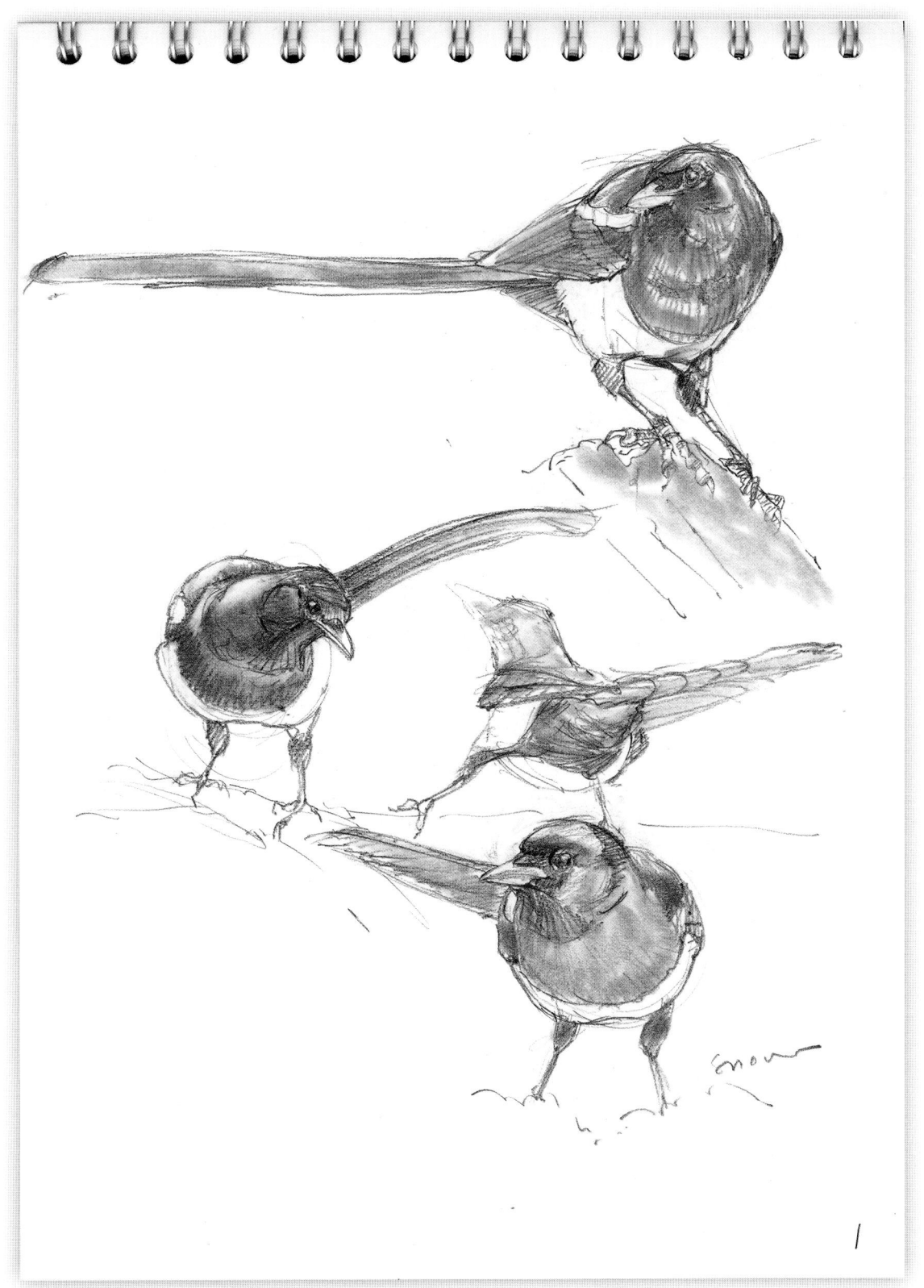

"Blue on Blue"

Airborne magpies always make me smile. Large and flashy, their bold black-and-white patterns capture my attention as they swoop across a field. When sun-struck, they gleam with iridescent blues and greens. Magpies are inspiring not only for their bright pattern but as highly inquisitive, intelligent, and social birds. I chose a single, swooping bird with an open, iridescent tail and bold wing patches of white. An intense, juicy wash of inky blue background harmonized with the overall movement of the bird pursuing a flash of blue—a Lupine Blue butterfly, another resident of the Western United States.

Black-billed Magpie (*Pica hudsonia*) and
Lupine Blue (*Plebejus lupini*)

Blue on Blue, 12 × 9 in (30.48 × 22.86 cm), watercolor and gouache.

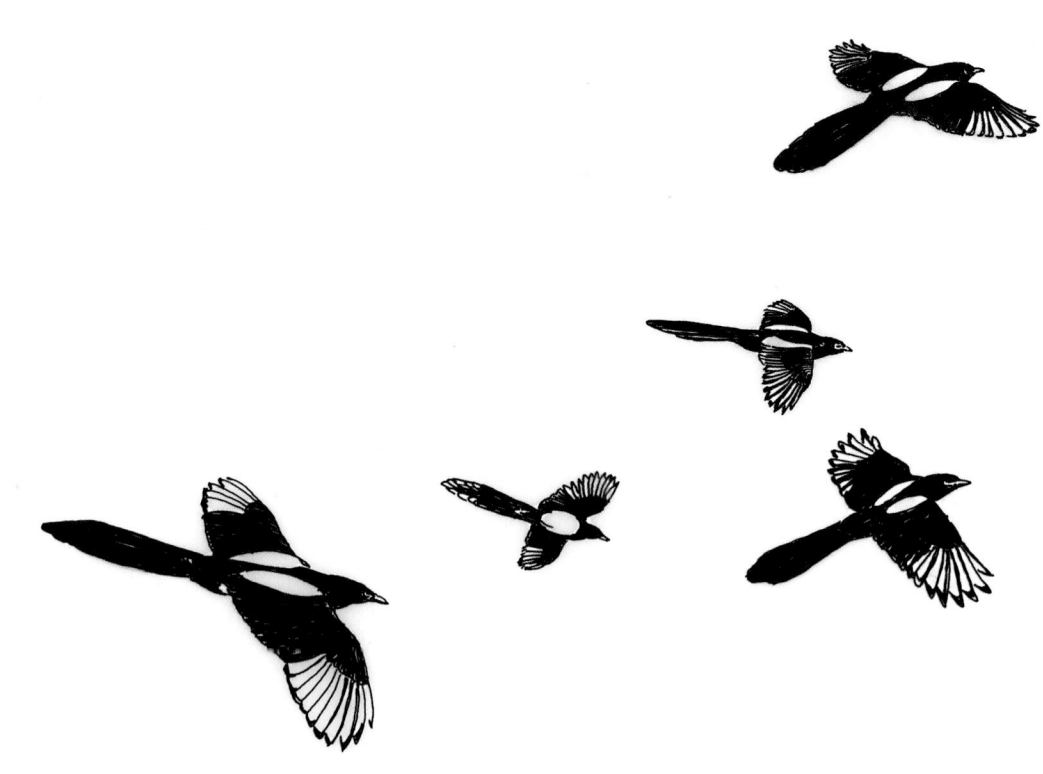

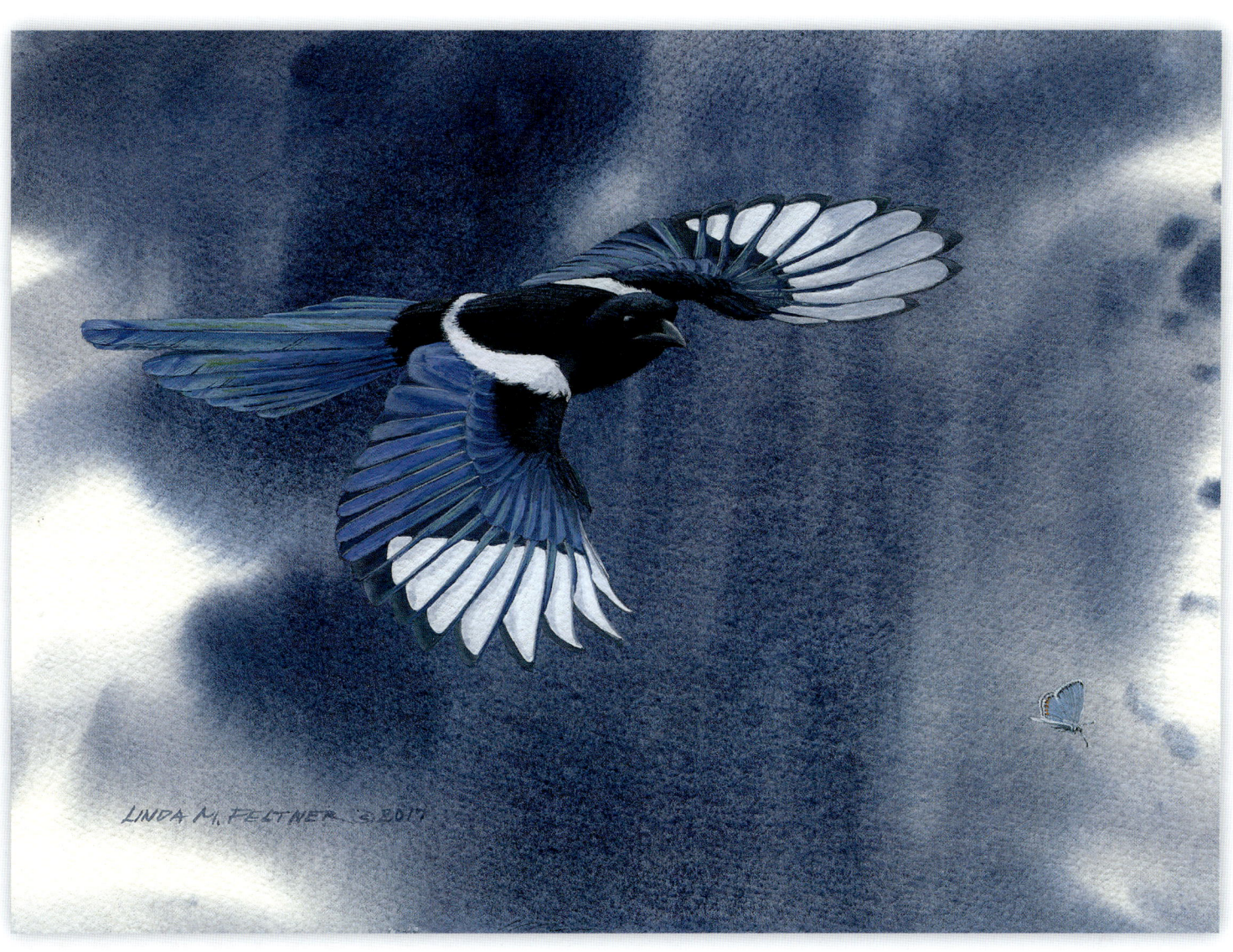

"Winged Mischief": Flying Sketches

Flying bird compositions start with sketches based on projections of still photos and videos. I sit back, capture the gestures, and don't bother with details. The goal is to capture the sweep of movement that comes naturally to the bird. Later, with several drawings to choose from, it becomes exciting to cut and paste and create a flock that exemplifies the species.

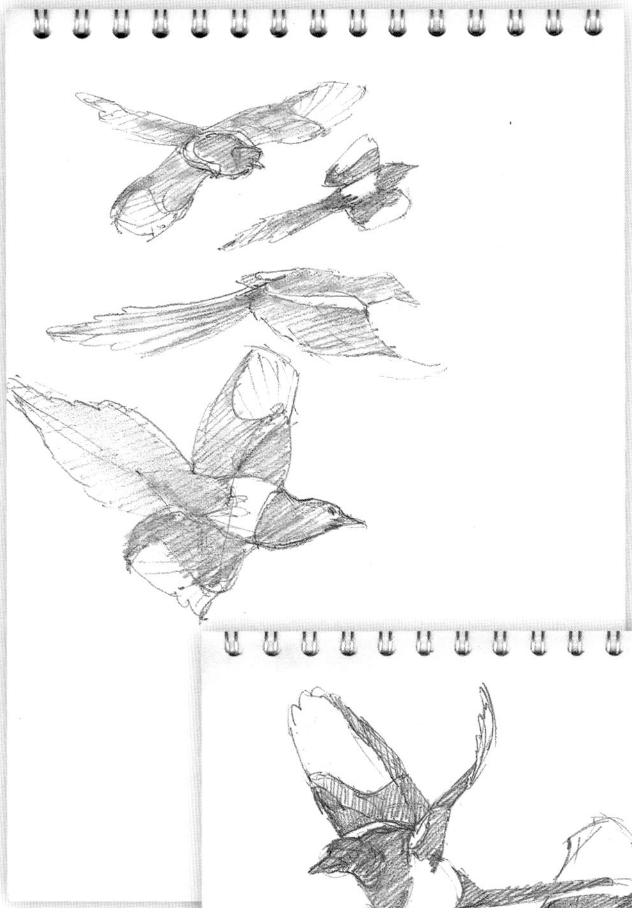

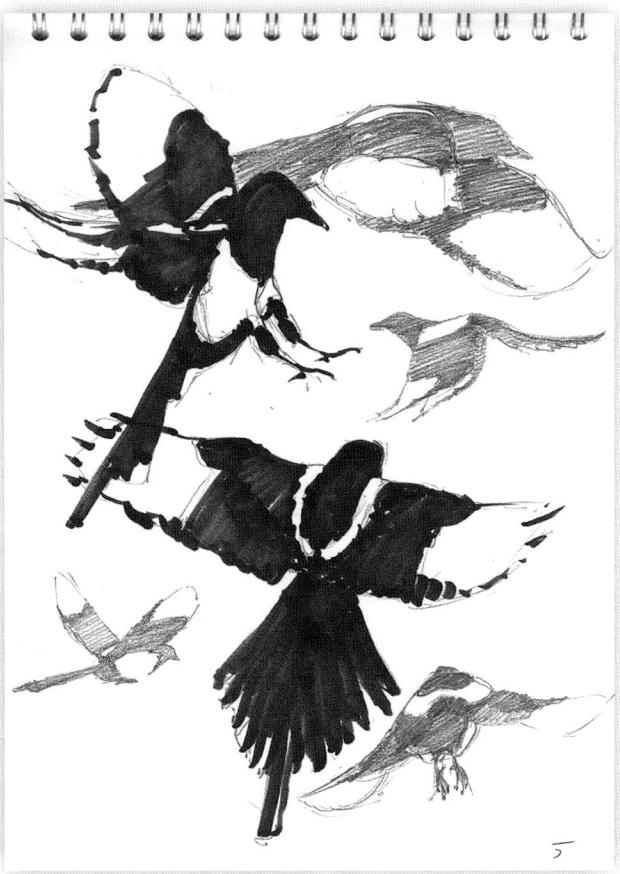

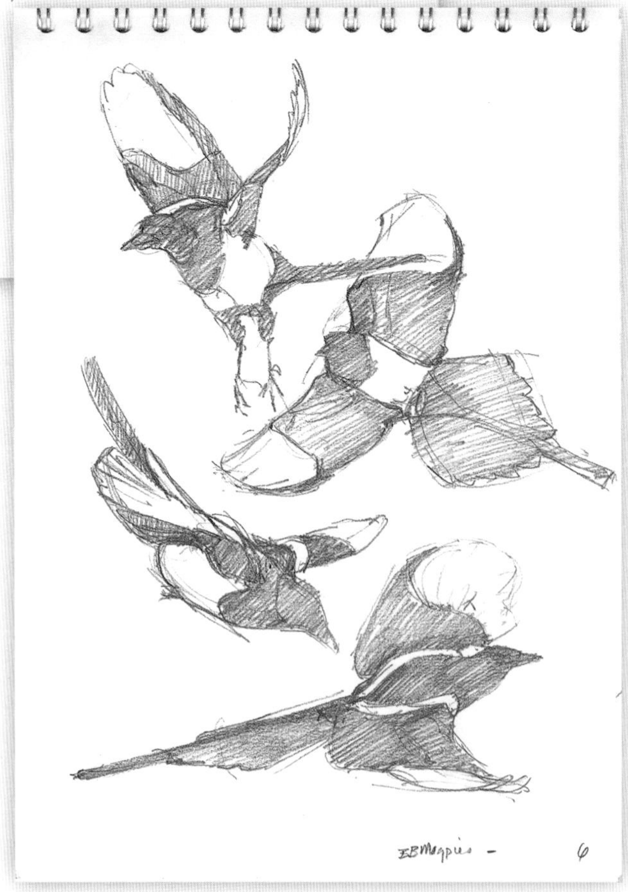

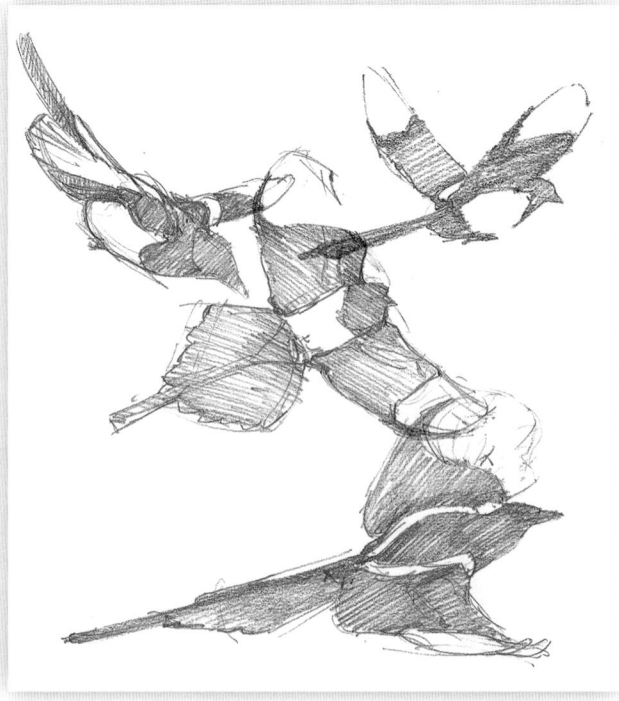

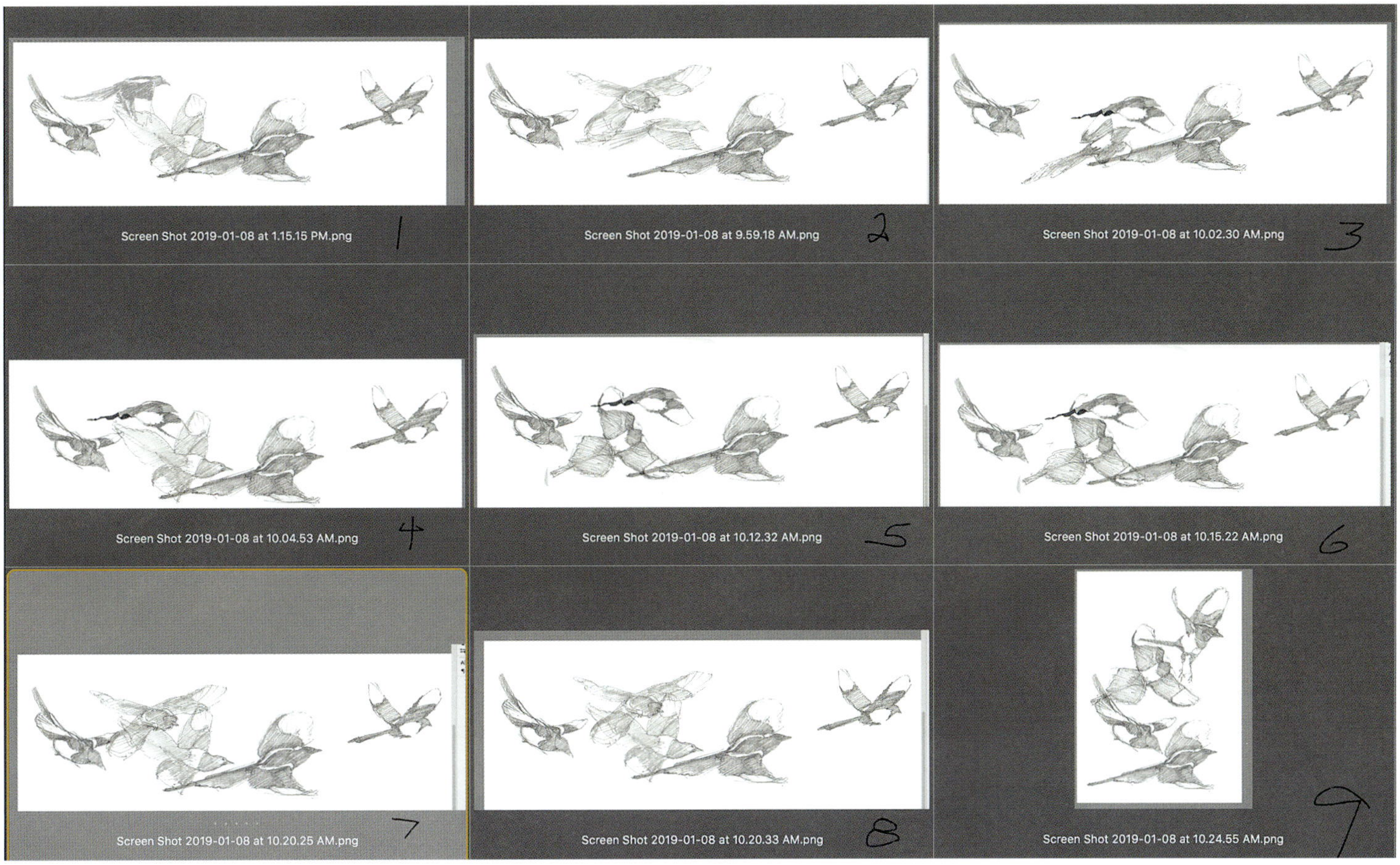

Place each bird on a layer in a paint program to shuffle them into a pattern easily. Saving the layers as a screenshot is a quick way of remembering what was created three steps ago.

Notan is a method using only black and white to determine how shapes relate. The background wash is considered part of the composition, reinforcing the rhythm.

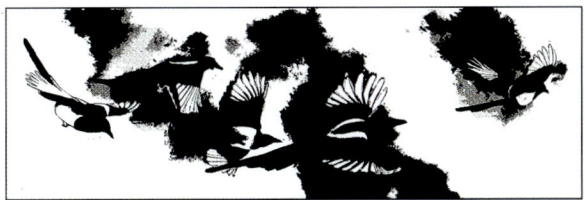

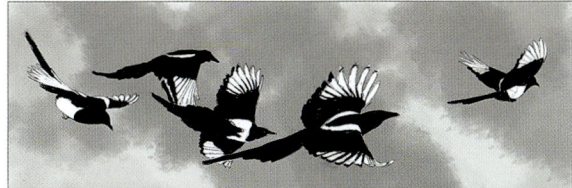

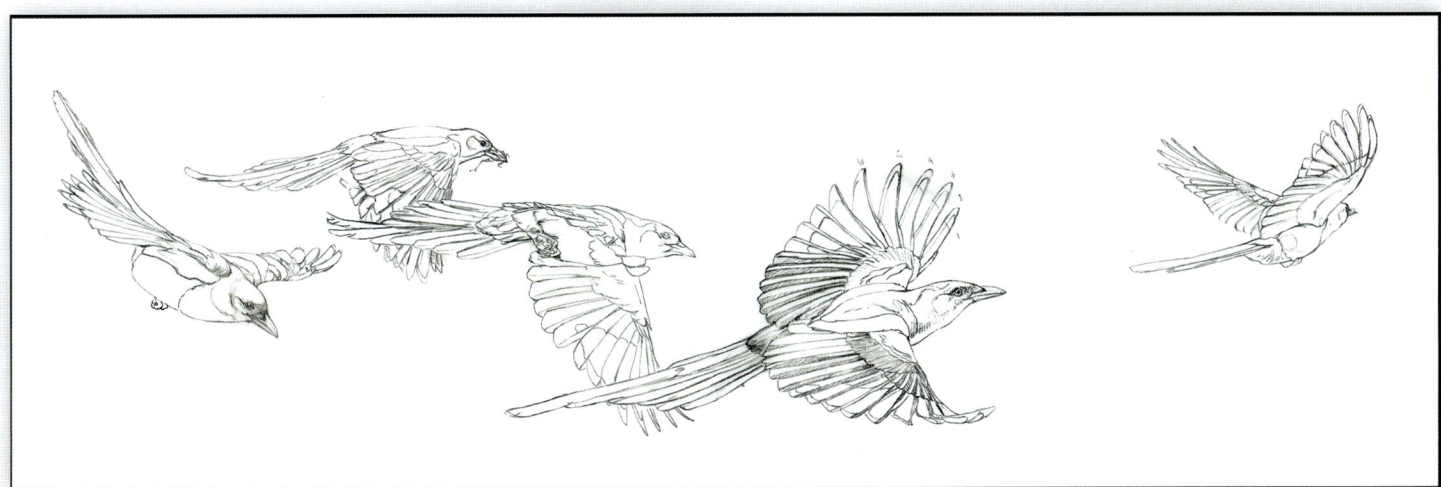

The final selection is prepared at 100 percent of the size of the painting (9 x 28 in) (22.86 x 71.12 cm). Each bird is drawn on tracing paper with precise details and combined on a single sheet, ready for transfer to watercolor paper.

"Winged Mischief"

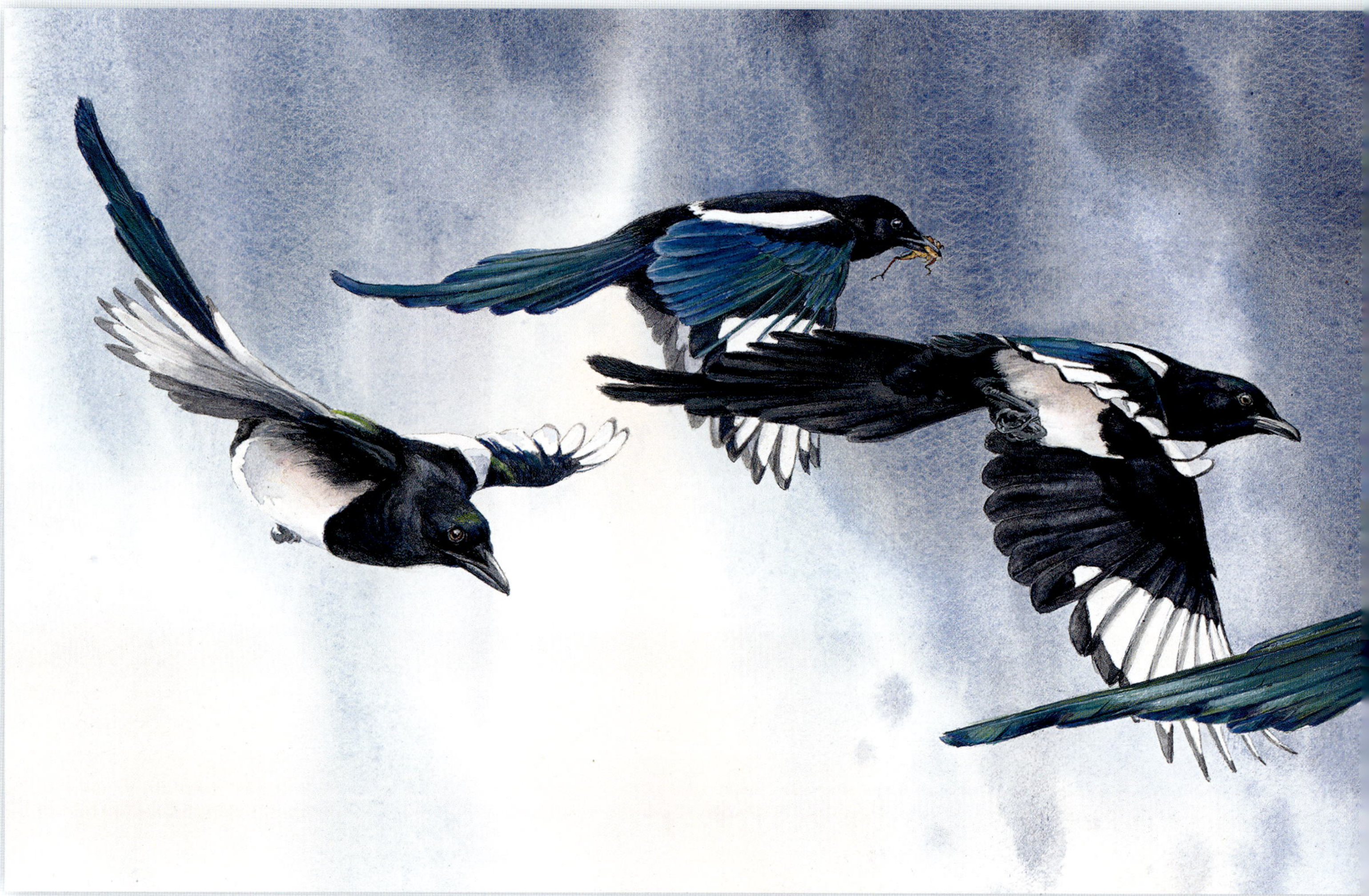

Iconic birds of the American West, Black-billed Magpies are bold and flashy members of the jay and raven family. The distinctive pattern appears black and white if seen across a distant field. Up close, a sun-struck bird's feathers will flash iridescent colors. They travel together in playful groups, sweeping across the landscape in waves of sapphire and emerald.

Black-billed Magpie (*Pica hudsonia*) and Red-legged Grasshopper (*Melanoplus femurrubrum*)

Winged Mischief, 9 × 28 in (22.86 × 71.12 cm), watercolor.

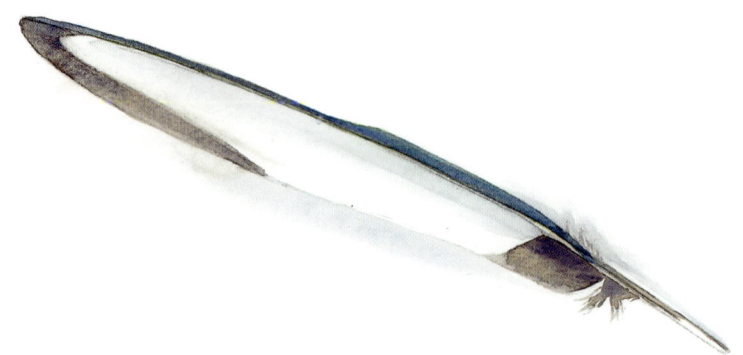

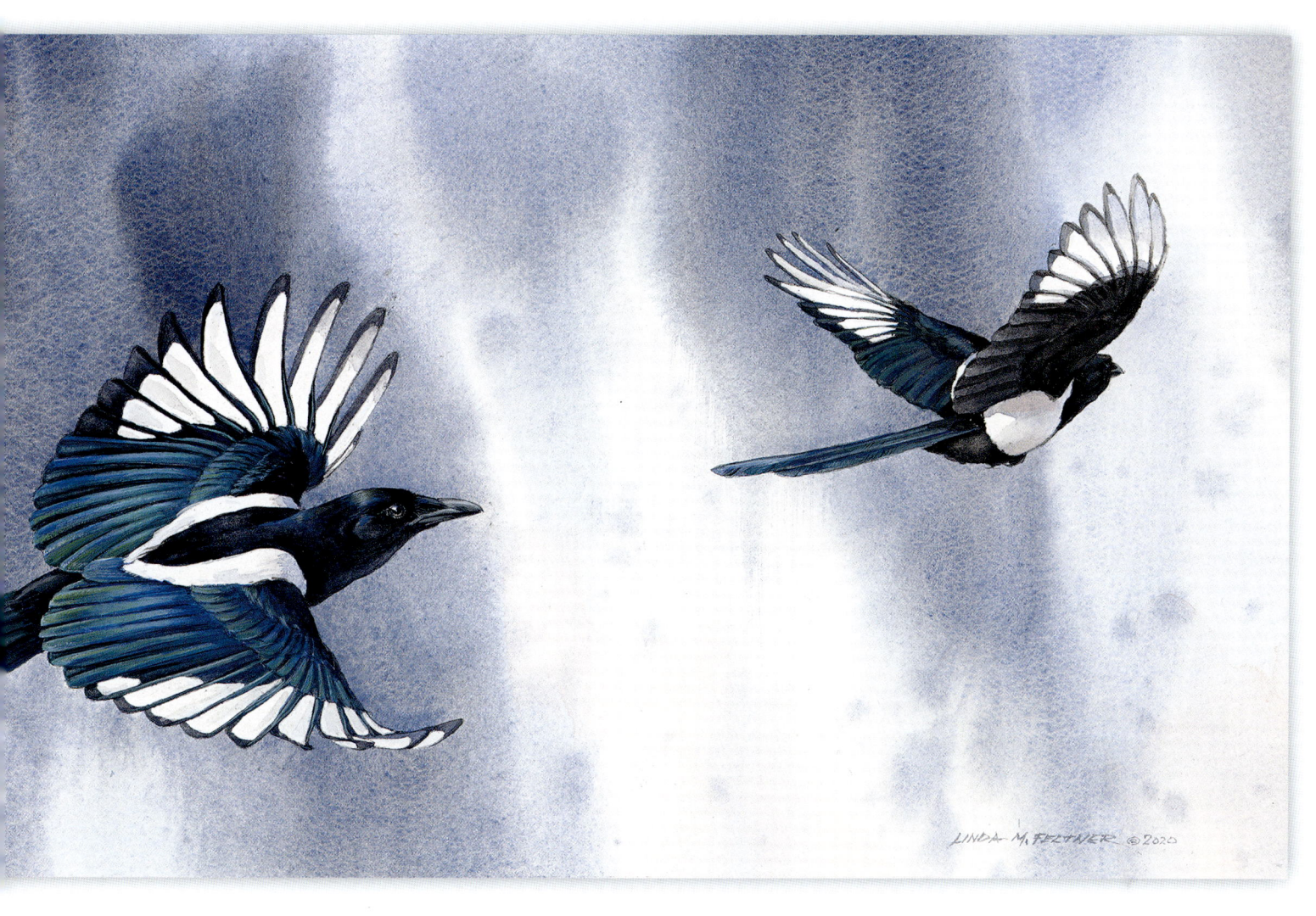

Eskimo Curlew: Gone but Not Forgotten

As a bird artist, I shall never paint this curlew from life. No one can, in all probability. Bringing an extinct bird back to life through scientific illustration was my way of paying homage.

My personal interest stemmed from my husband, T. Ben Feltner, who rediscovered the Eskimo Curlew (*Numenius borealis*) on Galveston Island on March 22, 1959, along with his friend Dudley A. Deaver. This sighting shocked the ornithological world and encouraged research for further evidence that the birds might have a viable population.

I began to work on this bird aided by museum specimens and the few photos of the last Galveston bird taken by Don Bleitz. Best of all, I listened to firsthand descriptions from one of the few people alive today who has intensely observed a living bird. Ben's knowledge and inspiration were invaluable.

The Whimbrel (*Numenius phaeopus*), a living relative, was a model for general body structure, balance, and posture. Anatomy elements were adjusted on nine layers of overlying tracing paper in order to transition and reshape it to a new species.

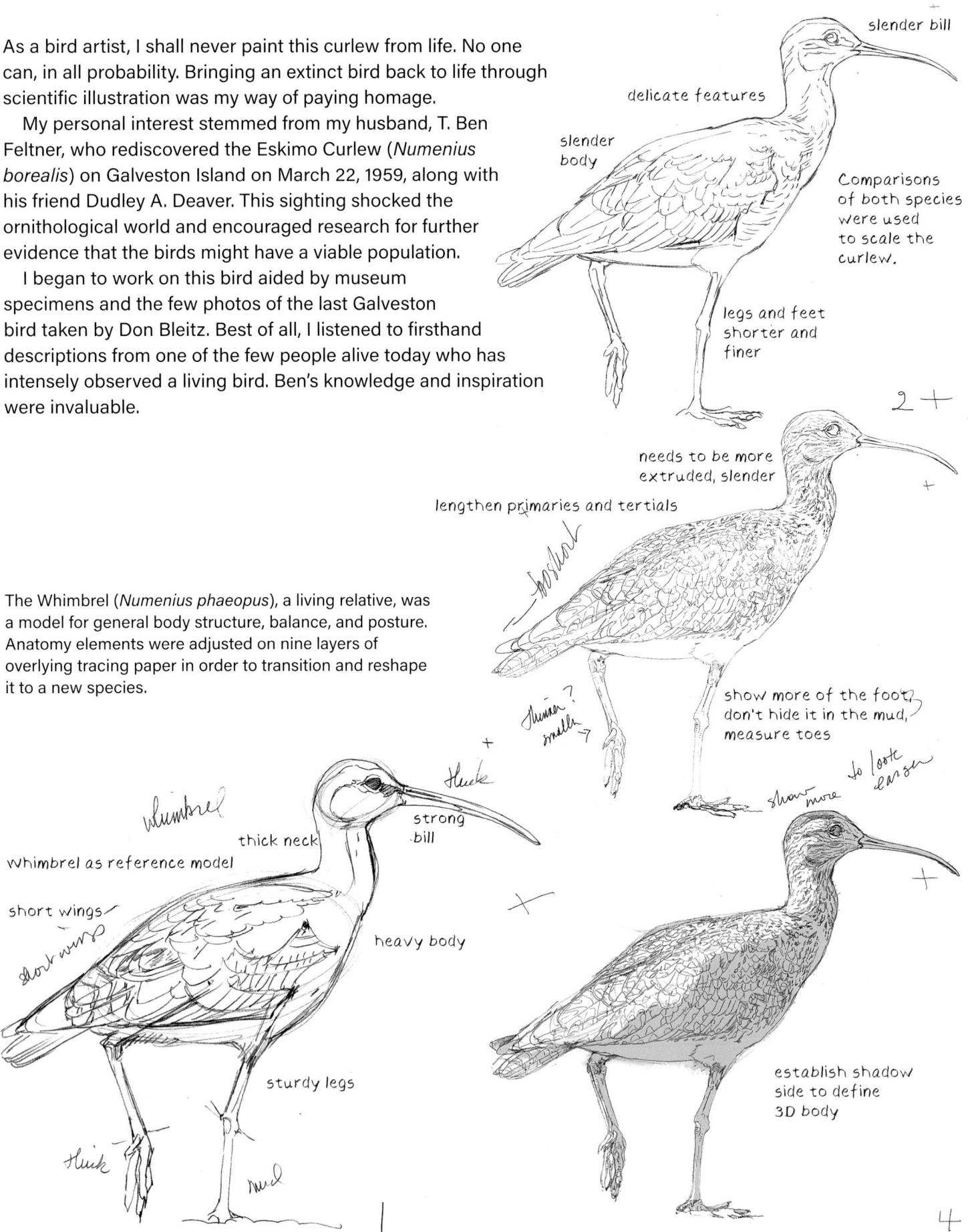

slender bill

delicate features

slender body

Comparisons of both species were used to scale the curlew.

legs and feet shorter and finer

2 +

needs to be more extruded, slender

lengthen primaries and tertials

show more of the foot, don't hide it in the mud, measure toes

whimbrel

thick neck

strong bill

whimbrel as reference model

short wings

heavy body

sturdy legs

show more to look larger

establish shadow side to define 3D body

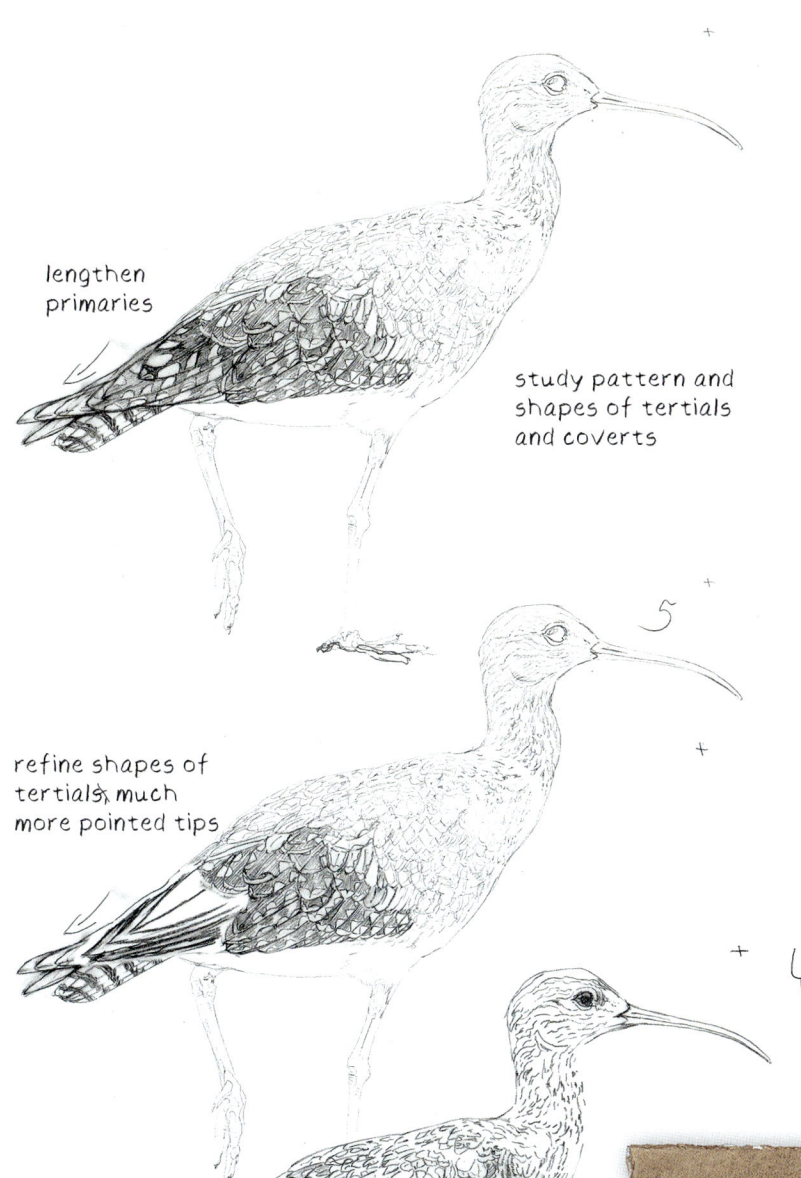

lengthen
primaries

study pattern and
shapes of tertials
and coverts

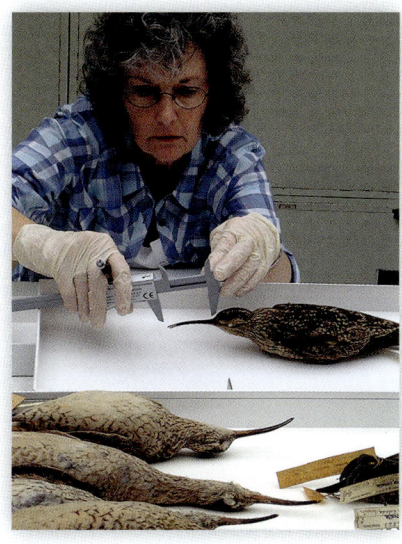

refine shapes of
tertials, much
more pointed tips

without personal knowledge of having seen a
living bird, my research began by investigating
resources that would supply crucial
information. Observing and measuring specimens
at the Smithsonian National Museum of
Natural History provided a heavy-hearted but
significant opportunity to get a feel for the
size, coloration, and variety. Photo courtesy of
Ikumi Kayama.

feather pattern
and shapes
refined

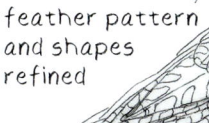

ready to
transfer to
good paper

Eskimo Curlew (*Numenius borealis*)

Eskimo Curlew, first rendition,
8 x 8 in (20.32 x 20.32 cm), transparent
watercolor on Fabriano Artistico paper.

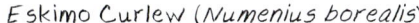

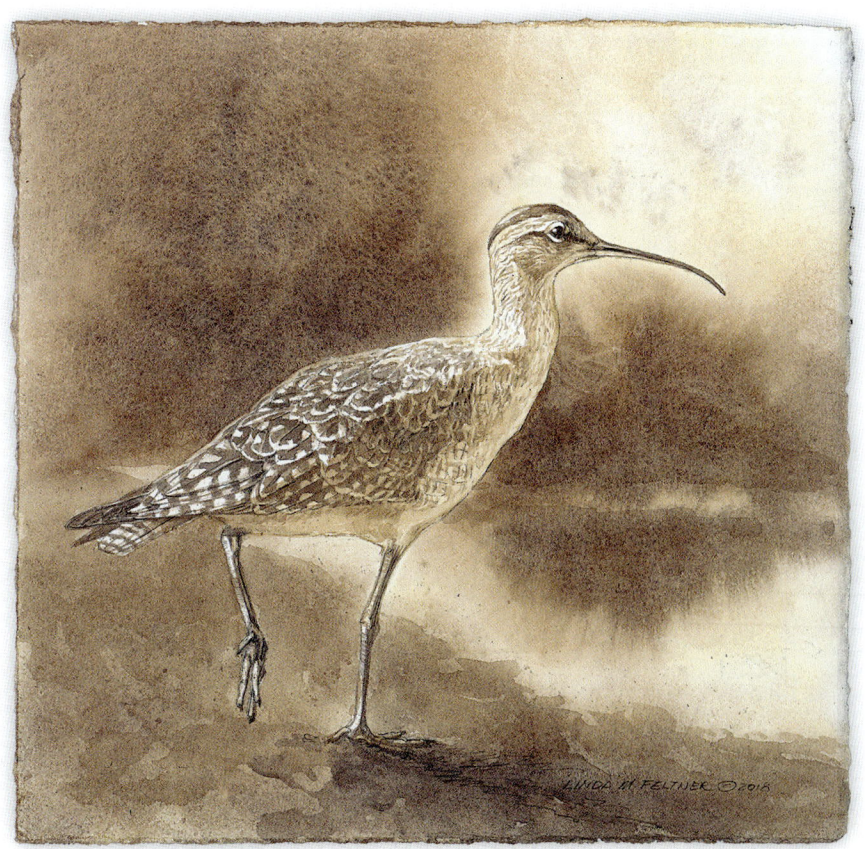

"20th Century Bird: Eskimo Curlew"

Formerly one of the most abundant birds in North America, the Eskimo Curlew is now listed as Critically Endangered on the IUCN Red List but is thought to be extinct.

   Immense flocks used to migrate, nesting in the arctic tundra of western Canada and Alaska and wintering in southern South America. They covered acres of grasslands, feasting on insects like grasshoppers. The conversion of native prairie to agricultural land contributed to a loss of food sources. Unafraid of humans, they fell in large numbers to the unregulated hunting in the mid-1800s and were called "dough-birds" for their fattened state. The once-massive population was unable to recover.

"After my involvement in the initial discovery of the Eskimo Curlew, it was my privilege to spend many hours observing the bird in the field. I often watched it feed, probing among grass clumps. It was more active in its movements than either the accompanying Whimbrel or Long-billed Curlews. It preferred the company of American Golden Plovers or at other times it fed alone. Small invertebrates seemed to be the primary prey items; occasionally small grasshoppers were identifiable.

   My friend Jerry Strickling, who was monitoring the bird's locations for visitors, asked me to keep tabs on the last known location of the bird before I left the island on the weekends. This happy task led to a singular event.

   Saturday at dusk, I was standing at the edge of a pasture watching the curlew as it fed alone. It worked the ground, moving towards me. Realizing the bird was on a contact trajectory with me, I started to back up slowly. At about ten yards, the bird stopped and looked directly at me. Slowly it sank to the ground and froze like a Snipe. For a few seconds we studied each other then I backed away still eye to eye with it. The next day it was found still in the same pasture and I had a photographic memory that will last at least in my lifetime.

   On 31 March 1962, I was again watching the curlew with Bill and Gene Petit, when a passing birder stopped to ask what was holding our attention. The Eskimo Curlew was our response. At that, the enquirer stated he had just seen it five miles to the east. How could this be? A terrifyingly fast drive ensued to the location he indicated. There we found Bob Deheyes looking at another Eskimo Curlew. Amazingly, it was established that least two birds still existed. A slight difference in bill curvature was noted by all present. This was a high count for a bird shortly to be extirpated. Subsequent trips on 1 April and 7 April revealed the two birds were still present. Sadly, they were never seen together. And then there were none!"

—Trevor Ben Feltner, Sr.

20th Century Bird: Eskimo Curlew, 11 × 15 in (27.94 × 38.1 cm), transparent watercolor on Fabriano Artistico paper.

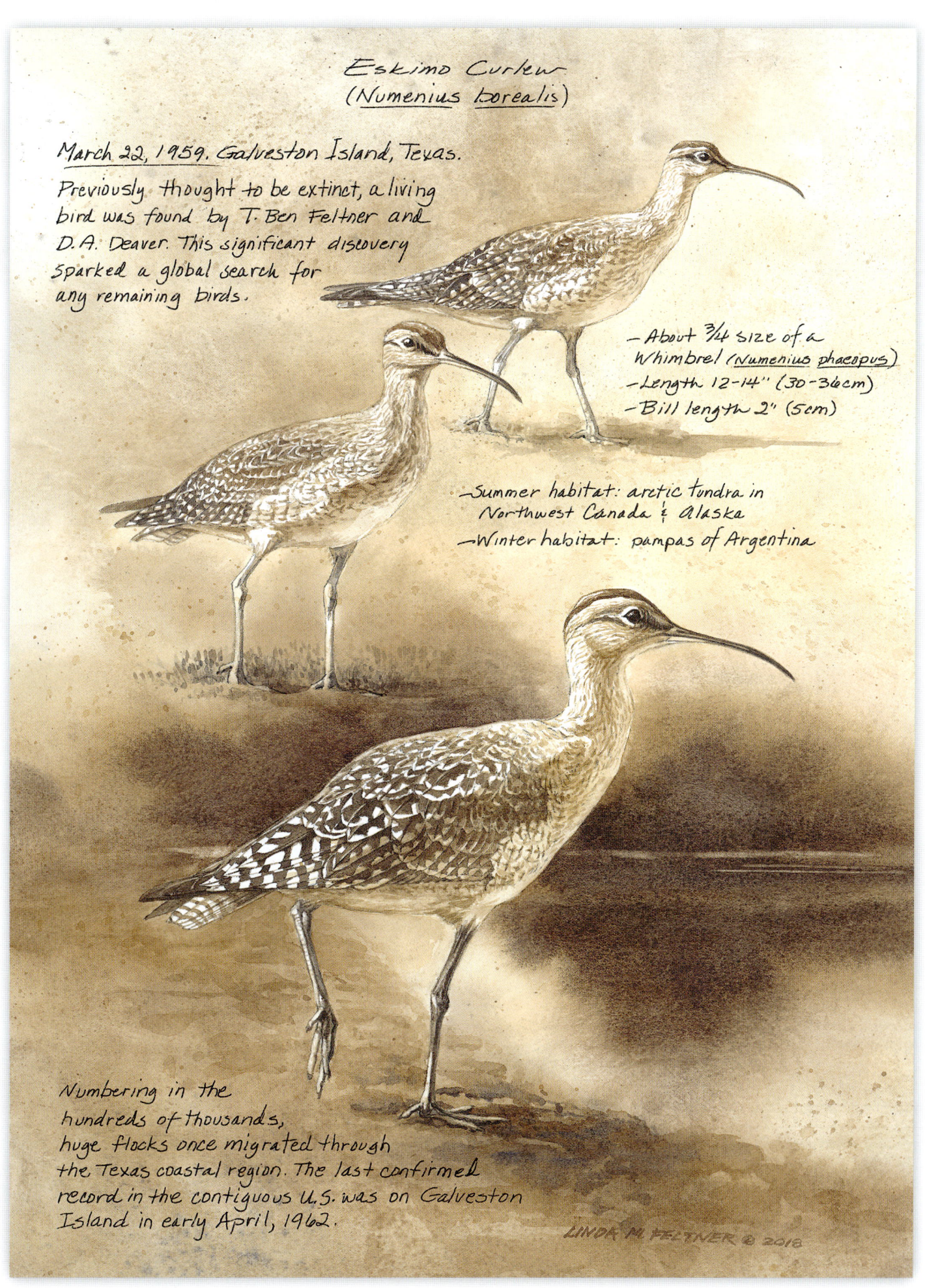

Eskimo Curlew
(_Numenius borealis_)

March 22, 1959. Galveston Island, Texas.
Previously thought to be extinct, a living
bird was found by T. Ben Feltner and
D.A. Deaver. This significant discovery
sparked a global search for
any remaining birds.

— About ¾ size of a
Whimbrel (_Numenius phaeopus_)
— Length 12-14'' (30-36cm)
— Bill length 2'' (5cm)

— Summer habitat: arctic tundra in
Northwest Canada & Alaska
— Winter habitat: pampas of Argentina

Numbering in the
hundreds of thousands,
huge flocks once migrated through
the Texas coastal region. The last confirmed
record in the contiguous U.S. was on Galveston
Island in early April, 1962.

LINDA M. FELTNER © 2018

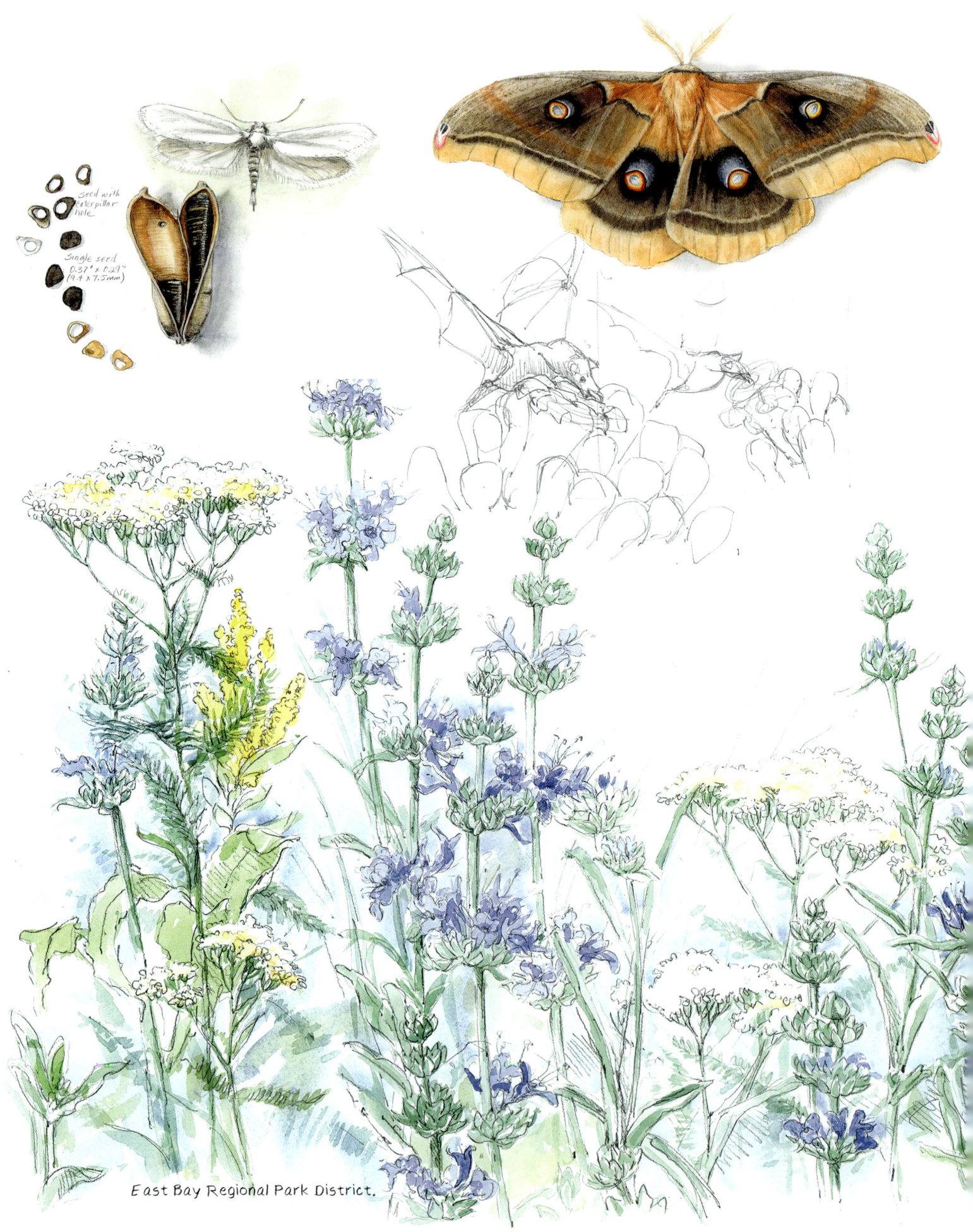

Seed with caterpillar hole

Single seed
0.37" x 0.29"
(9.4 x 7.5mm)

East Bay Regional Park District.

CHAPTER 3

Ancient Partnerships

Imagine a world without chocolate or coffee!

From the late Age of Dinosaurs, flowers began to explode and cover the earth, adapting to new conditions, with animal diversity developing in tandem. Walk around a yard, park, or city street and discover flowering, fruiting, and seeding plants. Listen for the vibrations of wings hovering over a flowering meadow.

Flowers exude sweet nectar to entice a visitor, where pollen sticks to feathers, fur, or insect bodies and becomes transferred to another flower. Animals transport seeds away from the parent plant. Hooked seeds cling to fur and clothing. Some are encased in juicy fruit to be eaten whole and voided undigested far away.

Wander along with me through fields of thistles, the southwestern deserts, and the diversity of my home biome. I take a close look at partnerships where one tiny creature leads to crucial connections in nature. What happens when insects just won't do?

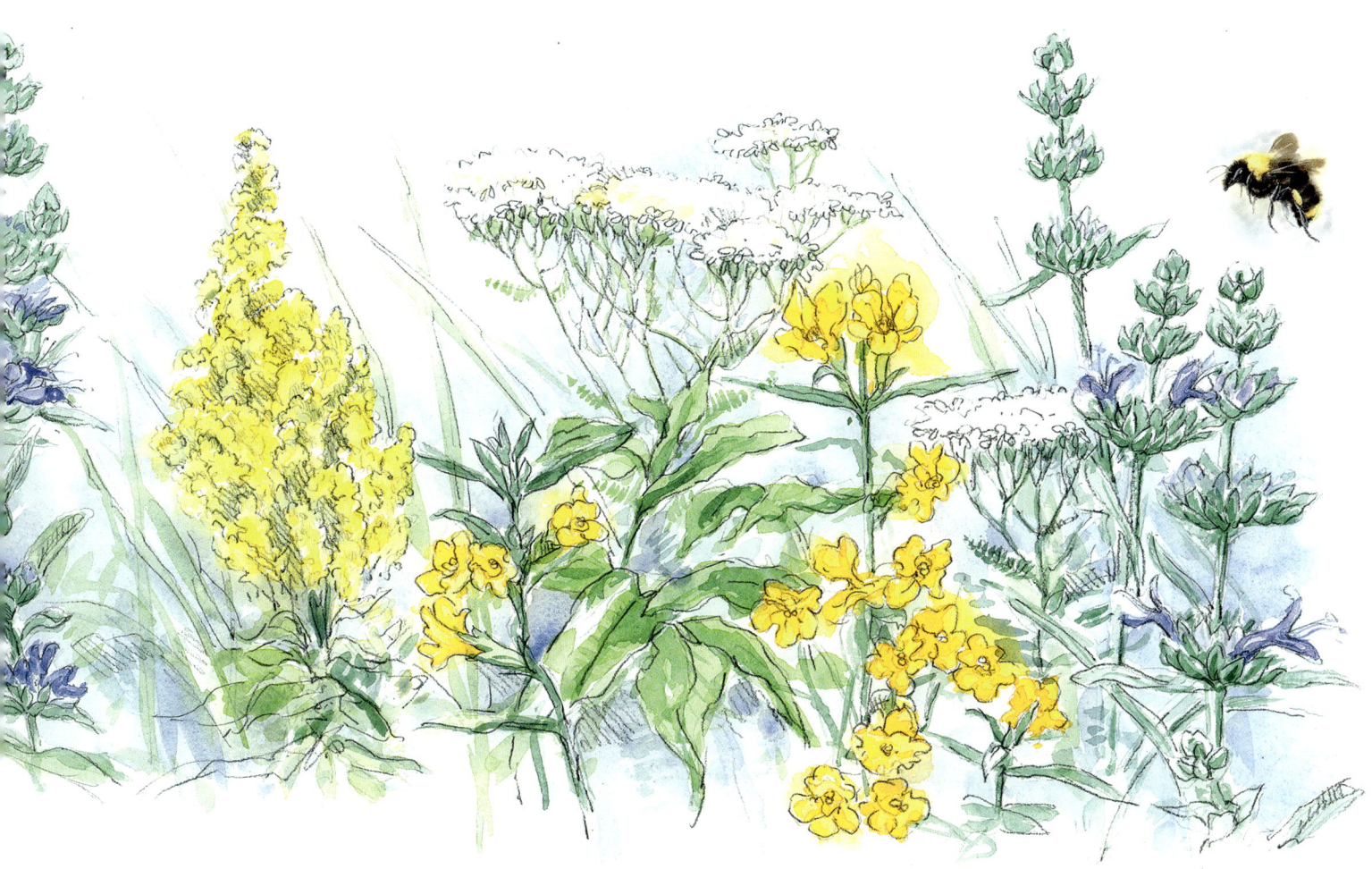

Contemplating Insects on a Thistle

A spring day in May found me wandering among thistles.
The flutter of insects and a mass of color captured my attention.

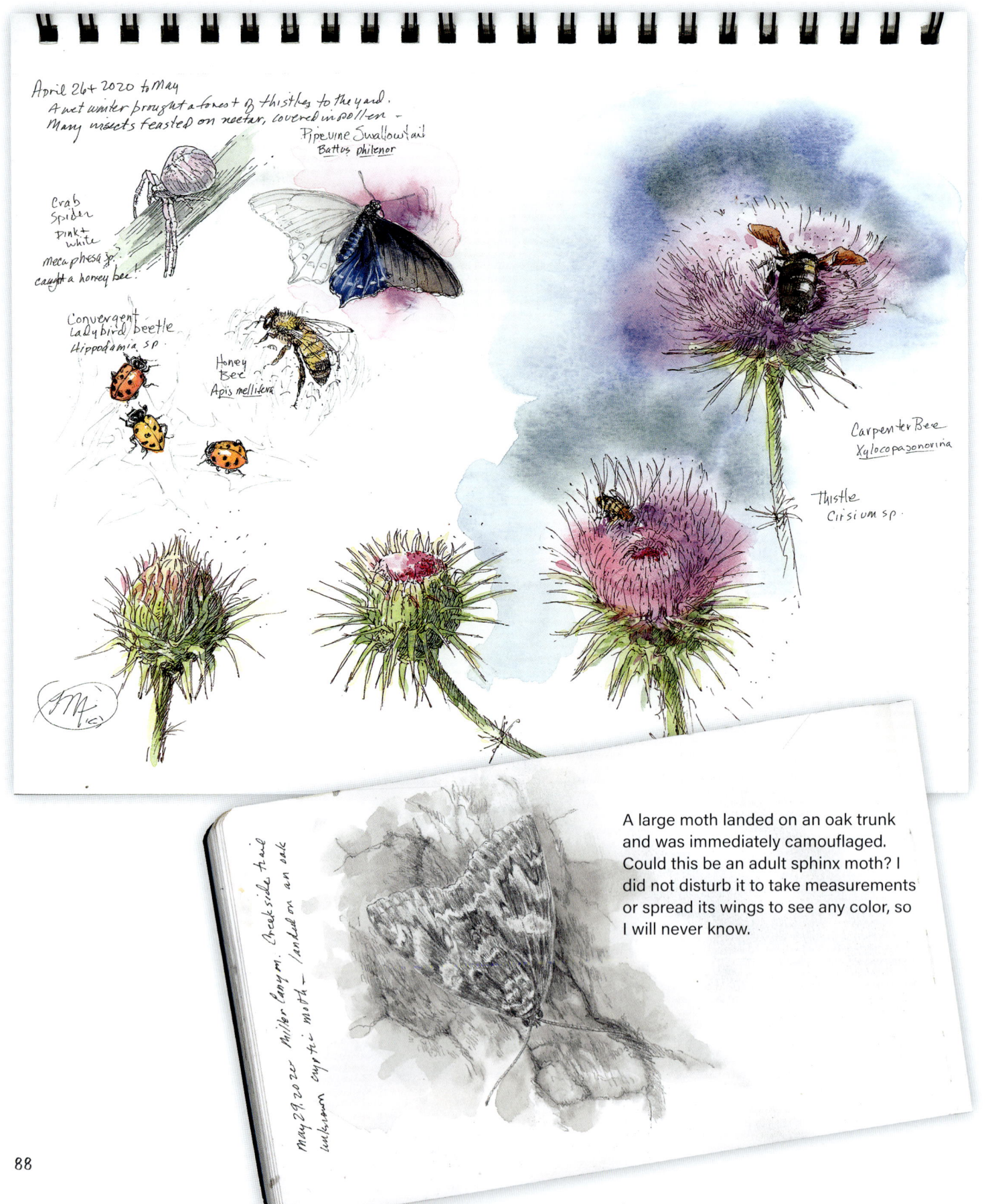

April 26th 2020 to May
A wet winter brought a forest of thistles to the yard.
Many insects feasted on nectar, covered in pollen —

Pipevine Swallowtail
Battus philenor

Crab
Spider
Pink +
white
mecaphesa sp.
caught a honey bee!

Convergent
ladybird beetle
Hippodamia. sp.

Honey
Bee
Apis mellifera

Carpenter Bee
Xylocopa sonorina

Thistle
Cirsium sp.

May 29 2020 Miller Canyon. Creekside trail
unknown cryptic moth — landed on an oak

A large moth landed on an oak trunk
and was immediately camouflaged.
Could this be an adult sphinx moth? I
did not disturb it to take measurements
or spread its wings to see any color, so
I will never know.

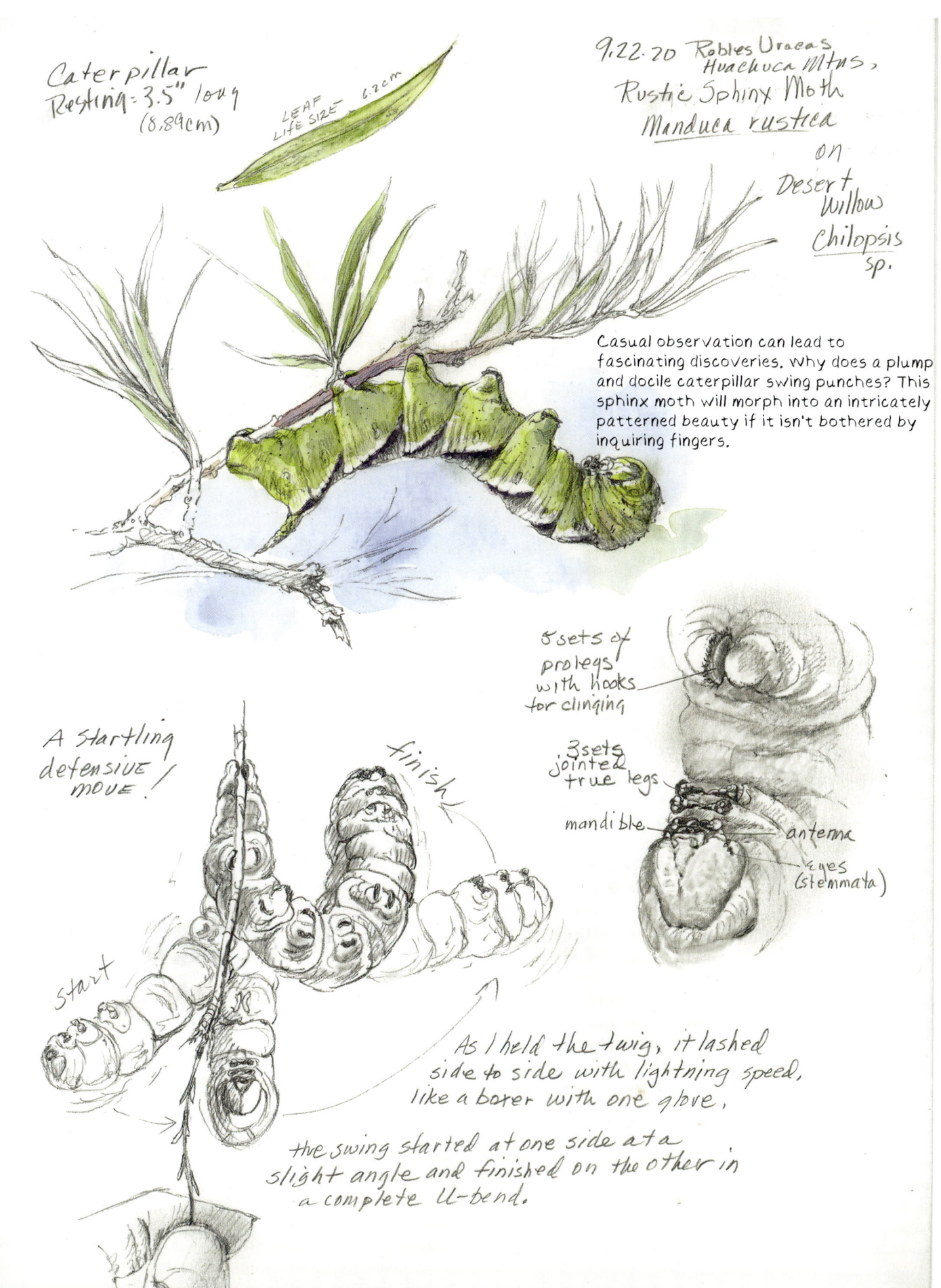

Caterpillar
Resting = 3.5" long
(8.89cm)

LEAF
LIFE SIZE   6.2cm

9.22.20 Robles Uraeas
Huachuca Mtns,
Rustic Sphinx Moth
Manduca rustica
on
Desert
Willow
Chilopsis
sp.

Casual observation can lead to
fascinating discoveries. Why does a plump
and docile caterpillar swing punches? This
sphinx moth will morph into an intricately
patterned beauty if it isn't bothered by
inquiring fingers.

5 sets of
prolegs
with hooks
for clinging

3 sets
jointed
true legs

mandible

antenna

eyes
(stemmata)

A startling
defensive
move!

finish

start

As I held the twig, it lashed
side to side with lightning speed,
like a boxer with one glove,

the swing started at one side at a
slight angle and finished on the other in
a complete U-bend.

A Much Closer Look …

My interest in insects on thistles kindled a fascination with local species of beetles. My class on sketching and nature journaling examined specimens loaned by a local entomologist.

The beetle collection presented the challenge of painting hard or soft reflections and iridescence. The fact that the subject didn't move provided an opportunity to create measured and detailed drawings.

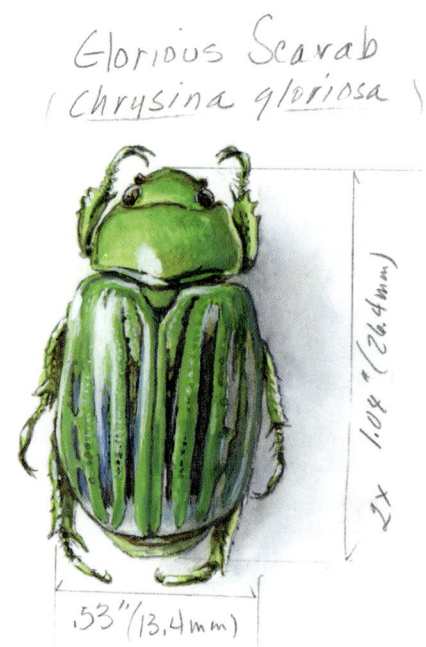

Glorious Scarab
(chrysina gloriosa)

1.08" (26.4mm) 2X

.53" (13.4mm)

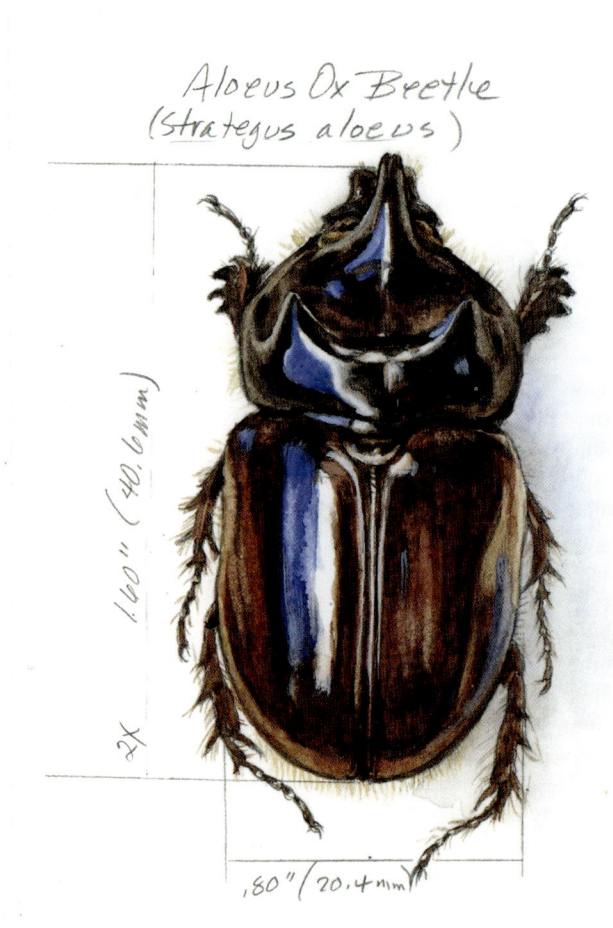

Aloeus Ox Beetle
(Strategus aloeus)

1.60" (40.6mm) 2X

.80" (20.4mm)

Studies of pinned specimens

"Beetles make up 25% of all animal life forms, with about 400,000 described species, and estimates for the number of species that actually exist range from 1 to 2 million. While some beetles are among the largest known insects, many are small to very tiny, and are poorly known scientifically, so that it is fairly easy to find unknown species in your backyard.

Many famous naturalists have had a fondness for beetles. Charles Darwin wrote in an 1858 letter to the botanist J. D. Hooker, 'I feel like an old war-horse at the sound of a trumpet when I read about the capture of rare beetles.'"

—Norman E. Woodley, Research Collaborator, Smithsonian Institution

Tools:

- A strong magnifier (mine is clamped to the table with an extendable arm)
- 10× loupe
- A light source coming from the upper left of the subject at a 45-degree angle (a scientific illustration convention)
- A precise ruler or calipers that measure both millimeter and inch

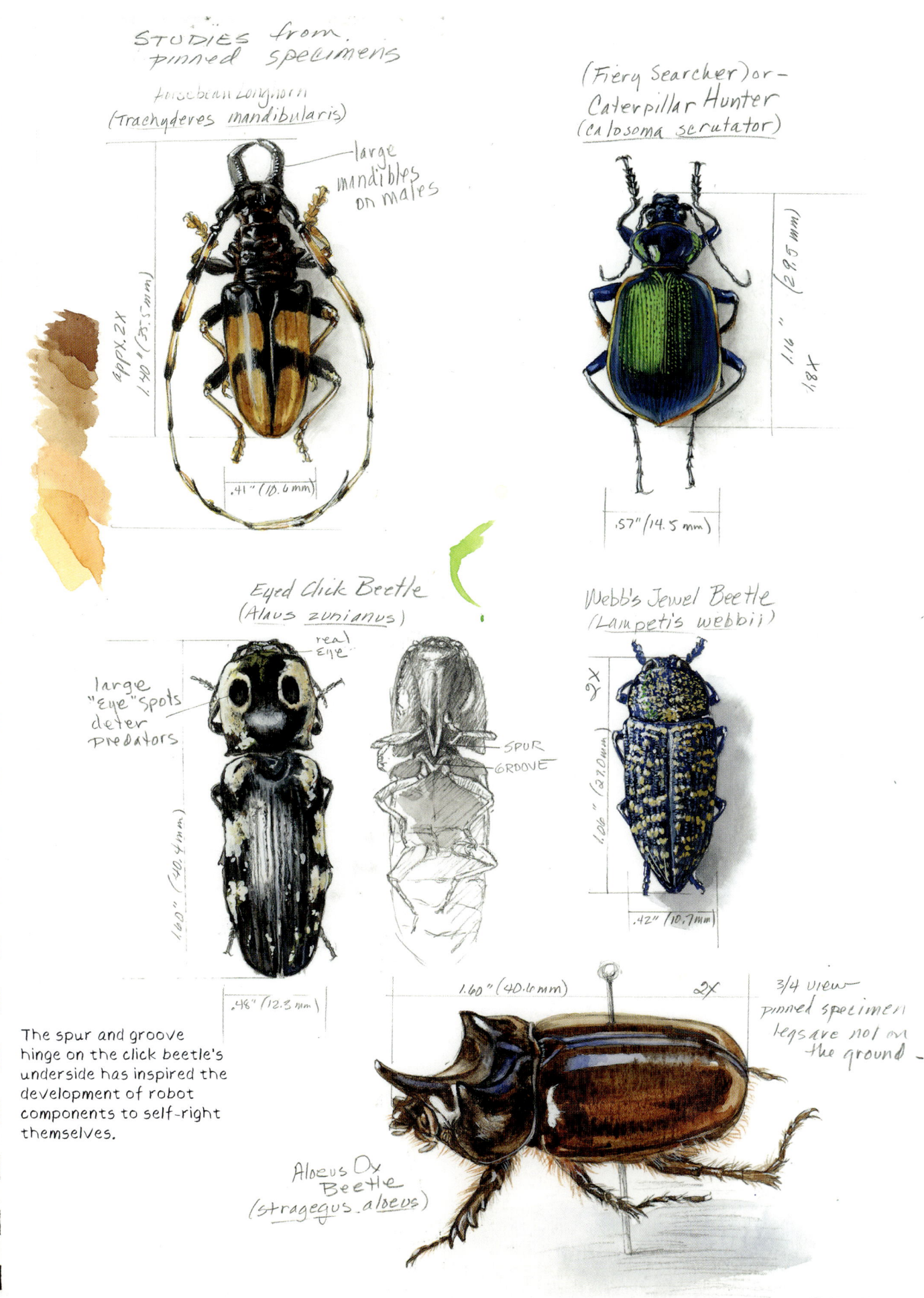

STUDIES from
pinned specimens

Harlequin Longhorn
(Trachyderes mandibularis)

large
mandibles
on males

appx 2X
1.40" (35.5 mm)

.41" (10.6 mm)

(Fiery Searcher) or—
Caterpillar Hunter
(calosoma scrutator)

1.12" (28.5 mm)

1.16"
1.8X

.57" (14.5 mm)

Eyed Click Beetle
(Alaus zunianus)

real
Eye

large
"Eye" spots
deter
predators

1.60" (40.4mm)

SPUR
GROOVE

.48" (12.3 mm)

Webb's Jewel Beetle
(Lampetis webbii)

2X

1.06" (27.0mm)

.42" (10.7mm)

The spur and groove
hinge on the click beetle's
underside has inspired the
development of robot
components to self-right
themselves.

1.60" (40.6mm)   2X

3/4 view
pinned specimen
legs are not on
the ground.

Aloeus Ox
Beetle
(stragegus aloeus)

Unexpected Directions

I planned to create a nocturnal painting with bats feeding among Saguaro cactus blossoms. An early morning drive around Saguaro National Park East found nighttime blossoms still open with daytime pollinators actively feeding. Honey Bees and tiny native bees buzzed over the flowers before they wilted from the sun's heat. I was impressed that such ordinary birds as White-winged Doves and Gila Woodpeckers were dominant daytime pollinators.

I became distracted by an extraordinary fan at the top of a single cactus. Crested cacti result from an unusual mutation on the growing tip. Quick sketches sparked a new idea and a new direction.

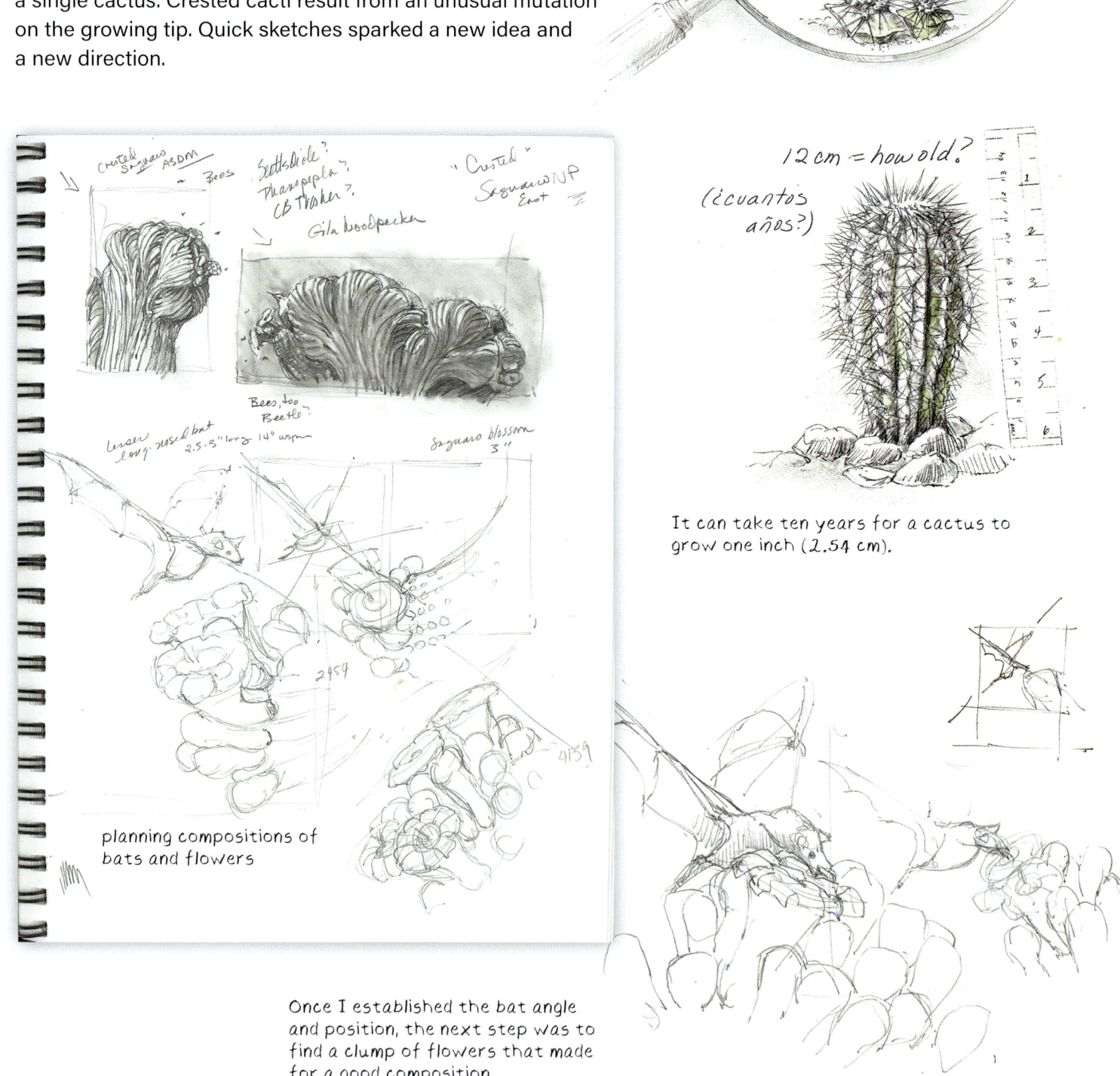

thousands of tiny black seeds (semillas)

seedlings (plantas de semillero)

tiny seedlings may be just months old

Crested Saguaro ASDM — Bees

Scottsdale? Phxpepla? CB Thrasher?

Gila Woodpecker

"Crested" Saguaro NP East

Bees, too Beetle?

lesser long-nosed bat 2.5-3" long, 14" wspn

Saguaro blossom 3"

2954

4159

planning compositions of bats and flowers

12 cm = how old? (¿cuantos años?)

It can take ten years for a cactus to grow one inch (2.54 cm).

Once I established the bat angle and position, the next step was to find a clump of flowers that made for a good composition.

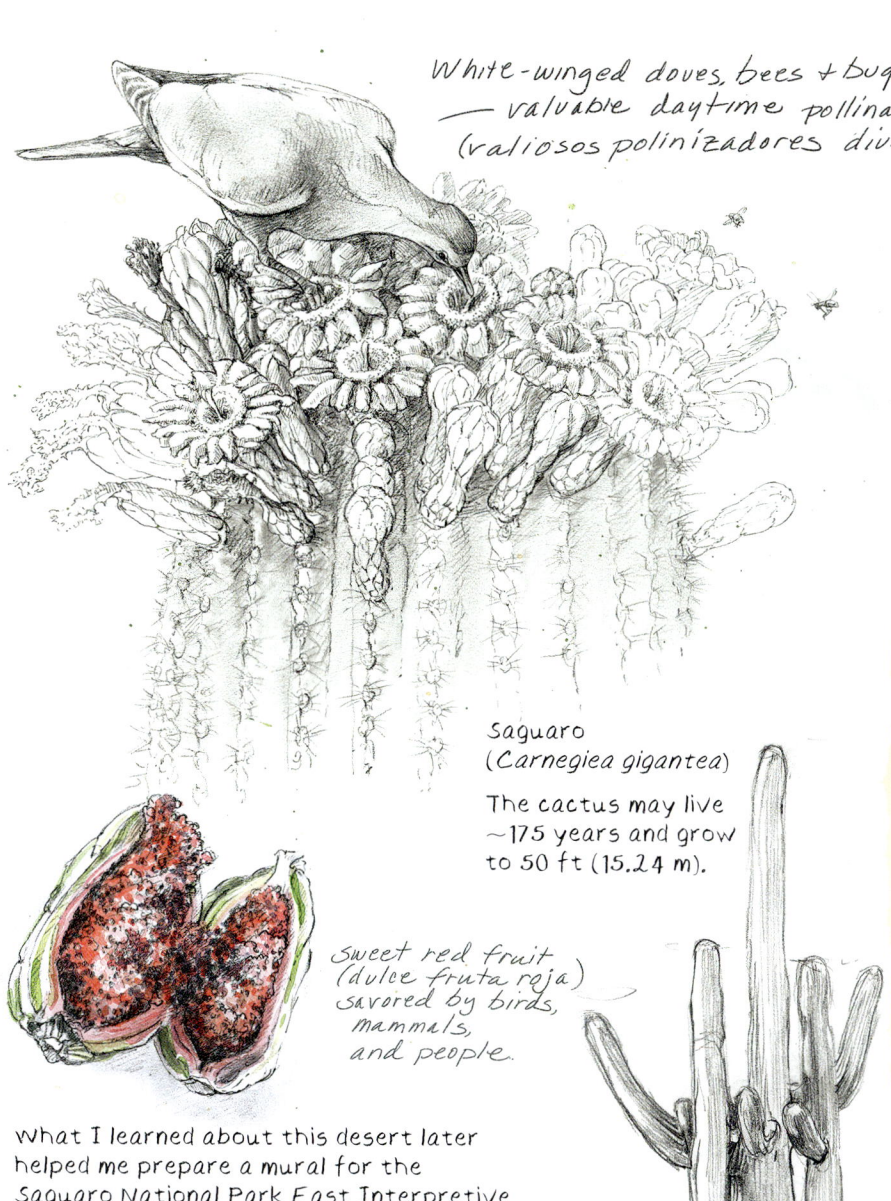

White-winged doves, bees + bugs
— valuable daytime pollinators
(valiosos polinizadores diurnos)

— nighttime pollinators
(polinizadores nocturnos)

lesser long-nosed bat
(murciélago)

Saguaro
(*Carnegiea gigantea*)

The cactus may live
~175 years and grow
to 50 ft (15.24 m).

sweet red fruit
(dulce fruta roja)
savored by birds,
mammals,
and people.

What I learned about this desert later
helped me prepare a mural for the
Saguaro National Park East Interpretive
Center, Tucson, Arizona.

"Many national parks are known for their grand and sweeping vistas, focusing on the enormity of a place. For me, at Saguaro National Park in the Sonoran Desert, the beauty is in the delicate details and relationships between species. This is a wilderness that requires cooperation and choreography to thrive and if you can slow down long enough and watch closely to observe the dance, you will see that the species here do thrive."

—Andy L. Fisher, Chief of Interpretation, Saguaro National Park

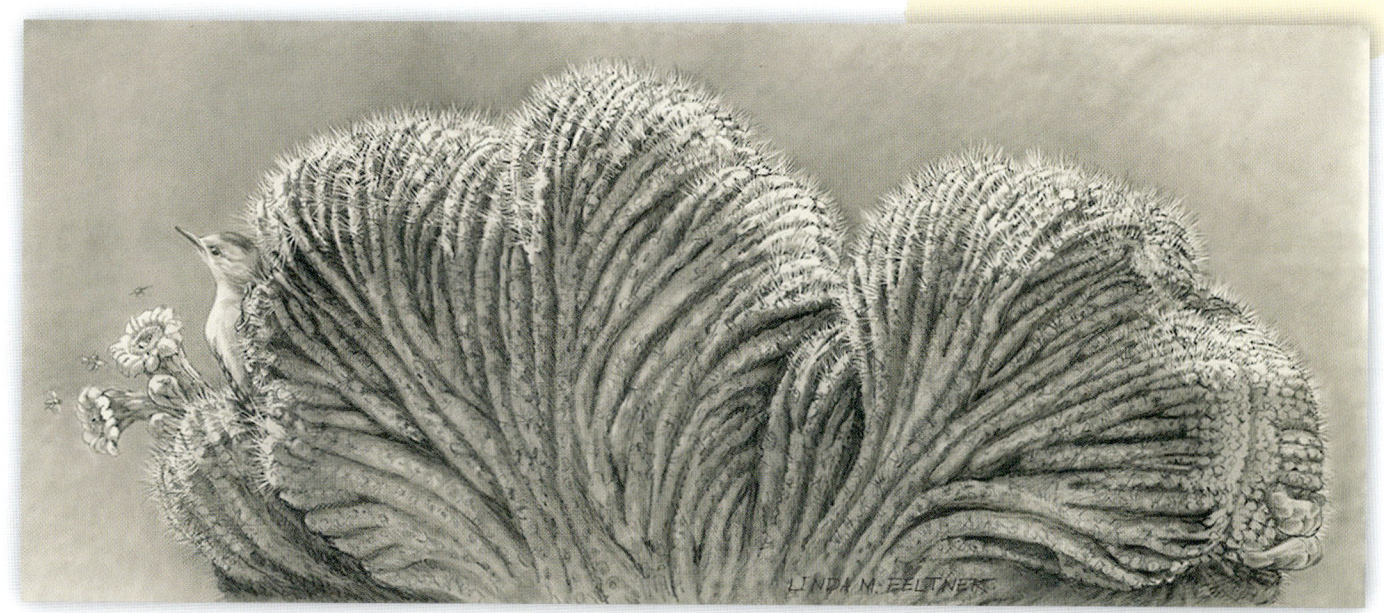

Preliminary study, 4.5 x 11 in (11.43 x 27.94 cm), graphite on Ampersand Claybord.

"Desert Fan-Crested Saguaro"

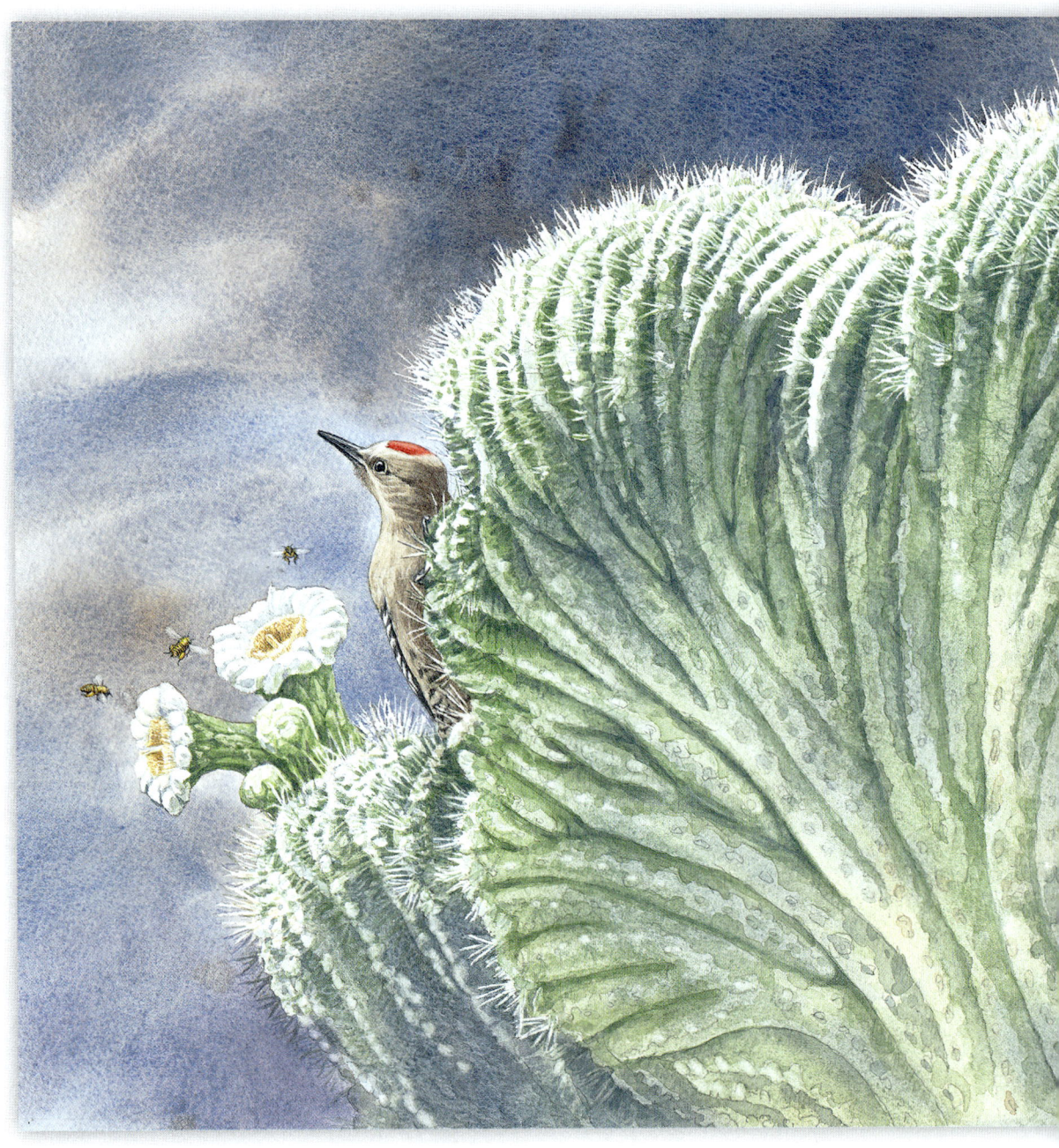

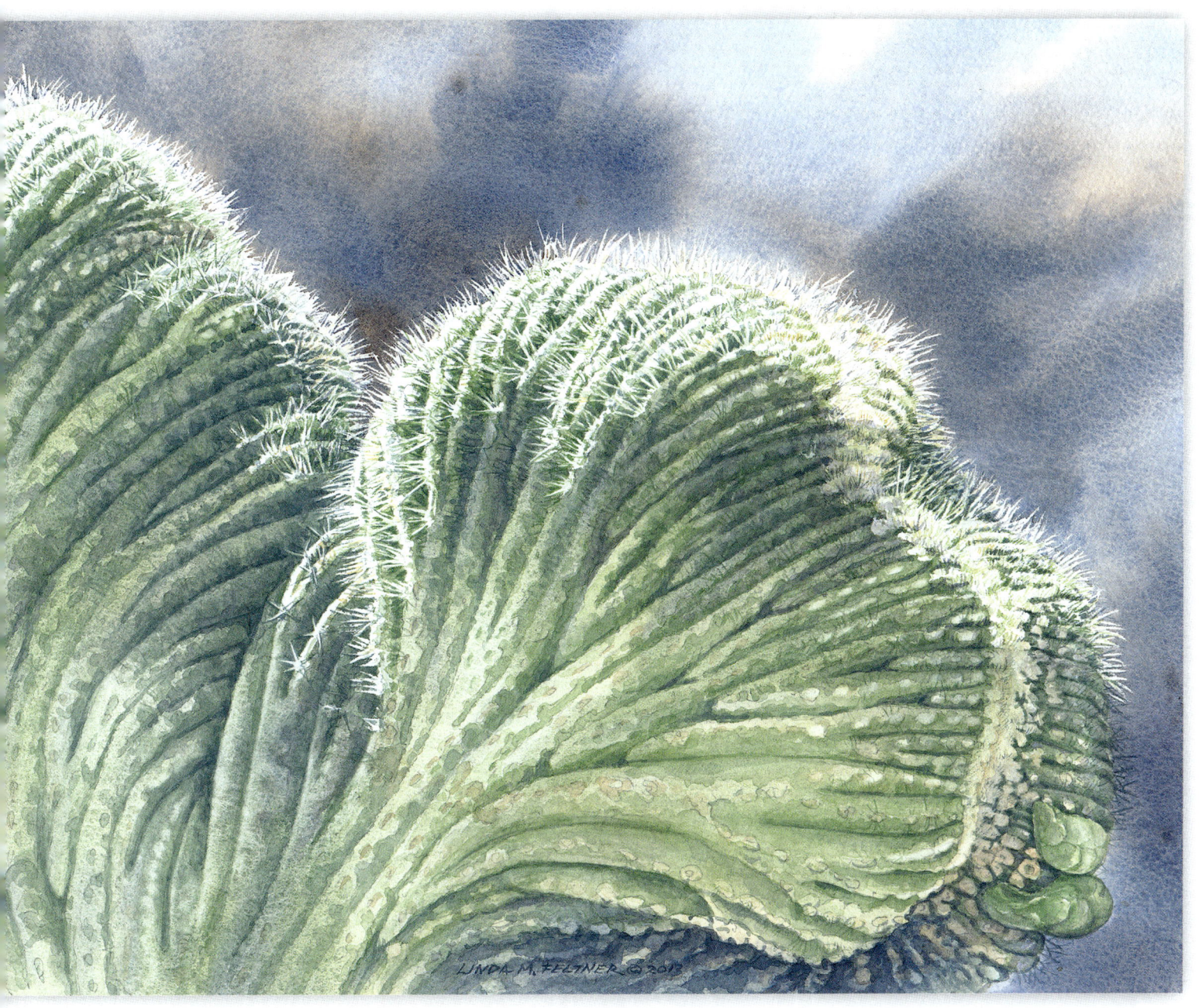

The iconic Saguaro cactus occasionally produces a rare, fan-shaped branching tip called "crested" or "cristate." As the sun rises, nighttime insects and bats give way to diurnal pollinators. Gila Woodpeckers thrust their heads into the flower, coating their faces with pollen, and quickly move among the blossoms extracting nectar. They also relish the bursting ripe fruit, revealing a thick mass of tiny seeds held within a sweet, delicious goo. The seeds are not digested and are distributed later throughout the desert. They provide other vital services by gobbling insects and removing damaged cactus tissue while chiseling holes. As a Saguaro forest provides tall standing trunks, desert birds and mammals find the chiseled cavities to be safe places for a home.

Saguaro (*Carnegiea gigantea*), Gila Woodpecker (*Melanerpes uropygialis*), and Honey Bee (*Apis mellifera*)

Desert Fan–Crested Saguaro, 12 × 25 in (30.48 × 63.5 cm), transparent watercolor, Sonoran Experience Collection, courtesy of the Arizona-Sonora Desert Museum Art Institute.

Adapting for Survival

Physical adaptations are all about survival. Specific body parts change to aid animals and plants in their survival. Slowly adapting over time, some collaborations are positive interactions that benefit both.

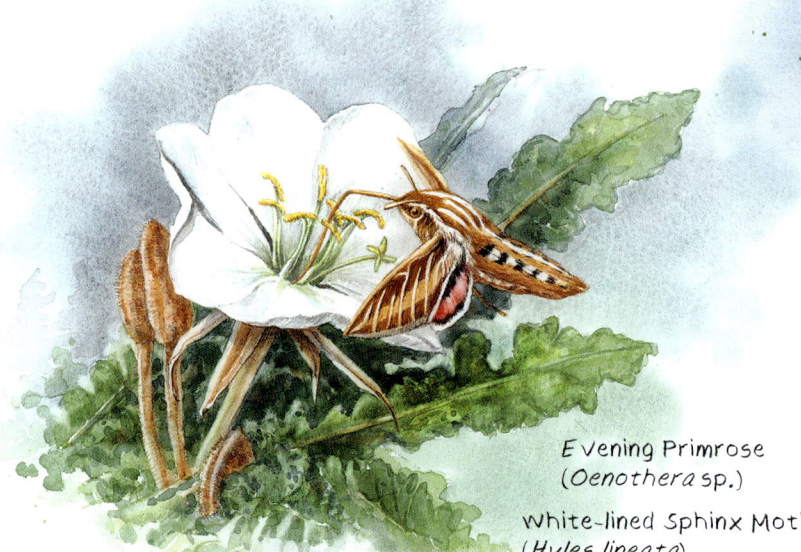

Evening Primrose
(*Oenothera* sp.)

White-lined Sphinx Moth
(*Hyles lineata*)

LINDA M. FELTNER

Nectar is found at the base of the long tube on the blossom. A long-tongued moth gets the reward.

lesser long-nosed bat
(murciélago)

(*Leptonycteris yerbabuena*)

The cutaway shows how the bat's long tongue licks up the nectar and its head becomes covered with pollen.

North American Beaver
(*Castor canadensis*)

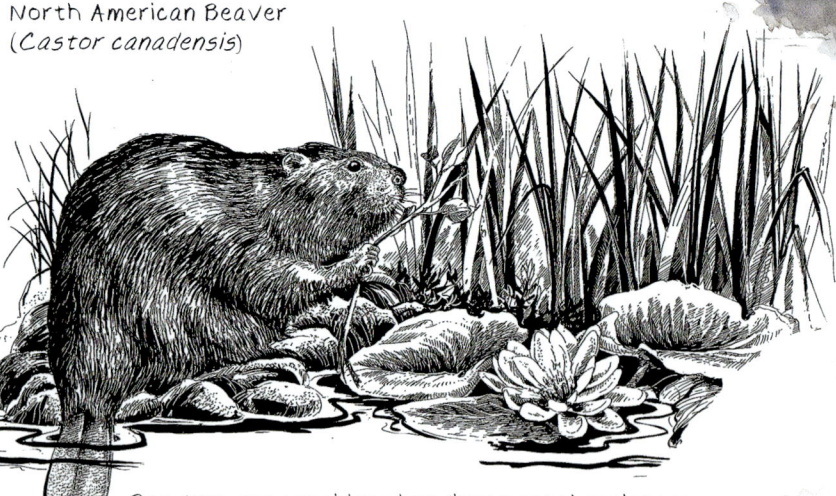

Beavers are considered environmental engineers because their dams alter the habitat, creating wetlands that become homes for an entire community of wetland plants and animals. Their dams filter and slow the water flow, allowing it to seep into and replenish a low water table.

saddleback type

Galapagos Tortoise
(*Chelonoidis niger*)

domed type

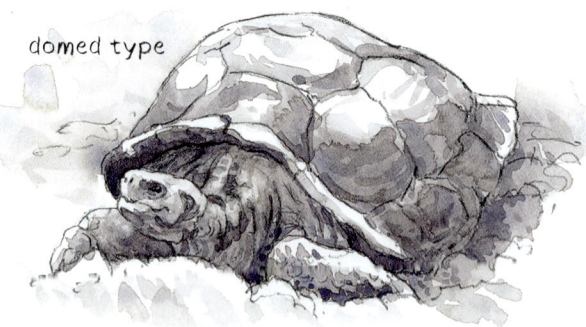

Compare two types of shells for Galapagos Tortoises. The "domed" type evolved for the tortoises who dine on islands with low grasses to graze. The "saddleback" shells developed a high curving shell that allows desert island tortoises to stretch their necks way up to eat cactus fruits.

A ripe, fruity seed casing provides nutrition to mammals and birds. The Cassowary gulps fruit down whole and later voids the seeds far away. Some seeds need to pass through their digestive system to germinate.

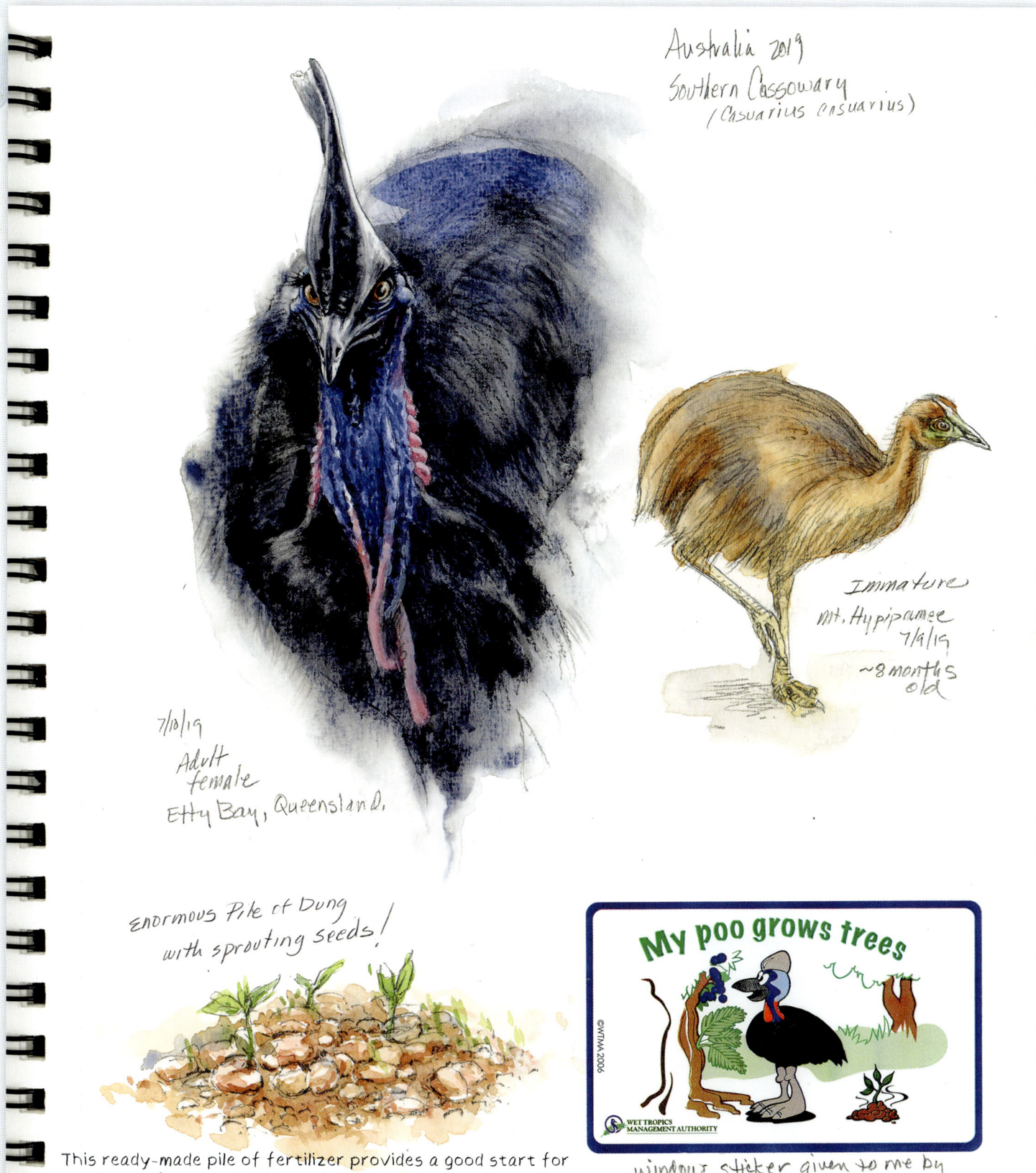

Australia 2019
Southern Cassowary
(Casuarius casuarius)

7/10/19
Adult female
Etty Bay, Queensland.

Immature
Mt. Hypipamee
7/9/19
~8 months old

Enormous Pile of Dung
with sprouting seeds!

This ready-made pile of fertilizer provides a good start for hundreds of seeds. Since the birds travel large distances, this process is crucial to maintaining a diversity of rainforest trees.

My poo grows trees
©WTMA 2006
WET TROPICS MANAGEMENT AUTHORITY

window sticker given to me by a teacher & naturalist.

Adapting for Survival: The Wild Ways of Seed Dispersal

They call it "The Great Escape" because plants adapted clever ways to move far beyond the parent plant to avoid competition for water, light, and soil nutrients.

One of the wildest methods uses wind and air currents. Aerodynamics plays a large part in how far seeds might travel. Lightweight, feathery seeds can parachute into the atmosphere and travel far. Try blowing on a dandelion seed head. Winged seeds, like those of maples, whirl like helicopter blades as they fall.

Floating on saltwater can transport seeds to new continents.

Hitchhiking seeds sport tiny hooks that cling to fur and clothing. The local deer are covered in clingy seeds from bedding down in grassy fields.

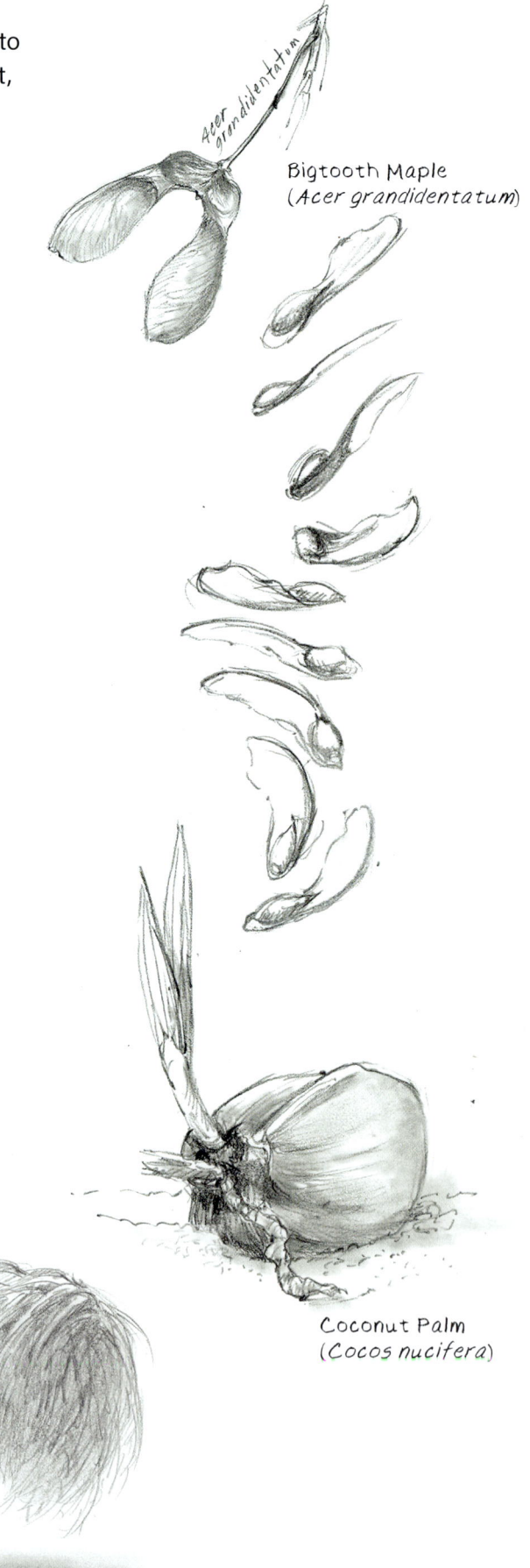

Bigtooth Maple
(*Acer grandidentatum*)

Coconut Palm
(*Cocos nucifera*)

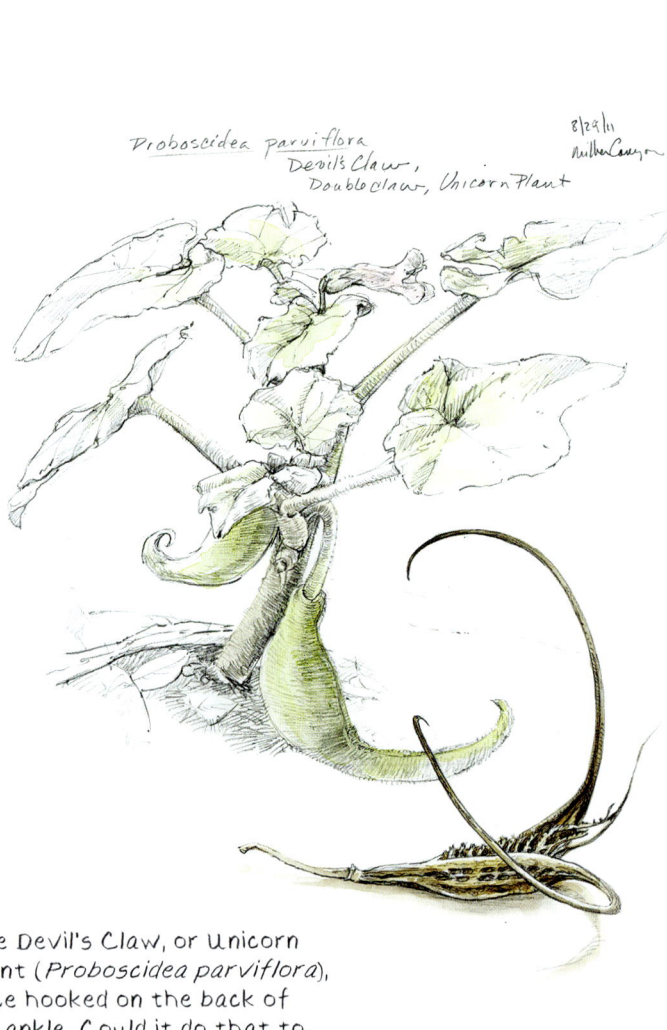

Proboscidea parviflora
Devil's Claw,
Doubleclaw, Unicorn Plant

8/29/11
Miller Canyon

The Devil's Claw, or Unicorn Plant (*Proboscidea parviflora*), once hooked on the back of my ankle. Could it do that to grazers, too?

And let's not forget the Tumbleweed or Russian Thistle (*Salsola tragus*), a Siberian plant whose seeds were found in livestock feed in the United States in the mid-1870s. It is highly invasive and a big problem, but a success story for prodigious seed dispersal, rolling across the iconic American West!

98

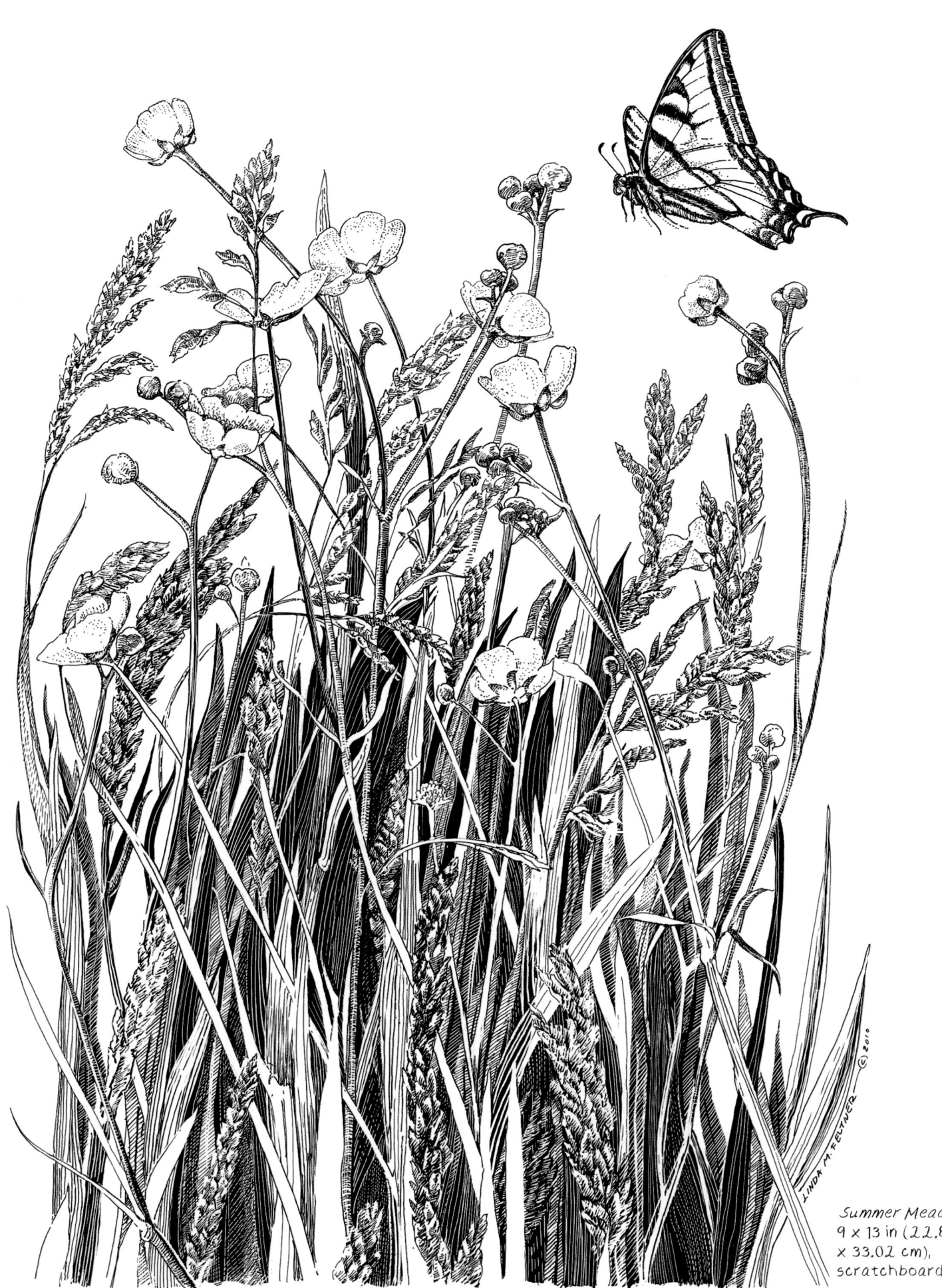

Summer Meadow,
9 x 13 in (22.86
x 33.02 cm),
scratchboard.

Special Relationships for Survival

When two organisms depend solely on one another to survive, it's called mutualism. An excellent example is the yucca and its moth.

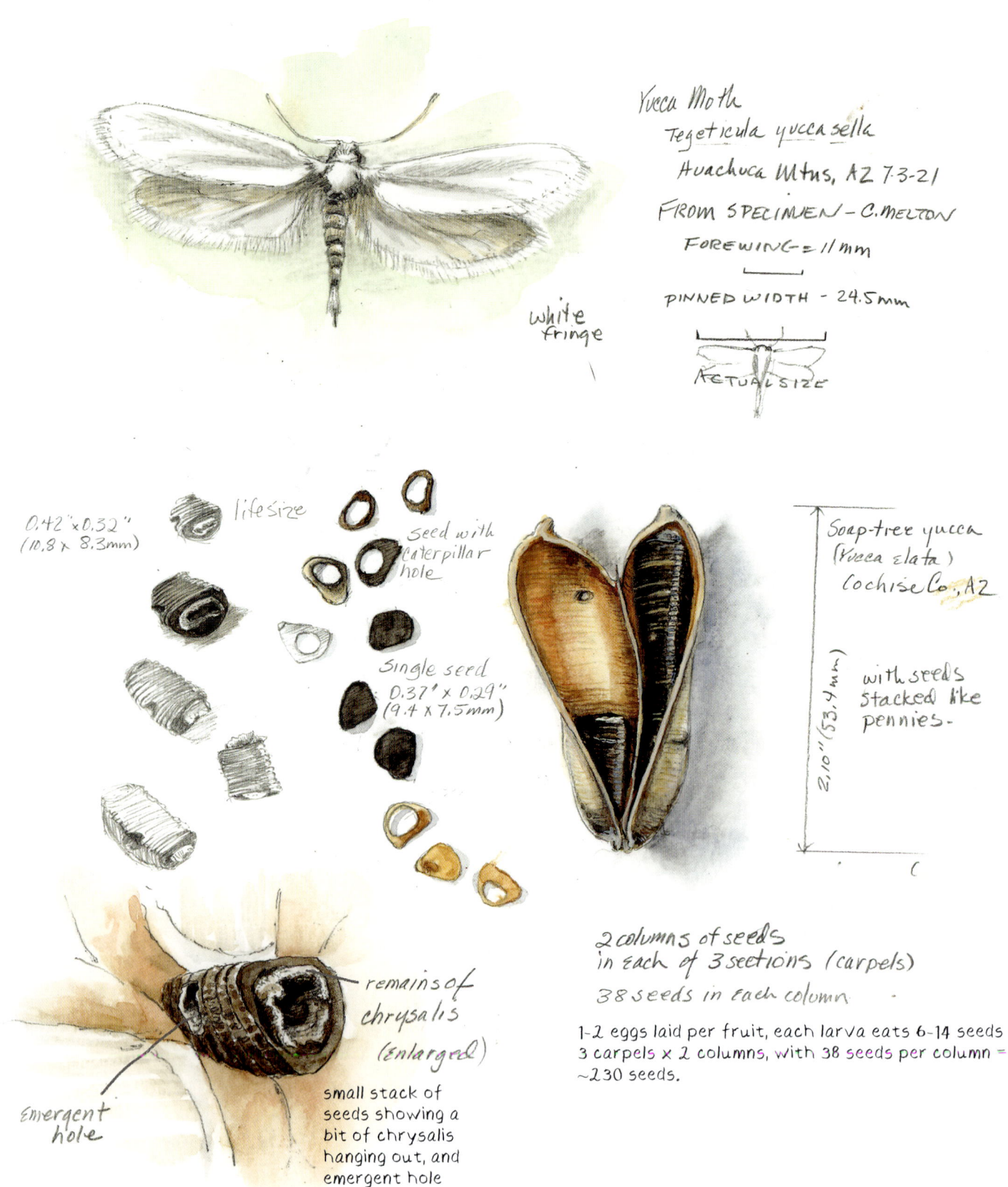

Yucca Moth
Tegeticula yuccasella
Huachuca Mtns, AZ 7-3-21
FROM SPECIMEN - C. MELTON
FOREWING = 11mm

PINNED WIDTH - 24.5mm

ACTUAL SIZE

white fringe

life size

0.42"x0.32"
(10.8 x 8.3mm)

Seed with caterpillar hole

Single seed
0.37" x 0.29"
(9.4 x 7.5mm)

Soap-tree yucca
(Yucca elata)
Cochise Co, AZ

2.10"(53.4mm)

with seeds stacked like pennies.

remains of chrysalis
(Enlarged)

emergent hole

small stack of seeds showing a bit of chrysalis hanging out, and emergent hole

2 columns of seeds
in each of 3 sections (carpels)
38 seeds in each column

1-2 eggs laid per fruit, each larva eats 6-14 seeds
3 carpels x 2 columns, with 38 seeds per column =
~230 seeds.

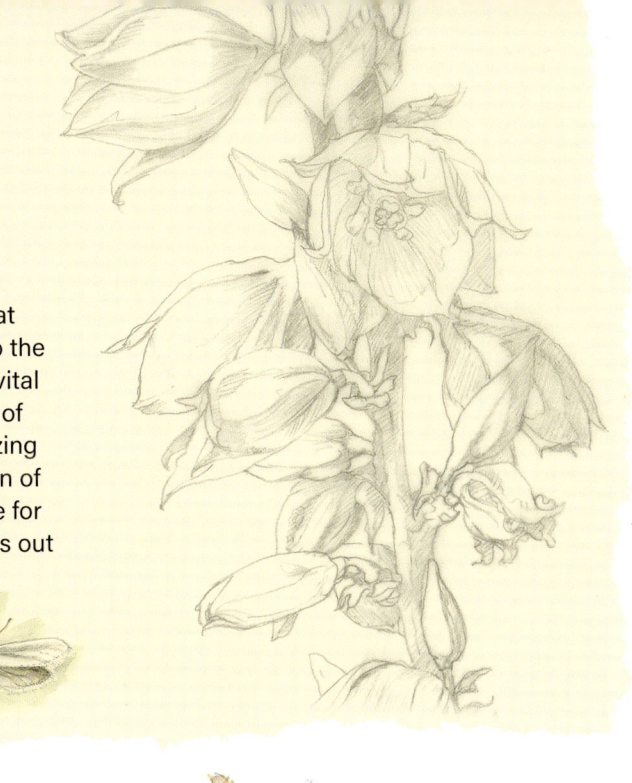

The moth pollinates the plant, and the yucca donates a few of its seeds to nourish and protect the larvae. The female employs a unique method of pollination. She has specialized, long, curved, flexible mouth parts that scoop up sticky pollen balls (pollinia). Afterward, she inserts an egg into the ovary wall with an egg-laying device (ovipositor). Then she performs a vital service to the plant, crucial to its survival. She shoves the amassed ball of pollen (sperm-bearing) into a cup depression on the stigma, thus fertilizing hundreds of immature seeds. The larva grows inside the stacked column of seeds and consumes six to fourteen seeds as it grows. It is a small price for the plant to pay in return for propagating the species. The larva emerges out of the pod in late fall and burrows in the ground to overwinter.

—Drawn from Wayne P. Armstrong, "The Yucca and Its Moth,"
ZooNooz 72, no. 4 (April 1999): 28–31. Paraphrased with permission.

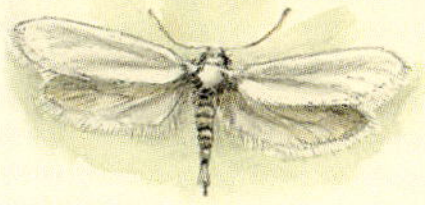

Watercolor pencil demonstration showing three stages of development. Each page, 7 × 11 in (17.78 × 27.94 cm), Faber-Castell Albrecht Dürer watercolor pencils on Bristol vellum.

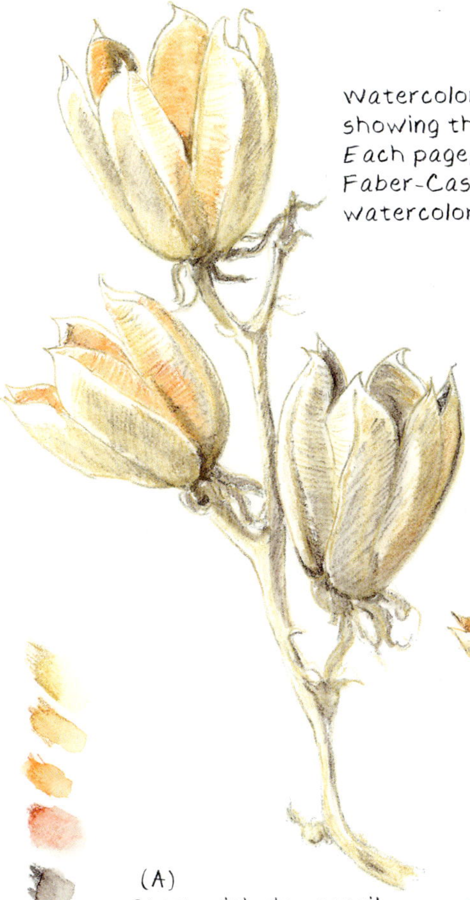

(A)
Start with dry pencil, apply like a colored pencil.

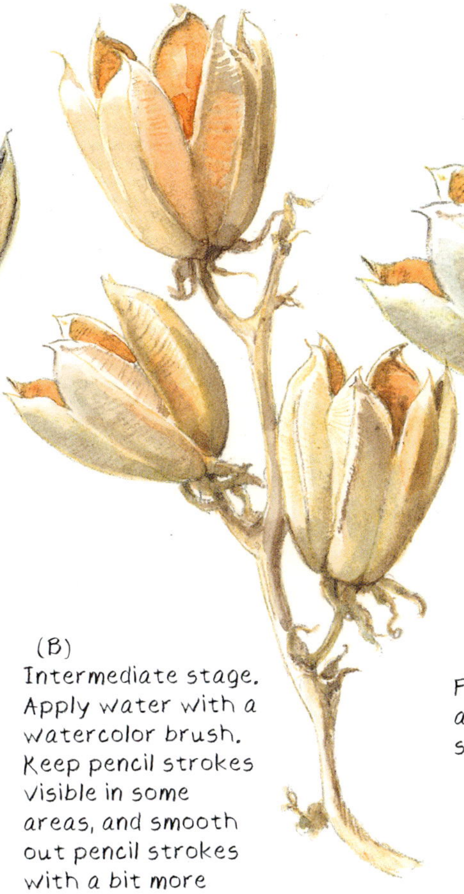

(B)
Intermediate stage. Apply water with a watercolor brush. Keep pencil strokes visible in some areas, and smooth out pencil strokes with a bit more brush blending.

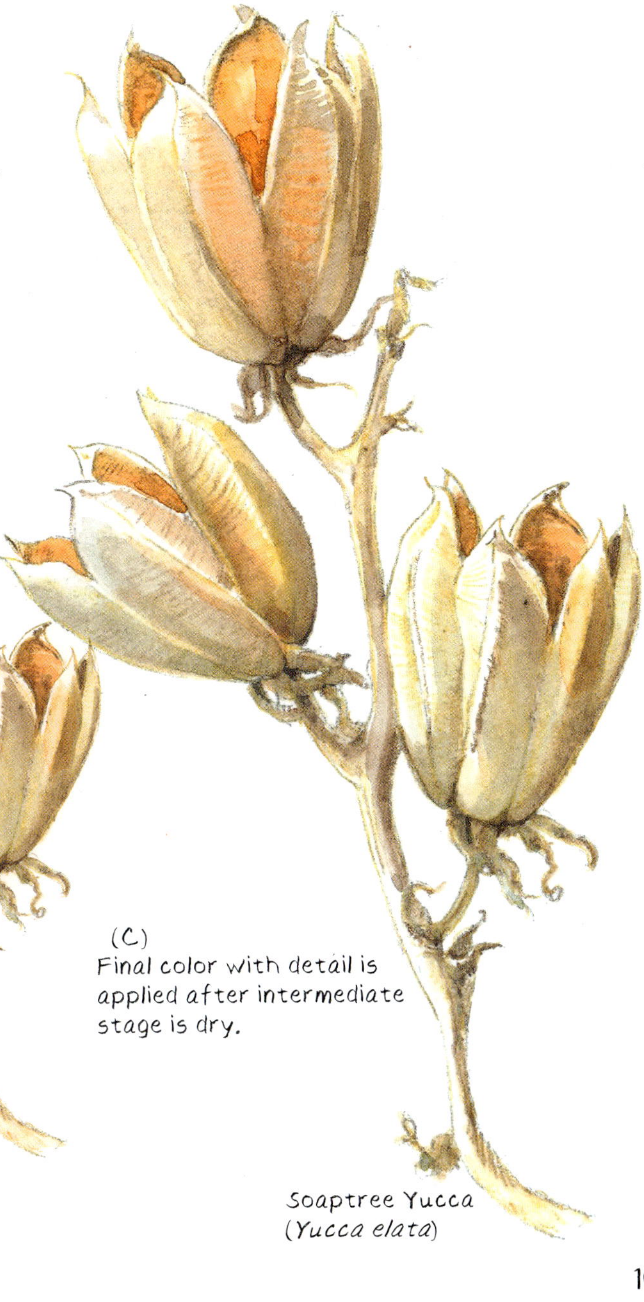

(C)
Final color with detail is applied after intermediate stage is dry.

Soaptree Yucca
(*Yucca elata*)

Emory Oak Woodland—Home Sweet Biome

It wasn't luck that brought us to this rich patch of paradise in southeast Arizona. The sky islands are renowned for biological diversity. World events discouraged travel and gave me reason to examine our nearby plant and animal neighborhood.

Biomes are loose ecological units based on plant descriptions. We live in the oak woodland-chaparral biome where Emory Oak is a keystone species. This belt of woodlands encircles the mountain foothills. It doesn't take much observation to see that acorns provide abundant food for quail, turkeys, woodpeckers, and jays along with squirrels, deer, and gray foxes. The oaks are host plants for butterflies and moths and their caterpillars. Gnarled branches and hollow trunks produce cavities for nesting and roosting for owls, woodpeckers, and small mammals.

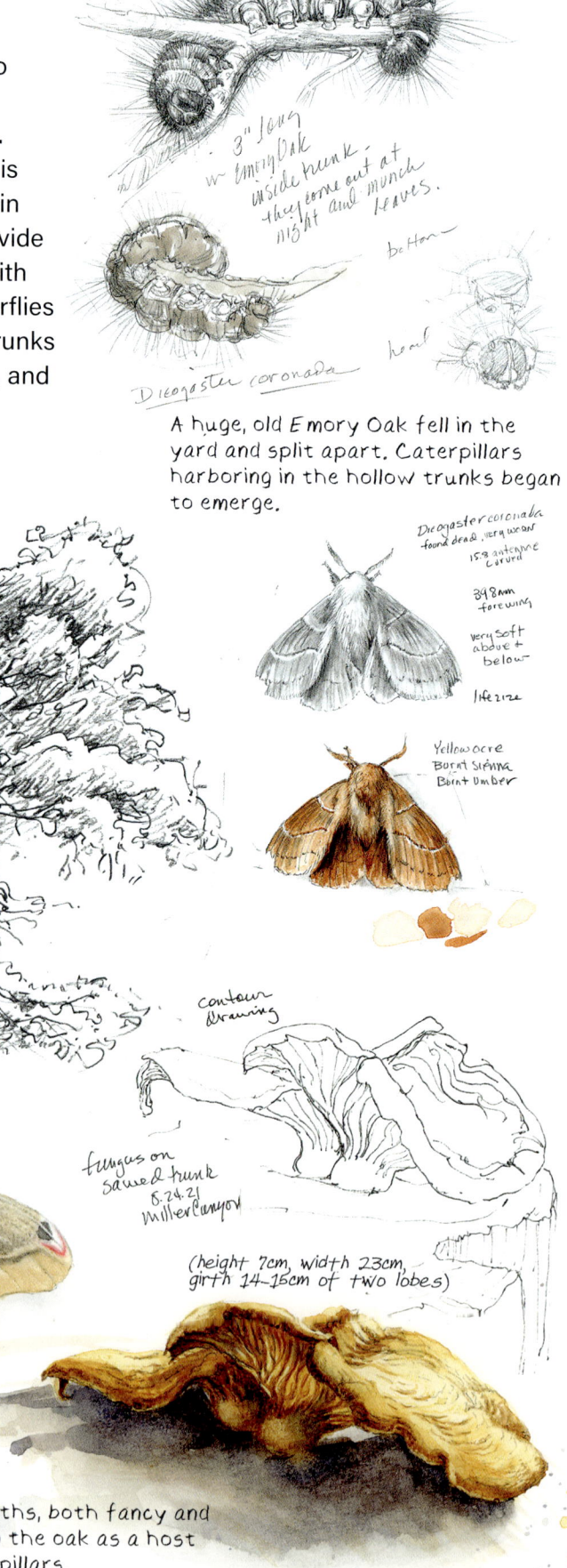

5/17/19

3" long on Emory Oak inside trunk. they come out at night and munch leaves.

be Hon

head

Dioogaster coronada

A huge, old Emory Oak fell in the yard and split apart. Caterpillars harboring in the hollow trunks began to emerge.

Dioogaster coronada found dead, very worn 15.8 antenne curved

34.8mm forewing

very soft above + below

life size

Yellow ocre Burnt sienna Burnt umber

contour drawing

fungus on sawed trunk 8.24.21 Miller Canyon

(height 7cm, width 23cm, girth 14-15cm of two lobes)

Emory Oak
(Quercus emoryi)

10-7-21
Robles Uracea's
Land

Oculea Silkmoth
(Antheraea oculea)

Many other moths, both fancy and plain, depend on the oak as a host for their caterpillars.

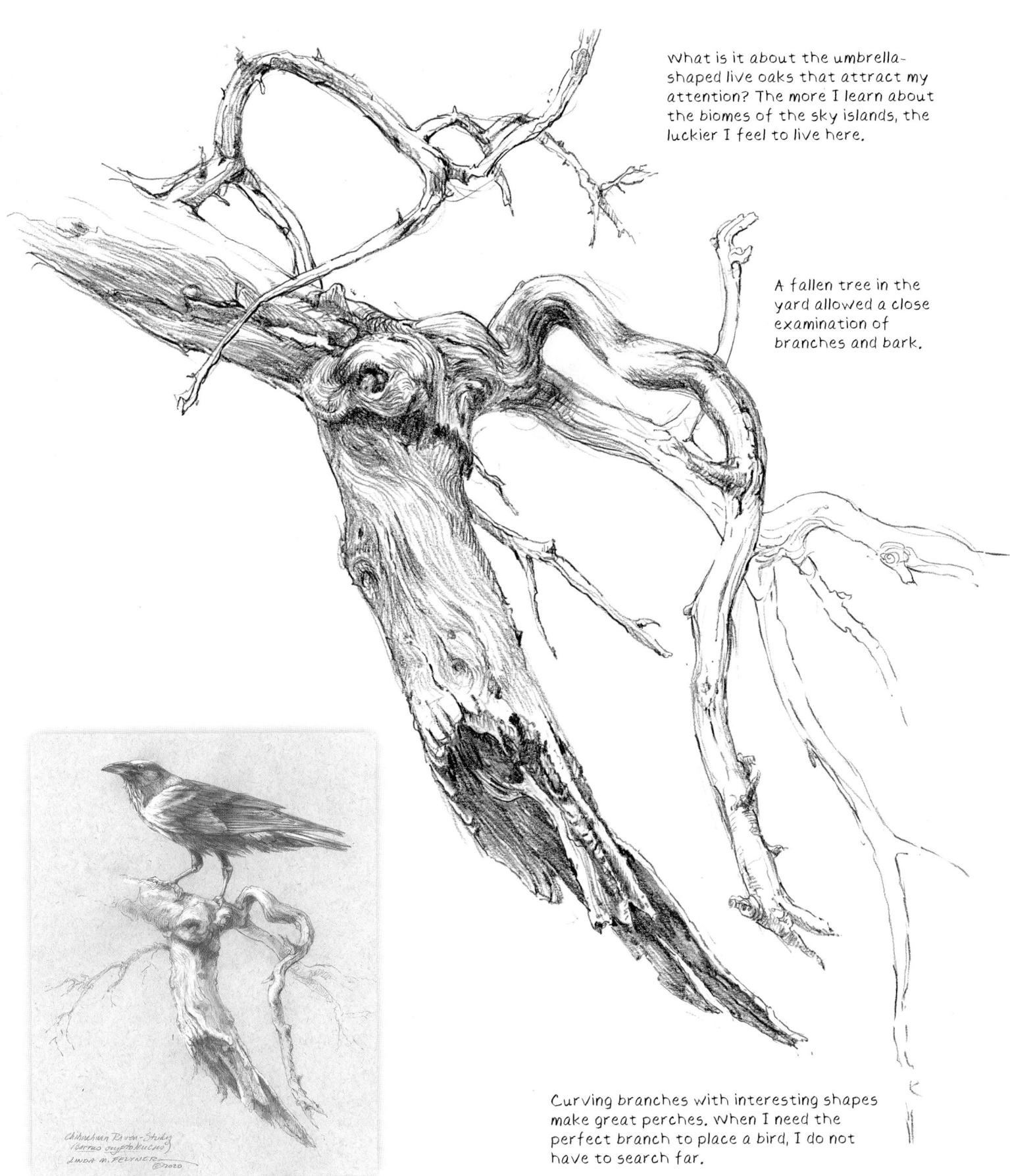

What is it about the umbrella-shaped live oaks that attract my attention? The more I learn about the biomes of the sky islands, the luckier I feel to live here.

A fallen tree in the yard allowed a close examination of branches and bark.

Curving branches with interesting shapes make great perches. When I need the perfect branch to place a bird, I do not have to search far.

Chihuahuan Raven (*Corvus cryptoleucus*)

Chihuahuan Raven, 8.5 x 11.7 in (21.59 x 29.72 cm), pencil and gouache on Strathmore toned gray paper.

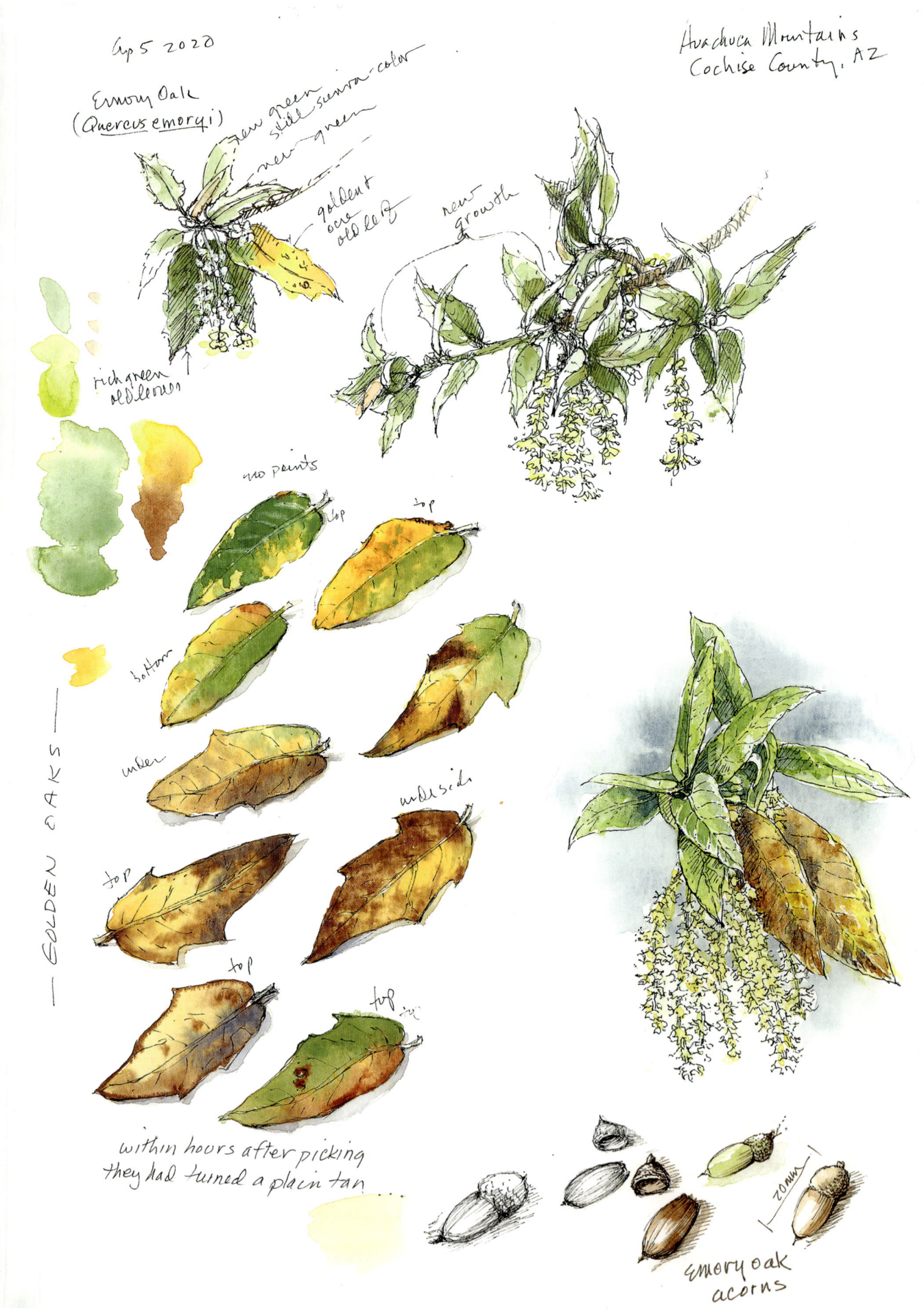

Sep 5 2020

Emory Oak
(Quercus emoryi)

Huachuca Mountains
Cochise County, AZ

new green
still sienna color
new green
new growth
golden ochre
old leaf

rich green
old leaves

no points
top
top
top
bottom
umber
top
underside
top
top in

GOLDEN OAKS

within hours after picking
they had turned a plain tan

20mm

emory oak
acorns

104

When Beetles Soar

Every three years, an exciting event occurs for only two days in the oak woodlands.

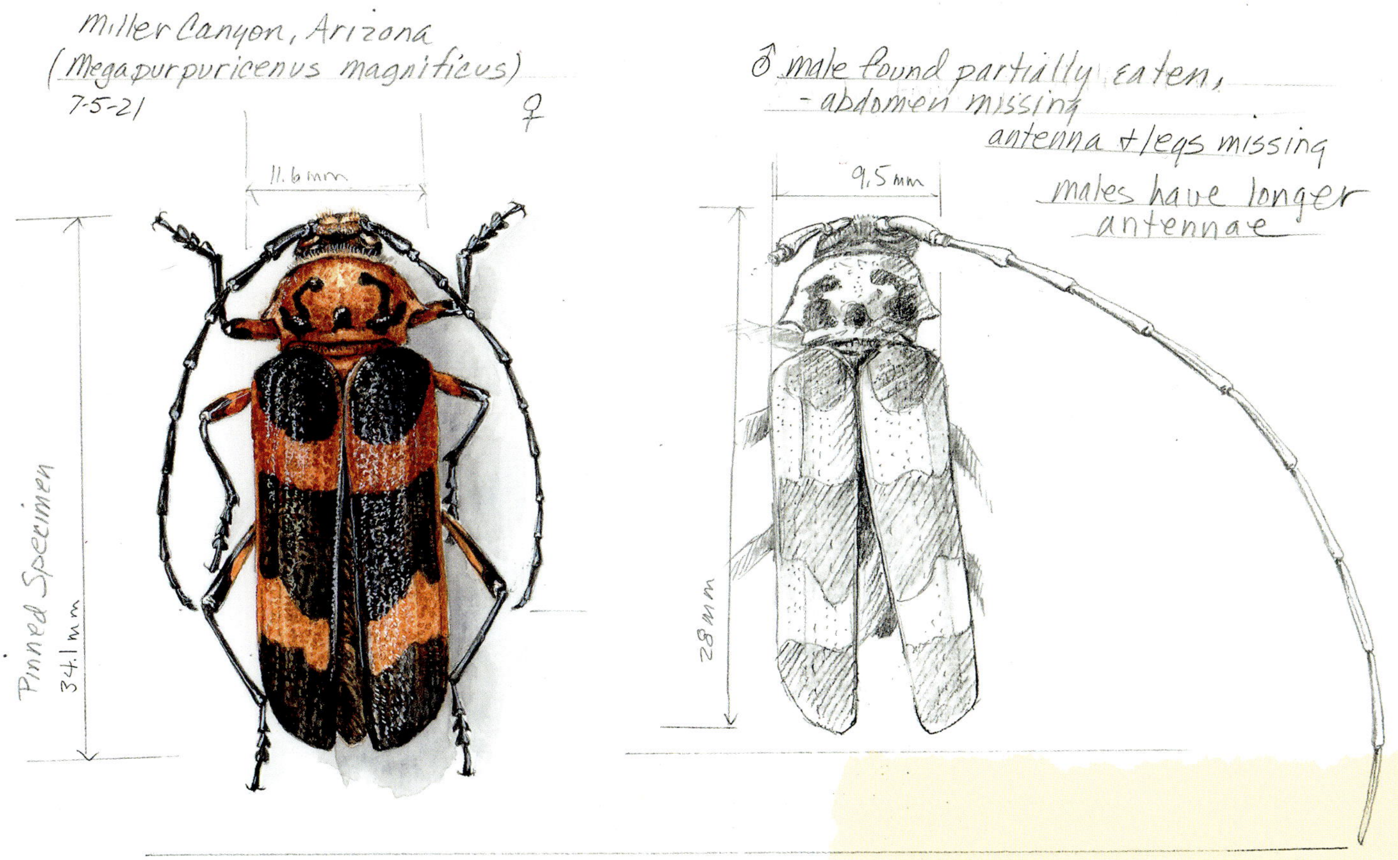

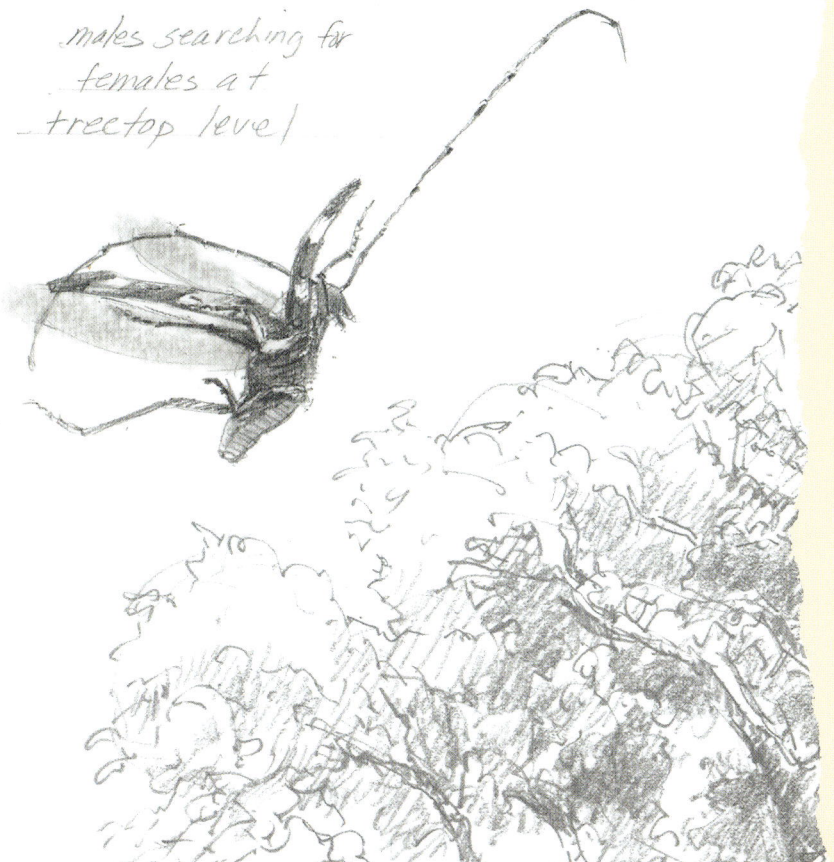

Miller Canyon, Arizona
(Megapurpuricenus magnificus)
7-5-21
♀

11.6 mm

Pinned Specimen
34.1 mm

♂ male found partially eaten,
– abdomen missing
antenna + legs missing
males have longer
antennae

9.5 mm

28 mm

males searching for
females at
treetop level

Megapurpuricenus magnificus

"This magnificent woodboring beetle species makes its home in southern Arizona. For three years, the larvae of these beetles feed and grow inside the trunks of living oak trees, especially Emory and Arizona oaks.

Early in their third year, the larvae transform into adult beetles and wait for their cue to emerge: the first monsoon rainfall. Over the next two or three days the beetles crawl out of the trees and engage in a frantic display of dispersal flights and mating.

Then, as quickly as they came, they are gone ... for another three years."

—Steven W. Lingafelter, PhD,
U.S. Department of Agriculture

Emory Oak Woodland and the Tropical Candle

From its winter home in Central America, the Painted Redstart migrates north to the Southwestern United States to breed. It prefers mid-altitude forested canyons. It is primarily a Mexican species called "Candelita," or "little torch."

Along with snappy, vibrant colors, its song and active pursuit of insects make it one of the most visible warblers in our oak woodlands.

Some think it should be called the "Painted Whitestart." They are closely related to the Whitestarts of South America and in the same genus. The name refers to the outer tail feathers that flick out in a flash of white. "Start" is an old word for tail.

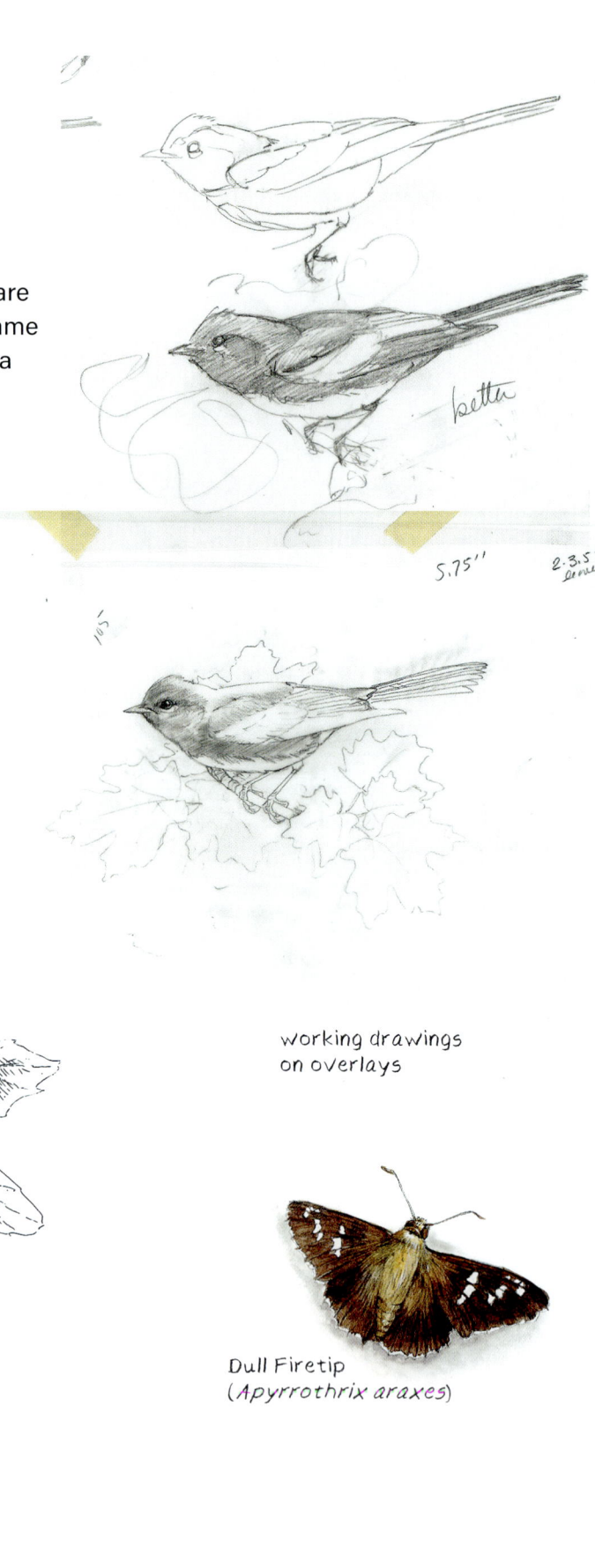

better

5.75"   2.3.5"
              leaves

working drawings
on overlays

while foraging, it flashes its white tail
and wing patches to flush insects.

Painted Redstart
(*Myioborus pictus*)

ink drawing, adapting
the composition of the
redstart, oak, and
butterfly

Dull Firetip
(*Apyrrothrix araxes*)

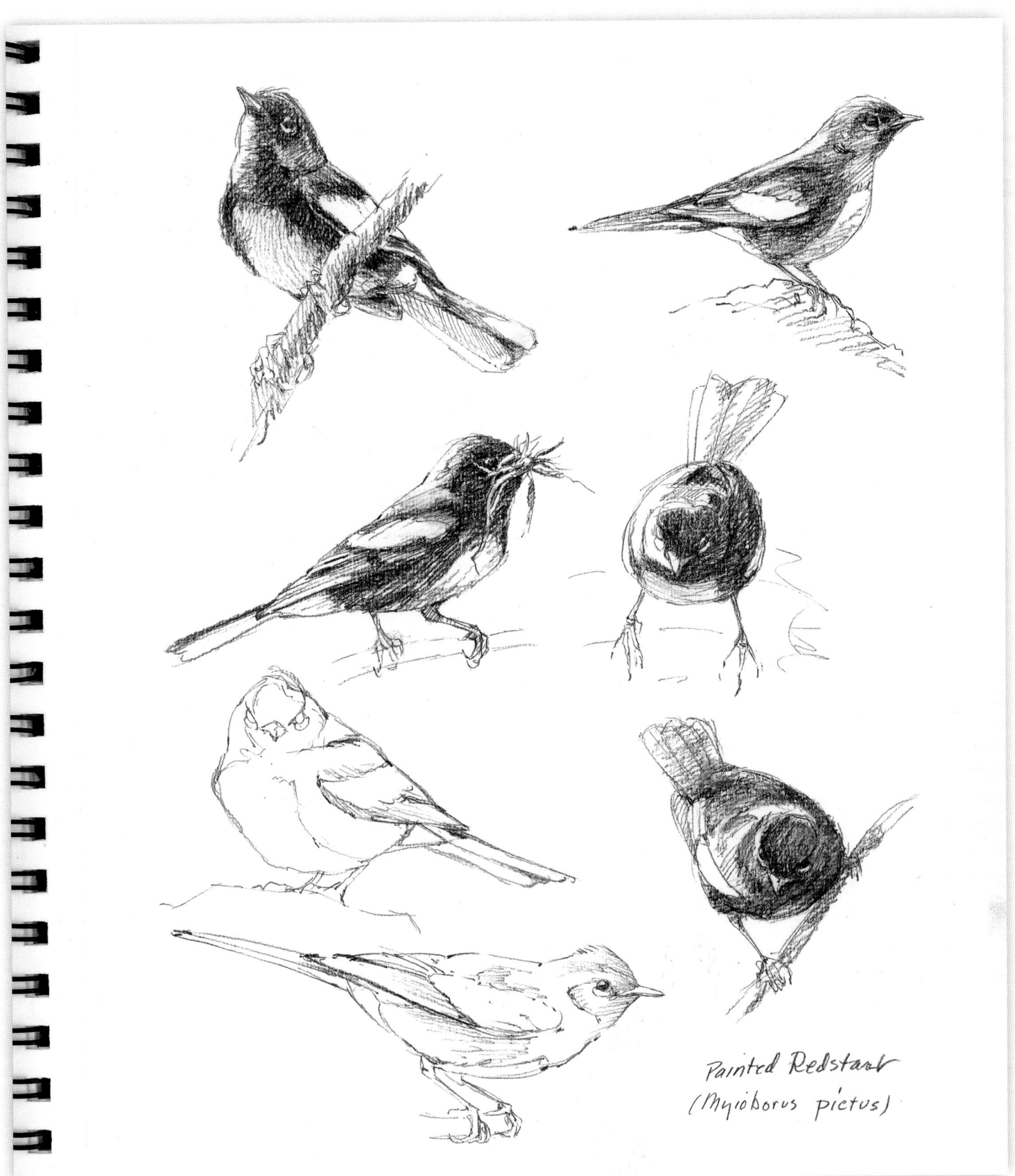

Painted Redstart
(Myioborus pictus)

"Huachuca Redstarts"

In the lower reaches of Miller Canyon, this pair of Painted Redstarts took grassy material into their hidden nest at the base of a tree. The Dull Firetip's caterpillars are specialized eaters and the Emory Oak is their host plant. The woodland biome provides year-round shelter and food for many types of animals and plants. Scientists, naturalists, and birders recognize the uniqueness and diversity of Arizona's southeastern sky islands. The Monument Fire in June 2011 destroyed this nesting site a few months after this painting was finished.

Painted Redstart (*Myioborus pictus*), Emory Oak (*Quercus emoryi*), and Dull Firetip (*Apyrrothrix araxes*)

Huachuca Redstarts, 18 × 12 in, (45.72 × 30.48 cm), transparent watercolor.

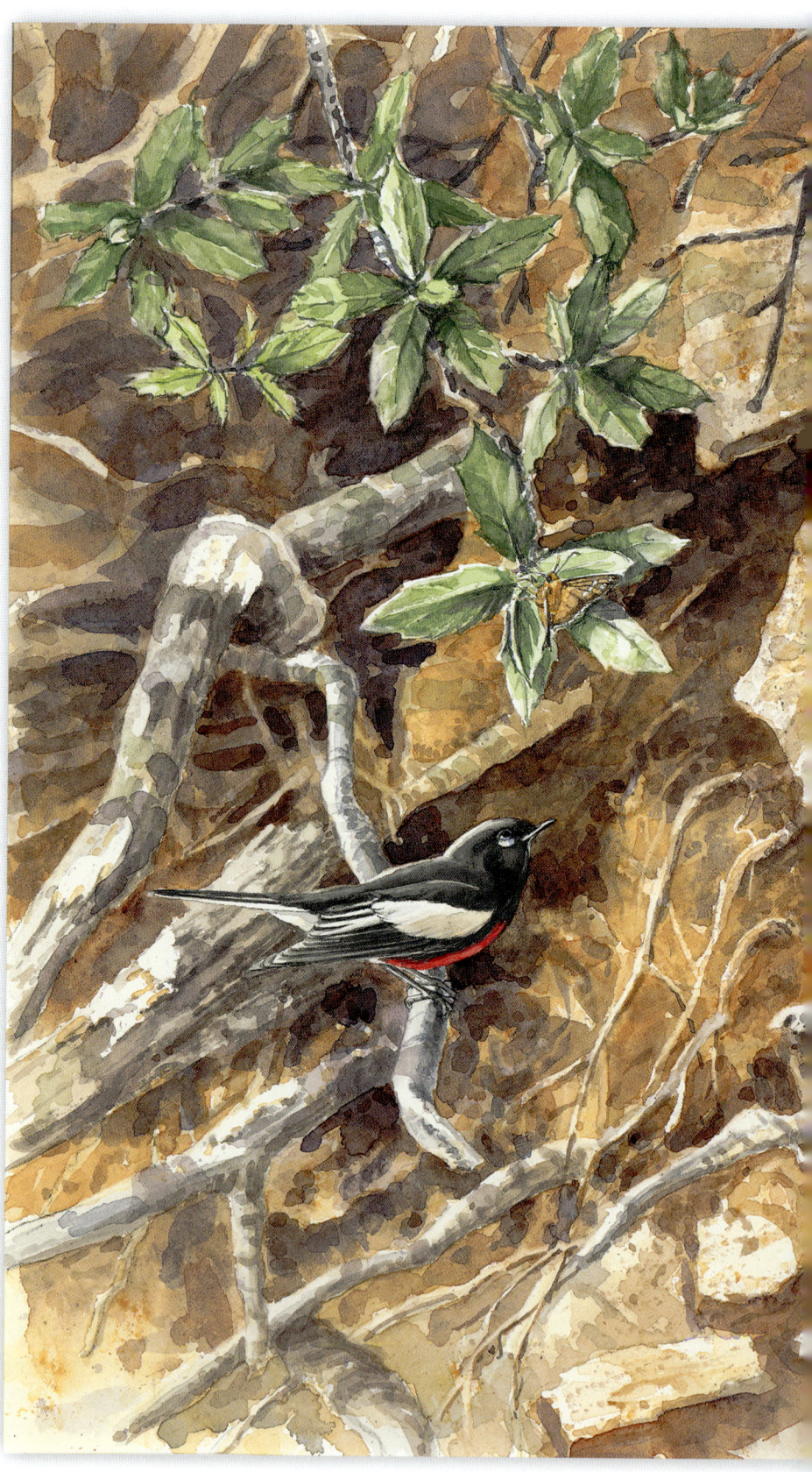

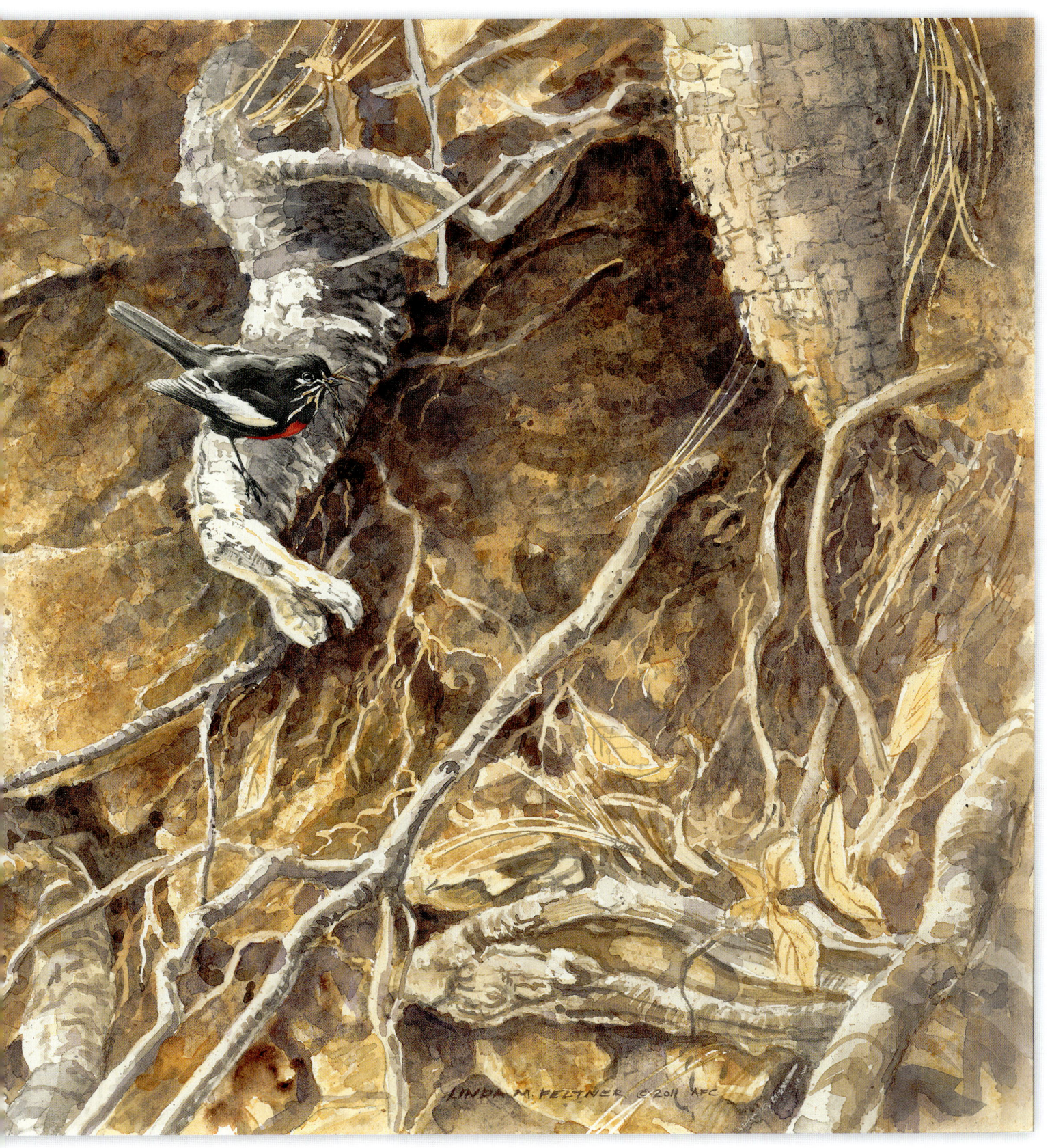

LINDA M. FELTNER ©2011 AFC

Hummingbirds—When Insects Just Won't Do ...

Living jewels sparkle among the wildflowers, often feeding where other pollinators cannot. The lengthy association of hummingbirds and plants developed in the American tropics where birds and flowers changed together over millennia, forming mutually beneficial relationships.

Why is there an advantage to discouraging insects as pollinators and favoring specialized birds?

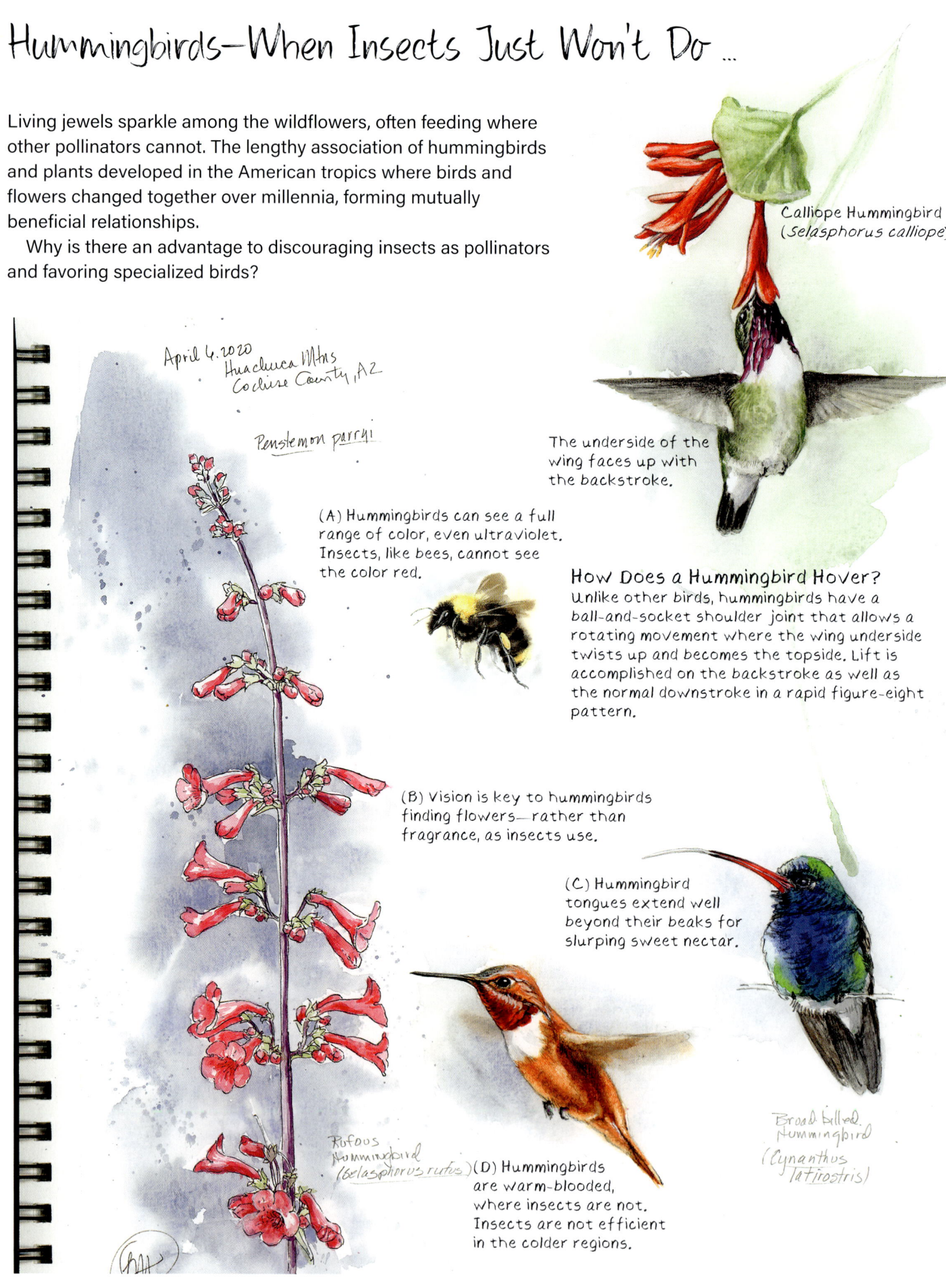

Calliope Hummingbird
(*Selasphorus calliope*)

April 4, 2020
Huachuca Mtns
Cochise County, AZ

Penstemon parryi

The underside of the wing faces up with the backstroke.

(A) Hummingbirds can see a full range of color, even ultraviolet. Insects, like bees, cannot see the color red.

How Does a Hummingbird Hover?
Unlike other birds, hummingbirds have a ball-and-socket shoulder joint that allows a rotating movement where the wing underside twists up and becomes the topside. Lift is accomplished on the backstroke as well as the normal downstroke in a rapid figure-eight pattern.

(B) Vision is key to hummingbirds finding flowers—rather than fragrance, as insects use.

(C) Hummingbird tongues extend well beyond their beaks for slurping sweet nectar.

Rufous Hummingbird
(*Selasphorus rufus*)

(D) Hummingbirds are warm-blooded, where insects are not. Insects are not efficient in the colder regions.

Broad-billed Hummingbird
(*Cynanthus latirostris*)

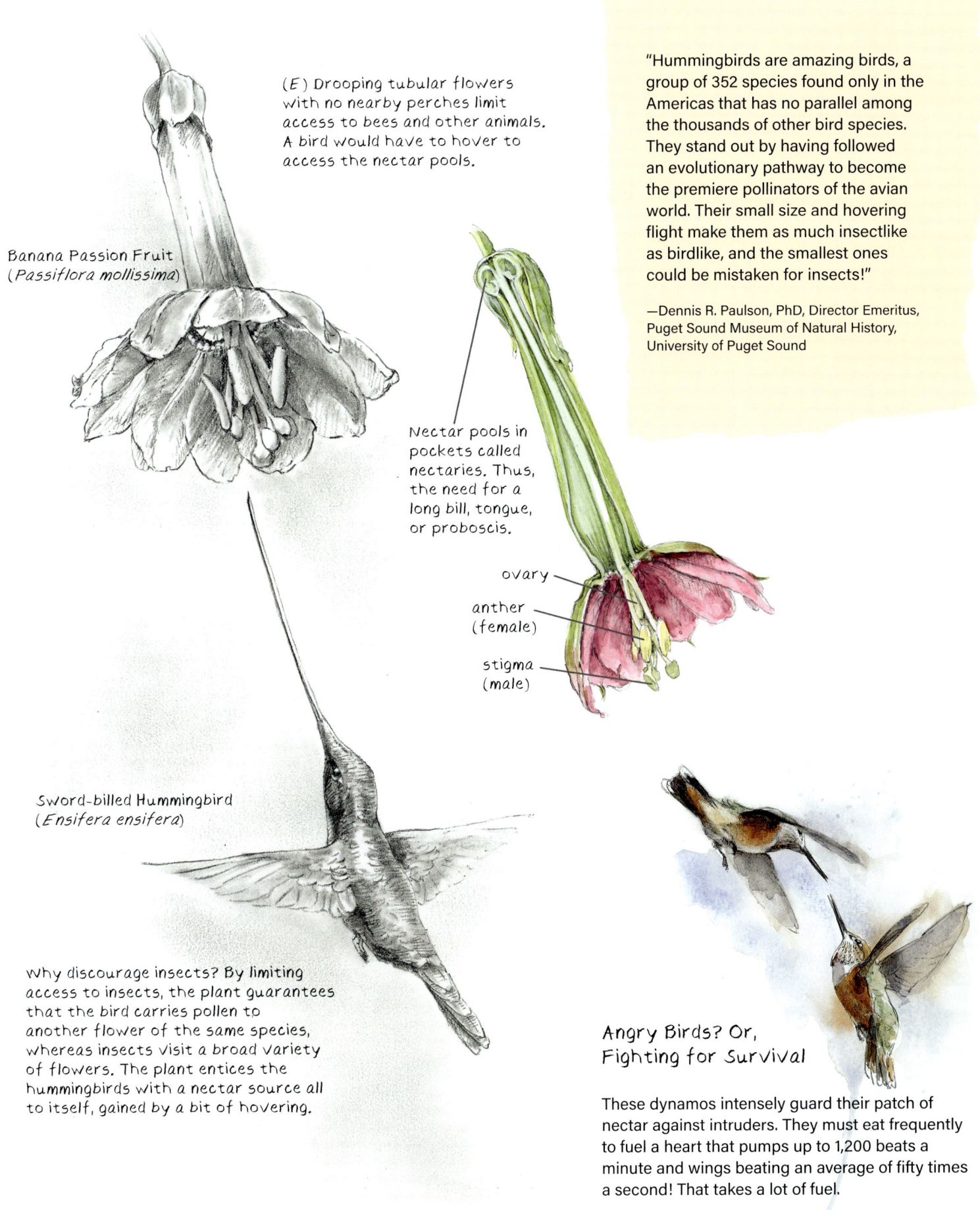

(E) Drooping tubular flowers with no nearby perches limit access to bees and other animals. A bird would have to hover to access the nectar pools.

Banana Passion Fruit (*Passiflora mollissima*)

Nectar pools in pockets called nectaries. Thus, the need for a long bill, tongue, or proboscis.

ovary

anther (female)

stigma (male)

"Hummingbirds are amazing birds, a group of 352 species found only in the Americas that has no parallel among the thousands of other bird species. They stand out by having followed an evolutionary pathway to become the premiere pollinators of the avian world. Their small size and hovering flight make them as much insectlike as birdlike, and the smallest ones could be mistaken for insects!"

—Dennis R. Paulson, PhD, Director Emeritus, Puget Sound Museum of Natural History, University of Puget Sound

Sword-billed Hummingbird (*Ensifera ensifera*)

Why discourage insects? By limiting access to insects, the plant guarantees that the bird carries pollen to another flower of the same species, whereas insects visit a broad variety of flowers. The plant entices the hummingbirds with a nectar source all to itself, gained by a bit of hovering.

Angry Birds? Or, Fighting for Survival

These dynamos intensely guard their patch of nectar against intruders. They must eat frequently to fuel a heart that pumps up to 1,200 beats a minute and wings beating an average of fifty times a second! That takes a lot of fuel.

Quick-Draw Moments

I didn't start to draw birds by sketching hummingbirds.
Hawks sat still a lot longer.

I know it's challenging to sketch hummers at feeders. But even the slightest mark may show angles of approach or the body's angle when paused before probing a flower. Studies of local species help train the eye to find behavior typical to each species. Which size of flower and height off the ground does each prefer?

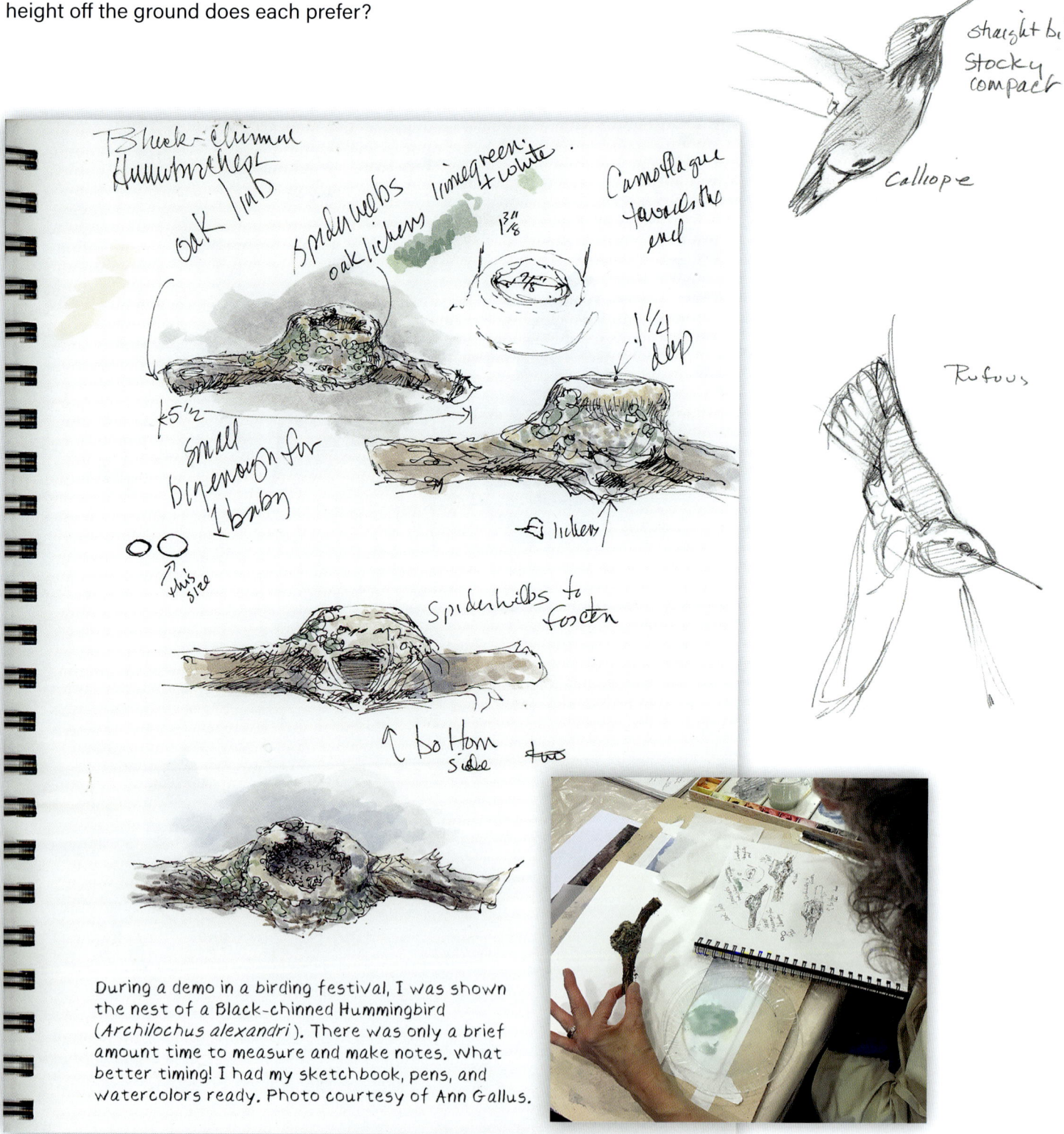

During a demo in a birding festival, I was shown the nest of a Black-chinned Hummingbird (*Archilochus alexandri*). There was only a brief amount time to measure and make notes. What better timing! I had my sketchbook, pens, and watercolors ready. Photo courtesy of Ann Gallus.

112

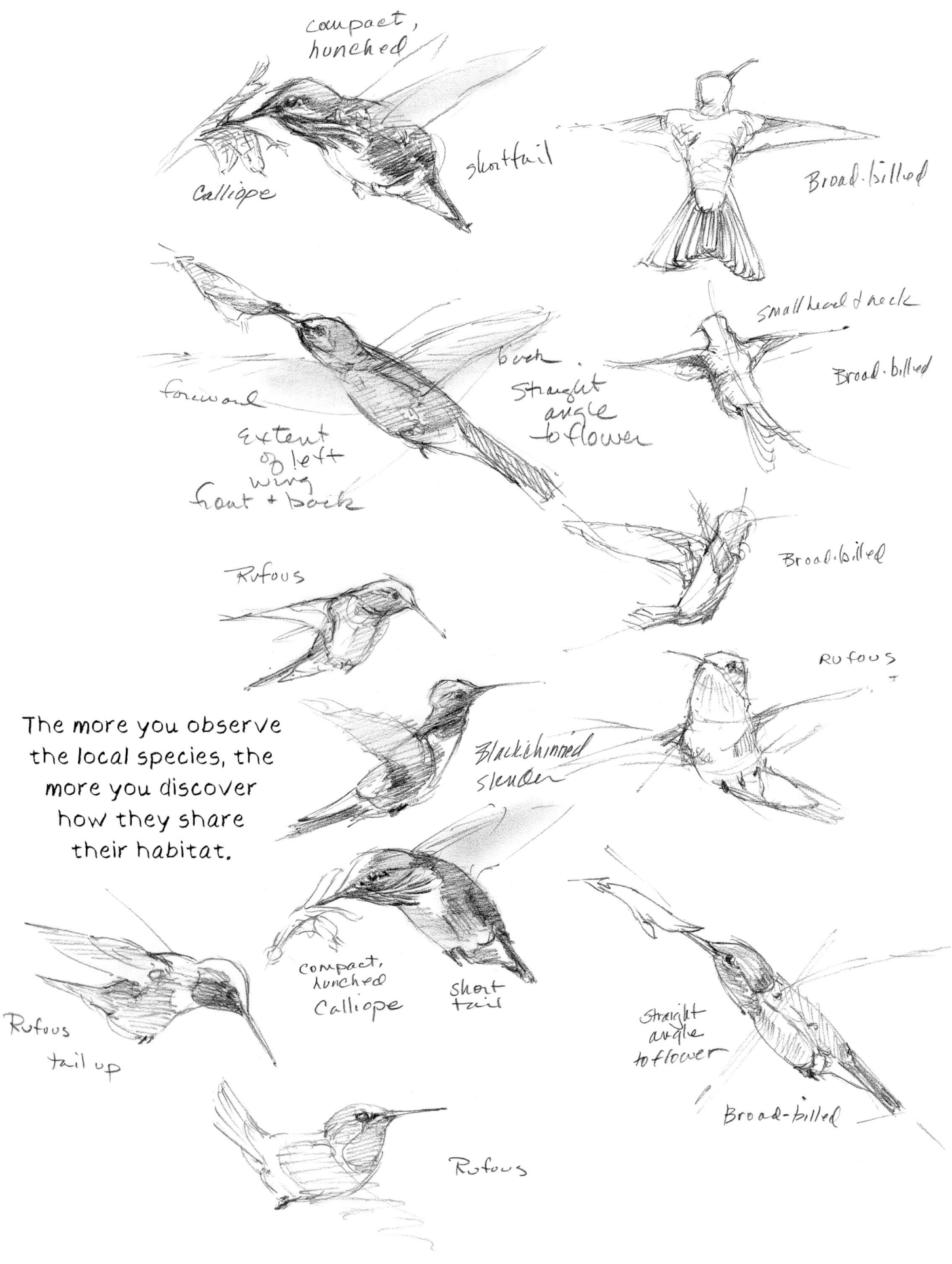

compact, hunched

Calliope

shorttail

Broad-billed

forward

Extent of left wing front + back

back. straight angle to flower

small head & neck

Broad-billed

Rufous

Broad-billed

Rufous

Black-chinned slender

The more you observe the local species, the more you discover how they share their habitat.

Rufous tail up

compact, hunched Calliope

short tail

straight angle to flower

Broad-billed

Rufous

Sketching Flying Darts

Dazzling white and violet combinations are unusual in hummingbirds. The Violet-crowned Hummingbird's brilliance is spectacular when seen feeding on pink penstemons against the ochre and sienna rocks.

Compare the flight styles of these large hummers with the small ones, such as the tiny Calliope Hummingbird. Observe the movement as well as the significant pauses. This behavior caught my attention while sketching live birds. Also, videos are handy for painting in winter when the birds are in more southern climes.

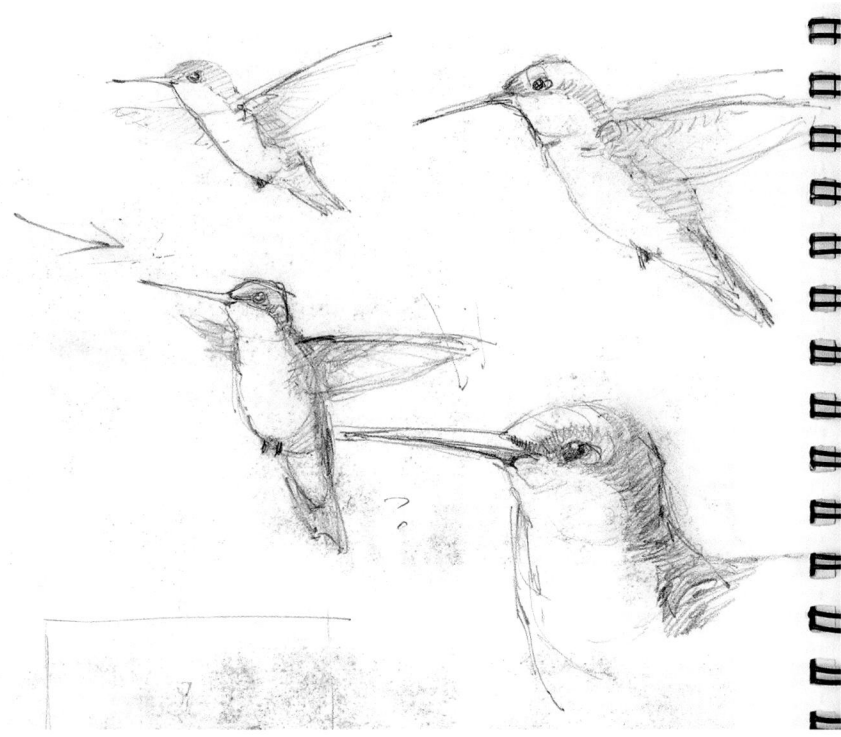

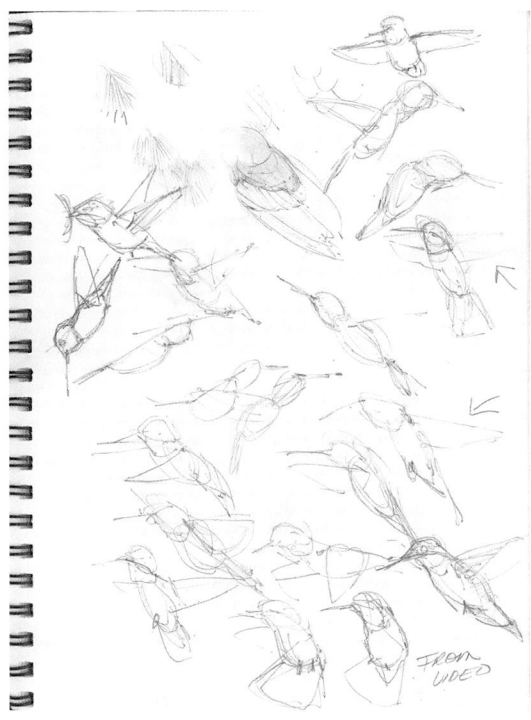

Warm-up gestures from a video called "Amazing Hummingbirds of the U.S.," by Charles W. Melton. The more I sketched, the more the bird's behavior began to show predictable moments that would make good poses.

When the bird probed the flower, its body was not entirely horizontal (perhaps because of its larger size?). I didn't want to hide its distinctive scarlet bill within a flower.

The hummingbird repeatedly backed a short distance away from the flower. As it moved forward and backward, it paused for a moment before diving into another flower or perhaps checking its surroundings.

Violet-crowned Hummingbird (*Amazilia violiceps*)

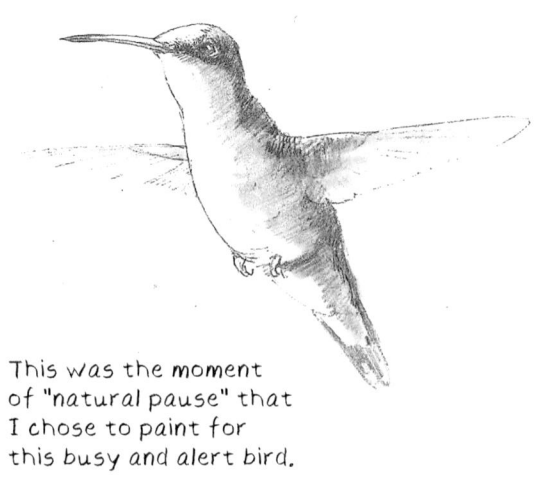

This was the moment of "natural pause" that I chose to paint for this busy and alert bird.

Thumbnail Sketches—A Valuable Step

Small thumbnail compositions are quick ideas placed on paper. Some are good, bad, or promising. Drawing quickly and not erasing but moving on to the next one allows the mind and hand to find an aesthetic balance. It takes ten to thirty seconds to do one thumbnail.

Some are instantly recognizable as unacceptable. Forget it and draw another. Once the composition is narrowed down, additional value studies with light and dark areas can be explored. Shape design comes first, without elements fighting one another. Shapes and values combine to achieve a balance that develops an image worth painting.

penstemon contour sketch

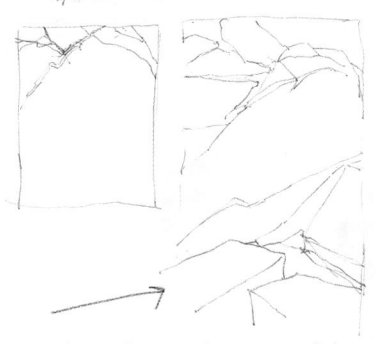

This is a nice rock composition that I might use in the future.

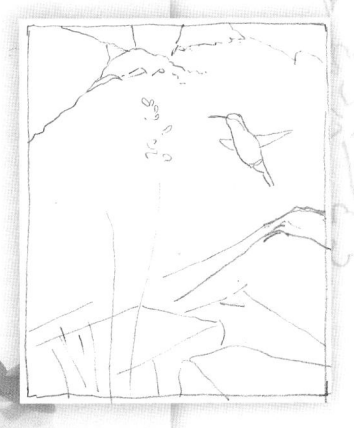

The first steps were to
(A) draw the bird and flowers,
(B) reposition the rocks to create the composition,
(C) transfer the final design to the good paper.

115

"Canyon Illumination": Work in Progress

The next step is testing. Rocky surfaces are so much fun in watercolor. I wanted to achieve the luminosity and intricate color of the shadowy rock face lying behind the main subject. Tests would provide answers for which colors would work well together.

I experimented with color mixing for each of the three separate wet-in-wet wash layers. Granular pigments would settle into the valleys of the cold pressed paper and create rocky textures. But which ones would hold up to multiple layers? Paint formulas are penciled in the margins for each layer. Some combos may look odd when wet, and I won't know until dry. Lunar Black super-granulation worked best on the top layer.

Fabriano Artistico, cold press watercolor paper, 140 lb (300 gsm). Small samples of the same paper give the best results.

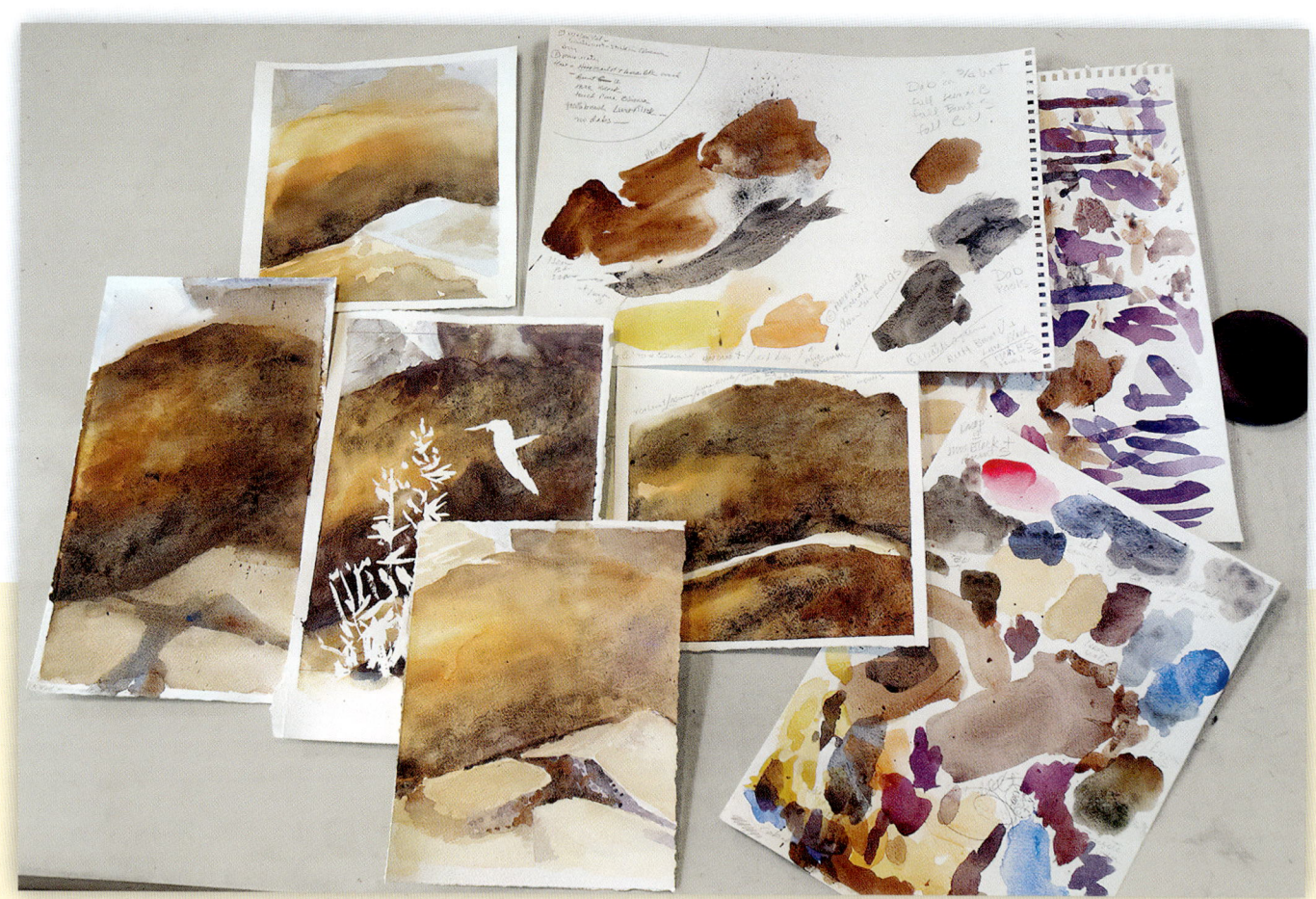

Notes to Self (From Formula Notes):

Layer 1: Brush pure water overall. Keep very wet. Add a thin mixture of Yellow Ochre + Lemon Yellow. Let dry thoroughly.

Layer 2: Lightly lay pure water over layer 1 with a 1.5 in super soft brush. While wet, add a thin layer of only Quinacridone Sienna. Leave some areas of the first layer to show through. Let dry thoroughly.

Layer 3: Gently lay water overall. Float in diluted Lunar Black tinged with Burnt Umber. WHILE 3/4 WET, touch in 100 percent (tube thick) Burnt Sienna + 100 percent Burnt Umber + 100 percent Lunar Black, separately. Dab with a soft paper towel in pools. The towel also creates interesting abstract patterns when the black granules are lifted from the paper. When dry, those organic patterns can be manipulated to create cool rock textures.

116

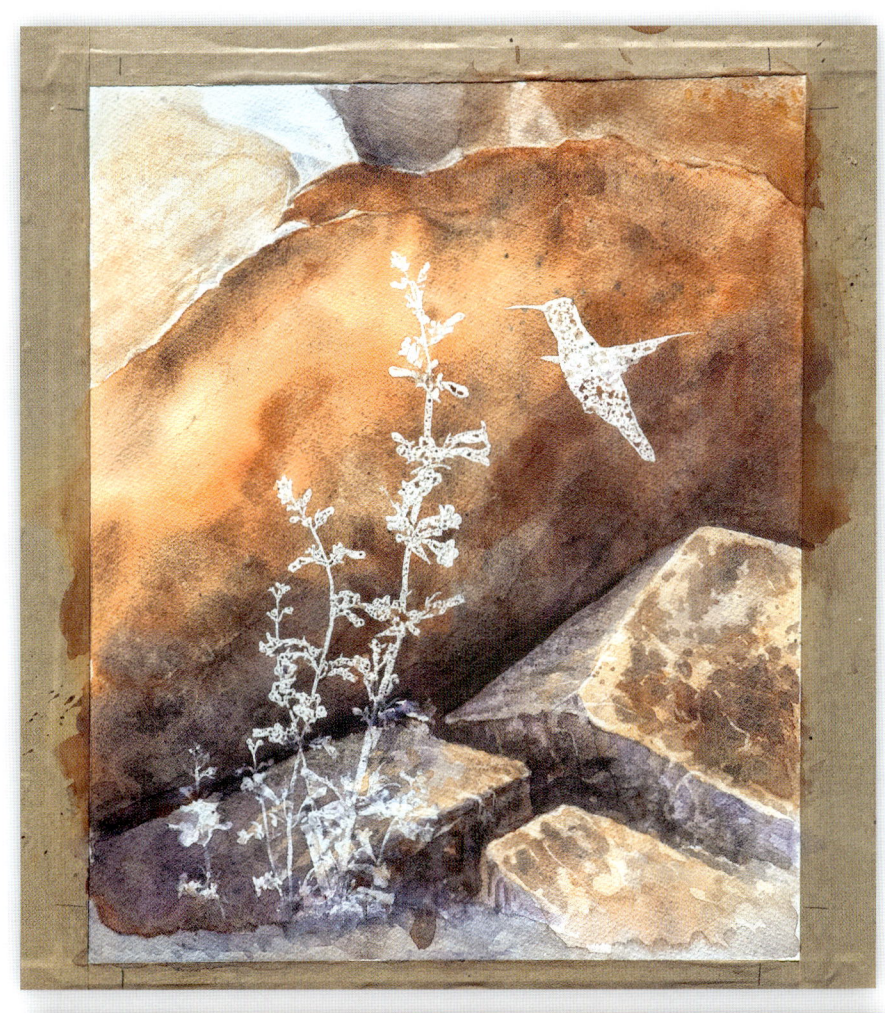

(A) The watercolor paper will receive several floods of washes and needs to remain flat, so it's stretched onto a board. The paper is gently painted with pure water and taped down with heavy-duty brown packaging tape moistened with a sponge. After it thoroughly dries, the paper is drum-tight.

(B) Arizona's dry air determined the use of masking fluid before painting. Water and paint dry too quickly to keep the wash consistently wet around each flower, stem, and bird. The fluid must dry thoroughly before paint is applied. The speckled pattern seen in the masking fluid covering the entire bird and flowers is where dimples in the dried fluid hold paint. The subjects are well sealed.

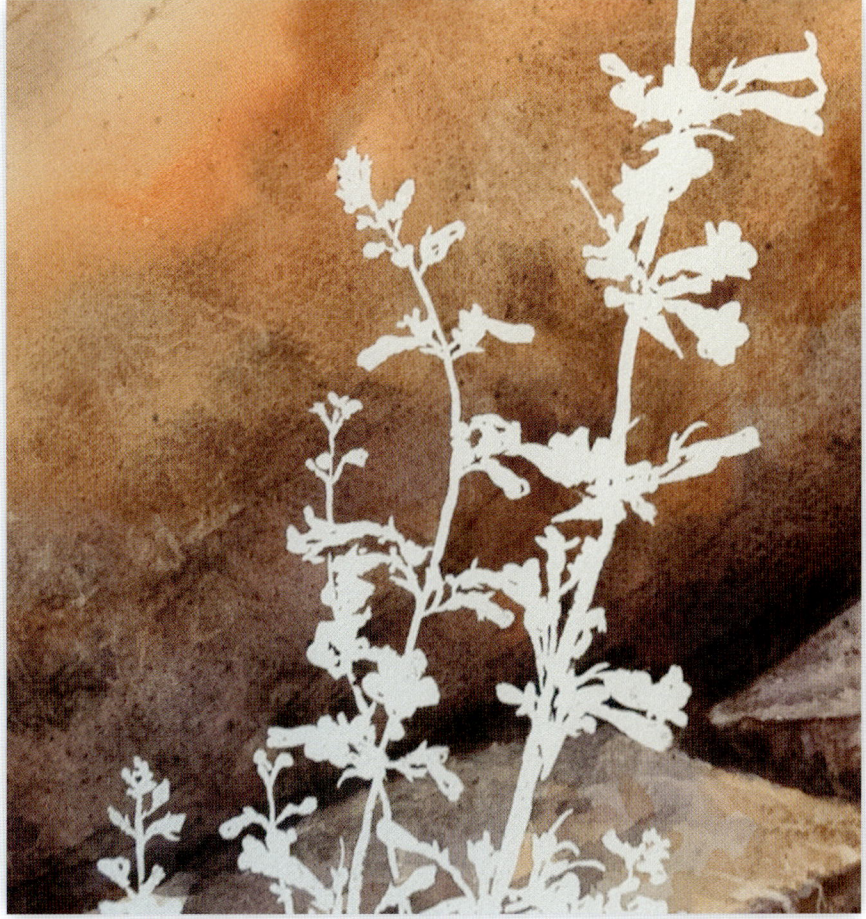

(C) Removing the masking fluid leaves the paper unstained with pigment. The latex material leaves super-harsh edges, requiring adjustment to every edge for each flower, stem, and bird by softening, blurring, painting, or lifting.

"Canyon Illumination"

Violet-crowned Hummingbirds are spectacular, with their snowy white underside and their brilliant violet crown. They favor southern Arizona riparian canyons of sycamores and cottonwoods. A hummingbird visited our yard in spring when the profusion of blooming penstemons echoed its pinkish-violet color. Low streaming sunlight across our rocky garden inspired my painting by illuminating the brilliant colors of birds and flowers. Creating an almost backlit effect, the lighting was crucial to placing the dazzling hummer in front of shadowy rocks. Rich gold and sienna color provided a compliment to the violet crown. A tiny insect on the plant's stalk suggested that there is more life visible in this habitat with closer observation.

Violet-crowned Hummingbird (*Amazilia violiceps*), Parry's Penstemon (*Penstemon parryi*), and Convergent Lady Bird Beetle (*Hippodamia convergens*)

Canyon Illumination, 10.25 × 12.75 in (26.04 × 32.39 cm), transparent watercolor.

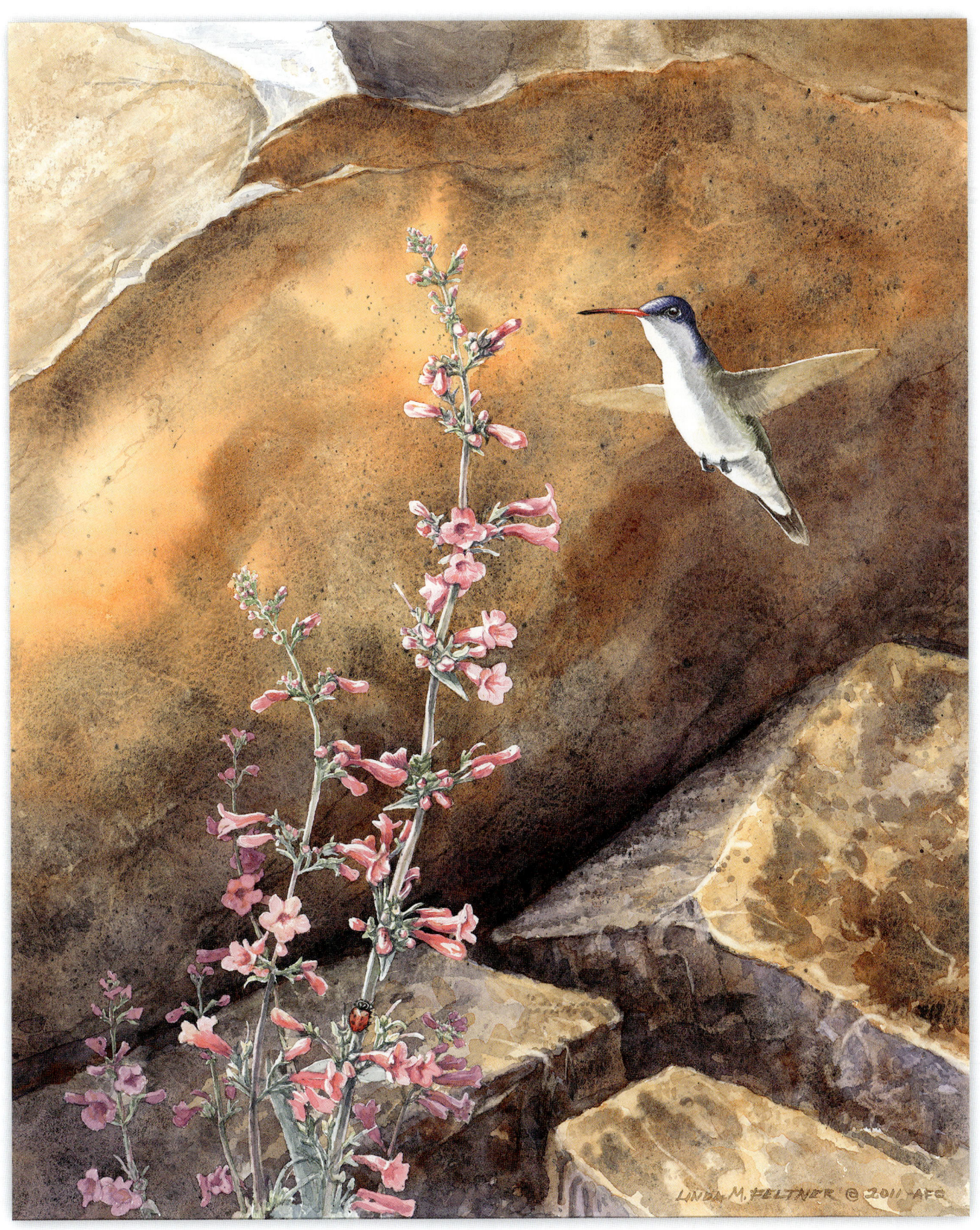

Linda M. Feltner © 2011 AFS

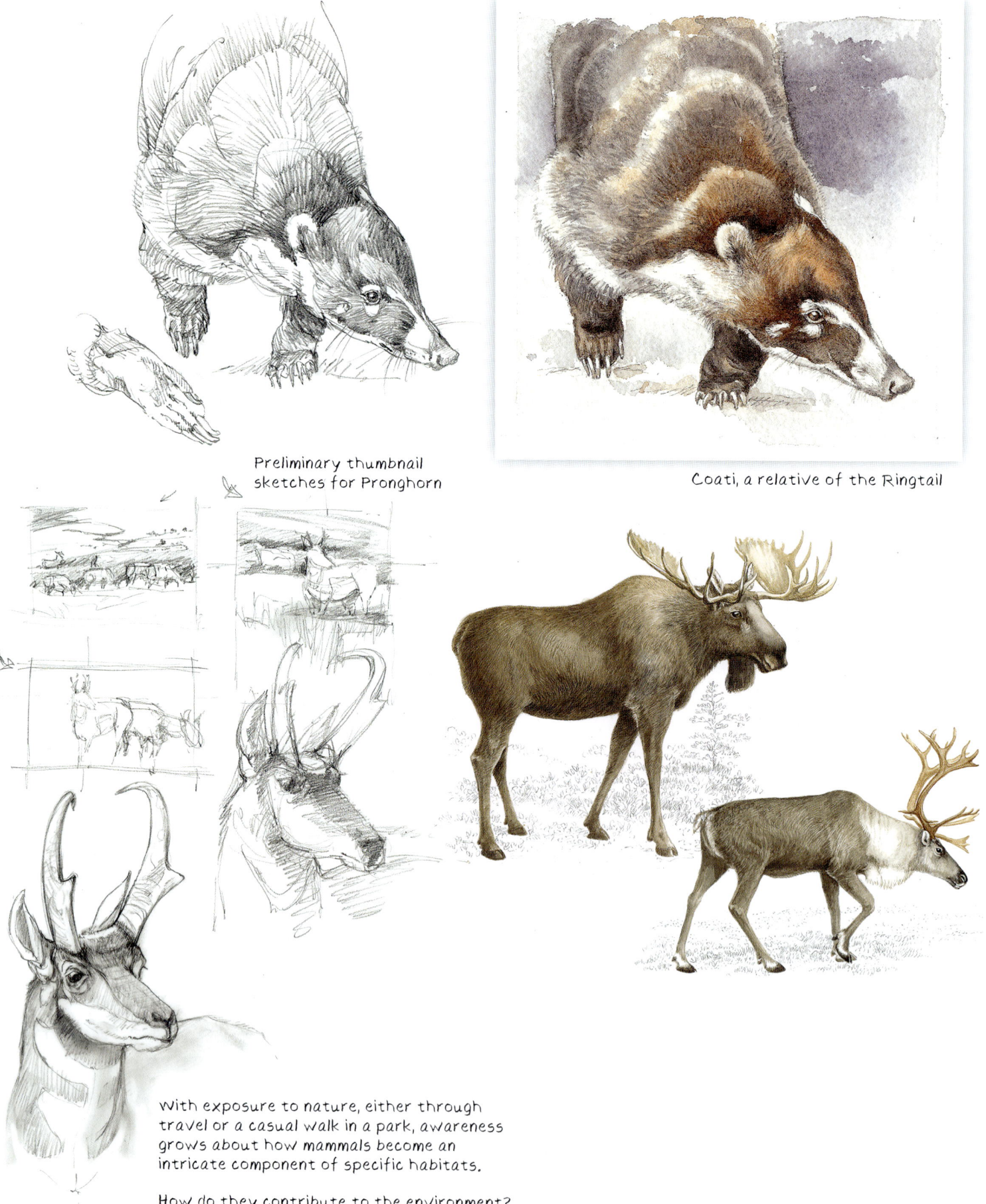

Preliminary thumbnail
sketches for Pronghorn

Coati, a relative of the Ringtail

With exposure to nature, either through
travel or a casual walk in a park, awareness
grows about how mammals become an
intricate component of specific habitats.

How do they contribute to the environment?

120

CHAPTER 4

Mammals: Miniscule to Massive

Consider the tiny Pygmy Shrew and the massive Blue Whale. Mammals are remarkably diverse in both body architecture and lifestyle. They have adapted to nearly all habitats on the planet.

Our most familiar mammals teach us a lot about the wilder ones. A sleeping housecat exhibits the characteristics of a lion. The grazing horse shows the structure of a zebra. Studying the motion of a dog inspires me when drawing a wolf or observing the lithe form of a fox. I often need to illustrate the details of an animal's lifestyle, which includes its strategies for survival. All animal activity deserves the artist's notice.

The following examples show distinct techniques for a diverse selection of artwork, ranging from fine art painting to interpretive illustration to field-guide illustrations. Building on the sketching and observation details in the previous chapters, I now move forward to present the story.

When working on a project, I consider the media options that best fit the message and audience. The "Naturalist's Notebook" style is more informal while still being accurate. It is visually engaging for all ages. Scratchboard, as an option, is perfect for creating detail, and its rich depths are suitable for illustrating underwater life. Field-guide illustrations require a distinct style that serves the purpose of identification and comparison.

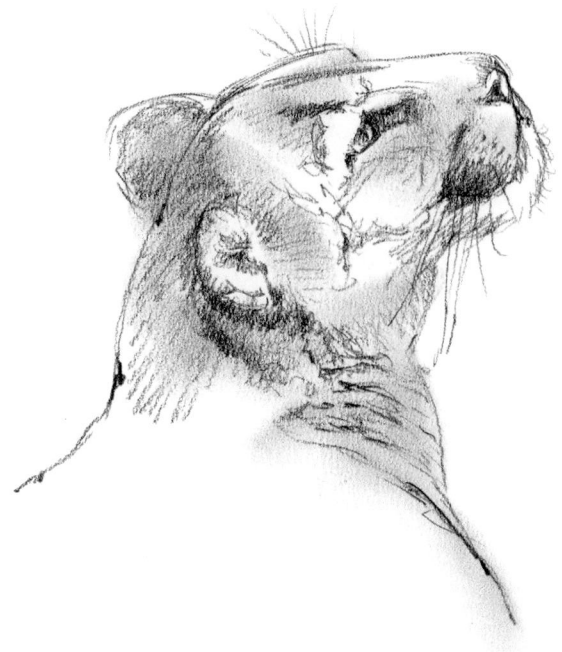

Nocturnal Native

I've had only a few glimpses of this nocturnal beauty in the wild, but I observed how amazing they are during a close encounter.

This female Ringtail was brought into one of my wildlife drawing classes at the Arizona-Sonora Desert Museum Art Institute. Animals in the class allow much closer observation of behavior and anatomical details. Climbing over a landscaping rock, the Ringtail demonstrated balance and movement. I was awestruck by her ballerina's grace, with smooth flowing lines and the balance of the soft, gentle tail.

"I have had several personal encounters with ringtails while camping or working in remote areas, and am constantly impressed by their curiosity and investigative nature. They demonstrate an engaging demeanor filled with playfulness and maybe even a bit of humor.

While camping atop a remote mountain, my wife and I awakened to noises at the foot of our sleeping bags. By the moonlight, we saw a bushy black and white tail extending out of my backpack while the rest of the ringtail was busily inspecting the contents inside. Chances are it had never seen newfound objects like people, backpacks, or sleeping bags. We soon became part of a ringtail playground as it ran back and forth across our sleeping bags and packs, exploring the scene. At one point, the ringtail ran onto my feet and rode along as I levitated my feet up and down, seemingly fascinated with this game. Finally satisfied with its exploration, it left us for the night.

As a Grand Canyon National Park Ranger stationed at the historic Yavapai Geology Museum, I knew ringtails visited the building's crawlspaces but were rarely seen. During an evening geology presentation for the public, a ringtail family emerged onto the large overhead beams supporting the ceiling, using these as "catwalks" and scampering to all corners of the building. Quiet and stealthy, they occasionally sat with their tails hanging below the beam, simply watching the audience or perhaps listening to the presentation. The audience never knew the ringtails were directly overhead, but the Rangers were fascinated by their fearless antics."

—William R. Radke, wildlife biologist (retired), Department of the Interior, Arizona

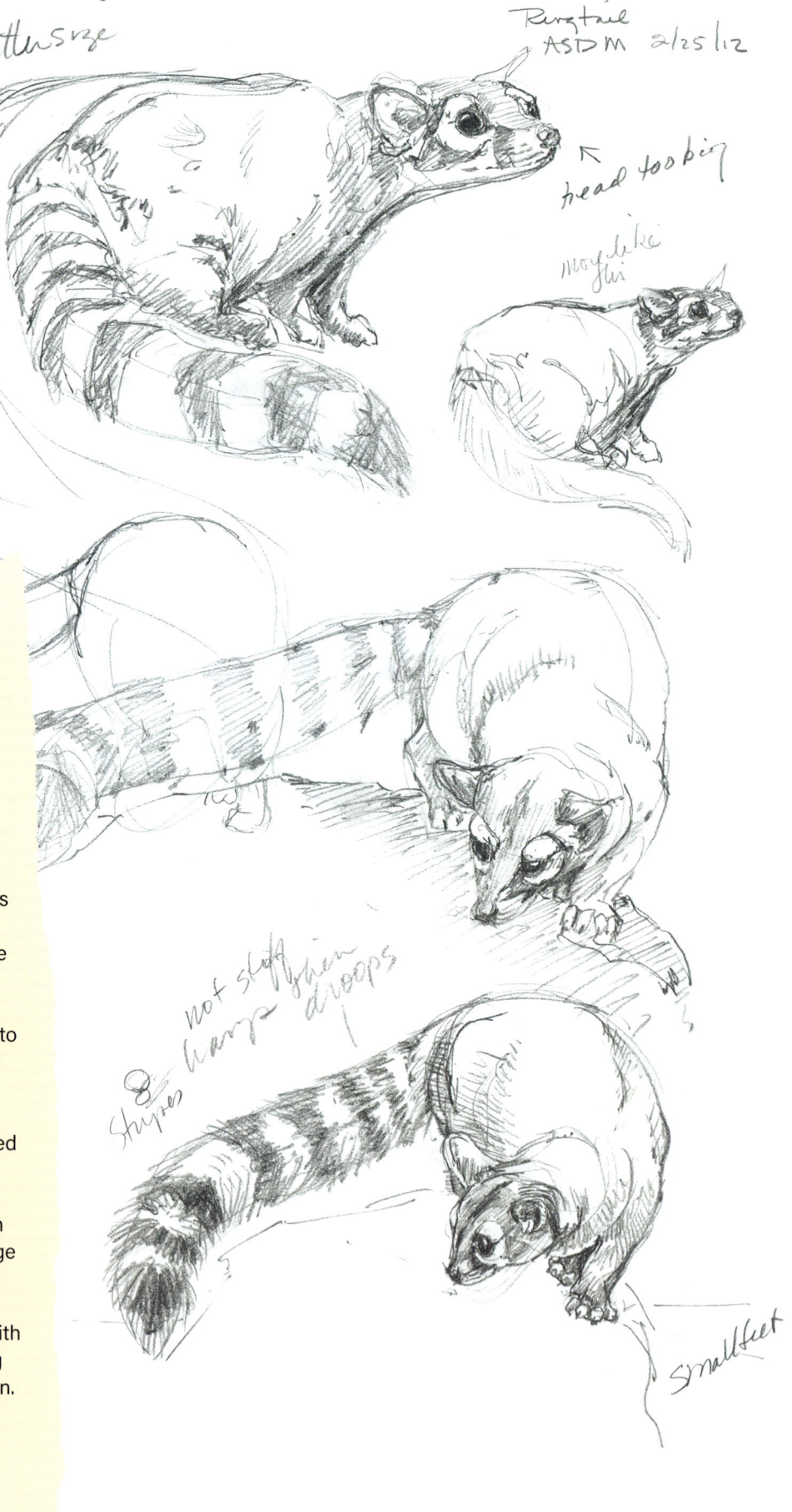

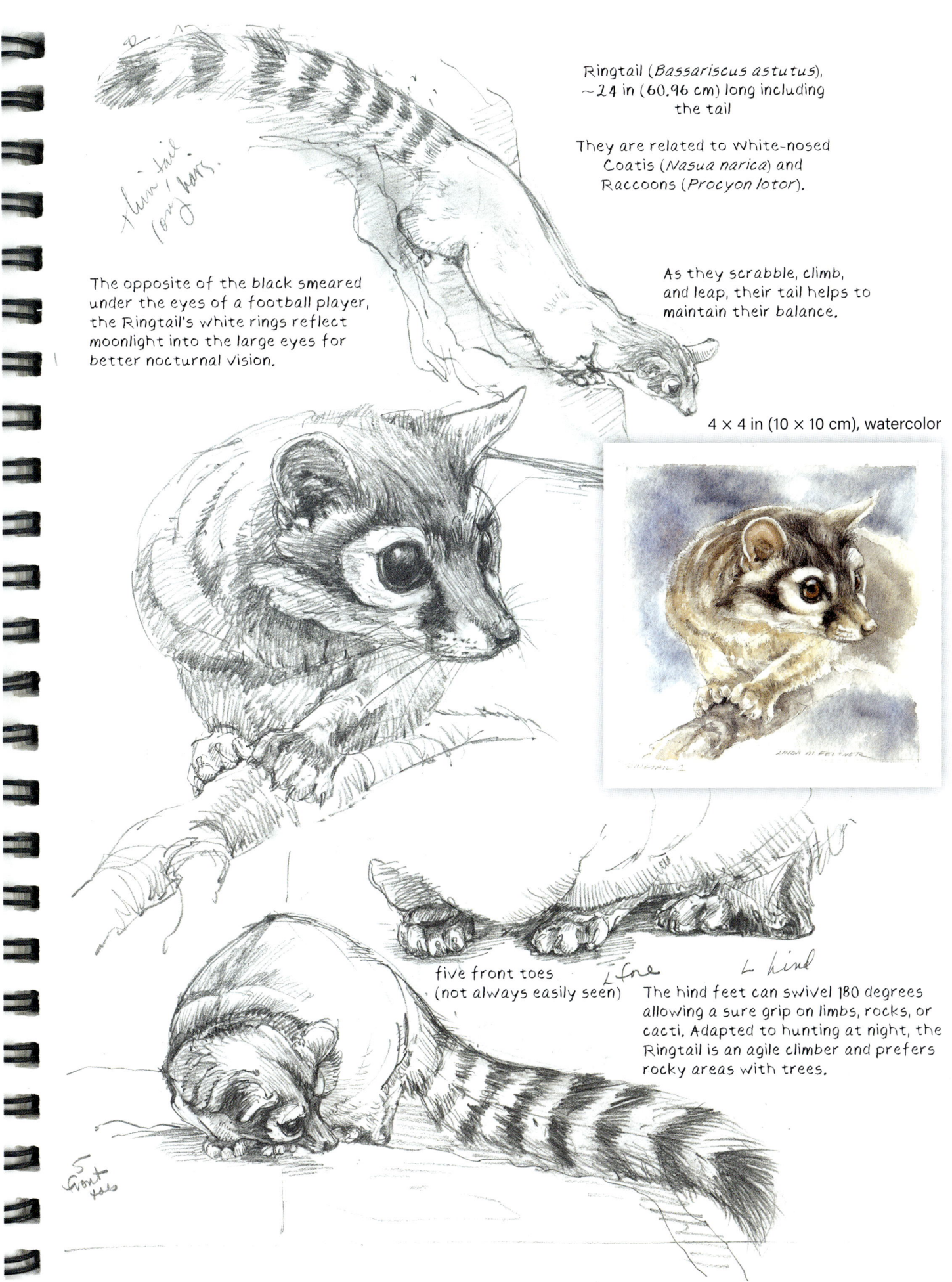

Thin tail long hairs.

Ringtail (*Bassariscus astutus*), ~24 in (60.96 cm) long including the tail

They are related to White-nosed Coatis (*Nasua narica*) and Raccoons (*Procyon lotor*).

The opposite of the black smeared under the eyes of a football player, the Ringtail's white rings reflect moonlight into the large eyes for better nocturnal vision.

As they scrabble, climb, and leap, their tail helps to maintain their balance.

4 × 4 in (10 × 10 cm), watercolor

five front toes (not always easily seen)

L fore   L hind

The hind feet can swivel 180 degrees allowing a sure grip on limbs, rocks, or cacti. Adapted to hunting at night, the Ringtail is an agile climber and prefers rocky areas with trees.

What Plant Unites the Scene?

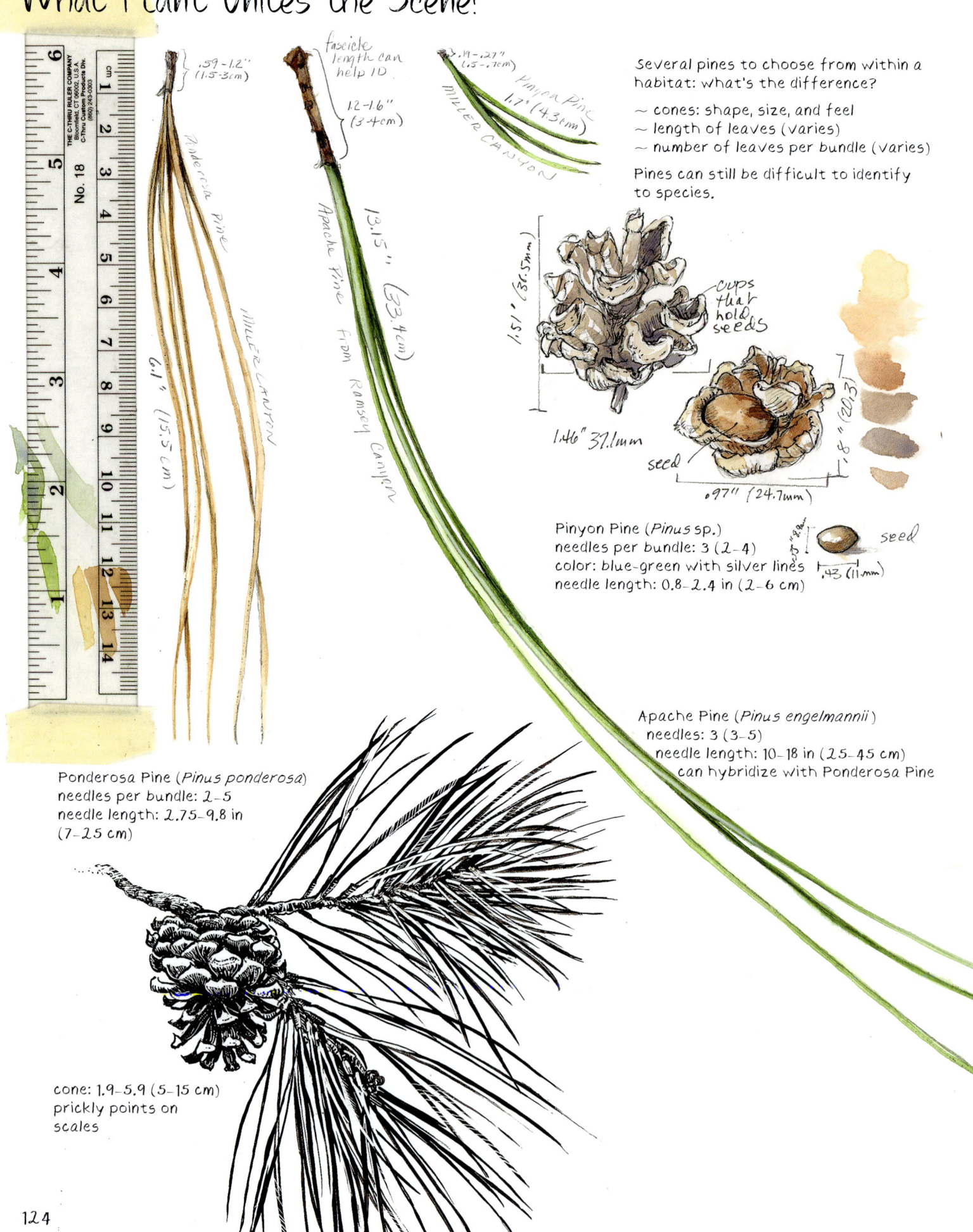

.59–1.2" (1.5–3 cm)

fascicle length can help ID.

1.2–1.6" (3–4 cm)

.19–.27" (.5–.7 cm)

Pinyon Pine 1.7" (4.3 cm)

MILLER CANYON

Ponderosa Pine

MILLER CANYON

6.1" (15.5 cm)

Apache Pine from Ramsey Canyon

13.15" (33.4 cm)

Several pines to choose from within a habitat: what's the difference?

~ cones: shape, size, and feel
~ length of leaves (varies)
~ number of leaves per bundle (varies)

Pines can still be difficult to identify to species.

1.51" (36.5 mm)

cups that hold seeds

1.46" 37.1 mm

seed

.97" (24.7 mm)

.8" (20.3)

Pinyon Pine (*Pinus* sp.)
needles per bundle: 3 (2–4)
color: blue-green with silver lines
needle length: 0.8–2.4 in (2–6 cm)

seed

.43 (11 mm)

Apache Pine (*Pinus engelmannii*)
needles: 3 (3–5)
needle length: 10–18 in (25–45 cm)
can hybridize with Ponderosa Pine

Ponderosa Pine (*Pinus ponderosa*)
needles per bundle: 2–5
needle length: 2.75–9.8 in
(7–25 cm)

cone: 1.9–5.9 (5–15 cm)
prickly points on scales

While investigating a background for an animal painting, I like to include plants, insects, or arachnids. As an interpreter of natural history, I want to visually describe their behavior or show how closely they are united to their surroundings. There may be a deeper story of how one can only survive because of the other. Geology and landscape also play a part in this story. These additional species can be small and nearly hidden under a leaf, but authenticity is crucial.

The canyon where I live at 5,000 ft (1,524 m), is home to Ringtails. There are rocky slopes in this mid-altitude forest where oaks, junipers, and pines overlap. The understory has a plentiful variety of plants providing year-round food sources. After comparing a dozen or more plant species, I chose the Pinyon Pine to add a subtle but significant element to the painting.

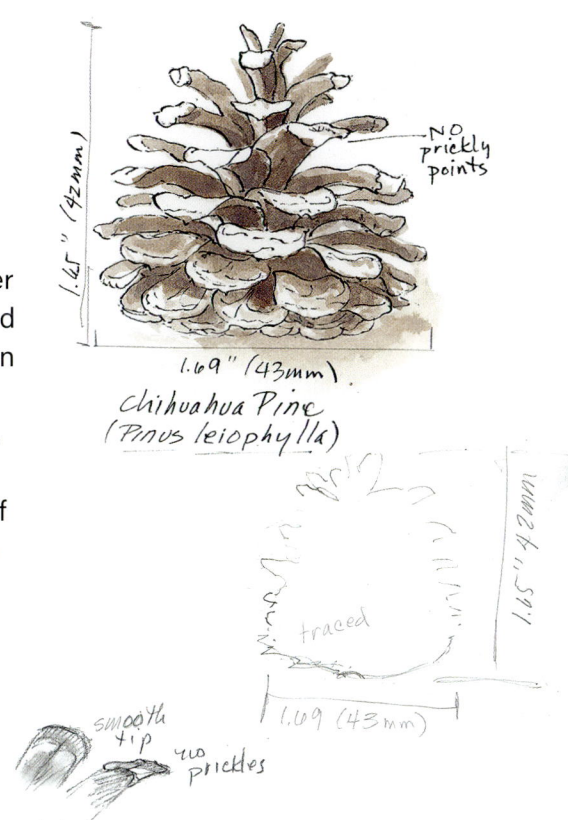

NO prickly points

1.65" (42mm)

1.69" (43mm)

Chihuahua Pine
(Pinus leiophylla)

1.65" (42mm)

traced

1.69 (43mm)

smooth tip

no prickles

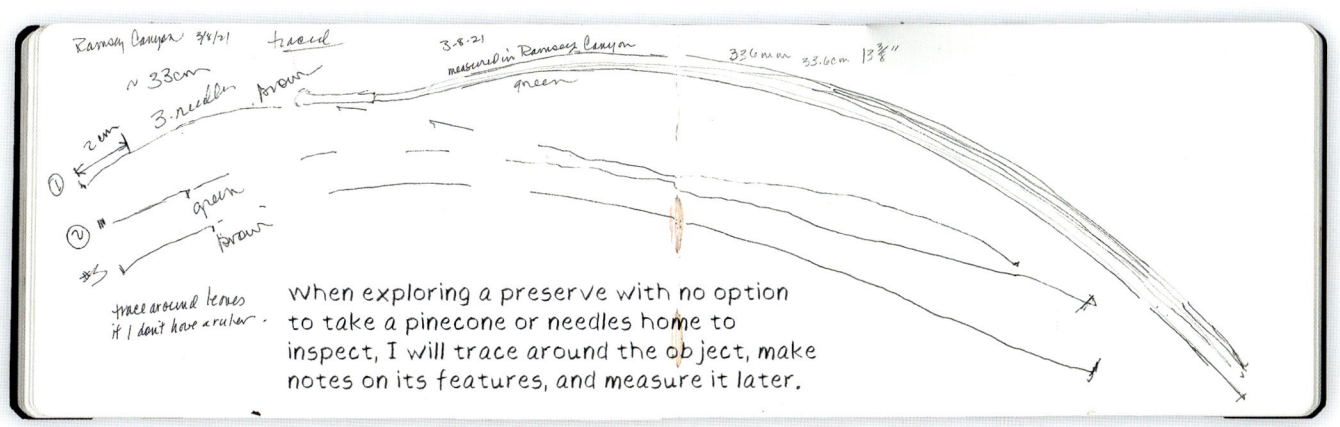

Ramsey Canyon 3/8/21 traced

~ 33cm

3-needle brown

2cm

green brown

measured in Ramsey Canyon green

336mm 33.6cm 13⅜"

trace around leaves if I don't have a ruler.

When exploring a preserve with no option to take a pinecone or needles home to inspect, I will trace around the object, make notes on its features, and measure it later.

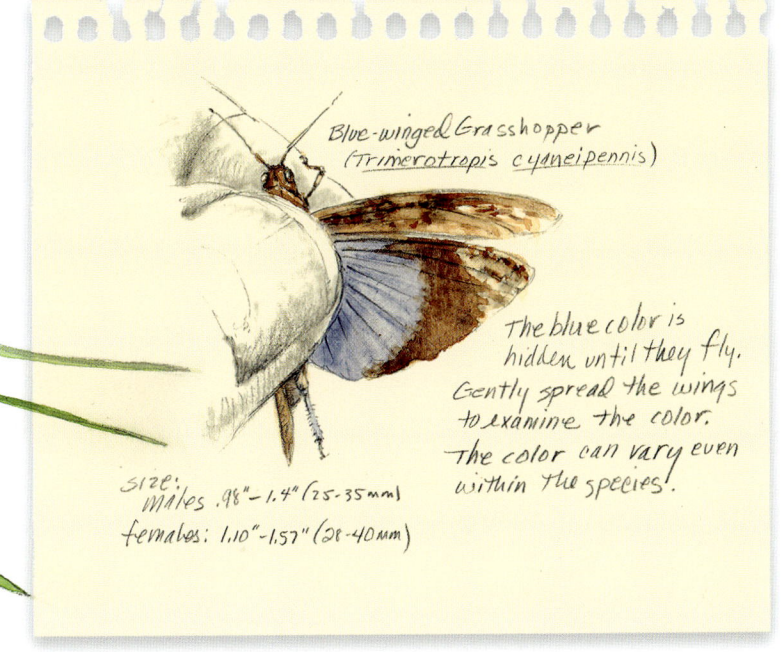

Blue-winged Grasshopper
(Trimerotropis cyaneipennis)

The blue color is hidden until they fly. Gently spread the wings to examine the color. The color can vary even within the species!

size: males .98"–1.4" (25-35mm)
females: 1.10"-1.57" (28-40mm)

Apache Pine
(Pinus engelmannii)

graceful, drooping. super-long leaves – distinctive in the forest.

needle bundle- 3 (up to 5)
long = 10-18" (25-45cm)
foliar sheath = 1.2-1.6" (3-4cm)
2.6cm long – 2.5cm fascicle
cones= often asymmetric
4.4-5.6" (11-14cm)
Elev. 4,500-9000' (1500-2400m)

when do they bear cones? how old?

"Evening Encounter"

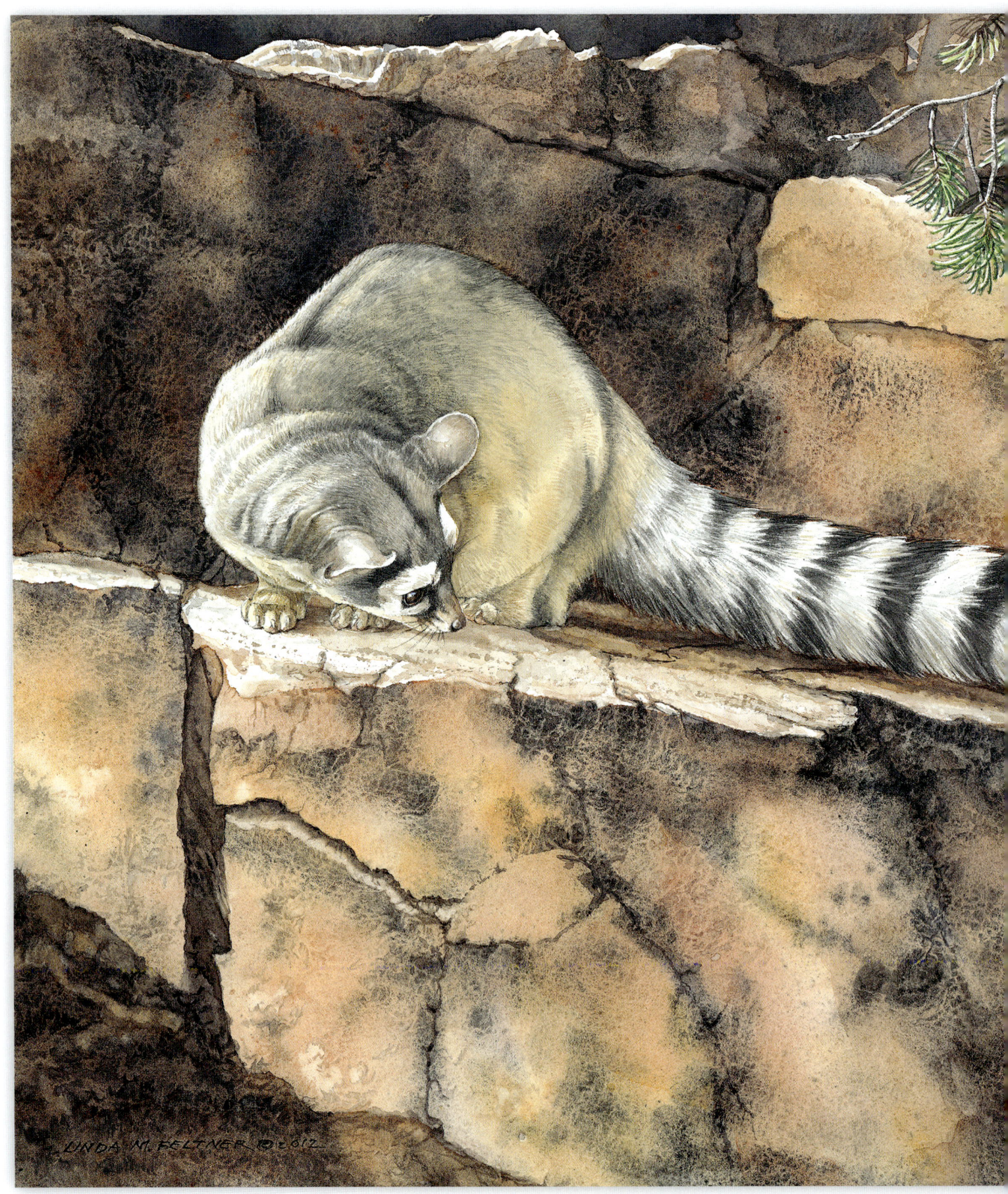

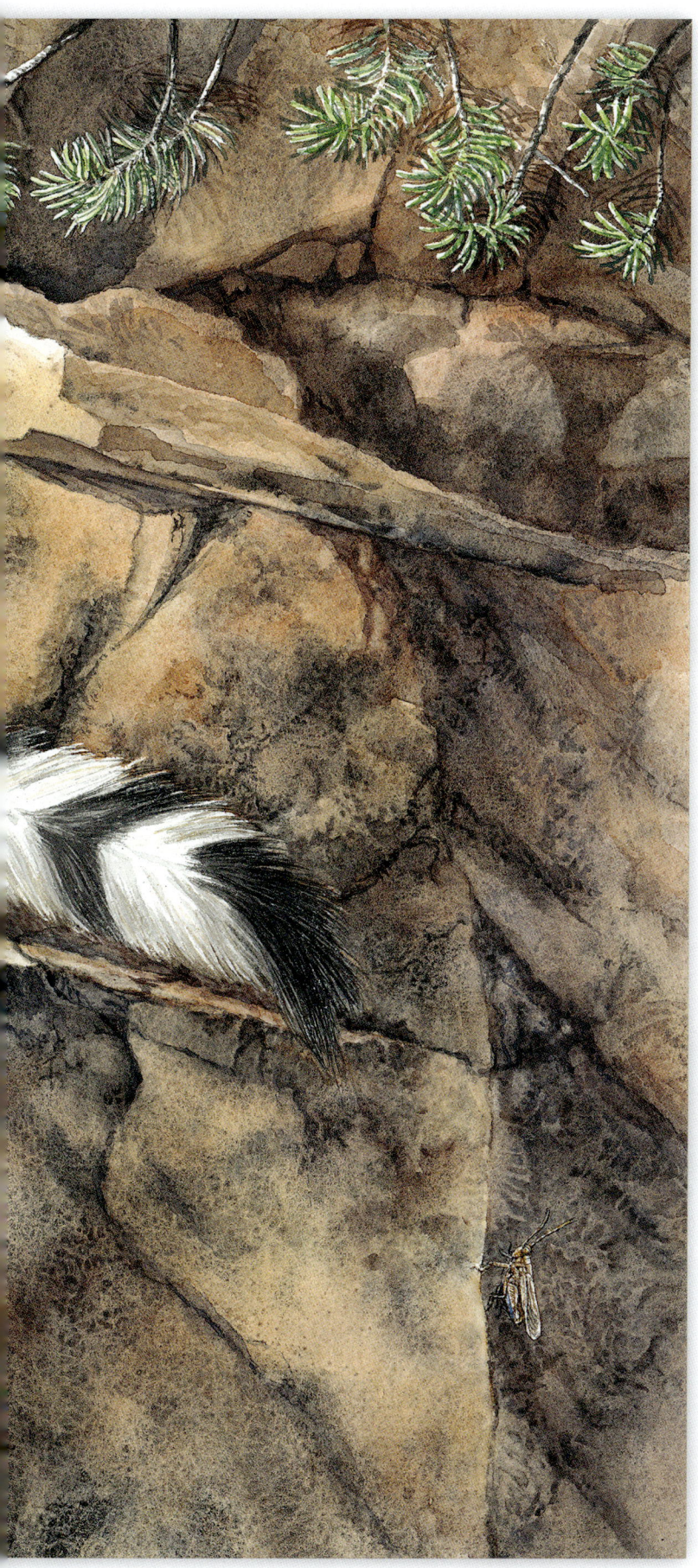

Admired for its large eyes and appealing demeanor, the Ringtail is among the nocturnal residents of the southwestern sky islands. It is an agile, expert climber in rocky terrain. Its diet includes insects, small mammals, and fruit.

Isolated by stretches of desert and grassland, these forested mountain ranges are internationally important for their outstanding biological diversity, supporting many species found nowhere else in the United States. The selected quartet of subjects shows their connections in this habitat. My developmental drawings were sparked by the graceful Ringtail model in the class. These led to curiosity about its food, its rocky forest habitat, and lifestyle in the wild. I pulled my car over on a dusty switchback road in the Chiricahua Mountains to discover the perfect rock ledge, slightly sun-struck with glowing reflected light, that appeared in the finished painting.

Ringtail (*Bassariscus astutus*), Blue-winged Grasshopper (*Trimerotropis cyaneipennis*), and Pinyon Pine (*Pinus* sp.)

Evening Encounter, 13.25 × 10.25 in (33.66 × 26.04 cm), transparent watercolor, Sonoran Experience Collection, courtesy of the Arizona-Sonora Desert Museum Art Institute.

Three Strategies for Winter Survival

High in the Cascade Mountains, three mammals are found that have developed different strategies for surviving the severe winters.

Creating the "Naturalist Notebooks" for the Cascade Crest Alpine Exhibit at the Oregon Zoo was a chance to show what extraordinary lengths these high-altitude mammals go to in order to survive the extreme cold. Strategy #1: Marmots. Strategy #2: Pikas. Strategy #3: Pocket Gophers.

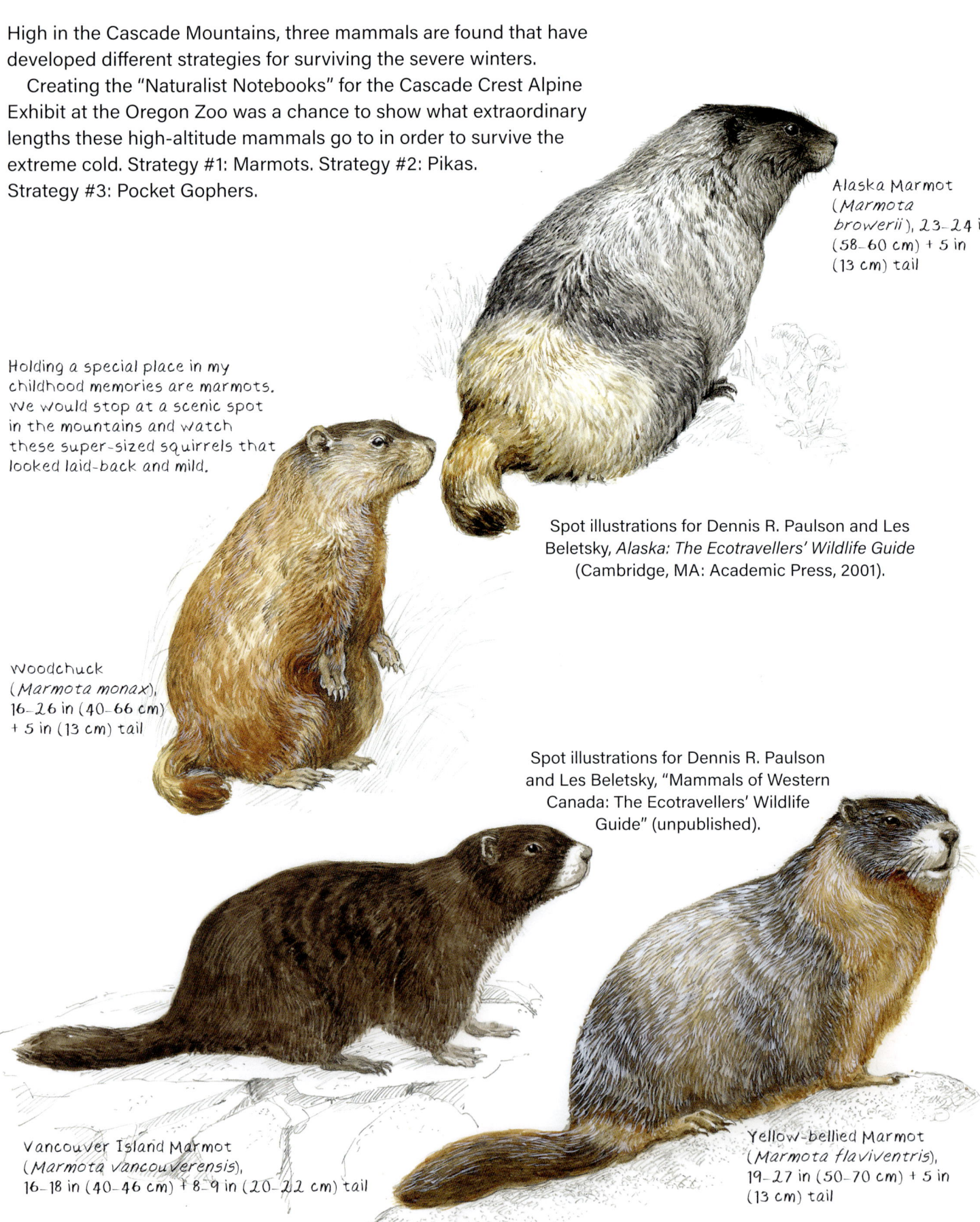

Alaska Marmot (*Marmota browerii*), 23–24 in (58–60 cm) + 5 in (13 cm) tail

Holding a special place in my childhood memories are marmots. We would stop at a scenic spot in the mountains and watch these super-sized squirrels that looked laid-back and mild.

Spot illustrations for Dennis R. Paulson and Les Beletsky, *Alaska: The Ecotravellers' Wildlife Guide* (Cambridge, MA: Academic Press, 2001).

Woodchuck (*Marmota monax*), 16–26 in (40–66 cm) + 5 in (13 cm) tail

Spot illustrations for Dennis R. Paulson and Les Beletsky, "Mammals of Western Canada: The Ecotravellers' Wildlife Guide" (unpublished).

Vancouver Island Marmot (*Marmota vancouverensis*), 16–18 in (40–46 cm) + 8–9 in (20–22 cm) tail

Yellow-bellied Marmot (*Marmota flaviventris*), 19–27 in (50–70 cm) + 5 in (13 cm) tail

Winter Survival Strategy #1: Marmots

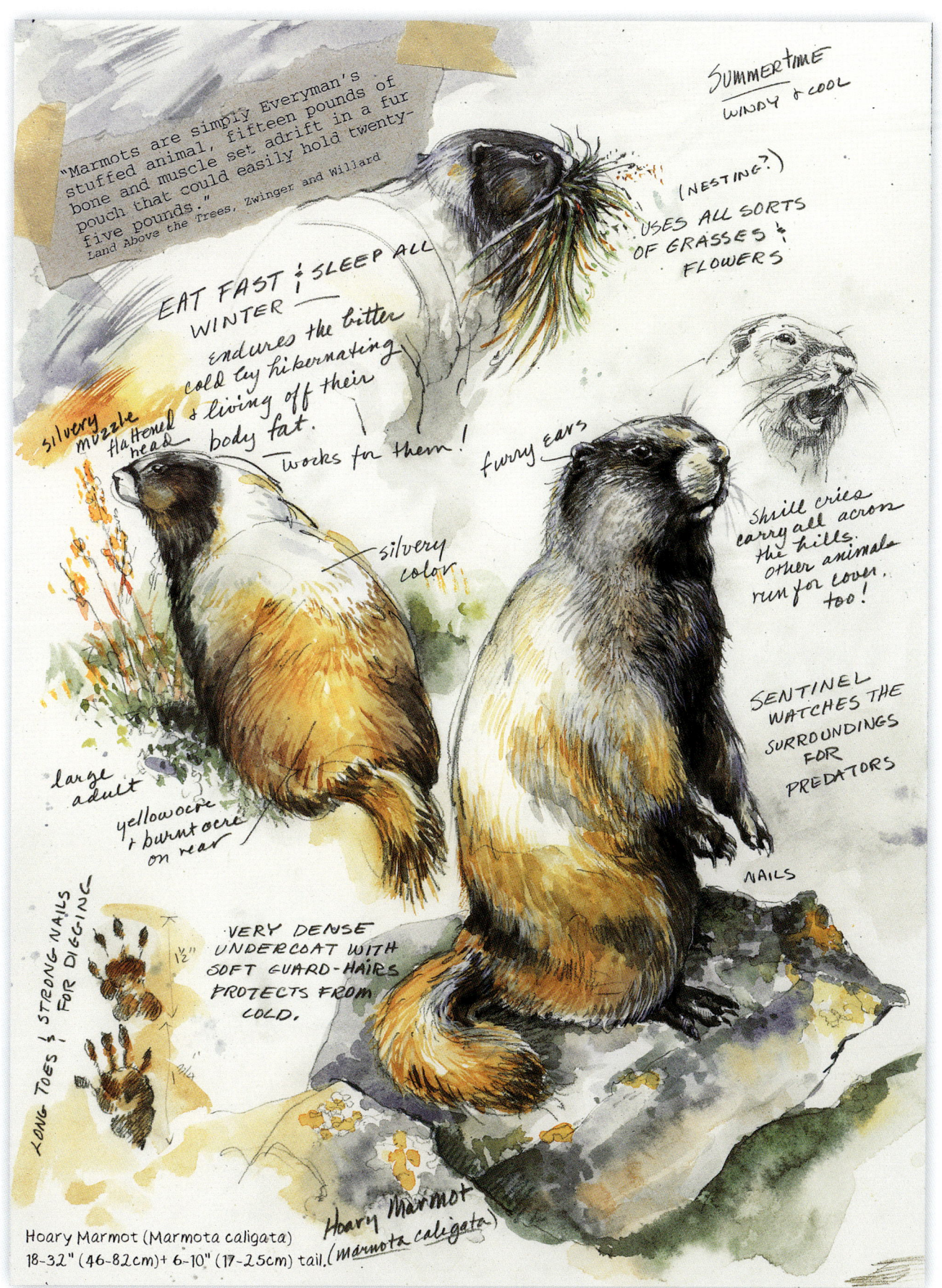

SUMMERTIME
WINDY & COOL

"Marmots are simply Everyman's stuffed animal, fifteen pounds of bone and muscle set adrift in a fur pouch that could easily hold twenty-five pounds."
Land Above the Trees, Zwinger and Willard

(NESTING?)
USES ALL SORTS OF GRASSES & FLOWERS

EAT FAST & SLEEP ALL WINTER — endures the bitter cold by hibernating & living off their body fat.
works for them!

silvery muzzle
flattened head

silvery color

furry ears

Shrill cries carry all across the hills. Other animals run for cover too!

large adult

yellow ocre & burnt ocre on rear

SENTINEL WATCHES THE SURROUNDINGS FOR PREDATORS

NAILS

LONG TOES & STRONG NAILS FOR DIGGING

1½"

VERY DENSE UNDERCOAT WITH SOFT GUARD-HAIRS PROTECTS FROM COLD.

Hoary Marmot (Marmota caligata)
18–32" (46–82cm) + 6–10" (17–25cm) tail.

Hoary Marmot (Marmota caligata)

11 × 14 in (27.94 × 35.56 cm), pencil and watercolor, high-pressure laminate, courtesy of The Oregon Zoo, Portland, Oregon.

Winter Survival Strategy #2: Pika

The Pika's closest relatives are hares and rabbits. They are tough little animals that spend their lives above the tree line and do not hibernate.

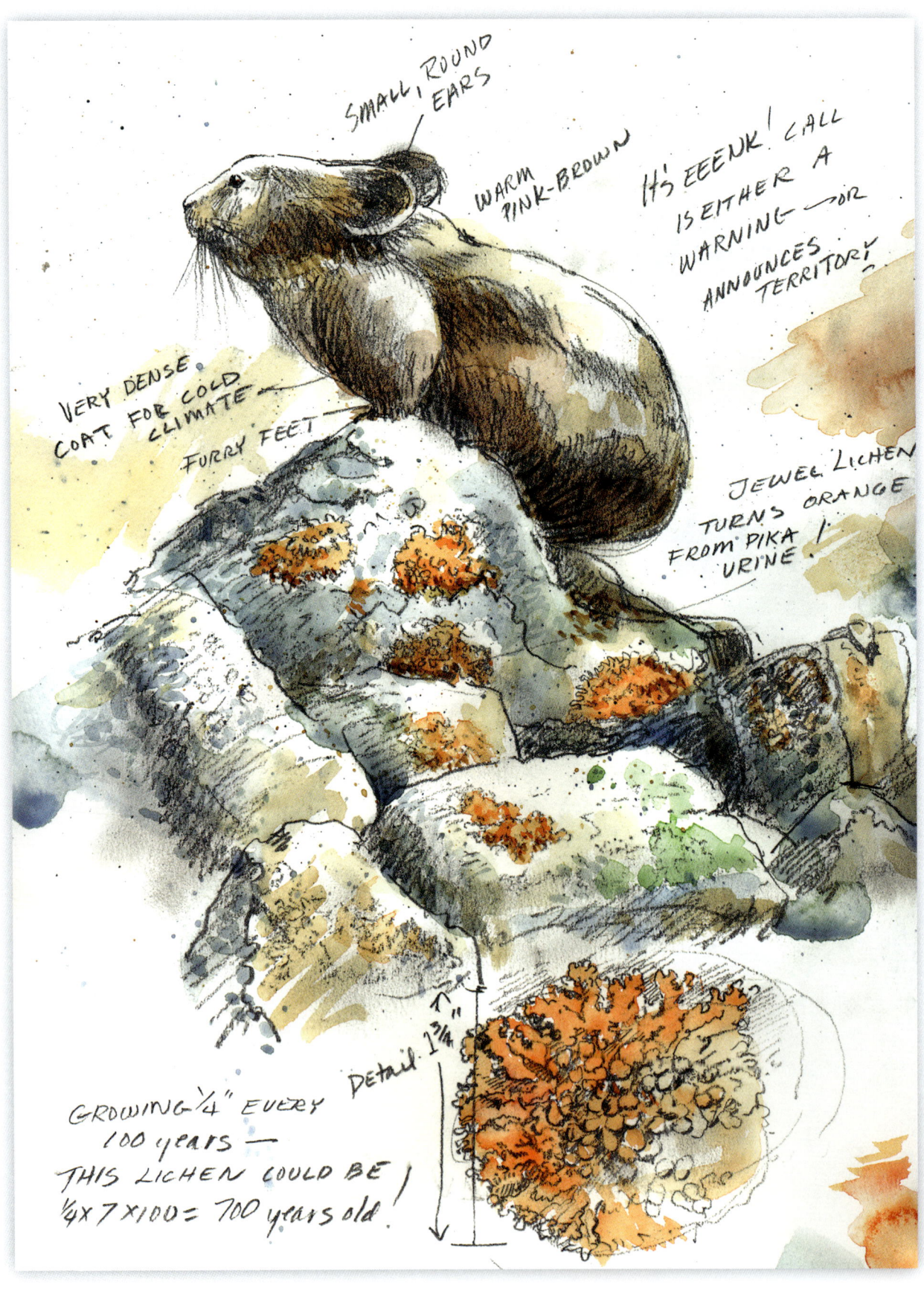

SMALL, ROUND EARS

WARM PINK-BROWN

It's EEENK! CALL IS EITHER A WARNING —OR ANNOUNCES TERRITORY

VERY DENSE COAT FOR COLD CLIMATE

FURRY FEET

JEWEL LICHEN TURNS ORANGE FROM PIKA URINE!

Detail: 1³/₁₆"

GROWING ¼" EVERY 100 years — THIS LICHEN COULD BE ¼ X 7 X 100 = 700 years old!

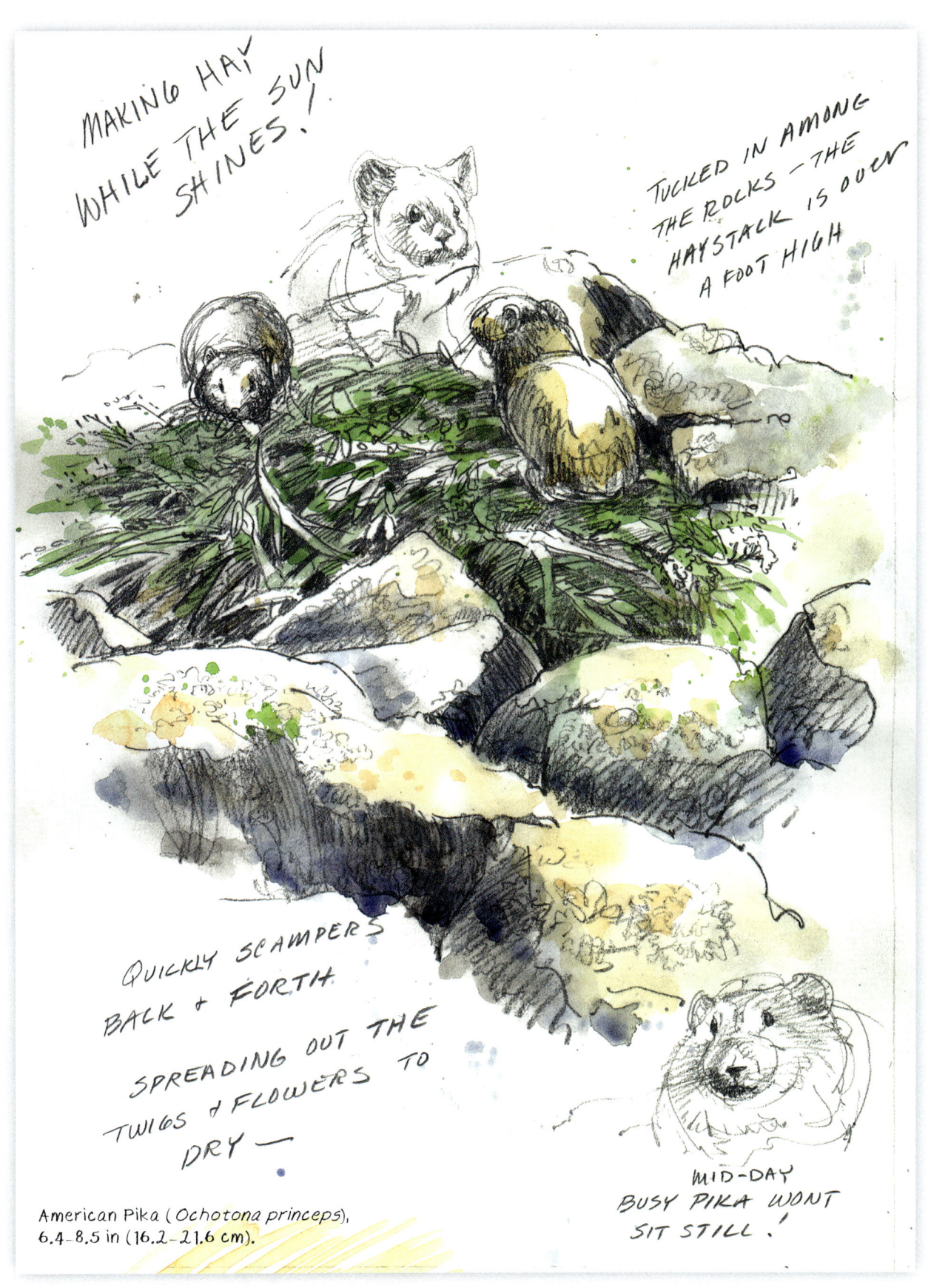

MAKING HAY WHILE THE SUN SHINES!

TUCKED IN AMONG THE ROCKS — THE HAYSTACK IS OVER A FOOT HIGH

QUICKLY SCAMPERS BACK & FORTH

SPREADING OUT THE TWIGS & FLOWERS TO DRY —

American Pika (*Ochotona princeps*), 6.4–8.5 in (16.2–21.6 cm).

MID-DAY BUSY PIKA WONT SIT STILL!

"Cascade Crest Alpine Exhibit Pika Flipbook," 12 × 14 in (30.48 × 35.56 cm), high-pressure laminate, courtesy of the Oregon Zoo, Portland, Oregon.

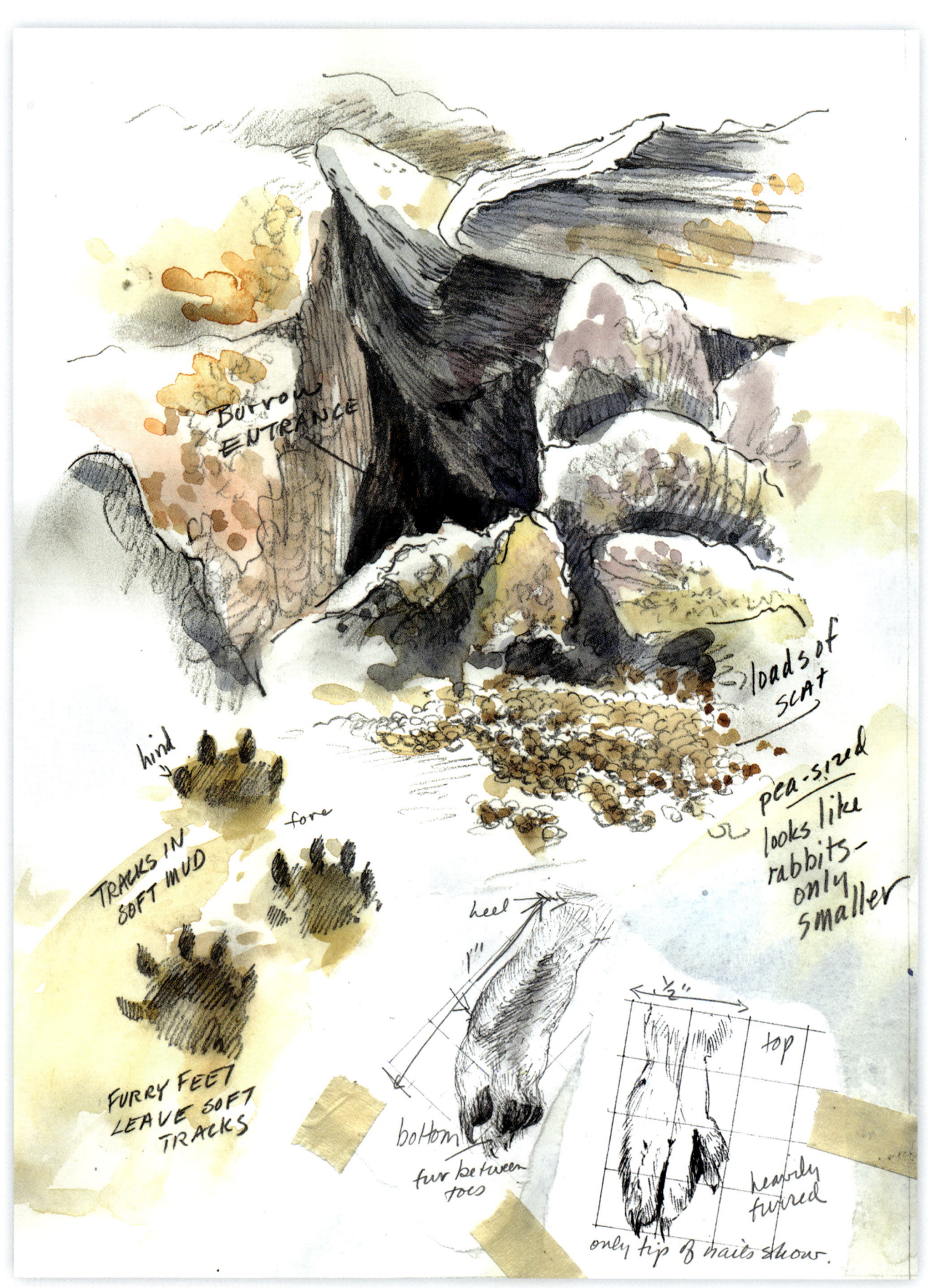

Borrow
ENTRANCE

loads of
scAt

pea-sized
looks like
rabbits-
only
smaller

hind

fore

TRACKS IN
SOFT MUD

FURRY FEET
LEAVE SOFT
TRACKS

heel

1"

bottom

fur between
toes

½"

top

heavily
furred

only tip of nails show.

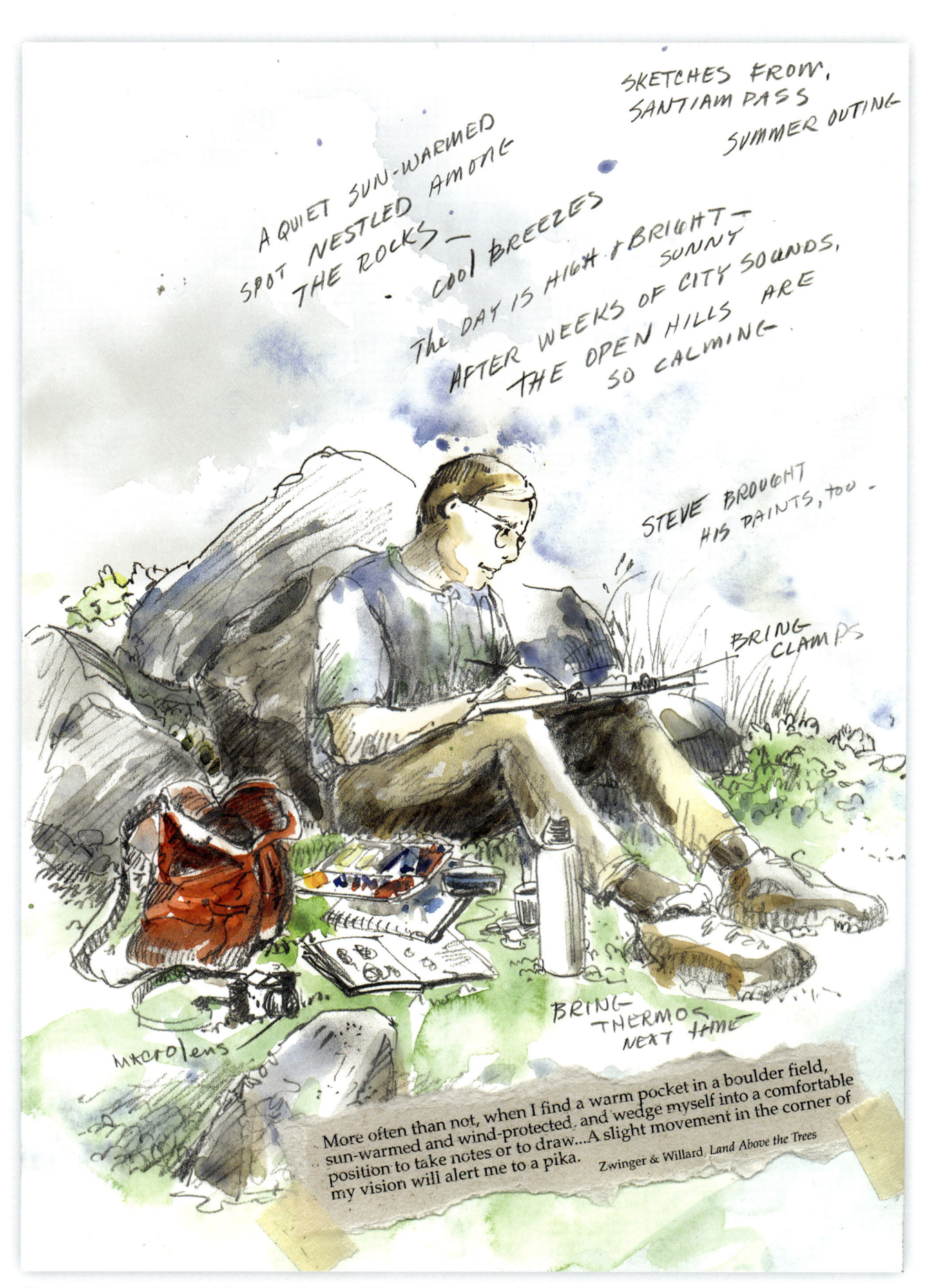

"Cascade Crest Alpine Exhibit Pika Flipbook," 12 × 14 in (30.48 × 35.56 cm),
high-pressure laminate, courtesy of the Oregon Zoo, Portland, Oregon.

Winter Survival Strategy #3: Pocket Gopher

Adapted for a lifetime underground and in the dark, Pocket Gophers stay active throughout the year. Burrowing a network of tunnels right under the surface allows access to yummy roots and tubers even beneath a snowy blanket.

A sleek body shape, tiny eyes, and small ears are perfect for tunnel life. Their strong front feet with long nails are excellent for digging. Fur-lined cheek pouches start with lips behind the large front teeth and extend to the shoulders. This is a convenient way to carry food underground and keep dirt out of the mouth while digging. The ears also have flaps to keep them clean.

Pocket Gopher
(*Thomomys* sp.)

exposed teeth

external
pocket
goes from
mouth to shoulder

They push dirt up while making the tunnels and create distinct humped ridges seen above ground. Sleeping chambers and food storage areas are roughly a foot deeper.

ridges seen from above

Several types of mountain species create shallow tunnels with vertical shafts to deeper burrows. Food storage, nests, and chambers for feces can be walled off from the system if needed.

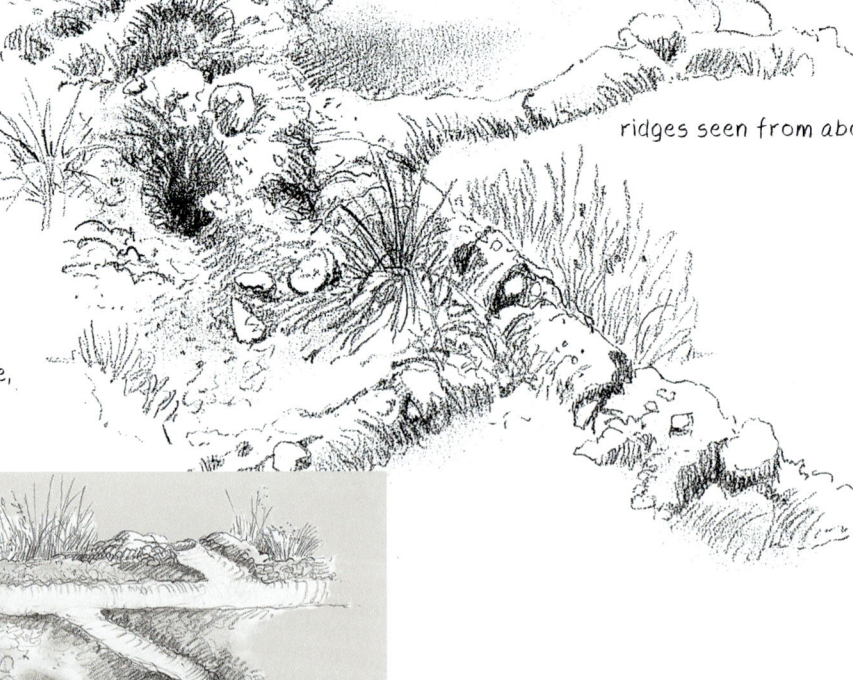

Cascade Crest Alpine Pocket Gopher Exhibit, 24 × 36 in (60.96 × 91.44 cm), pencil and watercolor, courtesy of the Oregon Zoo, Portland, Oregon.

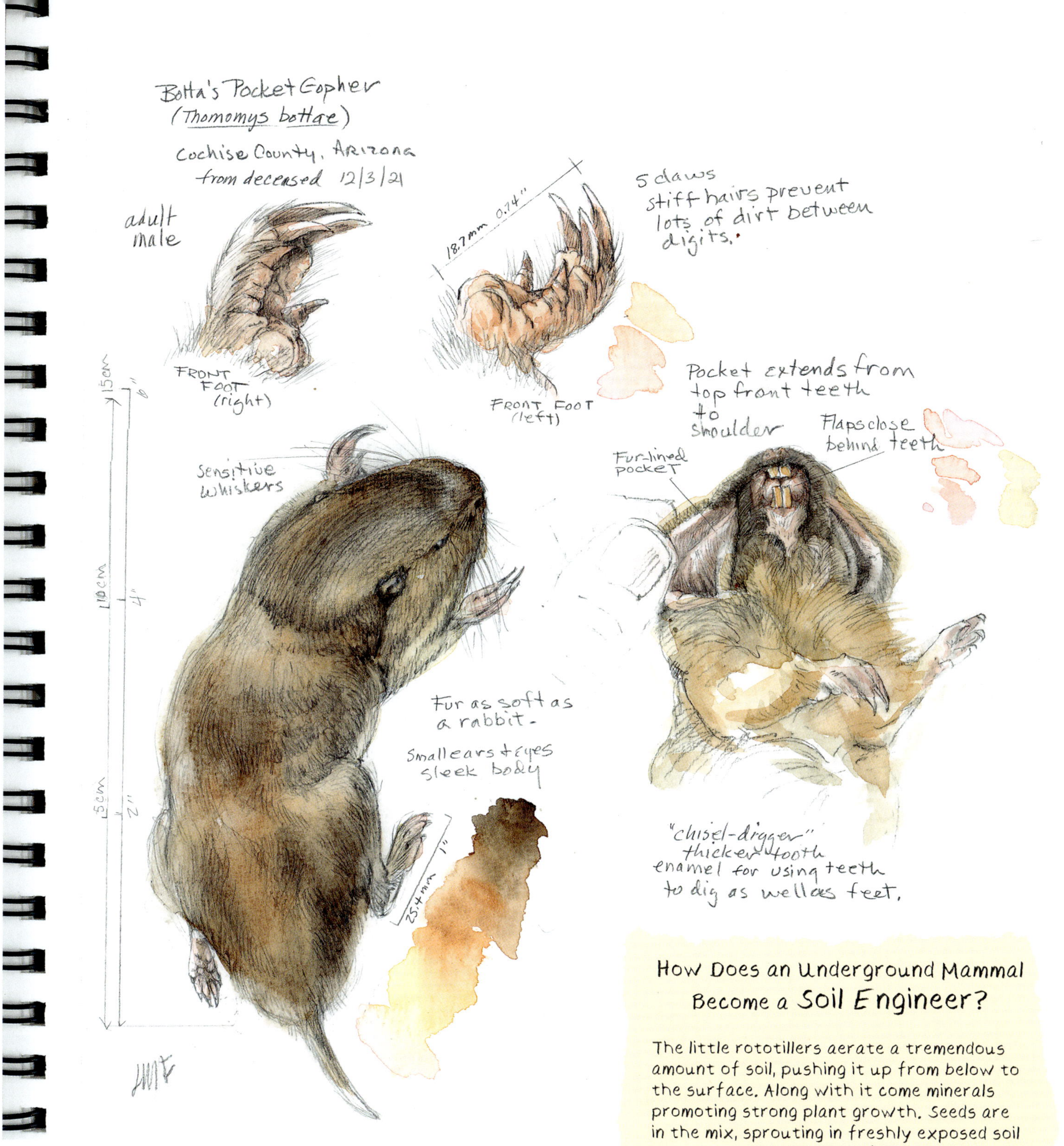

Botta's Pocket Gopher
(*Thomomys bottae*)

Cochise County, Arizona
from deceased 12/3/21

adult male

18.7mm 0.74"

FRONT FOOT (right)

FRONT FOOT (left)

5 claws
stiff hairs prevent lots of dirt between digits.

Pocket extends from top front teeth to shoulder

Flaps close behind teeth

Fur-lined pocket

Sensitive whiskers

15cm 6"
10cm 4"
5cm 2"

Fur as soft as a rabbit.

Small ears + eyes
sleek body

25.+mm 1"

"chisel-digger"
thicker tooth enamel for using teeth to dig as well as feet.

Botta's Pocket Gopher (*Thomomys bottae*), from my "Arizona sketchbook," December 12, 2021.

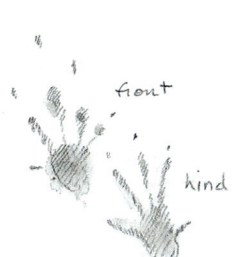

front

hind

How Does an Underground Mammal Become a Soil Engineer?

The little rototillers aerate a tremendous amount of soil, pushing it up from below to the surface. Along with it come minerals promoting strong plant growth. Seeds are in the mix, sprouting in freshly exposed soil and without competition from established plants. That results in an increased density of these plants, similar to farming.

In the rocky soil of mountains, the gopher's extensive labor loosens the earth. Over long periods, this creates meadows and alluvial fans. Snowmelt trickles downward and prevents run-off erosion.

Ongoing studies are discovering opportunities to restore native prairies and wild areas. Natural predators that control rodent populations are a significant contributor.

Seaworthy Mammals

Whether nearby or on the other side of the globe, exhilarating moments of wonder often inspire an idea that later becomes a picture.

This drawing celebrates the day I saw my first Sea Otter. Nestled among the offshore kelp carpet, a baby otter was firmly held in place by a snug blanket of kelp. Bobbing gently with the waves, it would tighten the blanket by rolling several times. The adults would surface around the young one held in place. I imagined the rocking activity beneath the surface with swaying algae fronds and graceful parents navigating the underwater forest.

Sea Otter (*Enhydra lutris*)

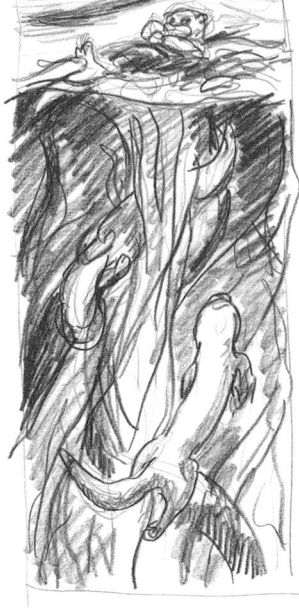
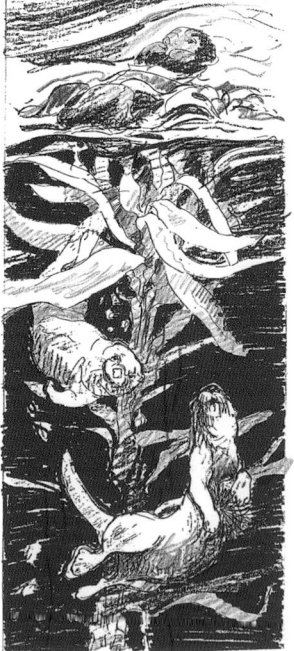

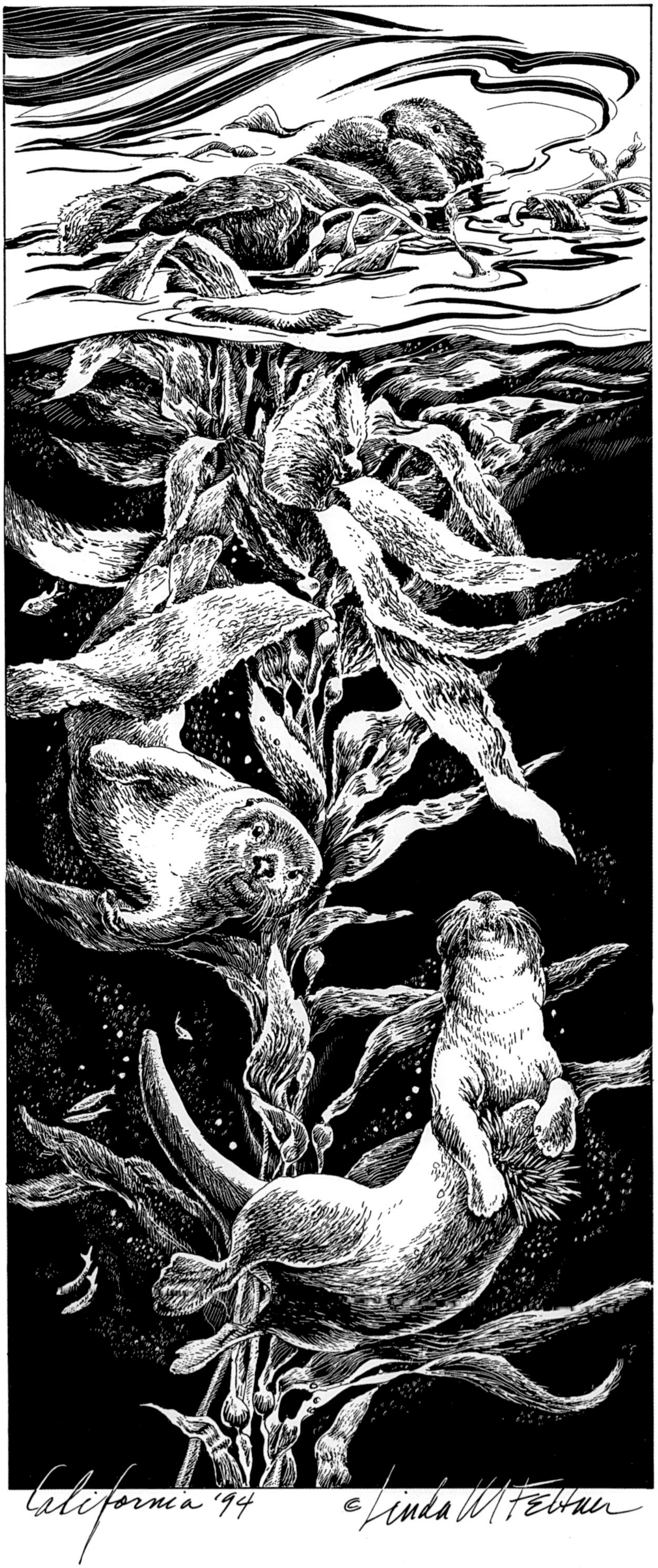

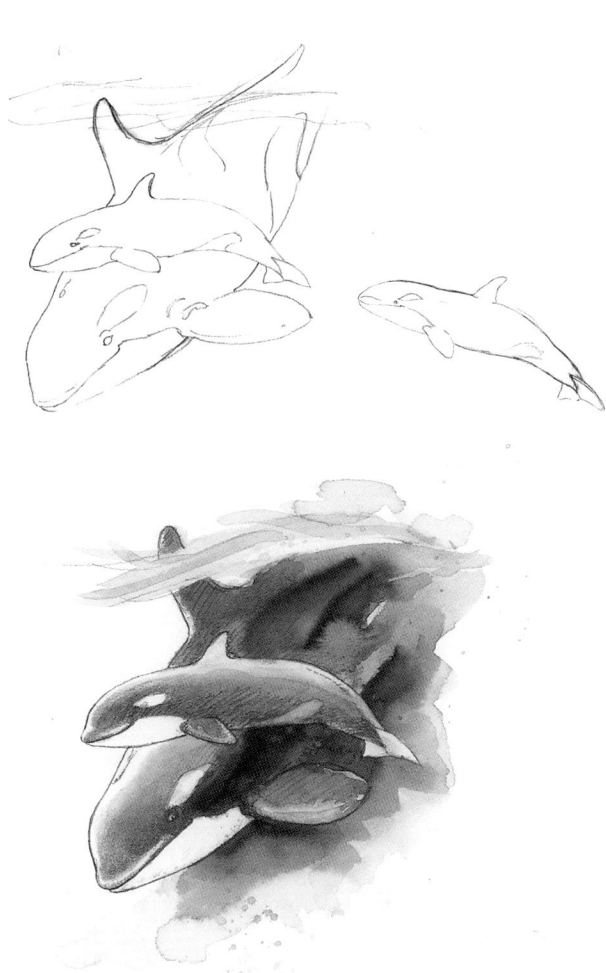

My first experience in Alaska included the remote Pribilof Islands. High above the ocean surface, we stood at the top of dizzying cliffs that held a thriving colony of nesting seabirds on the cliff face below. Looking straight down into the clear water, we saw a pod of Orcas sedately file past possibly to hunt for seals along the lower shoreline farther up the coast. Among them, a mother and baby came into view. It was a tender moment to see them swimming at ease together from such a viewpoint.

Orca (*Orcinus orca*)
Crested Auklet (*Aethia cristatella*)
Least Auklet (*Aethia pusilla*)
Dovekie (*Alle alle*)

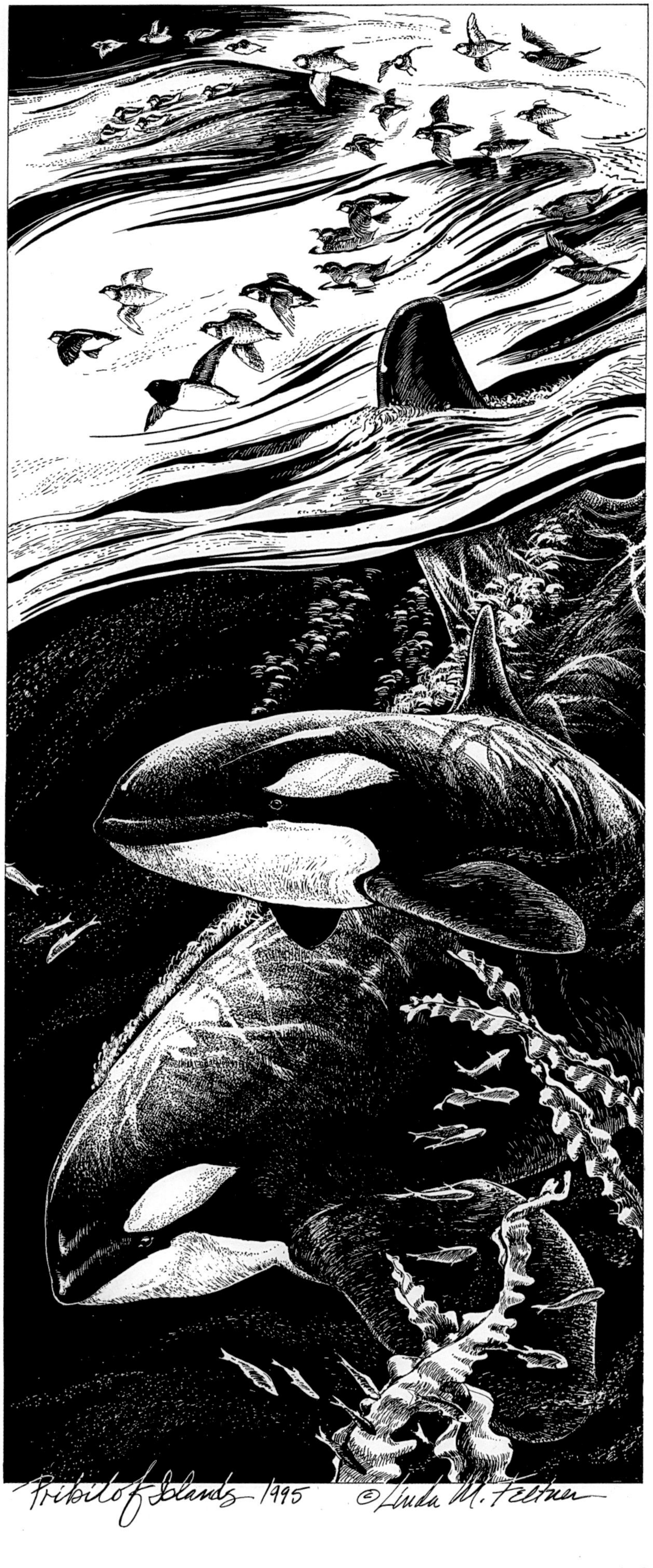

7 x 15 in (17.78 x 38.1 cm), ink on white Essdee Scraperboard.

Pribilof Islands 1995 ©*Linda M. Feltner*

Field-Guide Illustrations: Mammals

Field-guide illustrations serve a purpose other than fine art. Rather, this artwork shows direct comparison and anatomical details for species identification. Author and illustrator collaboration become crucial to providing the necessary information for the reader. The author might be a scientist who is often the best resource for the artist.

Each drawing progresses with revisions to achieve the best results. I dive into investigating and learning about each animal and its lifestyle. This adds to my knowledge of the diversity of animals sharing an environment, which makes the project enjoyable.

Pencil sketches show adjustments of body parts (the nose is blunter, the tail is thicker and bi-colored). Rough sketches show typical poses.

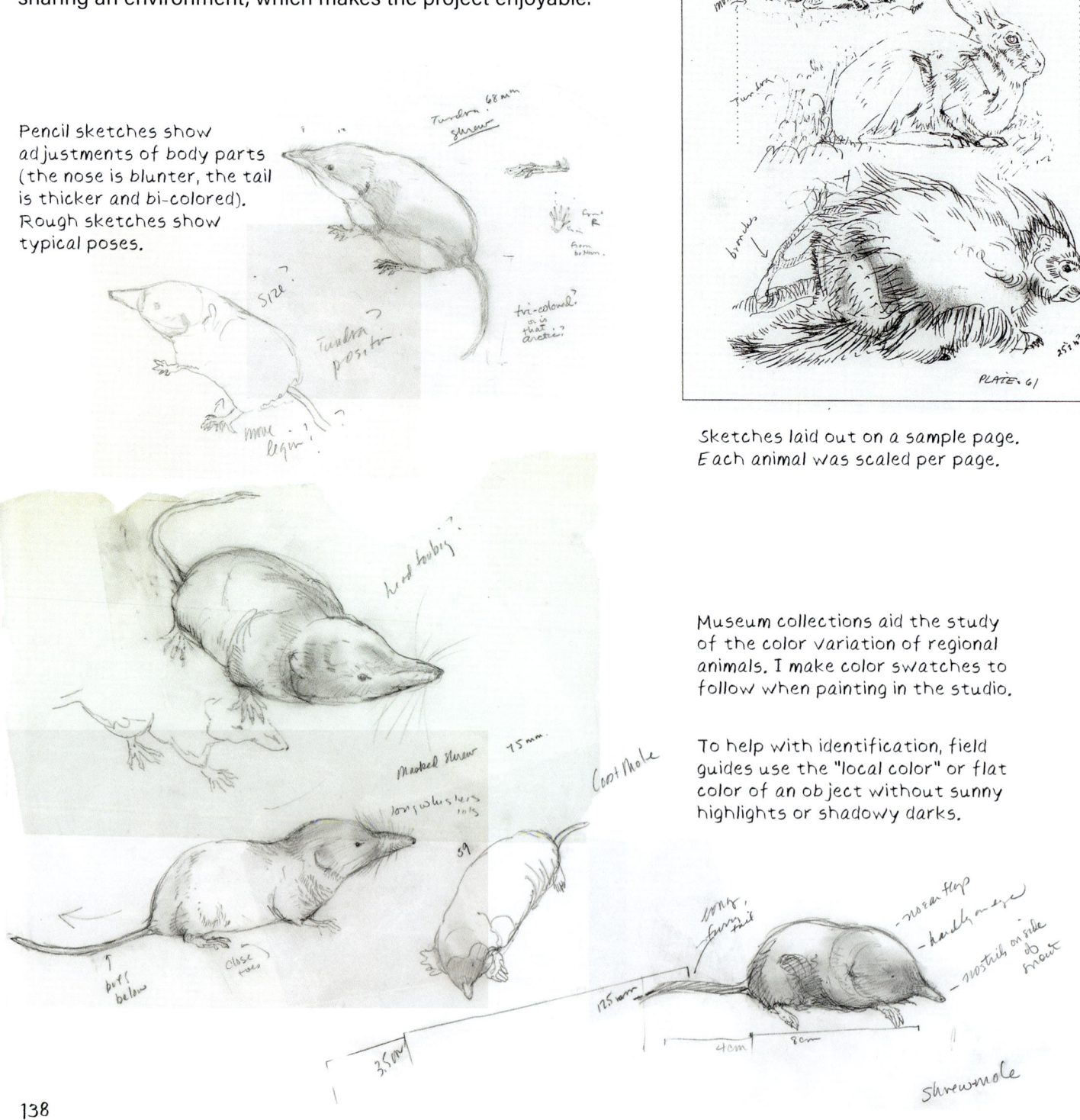

Sketches laid out on a sample page. Each animal was scaled per page.

Museum collections aid the study of the color variation of regional animals. I make color swatches to follow when painting in the studio.

To help with identification, field guides use the "local color" or flat color of an object without sunny highlights or shadowy darks.

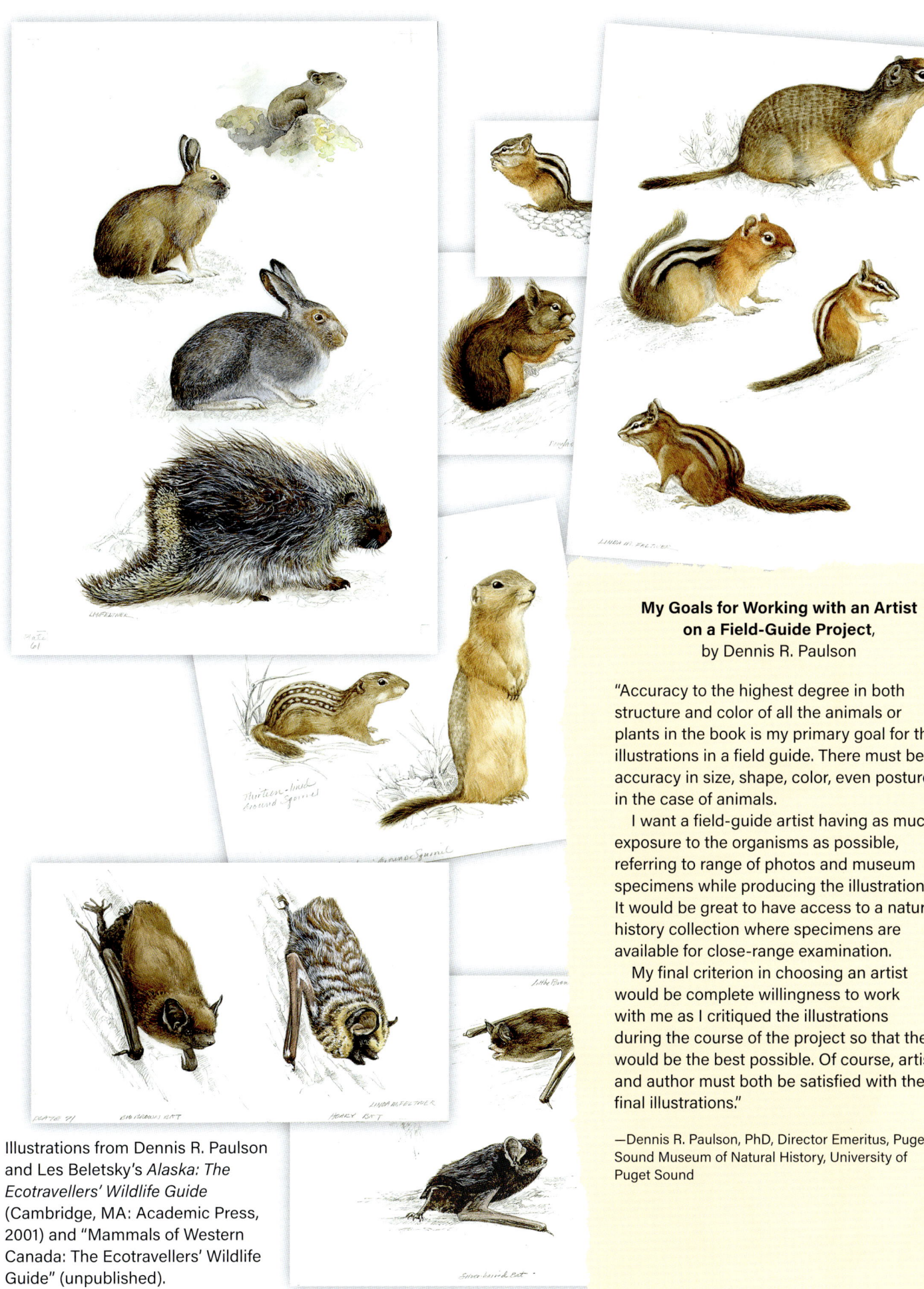

Illustrations from Dennis R. Paulson and Les Beletsky's *Alaska: The Ecotravellers' Wildlife Guide* (Cambridge, MA: Academic Press, 2001) and "Mammals of Western Canada: The Ecotravellers' Wildlife Guide" (unpublished).

My Goals for Working with an Artist on a Field-Guide Project,
by Dennis R. Paulson

"Accuracy to the highest degree in both structure and color of all the animals or plants in the book is my primary goal for the illustrations in a field guide. There must be accuracy in size, shape, color, even posture in the case of animals.

I want a field-guide artist having as much exposure to the organisms as possible, referring to range of photos and museum specimens while producing the illustrations. It would be great to have access to a natural history collection where specimens are available for close-range examination.

My final criterion in choosing an artist would be complete willingness to work with me as I critiqued the illustrations during the course of the project so that they would be the best possible. Of course, artist and author must both be satisfied with the final illustrations."

—Dennis R. Paulson, PhD, Director Emeritus, Puget Sound Museum of Natural History, University of Puget Sound

Field-Guide Illustrations for Alaskan Mammals

I had the pleasure of creating sixty-four mammal illustrations on fifteen plates for *Alaska: The Ecotravellers' Wildlife Guide*.

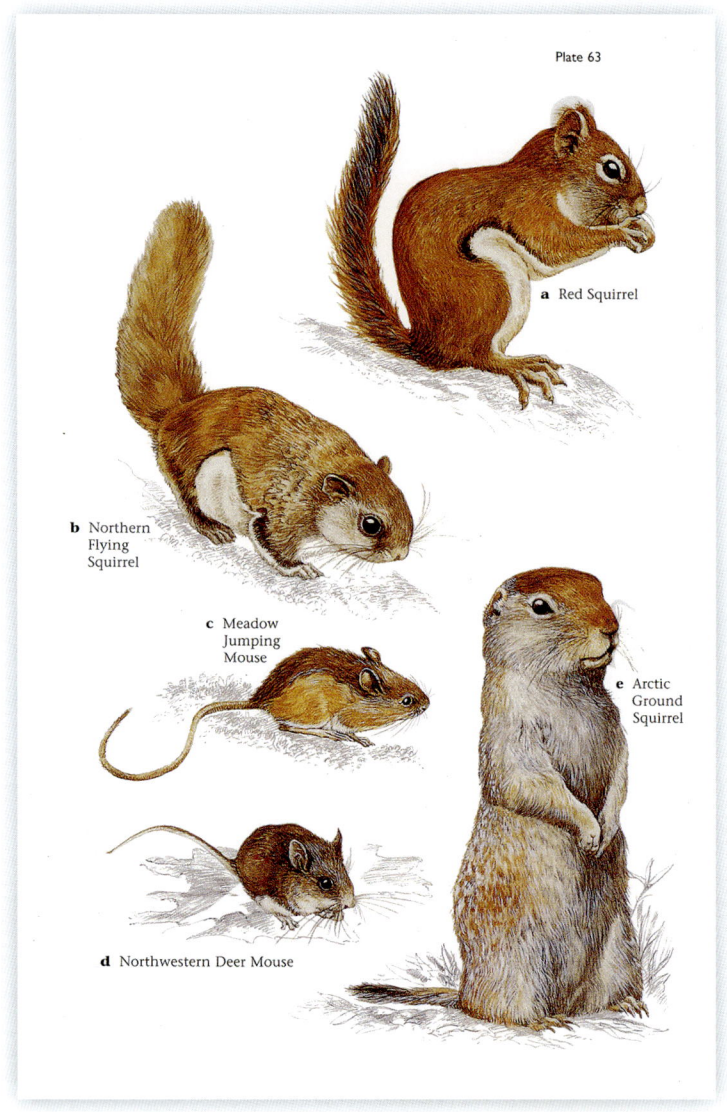

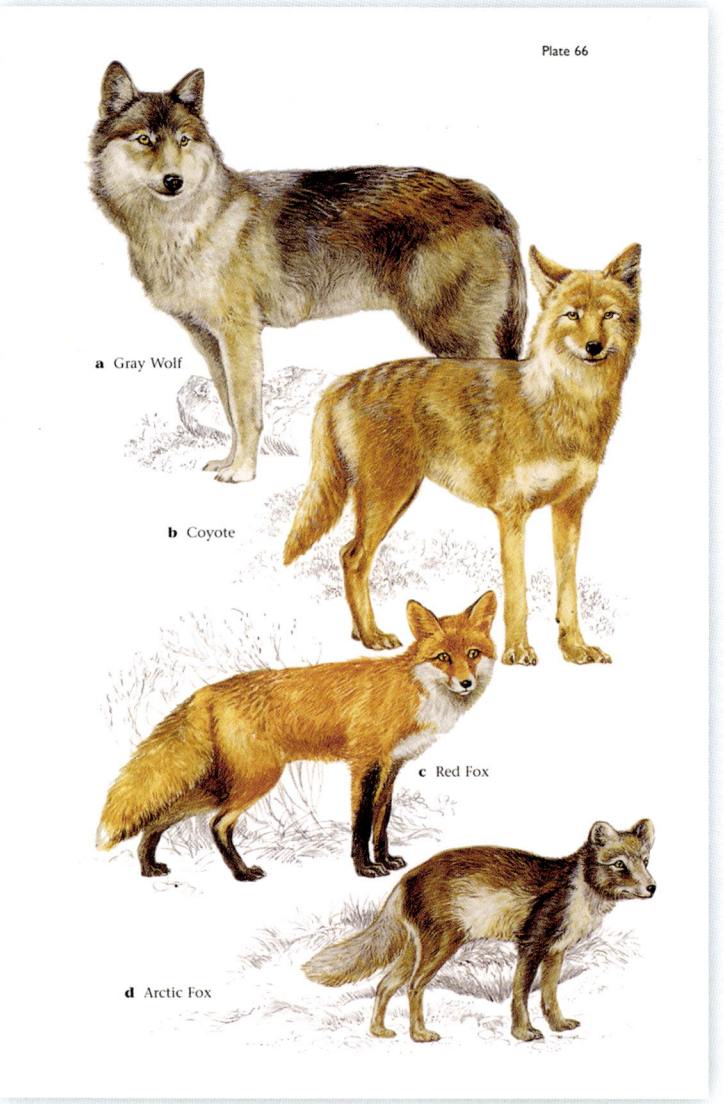

Dennis R. Paulson and Les Beletsky, *Alaska: The Ecotravellers' Wildlife Guide* (Cambridge, MA: Academic Press, 2001).

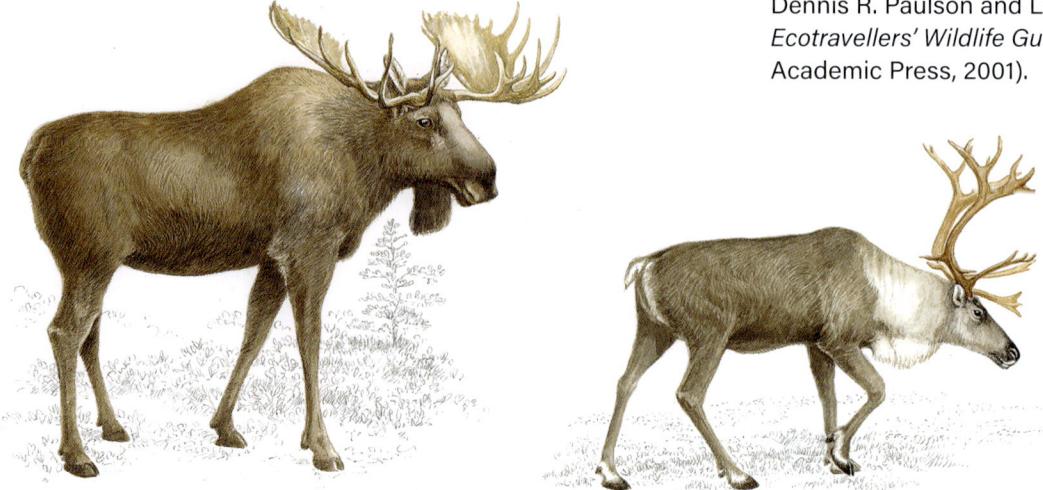

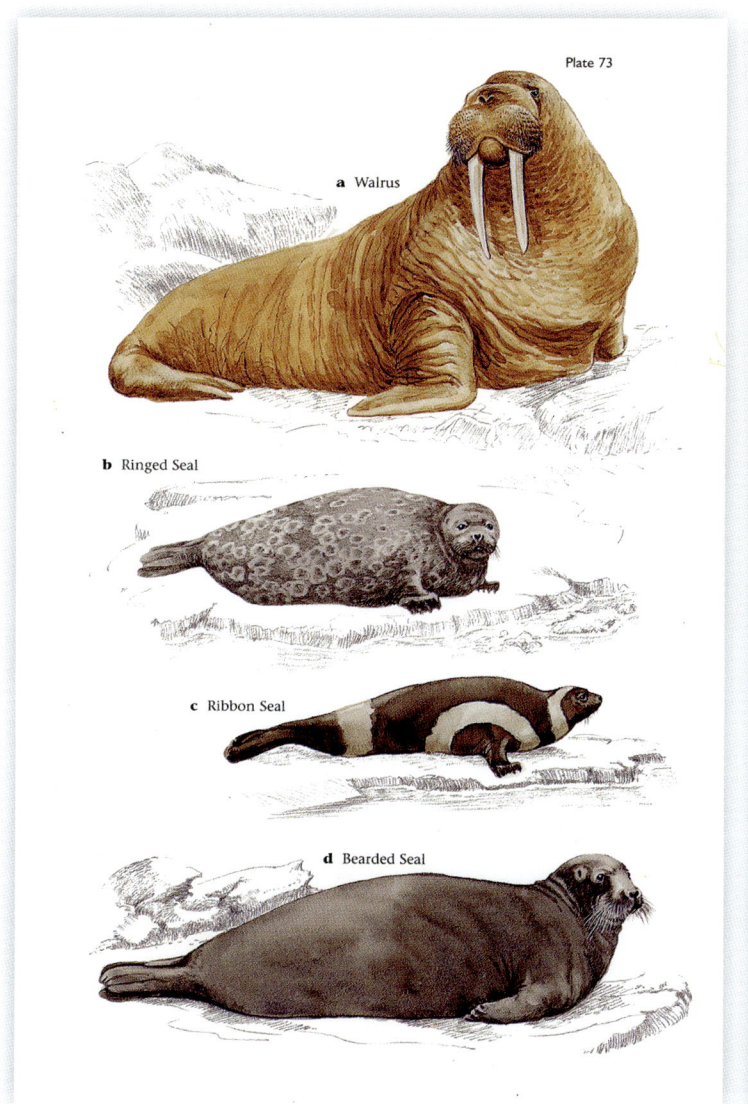

a Walrus

Plate 73

b Ringed Seal

c Ribbon Seal

d Bearded Seal

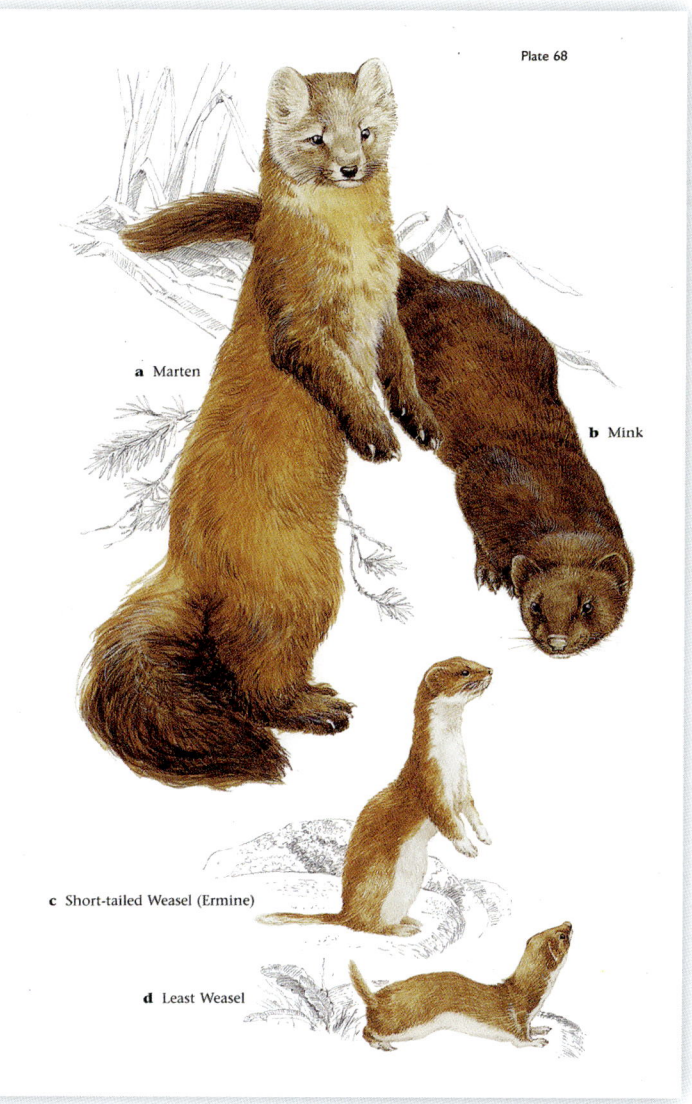

Plate 68

a Marten

b Mink

c Short-tailed Weasel (Ermine)

d Least Weasel

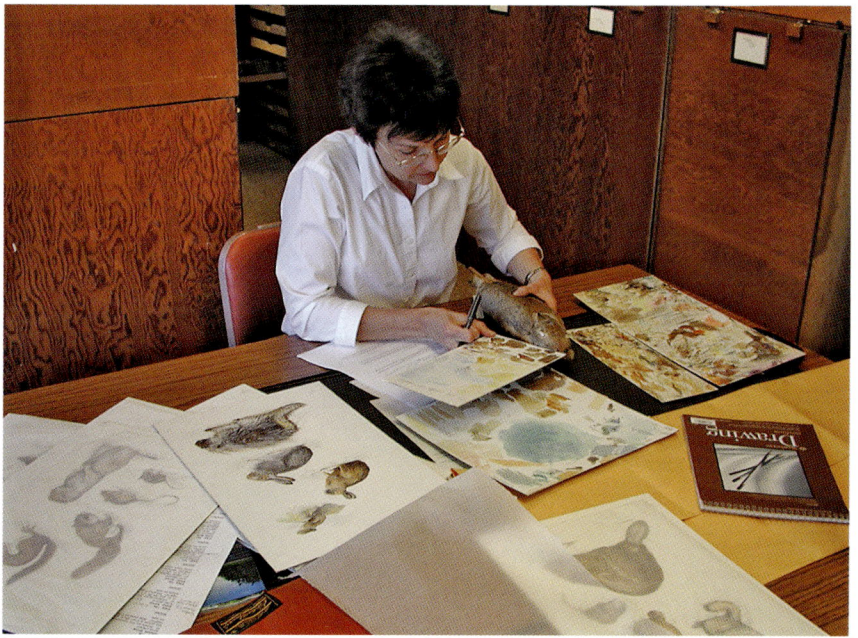

Dennis Paulson, the Director of the Puget Sound Museum of Natural History, selected specimens from the collection for me to use as typical of the Alaskan species. Color swatches made at the museum formed a guide for later painting the animal back in the studio. After painting the plates, I checked the colors against the specimens. Photo courtesy of Dennis Paulson.

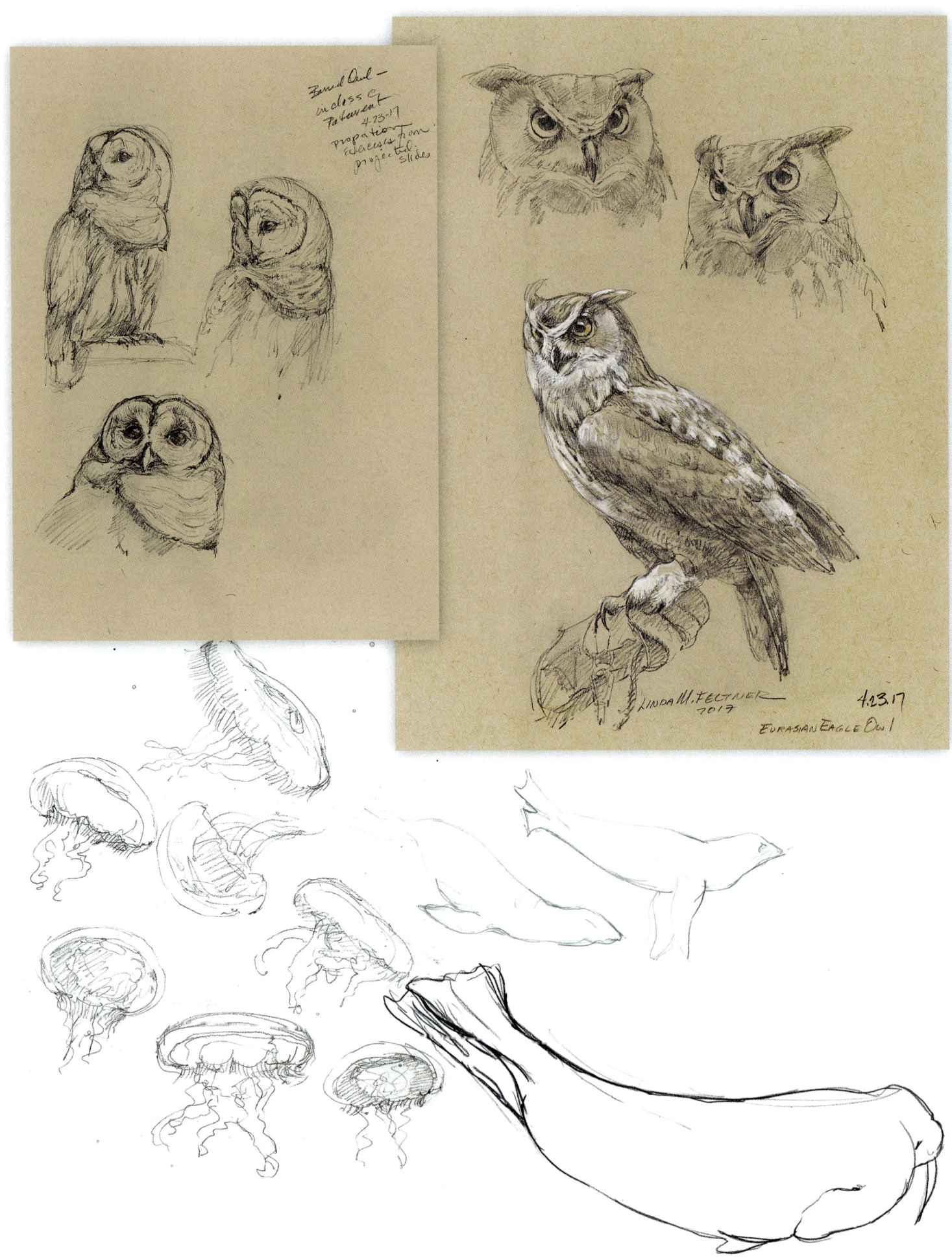

142

CHAPTER 5

Educational Animals

From the first moment a falconer walked into my classroom with live birds at the University of Washington Scientific Illustration Certification Program, I knew this was a golden moment for students. I remember my first experience sketching a live bird. From the beginning, it was an enchanting encounter with a bird that was sitting quite close, breathing, moving, and intensely looking around. My admiration grew with each bird.

Educational animals may not be releasable back into the wild, whether they are Gila Monsters, tortoises, or birds. They become accustomed to people staring at them and schoolchildren's squeals. Some have fallen asleep as I sketch. Animals not distressed by our closeness demonstrate actions hard to glimpse in the wild.

Zoo and aquarium animals are usually uninjured and offer characteristic postures to study. Sometimes I scribble the quick dash of a disappearing lizard. Sometimes all I get is a long tail hanging out and a backside view of a large cat asleep in a niche to avoid the hot sun. I was lucky to live near an aquarium and study underwater diving murres, floating jellyfish, and feeding crustaceans while illustrating a book on marine life in the Pacific Northwest.

This chapter shows a variety of animals sketched to gain a further understanding of body movement and structure. Some anatomy research usually follows to explain why the subject stands or sits in a typical manner. Through drawing iterations, I develop a series of sketches from the close encounter and inspiration that zoos and educational animals provide.

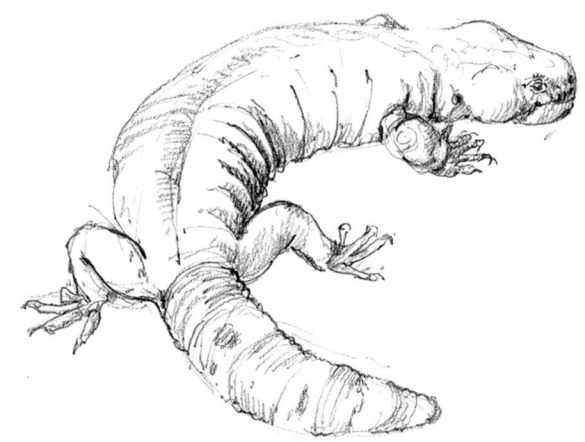

An Injured Falcon

Often educational animals are injured, healed but not releasable.
They become ambassadors of the natural world, allowing people to
look closer. Raptors are often iconic and admired for their beauty.
Peregrine Falcons are noble and renowned for their flying speeds
and skills. The audience is captivated.

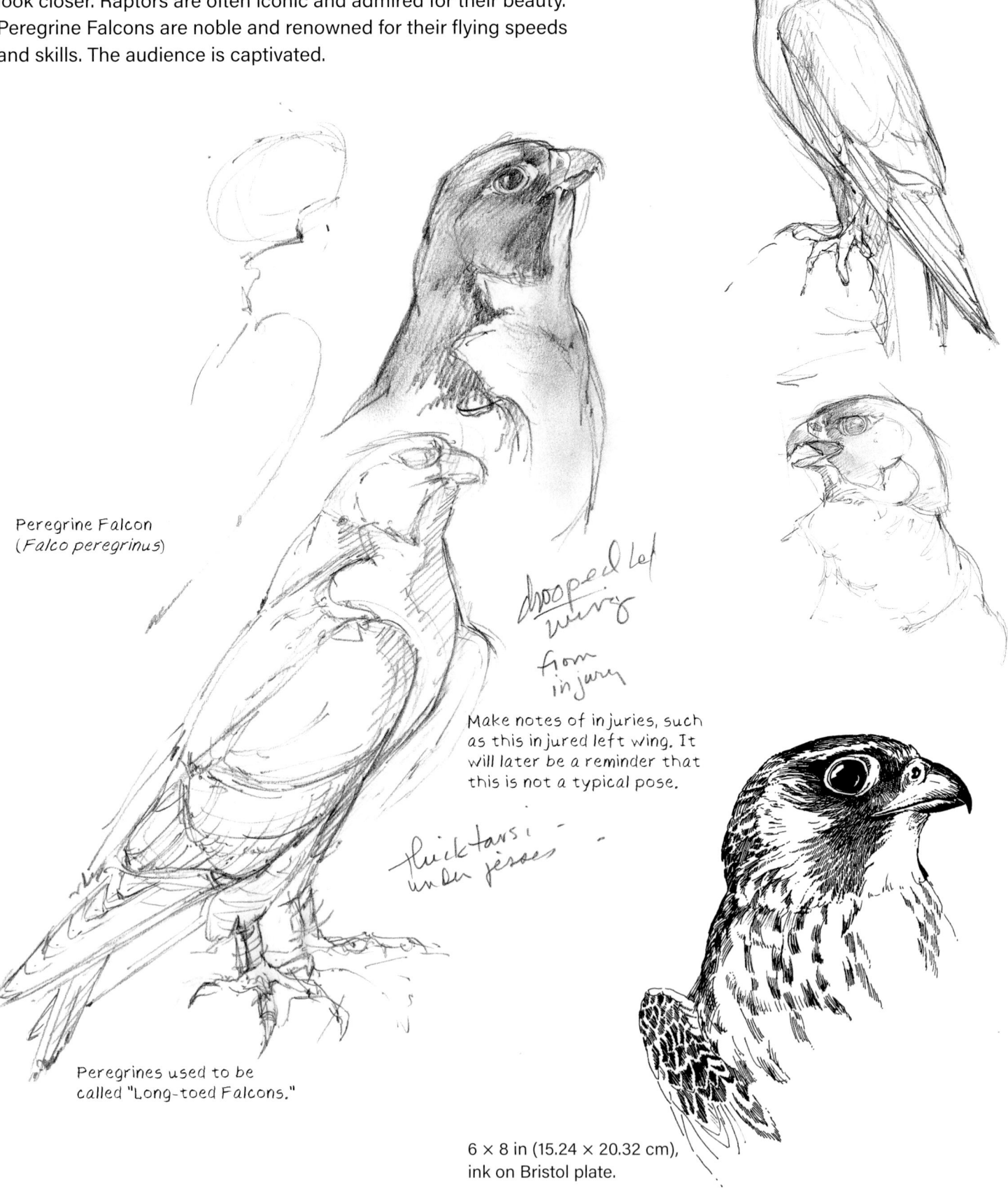

Peregrine Falcon
(*Falco peregrinus*)

drooped left
wing

from
injury

Make notes of injuries, such
as this injured left wing. It
will later be a reminder that
this is not a typical pose.

thick tarsi —
under jesses

Peregrines used to be
called "Long-toed Falcons."

6 × 8 in (15.24 × 20.32 cm),
ink on Bristol plate.

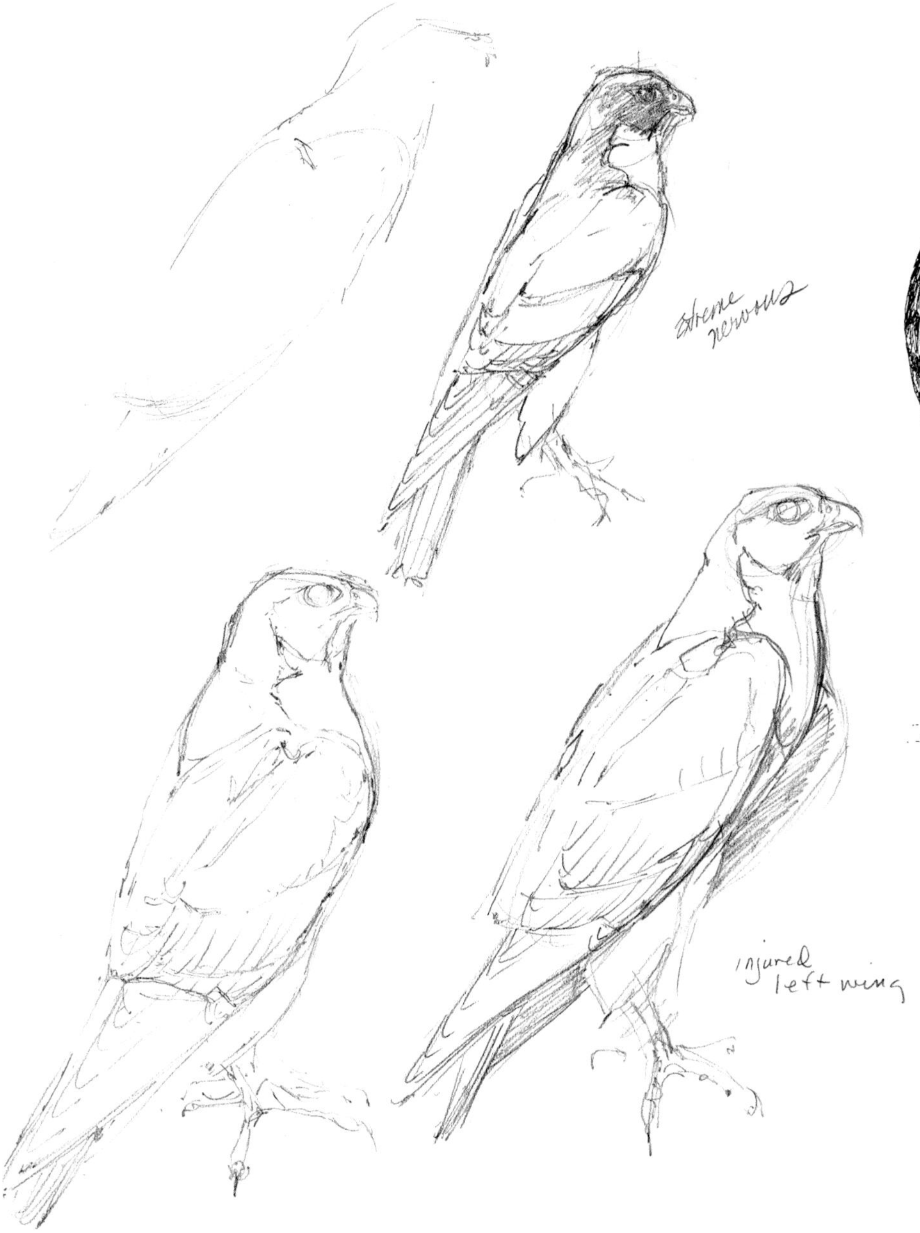

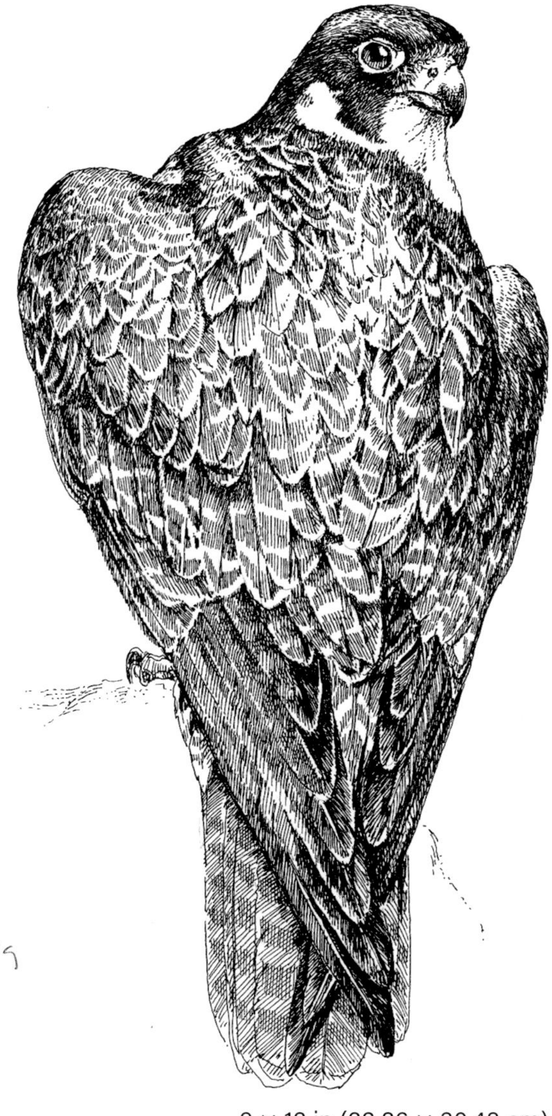

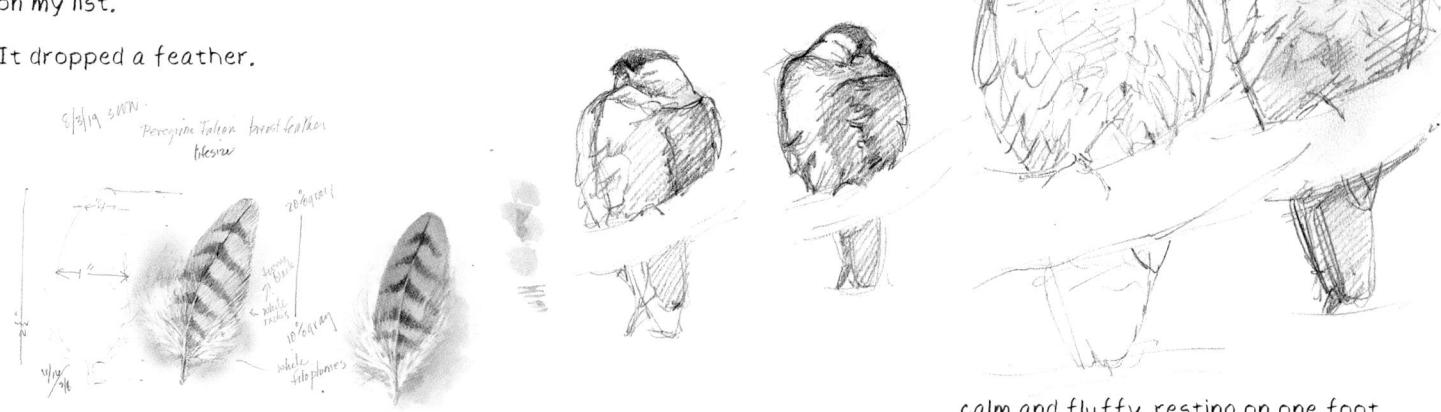

9 × 12 in (22.86 × 30.48 cm), ink on Bristol plate.

This Peregrine posed during a sketching session. When it first met the class, it was slim and sleek. Along with its panting, this slimness showed that it was nervous. Notations remind me later that this is not a typical calm position. When outdoors, the falcon never stopped looking up and around. As it became comfortable, sketches show it relaxed and fluffed out. I have yet to paint from these sketches, but they are high on my list.

It dropped a feather.

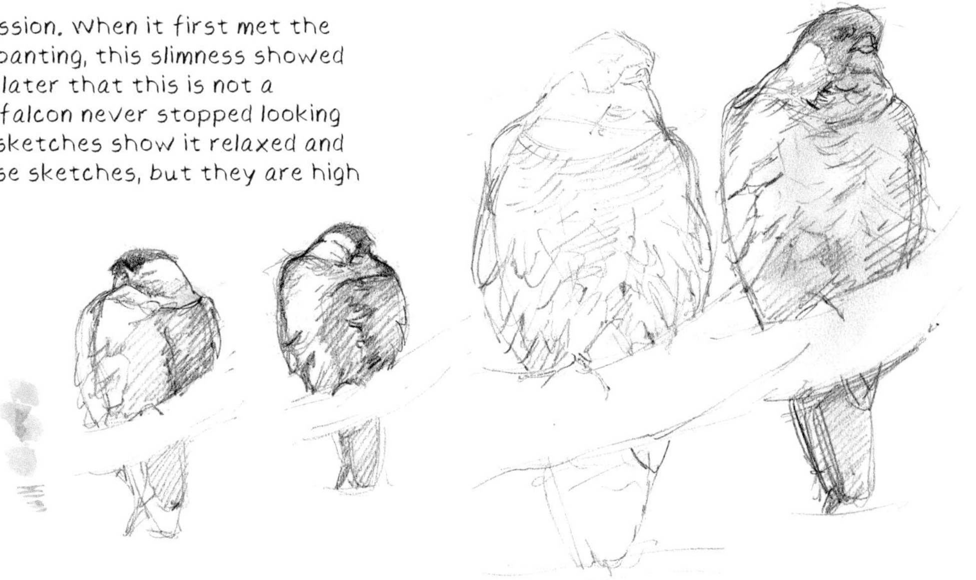

calm and fluffy, resting on one foot

Scales and Scutes

A variety of animals can be brought into the classroom by rehabilitators and educational organizations. Animals other than birds can provide a creative experience. Usually quiet and allowing longer sketching time, reptiles are great models.

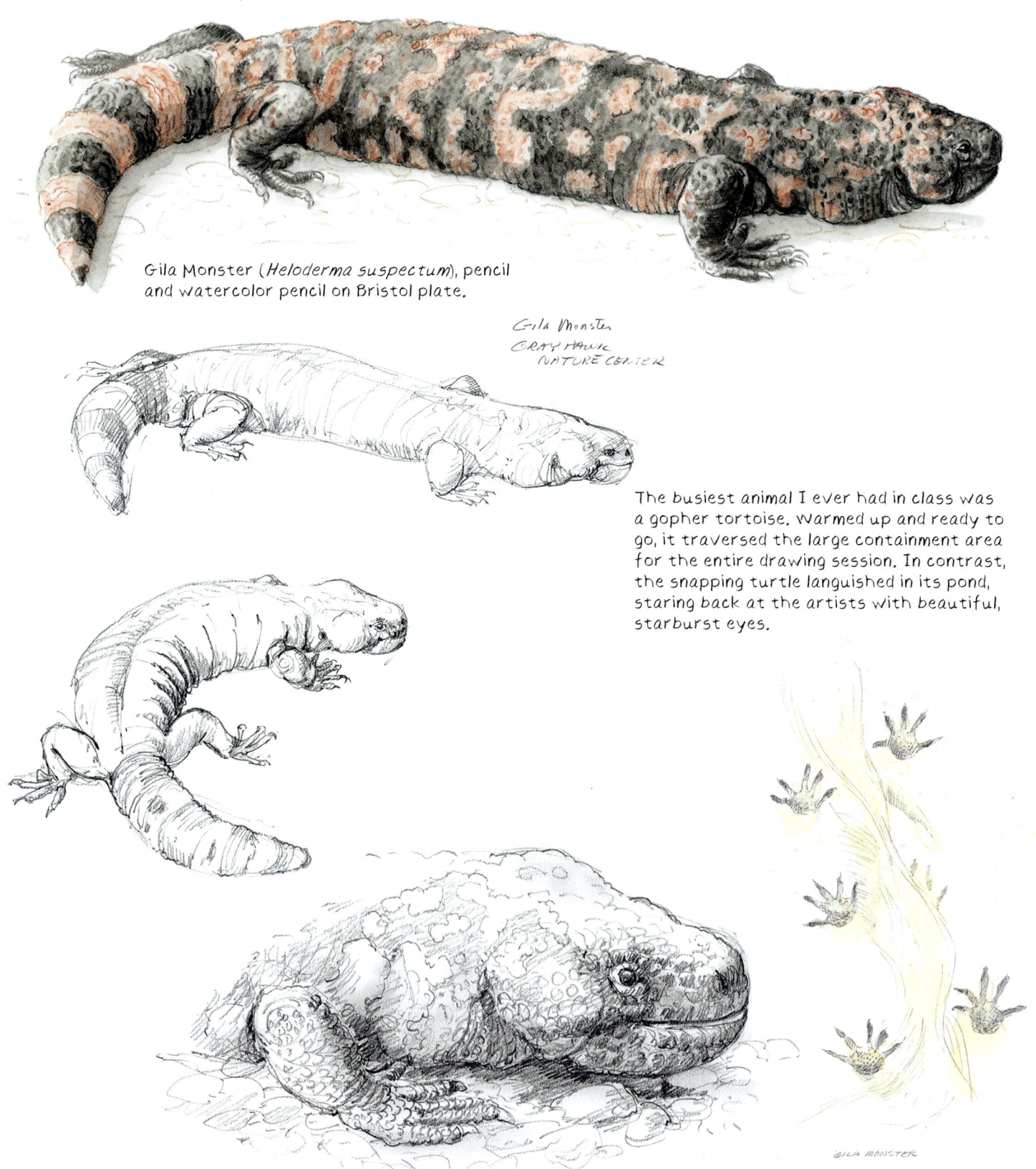

Gila Monster (*Heloderma suspectum*), pencil and watercolor pencil on Bristol plate.

Gila Monster
GRAY HAWK
NATURE CENTER

The busiest animal I ever had in class was a gopher tortoise. Warmed up and ready to go, it traversed the large containment area for the entire drawing session. In contrast, the snapping turtle languished in its pond, staring back at the artists with beautiful, starburst eyes.

GILA MONSTER

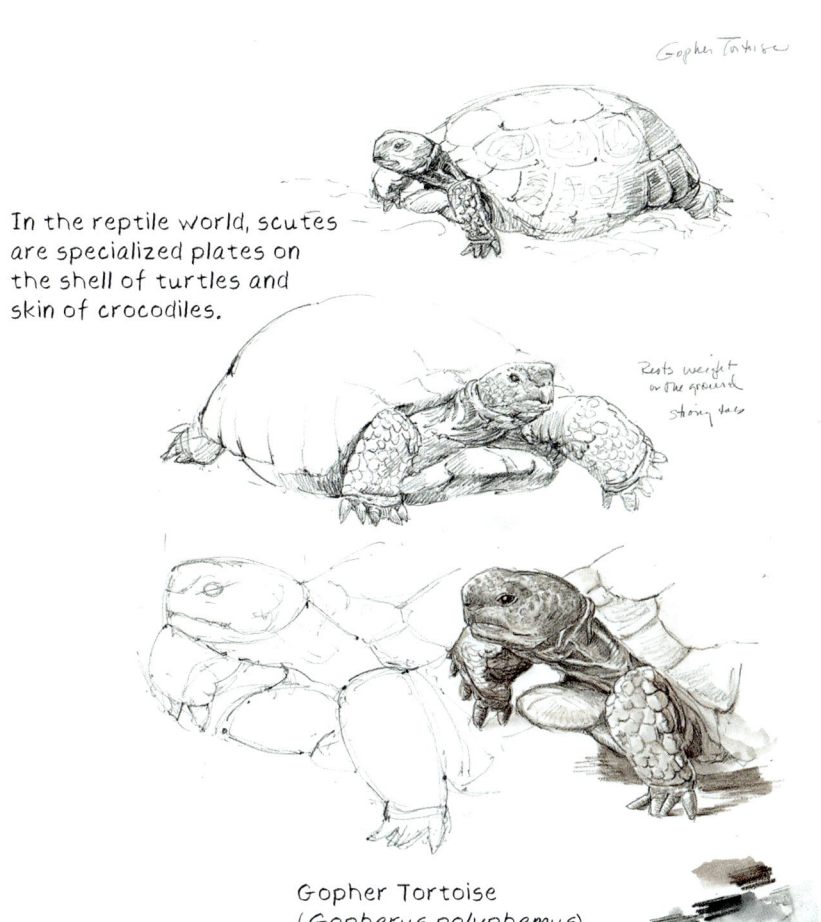

In the reptile world, scutes are specialized plates on the shell of turtles and skin of crocodiles.

Gopher Tortoise
(*Gopherus polyphemus*)

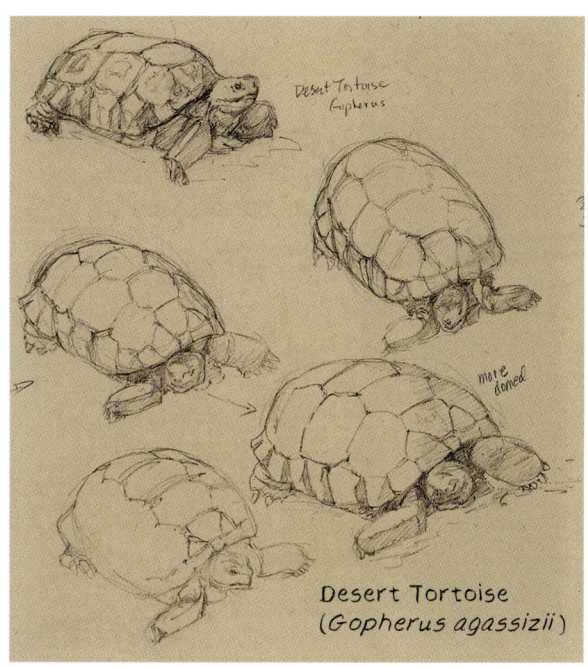

Desert Tortoise
(*Gopherus agassizii*)

Hey, sweetie, what do you think of your portrait? Meet Lateesha, a Boa Constrictor at the Southwest Wings Birding and Nature Festival. She is a reptile ambassador with the Huachuca Area Herpetological Association. She was warm and moved gently, so I made quick gesture sketches! Photo courtesy of Jo Ann Woodley.

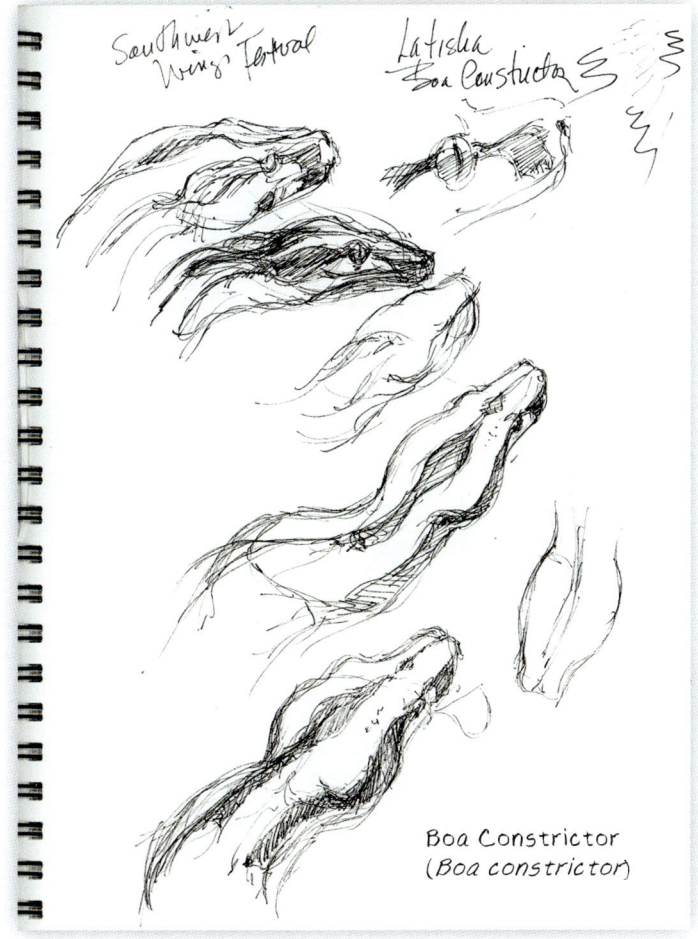

Boa Constrictor
(*Boa constrictor*)

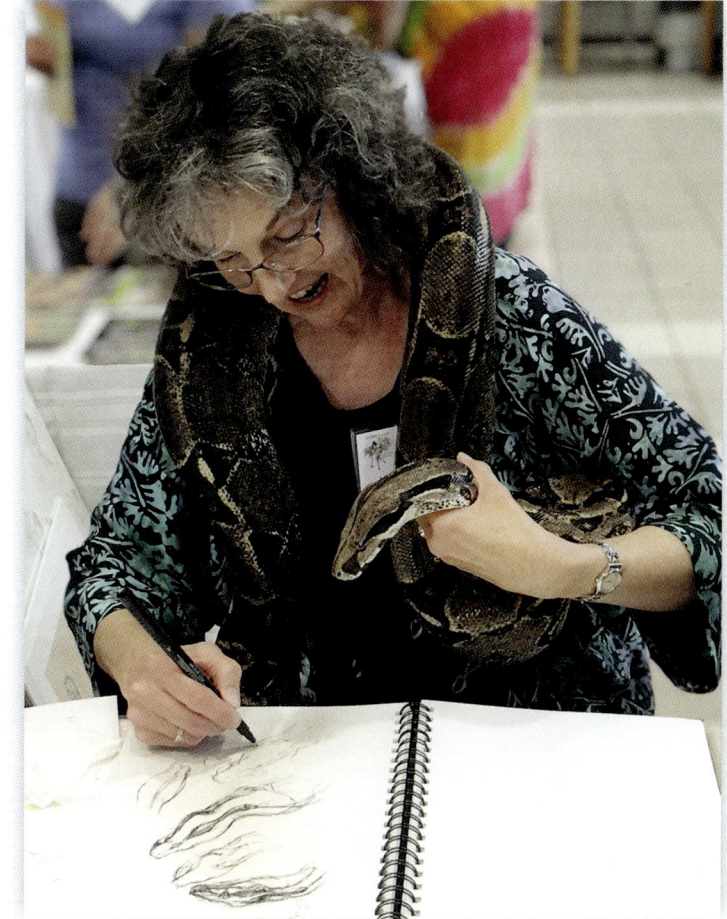

Scales and Scutes, Continued

Most reptiles I draw are educational animals or from zoos. Projects often request species not found in zoos. Those require research from museums or references to illustrate their unique features. Sometimes, I am fortunate that other projects feature reptiles found in my yard.

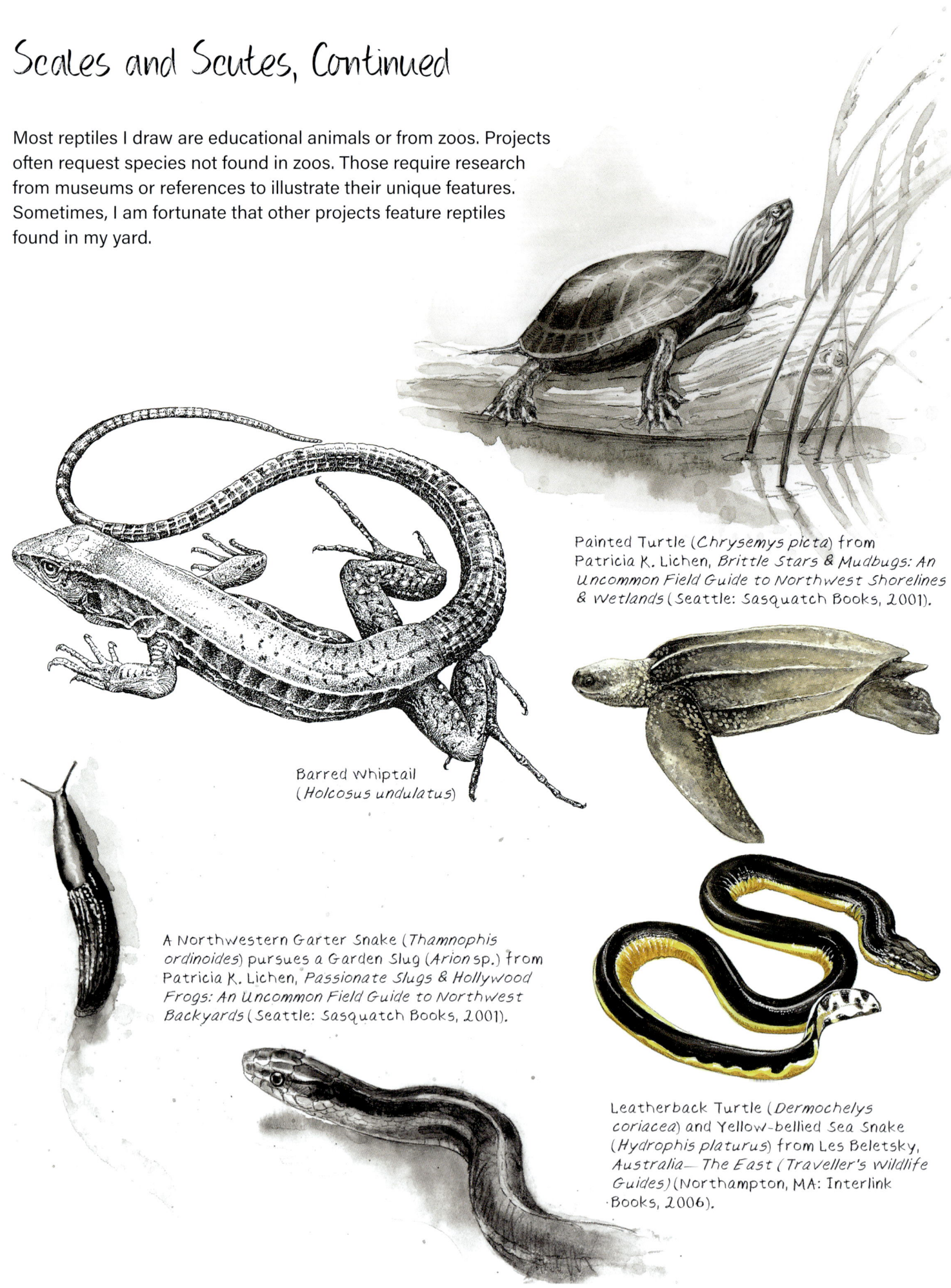

Painted Turtle (*Chrysemys picta*) from Patricia K. Lichen, *Brittle Stars & Mudbugs: An Uncommon Field Guide to Northwest Shorelines & Wetlands* (Seattle: Sasquatch Books, 2001).

Barred Whiptail (*Holcosus undulatus*)

A Northwestern Garter Snake (*Thamnophis ordinoides*) pursues a Garden Slug (*Arion* sp.) from Patricia K. Lichen, *Passionate Slugs & Hollywood Frogs: An Uncommon Field Guide to Northwest Backyards* (Seattle: Sasquatch Books, 2001).

Leatherback Turtle (*Dermochelys coriacea*) and Yellow-bellied Sea Snake (*Hydrophis platurus*) from Les Beletsky, *Australia—The East (Traveller's Wildlife Guides)* (Northampton, MA: Interlink Books, 2006).

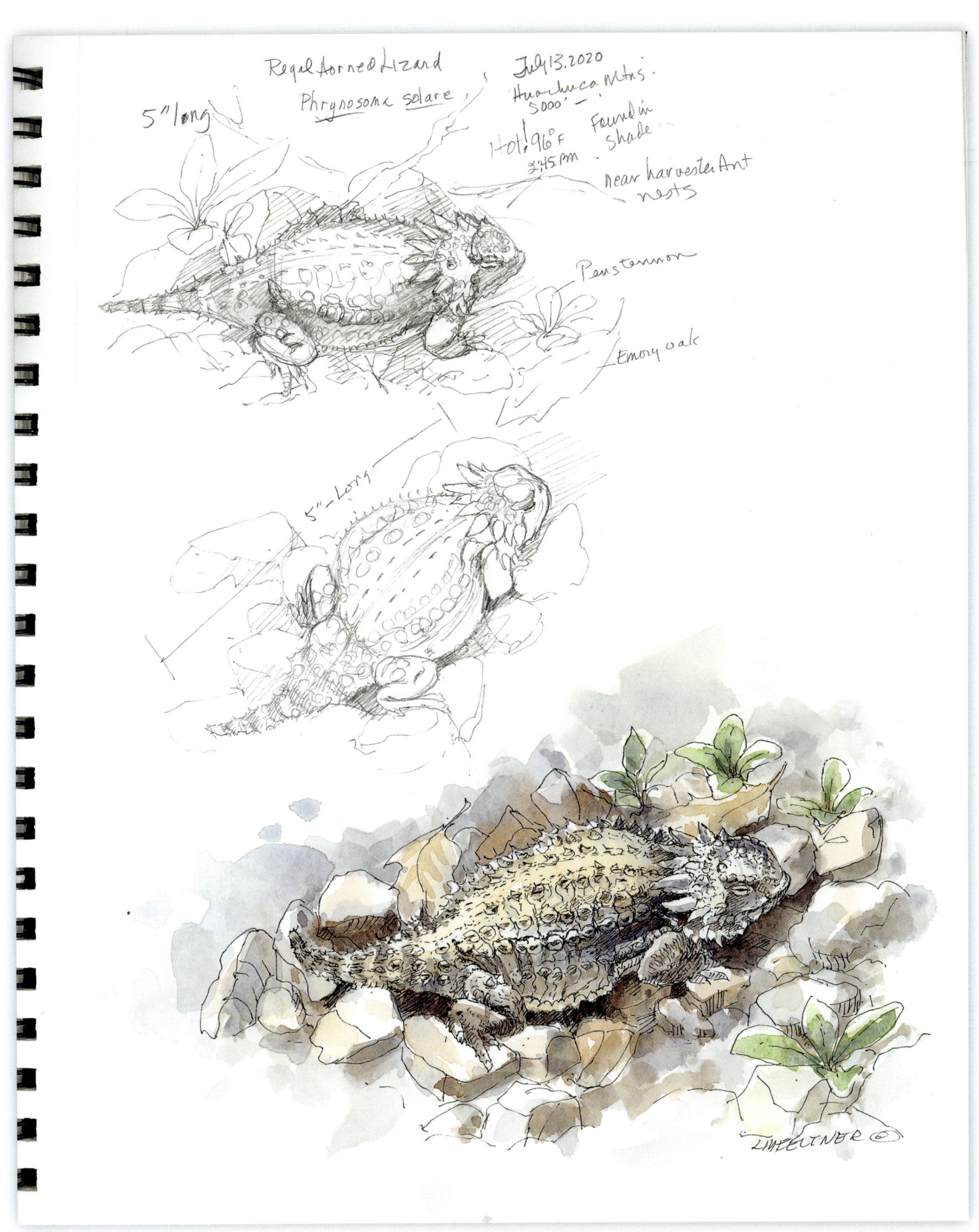

Regal Horned Lizard
Phrynosoma solare

July 13, 2020
Huachuca Mtns.
5000'—

5" long

Hot! 96°F
2:45 PM

Found in
Shade

near harvester Ant
nests

Penstemon

Emory oak

5"—Long

"LIHEELTNER" ©

The Regal Horned Lizard (*Phrynosoma solare*) is often encountered in the yard. Always a delight to find and sketch.

Zoos: Places to Become Inspired

Where would you find unique poses of an iconic animal already portrayed a zillion times? My choice would be to find a living animal and observe it. If direct observation is not possible, online videos provide much more information to the visual artist than a still photo. Look for a position that demonstrates behavior or traits. Zoos are a valuable asset to the artist. How can we determine if a stop-motion photograph is an awkward pose if we do not observe the living animal?

Observe and sketch with what time is allowed. Make notations if anything seems unusual. Zoo animals are well-fed and do not experience the stress of living in the wild. They may gain weight and act differently.

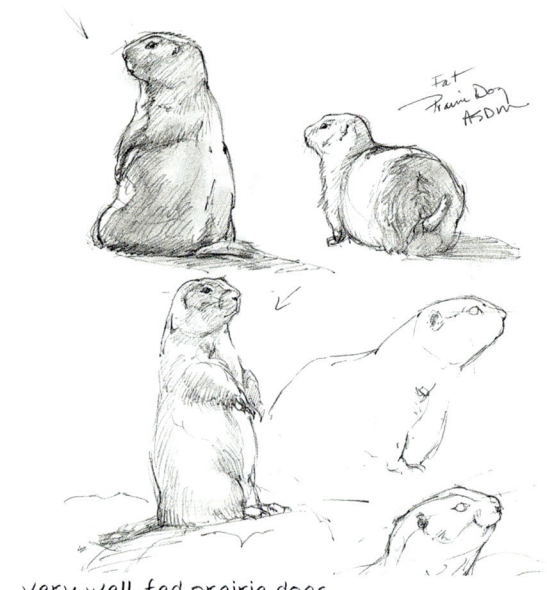

very well-fed prairie dogs

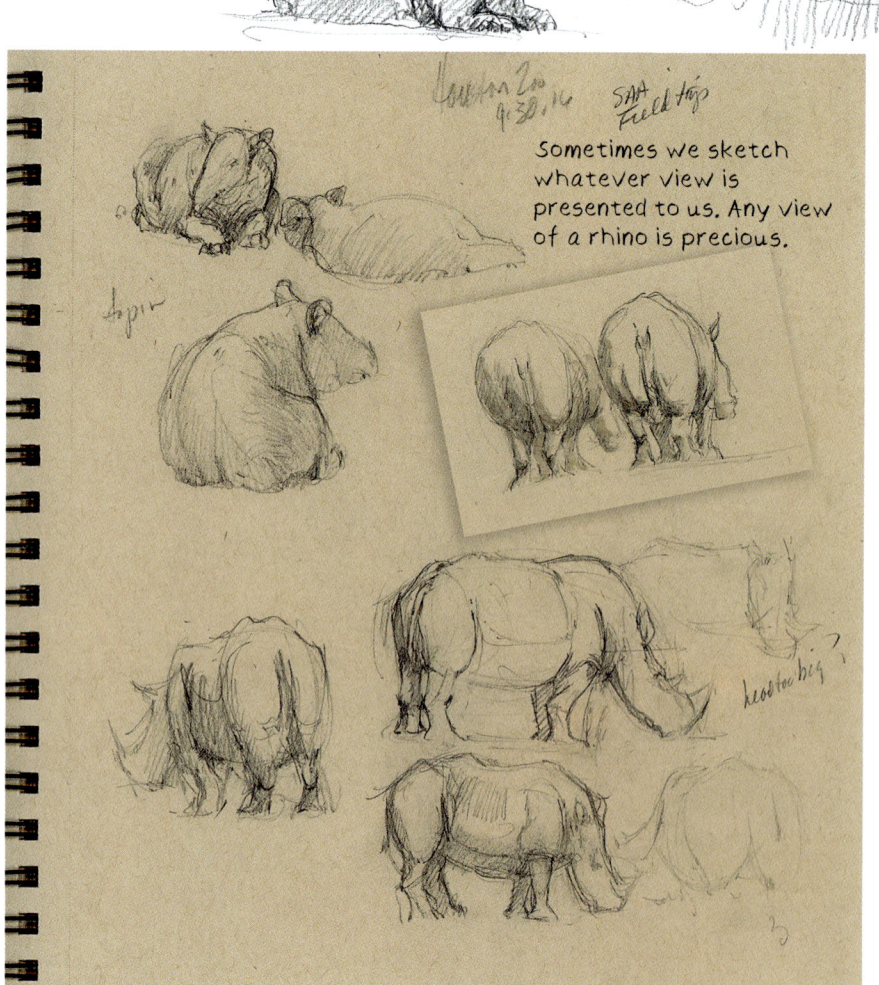

Sometimes we sketch whatever view is presented to us. Any view of a rhino is precious.

If I cannot find the same species as the project requires, it helps to study a close relative for movement, balance, and behavioral characteristics.

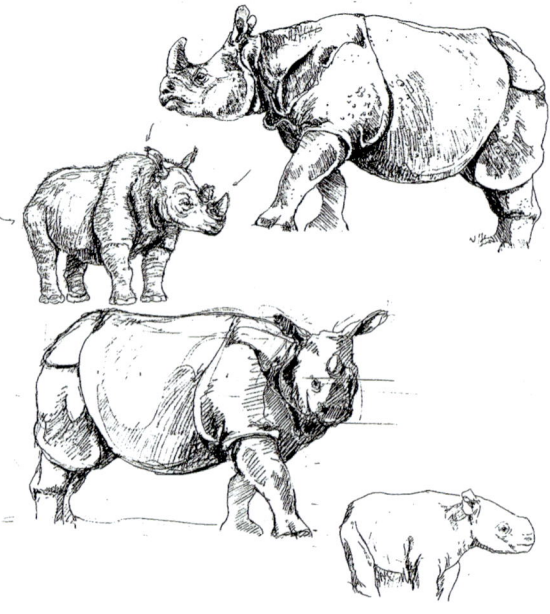

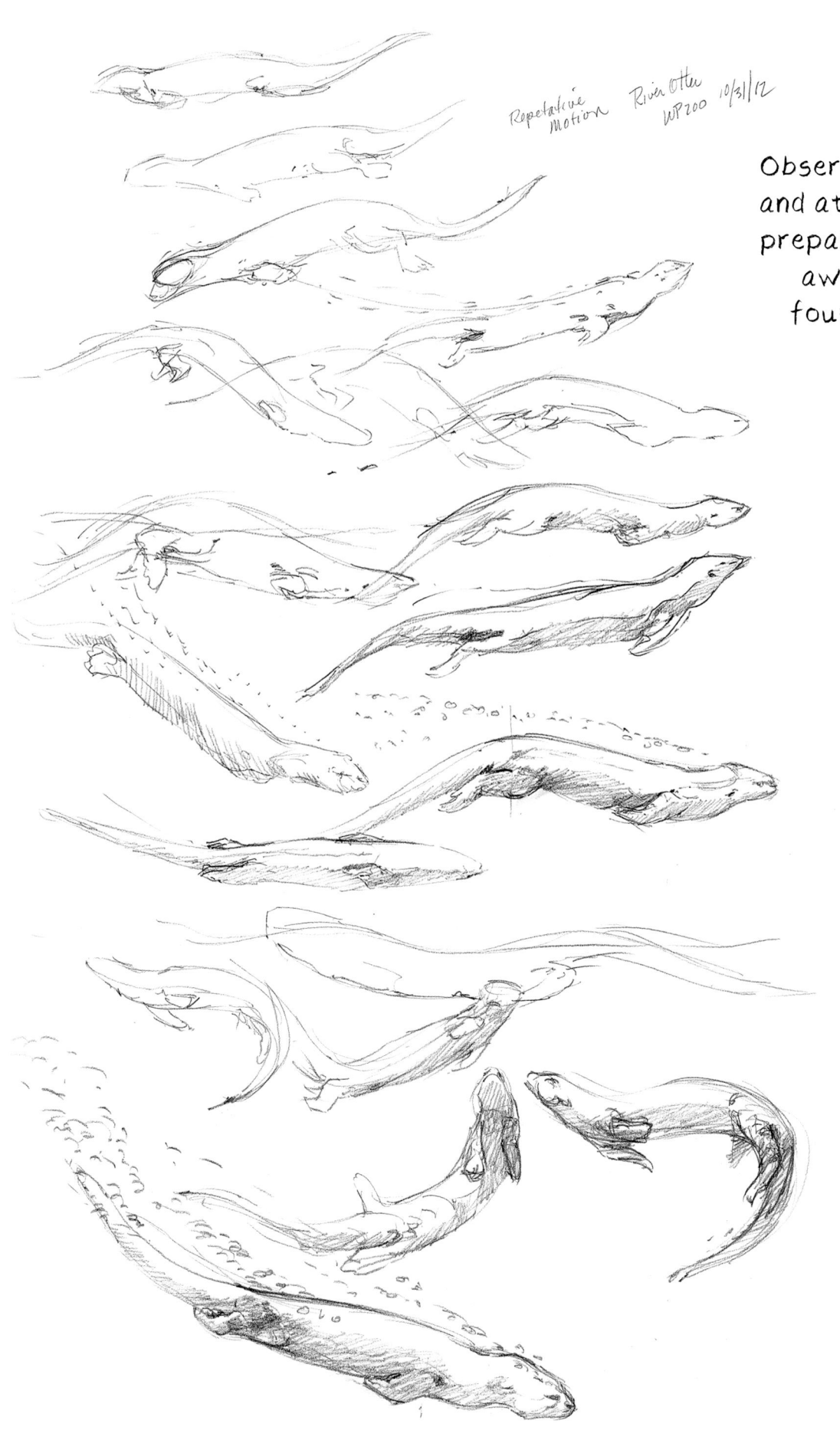

Repetitive Motion   River Otter WP200 10/31/12

Observing the movement
and attitude of an animal
prepares us to recognize
awkward positions
found in still photos.

Zoos: Time and Opportunity

A day at the zoo has its challenges. Misty rain, blistering sun, and crowds affect the amount of time spent. I choose a technique and paper to suit the occasion. Toned paper reduces glaring sunshine. I seldom allot time to a full-color painting. When time or weather does not permit lengthy study, photos are a great asset.

Take your own photos if possible. My archives bulge from more blurry, imperfect photos than perfect ones. I keep blurry ones that show a natural position or the leg extension of a moving animal. Sketches combined with photos provide ample information to create an image later.

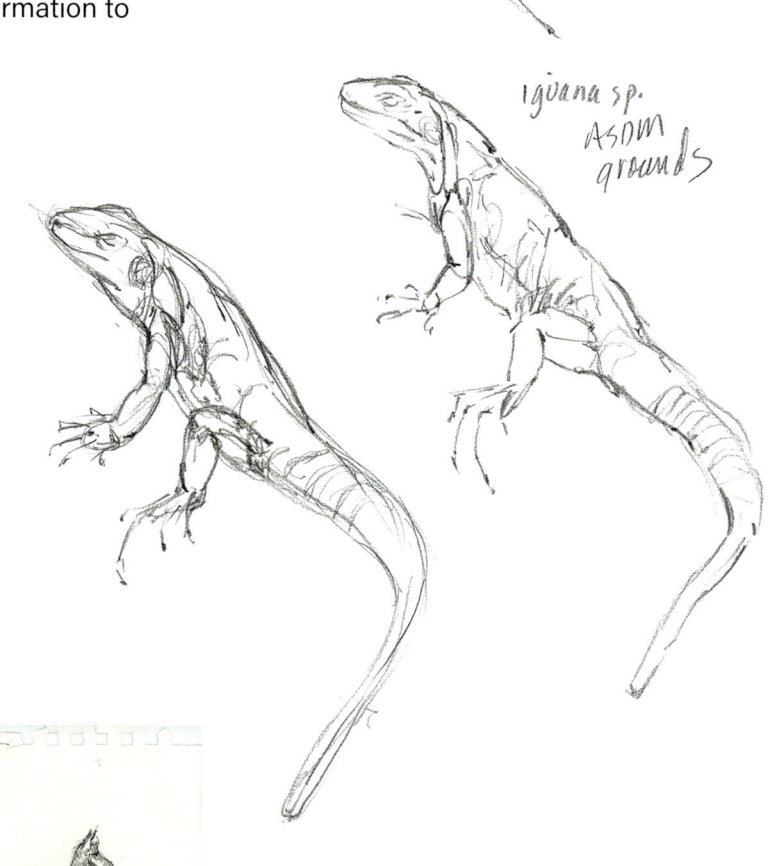

Yarrow's Spiny Lizard

iguana sp.
ASDM
grounds

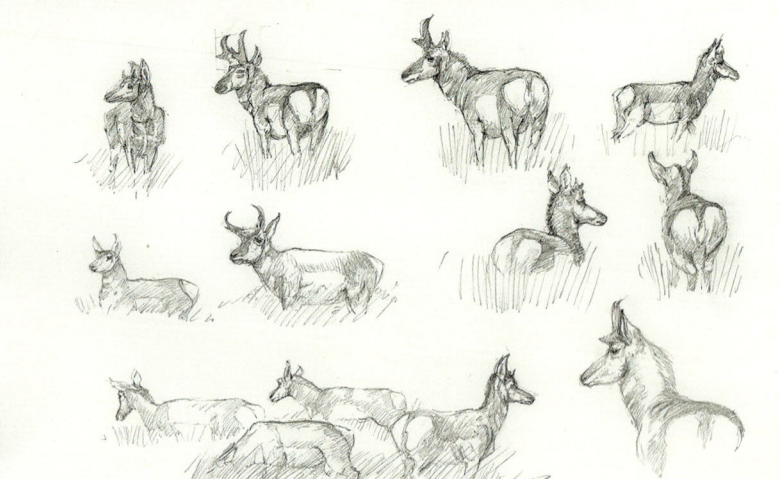

Pronghorn Antelope

Searching the web for reference photos has several disadvantages. Those lovely poses have all been preselected for the photographer's usage, not mine.

Avoid copyright infringement by obtaining permission to use a photo reference.

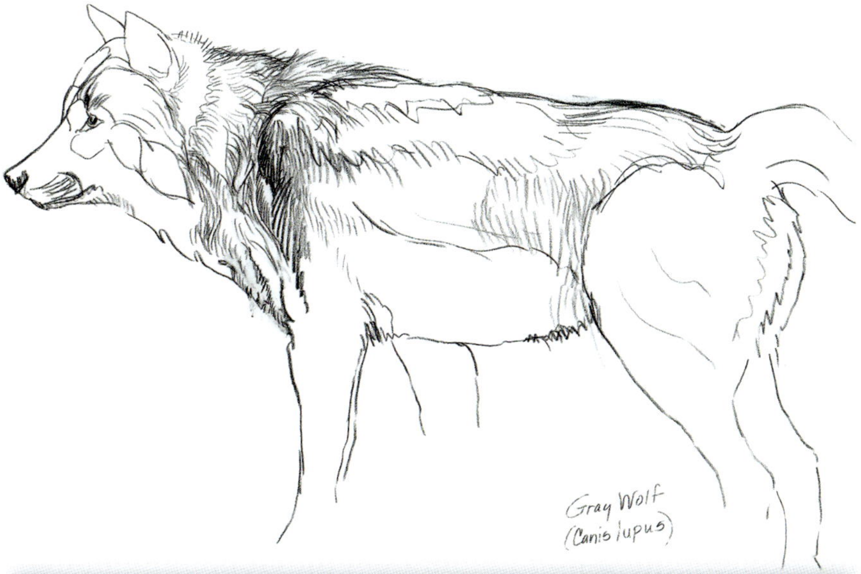

Gray Wolf
(Canis lupus)

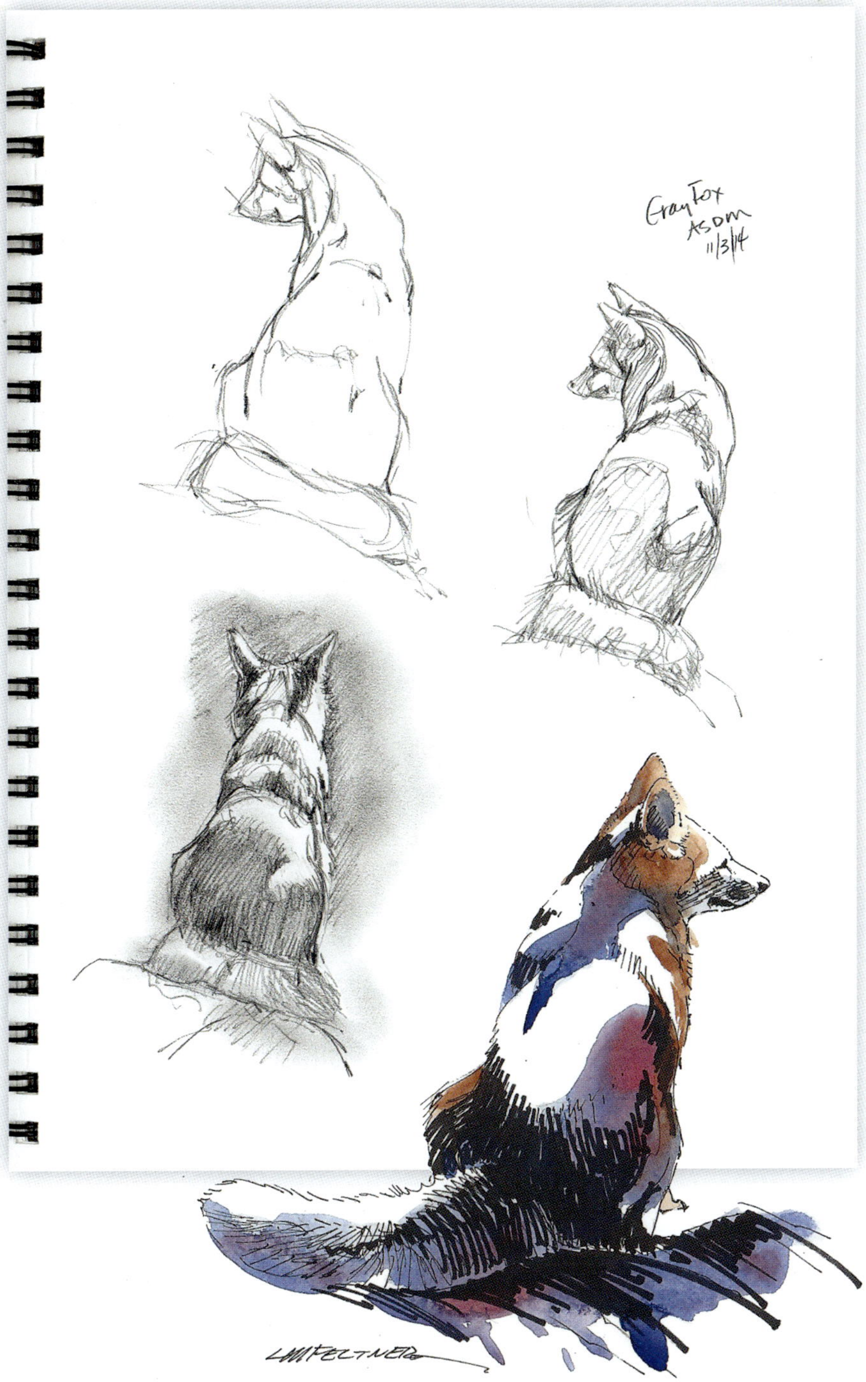

Gray Fox
ASDM
11/3/14

LMFELTNER

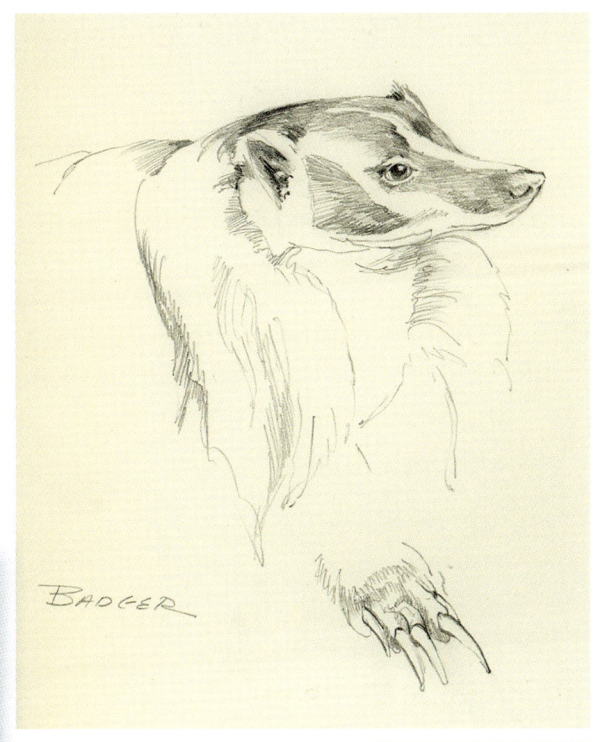

BADGER

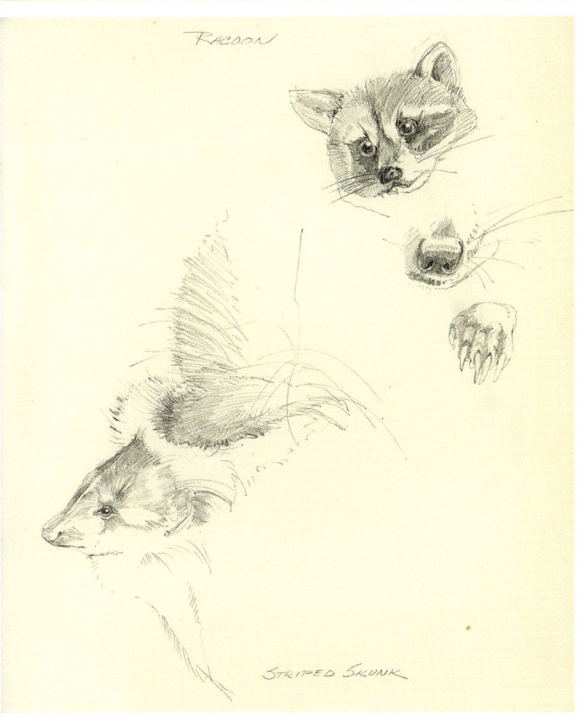

RACOON

STRIPED SKUNK

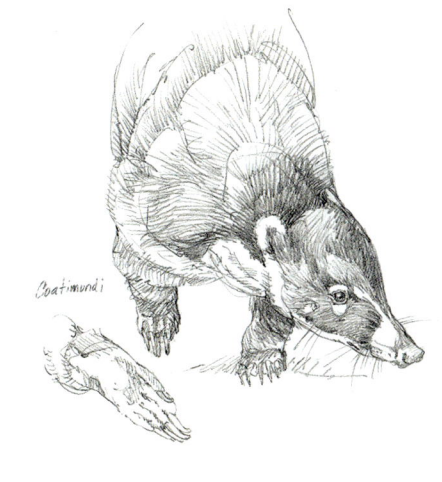

Coatimundi

Zoos: The Iconic Cougar

The Arizona-Sonora Desert Museum adopted a young Cougar (*Puma concolor*), a five-and-a-half-month-old male. This fellow was lean and lithe, finding his new home to be spacious and a curious place. The website reported his favorite activity was "chasing rock squirrels and lazing in the shade." Over the past few years, this youngster has been the model for many wildlife artists visiting the desert museum.

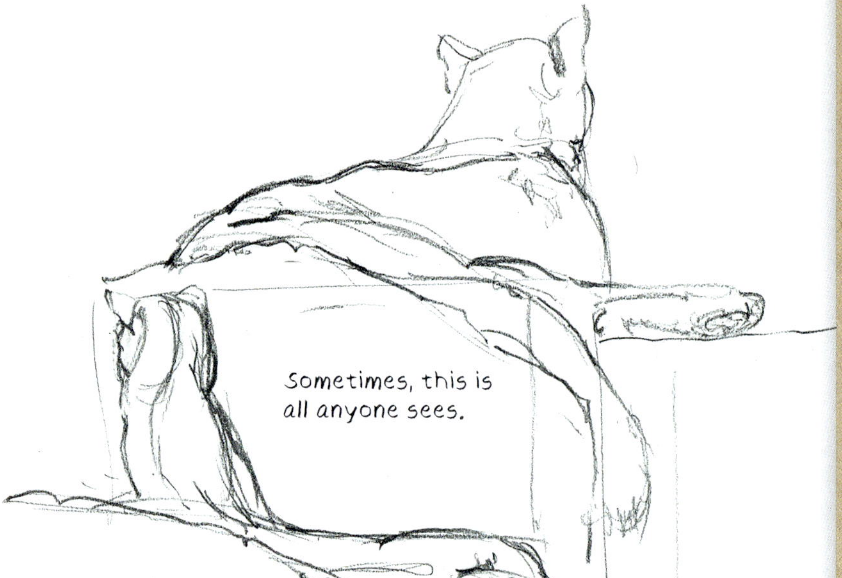

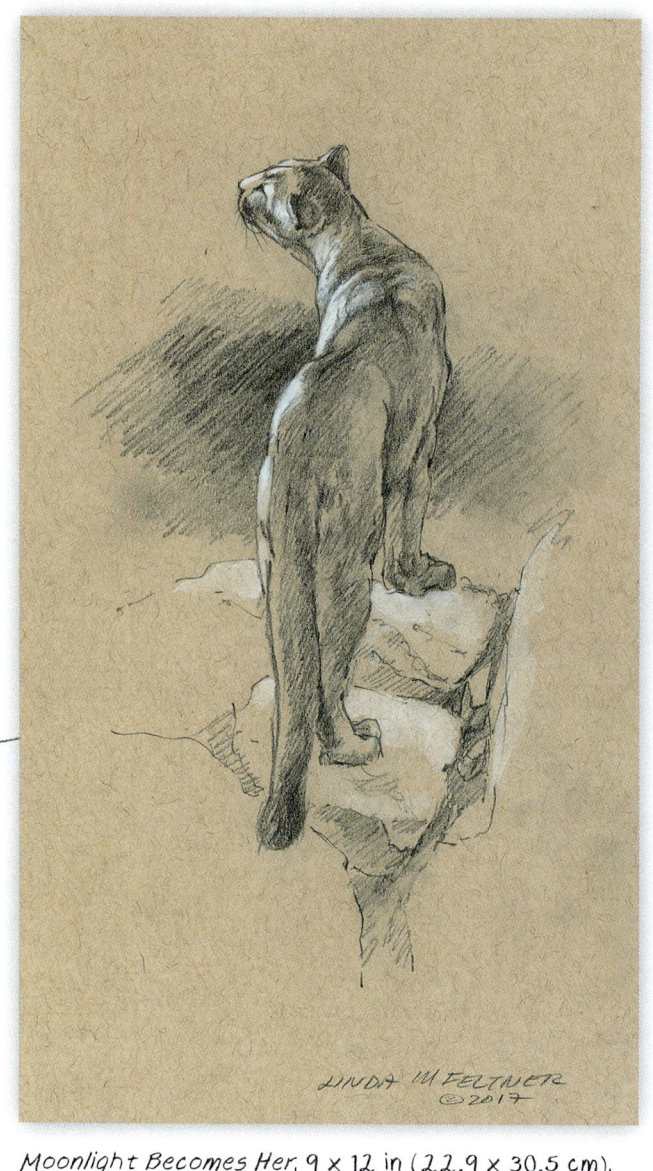

Sometimes, this is all anyone sees.

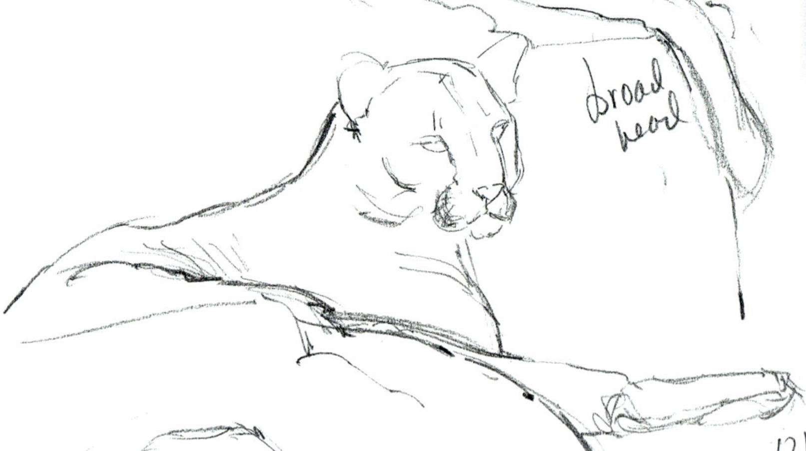

broad head

Moonlight Becomes Her, 9 x 12 in (22.9 x 30.5 cm), graphite and gouache on Strathmore toned tan sketch paper.

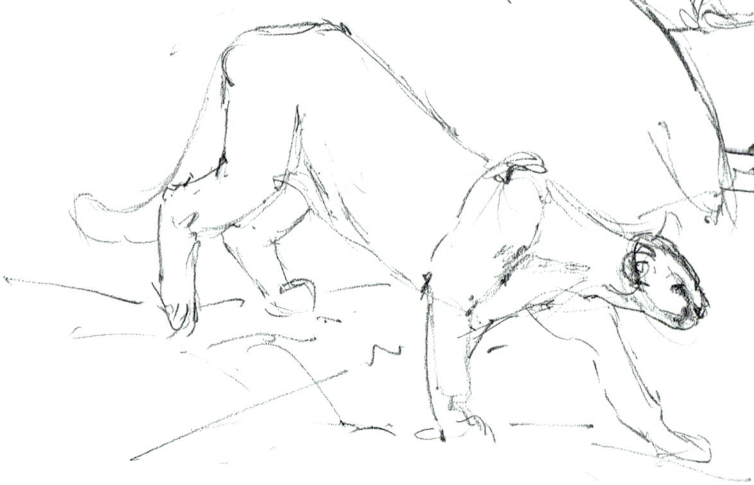

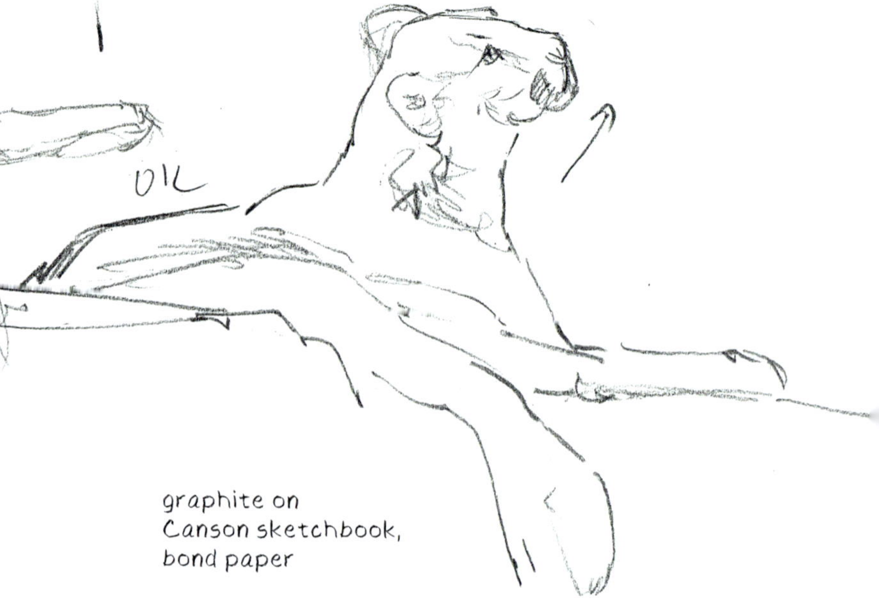

OIL

graphite on Canson sketchbook, bond paper

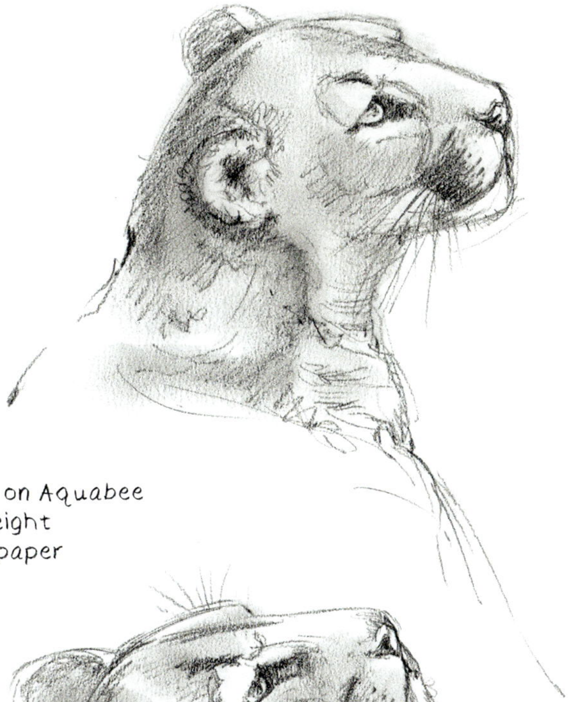

graphite on Aquabee
heavyweight
drawing paper

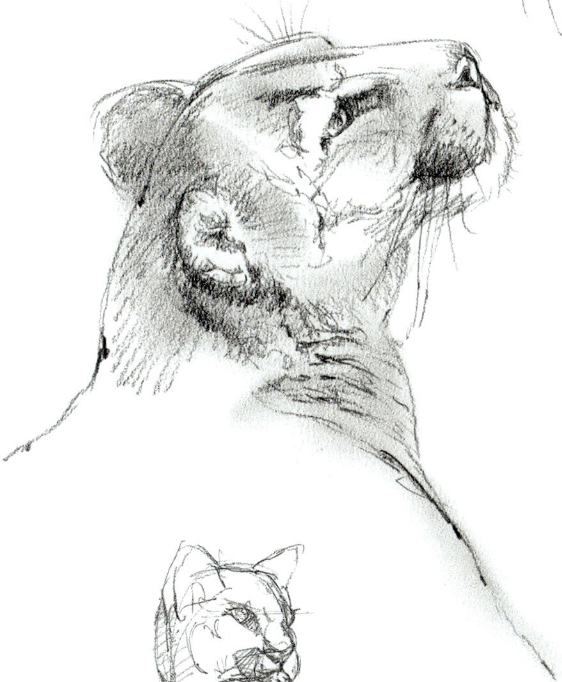

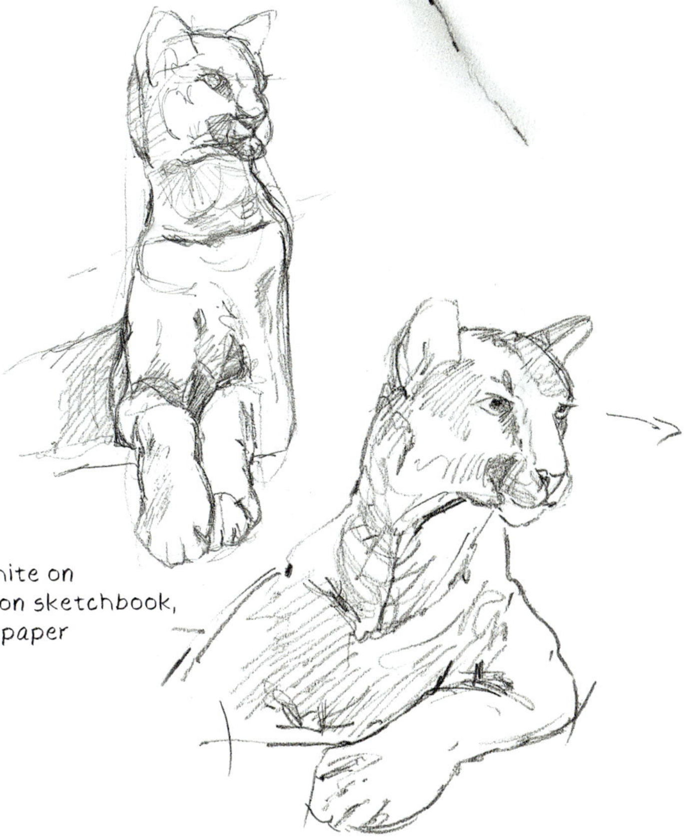

graphite on
Canson sketchbook,
bond paper

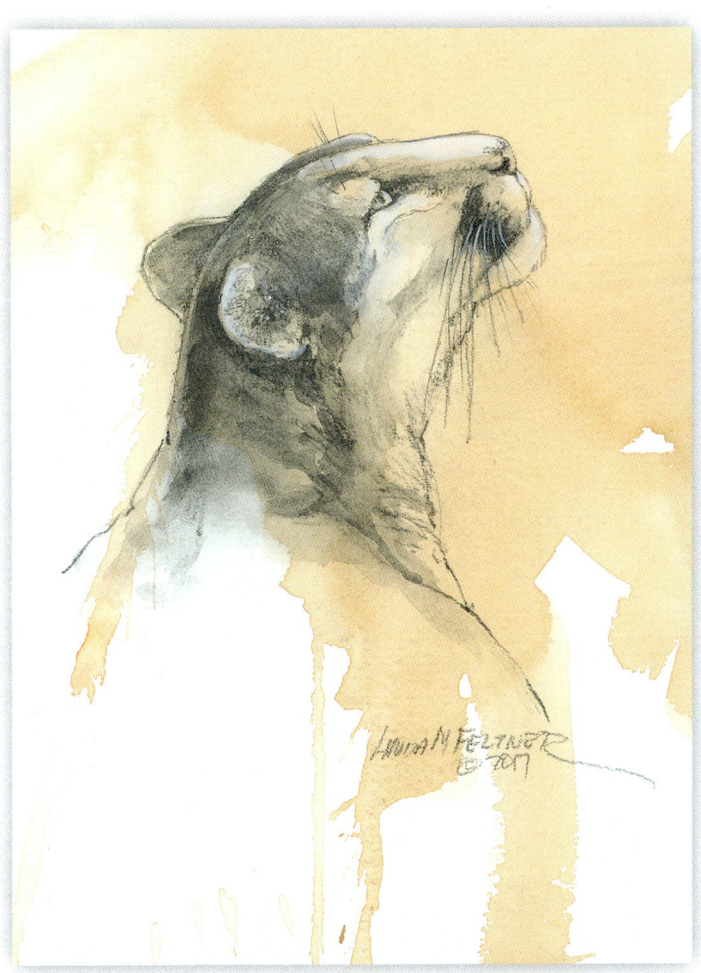

Something on the wind, 9 x 14 in (22.9 x 35.5 cm),
graphite and watercolor on Fabriano Artistico
watercolor paper.

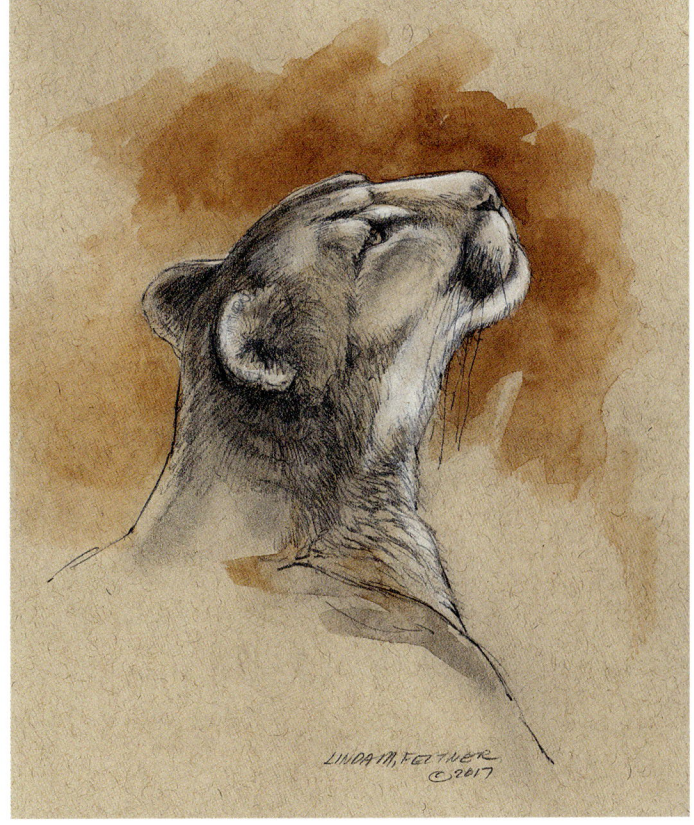

Cougar Study, 9 x 12 in (22.9 x 30.5 cm), Strathmore
toned tan sketch paper.

Zoos and Aquaria

I brought students to a nearby aquarium to experience an underwater world. Whether marine or freshwater, we peek into a world most of us cannot often visit. Although aquariums are not natural environments, they offer insights into marine and freshwater life. From small displays to grand tanks with schools of varied creatures, the artist has opportunities to experience aesthetic and scientific goals.

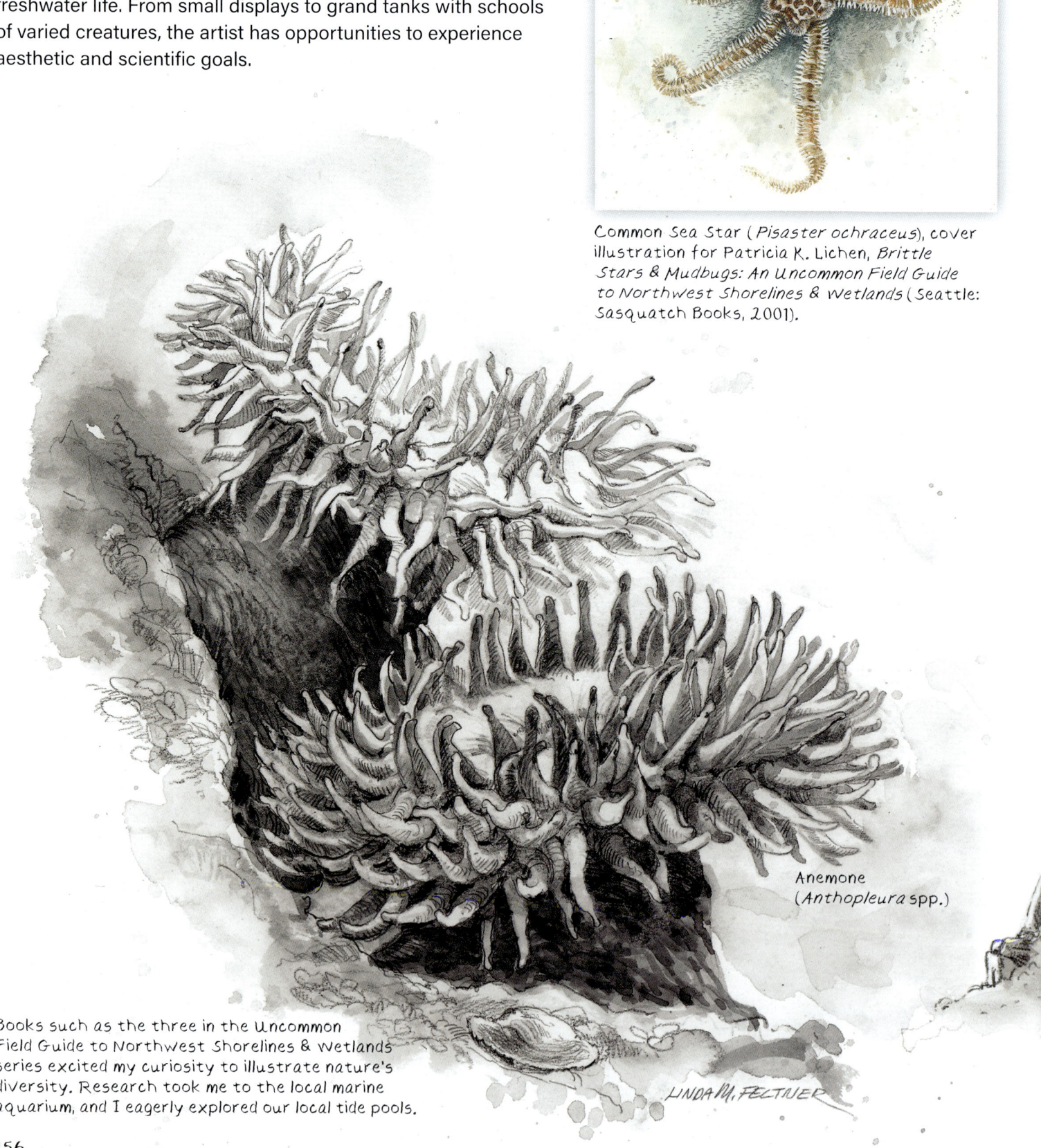

Common Sea Star (*Pisaster ochraceus*), cover illustration for Patricia K. Lichen, *Brittle Stars & Mudbugs: An Uncommon Field Guide to Northwest Shorelines & Wetlands* (Seattle: Sasquatch Books, 2001).

Anemone (*Anthopleura* spp.)

Books such as the three in the Uncommon Field Guide to Northwest Shorelines & Wetlands series excited my curiosity to illustrate nature's diversity. Research took me to the local marine aquarium, and I eagerly explored our local tide pools.

LINDA M. FELTNER

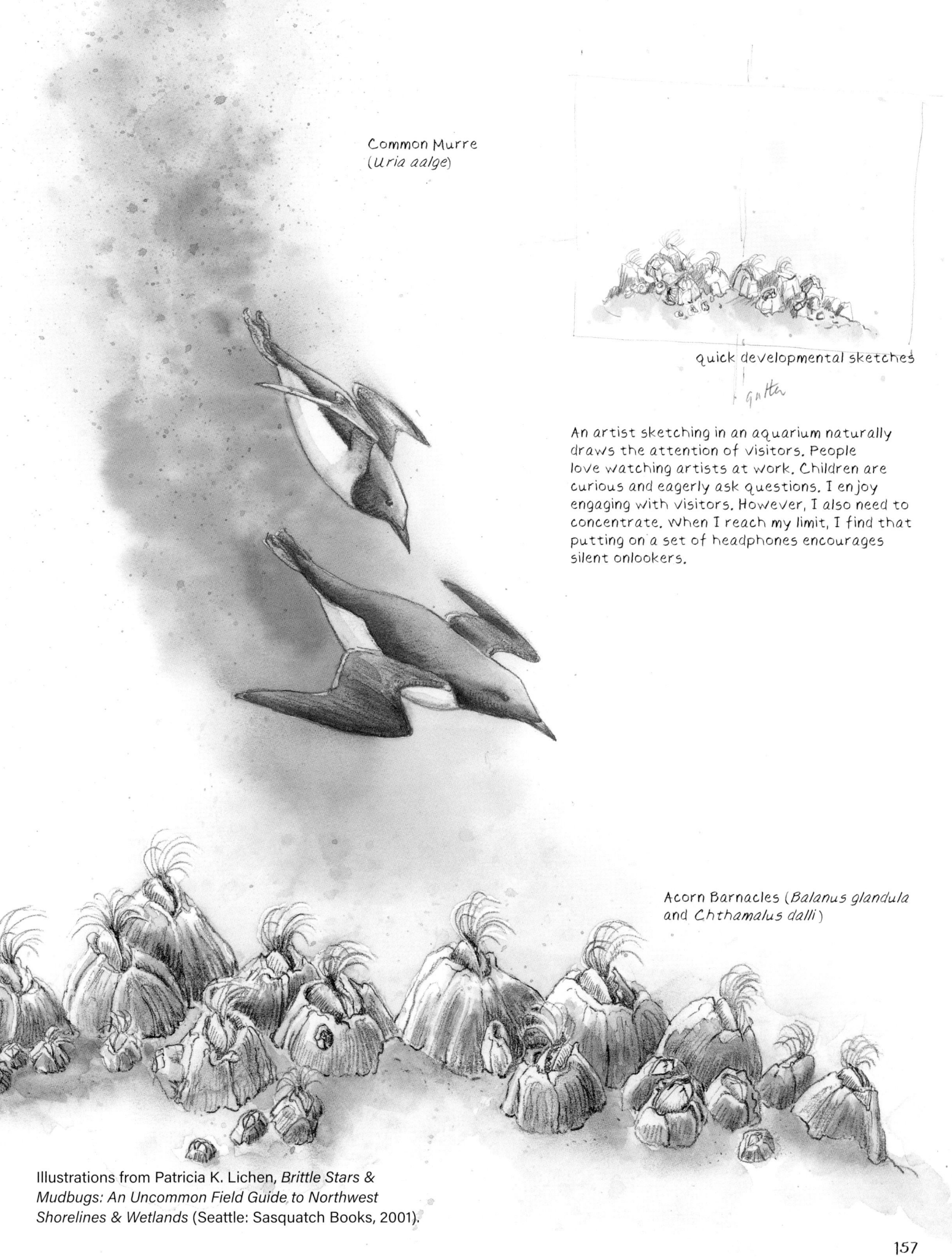

Common Murre
(*Uria aalge*)

quick developmental sketches

gutter

An artist sketching in an aquarium naturally draws the attention of visitors. People love watching artists at work. Children are curious and eagerly ask questions. I enjoy engaging with visitors. However, I also need to concentrate. When I reach my limit, I find that putting on a set of headphones encourages silent onlookers.

Acorn Barnacles (*Balanus glandula* and *Chthamalus dalli*)

Illustrations from Patricia K. Lichen, *Brittle Stars & Mudbugs: An Uncommon Field Guide to Northwest Shorelines & Wetlands* (Seattle: Sasquatch Books, 2001).

Zoos and Aquaria, Continued

Observing aquatic mammals gracefully moving, swimming, and floating is a soothing experience. Loose gesture sketches give me a sense of proportions and characteristic movements. The study of foreshortening takes practice as the artist learns to identify shapes. While sitting on a portable stool, I become comfortable using a soft pencil and starting bold contour drawings. Now is the time to draw freely and take pleasure in the hand following the animal's movement. Details can be researched later in the studio.

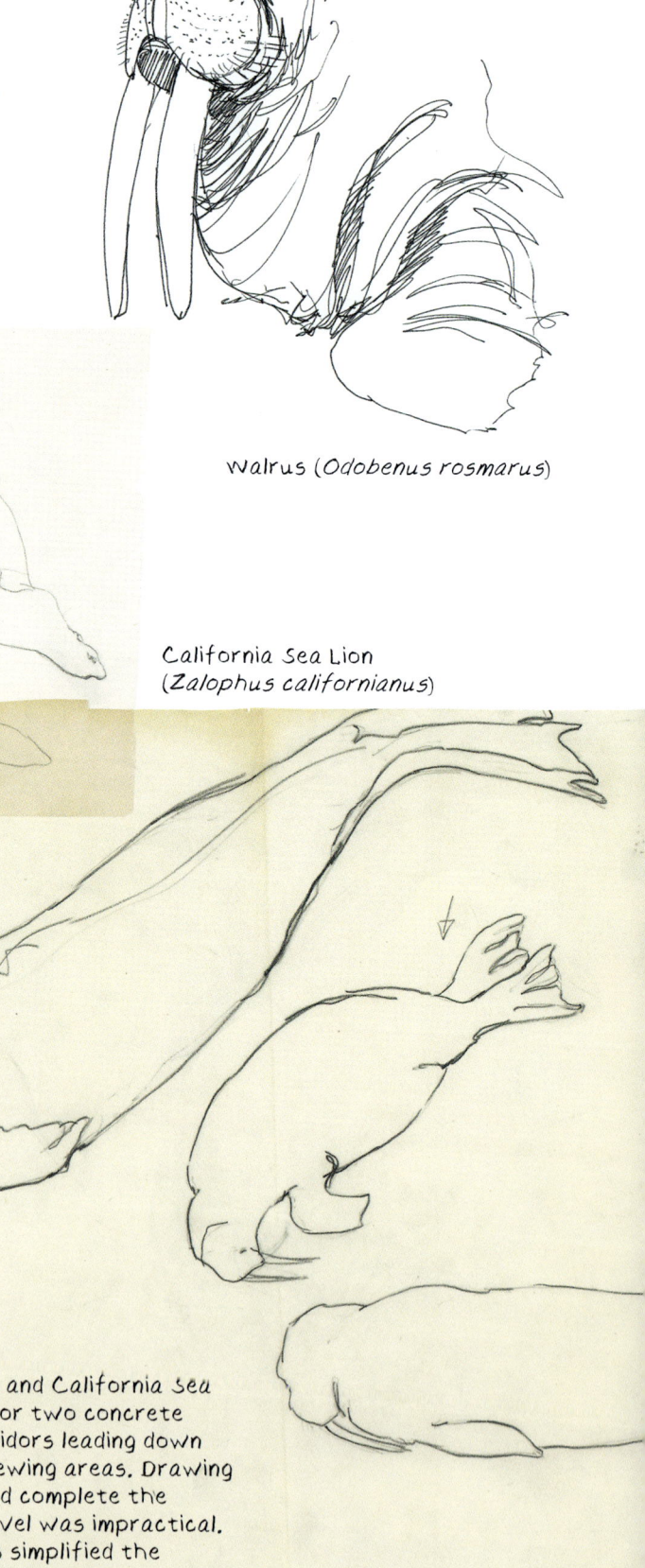

Walrus (*Odobenus rosmarus*)

California Sea Lion
(*Zalophus californianus*)

I designed Walrus and California Sea Lion silhouettes for two concrete friezes along corridors leading down to underwater viewing areas. Drawing from videos helped complete the project when travel was impractical. Contour drawings simplified the shapes for concrete casting.

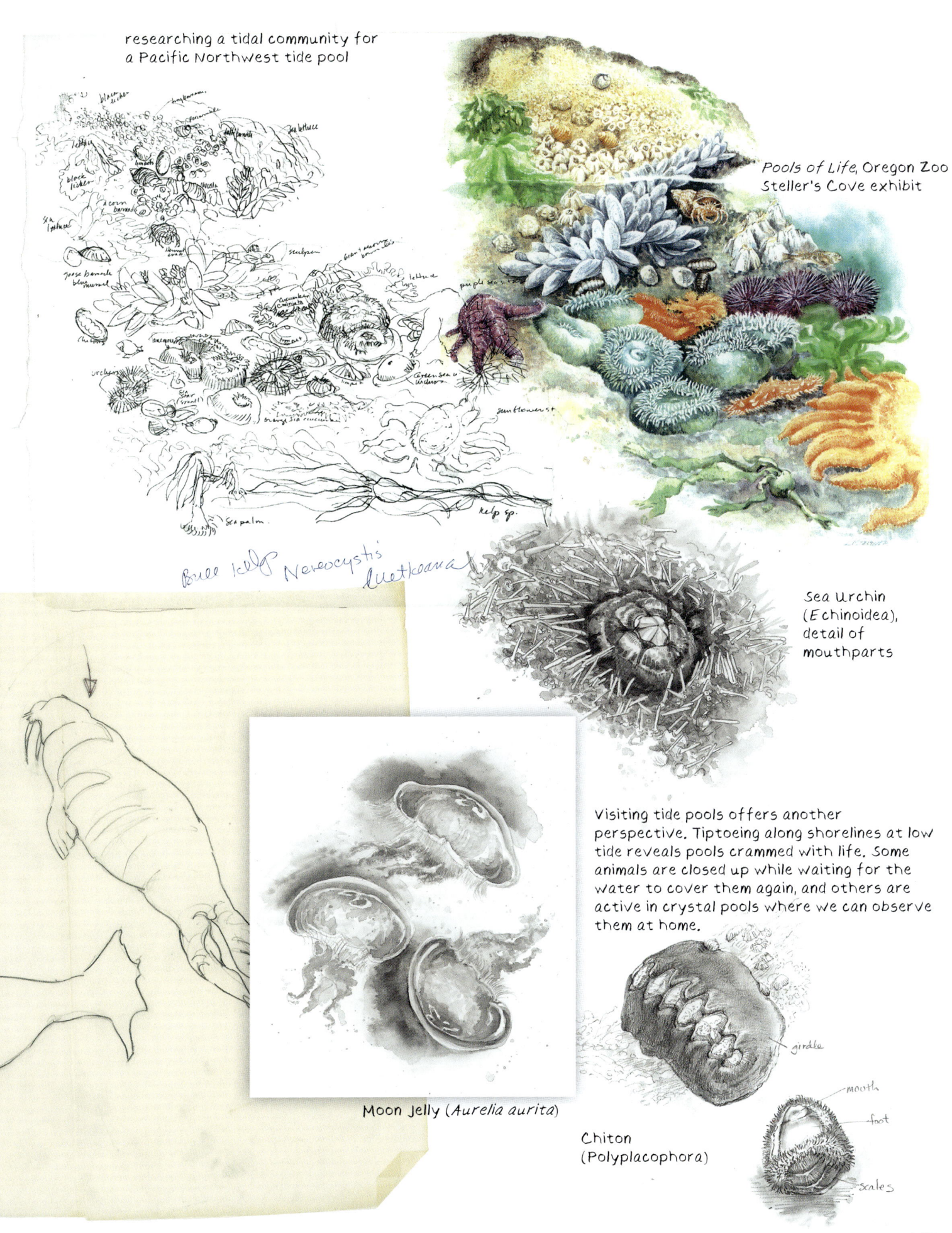

researching a tidal community for
a Pacific Northwest tide pool

Pools of Life, Oregon Zoo
Steller's Cove exhibit

Bull kelp *Nereocystis luetkeana*

Sea Urchin
(*Echinoidea*),
detail of
mouthparts

Visiting tide pools offers another
perspective. Tiptoeing along shorelines at low
tide reveals pools crammed with life. Some
animals are closed up while waiting for the
water to cover them again, and others are
active in crystal pools where we can observe
them at home.

girdle

mouth

foot

scales

Moon Jelly (*Aurelia aurita*)

Chiton
(*Polyplacophora*)

Educational Animals Help Transform Species

Often a species needed for a project is unavailable for live drawing studies. I start with sketches of a close relative and make anatomical adjustments to create the new bird. My assignment was a White-tailed Hawk for a book cover for nature writer B. C. Robison's *A Haven in the Sun: Five Stories of Bird Life and Its Future on the Texas Coast*. This hawk is a personal favorite observed and painted in Texas in years past.

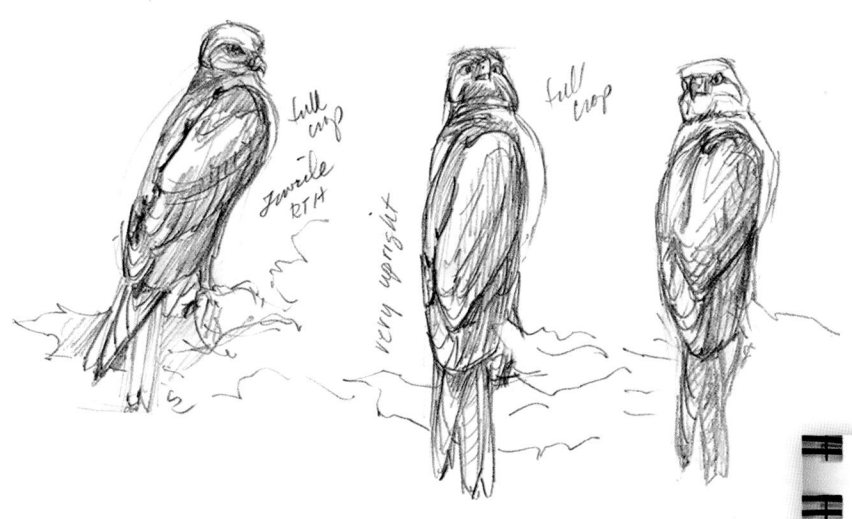

Sketches of a juvenile Red-tailed Hawk (*Buteo jamaicensis*) in class provided potential poses. The young bird was nervous at first and in an upright, slender pose but began to relax. The Red-tail's wings do not extend beyond the tail when perched. Photo references from a friend provided small details necessary for the transformation from one species to another.

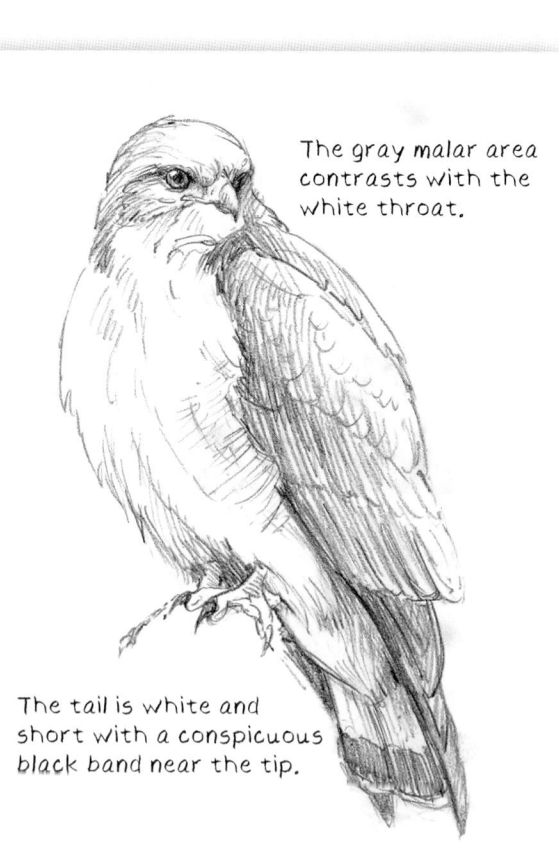

The gray malar area contrasts with the white throat.

The tail is white and short with a conspicuous black band near the tip.

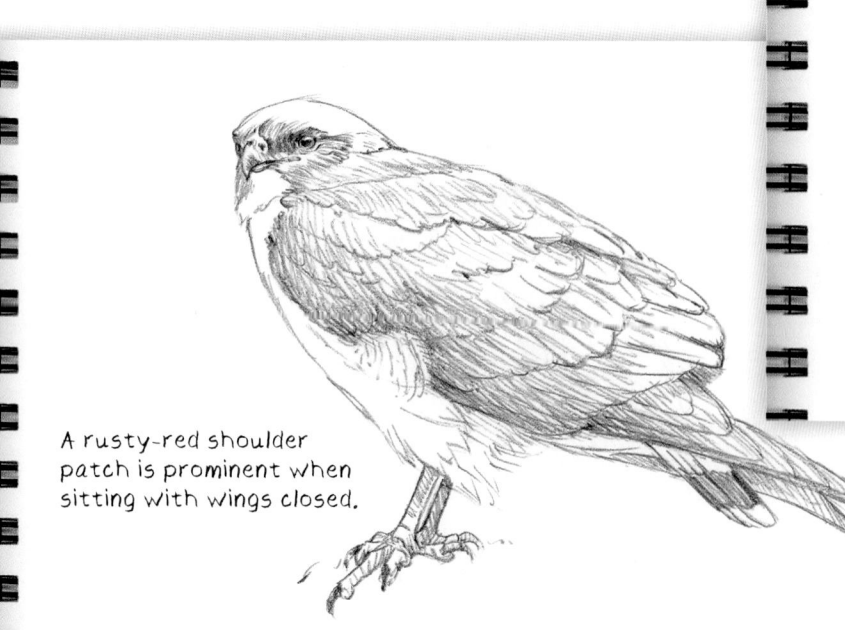

A rusty-red shoulder patch is prominent when sitting with wings closed.

These two sketchpages depict two poses for the White-tailed Hawk, highlighting diagnostic features needed for the illustration.

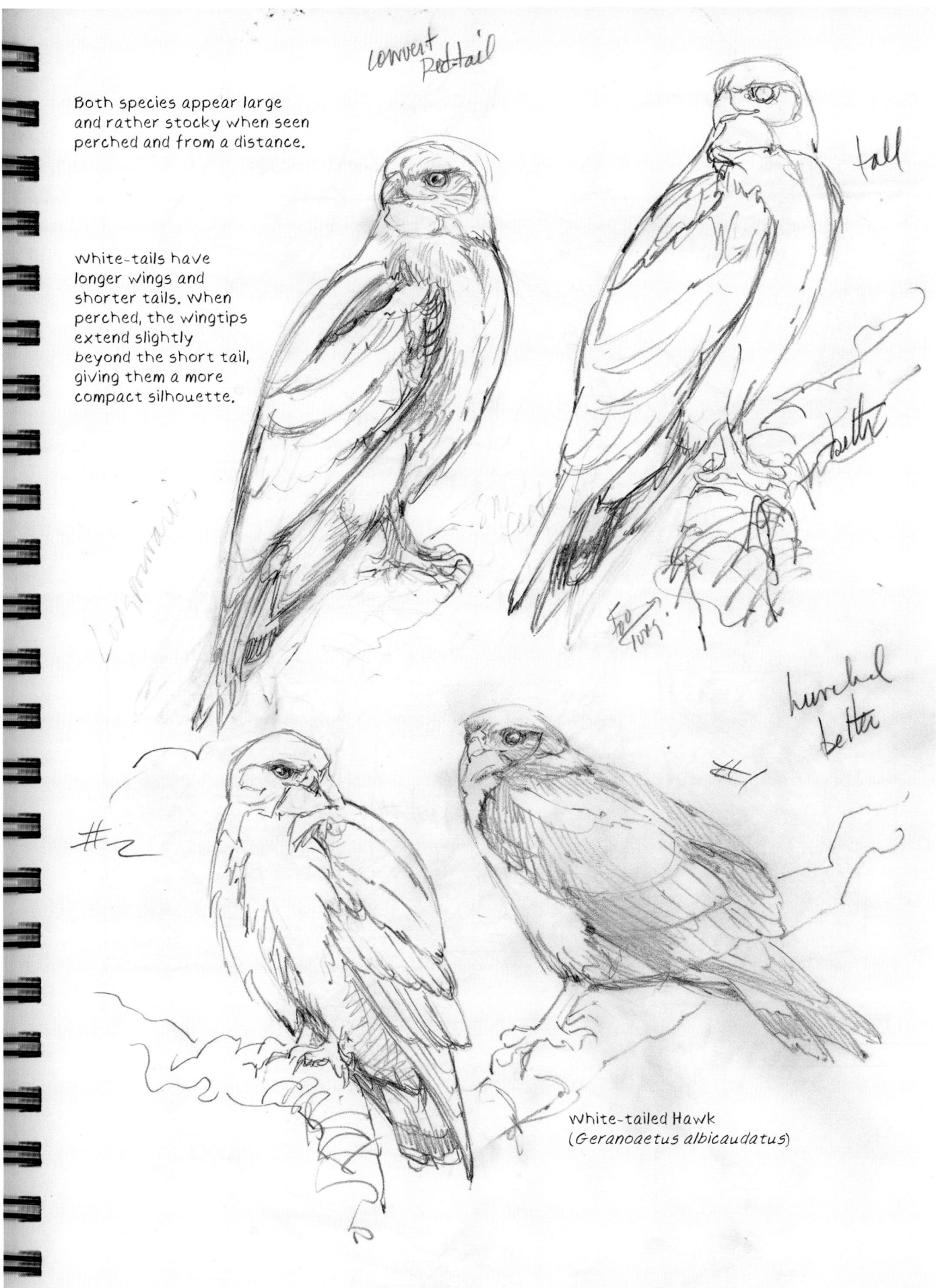

convert
Red-tail

tall

Both species appear large
and rather stocky when seen
perched and from a distance.

white-tails have
longer wings and
shorter tails. when
perched, the wingtips
extend slightly
beyond the short tail,
giving them a more
compact silhouette.

lurched
better

#1

#2

White-tailed Hawk
(*Geranoaetus albicaudatus*)

"A Haven in the Sun ... ": Work in Progress

Compose and Find the Perfect Branch

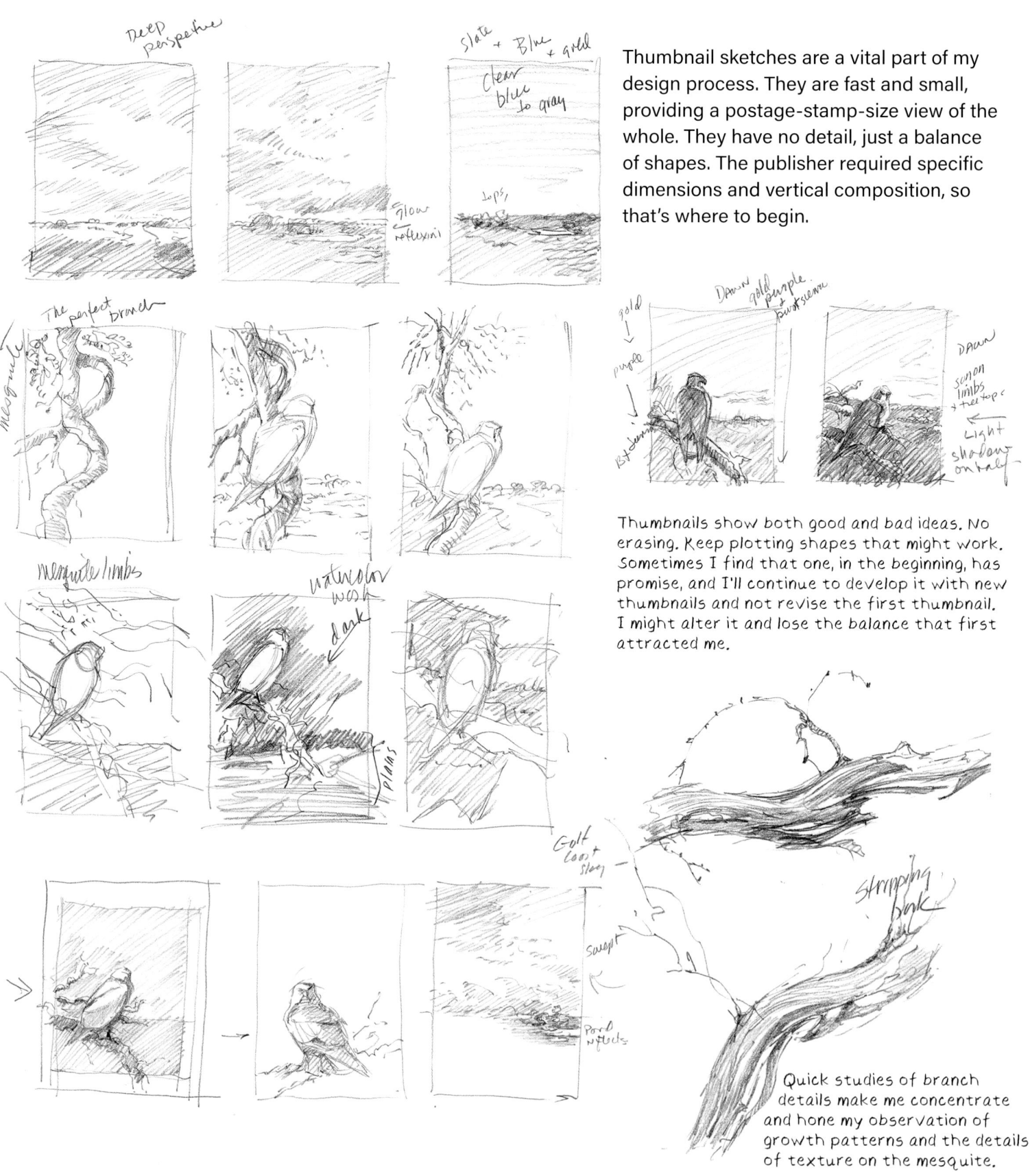

Thumbnail sketches are a vital part of my design process. They are fast and small, providing a postage-stamp-size view of the whole. They have no detail, just a balance of shapes. The publisher required specific dimensions and vertical composition, so that's where to begin.

Thumbnails show both good and bad ideas. No erasing. Keep plotting shapes that might work. Sometimes I find that one, in the beginning, has promise, and I'll continue to develop it with new thumbnails and not revise the first thumbnail. I might alter it and lose the balance that first attracted me.

Quick studies of branch details make me concentrate and hone my observation of growth patterns and the details of texture on the mesquite.

162

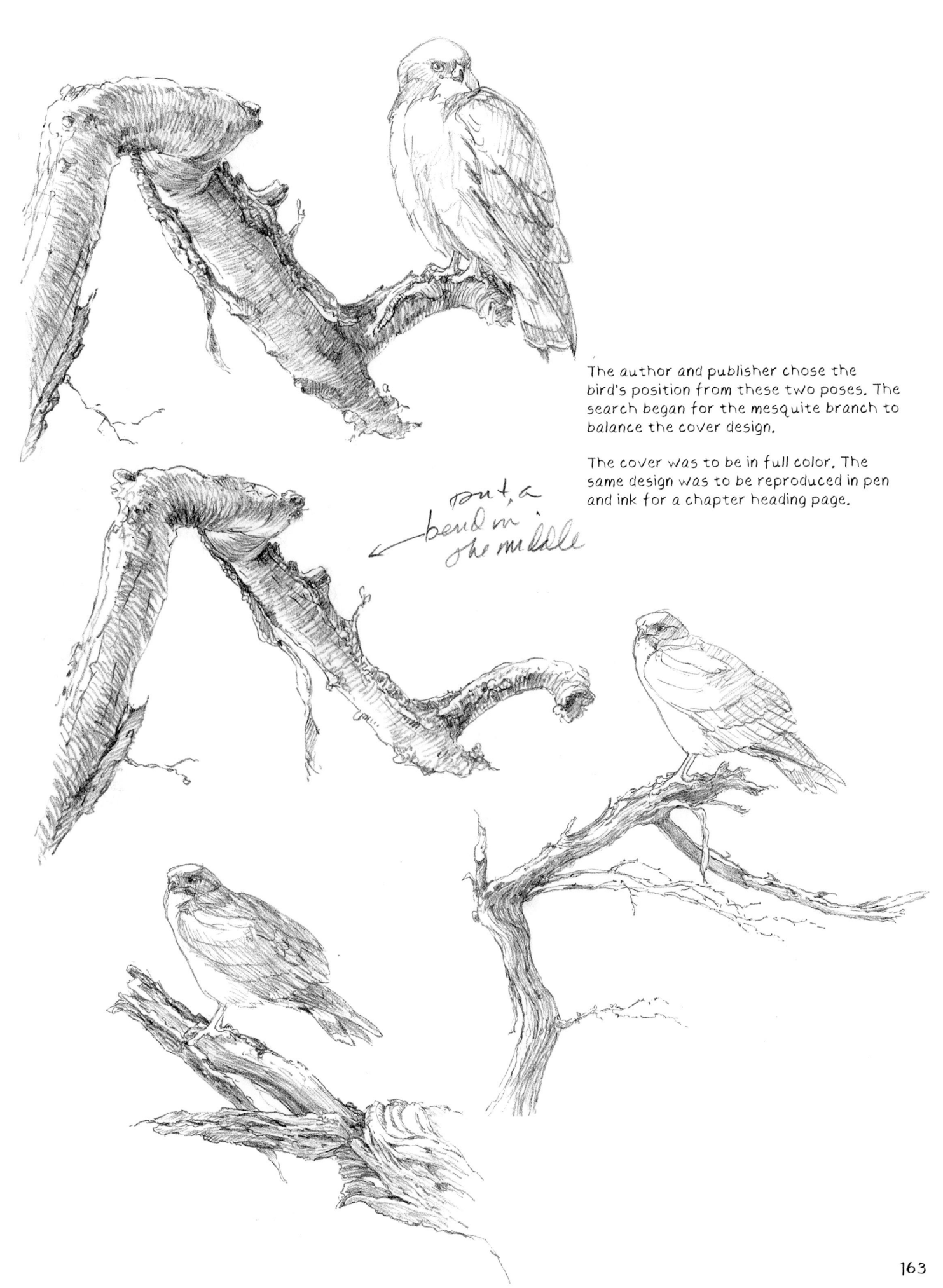

The author and publisher chose the bird's position from these two poses. The search began for the mesquite branch to balance the cover design.

The cover was to be in full color. The same design was to be reproduced in pen and ink for a chapter heading page.

put a bend in the middle

163

"A Haven in the Sun ...": Final Art

Nature writer B. C. Robison presents stories of five birds that have a special bond with coastal Texas. He portrays not only the importance of the Texas Coast to North American bird life but also the intimate dependence of coastal birds on our use of the land.

When I lived in Houston, B. C. wrote the "Texas Naturalist" for the *Houston Post* and invited me to illustrate his column for several years. It was a delight to work with him again on this wonderful portrayal of his selection of iconic birds and landscape.

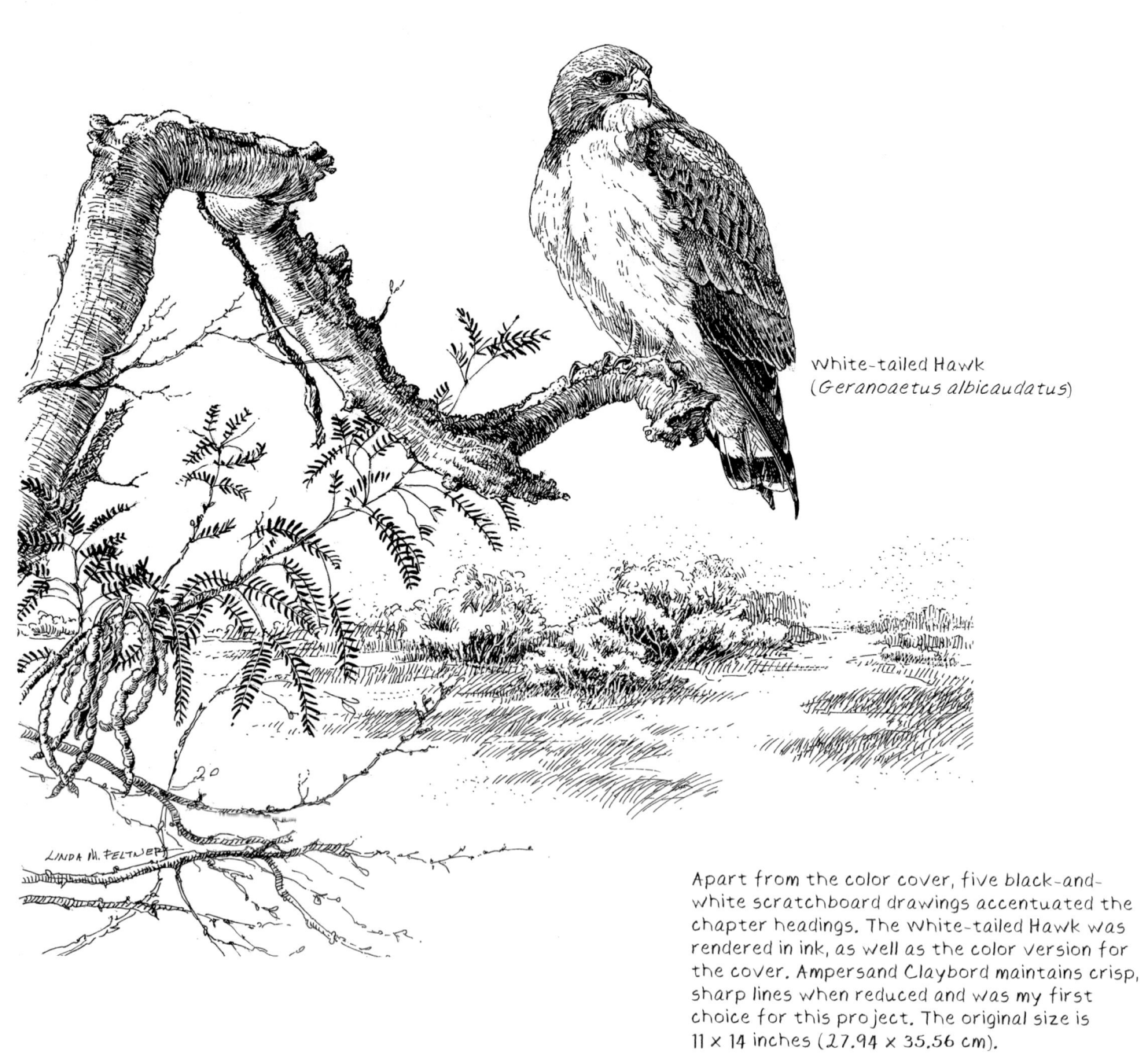

White-tailed Hawk
(*Geranoaetus albicaudatus*)

Apart from the color cover, five black-and-white scratchboard drawings accentuated the chapter headings. The White-tailed Hawk was rendered in ink, as well as the color version for the cover. Ampersand Claybord maintains crisp, sharp lines when reduced and was my first choice for this project. The original size is 11 x 14 inches (27.94 x 35.56 cm).

164

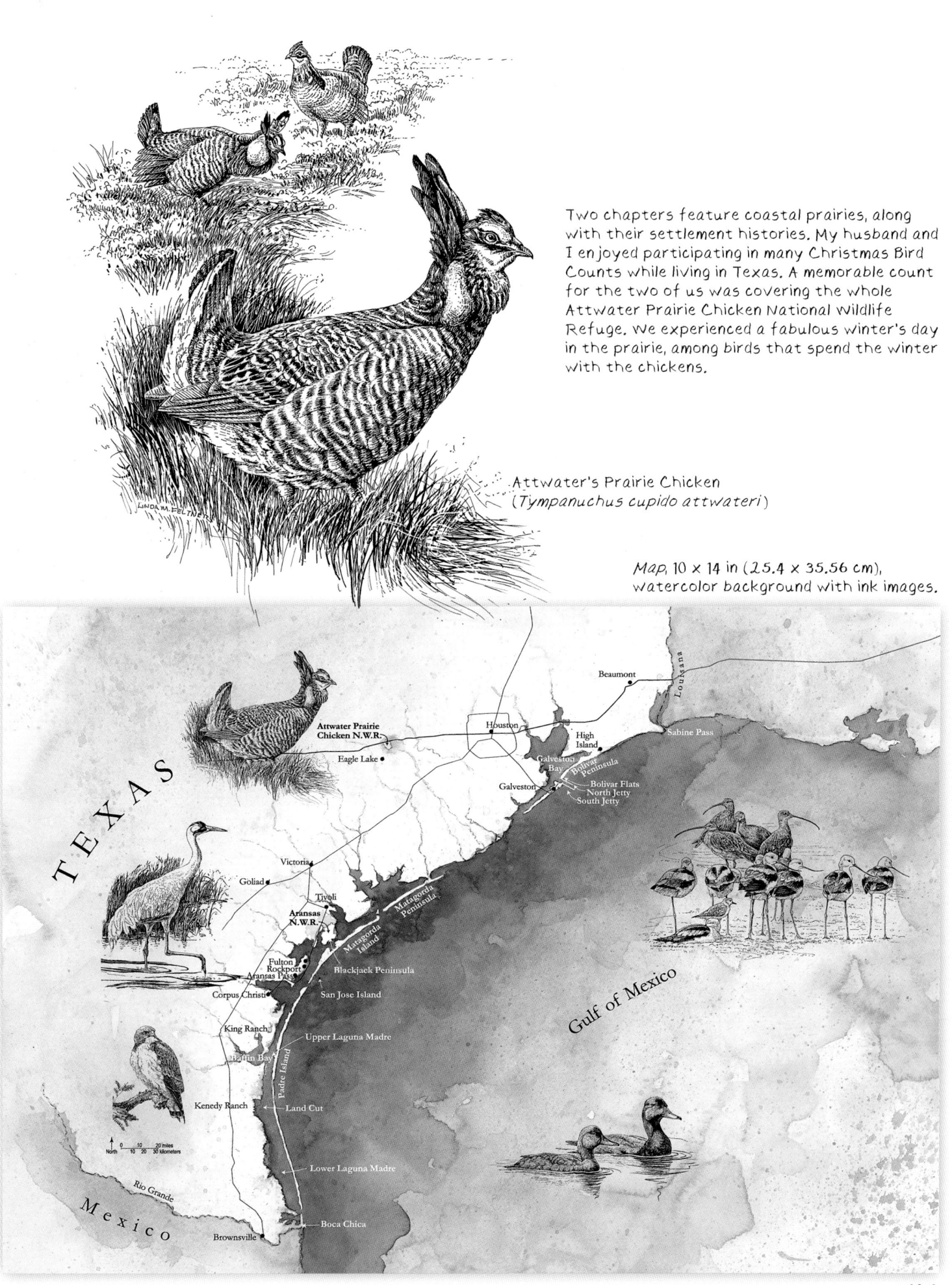

Two chapters feature coastal prairies, along with their settlement histories. My husband and I enjoyed participating in many Christmas Bird Counts while living in Texas. A memorable count for the two of us was covering the whole Attwater Prairie Chicken National Wildlife Refuge. We experienced a fabulous winter's day in the prairie, among birds that spend the winter with the chickens.

Attwater's Prairie Chicken
(*Tympanuchus cupido attwateri*)

Map, 10 x 14 in (25.4 x 35.56 cm), watercolor background with ink images.

TEXAS

Beaumont

Houston

Attwater Prairie Chicken N.W.R.

Eagle Lake

High Island

Sabine Pass

Galveston Bay

Bolivar Peninsula

Galveston

Bolivar Flats
North Jetty
South Jetty

Victoria

Goliad

Tivoli

Aransas N.W.R.

Matagorda Island

Matagorda Peninsula

Fulton
Rockport
Aransas Pass

Blackjack Peninsula

San Jose Island

Corpus Christi

King Ranch

Upper Laguna Madre

Baffin Bay

Padre Island

Kenedy Ranch

Land Cut

0   10   20 miles
North   10   20   30 kilometers

Gulf of Mexico

Lower Laguna Madre

Rio Grande

Mexico

Brownsville

Boca Chica

Louisiana

165

"A Haven in the Sun ...": Final Art, Continued

While standing at the flat Texas coastline, the view of mudflats and vegetation stretches horizontally. The book format was vertical, which directed the design flow. From a shifted viewpoint, the drawings maintain the sensation of extensive beaches and dense, vast wetlands.

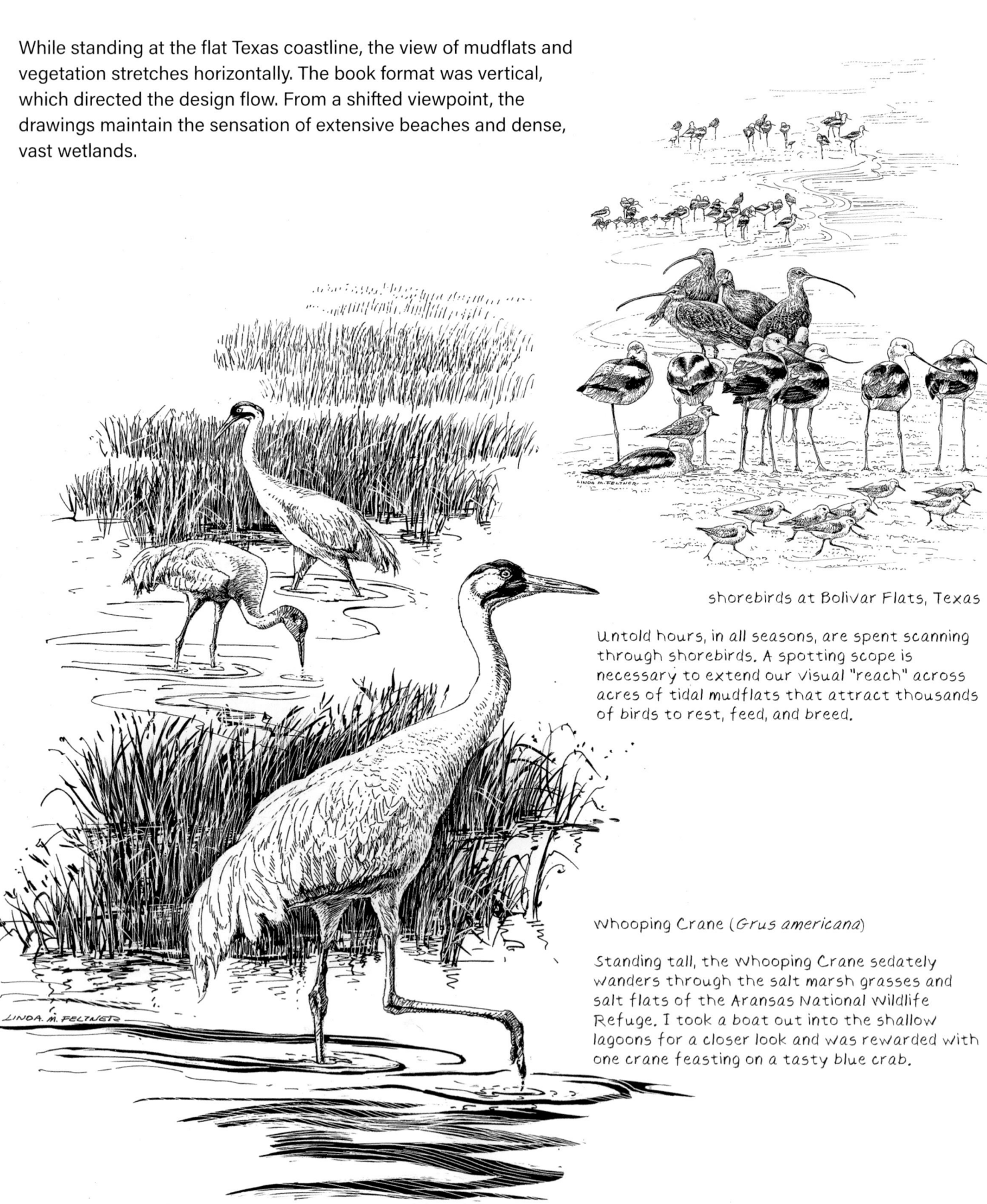

shorebirds at Bolivar Flats, Texas

Untold hours, in all seasons, are spent scanning through shorebirds. A spotting scope is necessary to extend our visual "reach" across acres of tidal mudflats that attract thousands of birds to rest, feed, and breed.

Whooping Crane (*Grus americana*)

Standing tall, the Whooping Crane sedately wanders through the salt marsh grasses and salt flats of the Aransas National Wildlife Refuge. I took a boat out into the shallow lagoons for a closer look and was rewarded with one crane feasting on a tasty blue crab.

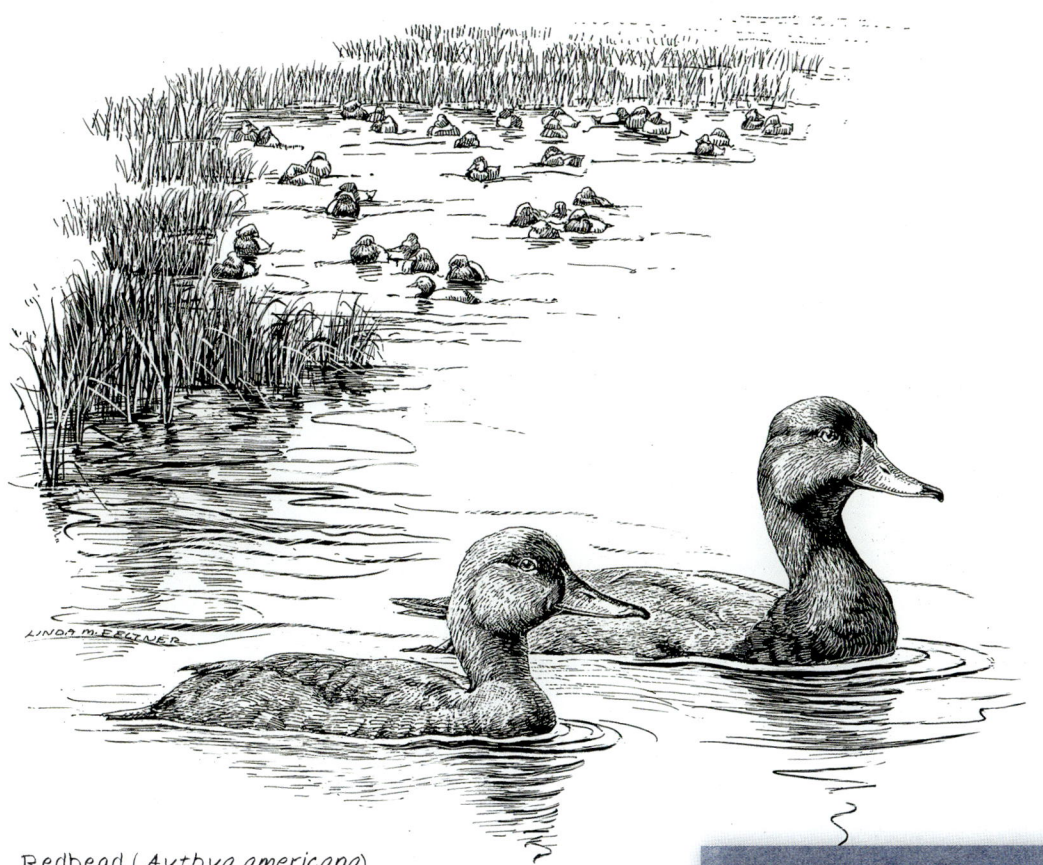

Redhead (*Aythya americana*)

Scanning the lagoons, we find wintering ducks with heads of burnished sienna glowing across the water's surface. These social Redheads gather and feed in large numbers in the salty lagoons and freshwater wetlands of the lower Texas coastal bend.

A Haven in the Sun

Five Stories of Bird Life and Its Future on the Texas Coast

B.C. Robison

Illustrations by Linda M. Feltner

Cover illustration for B. C. Robison, *A Haven in the Sun: Five Stories of Bird Life and Its Future on the Texas Coast* (Lubbock, TX: Texas Tech University Press, 2020), 11 × 15 (27.94 × 38.1 cm), transparent watercolor on 300 lb (640 gsm) cold press Fabriano Artistico watercolor paper.

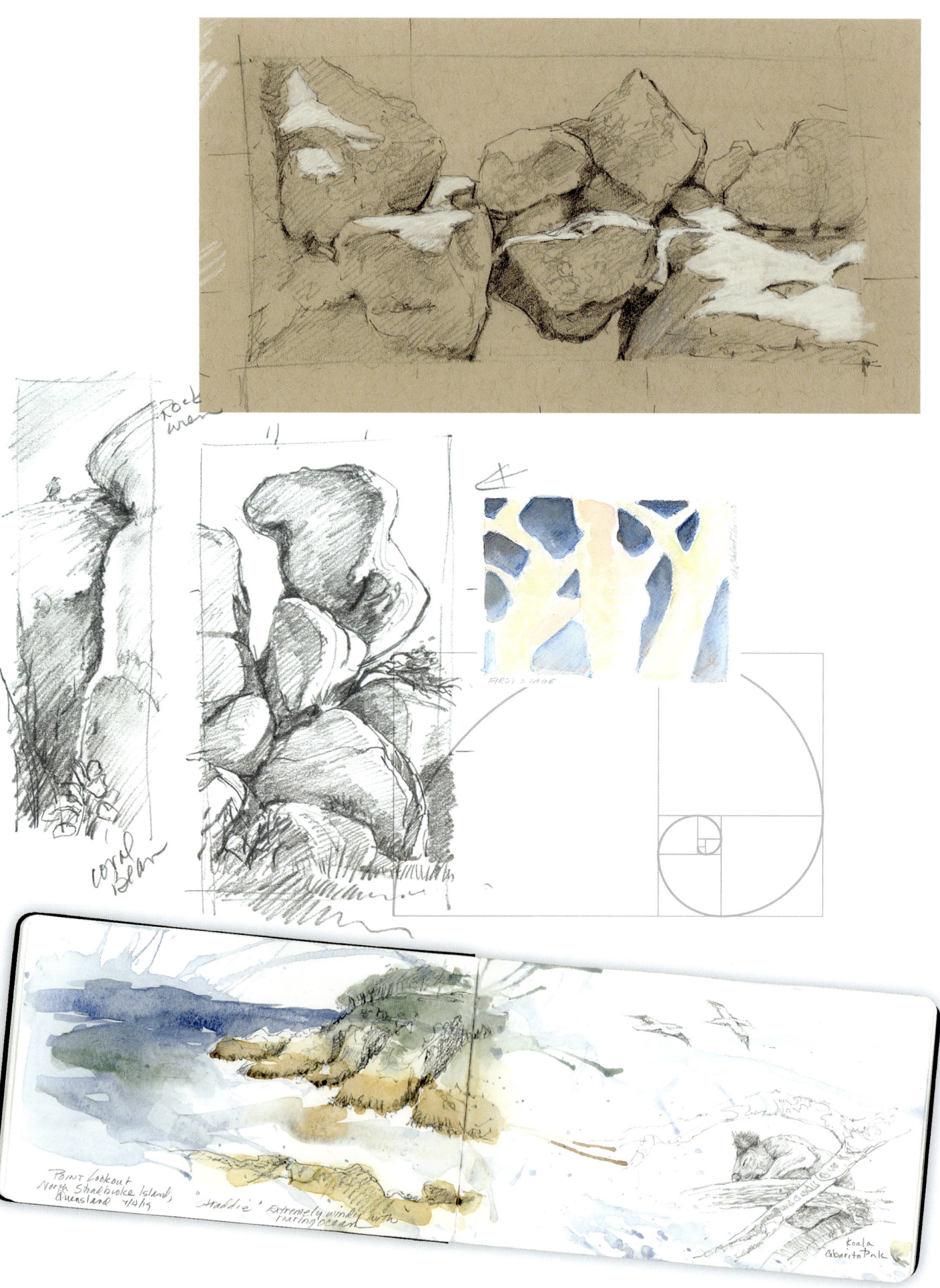

Point Lookout
North Stradbroke Island,
Queensland 7/4/19   "Maddie" Extremely windy with
                      roaring ocean

Koala
Cabarita Park

CHAPTER 6

From Spark to Finish

As a watercolor painter, if I'm not happy with an area of a painting, I can't completely wipe it off and do something different. Planning the design is essential to building the message and presenting the layout. Plus, it saves a lot of wasted handmade paper.

This chapter presents essential methods for creating finished art. Among them are techniques for composing images and simplifying the focus while sketching outdoors amid the cacophony of nature's details.

Once I render a subject to my satisfaction, the next step is placing it on the page with other elements to enhance the story. The process achieves an aesthetic balance that composes the scene, determines where the eye travels, and plans an appropriate grayscale value balance.

I mosey through a landscape with a pocket-sized sketchbook. Here, the sketches remain quick, unfinished sparks. Planning and composition have become intuitive from much practice. A travel sketchbook or journal is a lightweight and practical tool for recording ideas. While traveling, I discovered that sometimes written impressions are the only way to capture the moment. It does not matter in what manner it's put on paper. It matters that my eyes remain open and curious.

No matter what sparks my interest, what takes me to the finish is a few deliberate decisions.

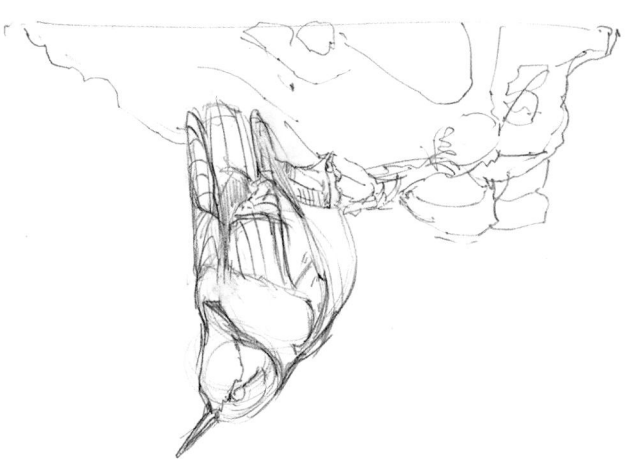

Finding the Balance: Notan

Notan is an ancient Asian balance of harmony using only black and white. It's not a value study. It is the underpinning of what follows, and sets the stage by first recognizing shapes and patterns. By adjusting shapes against each other, a compositional balance emerges.

Notan studies create the bare bones of balance. Decisions on applying values are made in the next stage. Value studies contain a variety of tones within a dark or a light shape. Even with values established, the initial structural harmony is maintained.

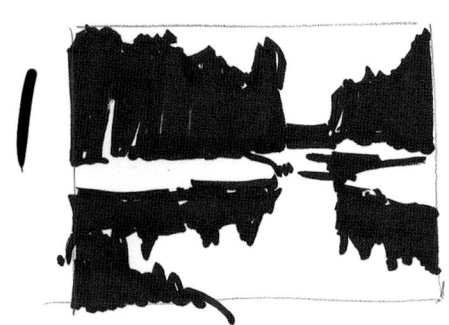
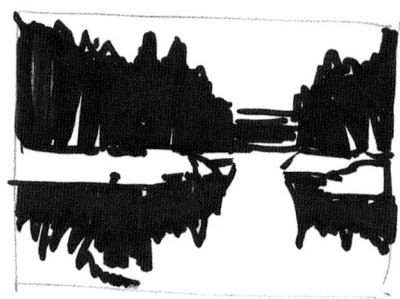

MAINE POND

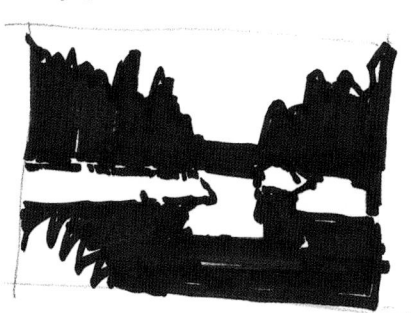

from two photos of a quiet pond in Maine

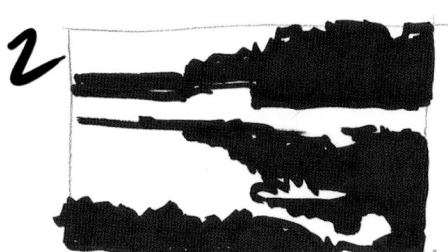
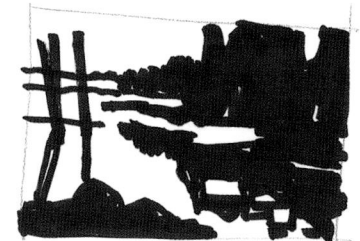
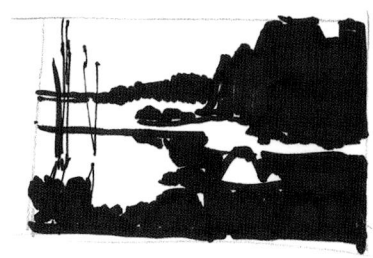

Counterpoint is a term I define as an area that balances out a larger mass. It can be a single shape or a grouping of small marks. The smaller ones act in concert to create a visual dazzle that should balance the larger mass. Rotate the study sideways to determine if the balance remains. This action helps to see it as shape and not as an object.

Essential considerations to simplify the visual chaos of landscape detail:

- Recognize shapes and patterns without giving a name to the object.
- View the landscape before you. Pick an area of similar grayscale value and make it either a black or white shape.
- Simplify the larger shapes.
- Can smaller shapes connect to make a larger shape?
- Where is the best place to put a counterpoint to the larger shape?

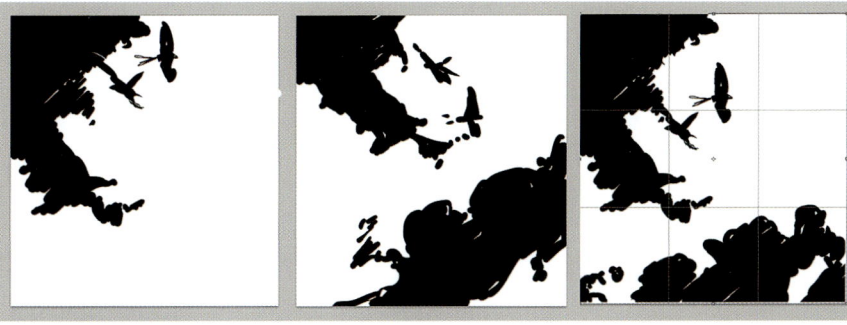

Screenshots created to plan the cloud shapes for *Kites Ascending Before a Storm*.

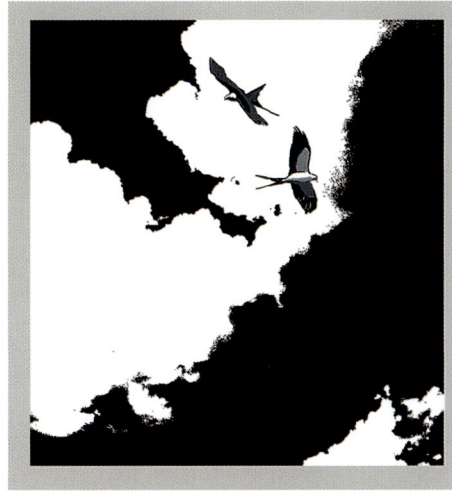

Once the balance is determined and composition guidelines are fixed in my mind, I do not have to stick to precise edges. I can let watercolor flow with a touch of each brushstroke and allow a wet-in-wet technique to flow with a freshness that is quintessentially watercolor.

How often have I gone back through old thumbnails to discover a jewel that appeals because of its simple elegance? Here, I experimented with a warm Gray Copic sketch pen. It borrowed the bones of the black-and-white notan. With a few simple strokes, it immediately has potential atmosphere with a strong composition.

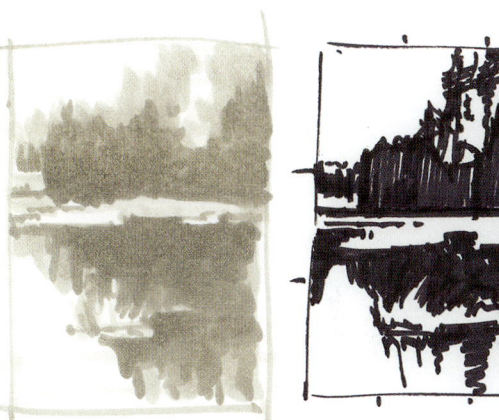

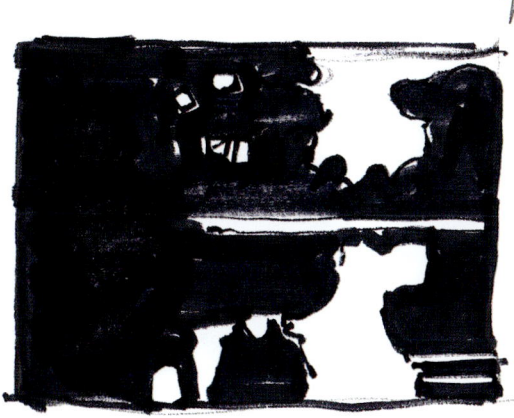

Monet
Many variations on
atmosphere, +
time of Day —
but FOUNDATION
remains the
same

Color shapes

Look up Claude Monet's "Morning on the Seine" series, painted near Giverny. This will show at least twenty engaging variations together on the screen. Each painting represents a different atmosphere, time of day, and warm or cool palette. All use the same harmony of composition, but the shift of values within the shapes provides a different atmosphere.

The Shape of Color

Notan also applies to warm and cool colors. Even if they are the same value, a warm or cool area has a shape that affects the composition.

"Kites Ascending Before a Storm"

A friend mentioned that Swallow-tailed Kites were their favorite birds. This sparked a vivid memory of an exhilarating moment of joy one day as I witnessed the spiraling grace of these birds up close. The birds lifted upward with wings out and tails spread in effortless movement. Cumulus clouds echoed their rising motion. Inspired by this experience, my painting focused equally on the soaring pair and the force of the swelling clouds.

Rather than painting the precise details of billowing clouds, I felt watercolor was the ideal medium to suggest loose movement in contrast to the birds. The natural flowing ability of a wet-in-wet wash implies freshness and moisture within the growing clouds. The experimentation with notan studies helped me to visualize a successful pattern of light and dark shapes. I did not have to follow the exact notan edges but only used them as a guide. With the pattern fixed in my mind, I applied the paint in a controlled way, but allowing the watercolor to flow with the same buoyant spontaneity.

Swallow-tailed Kite (*Elanoides forficatus*)

Kites Ascending Before a Storm, 10 × 14 in (25.4 × 35.56 cm), transparent watercolor.

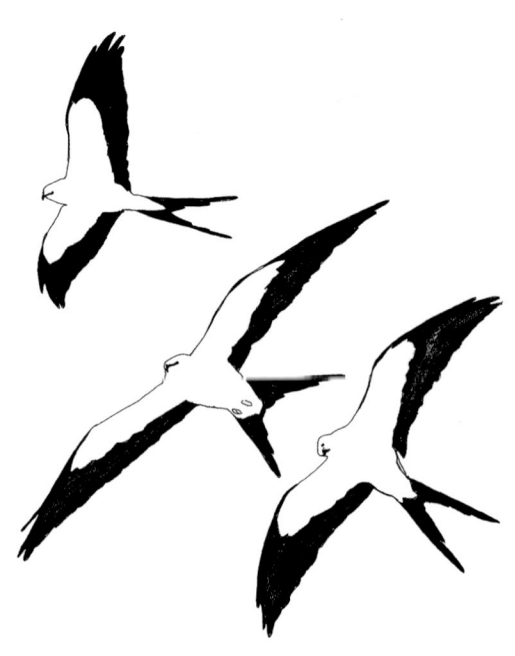

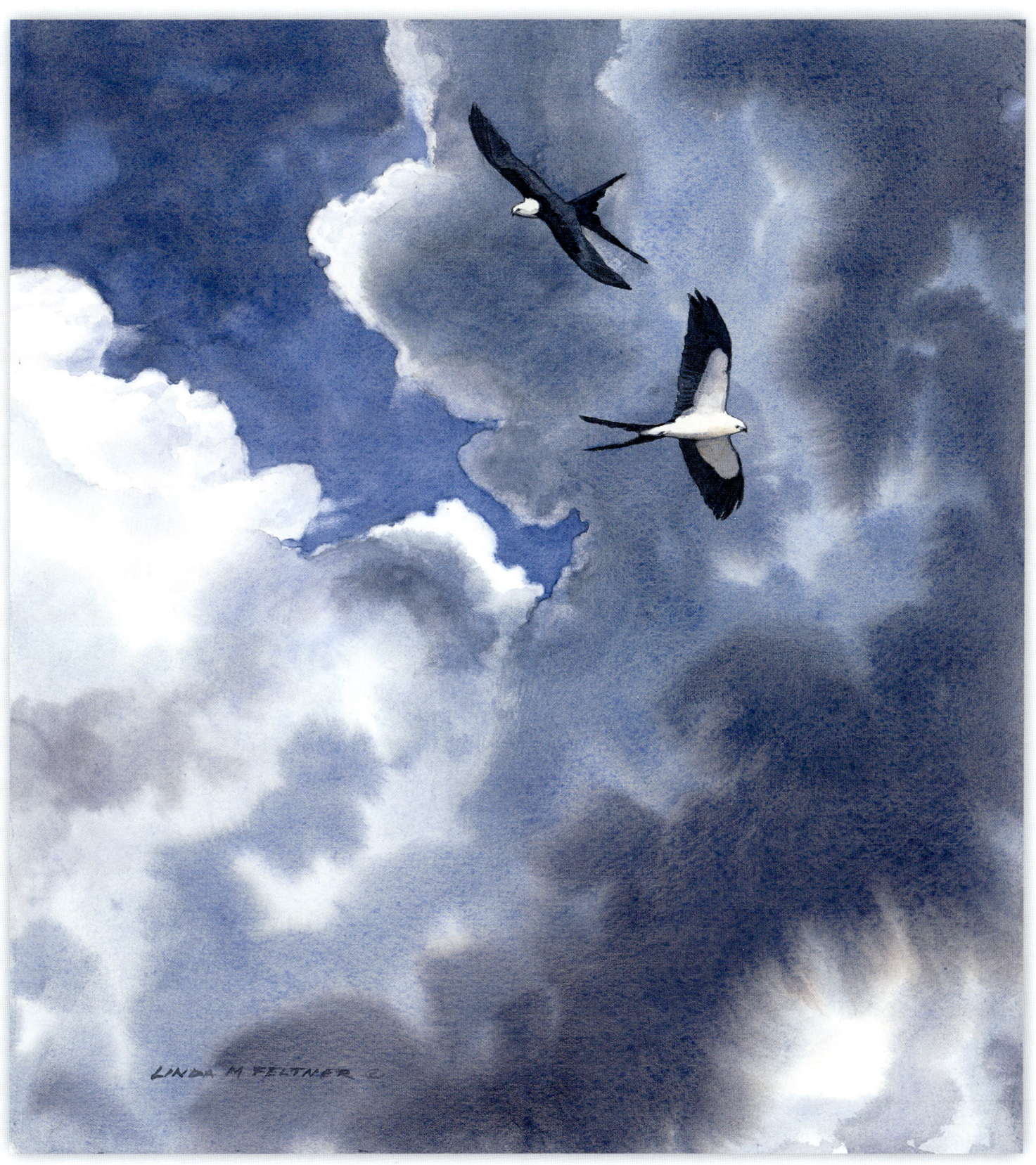

Linda M Feltner ©

From Bare Essentials to Adding Values

Why create so many thumbnail sketches? It is fun, fast, and helpful. Perhaps I am one of those who enjoy experimentation and pushing the limits of preconceived ideas. The studies are usually small, 2 x 3 in, and therefore it is easy to visualize the whole. It removes the "stepping back and squinting" process. It's very easy to rotate the studies upside down and sideways or view in a mirror. If created with the computer, the studies can even be inverted so light becomes dark.

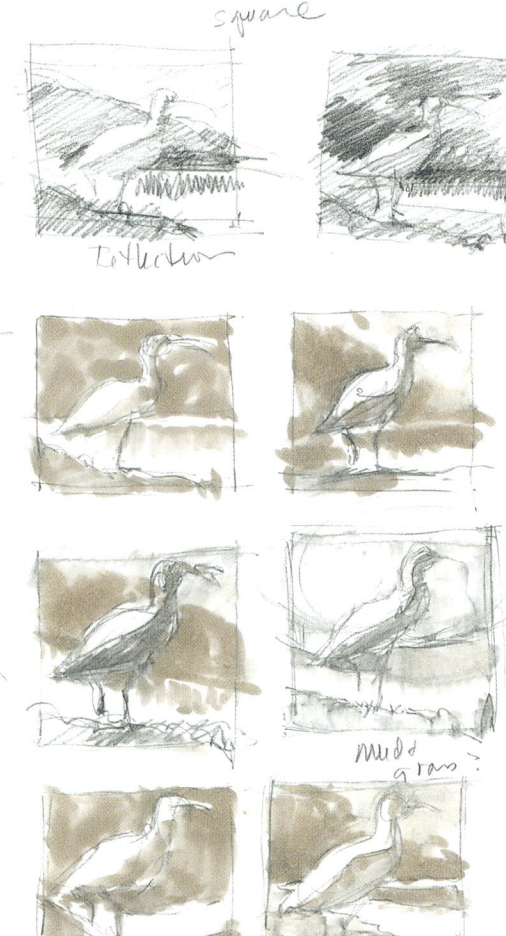

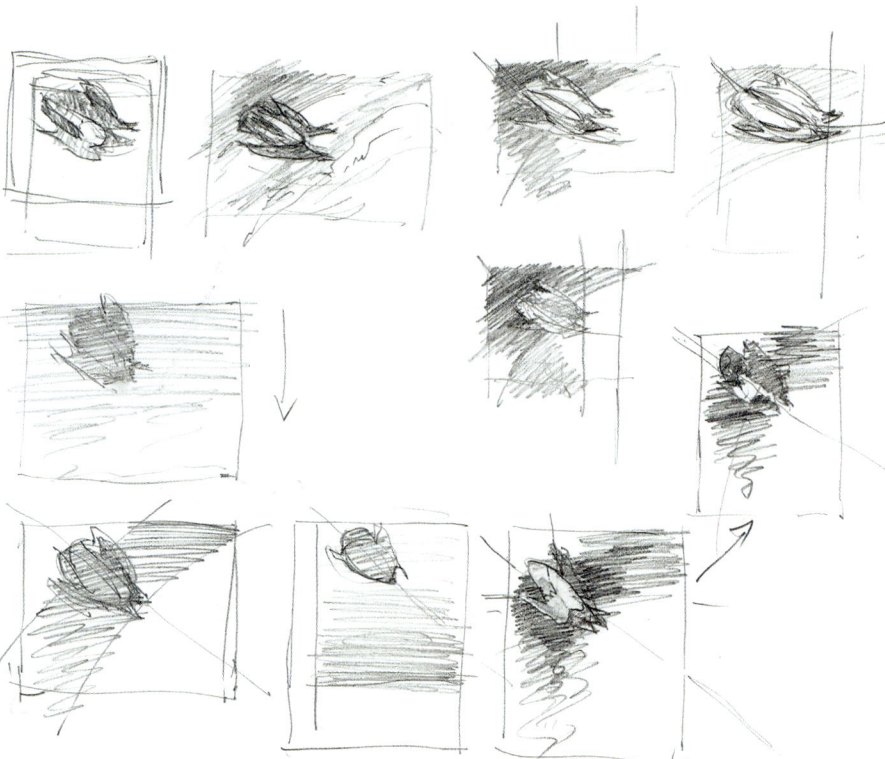

airborne thumbnails for *Love at First Flight*

Spontaneous value studies experiment with directing the viewer's eye through the painting. Background shading directly supports the tumbling action of the birds. For this subject, the composition needed buoyancy and dramatic motion. Value studies, with options for cropping, quickly solve several compositional issues at once, and inspire the perfect solution.

No matter how rough the thumbnail sketch, each version has an adjustment, often a very tiny tweak.

Seeing it on the page gives me more information about the whole composition than tweaking it in my imagination would.

It's faster to do another thumbnail than erase and alter one.

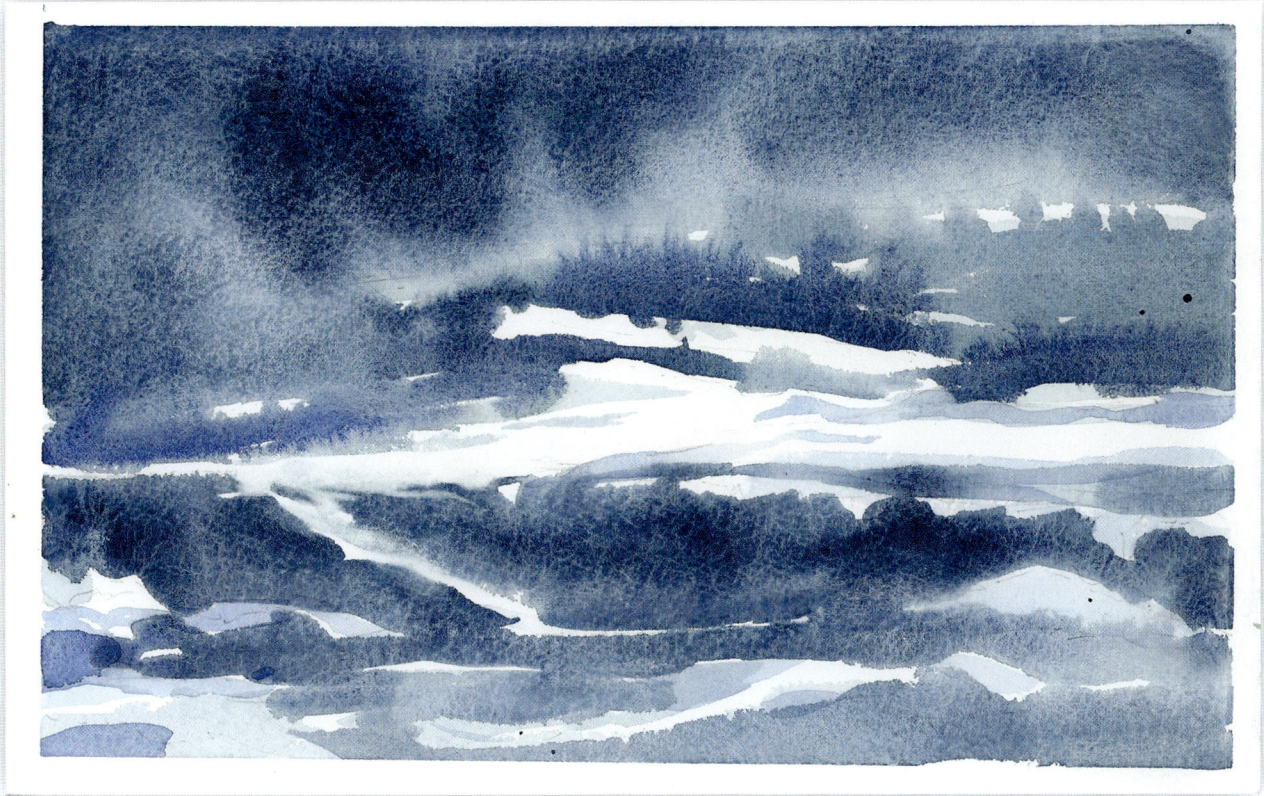

This experiment surprised me. I introduced grayscale values within large dark and light shapes. Using a juicy brush and creating random patterns caused the thicker pigment to mingle with water, creating a luscious wet-in-wet technique. When dry, I rotated it on all sides to see if the design was harmonious. To my astonishment, when turned upside down, the image resembled a snowy landscape. Does it have the potential for a larger painting? Perhaps. However, I did not alter it or place any other stroke on it. Long ago, I learned to keep that first study untouched to remind myself that I did it once and can do it again.

6.5 x 10.5 in (16.51 x 26.67 cm), transparent watercolor, on 300 lb (640 gsm) cold press Fabriano Artistico paper.

four-value digital study for a larger painting

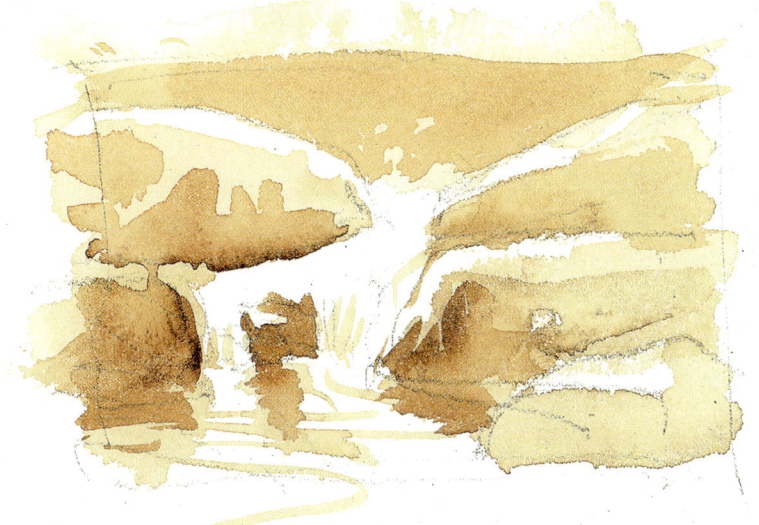

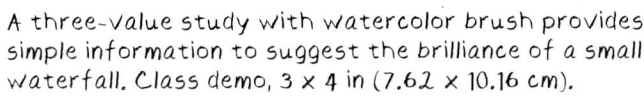

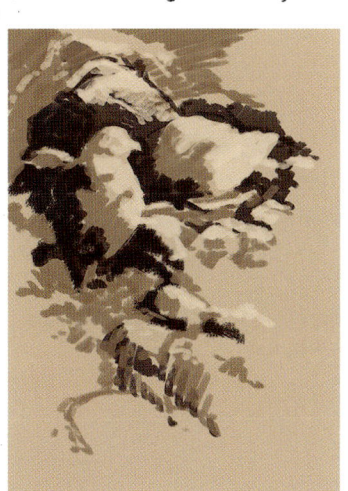

A three-value study with watercolor brush provides simple information to suggest the brilliance of a small waterfall. Class demo, 3 x 4 in (7.62 x 10.16 cm).

The Value of Value Studies

I learned very early how important it is for a two-dimensional artist to understand value and shading. "Value" is the level of lightness or darkness of a color. It is essential for depicting three-dimensional objects.

Our eyes are capable of detecting a great deal of detail. An artist uses value studies to simplify the visual cacophony to its essence. Reducing the range to three or four values is sufficient for this type of sketch.

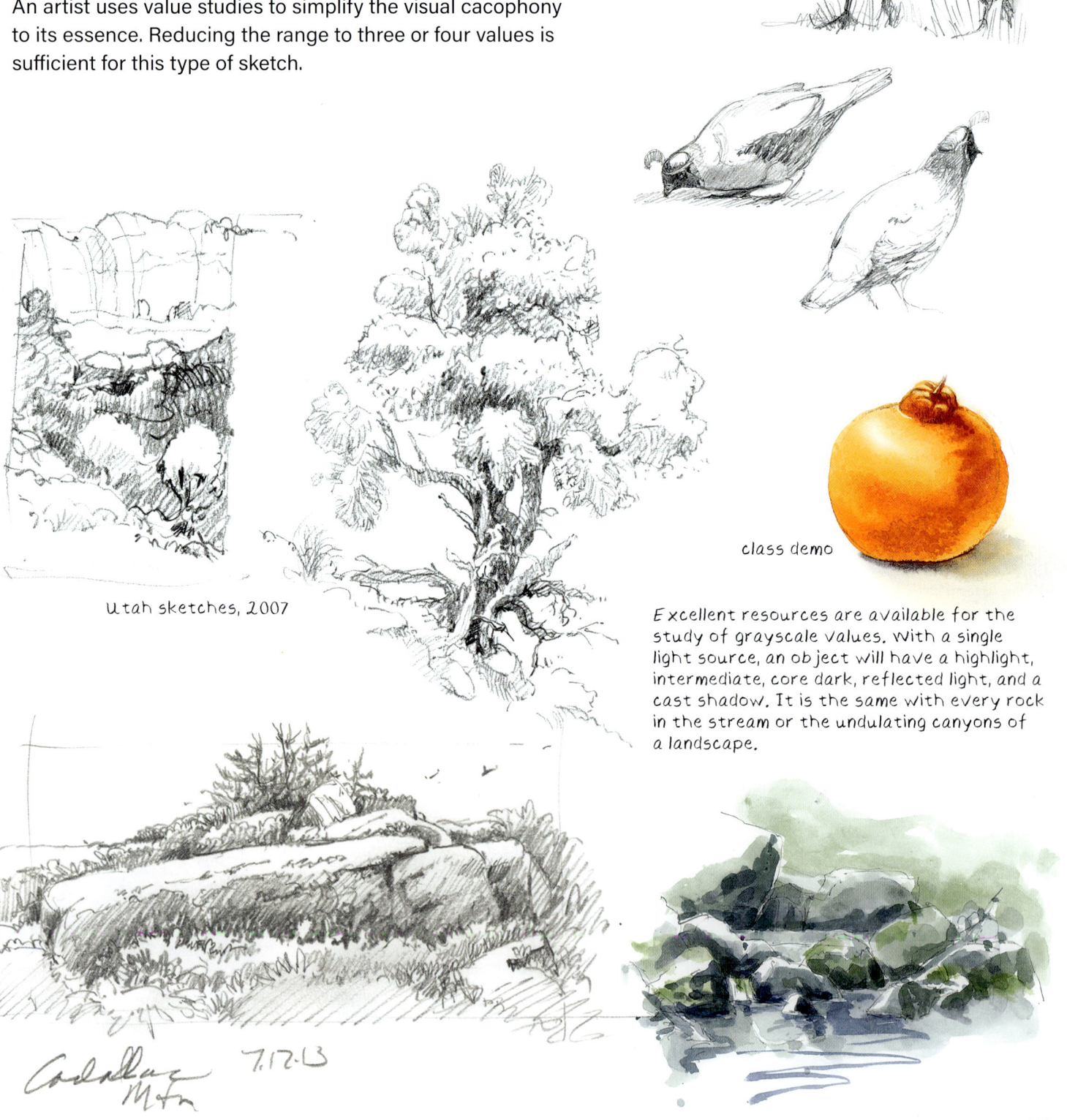

Utah sketches, 2007

class demo

Excellent resources are available for the study of grayscale values. With a single light source, an object will have a highlight, intermediate, core dark, reflected light, and a cast shadow. It is the same with every rock in the stream or the undulating canyons of a landscape.

Cadillac Mtn   7.12.13

Ramsey Canyon class demo, 2020

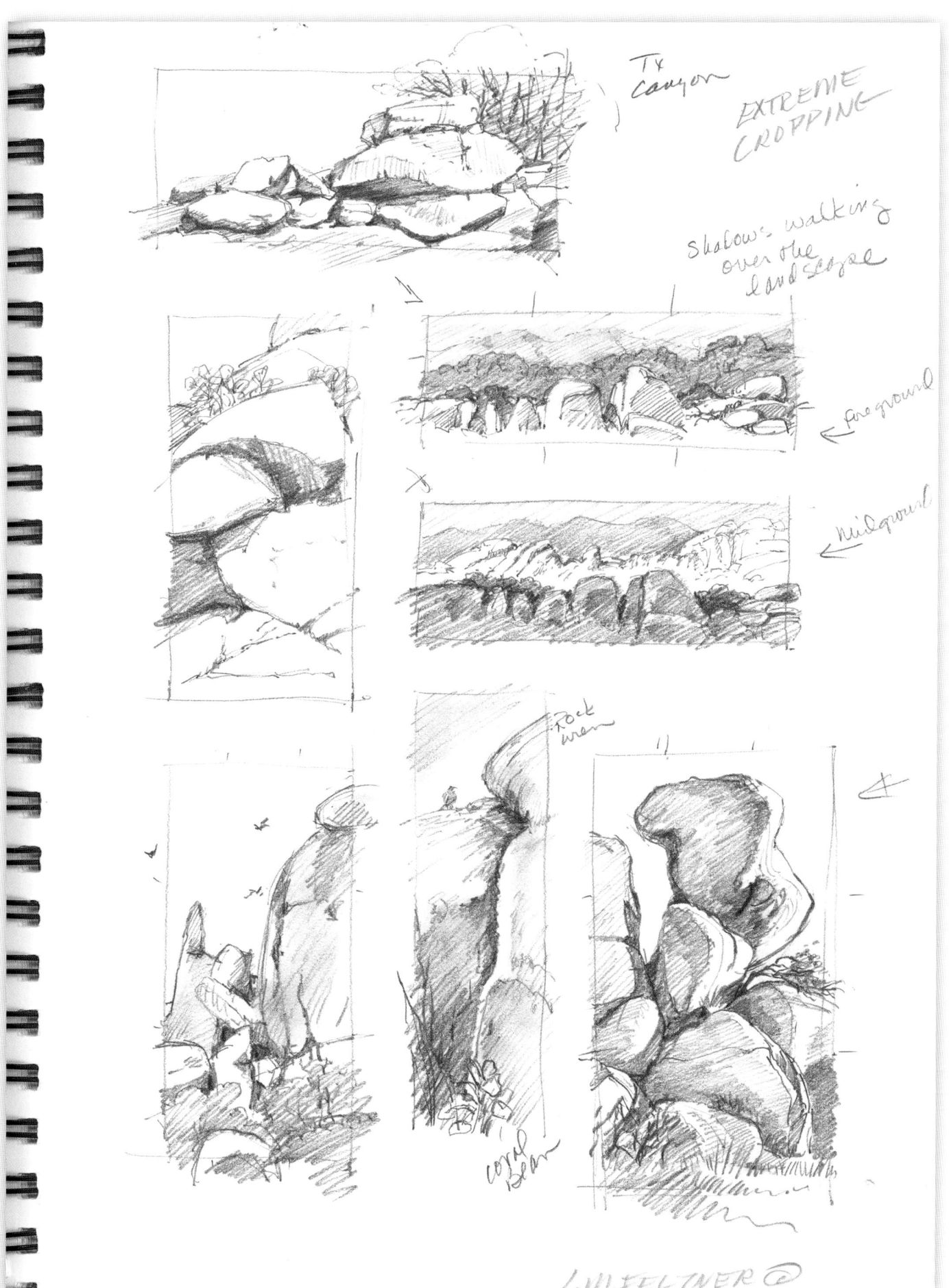

Tx
Canyon

EXTREME
CROPPING

Shadows walking
over the
landscape

←foreground

←midground

Rock
wren

coral
bean

L.M.FELTNER ©

The Power of Cropping

Many students are focused on the exquisite execution of fur, feathers, or landscapes. As a tool to improve composition, cropping is often not considered as valuable as the drawing or painting technique.

Cropping the design maximizes the focus on what the artist wants the viewer to see. It sets the stage for the presentation.

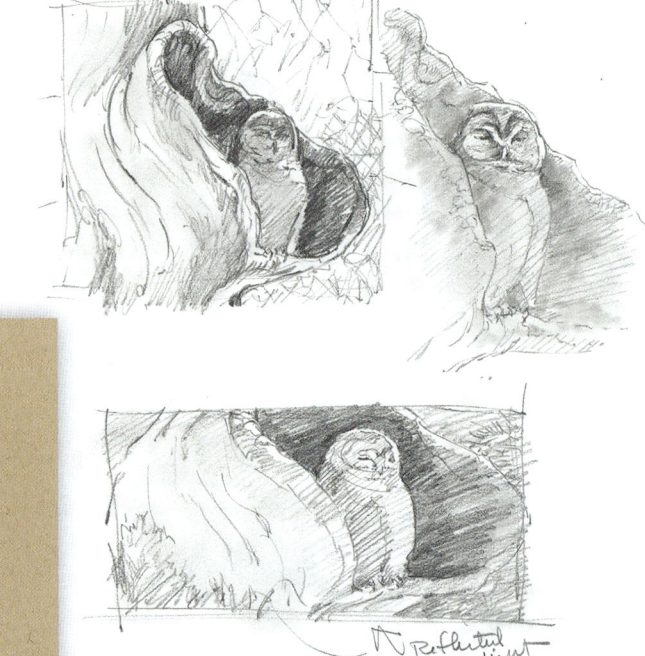

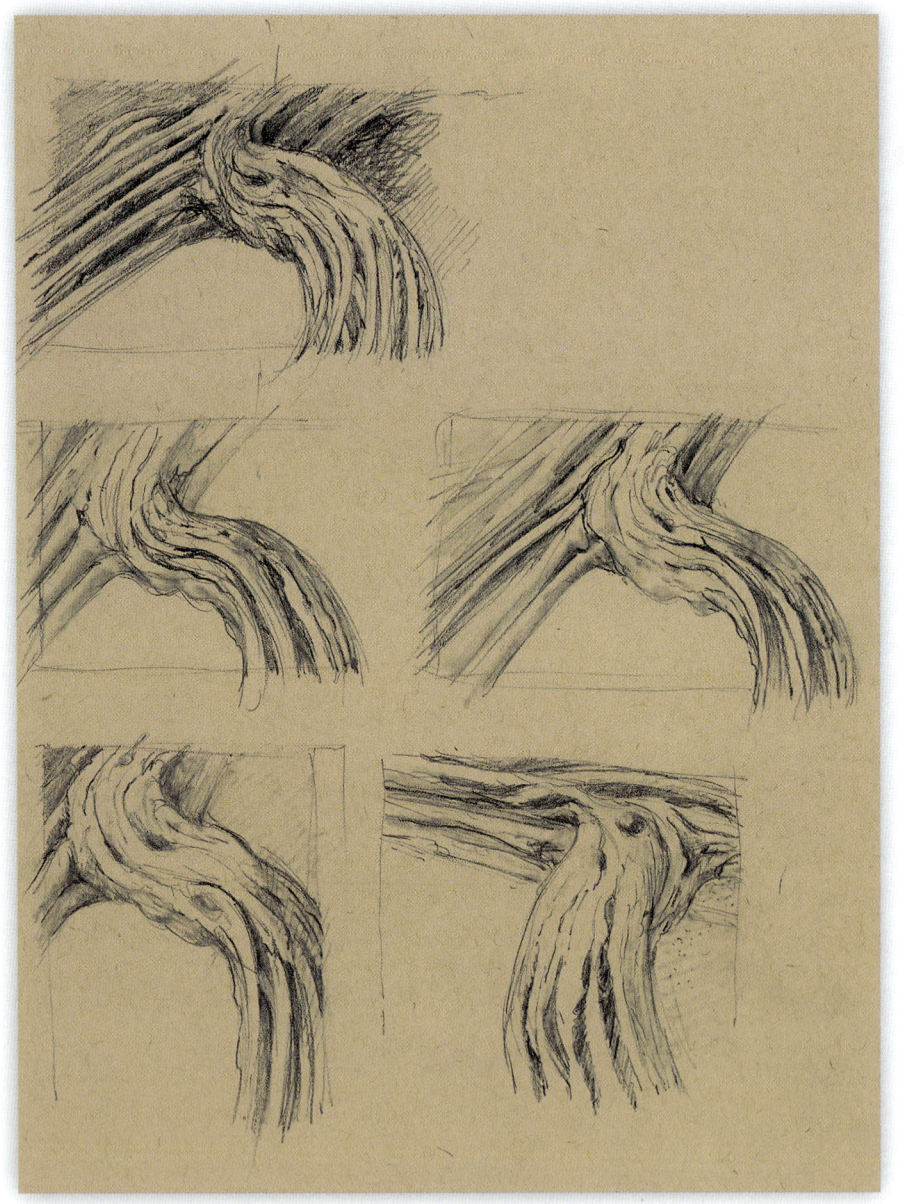

A Mexican Spotted Owl (*Strix occidentalis lucida*) rests in a well-known roost in the broken limb cavity of an Arizona Sycamore (*Platanus wrightii*). Many cropping possibilities focus our attention while adding intriguing elements to the subject's surroundings.

A "skeleton" of a Saguaro cactus (*Carnegiea gigantea*) lying on the ground in the desert. Where would you place an animal or flowering cactus for the strongest composition?

Never underestimate what good composition can do for the impact of a well-executed technique.

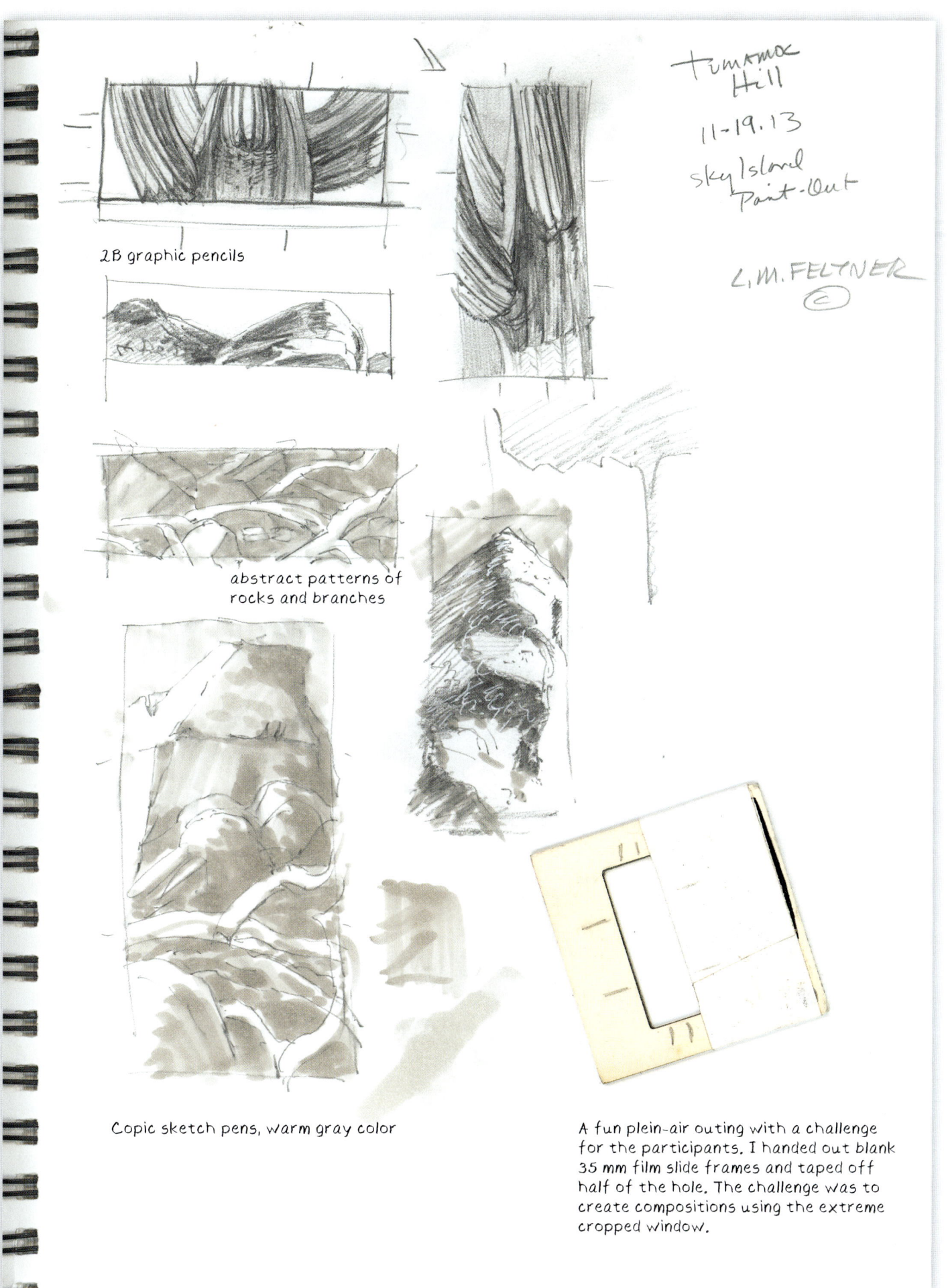

Tumamox
Hill
11-19-13
Sky Island
Paint-Out

L.M. FELTNER ©

2B graphic pencils

abstract patterns of
rocks and branches

Copic sketch pens, warm gray color

A fun plein-air outing with a challenge
for the participants. I handed out blank
35 mm film slide frames and taped off
half of the hole. The challenge was to
create compositions using the extreme
cropped window.

"Texas Canyon Wren"

I love rocks. The abstract nature of cracks, lichen, and overlapping limbs have become essential to my paintings. An unusual rocky landscape in the Little Dragoon Mountains of Arizona intrigues many artists. Texas Canyon displays prominent and curious geological formations: the rocks formed from magma that never made it to the surface. It cooled 50 million years ago, long after dinosaurs became extinct. Natural weathering has left distinctive pedestals and balanced boulders exposed. On my visit, dawn light accentuated the sculpted shapes while their ochre colors glowed. The dramatic spires and pedestals dwarfed the tiny Canyon Wren, whose song echoed from a hidden crevice. My painting shows powerful rock forms accented by the smallest bird I've painted as its shape and shadow fly against the balanced boulders.

Canyon Wren (*Catherpes mexicanus*)

Texas Canyon Wren, 9.75 × 16 in (24.76 × 40.64 cm), gouache on black museum board.

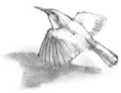

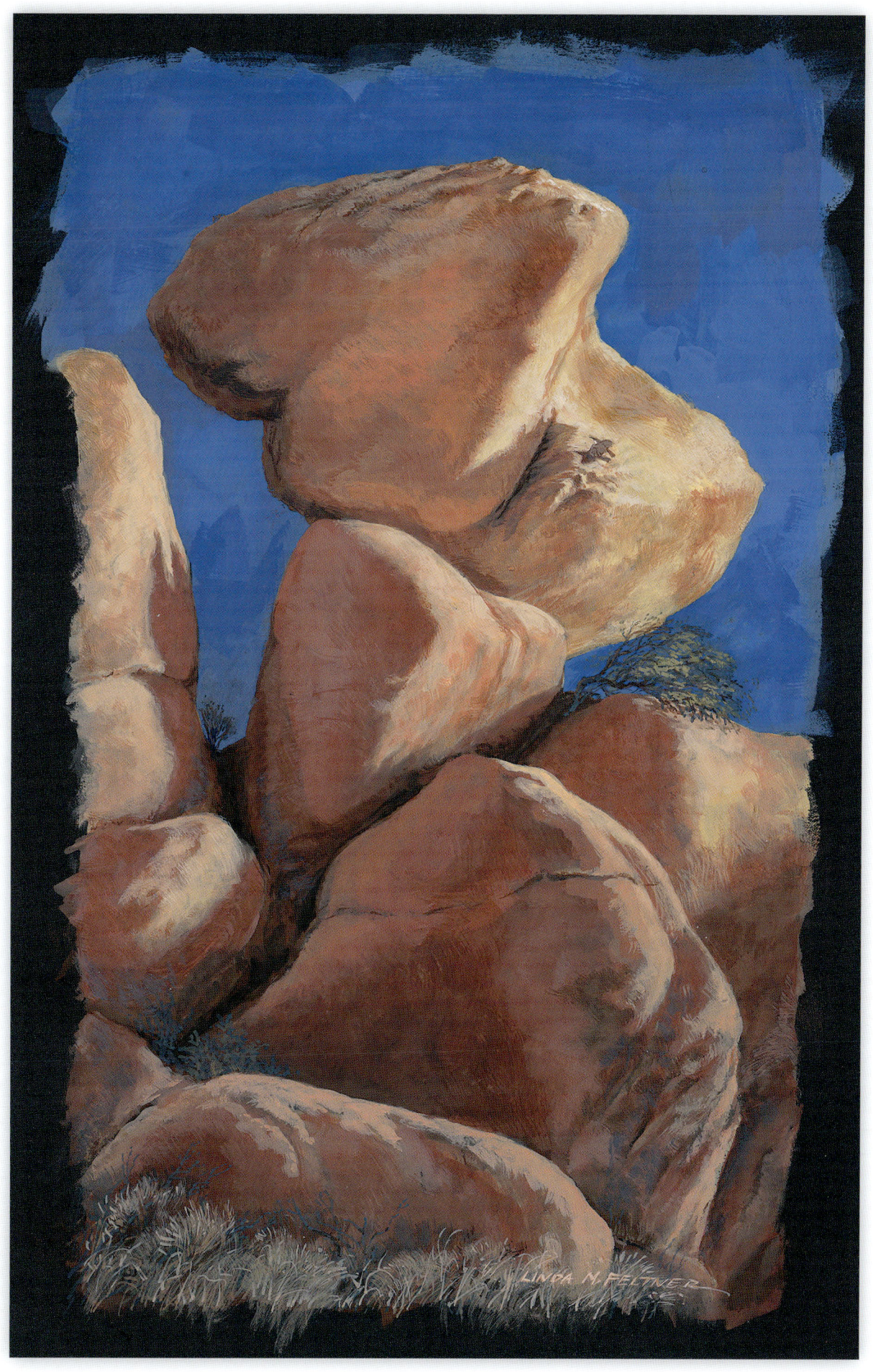

Visual Movement: Action and Stability

The artist controls eye movement through the image by deliberately applying elements for movement and energy. Using design elements and often geometry, the image can evoke emotions ranging from tension to serenity. For centuries, artists have employed various strategies to reveal a story.

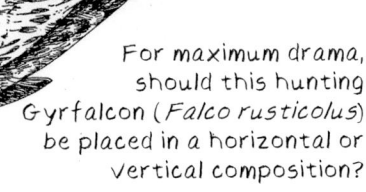

For maximum drama, should this hunting Gyrfalcon (*Falco rusticolus*) be placed in a horizontal or vertical composition?

Consider:

- What impact do angles have on our perception of action?
- Do some angles work better than others?
- Can the edges of two values have the same effect as a drawn line?
- What is suggested when a round shape is pressed near a flat shape or an edge?

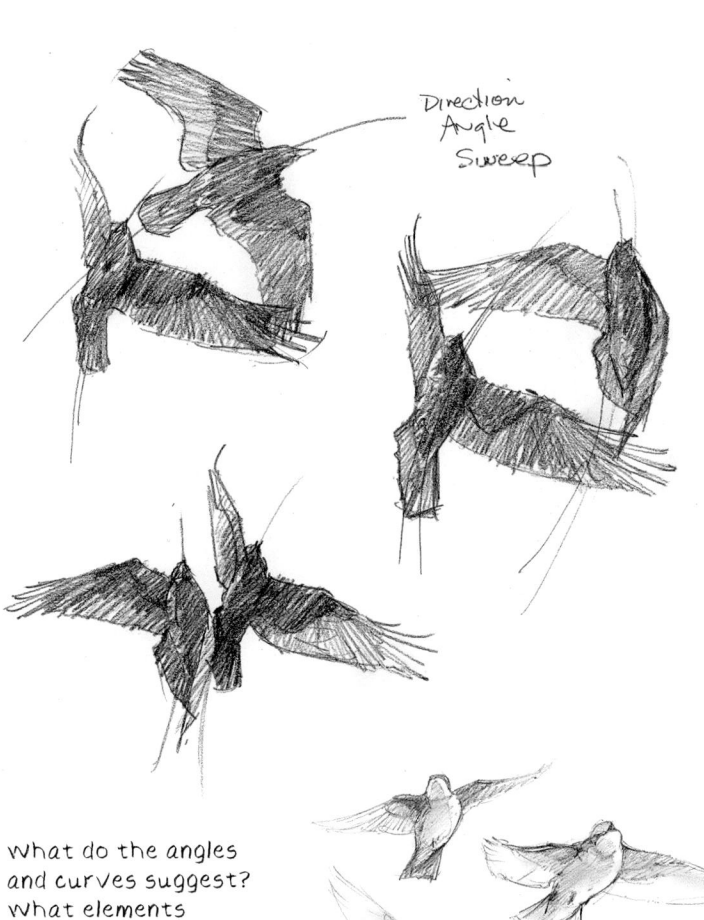

Direction
Angle
Sweep

What do the angles and curves suggest? What elements suggest buoyancy?

I made quick sketches of flying swallows while considering the flight of small, migrating birds.

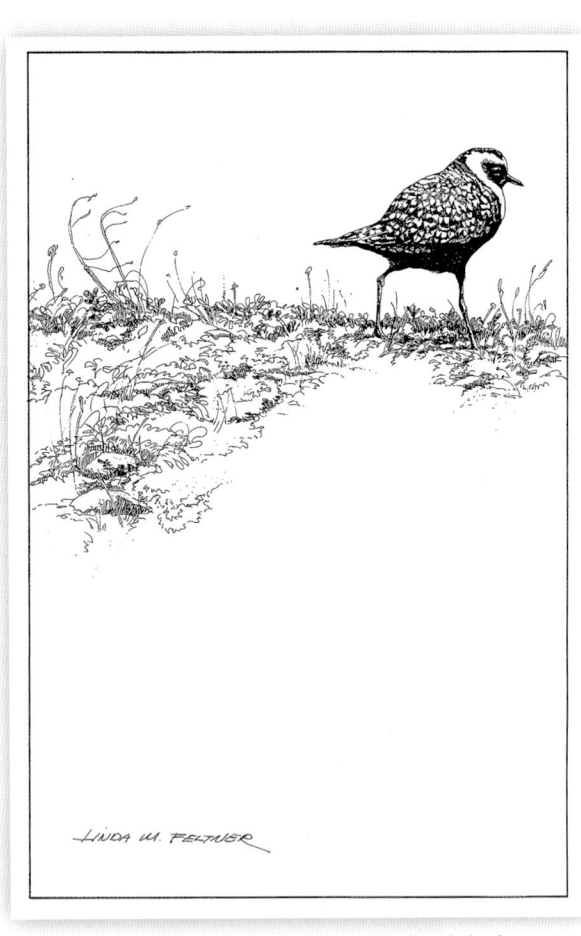

American Golden Plover (*Pluvialis dominica*), Churchill, Manitoba, Canada, from Noel Pettingell and David M. Mark, *The Pettingell Book of Birding Records* (Austin, TX: The American Birding Association, 1986).

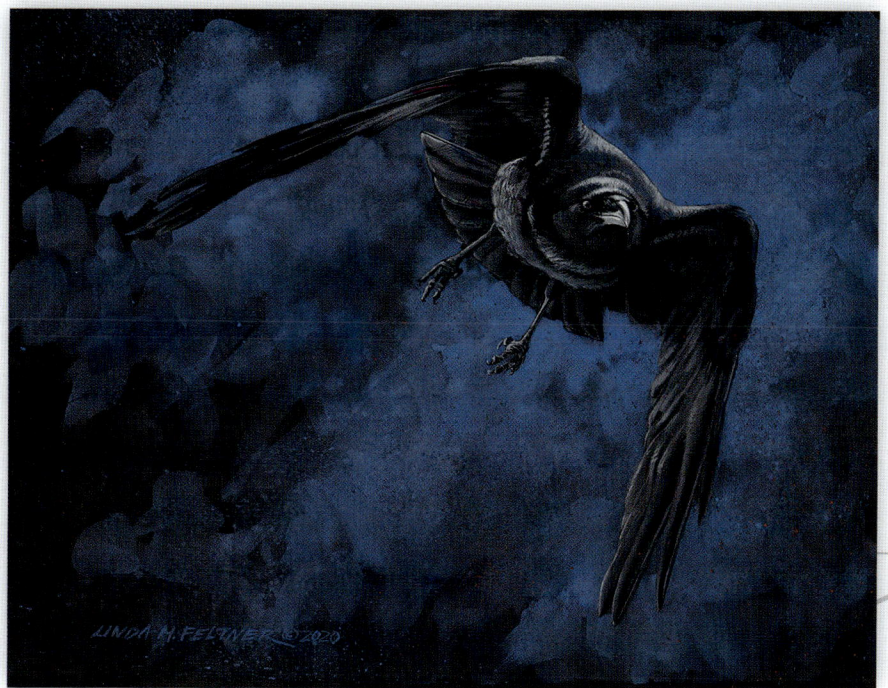

Raven Resolve, 8 × 10 in (20.32 × 25.4 cm), gouache on black museum board.

Art and design education often teach centuries-old definitions of good design. Students may encounter the "Golden Mean," "Fibonacci Spiral," and "Rule of Thirds." Many artists accept that information and it subconsciously guides their decisions. Self-taught artists establish pleasing compositions through experience, reaching similar conclusions.

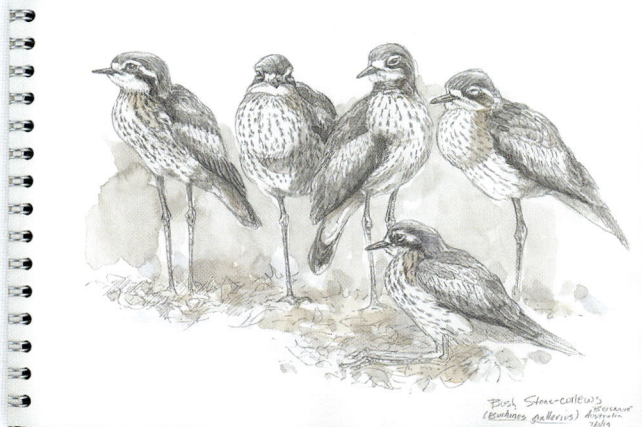

The horizontal ground plane and repetitive horizontal shapes imply stability. What about an ocean-going bird? The horizon line reinforces the angle of the body's axis.

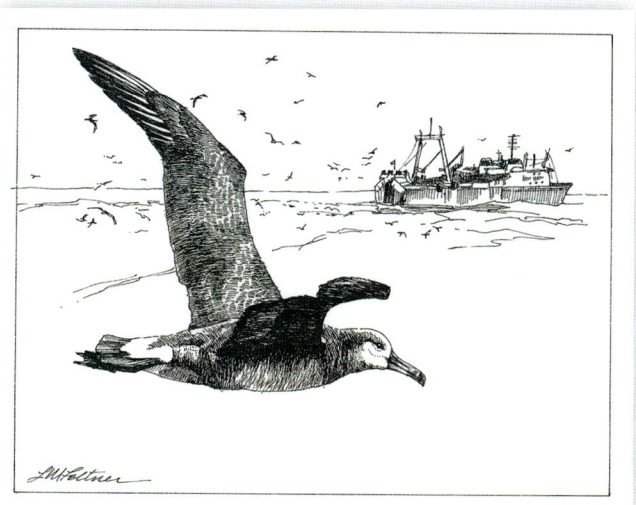

Black-footed Albatross (*Phoebastria nigripes*), from David M. Mark, *Where to Find Birds in British Columbia* (New Westminster, BC, Canada: Kestrel Press, 1984).

Math is Creative ...

I use math in art every day. An understanding of shapes, patterns, symmetry, and geometry underlies an aesthetic balance. The use of proportion, measurement, and linear perspective makes art more realistic.

Observe any type of art form. Mathematical relationships are present in dance, music, sculpture, architecture, textiles, and painting.

From Stonehenge or the Aztec Calendar to computer art, geometry and symmetry have been paramount in creative endeavors. Recent analysis demonstrates how some of my favorite artists through the ages used fractals, tessellations, geometrics, and kineticism.

Drawing a Breath of Fresh Air

Step outside, mosey along a trail, breathe deeply, and enjoy sketching. I find comfort and calm in outdoor sketching. Whether it is a quick sketch or a detailed study, the inspiration is always there. I used to carry a large sketchbook in a backpack. Forcing myself to travel lighter with only a pocket-sized book, I adapted to a 5 × 8 in (12.7 × 20.32 cm) book with watercolor paper. It proved to work well with my painting style and note-taking.

I may always search for the perfect sketchbook. Perhaps this is simply a desire to try more art supplies! But like any tool, a sketchbook is personal. Preferences include quality, paper type, weight, and size for comfortable drawing. For me, the paper should take watercolor, ink, and pencil, a practical surface for whatever variety of tools is found in my vest pockets. I have found some practical sketchbooks through the generosity of sketchbook distributors.

One way to learn if you like a paper is to try the same scene and medium in each book.

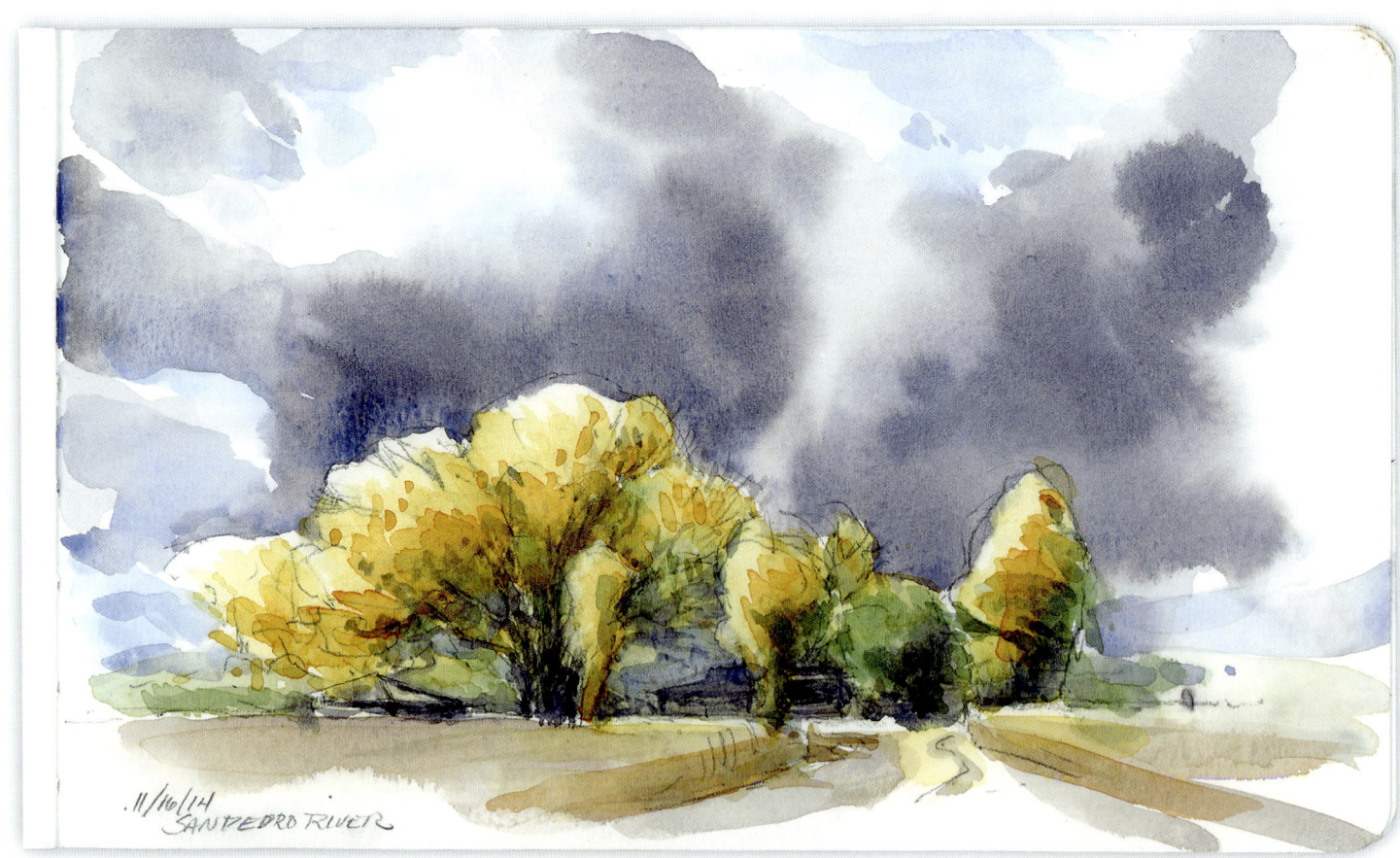

.11/16/14 SAN PEDRO RIVER

San Pedro House, Sierra Vista, Arizona, 5 x 8 in (12.5 x 20.3 cm), watercolor on 100 lb (200 gsm) Moleskine watercolor paper.

These three examples are on heavier watercolor and sketch paper. I used juicy washes, a typical technique for traditional handmade watercolor paper. The same palette with similar loads of water and saturated color were used on all three. It proved to be a fun experiment.

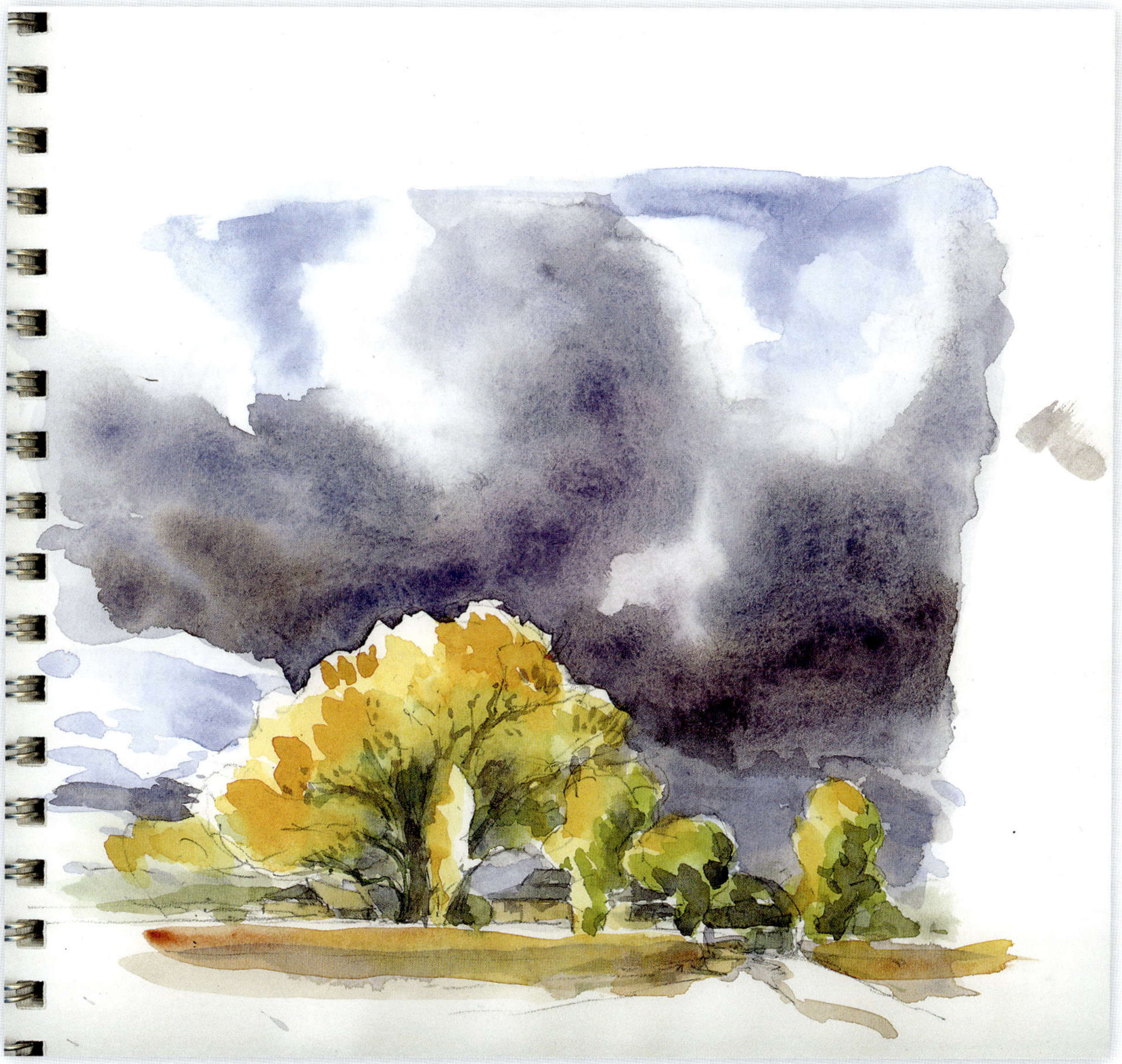

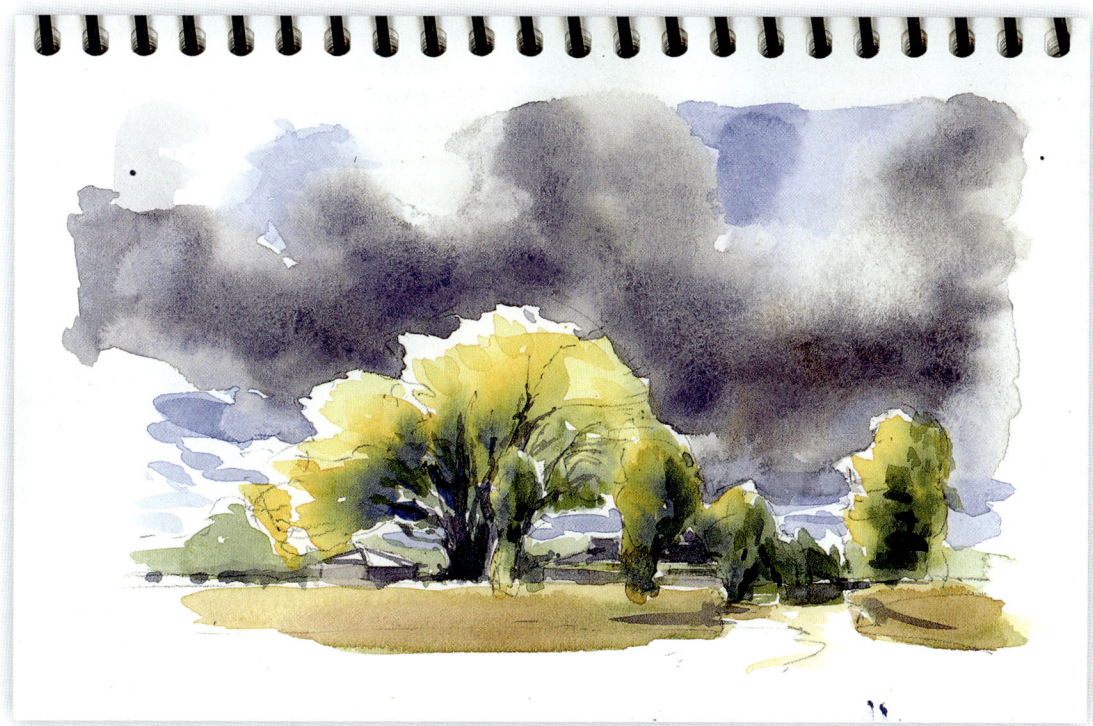

9 x 9 in (22.86 x
22.86 cm), watercolor on
93 lb (150 gsm) Aquabee
heavyweight drawing
paper, super deluxe.

9 x 6 in (22.86 x 15.24 cm),
watercolor on 130 lb
(212 gsm) Pentalic
nature sketch,
heavyweight natural
white drawing paper.

Field Notes

Leonardo da Vinci took notebooks outdoors, drawing from life as he encountered it. The artist J.M.W. Turner carried custom notebooks and a portable painting kit, creating over thirty thousand watercolors throughout his travels. Today, plein-air painting and sketching have given us the freedom to spend minutes or hours in outdoor creative endeavors.

For those who prefer to carry less weight, a small notebook and fewer tools is sufficient to satisfy the need to record whatever catches your eye. A minimum tool kit in my pockets has a small sketchbook, a permanent ink pen, a 2B mechanical pencil, a black watercolor pencil, and a water brush. I often add a few colored watercolor pencils or a small folding tin of watercolor pans. Many artists have cleverly made tiny kits that suit their needs. Other times may call for a bulkier outfit with a pochade box, a full palette, and a folding chair. Find your personal choice for your outdoor adventures.

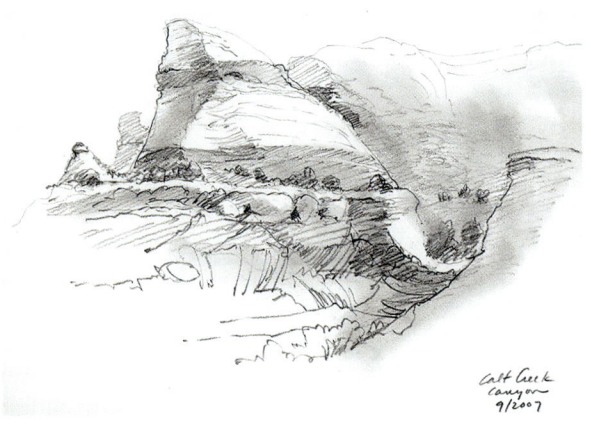

Calf Creek Canyon
9/2007

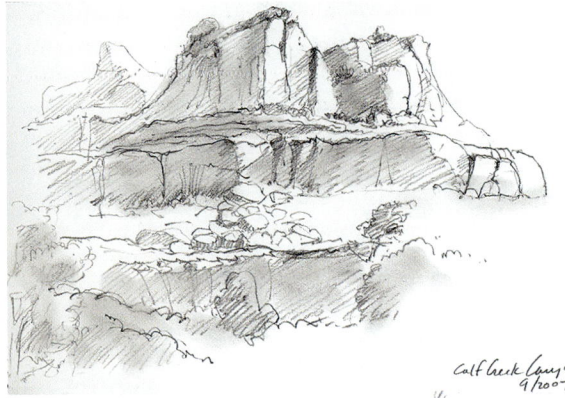

Calf Creek Canyon
9/2007

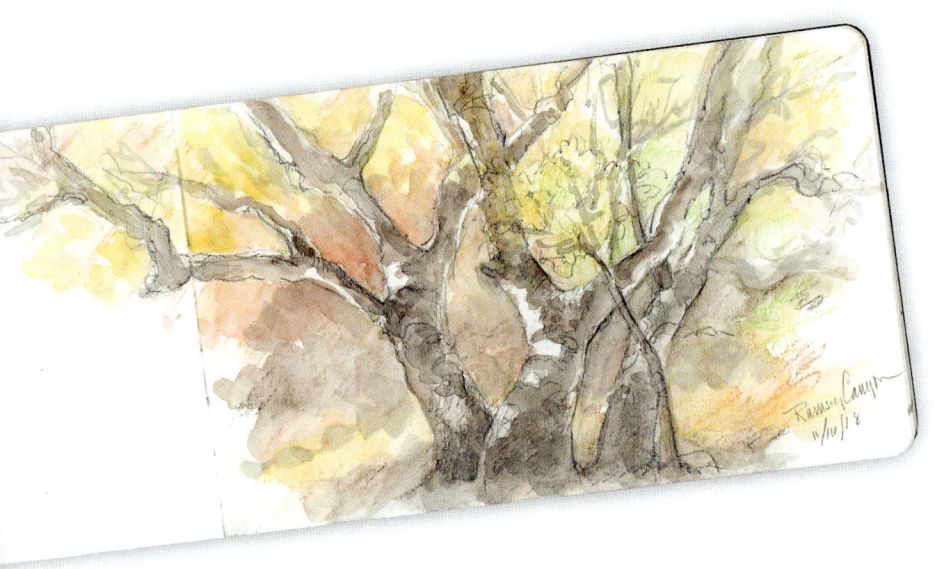

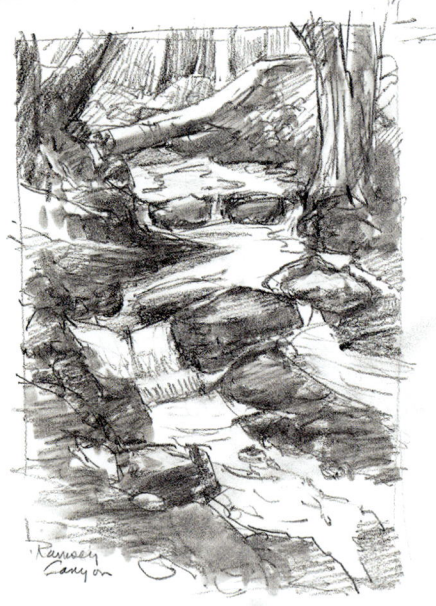

Ramsey Canyon

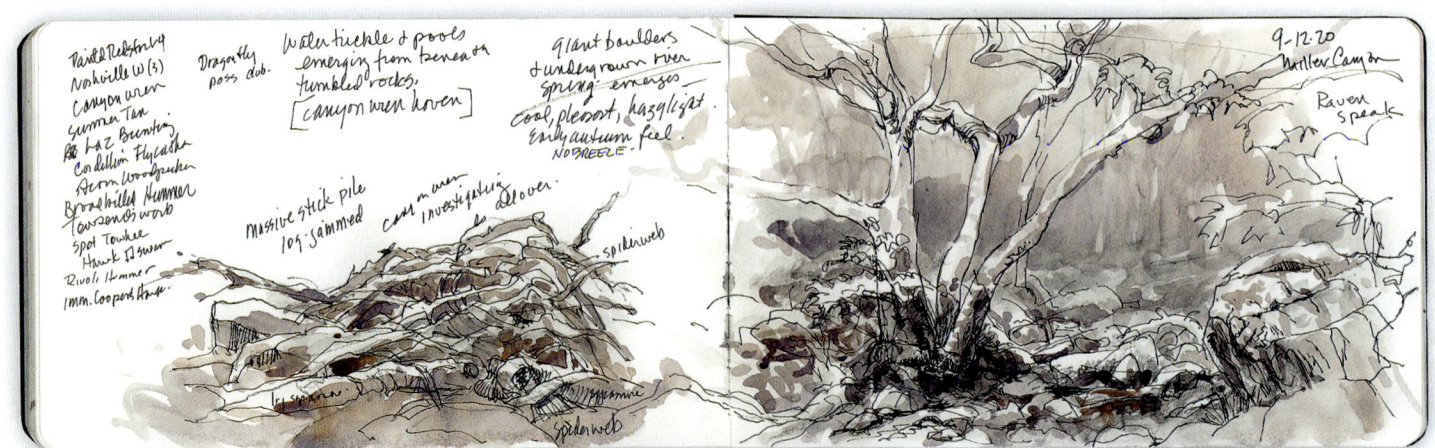

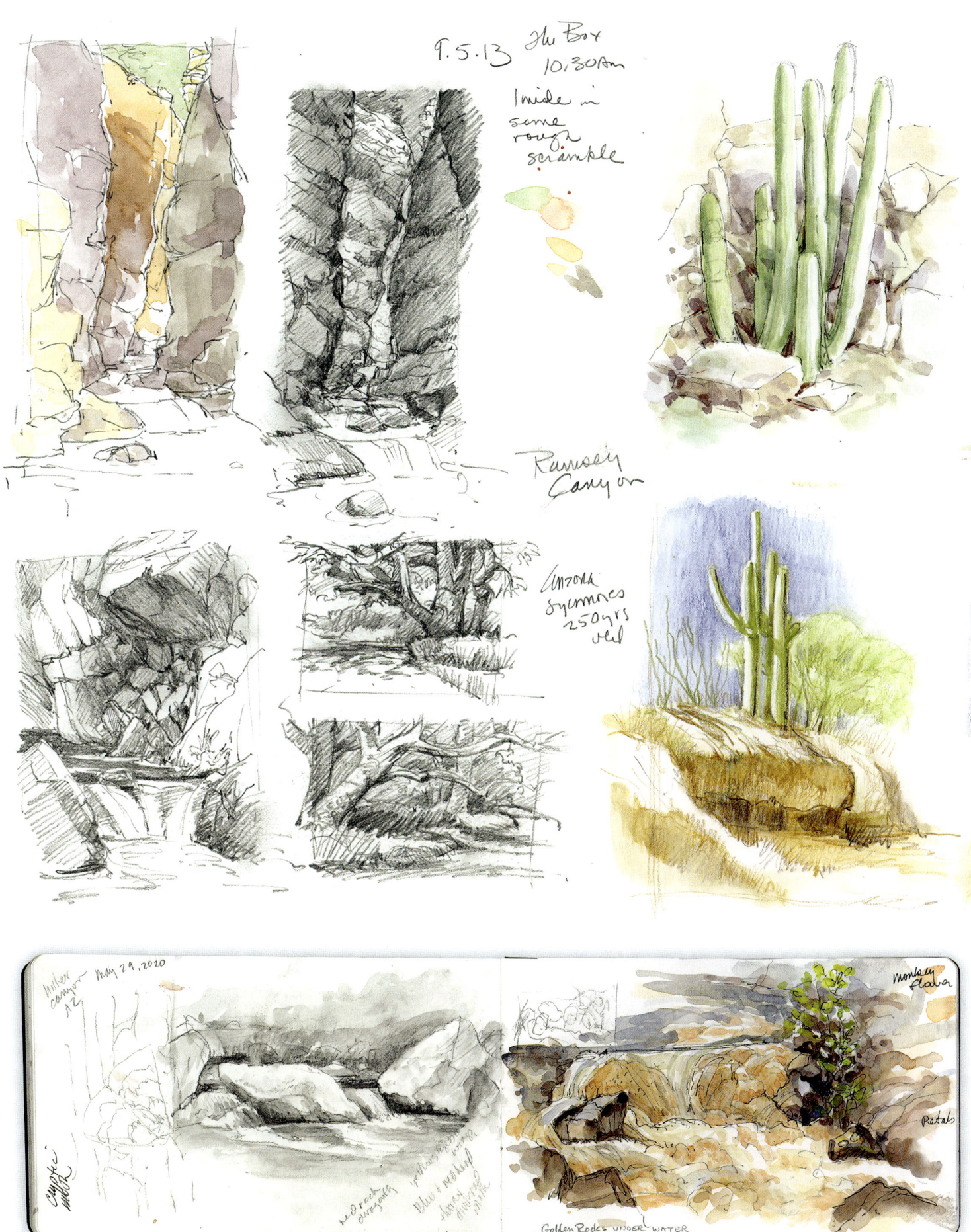

9.5.13 The Box
10:30 Am

Inside in
some
rough
scramble

Ramsey
Canyon

Arizona
sycamores
250 yrs
old

Wilson canyon AZ May 29, 2020

Golden Rocks under water

Monkey flower

Petals

Capturing the Moment

A sketchbook, notebook, or journal allows the pleasure of observation that does not have to be turned into a finished painting. You can either share your drawings with others or keep them private while preserving your personal experience.

If outdoors, noting the date, place, and weather will be helpful later to enhance the memory of the occasion. Add any pertinent comment that is meaningful. Was it windy, foggy, or full of blazing sun? The notebook is what you want it to be.

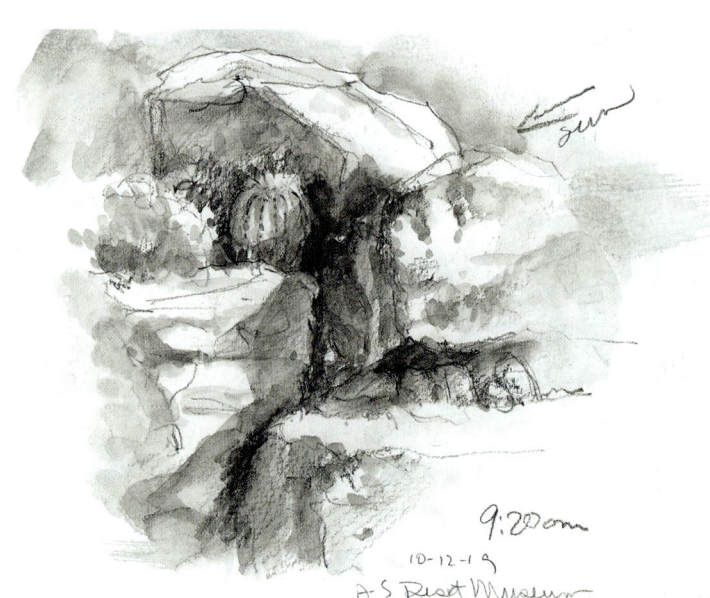

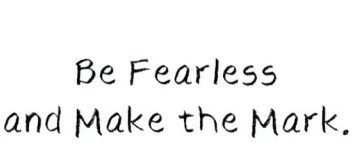

Be Fearless
and Make the Mark.

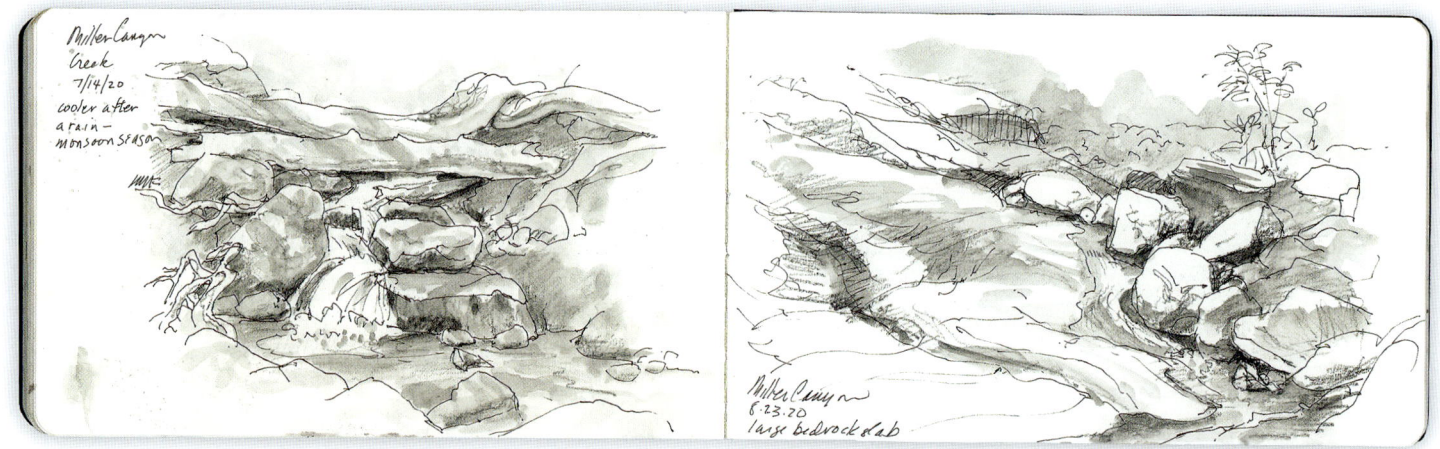

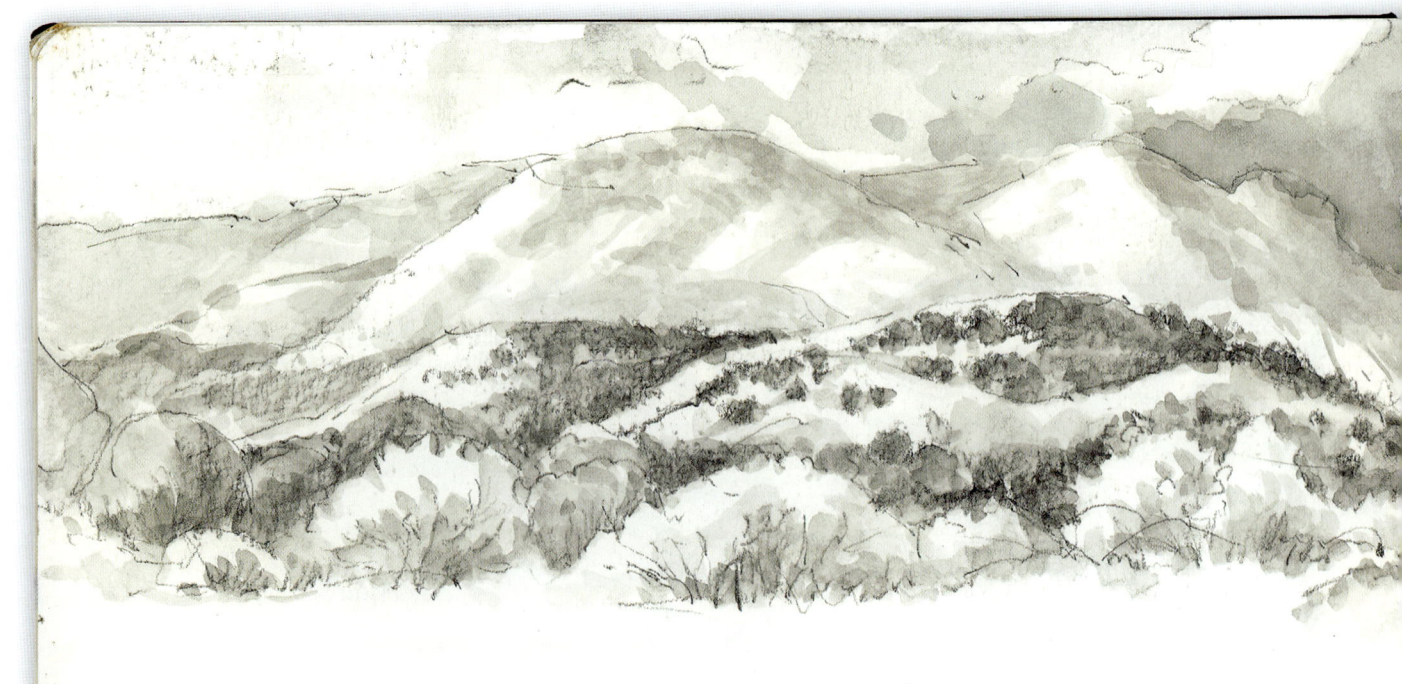

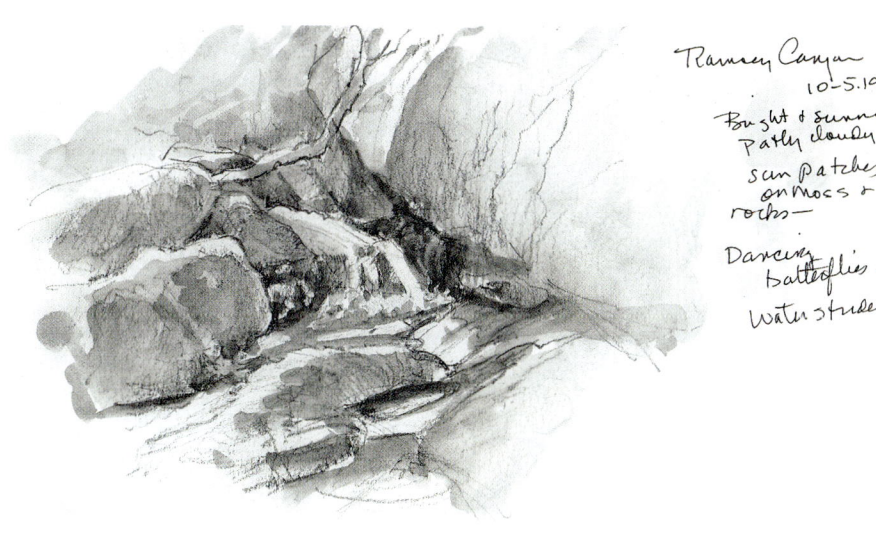

Ramsey Canyon
10-5-19
Bright & Sunny &
Partly cloudy
sun patches
on moss &
rocks—

Dancing
butterflies—

Water striders

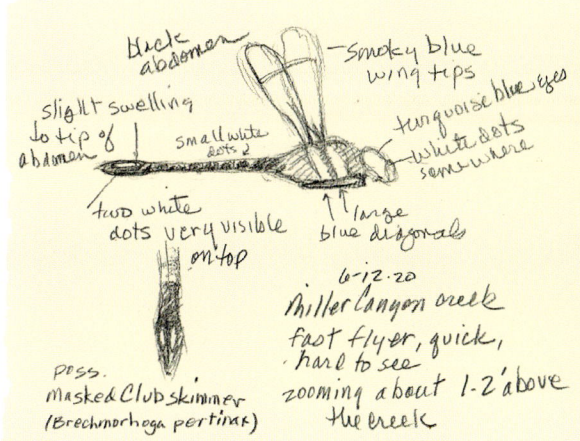

thick
abdomen
—smoky blue
wing tips
slight swelling
to tip of
abdomen
small white
dots?
turquoise blue eyes
white dots
some where
two white
dots very visible
on top
large
blue diagonals

poss.
Masked Club skimmer
(Brechmorhoga pertinax)

6-12-20
Miller Canyon creek
fast flyer, quick,
hard to see
zooming about 1-2' above
the creek

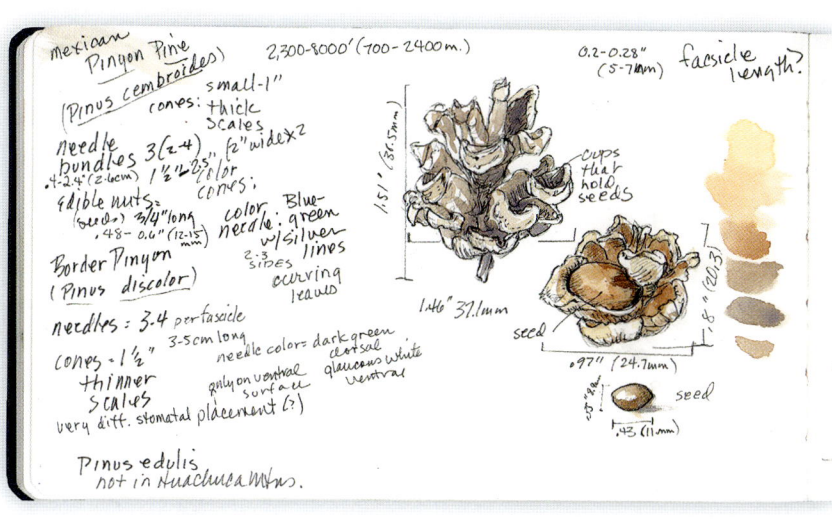

Mexican
Pinyon Pine)
(Pinus cembroides)   2,300-8000' (700-2400 m.)

cones: small-1"
thick
scales
needle
bundles 3(2-4), 1/2" wide x 2
.4-2.4" (2-6cm) 1 1/2"-2.3"
color:
edible nuts=
(seeds) 3/4" long cones:
.48 - 0.6" (12-15 color: Blue-
mm) needle: green
w/silver
Border Pinyon 2-3 sides lines
(Pinus discolor) curving
leaves
needles: 3-4 per fascicle
3-5cm long
cones = 1 1/2" needle color= dark green
thinner dorsal
scales only on ventral glaucous white
surface ventral
very diff. stomatal placement (?)

Pinus edulis
not in Huachuca Mtns.

0.2-0.28"
(5-7mm) fascicle
length?

1.51" (38.5mm)
1.46" 37.1mm
cups
that
hold
seeds
seed
.97" (24.7mm)

1.8" (203)
15.5 cm

seed
.43, (11mm)

Oct 26.20 Ramsey Canyon
Preserve
possible puma poop? full of hair

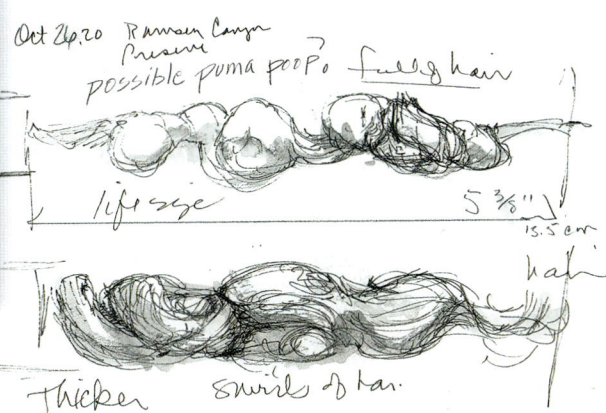

life size 5 3/8"
15.5 cm
hair
Thicker swirls of hair.

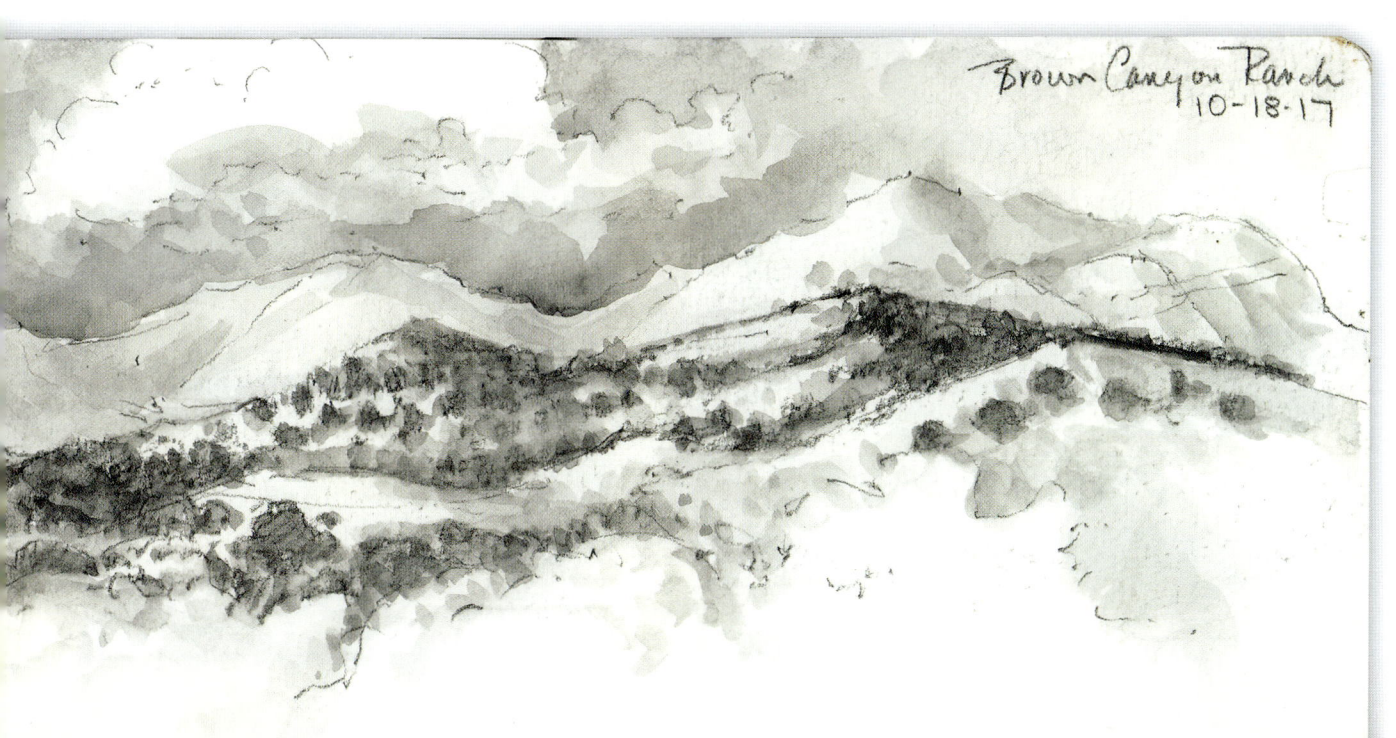

Brown Canyon Ranch
10-18-17

Familiar Places

Visiting the same area throughout the seasons yields new insights with each visit. Leafless trees provide a different view than the same scene with full, green boughs. A carpet of autumn leaves presents a palette of color not found in spring.

In Ramsey Canyon Preserve, the Arizona Sycamore trees are historically famous. Their spectacular sinuous shapes are white against a deep winter sky and a background of dark evergreen hillsides.

A young lad, walking in the winter canyons, once remarked that the sycamores, without leaves, looked like upside-down lightning. Now, I cannot walk these canyons without thinking the same. Encouraging young people to experience the outdoors can open our eyes as well.

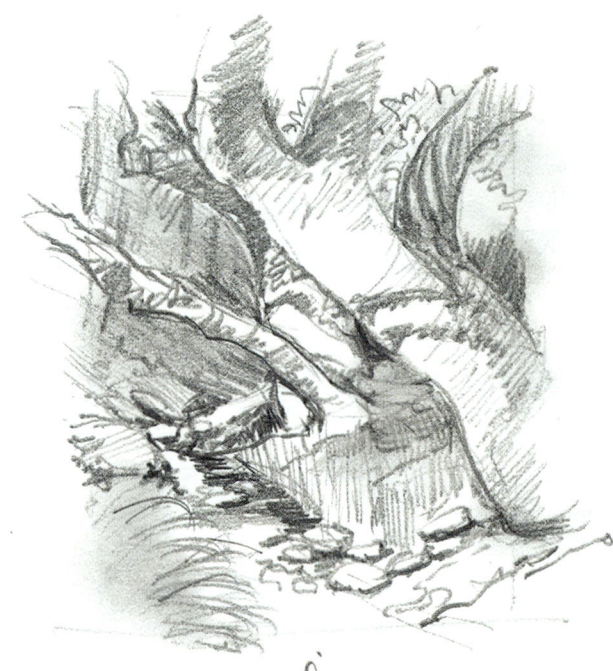

Ramsey canyon cont'd
AZ sycamores

Chaotic forest details are simplified in thumbnails that capture the essential elements of the scene.

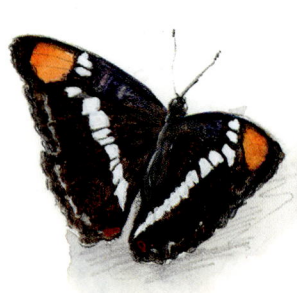

Sun through dappled leaves

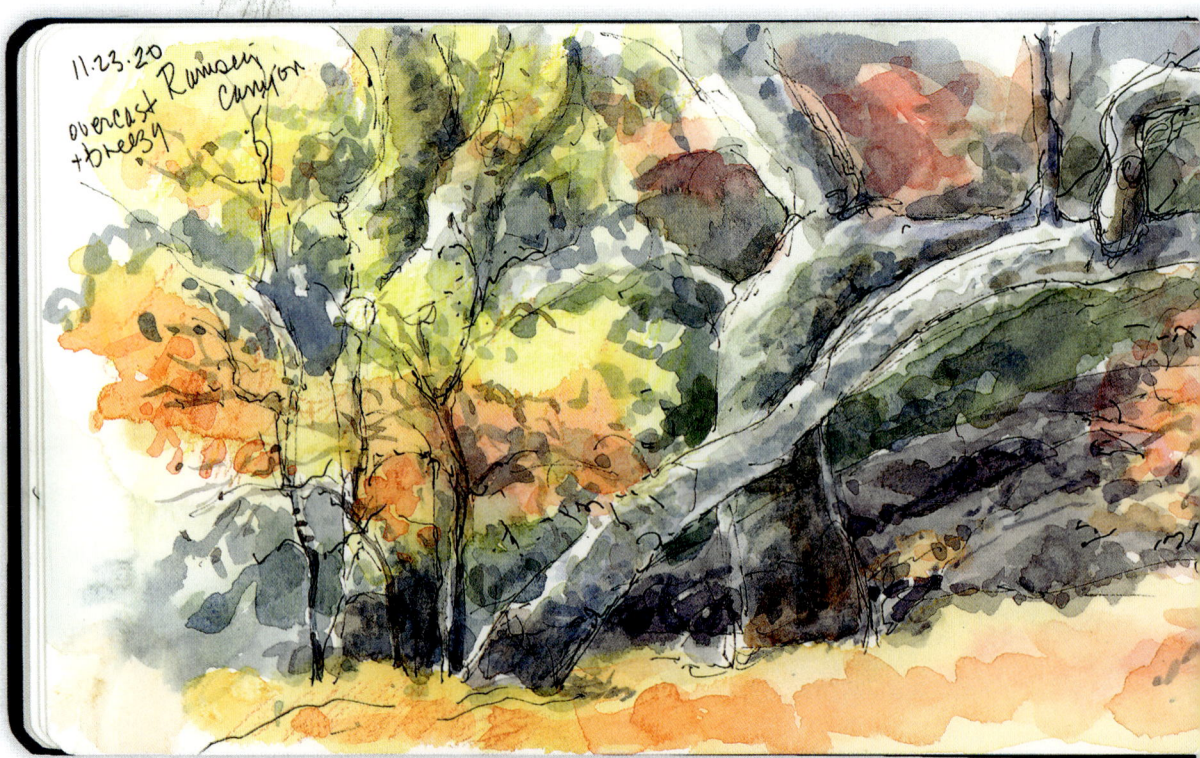

11.23.20 Ramsey Canyon
overcast + breezy

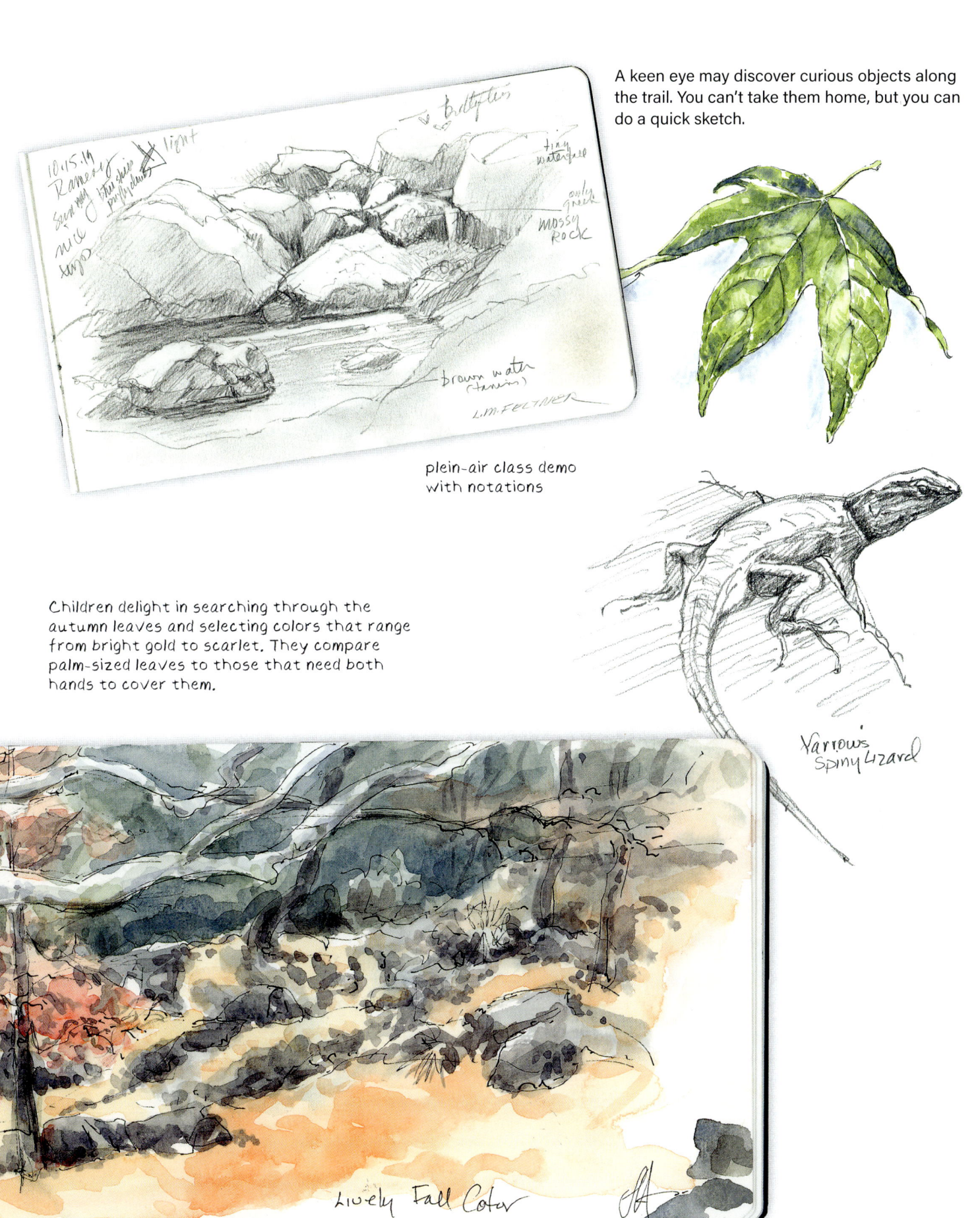

A keen eye may discover curious objects along the trail. You can't take them home, but you can do a quick sketch.

plein-air class demo
with notations

Children delight in searching through the autumn leaves and selecting colors that range from bright gold to scarlet. They compare palm-sized leaves to those that need both hands to cover them.

Yarrow's Spiny Lizard

Lively Fall Color

Familiar Places Spark New Ideas

Look at a familiar scene with a fresh eye and possibilities will open for new angles, colors, or viewpoints. Knowing I am likely to return eliminates pressure to make the one perfect painting. I become comfortable and ideas both big and small emerge.

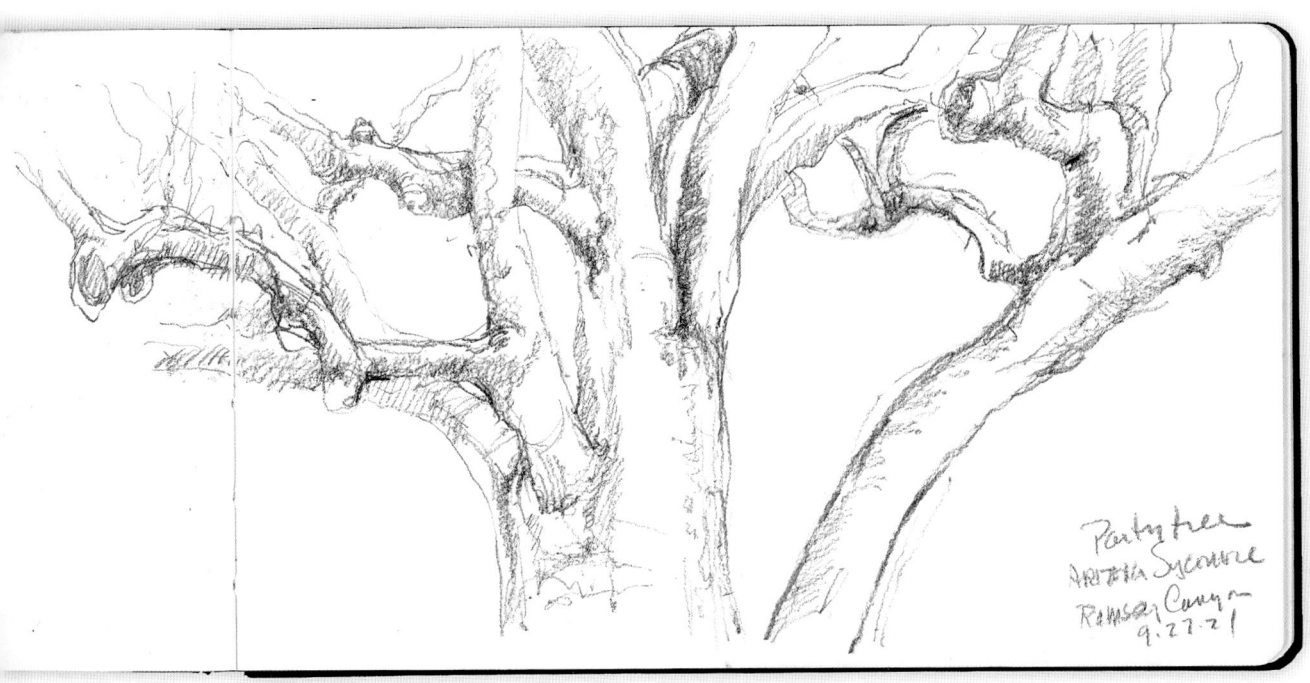

The Ramsey Canyon 250-year-old "Party Tree." Arizona Sycamores are magnificent to draw.

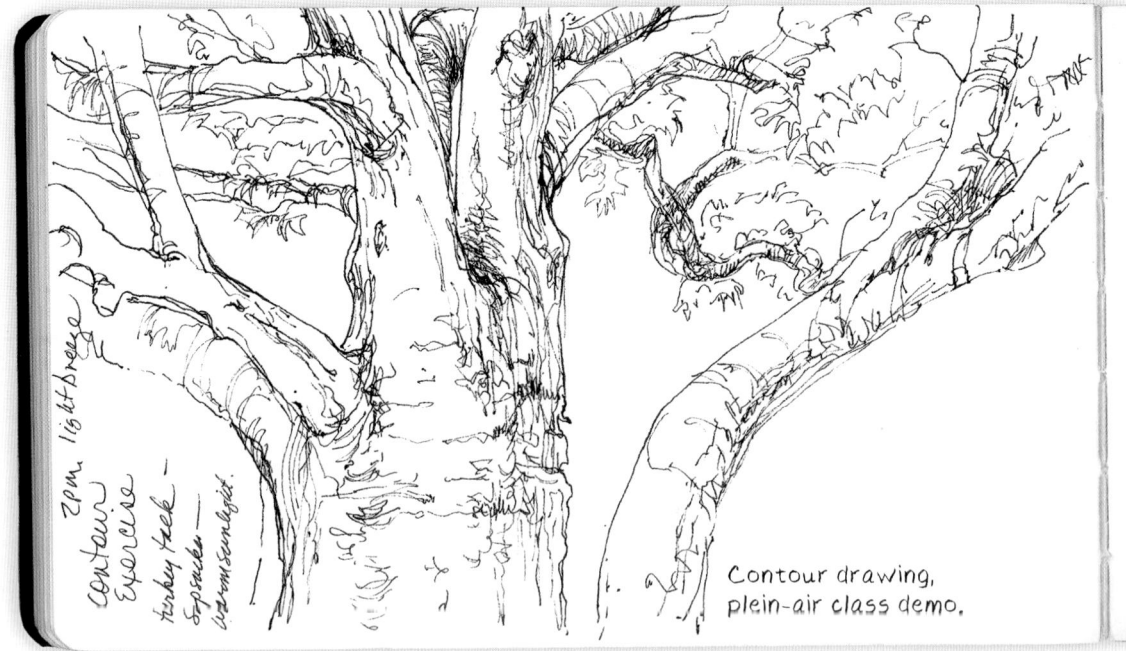

Contour drawing, plein-air class demo.

Experiment with new media on familiar subjects. Pull out the odd scraps and see what happens. It may surprise you!

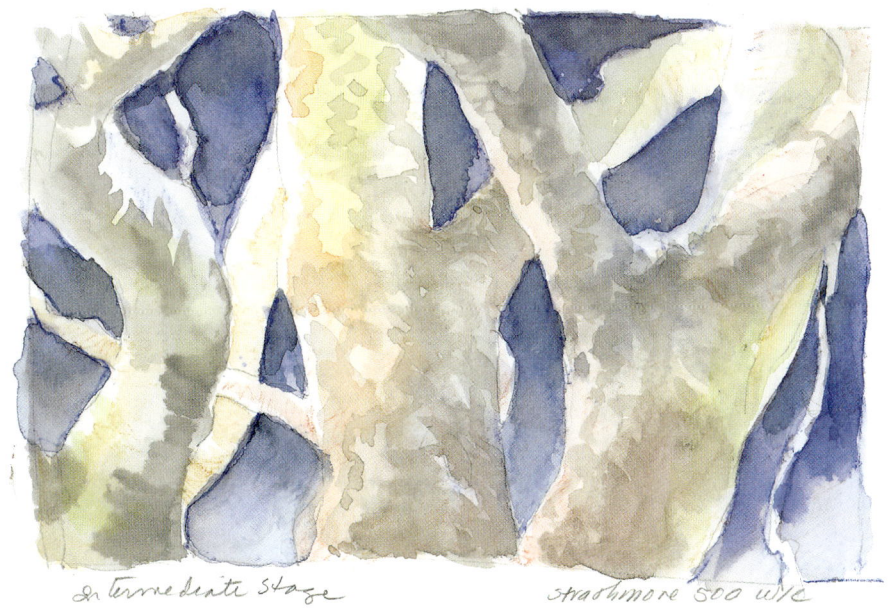

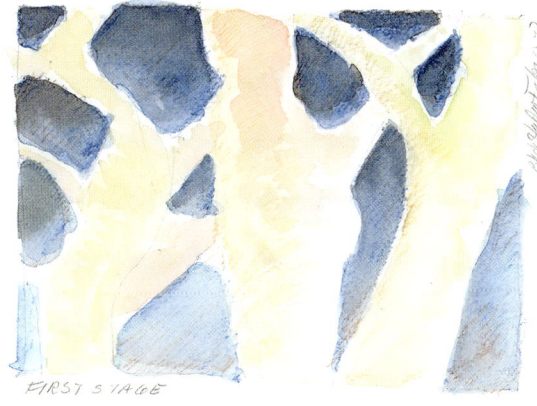

FIRST STAGE

Intermediate Stage   *strathmore 500 W/C*

These four images are experiments using different paper brands and surfaces.

Watercolor pencils have the advantage of serving double duty in the travel kit. When used dry, they are like colored pencils. Brush on water, and they become watercolor!

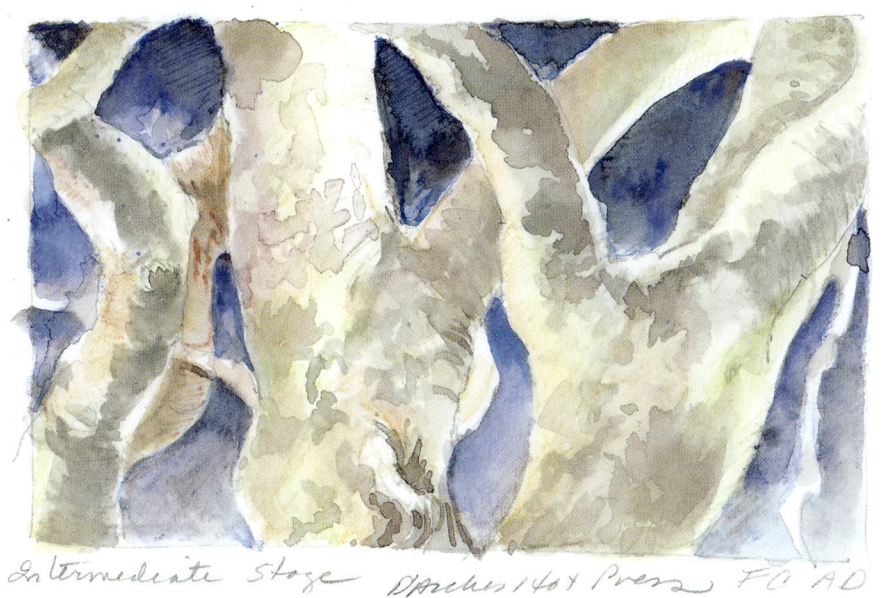

Intermediate Stage   *D'Arches Hot Press*   *FC AD*

I made a surprising discovery while experimenting with papers I seldom use. Student-grade paper, with its heavy sizing, performed far better than expected while still absorbing wet brushstrokes and maintaining pencil texture. When it comes to traditional watercolors, my preference is for hand-made, cold pressed watercolor paper. However, the paper I liked best for these studies turned out to be a paper I hardly ever used.

This experiment inspired a class exercise using simple, free-hand shapes and varied negative spaces— and it gave students the freedom to use fun colors. We used two brands of watercolor pencils, Faber-Castell's Albrecht Dürer (soft) and Derwent (hard).

In the first stage, graded washes were used in the background negative spaces. In the intermediate stage, color was applied inside the trees. In the final stage, dry watercolor pencils added finishing touches.

While walking around the class and looking at student work upside down, the lively shapes reminded me of Henri Matisse's *Dance* (*La Danse*).

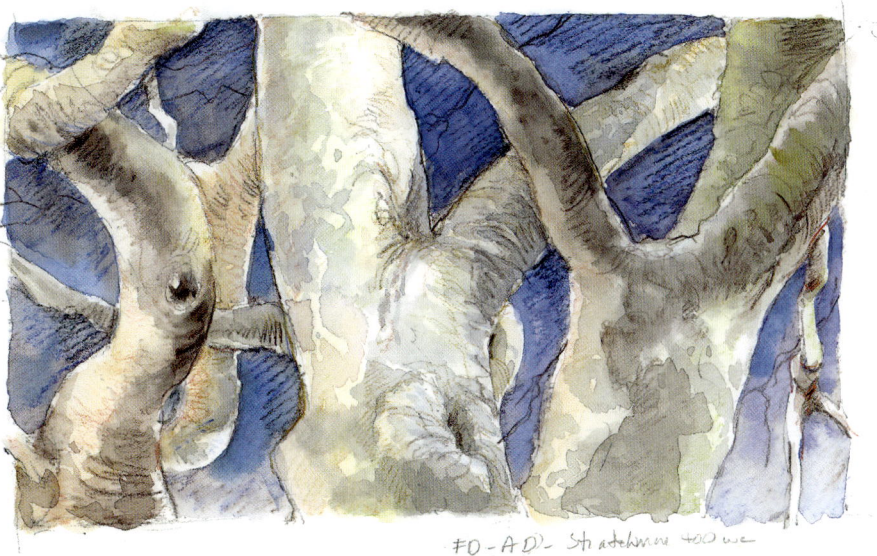

FC-AD - Strathmore 400 w/c

Traveling Memories

Quick sketches are a genuine record of the movement you have seen. After the animal has moved or disappeared entirely, leave the drawing alone. The spontaneous mark is lost when we erase and "improve." Later, when there is time, build the drawing on another page or overlay.

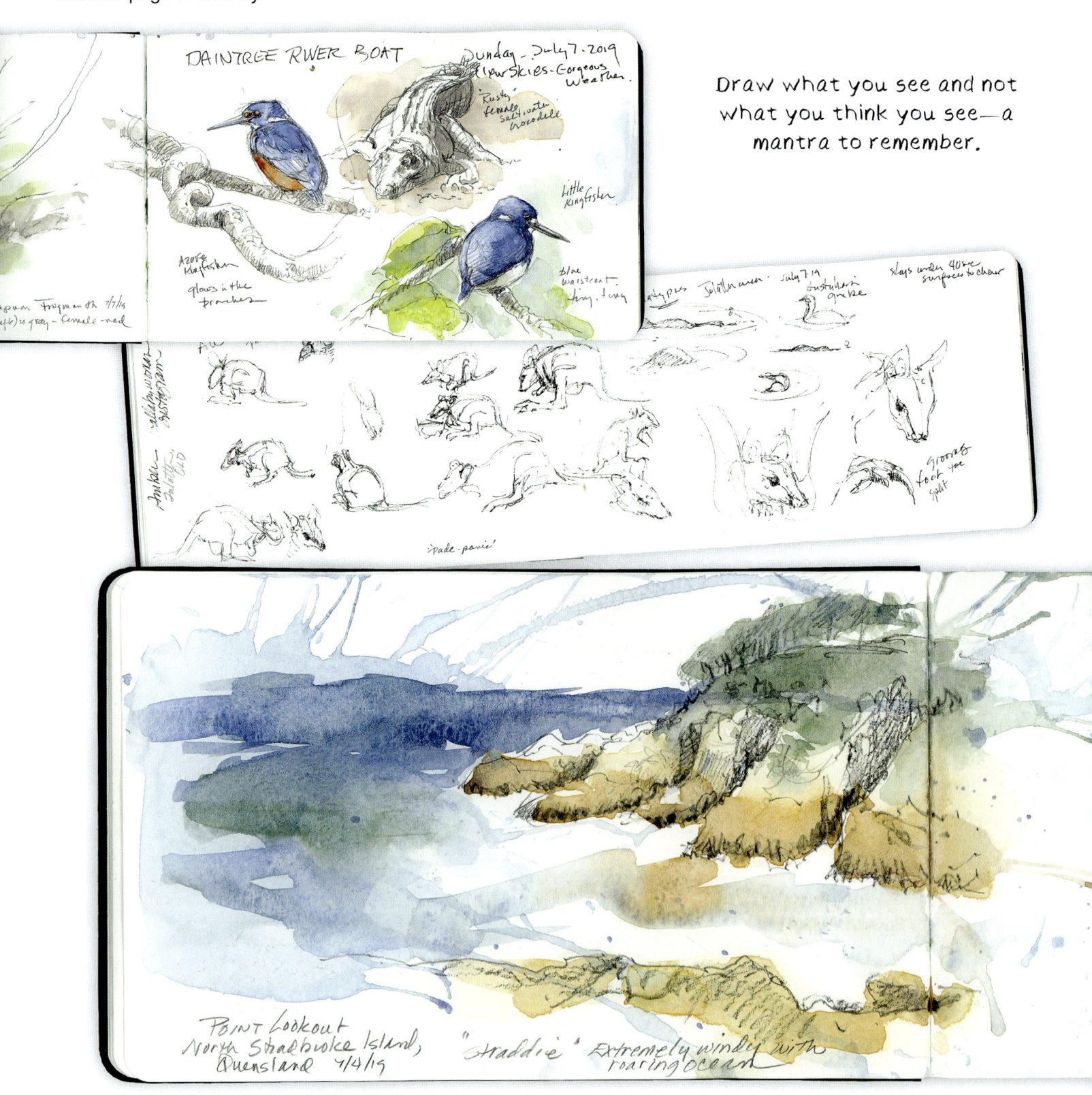

Draw what you see and not what you think you see—a mantra to remember.

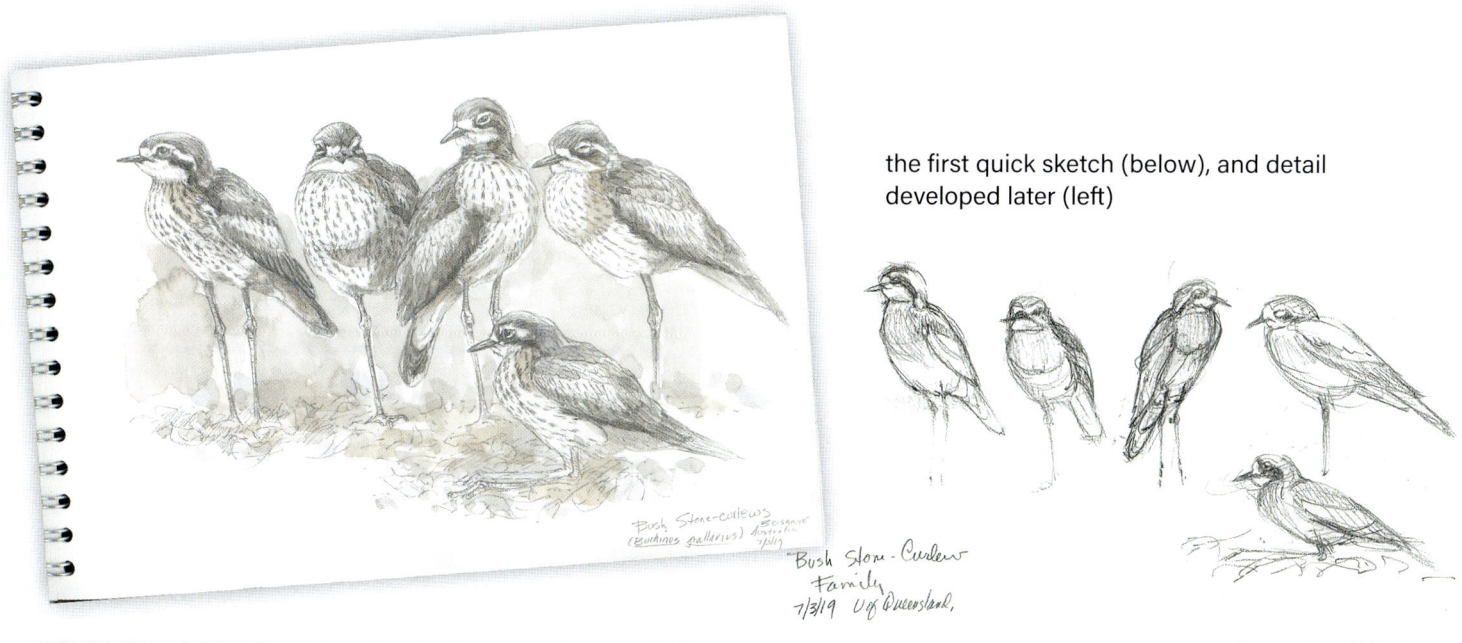

the first quick sketch (below), and detail
developed later (left)

Bush Stone-Curlews
(Burhinus grallarius) *southern Australia*
Bush Stone-Curlew
Family
7/3/19 USA Queensland,

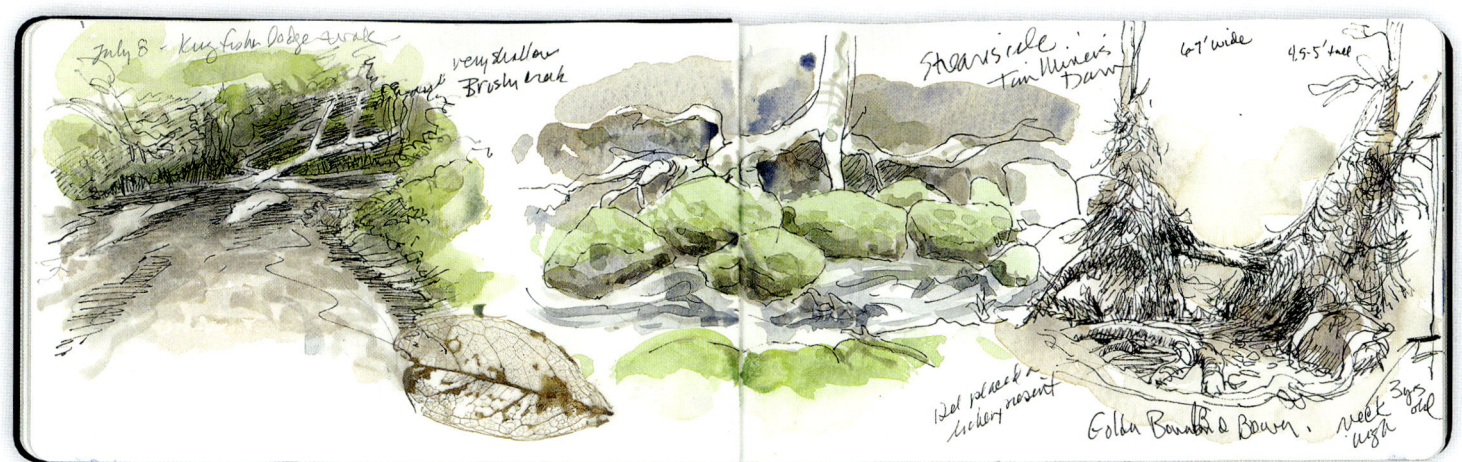

July 8 - Kingfisher Lodge trail
very shallow
Brush trail
Shearscale
Tin Miners
Dam
60' wide
4.5-5' tall
Well placed in
lichery present
Golden Bowerbird Bower, week 3yrs
USA old

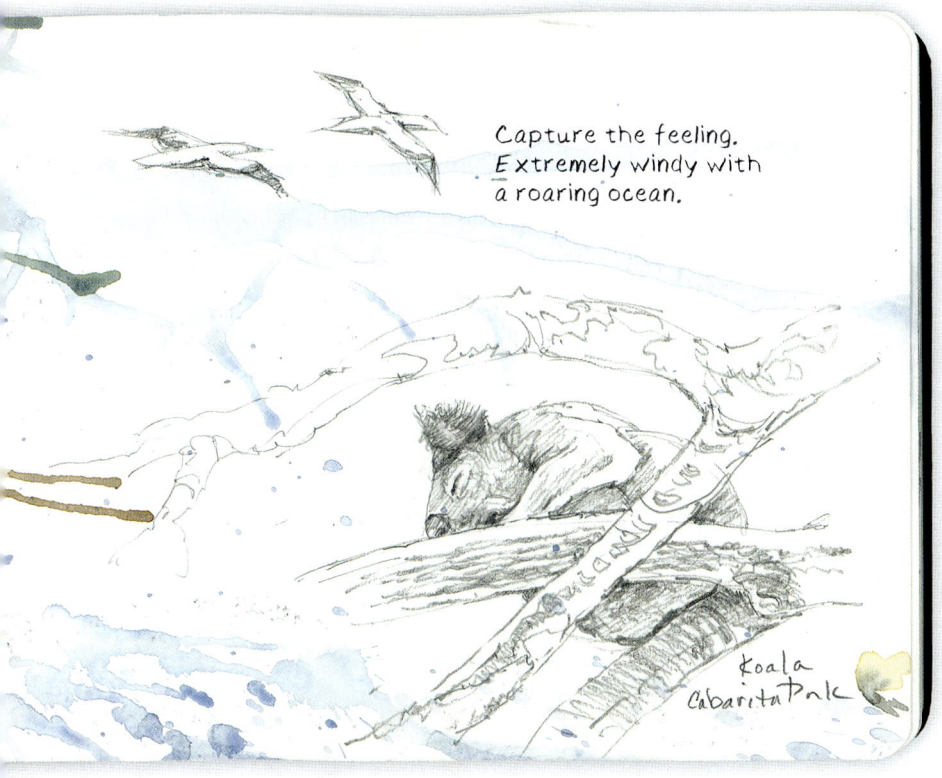

Capture the feeling.
Extremely windy with
a roaring ocean.

Koala
Cabarita Park

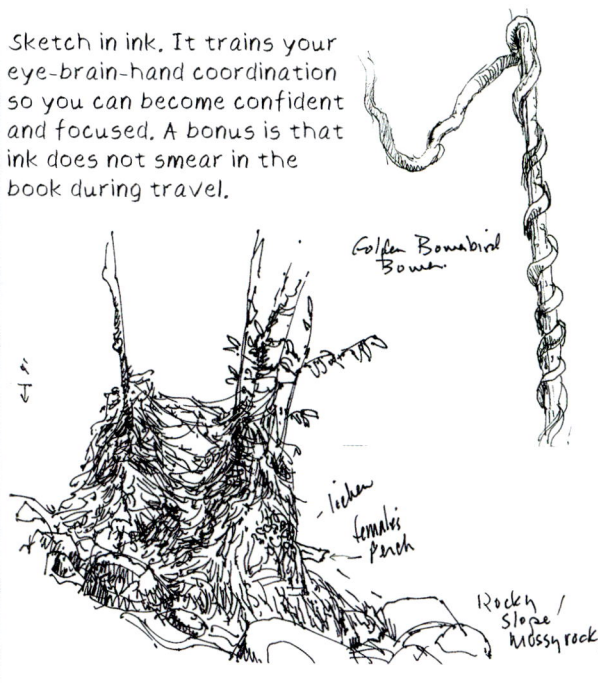

Sketch in ink. It trains your
eye-brain-hand coordination
so you can become confident
and focused. A bonus is that
ink does not smear in the
book during travel.

Golden Bowerbird
Bower.

lichen
females
Perch

Rocky
slope
mossy rocks

Without a Sketchbook at Hand

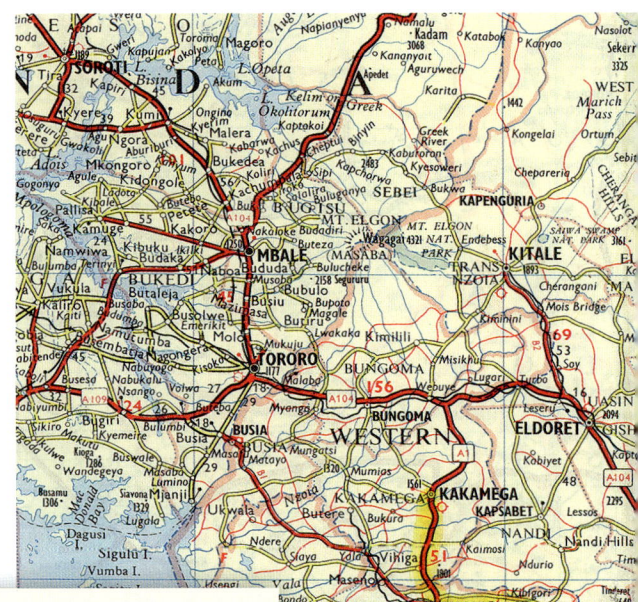

I was never good at writing a comprehensive journal entry at the end of a long birding tour day. As I was usually too tired to hold a pencil, most of the notes from 1986 in Kenya record only place names and singular events. A disturbing guest in the safari jeep was doing a fine job of playing the spoiled tourist. I was determined to shift my focus toward the unfolding adventure of each day. I tried something different to record my experiences. With a small notepad in my pocket, I jotted written images of what I saw and felt throughout the day. Years later, the words have brought it back, even the feel of sand in my teeth.

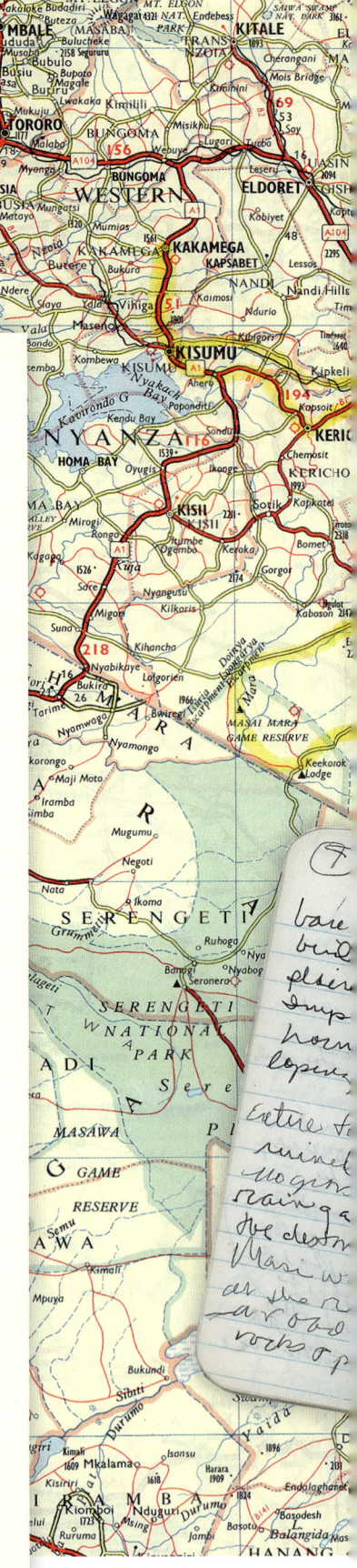

Notepad from the Serengeti— Scribbles Translated

Impressions driving through the Serengeti, November 19, 1986

"Serengeti morning, the edge of the Masai world
Cool dawn, long-sleeved cotton billowing
Wind pressing hair and eyeglasses flat—no air could be fresher
Close-cropped plains, left-overs from the millions of wildebeests who passed before
Zebra, topi, warthogs, and piglets—tails held high
Hyena with full bellies
Jackal peeking out of the burrow
Mongeese scamper toward the den
Baby Tommie on its first run—bouncing and semi-pronking
Lions asleep in the bushes
Grey Flycatcher scolds a snake
Gritty teeth
Last minute search under every bush—look for the place with no impalas or Tommies
Streaking across the Serengeti, impalas scatter, buffalo snorts and retreats into the brush
A rock under a bush— no, the eye, cheek, and ear of a cheetah
One—then two

Endless miles of green-riverine belts amble through the slightly rolling countryside, dotted with those lanky limbs of the acacia, much like the Masai—spreading their canopy evenly toward the clouds.

Dappling the hillsides, shadows calmly walk the Serengeti
Giraffe heads appear above the acacia
Dust devils cross the overgrazed plains
Two-banded Courser hides in the grass
Tommies flick
Blue sky—clouds forming
Choking dust
Red bandana
Wildebeest turn to stare—
One-horned Tommie stamps the ground
Bare-faced Go-away-bird
Seas of Serengeti grass
Impala with impressive horns and his harem
Loping giraffe
Entire forests of trees ruined by elephants, no grass to eat
Rain gathering on the distant hills of dusky purple
Masai waiting patiently by the side of the track
A road of endless rocks and holes
Bumps on the head
Trees are dusted with tawny sand."

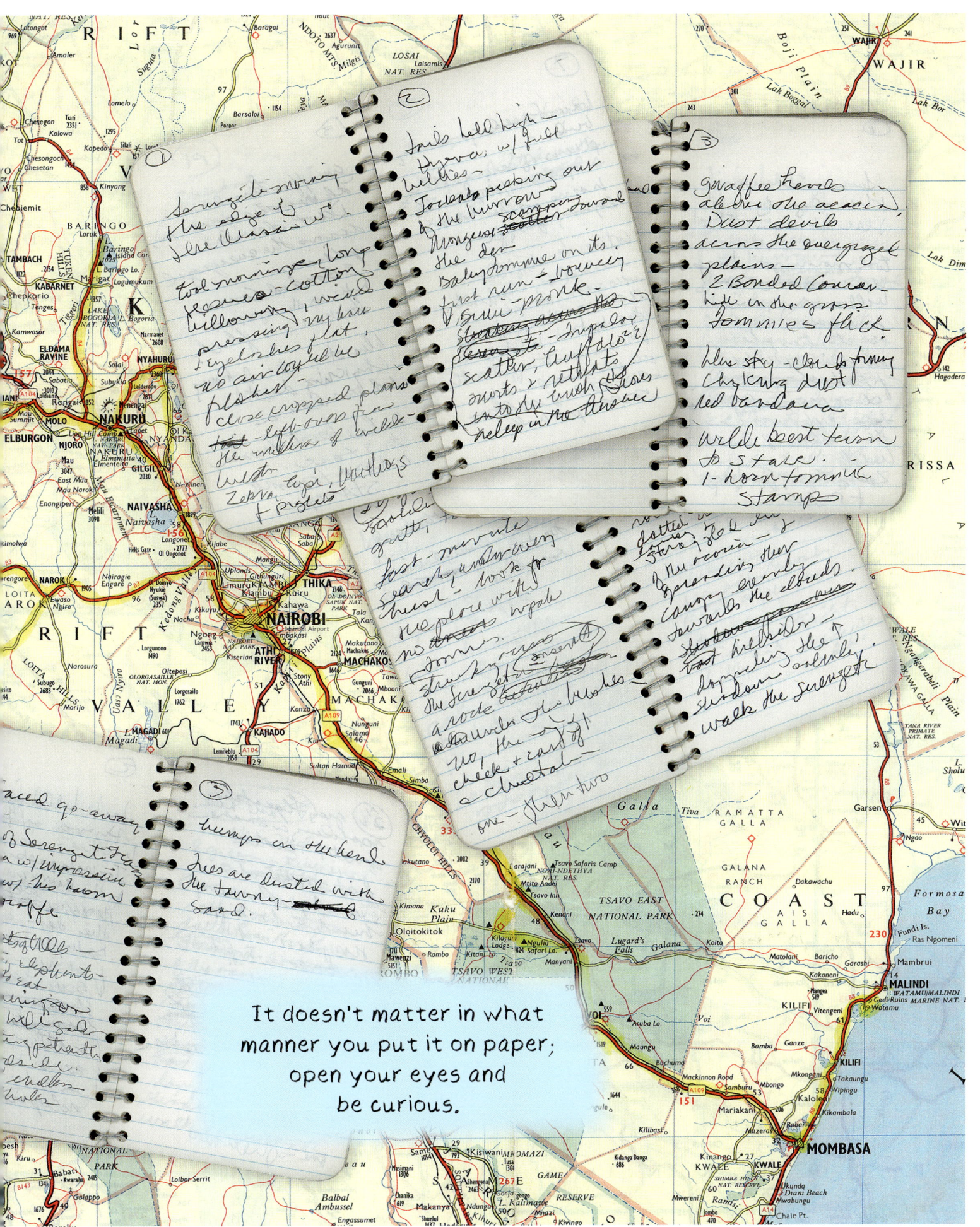

It doesn't matter in what manner you put it on paper; open your eyes and be curious.

Without a Sketchbook or Camera, Again

It was a once-in-a-lifetime experience, and one where a memory trained for detail could help construct the illustration.

On May 20, 1984, I rode with our good friend Jim Morgan. With little room for bulging camera bags in his truck, I made a last-second decision and left my cameras at home.

We wandered the trails of Houston Audubon's Louis B. Smith Bird Sanctuary, avoiding spider webs and sharing our walk with mosquitos. In an open area of the woodland, we noticed a small bird flycatching among the lower branches of the canopy. Its muted greens and yellows seemed oddly familiar. After about twenty seconds of observation, Jim thought it was a Greenish Elaenia, a bird he was familiar with in Mexico. I agreed. We both had observed them in Central America but were shocked to see one in the United States.

Jim took photos, finding it challenging under a dark canopy through small branches and vines. Regretting leaving behind my beloved cameras, I sketched in a spiral pocket notebook while we made identification notes.

While I kept an eye on the bird, Jim drove to telephone two seasoned Central American birders and bird banders. They arrived from Houston about two and a half hours later and set up mist nets. They photographed the bird while it was hand-held. After measurements and banding, I was the last person to hold it and I released it. About seventy-five birders observed the bird over the next three days. That evening, I telephoned my husband, Ben, in Big Bend National Park. There was a long silence on the phone, then a heavy sigh, with the realization that he and his birding group were 650 miles away.

Jim wrote an article for *American Birds* magazine, "A Neotropical Bird Flies North: The Greenish Elaenia." It described the review process and the confirmation by noted ornithologists.

The descriptions, photos, and measurements were accepted as the first United States record for the Greenish Elaenia (*Myiopagis viridicata*).

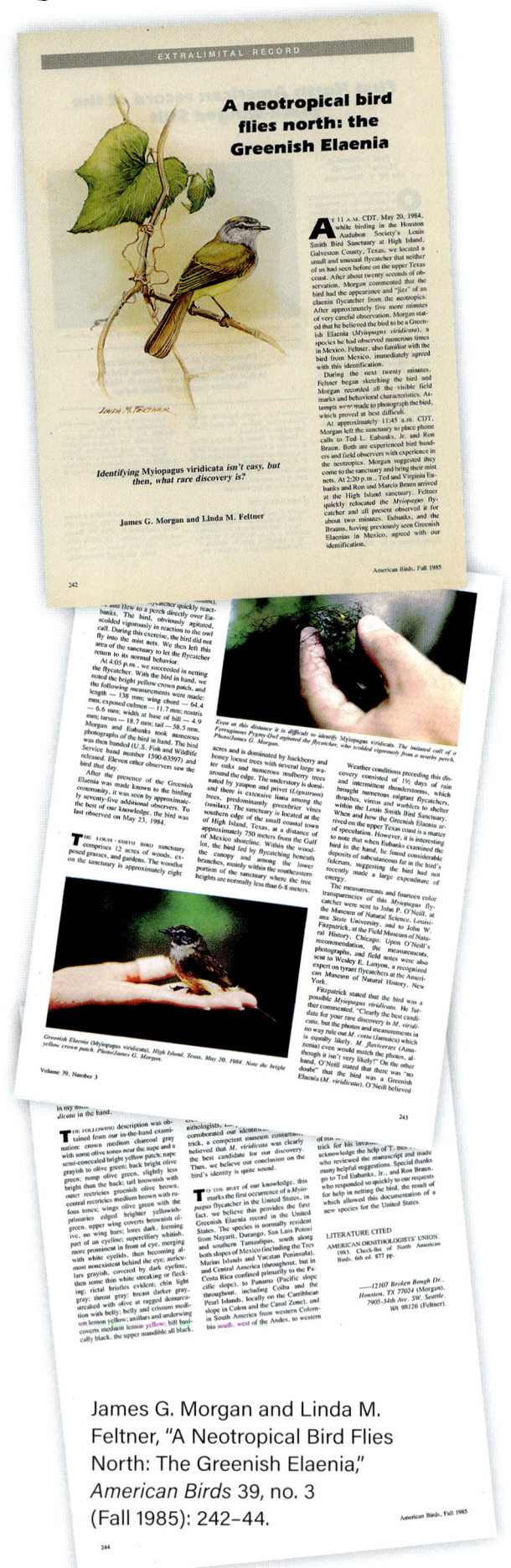

James G. Morgan and Linda M. Feltner, "A Neotropical Bird Flies North: The Greenish Elaenia," *American Birds* 39, no. 3 (Fall 1985): 242–44.

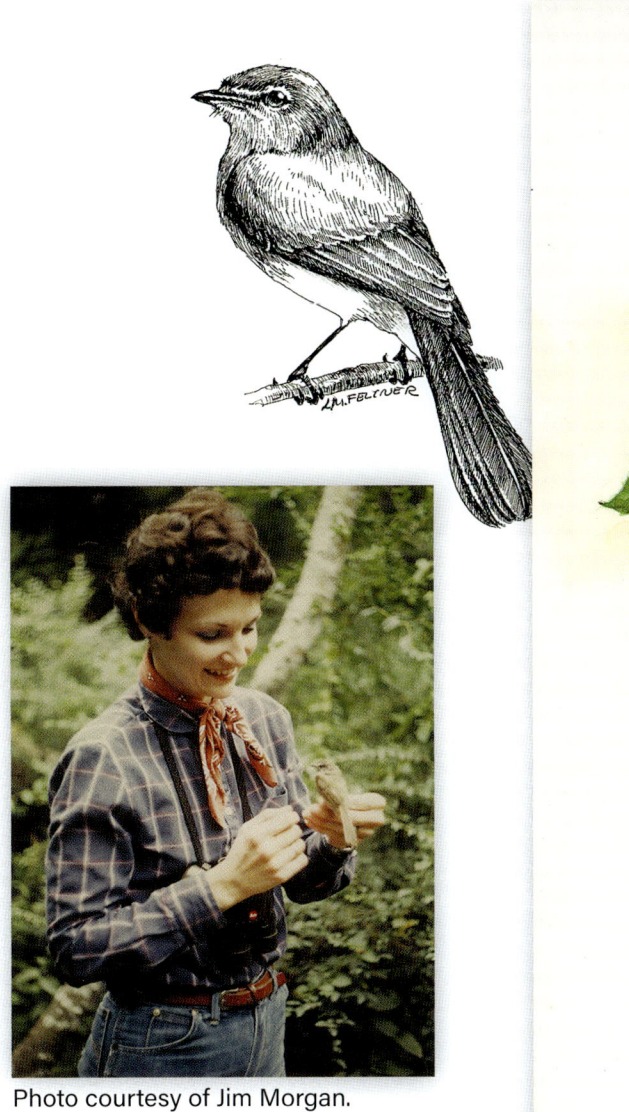

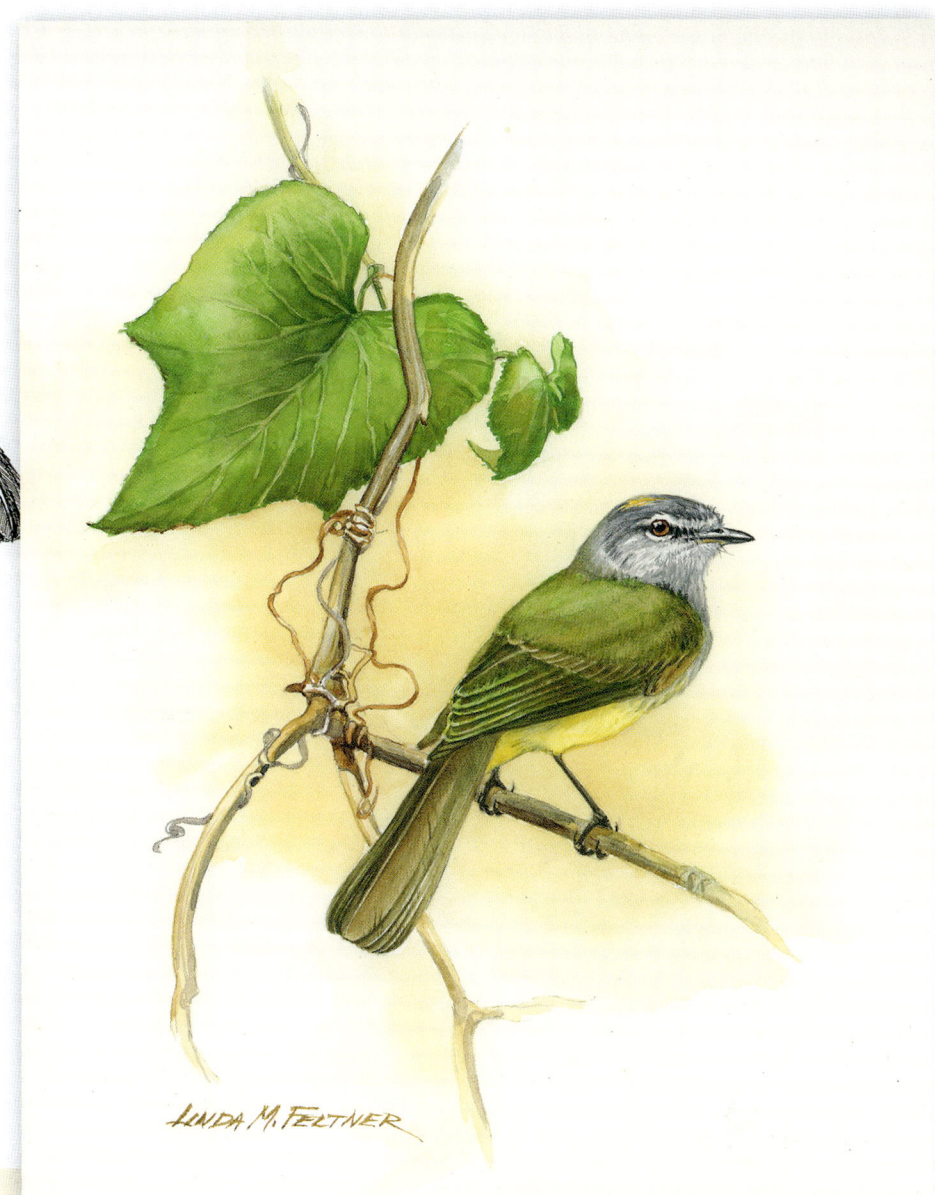

Photo courtesy of Jim Morgan.

Greenish Elaenia (*Myiopagis viridicata*)

LINDA M. FELTNER

I searched for my original field sketches with no success. All I found was the preparatory drawing for the design. The watercolor created for the magazine article was on an illustration board. It is slightly yellowed now, but I was happy with the outcome of the bird portrait at the time. Looking back, I am still pleased with it. It brings a smile and long-distant memories of unexpected thrills while slowly walking through nature.

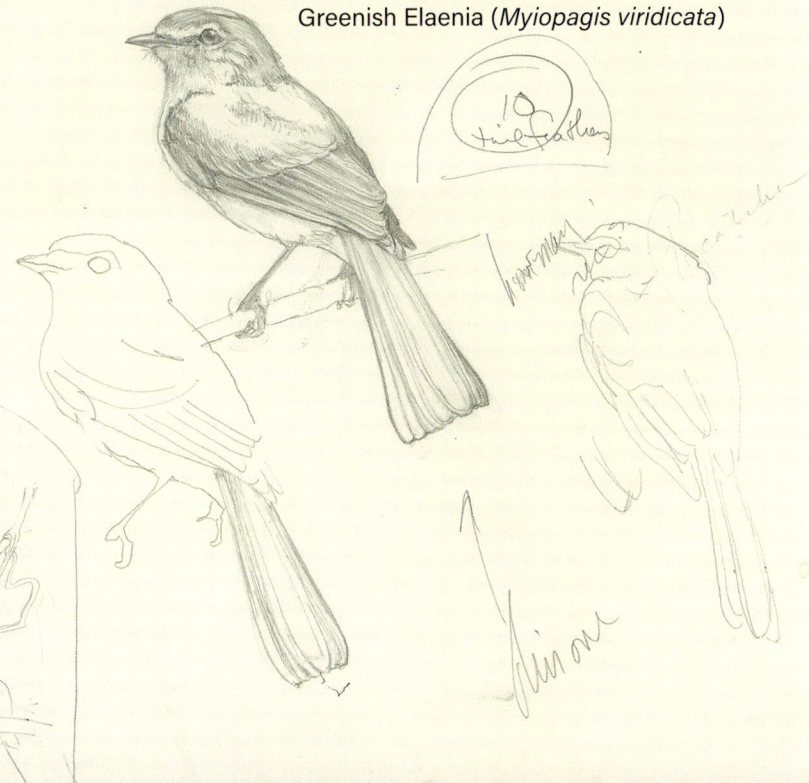

Iterations Are Gold

A photographer friend sent me this photo and permitted its use as a class exercise. Watercolorists seek areas in a landscape where pigment and water combine to create rich textures and atmosphere. Having spent a lot of time in wetlands, I love to get my feet wet. Evocative of many places where I've waded, this photo sparked memories for me.

In my Advanced Watercolor class, the assignment was for each participant to take the idea and "do something interesting with it." Three demos showed ways to alter the composition, use the flat black areas to apply lush pigment, and harmonize color. Each iteration allowed me to experiment and play.

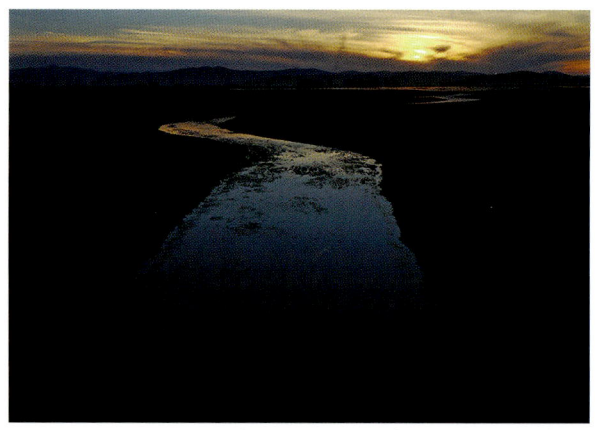

Photo courtesy of A. Eugene Beckes.

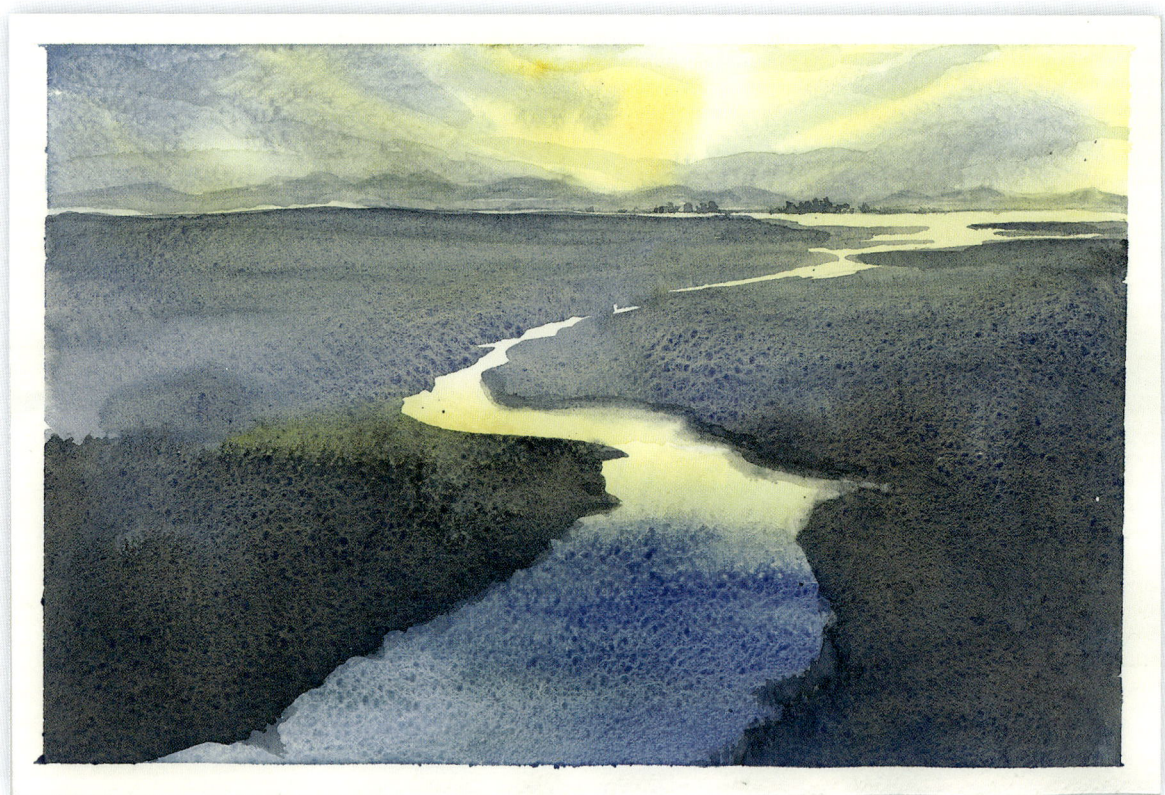

Demo 1: 7 x 10 in (17.78 x 25.4 cm) rough 140 lb (300 gsm) Fabriano Artistico paper. Rough watercolor paper allows a soft bleeding of pigments within wet-in-wet washes. Granular pigments such as ultramarine blue and burnt umber create an organic texture on the rough paper.

Class demonstrations like these are about fifteen minutes long. I demonstrate how to approach the lesson, painting only enough to encourage the student's inner creative voice to guide them.

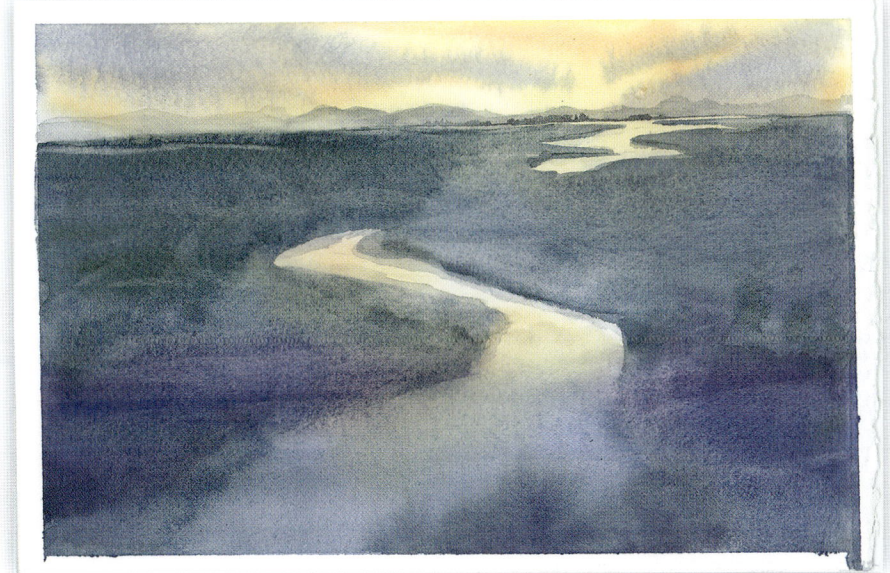

Demo 2: 7 x 10 in (17.78 x 25.4 cm) cold press 300 lb (640 gsm) Fabriano Artistico paper. With the use of a lot of water, the heavier paper reduced buckling. The moderately-textured paper added a new element to the experiment.

While the first version was drying, I took a different approach with the second. When I felt the time was right to leave the foreground wash alone, I paused to let it dry. Saying to the class that a bit of purple might harmonize well in that wet wash, my gut told me to "leave it alone" at this stage of drying. One student said, "Oh, go ahead. Do it." I did it. I was right. It was a spectacular mess. However, it was a perfect lesson. One of the hardest lessons in watercolor is judging when not to add pigment to a wash, so: "Leave It Alone!" I'm like a broken record in class.

The hardest lesson in watercolor is judging when to "Leave It Alone!"

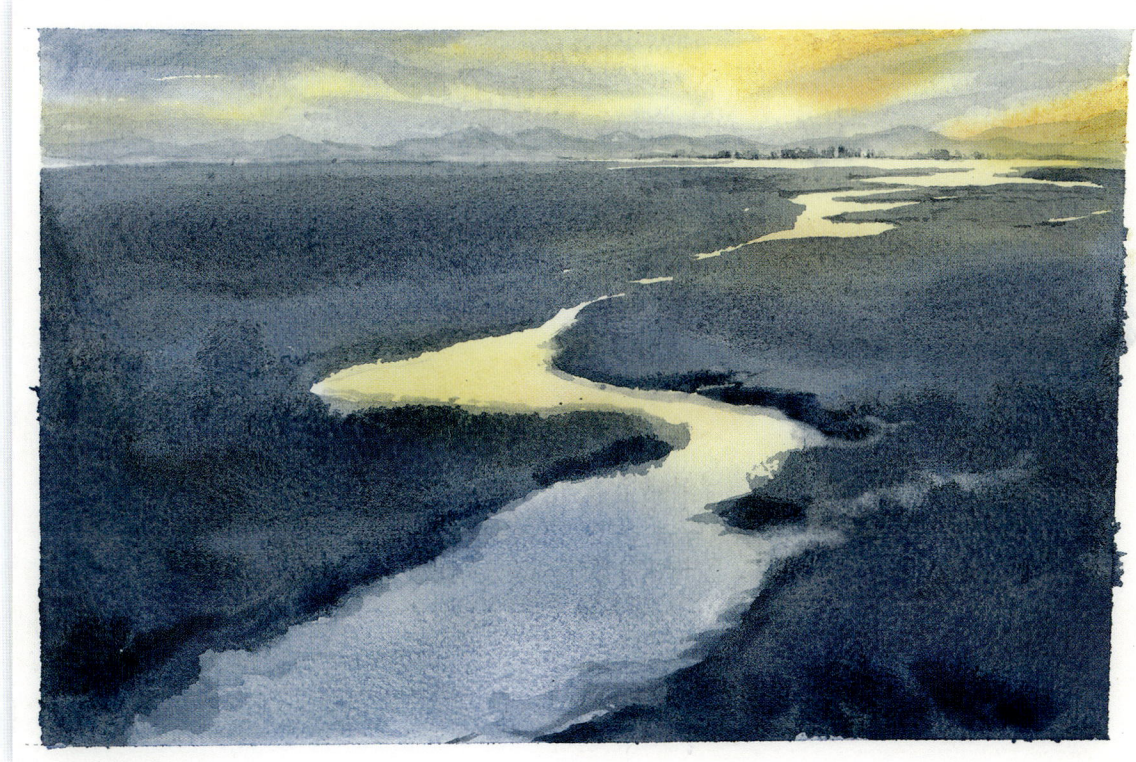

Demo 3: 7 x 10 in (17.78 x 25.4 cm), rough 300 lb (640 gsm) Fabriano Artistico paper.

No worries— it was very instructive. It showed two valuable things: the purple color didn't do anything significant for the color harmony, and it's fine to throw out that version and paint another. With the knowledge of that experience, I approached the next version with the fun and spontaneous interaction of water and paint— the essence of watercolor painting.

"Swallows over Gold"

The concept, initiated by the class demo, continued to tug at my memory. It evoked strong emotions associated with pleasurable hours spent birding in marshes. Weeks later, but not long enough to forget the lessons of flowing pigment and water, the unfinished concept pulled me toward the drawing table. Another version in the studio resulted in *Swallows Over Gold*. The composition stood alone as successful, and I mulled over whether to add birds. I rejected placing a flying bird against the sky because it would entirely alter the center of interest. Deliberately distributed below the horizon, the low sweeping flight of swallows at dusk felt perfect. The theme emerged as a stronger connection between nature and landscape. Imagine the delicate sound of chittering Barn Swallows sweeping across the wetlands toward their evening roost. Wetlands are among the most threatened ecosystems. They are biodiverse communities of plants and animals that deserve worldwide protection.

Barn Swallow (*Hirundo rustica*)

Swallows Over Gold, 7 × 10 in (17.8 × 25.4 cm)
transparent watercolor.

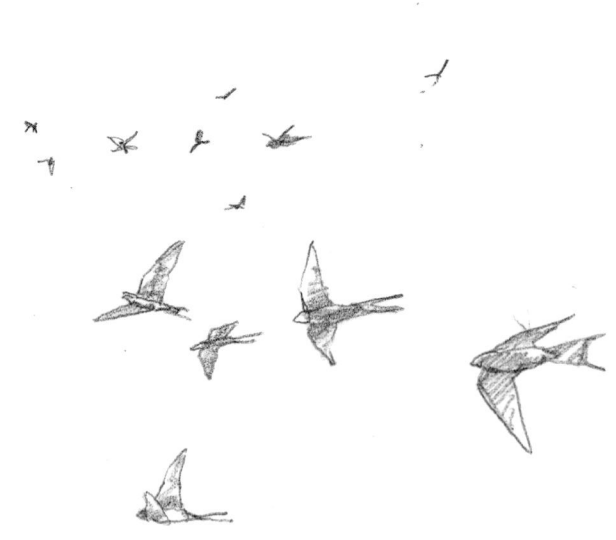

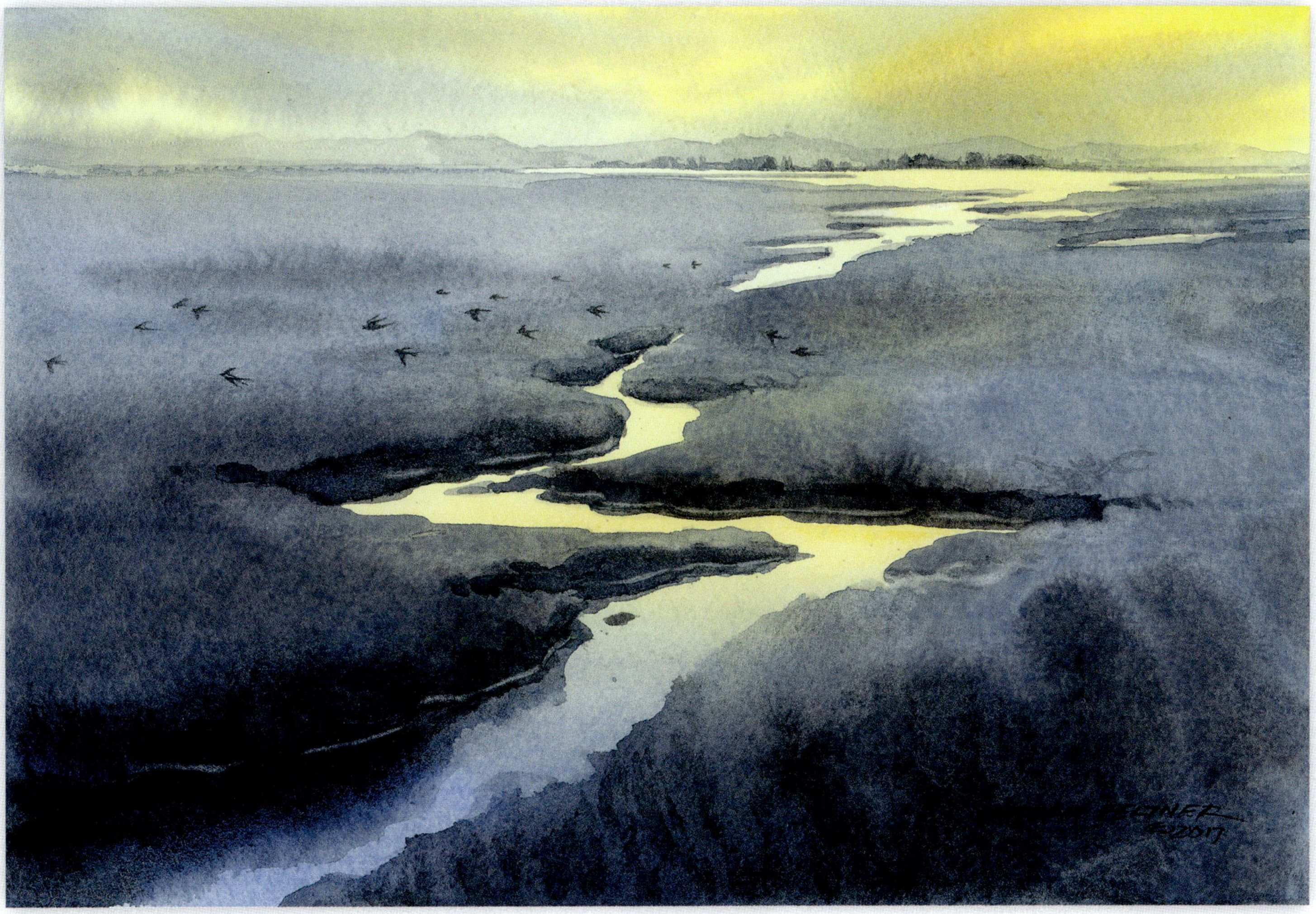

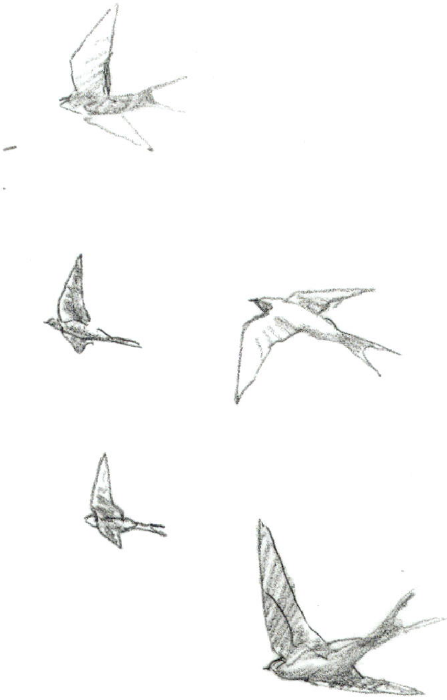

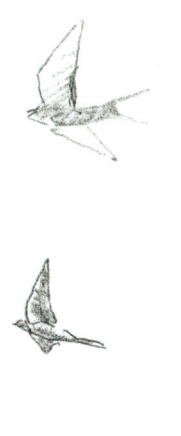

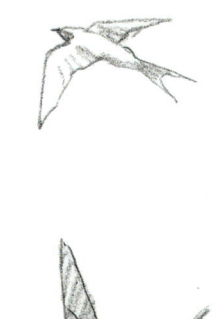

"Late Light—Huachuca Migrant": Inception

Migratory birds pass through all sorts of habitats on their journey to where they will spend the winter. This Green-tailed Towhee hopped up on a sunstruck agave with perfect timing, as the low angle of light illuminated the greens of the plant and bird in striking harmony. Palmer Agaves dot the grassy slopes of the mountain foothills. Perhaps the towhee had arrived for the winter.

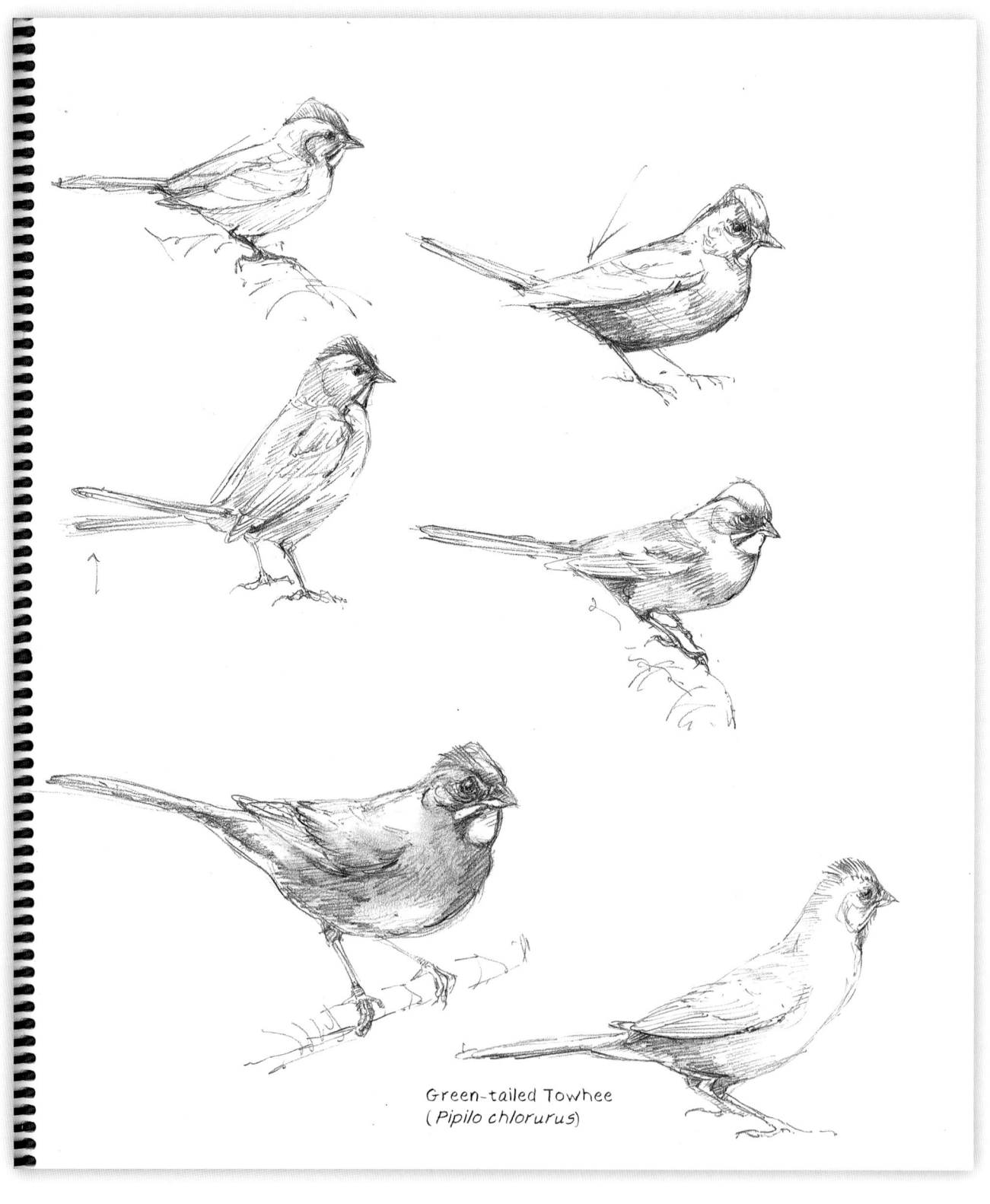

Green-tailed Towhee
(*Pipilo chlorurus*)

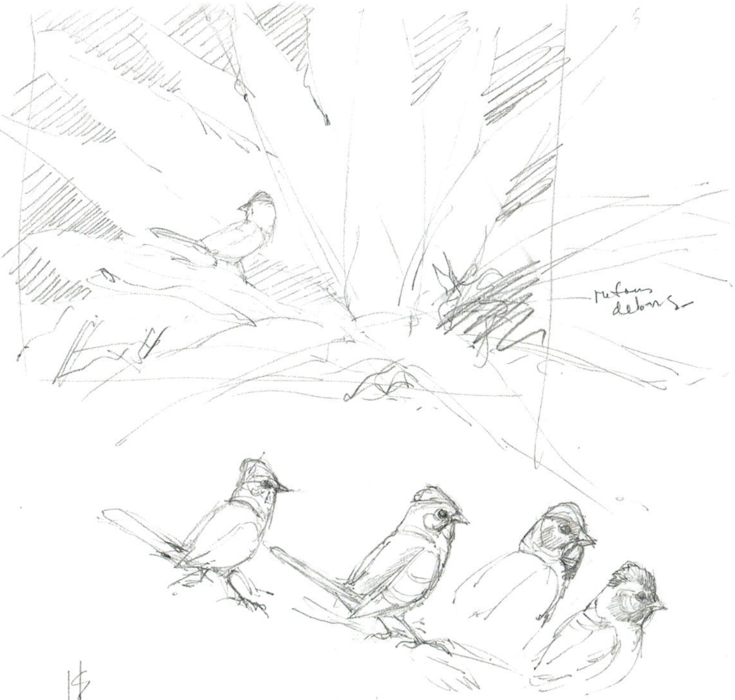

The first scribble of an idea
with gesture sketches.

I drew the pose with greater detail,
using overlays to make adjustments.

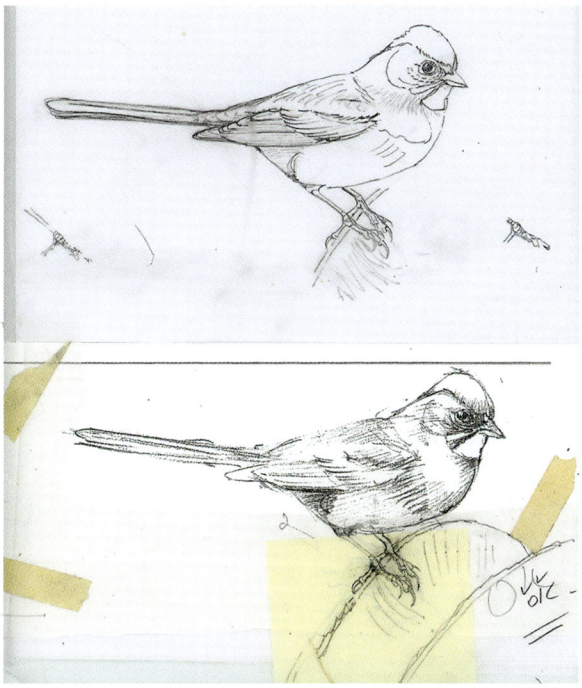

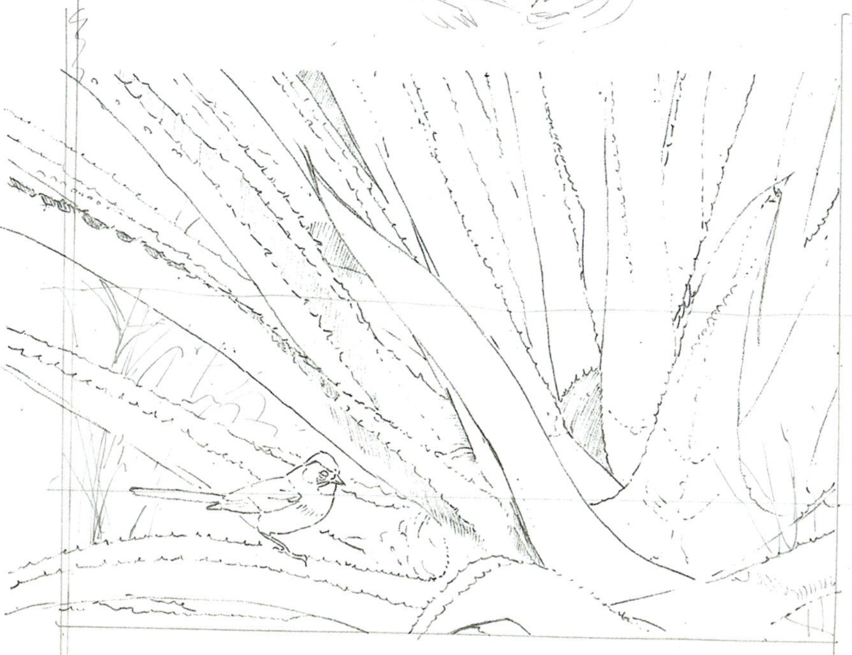

The working drawing with agave details and the
bird in position was drawn on 8 x 10 in (20.32
x 25.4 cm) bond sketch paper. I scanned the
image and enlarged it to fit the good paper.

I printed a letter-sized copy and added
grayscale values with a soft pencil.

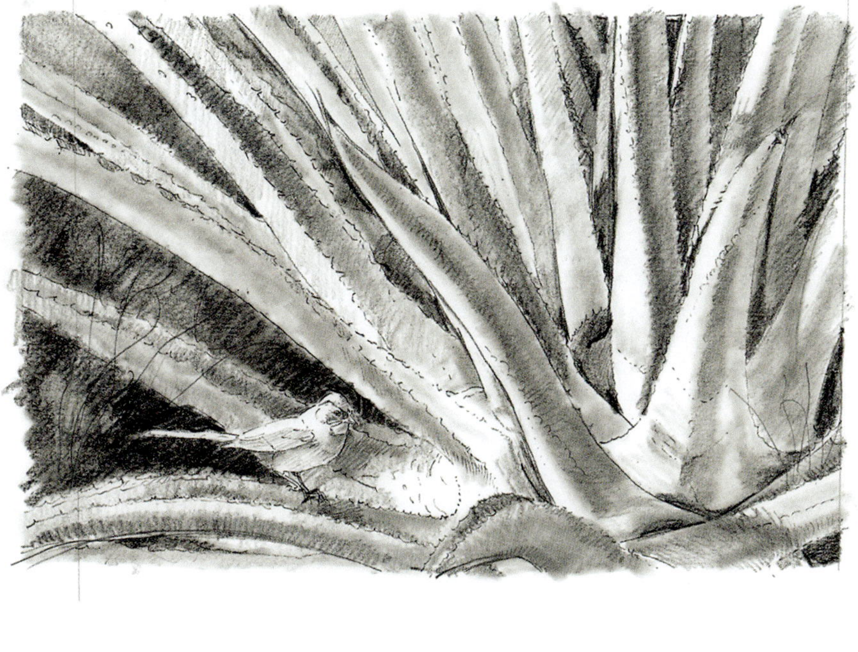

Palmer Agave (*Agave palmeri*)

"Late Light—Huachuca Migrant"

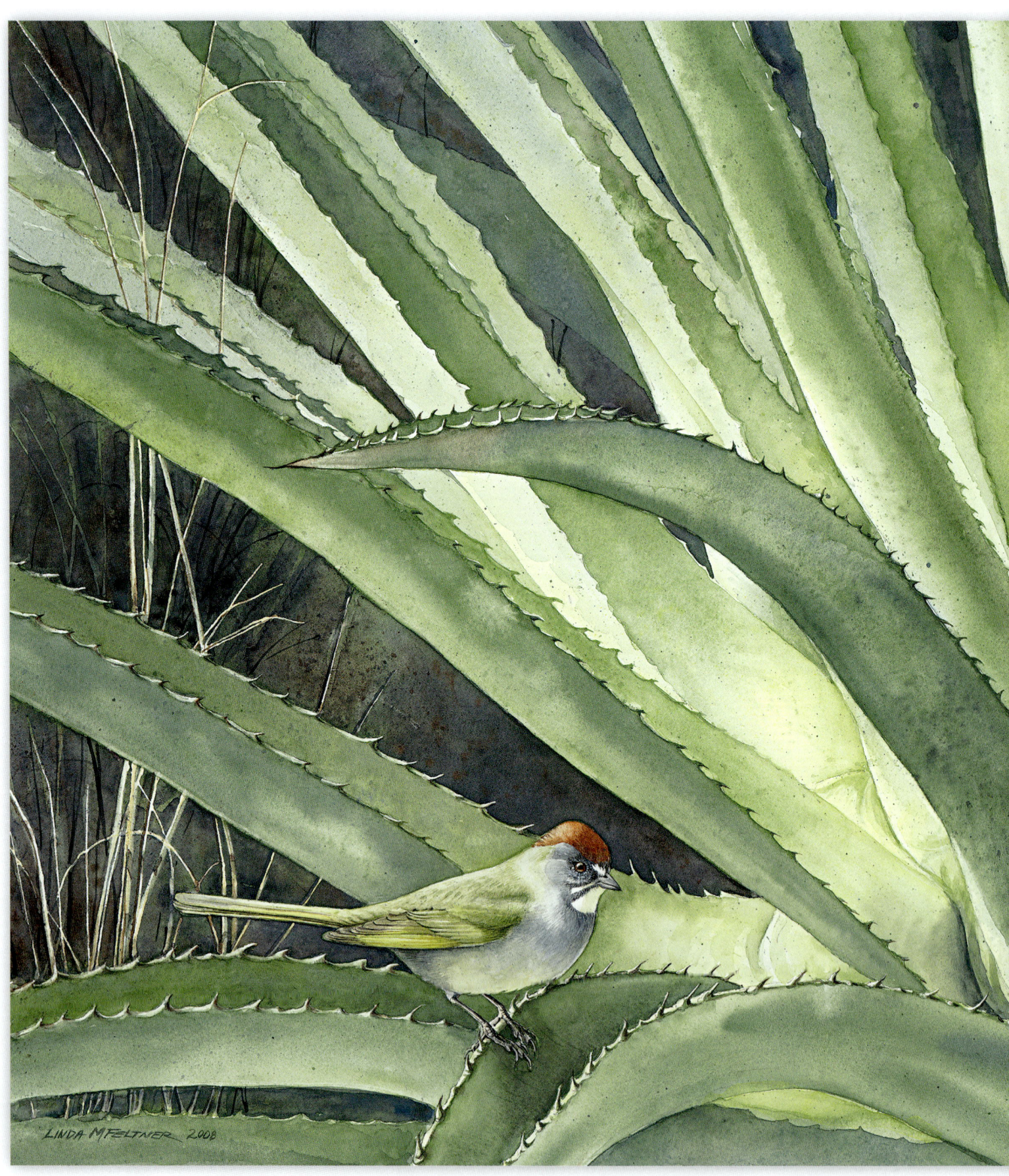

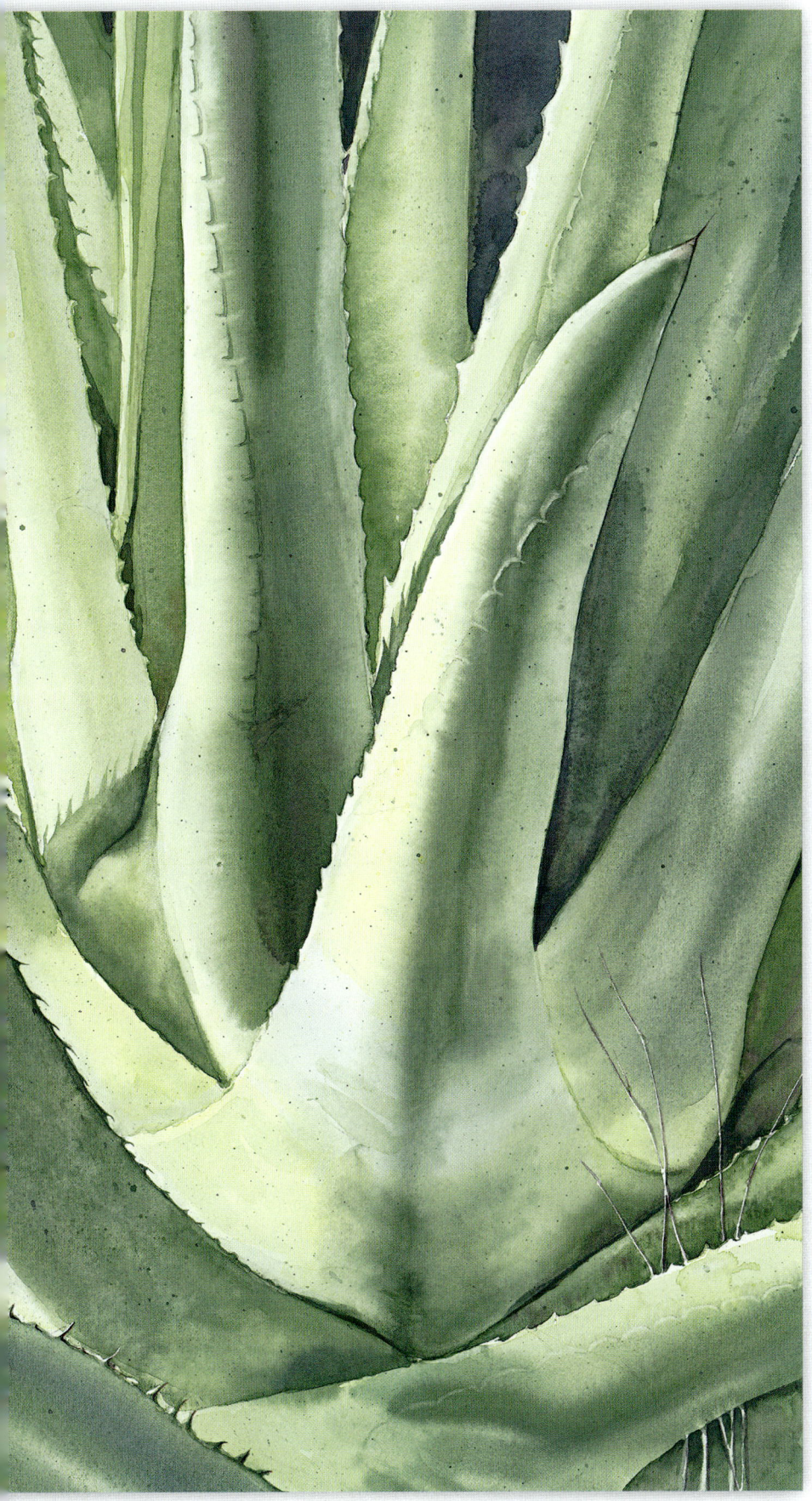

Agaves dot the oak woodlands and grasslands in the southwest. While I enjoyed a late afternoon walk, a Green-tailed Towhee paused in its foraging and perched on the agave leaves. The low angle of streaked sunlight enhanced the various greens, maroons, and rust colors of both plant and bird. Radiating leaves provided rhythm to the composition and allowed each fleshy leaf to exhibit subtle blended color and texture, well suited to watercolor. This painting represents what I like about observing nature. It's not only about a single species but about the time, place, and inspiration of observing the natural world.

Palmer Agave (*Agave palmeri*) and Green-tailed Towhee (*Pipilo chlorurus*)

Late Light–Huachuca Migrant, 22 × 30 in (55.9 × 76.2 cm), transparent watercolor.

"On the Downside": Work in Progress

Called the "Upside-Down Bird," nuthatches search up and down the trunks, as well as under and over large limbs. No crevice goes unexamined in their search. They might find juicy insects and seeds that other birds have missed. With a sturdy and narrow bill, they pry food from tiny cracks as they cling to the underside with their strong toes. An endearing bird for many, their gentle nature brings them to seed feeders in cold weather. We watch as they toss aside seemingly inferior seeds and select the perfect one, often flying to a hidden location to cache it away for the future.

Anadarka Mts.
4-28-14

White-breasted Nuthatch
(*Sitta carolinensis*)

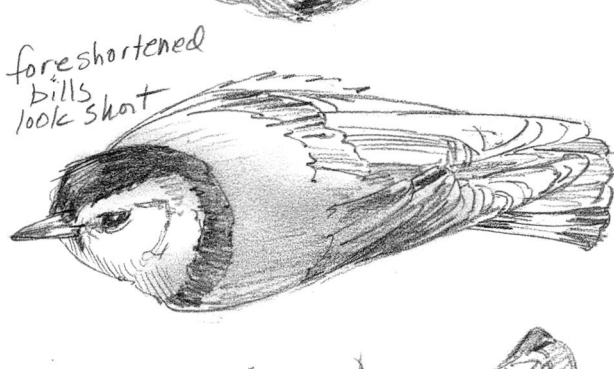

Madera Canyon, AZ
6-20-2021

very slender bill

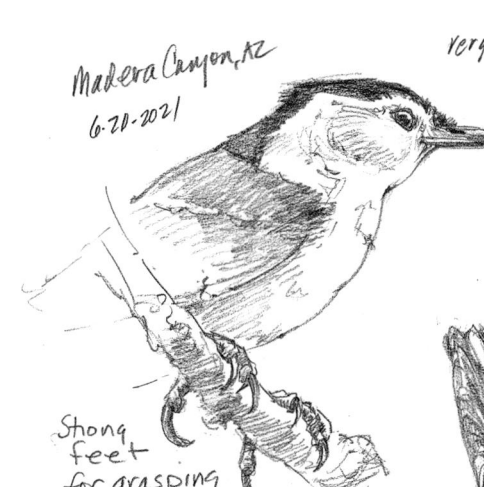

Strong feet for grasping bark

foreshortened bills look short

I chose the typical curving, crescent body posture with a straight back and lifted head. The black-and-white head pattern makes a unique shape with different head positions. The bill shape visually alters from a foreshortened view. Some subspecies have longer and more slender bills.

black on head takes different shape with new angles

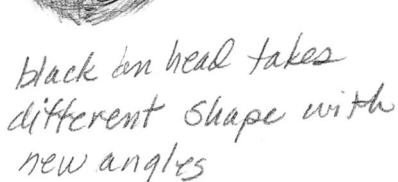

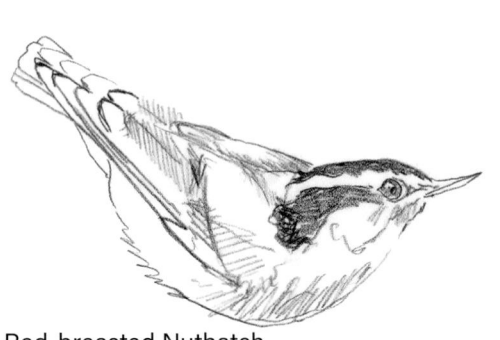

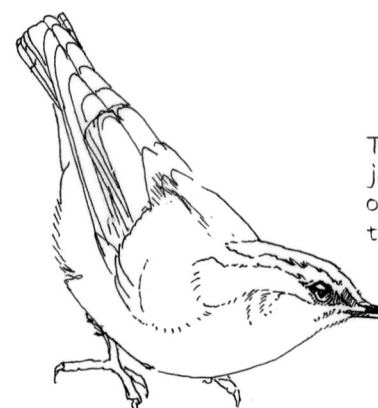

Red-breasted Nuthatch
(*Sitta canadensis*)

The Red-breasted Nuthatch also carries this jaunty posture. Their bill is slightly more curved on the lower mandible at the tip, creating a tweezer-like probe into tiny bark crevices.

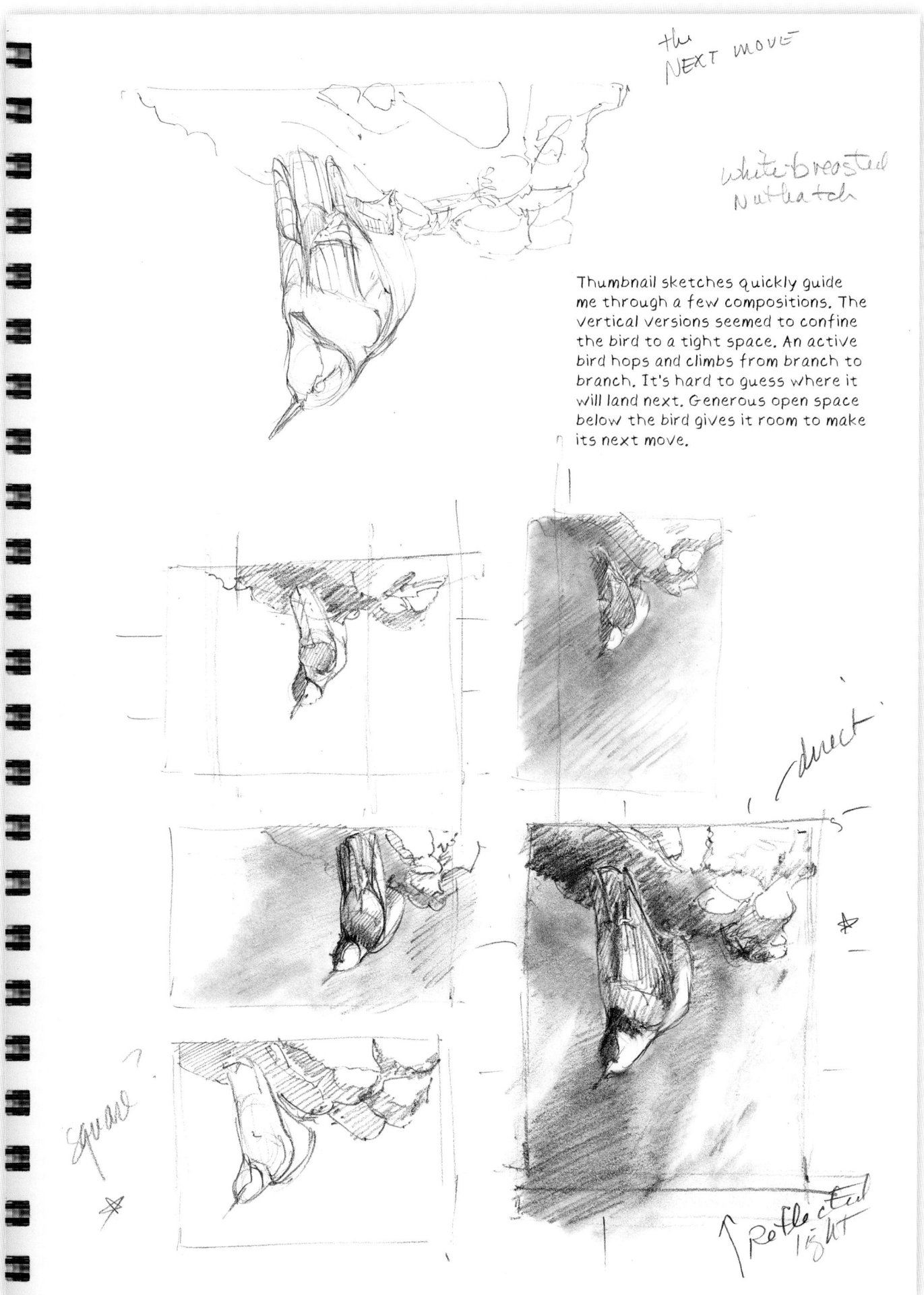

the
NEXT MOVE

White-Breasted
Nuthatch

Thumbnail sketches quickly guide
me through a few compositions. The
vertical versions seemed to confine
the bird to a tight space. An active
bird hops and climbs from branch to
branch. It's hard to guess where it
will land next. Generous open space
below the bird gives it room to make
its next move.

direct

square ?

Reflected
light

209

"On the Downside"

Hanging upside down is no strange feat for this small bird. An agile and active climber, it combs limbs and tree trunks for hearty seeds, nuts, and insects. The long and slightly upturned lower bill acts as a lever, prying in crevices in search of food. It seeks suitable cracks along the bark where it can jam a seed tightly in place while it pounds it open with its beak. The origin of the name comes from the pounding of the seed case and therefore "hatching" the seeds. The White-breasted Nuthatch is a welcome bird in our yard year-round where we hear its nasal call from a distance, and its whisper-quiet notes to its mate in spring.

White-breasted Nuthatch (*Sitta carolinensis*) and Tolype Moth (*Tolype* sp.)

On the Downside, 7.5 × 10.5 in (19.05 × 26.67 cm), transparent watercolor.

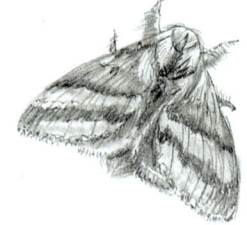

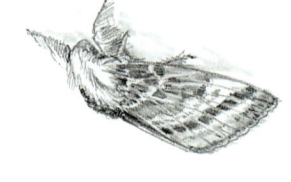

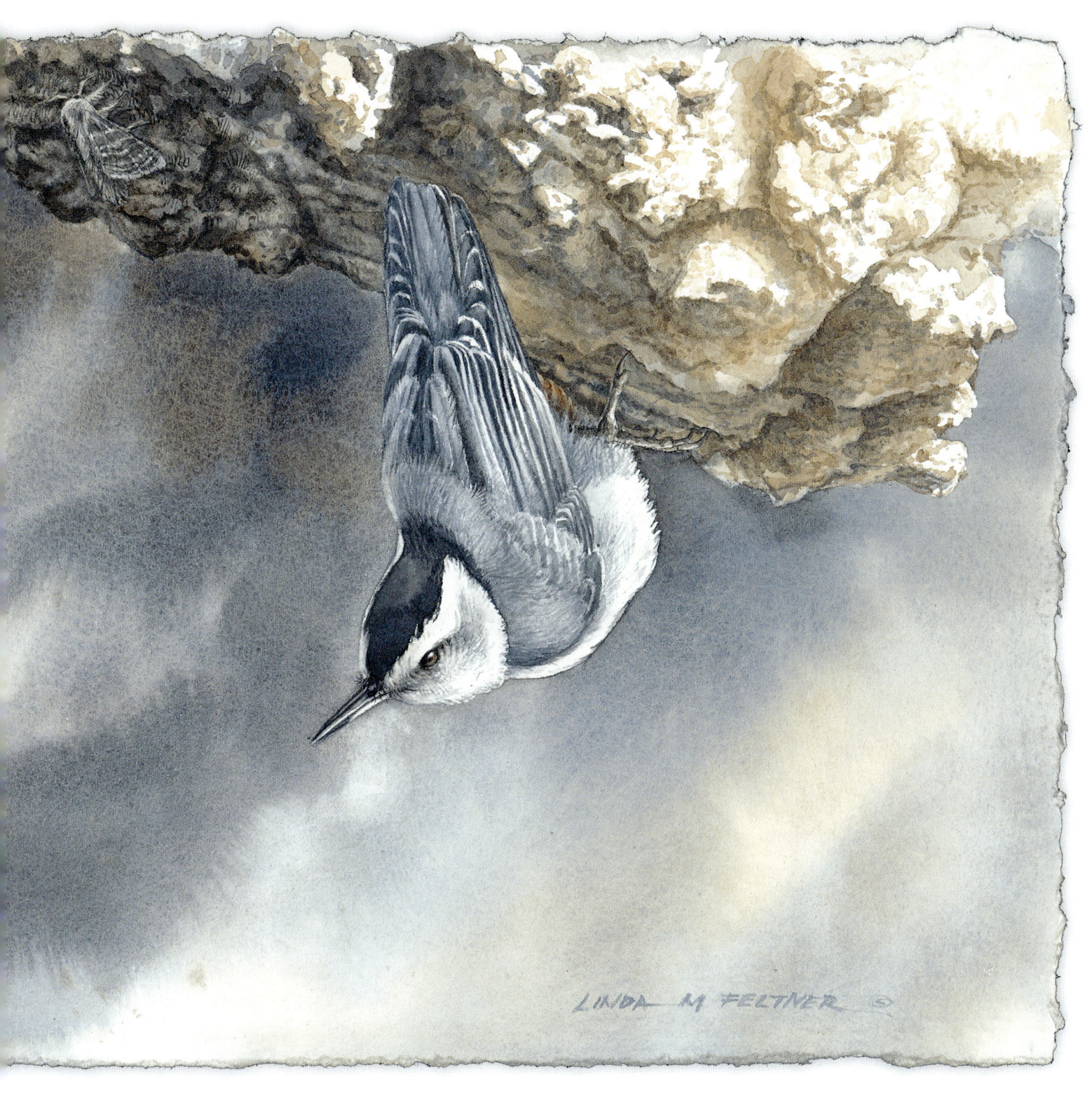

LINDA M FELTNER ©

Where Balance Counts

From an early age, I have been fascinated with geology. The columnar hoodoos at the Chiricahua National Monument provide abundant opportunities for an artist. The wind-etched and eroded columns are enchanting. The Massai Point Overlook is the apex of the drive through the monument. Staying close among the rocks or looking out across the valley provides many painting ideas.

In March, snow lingered in shady patches, providing a dramatic accent against the earthen tones. A tumble of massive boulders was precariously held between two columns. Was it unstable? How many decades had they rested there? What might perch upon those rocks?

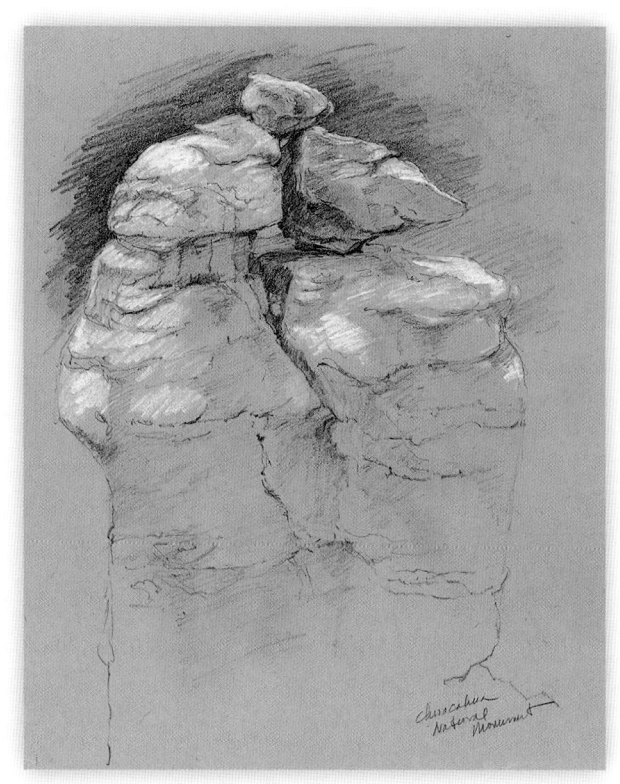

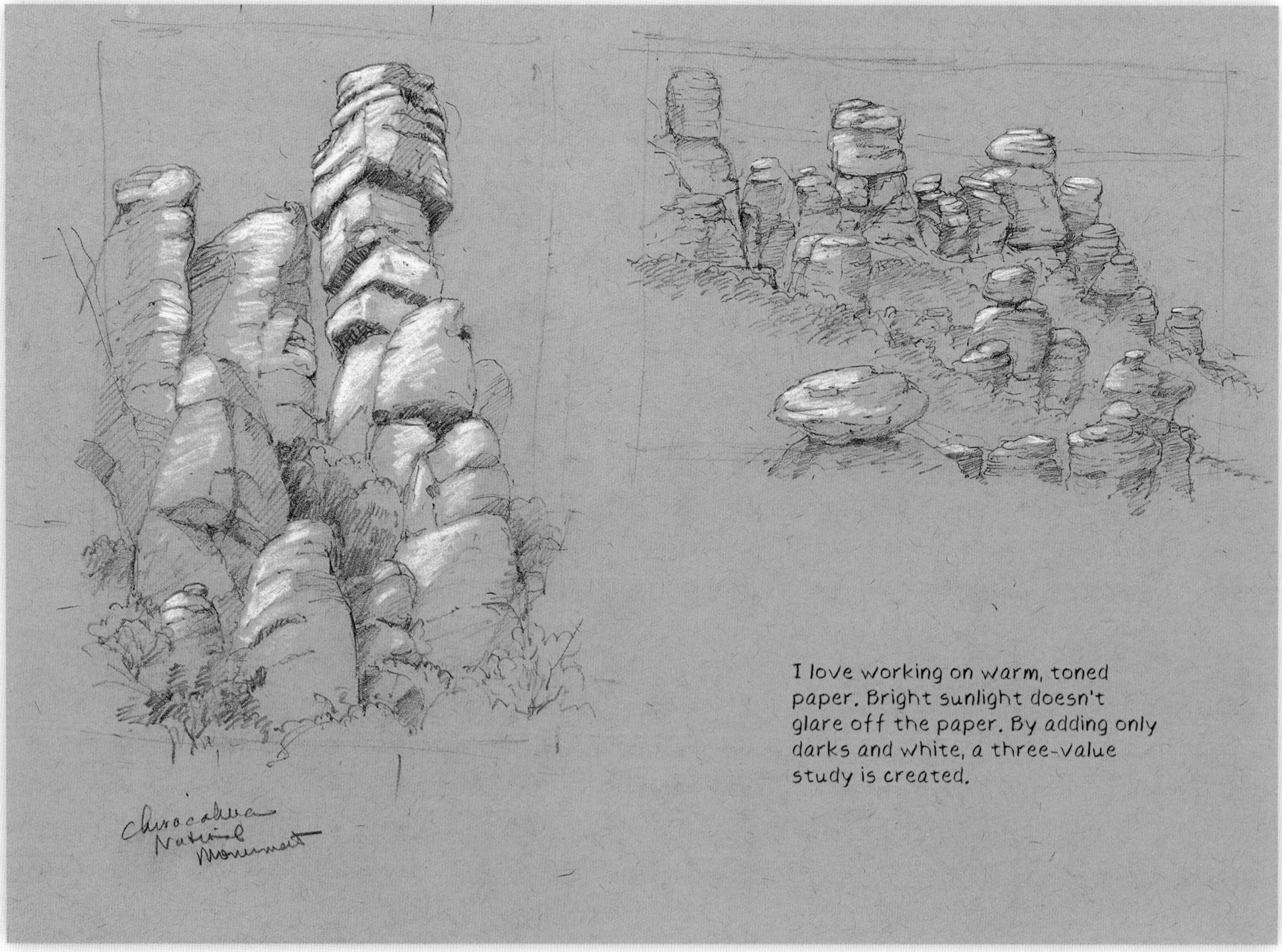

Chiricahua
National Monument

Chiricahua
National
Monument

I love working on warm, toned paper. Bright sunlight doesn't glare off the paper. By adding only darks and white, a three-value study is created.

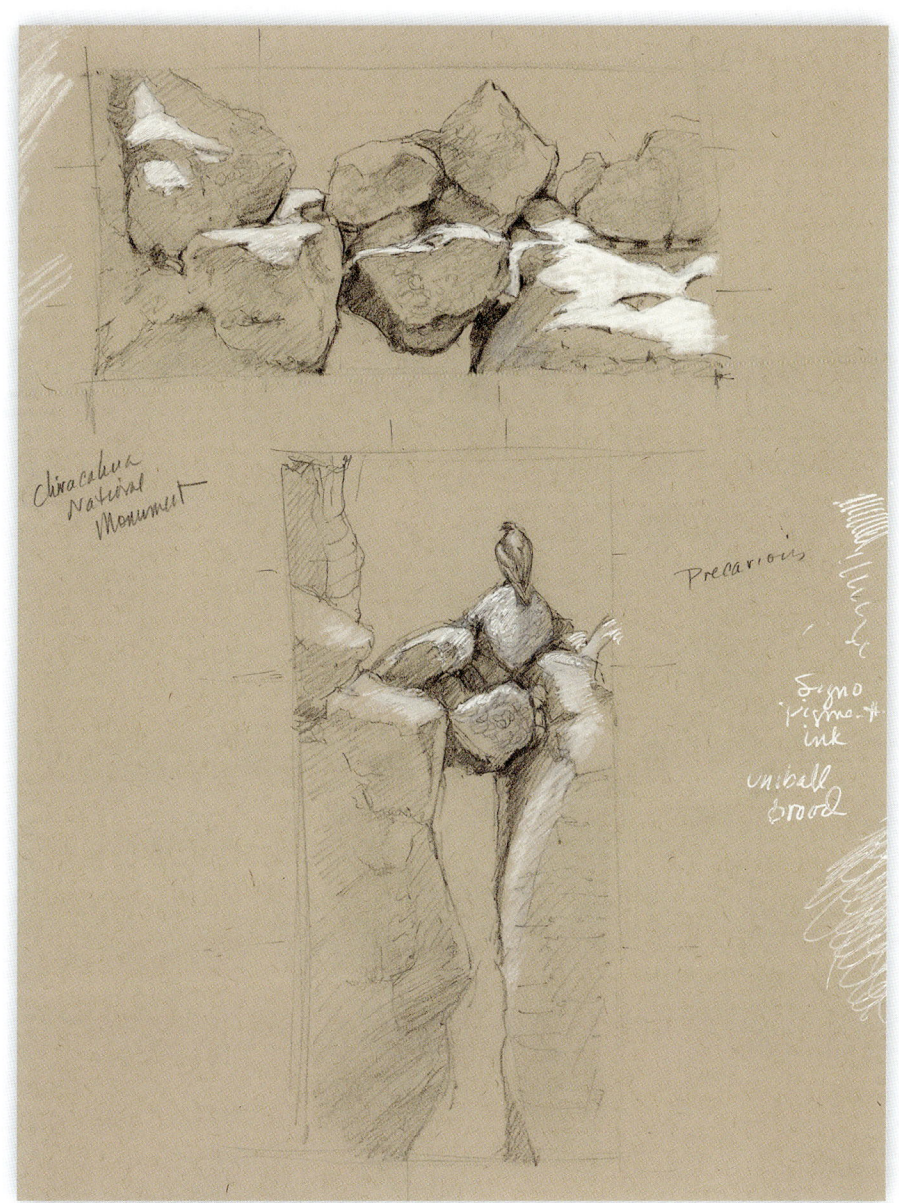

A horizontal study offers a potential design.

A slender vertical composition gives the illusion of height and emphasizes the transitory nature of the hoodoos.

The smooth surface of Strathmore toned tan paper takes ink and graphite beautifully. Try permanent ink pens and white gel ink pens for crisp lines. White colored pencils or watercolor pencils work well over ink.

However, I discovered the whites do not stick to the drawing when applied over burnished or rubbed graphite pencil. A little experimentation showed that white gouache covered well over the burnished areas.

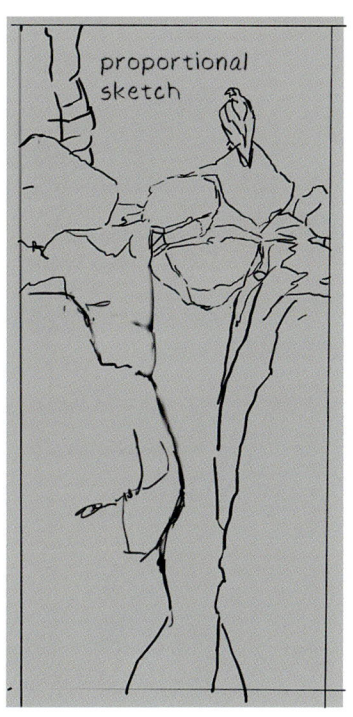

proportional sketch

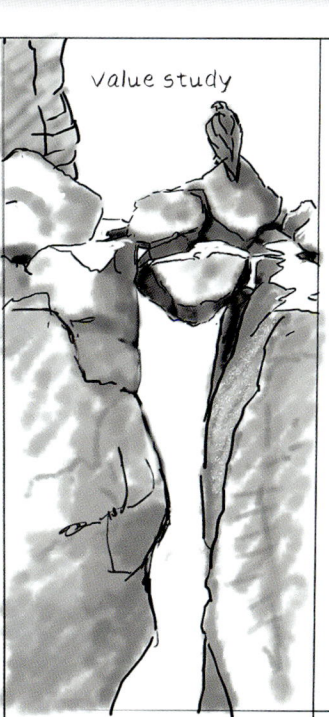

value study

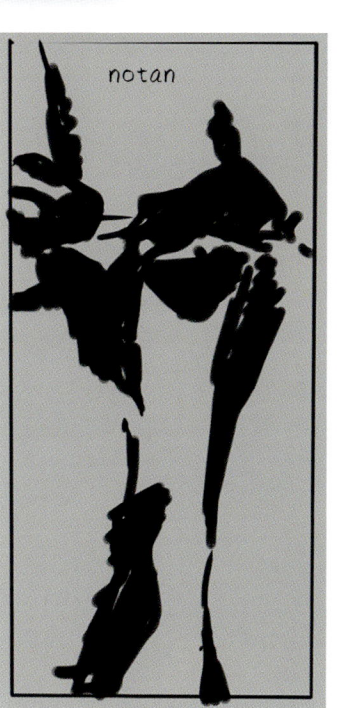

notan

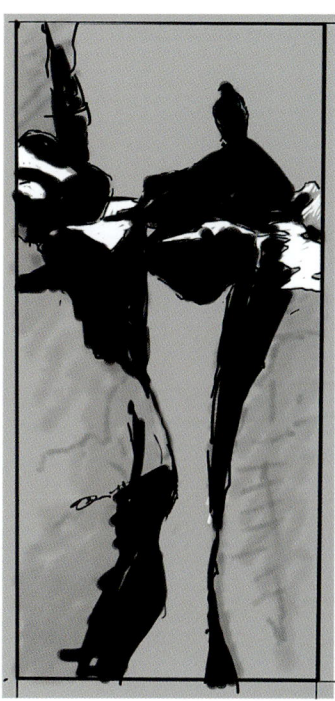

"Where Eagles Dare"

There were no insects or lizards out in the chilled air on that day, and that led me to use White-throated Swifts as my secondary species for this painting.

Years ago, I began discretely to place an insect or arthropod and plant, if possible, into each painting. Tightly connected to its habitat, the primary subject always lives among other animals and plants and shares the habitat.

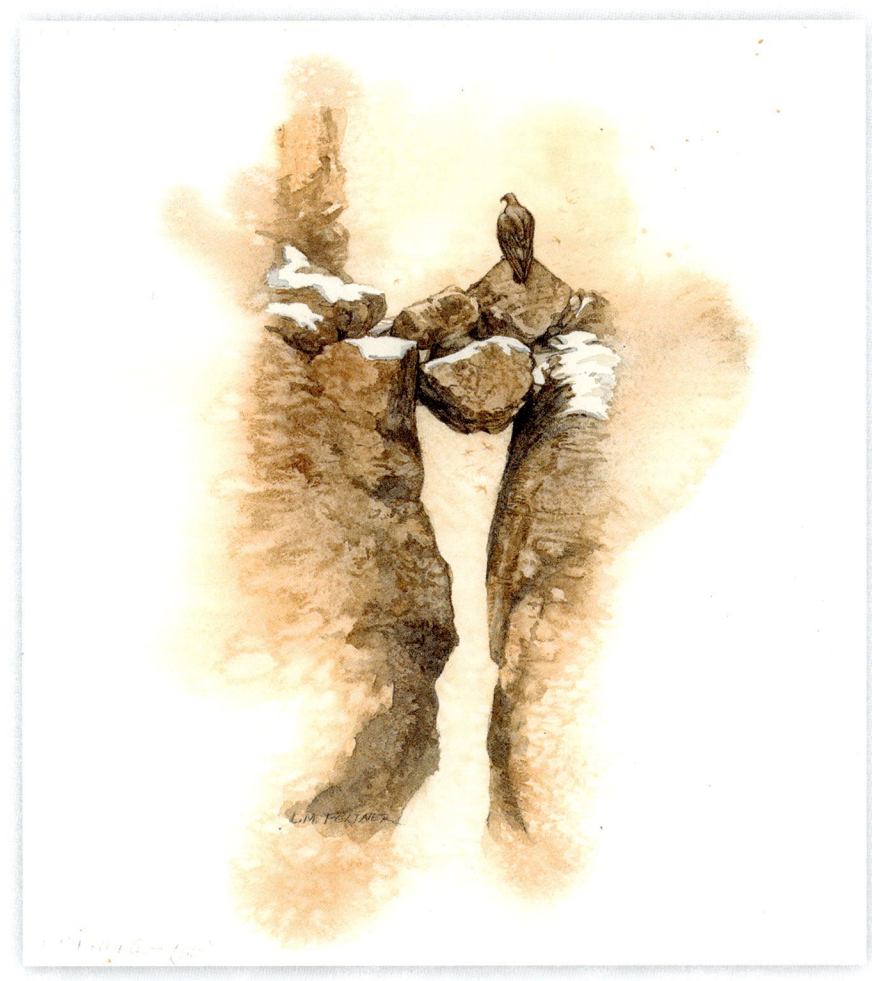

Study for *Where Eagles Dare*, 8.5 x 9.5 in (21.59 x 24.13 cm), 140 lb (300 gsm) cold press Fabriano Artistico paper. Notes in corner indicate color formula: BU (burnt umber) + YO (yellow ocre) + QG (quinacradone gold) + ULT (ultramarine blue). The final painting is on rough 400 lb (850 gsm) Arches watercolor paper.

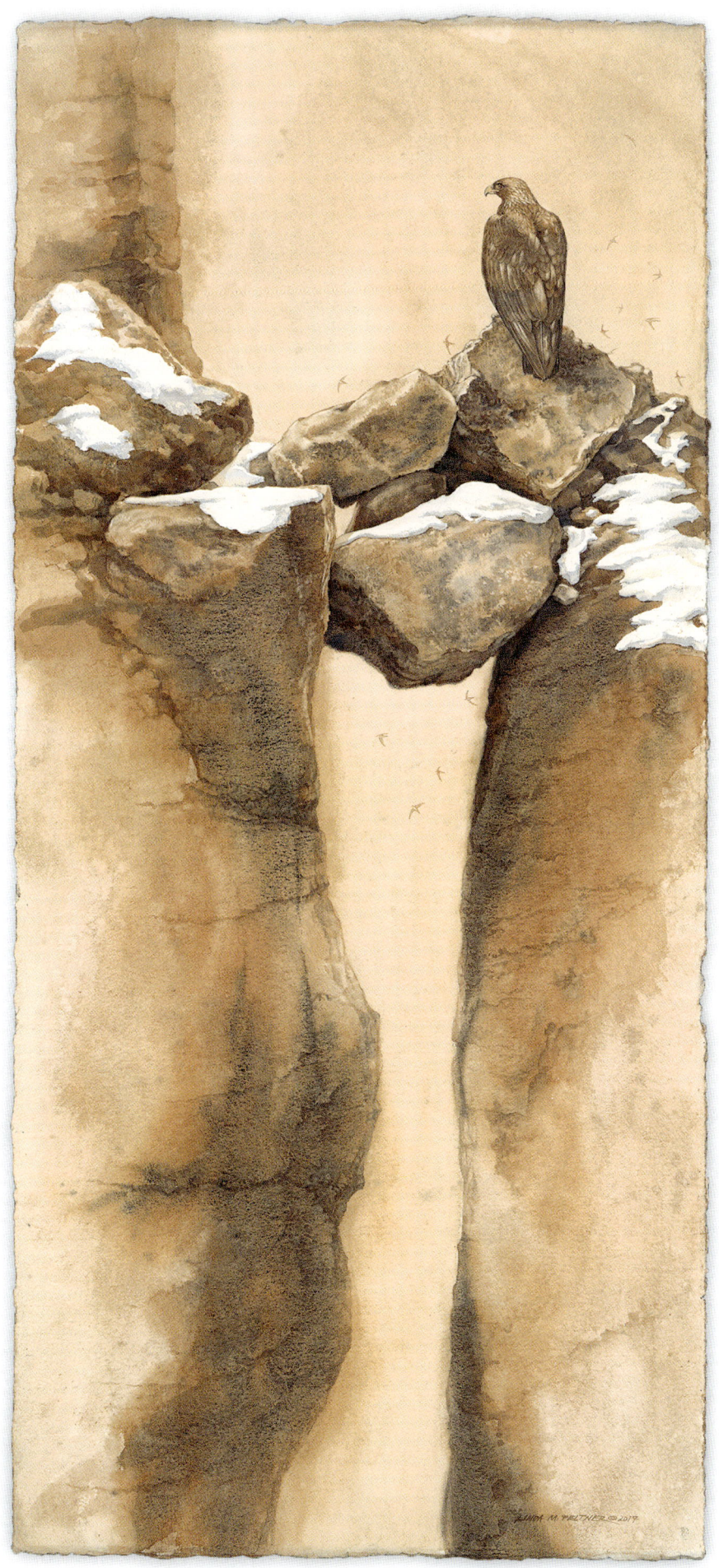

A winding road leads to a mountain vista across the "Land of Standing-Up Rocks," providing an eagle's-eye view of extraordinary rock formations and the valley below Chiricahua National Monument. Massive stone columns and balanced rocks attest to the work of wind, water, and time. Crumbled pillars create improbable sculptures, offering a transitory throne for a Golden Eagle. Swifts gracefully career among stately towers, ignored by the solitary monarch.

Golden Eagle (*Aquila chrysaetos*) and White-throated Swift (*Aeronautes saxatalis*)

Where Eagles Dare, 18.5 × 41.5 in (46.99 × 105.41 cm), transparent watercolor, permanent collection of the Zhejiang Museum of Natural History, Hangzhou, China.

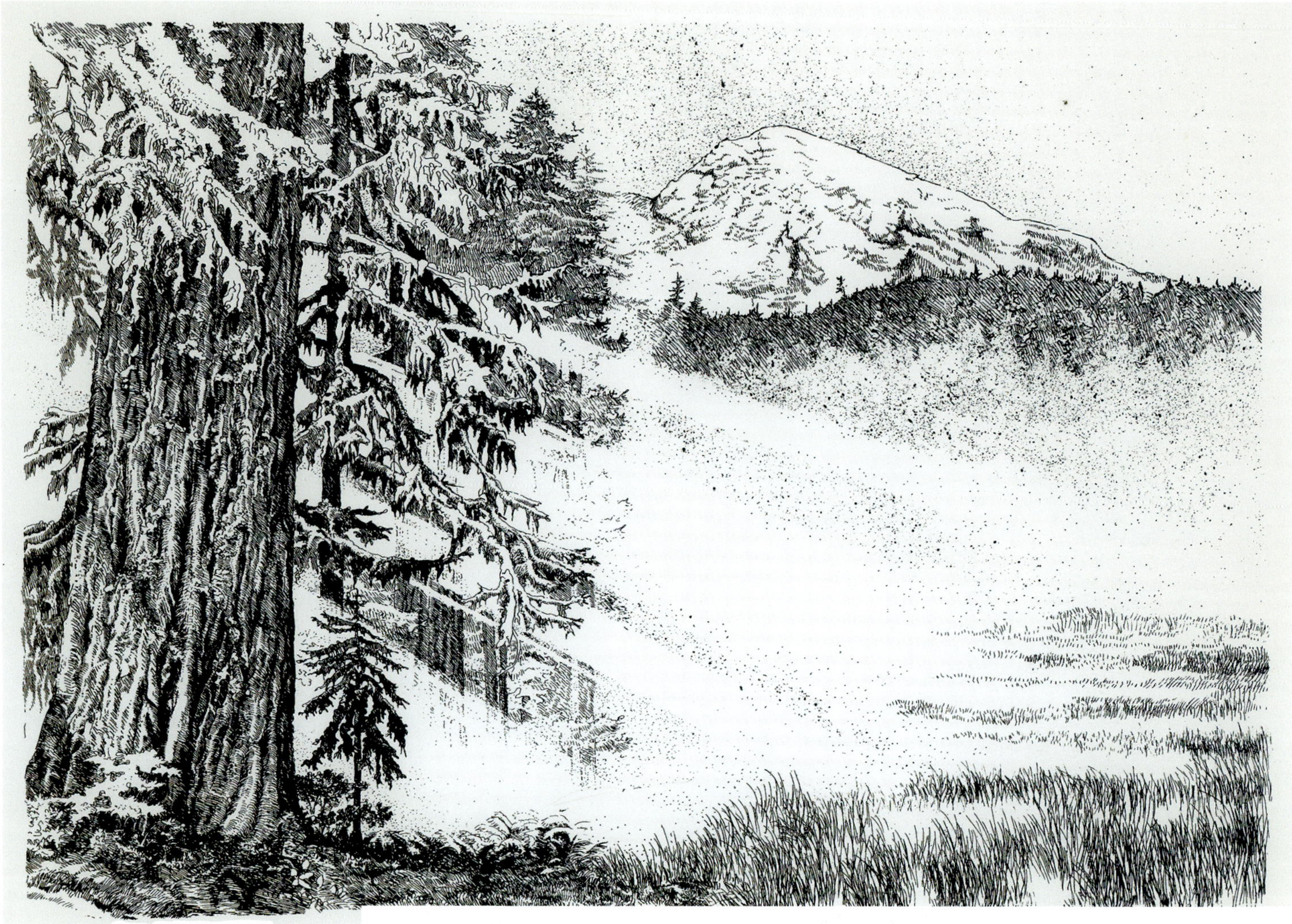

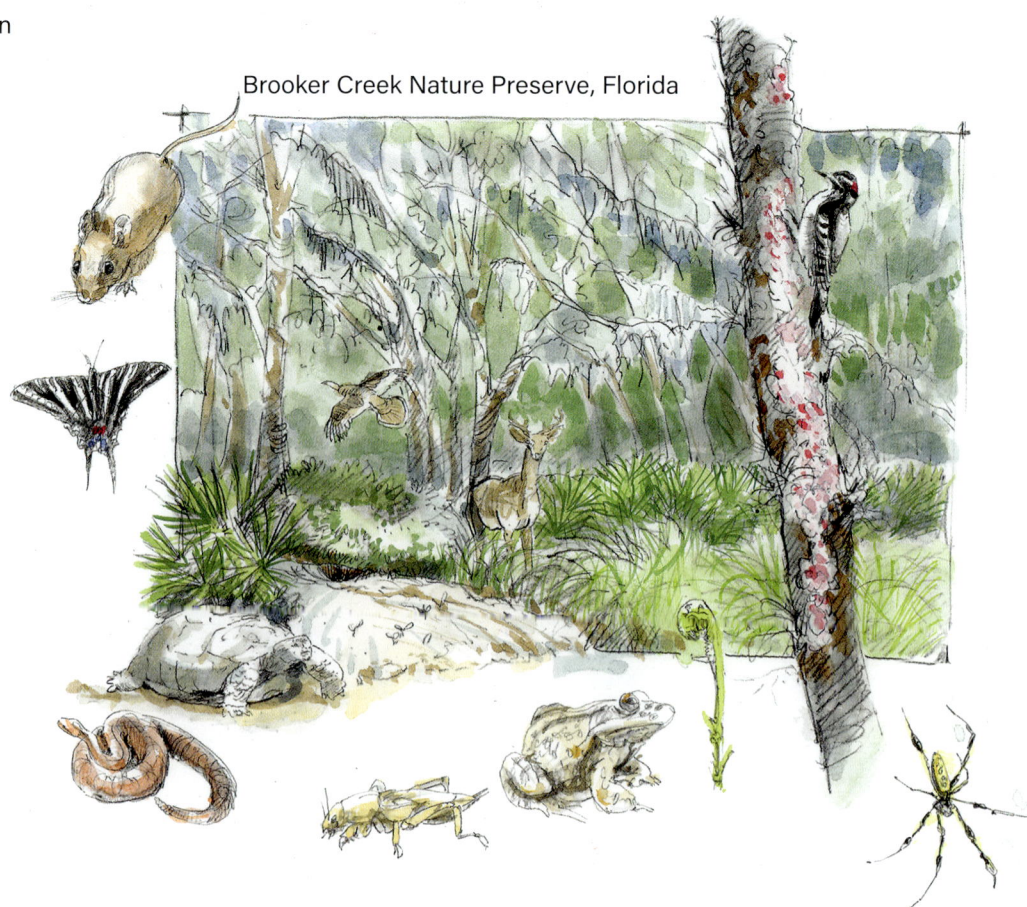

Mt. Rainier National Park, Washington

Brooker Creek Nature Preserve, Florida

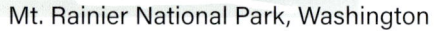

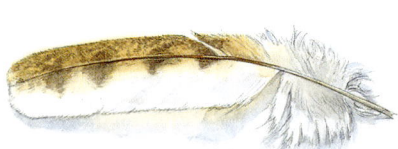

If one feather can
stir curiosity, where
will that story lead?

CHAPTER 7

Interpreting Nature's Connections

Throughout my career, my focus has always been on natural history interpretation, specializing in fine art and scientific illustration. Artwork for educational graphics inspires people of all ages and backgrounds, regardless of language. The following pages show artwork created for National Parks and Monuments, wilderness and city trails, and zoos. I aim to awaken curiosity about the interconnected relationships found in nature and foster a desire to protect them. What good is that creepy bug? The smallest creatures have a significant impact and can help us connect the dots in nature.

My first job was with a zoo, where creating images of animal lifestyles served to inspire the public and raise awareness. Later on, as an independent contractor, I thrived telling visual stories of the interconnections in nature. Fed by my childhood curiosity about wetlands, forests, geology, archeology, and wildlife, I relished drawing natural postures and behaviors. Extensive travels and birding through North and Central American habitats immersed me in the connections within ecological systems.

In this chapter, I explain what factors influenced my decisions for the developmental process. I discuss black-and-white or color choices, and how digital color fabrication factored into my design decisions.

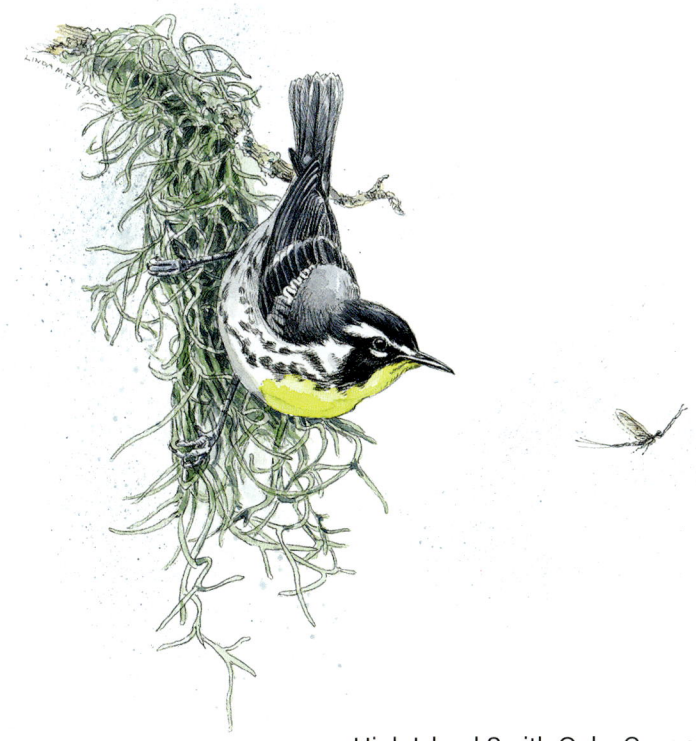

High Island Smith Oaks Canopy Walk, Texas

Mount St. Helens National Volcanic Monument

Mount St. Helens National Volcanic Monument, Washington, USDA Forest Service, Pacific Northwest Region.

On May 18, 1980, Mount St. Helens erupted, altering a vast area of forest, streams, and lakes. Scientists began the study of the devastation as a living laboratory. My projects interpreted the regrowth of landscapes and lakes. Geology was, of course, a primary focus in telling the story of a world transformed.

My creation of the story grew from the scientific research findings and interpretive writing. Aerial photos provided resources for illustrating the alterations to the landscape. As I collaborated with the park rangers and the interpretive writer, I became fascinated with the ways in which a diversity of lifeforms adapt during the recovery of the habitat. Life returned with the help of microorganisms, wind, rain, insects, plants, birds, and mammals.

I've always loved aquatic habitats, busy with life and action. I became engrossed by the newly formed Coldwater Lake. It transformed from a murky, methane-stinking soup into clear water through the action of oxygen-gulping bacteria and those that thrive without oxygen. One drop of water contained 50 million bacteria! These organisms were vital to the lake's conversion in only three years to a healthy environment and a haven for wildlife.

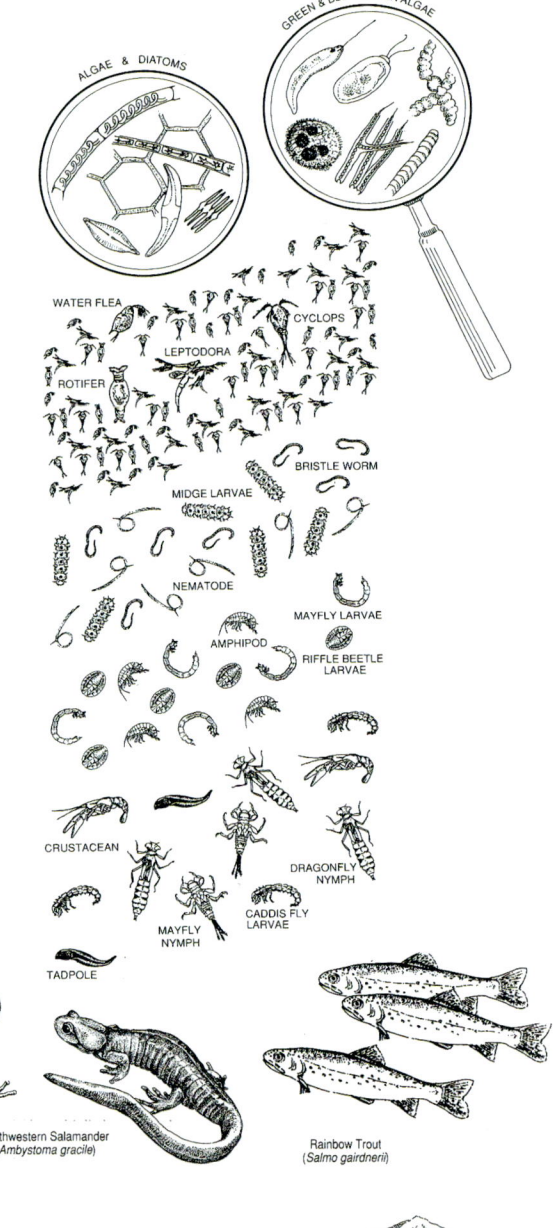

Pacific Treefrog
(*Hyla regilla*)

Northwestern Salamander
(*Ambystoma gracile*)

Rainbow Trout
(*Salmo gairdnerii*)

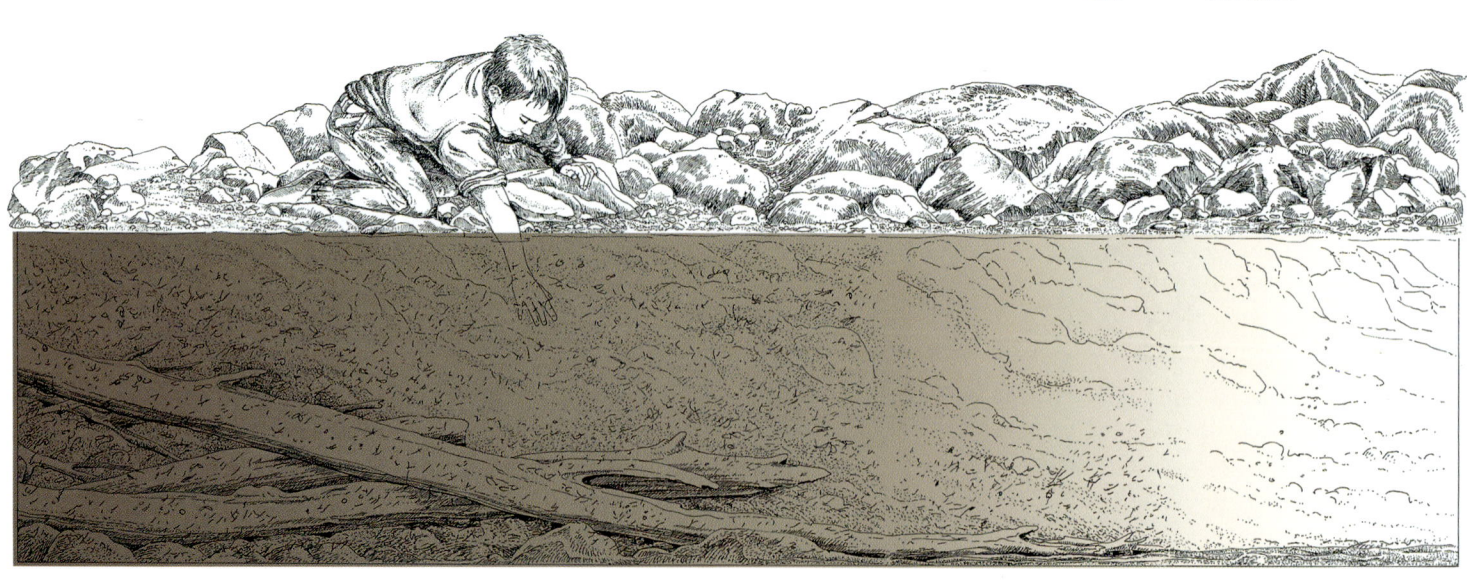

June, 1980　　　*April, 1981*　　　*April, 1983 - present*

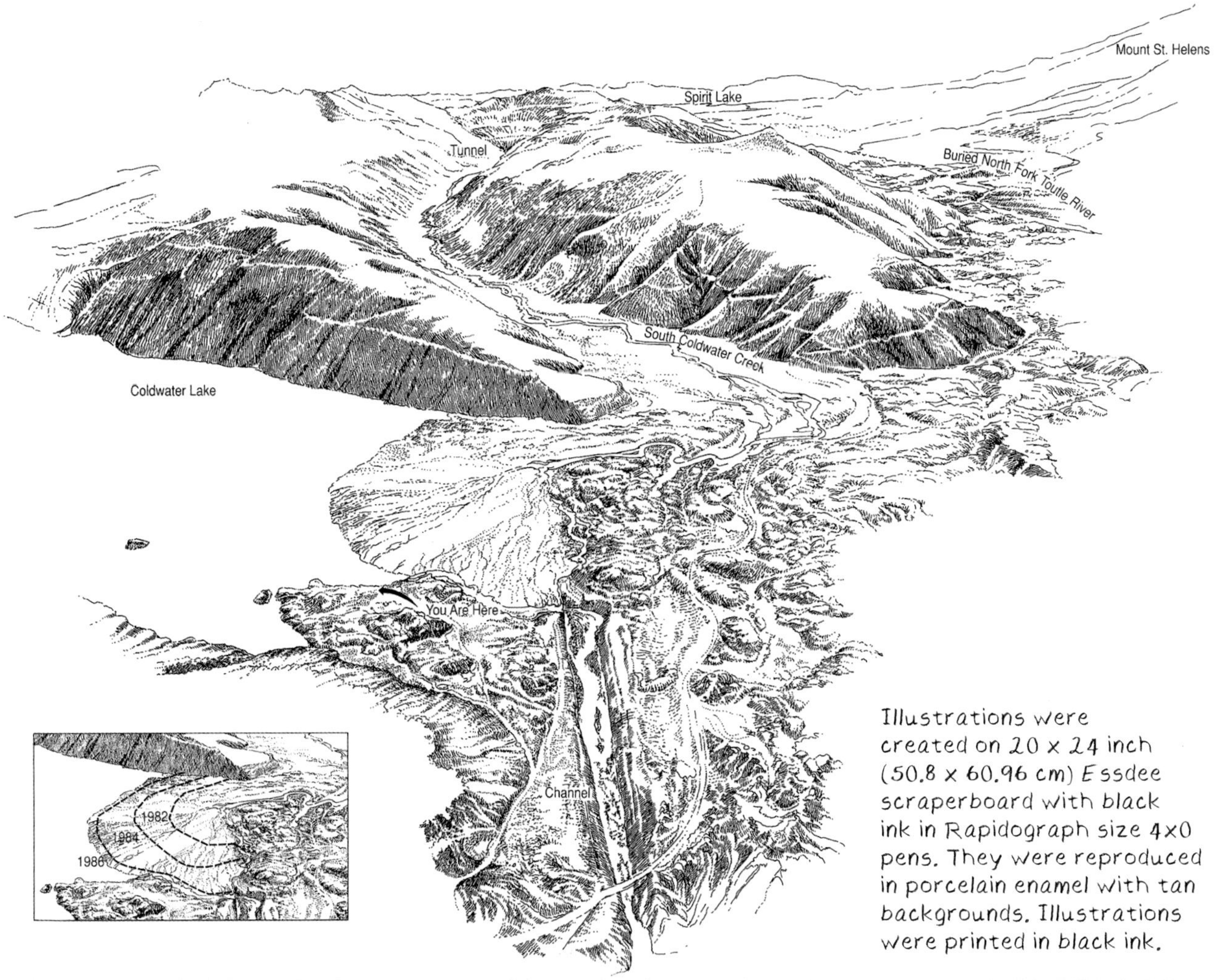

Labels on top illustration: Mount St. Helens, Spirit Lake, Tunnel, Buried North Fork Toutle River, South Coldwater Creek, Coldwater Lake, You Are Here, Channel

Inset map labels: 1982, 1984, 1986

Illustrations were created on 20 x 24 inch (50.8 x 60.96 cm) Essdee scraperboard with black ink in Rapidograph size 4x0 pens. They were reproduced in porcelain enamel with tan backgrounds. Illustrations were printed in black ink.

A Fiery Mountain Of Many Names

Throughout time, many names have been given and stories told about the mountain that stands before you. In the 1700's, Captain George Vancouver named it Mount St. Helens, after a British diplomat.

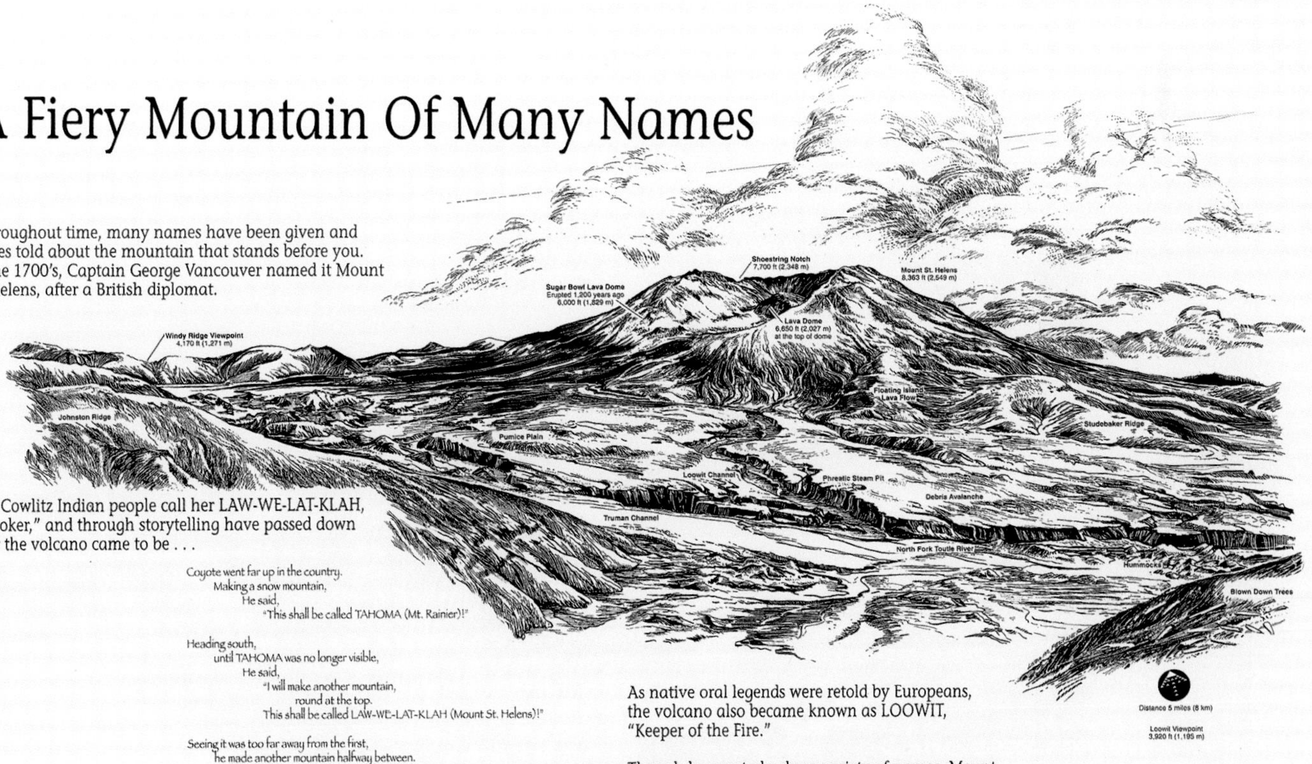

The Cowlitz Indian people call her LAW-WE-LAT-KLAH, "Smoker," and through storytelling have passed down how the volcano came to be . . .

Coyote went far up in the country.
Making a snow mountain,
He said,
"This shall be called TAHOMA (Mt. Rainier)!"

Heading south,
until TAHOMA was no longer visible,
He said,
"I will make another mountain,
round at the top.
This shall be called LAW-WE-LAT-KLAH (Mount St. Helens)!"

Seeing it was too far away from the first,
he made another mountain halfway between.
He said,
"This one shall be called PATU (Mt. Adams)!
This shall be the husband of the two others."

They say that LAW-WE-LAT-KLAH got jealous of TAHOMA,
and threw fire at her.
She burnt TAHOMA's head off,
burnt her backbone and shoulders, too.

As native oral legends were retold by Europeans, the volcano also became known as LOOWIT, "Keeper of the Fire."

Though known today by a variety of names, Mount St. Helens is recognized for its awe-inspiring beauty and is respected for its fiery temperament.

Labels on lower illustration: Windy Ridge Viewpoint 4,170 ft (1,271 m); Sugar Bowl Lava Dome Erupted 1,200 years ago 6,000 ft (1,829 m); Shoestring Notch 7,700 ft (2,348 m); Mount St. Helens 8,363 ft (2,549 m); Lava Dome 6,650 ft (2,027 m) at the top of dome; Floating Island Lava Flow; Johnston Ridge; Pumice Plain; Loowit Channel; Phreatic Steam Pit; Studebaker Ridge; Debris Avalanche; Truman Channel; North Fork Toutle River; Hummocks; Blown Down Trees; Distance 5 miles (8 km); Loowit Viewpoint 3,920 ft (1,195 m)

Mount St. Helens: Wetland Restoration

Lakes and wetlands downstream from the volcano improved with the nutrients from ash and displaced soil, returning to near-original conditions. Interpretive panels for the boardwalk trail at the Silver Lake Visitor Center introduced visitors to the wetland ecosystem and its history of use.

Research and sketches start with plant and animal species fitting together like puzzle pieces to form a whole scene. I enjoy creating above- and below-water views as these illustrate the unseen elements as well as the complexity of the habitat.

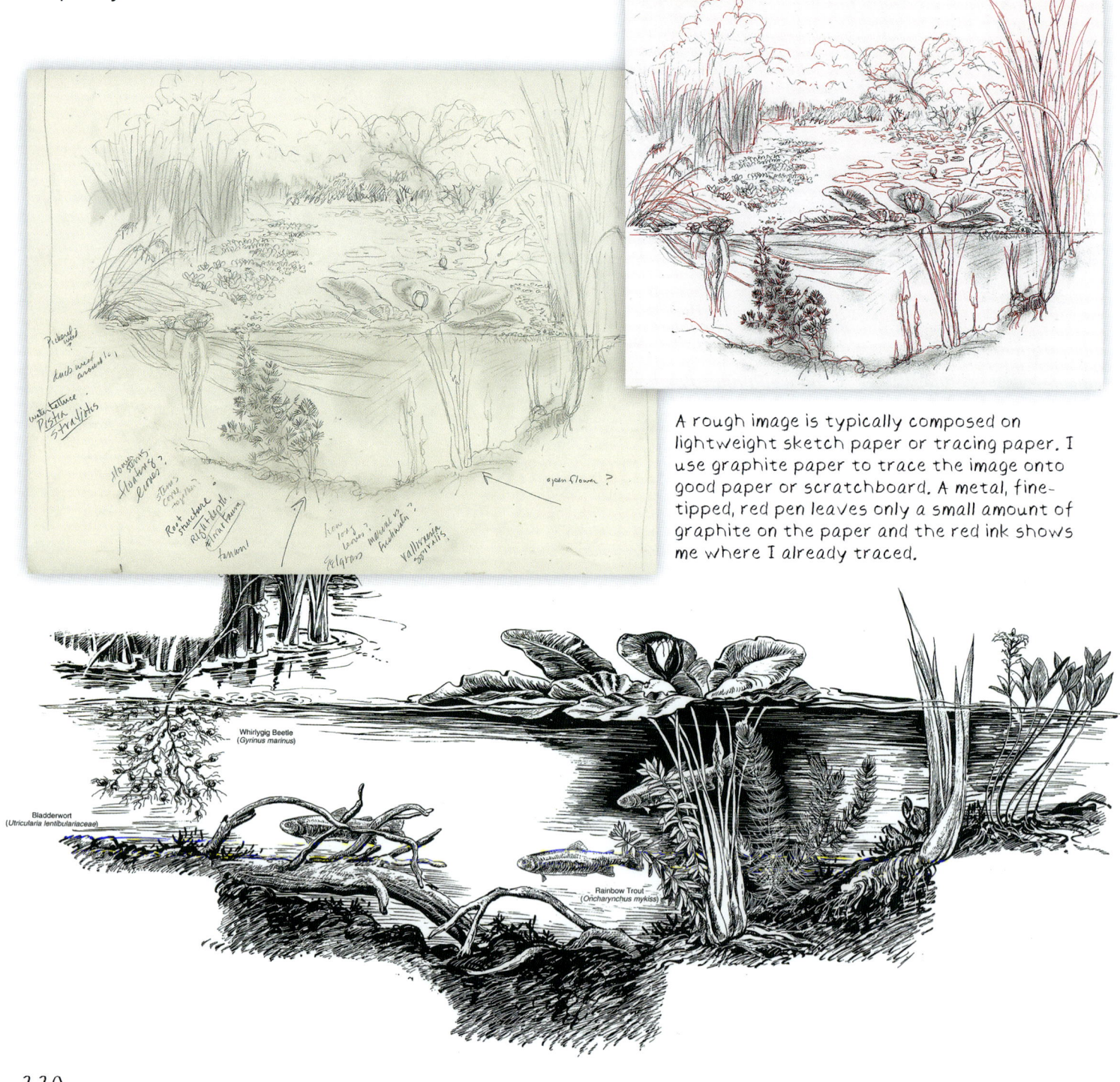

A rough image is typically composed on lightweight sketch paper or tracing paper. I use graphite paper to trace the image onto good paper or scratchboard. A metal, fine-tipped, red pen leaves only a small amount of graphite on the paper and the red ink shows me where I already traced.

Whirlygig Beetle
(*Gyrinus marinus*)

Bladderwort
(*Utricularia lentibulariaceae*)

Rainbow Trout
(*Oricharynchus mykiss*)

A Wetland Haven

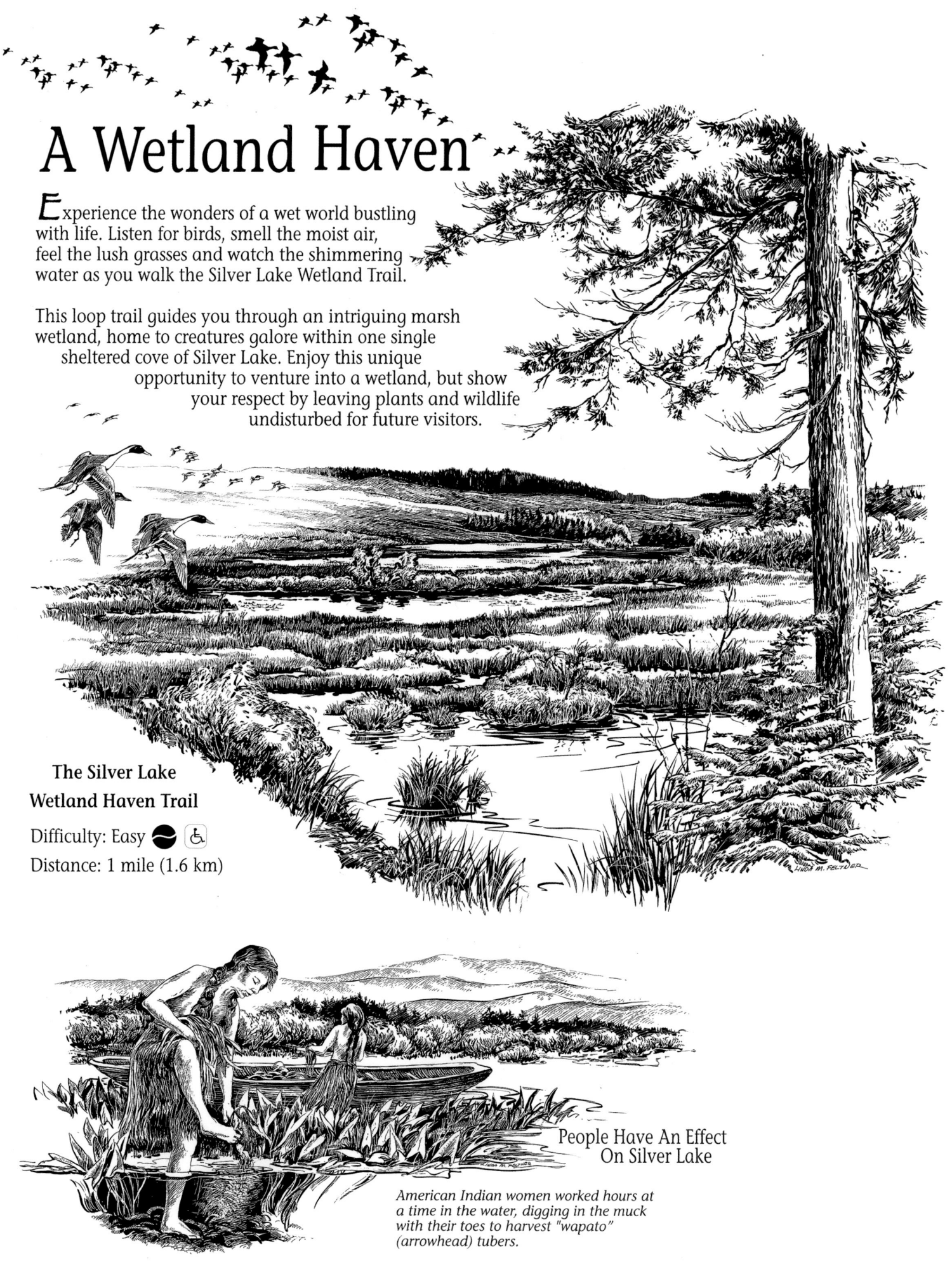

*E*xperience the wonders of a wet world bustling with life. Listen for birds, smell the moist air, feel the lush grasses and watch the shimmering water as you walk the Silver Lake Wetland Trail.

This loop trail guides you through an intriguing marsh wetland, home to creatures galore within one single sheltered cove of Silver Lake. Enjoy this unique opportunity to venture into a wetland, but show your respect by leaving plants and wildlife undisturbed for future visitors.

The Silver Lake Wetland Haven Trail

Difficulty: Easy

Distance: 1 mile (1.6 km)

People Have An Effect On Silver Lake

American Indian women worked hours at a time in the water, digging in the muck with their toes to harvest "wapato" (arrowhead) tubers.

221

"A Race for Refuge": Preliminary Research

As a birder growing up in Texas, I relished the opportunity to paint a commission that epitomized the challenging journey that tiny warblers endure in their migration across the Gulf of Mexico. The birds seek landfall where they can rest, eat, and bathe before continuing on their journey to their breeding grounds. The client wanted me to show warblers in their determined struggle to reach land with vegetation.

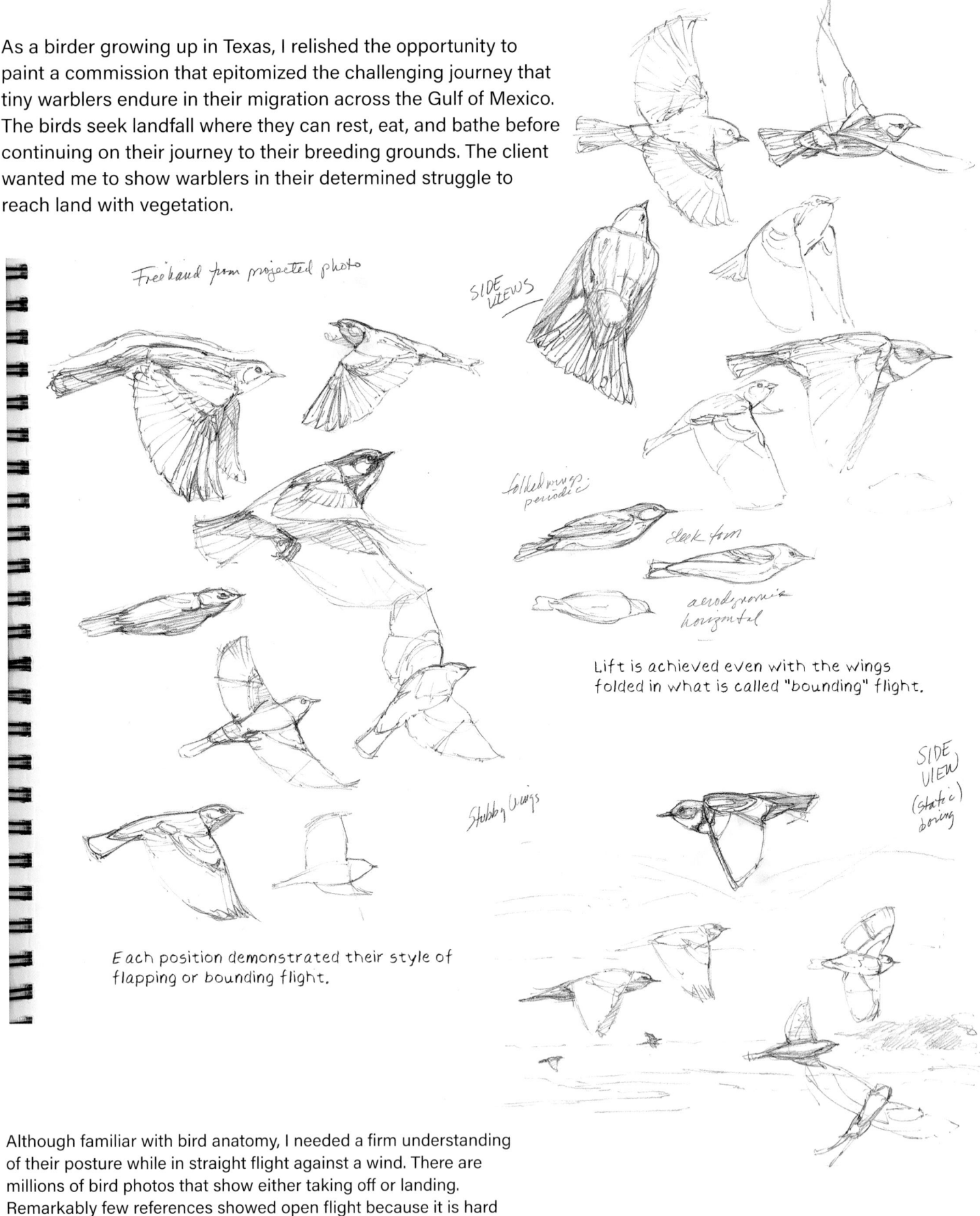

Freehand from projected photo

SIDE VIEWS

folded wings: periodic

sleek form

aerodynamic horizontal

Lift is achieved even with the wings folded in what is called "bounding" flight.

Stubby wings

SIDE VIEW (static) boring

Each position demonstrated their style of flapping or bounding flight.

Although familiar with bird anatomy, I needed a firm understanding of their posture while in straight flight against a wind. There are millions of bird photos that show either taking off or landing. Remarkably few references showed open flight because it is hard to photograph warblers flying high.

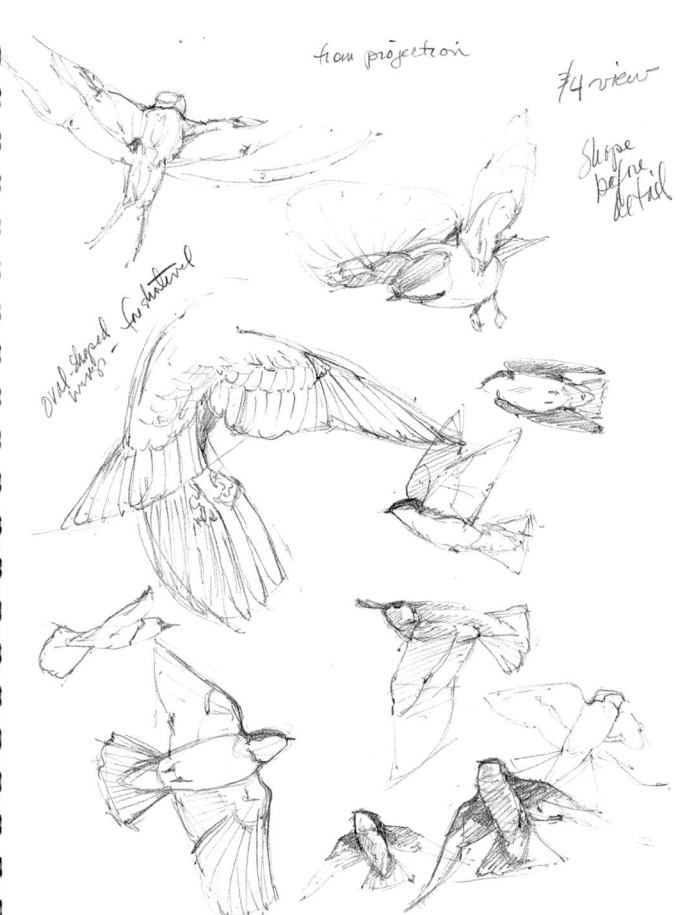

from projection

3/4 view

Shape before detail

Oval-shaped wings—foreshortened

Freehand drawings from projected photos of birds other than warblers provided active gesture drawings for shapes and wing positions.

I found a short video from an offshore oil rig whose bright lights illuminated a warbler migrating north at night against the wind. It was very informative. The Macaulay Library of The Cornell Lab of Ornithology online videos were also helpful. Generous friends sent me flight photos of small species, mostly swallows, waxwings, blackbirds, and tanagers. I eagerly studied any small bird in straight flight to determine if I could later adapt it for warblers.

I draw the shape before detail.

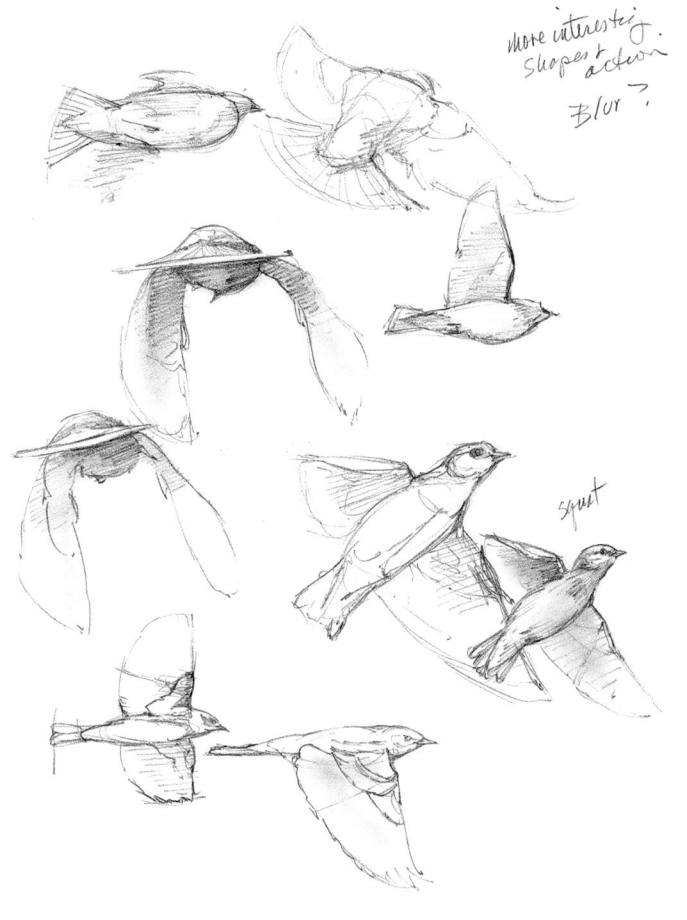

more interesting. Shapes + action

Blur

squat

Freehand drawing from projected 3/4 view shape only detail later

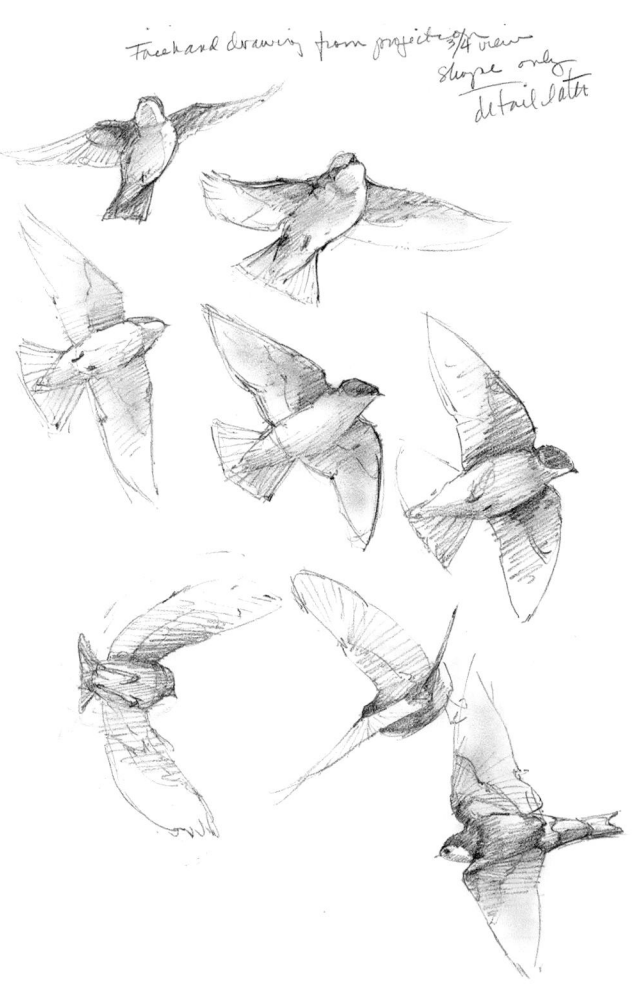

The wings and body in direct and struggling flight present a different shape than during landing or taking off.

"A Race for Refuge": Development

The mission statement of the Gulf Coast Bird Observatory in Lake Jackson, Texas, is: "Protect birds and their habitats around the Gulf of Mexico and beyond." The painting was commissioned to raise awareness, as well as help fund conservation.

Springtime thunderstorms hinder the tired birds as they approach the coastal edge. Migrating birds face these local downbursts and maneuver around them to find a place to land.

The Cerulean Warbler was requested as the primary species, along with a mixed flock of warbler species that migrate together in early spring.

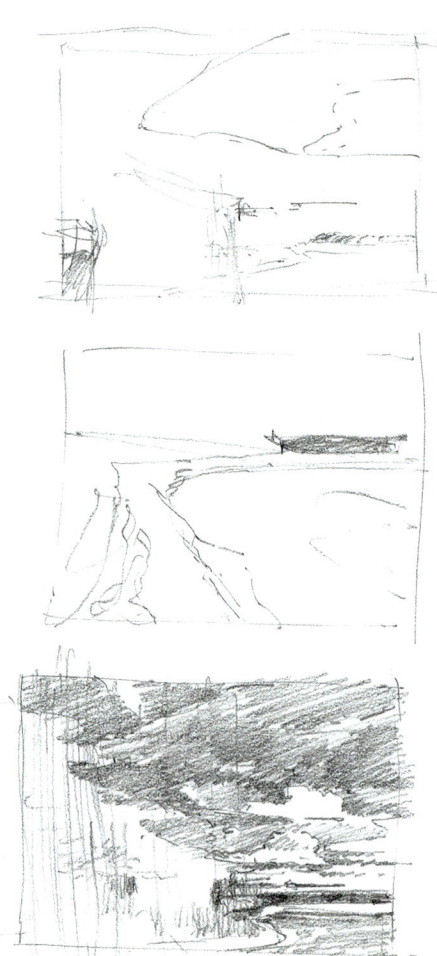

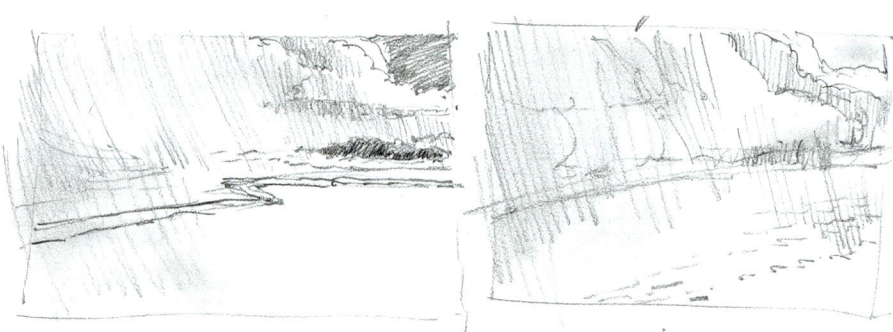

Compositional sketches show the coastal edge with localized thundershowers.

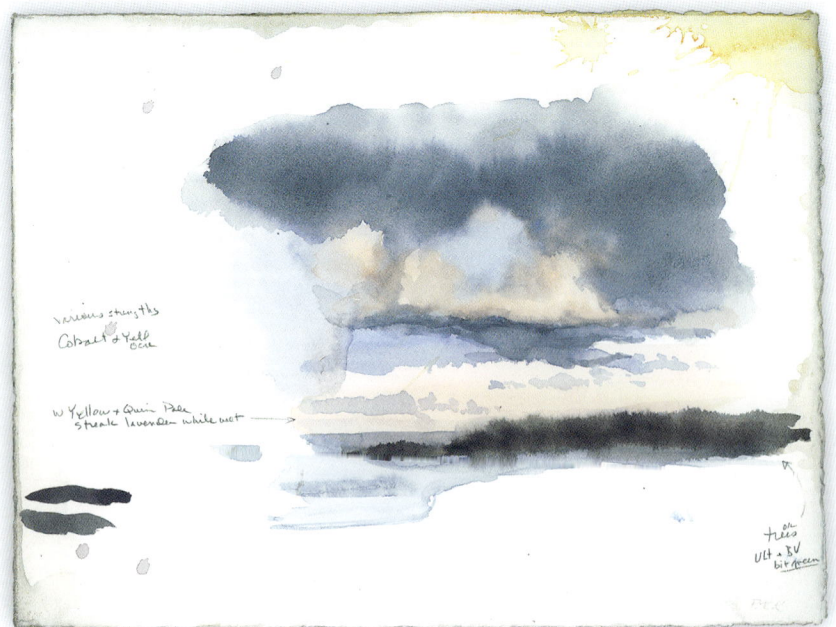

Testing the paper for humidity and colors. 8.5 × 11 in (21.59 × 27.94 cm), 140 lb (300 gsm) cold press Fabriano Artistico paper.

The background scene is a crucial part of the story. Its painting technique is as important as the birds. I did a test to determine how both transparent and opaque watercolor (gouache) would perform. The dry Arizona air is a constant consideration. I tried two methods, the first using only transparent watercolor with wet washes around the bird. The tricky part was painting around each feather tip of the open wing while the paint was quickly drying. It did not achieve a background to my satisfaction. It would be easy if it were a rocky textured background, but smooth, billowy clouds were necessary.

The second option was to use both media, seamlessly blended together and balanced throughout both birds and background. This proved to be the best of both worlds, achieving the ominous and spontaneous action of the message.

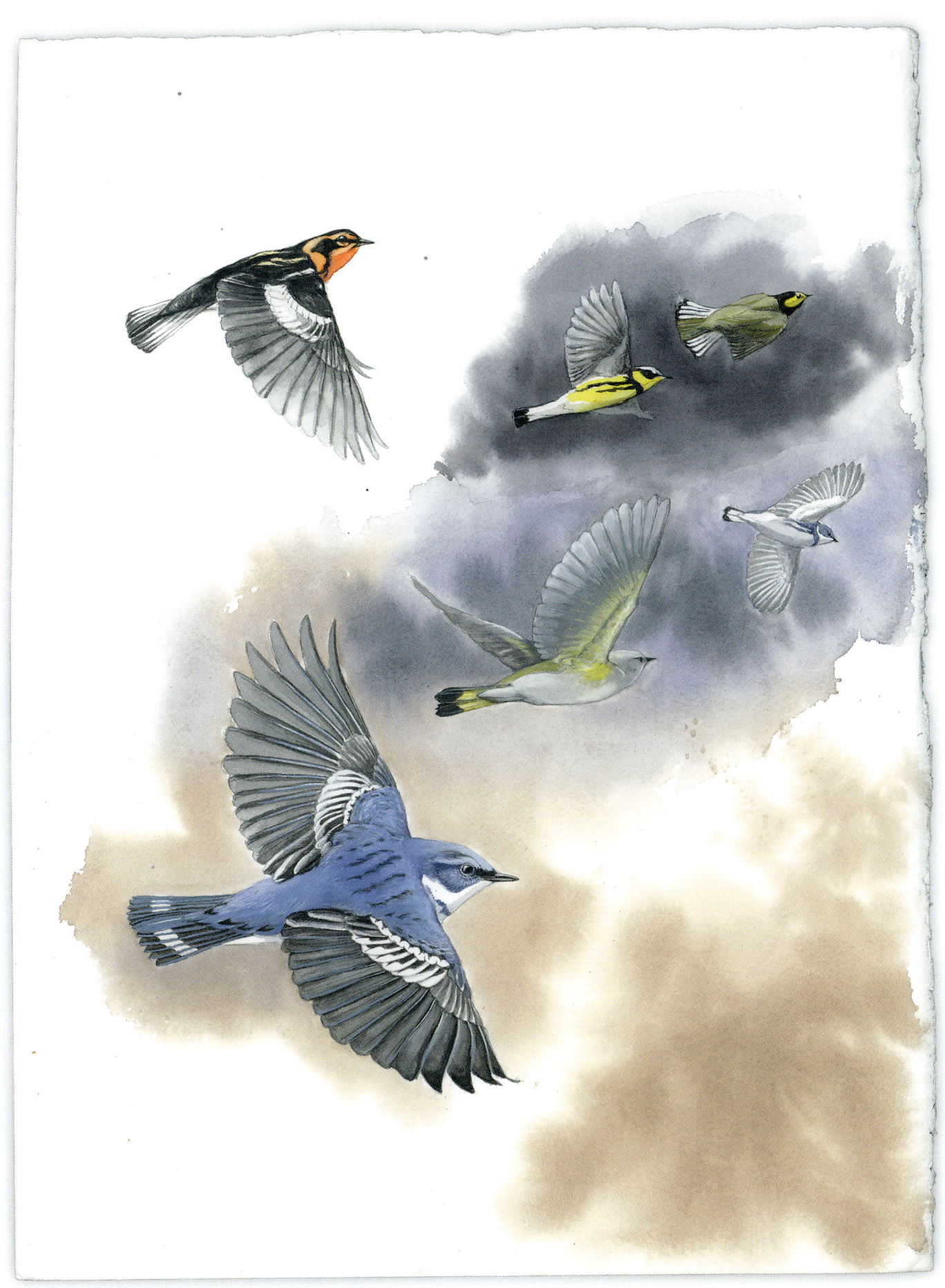

Practice test for harmonizing transparency and opacity. 11 x 15 in
(27.94 x 38.1 cm), 300 lb (640 gsm) cold press Fabriano Artistico paper.

"A Race for Refuge"

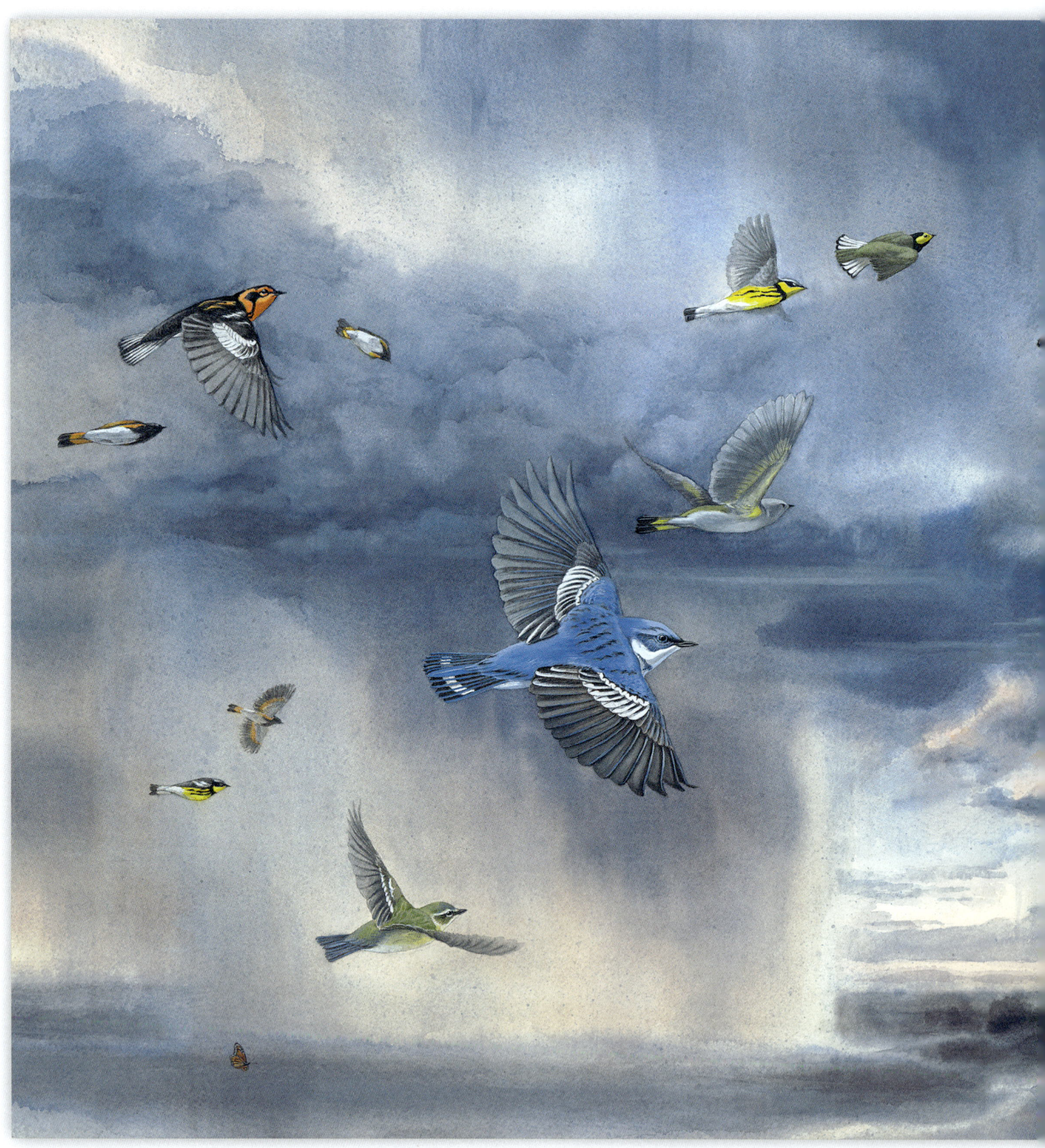

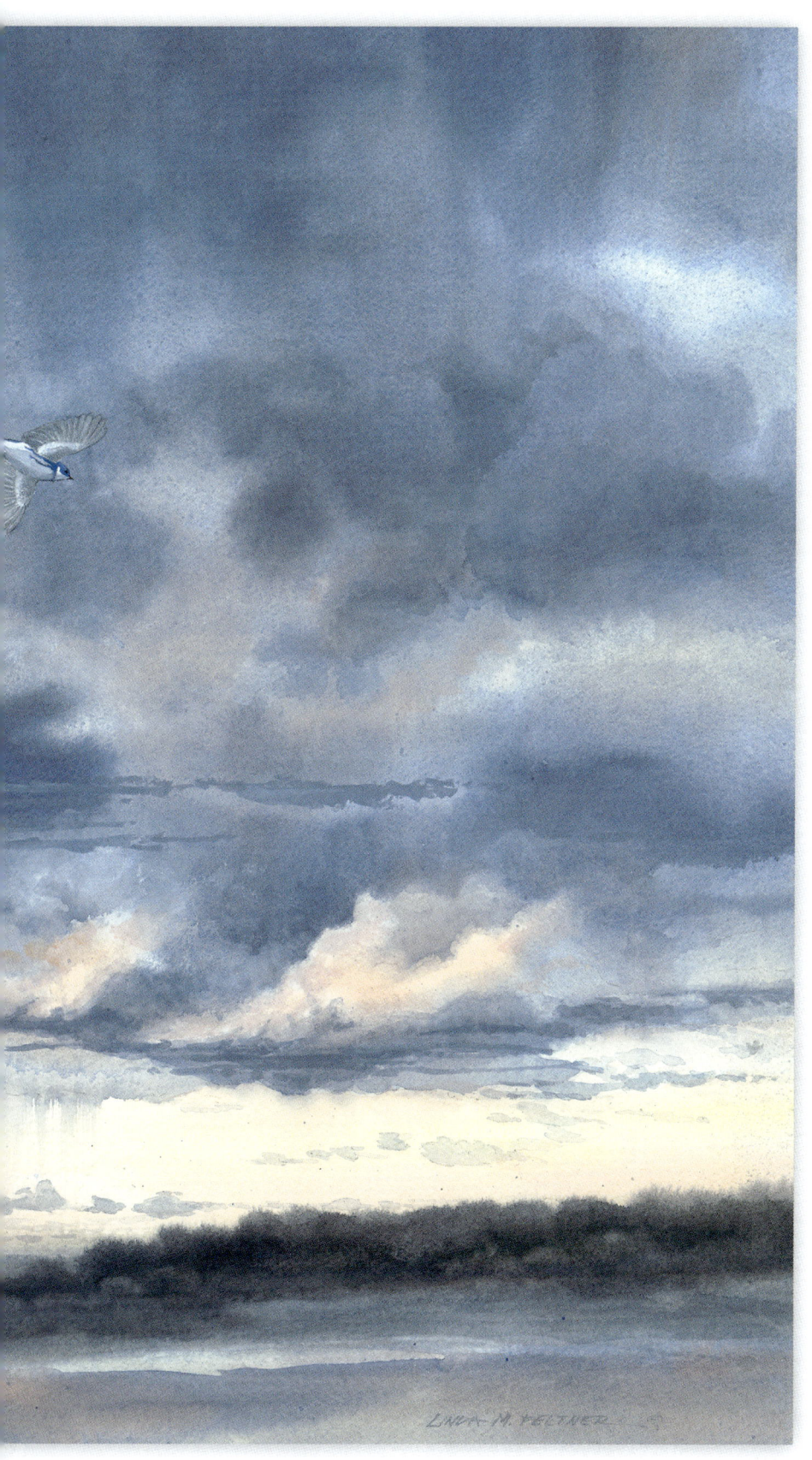

If you had wings, imagine flapping for five hundred miles nonstop over water. Bird migration across the Gulf of Mexico is strenuous and ventured twice a year. The birds' springtime journey can be met with tempestuous rainstorms and high winds, creating hazards they must avoid. Coastal lands are the first they encounter, providing refuge for the tired and hungry birds. Preservation of coastal habitat is vital to the success of the journey for thousands of tiny migrants.

Cerulean Warbler (*Setophaga cerulea*), American Redstart (*Setophaga ruticilla*), Blackburnian Warbler (*Setophaga fusca*), Magnolia Warbler (*Setophaga magnolia*), Hooded Warbler (*Setophaga citrina*), and Monarch Butterfly (*Danaus plexippus*)

A Race for Refuge, 28.5 × 19 in (72.39 × 48.26 cm), watercolor on 300 lb (640 gsm) cold press Fabriano Artistico paper.

High Island Smith Oaks Canopy Walk

The Kathrine G. McGovern Canopy Walkway provides an elevated canopy experience in the world-famous bird migration stopover on the Gulf of Mexico in High Island, Texas. Houston Audubon Society commissioned the illustrated notebook-style panels to spark interest in these critical sanctuaries.

   The dedicated conservation managers guided the team writer, Wendy Walker, and me through an on-site tour of the woodland. Wendy was a first-time visitor, while I have been birding in these woods for decades. I sketched loose impressions as if I were a new visitor, noting things that caught my attention and were curious.

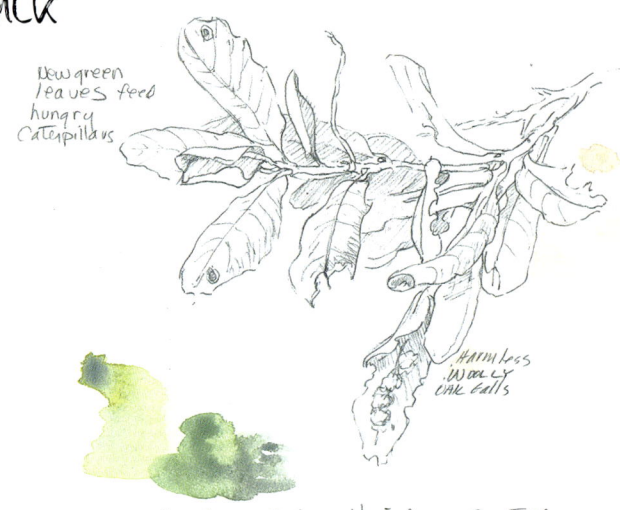

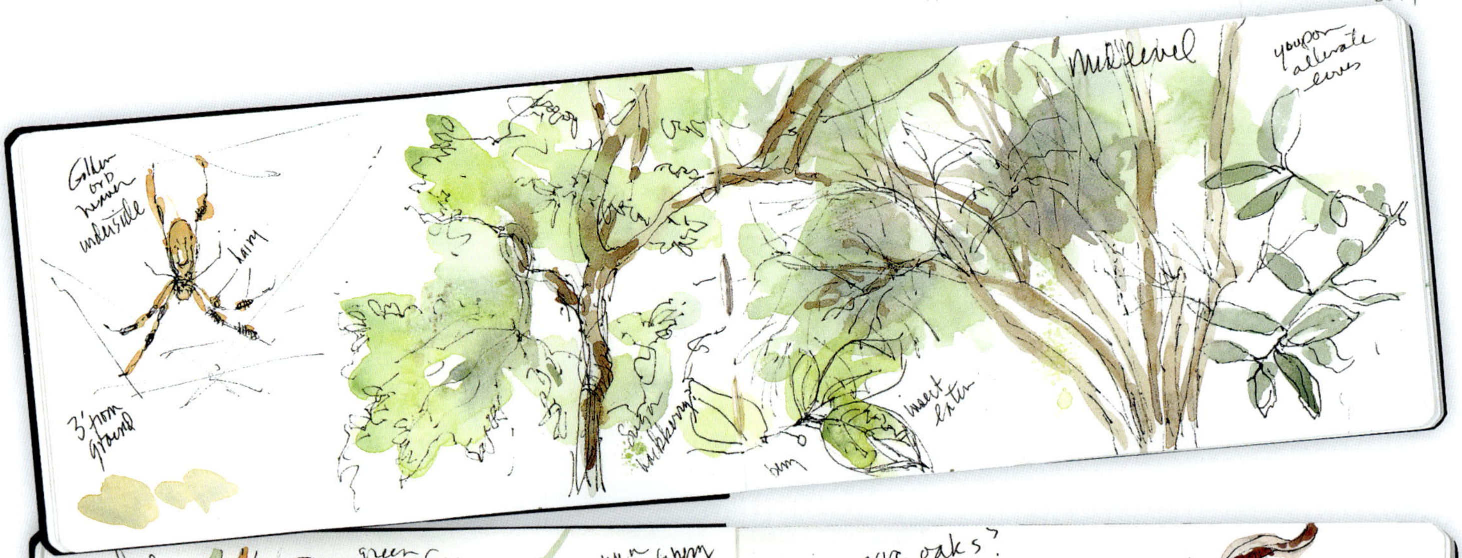

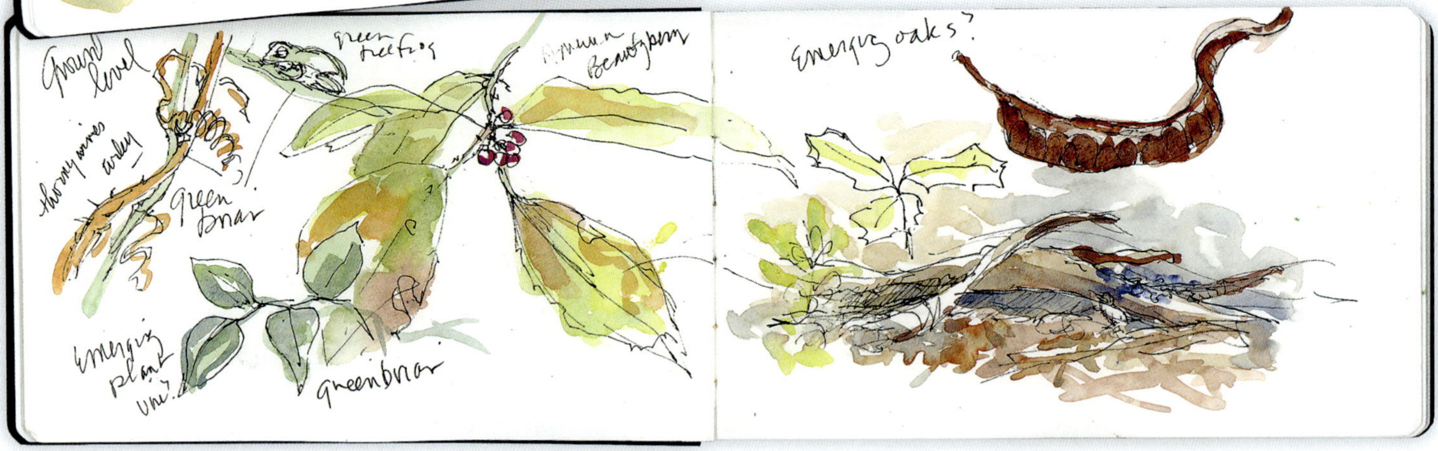

New green leaves feed hungry Caterpillars

Harmless Wooly Oak Galls

studies for Smith Oaks, High Island Fall 2019

Midlevel

youpon alternate leaves

Golden orb weaver underside

hairy

3' from ground

Sandy wildberry

insect eater

Ground level

Green treefrog

Common Beautyberry

Emerging oaks?

thorny vines early

Green briar

Emerging plant vine

greenbriar

Jot down things that catch your attention and ask questions as if you were walking there for the first time.

Acorns

What captures my attention? I admire the dark umbrella of the gnarly oaks that shelter broad-leaved bushes with beautiful berries. Elegant twisting vines hang from the trees and camouflage a clinging tree frog. Impressive spiders stretch their webs across the woodland trails. What might I find in the upper canopy foliage, the understory, or the ground?

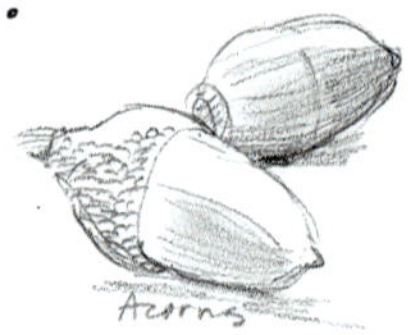

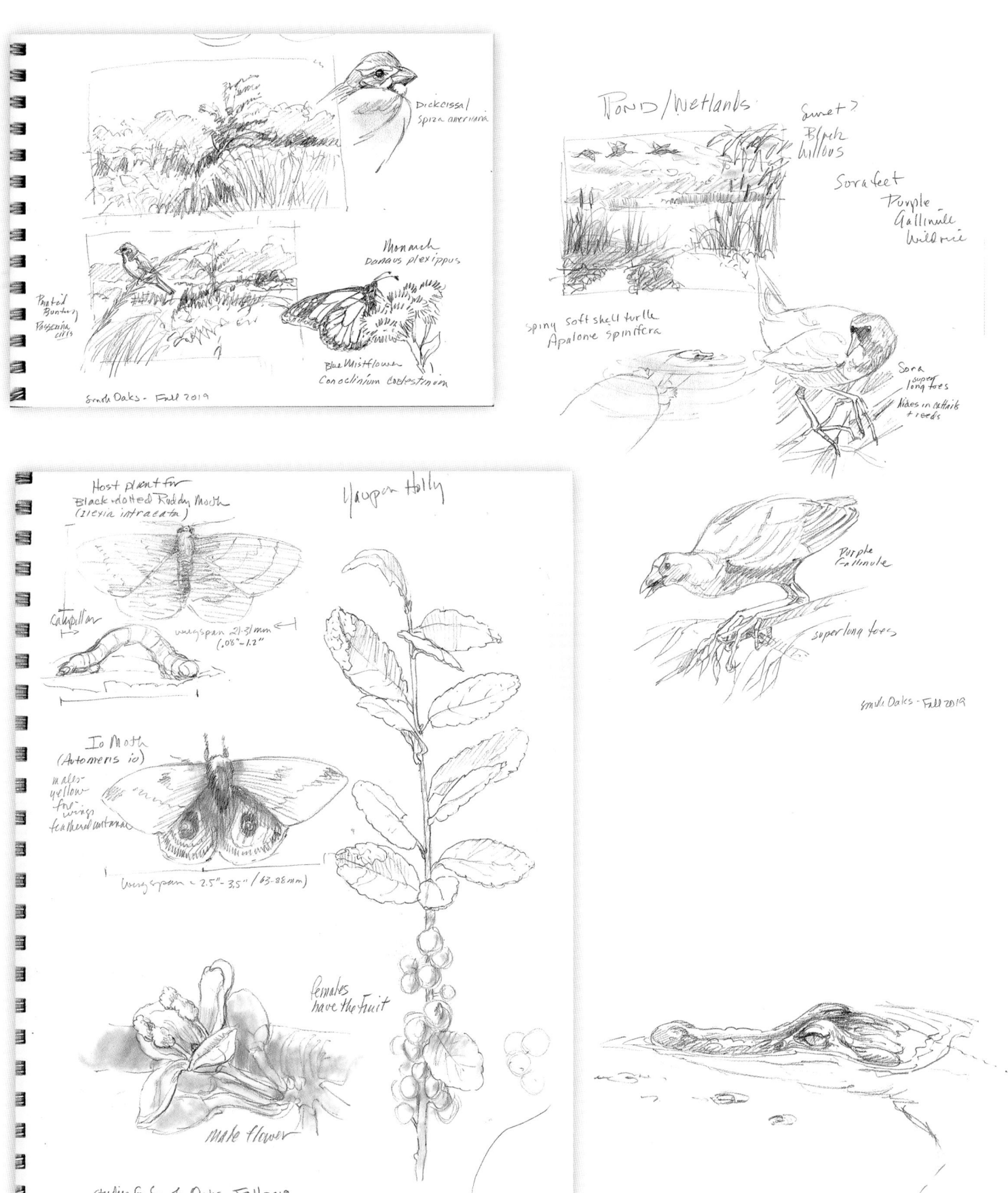

As ideas grow and are added to the story, studies are drawn in greater detail.

The following four panels are high-pressure laminate reproductions, 20 × 30 in (51 × 76 cm), courtesy of the Houston Audubon Society, Houston, Texas.

Welcome to the Kathrine G. McGovern Canopy Walkway

Come and travel this boardwalk trail up into the treetops. Try to slow down and open your eyes and ears to explore like a naturalist. Notice the connections between organisms. You may discover new perspectives through the lives of birds, butterflies, reptiles, and other wildlife in this place of rest and refuge.

Yellow-throated Warbler & Mayfly

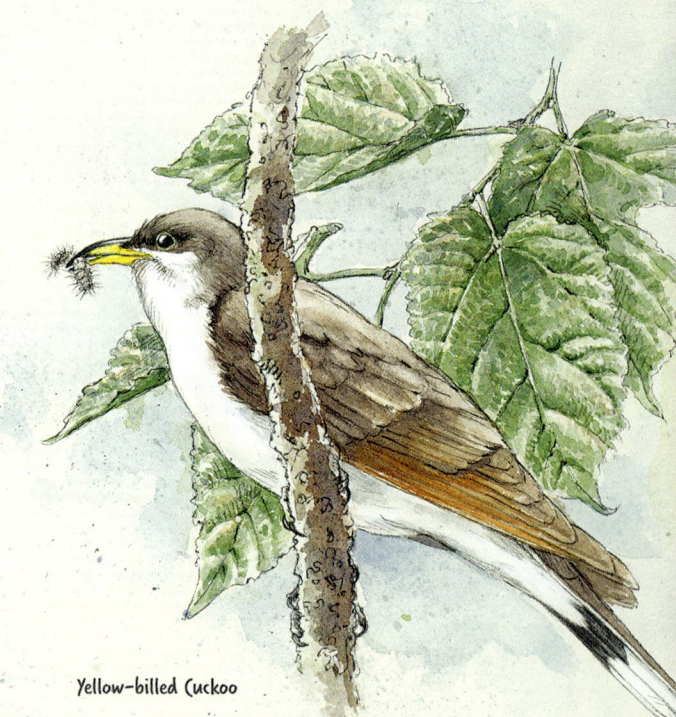

Imagine being a small forest bird flying north more than a mile high over the Gulf of Mexico on a spring day. You launched from Mexico 18 hours and 600 miles ago. Exhausted, you need at least a patch of wooded habitat to rest and refuel before continuing on to your breeding grounds far to the north.

Yellow-billed Cuckoo

Kentucky Warbler

Land ahead! Scan the flat, marshy coast and fly toward the only forested hill... High Island. Glide down into the branches of a live oak. A caterpillar inches along on a leaf. Yum! A small pool on the forest floor glistens. Flutter down for a drink and a refreshing bath. Ah!

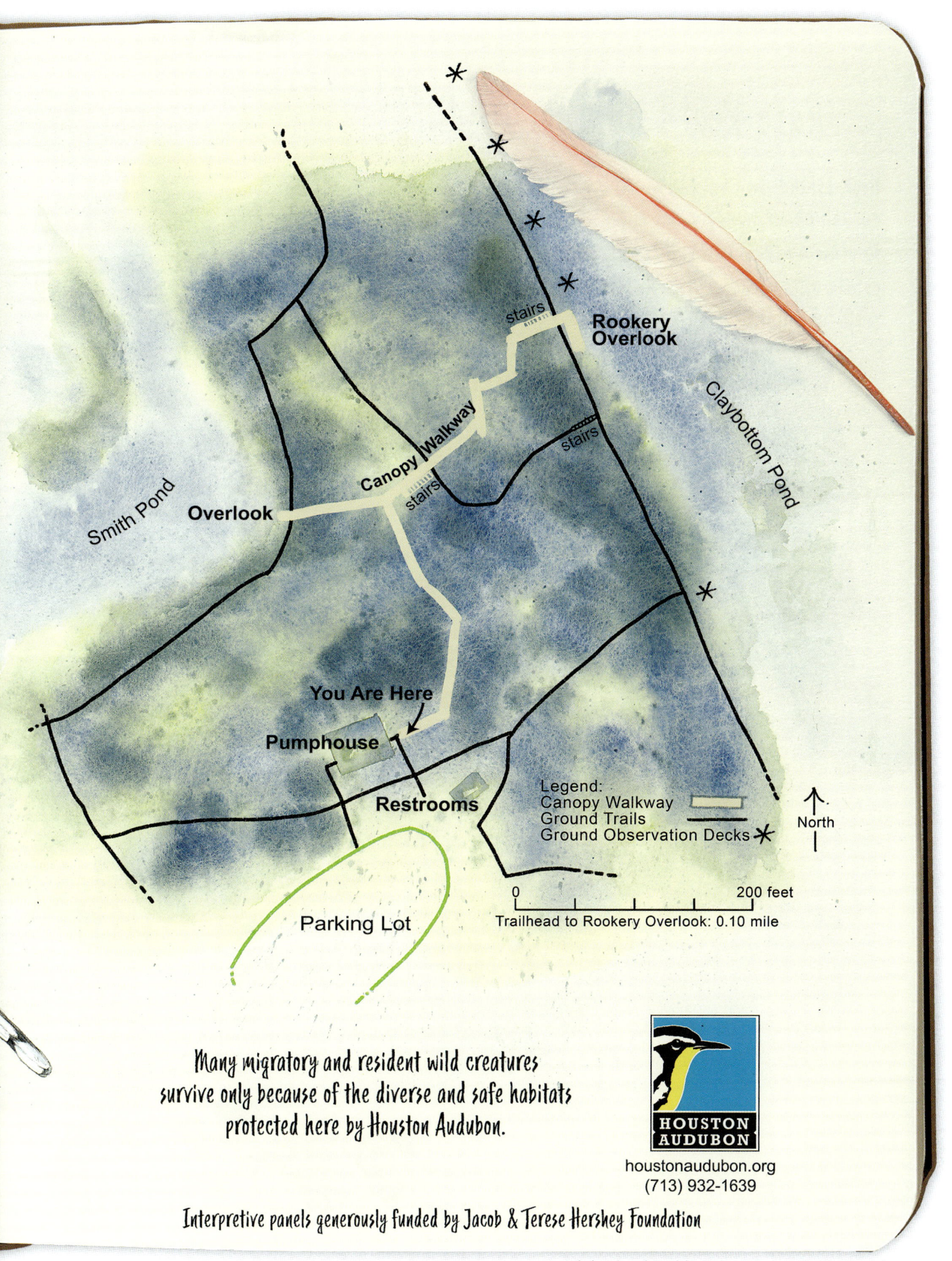

Smith Pond

Overlook

Canopy Walkway

stairs

stairs

stairs

Rookery Overlook

Claybottom Pond

You Are Here

Pumphouse

Restrooms

Legend:
Canopy Walkway
Ground Trails
Ground Observation Decks ✳

↑
North

0   200 feet

Trailhead to Rookery Overlook: 0.10 mile

Parking Lot

Many migratory and resident wild creatures
survive only because of the diverse and safe habitats
protected here by Houston Audubon.

**HOUSTON
AUDUBON**

houstonaudubon.org
(713) 932-1639

Interpretive panels generously funded by Jacob & Terese Hershey Foundation

High Island Smith Oaks Canopy Walk: Panel 1

Rare Real Estate for Wildlife

High Island isn't very high. At 25 feet, it rises just enough above hundreds of miles of flat coastal wetlands to grow a precious woodland ecosystem. This rare real estate offers food, water, and shelter to migratory and resident wildlife.

Here an exhausted migrating warbler can fly into the forest to rest, eat, and bathe before the long flight north. An egret can build a nest on a pond island, with little threat from disturbance or predators. Native plants like live oak, mulberry, and greenbriar thrive with little competition from invasive species. Each plant hosts a world of insects, spiders, lichen, and fungi.

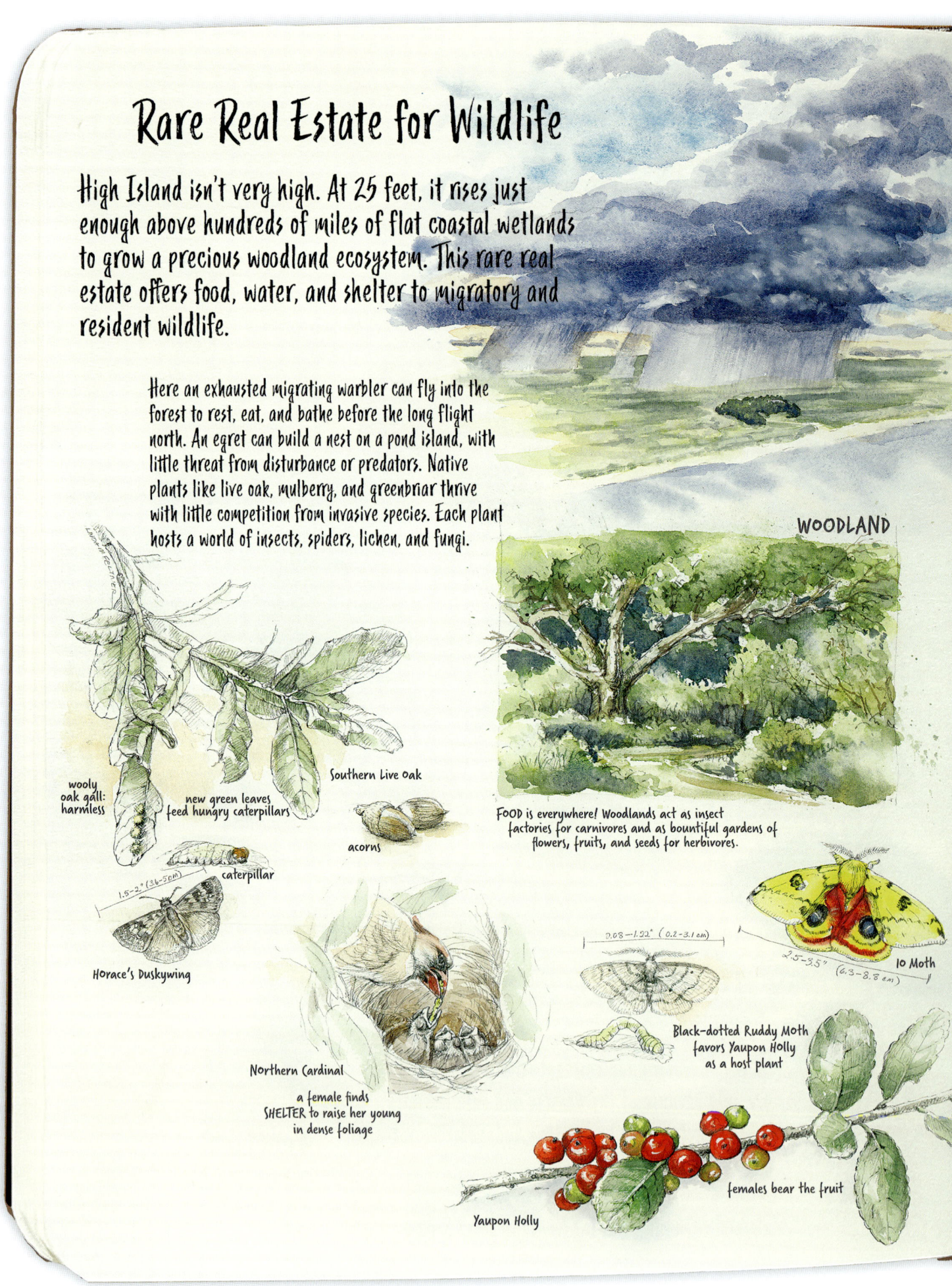

WOODLAND

wooly oak gall: harmless

Southern Live Oak

new green leaves feed hungry caterpillars

acorns

caterpillar

1.5–2" (3.6–5cm)

Horace's Duskywing

FOOD is everywhere! Woodlands act as insect factories for carnivores and as bountiful gardens of flowers, fruits, and seeds for herbivores.

0.08–1.22" (0.2–3.1 cm)

2.5–3.5" (6.3–8.8 cm)

IO Moth

Black-dotted Ruddy Moth favors Yaupon Holly as a host plant

Northern Cardinal

a female finds SHELTER to raise her young in dense foliage

Yaupon Holly

females bear the fruit

Reptiles like alligators, turtles, and snakes share the wetlands with amphibians such as salamanders and frogs. This food web supports bobcats, raccoons, and other mammals.

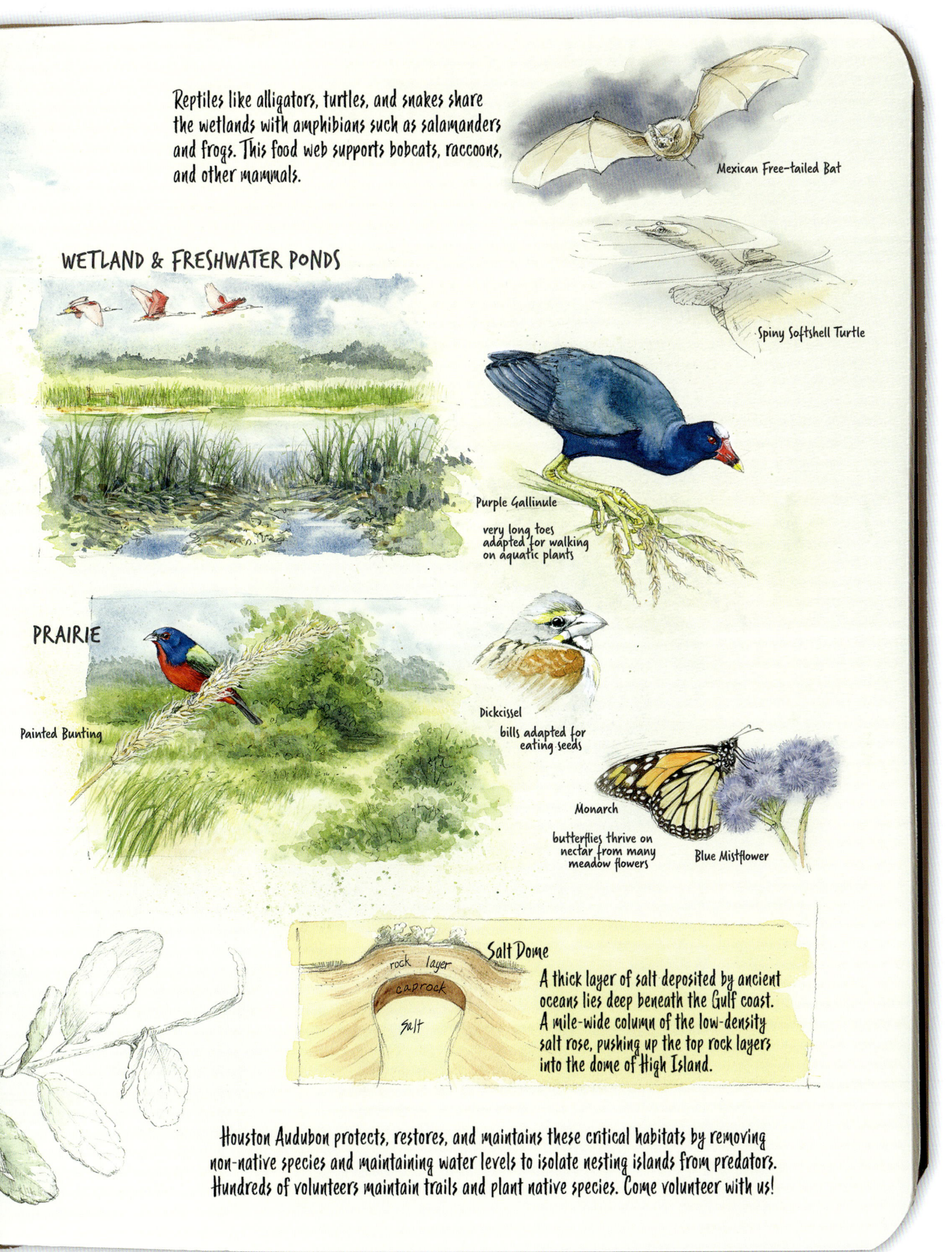

Mexican Free-tailed Bat

Spiny Softshell Turtle

WETLAND & FRESHWATER PONDS

Purple Gallinule

very long toes adapted for walking on aquatic plants

PRAIRIE

Painted Bunting

Dickcissel

bills adapted for eating seeds

Monarch

butterflies thrive on nectar from many meadow flowers

Blue Mistflower

Salt Dome

rock layer
caprock
salt

A thick layer of salt deposited by ancient oceans lies deep beneath the Gulf coast. A mile-wide column of the low-density salt rose, pushing up the top rock layers into the dome of High Island.

Houston Audubon protects, restores, and maintains these critical habitats by removing non-native species and maintaining water levels to isolate nesting islands from predators. Hundreds of volunteers maintain trails and plant native species. Come volunteer with us!

High Island Smith Oaks Canopy Walk: Panel 2

Rest Stop for Weary Migrants

Look out into the forest canopy. The vertical layers of habitat offer birds many levels for perching, roosting, feeding, drinking, and bathing. This protected rest stop can mean the difference between life and death for migrating birds.

A Spring Day in the Forest

Treetops: A tiny blue-green and yellow Northern Parula darts among the oak leaves, plucking insects with its thin beak. She flew in from Mexico yesterday and instinct will propel her north toward Minnesota tonight. Catch a glint of blue in the canopy as a Cerulean Warbler gorges on a caterpillar. He winters in the Andes and nests in the Appalachians.

Cerulean Warbler
in Southern Live Oak

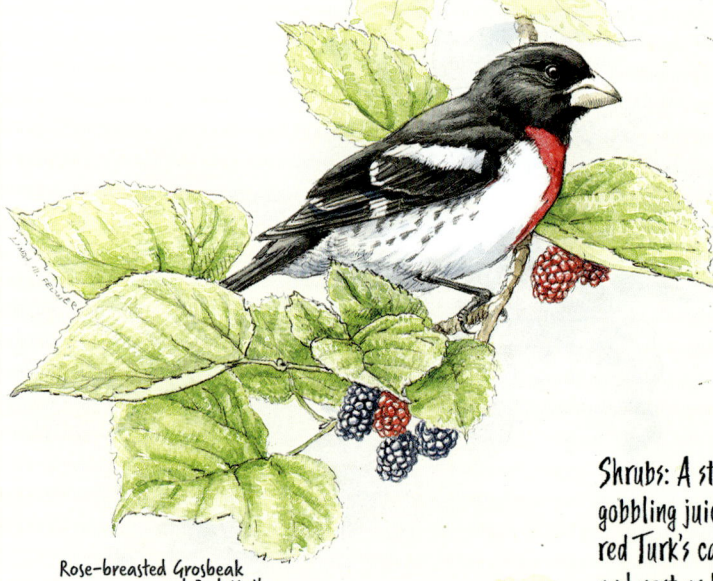

Rose-breasted Grosbeak
and Red Mulberry

Shrubs: A stocky Rose-breasted Grosbeak hops along a mulberry branch gobbling juicy purple berries. A Ruby-throated Hummingbird hovers over red Turk's cap flowers, sipping nectar. Both winter in Central America and nest as far north as Canada.

Forest Floor: A Swainson's Warbler tosses leaf litter with its stout beak, probing for a spider lunch. A Wood Thrush hops about, stalking worms. Both wintered in Central America and will fly north tonight, well fed.

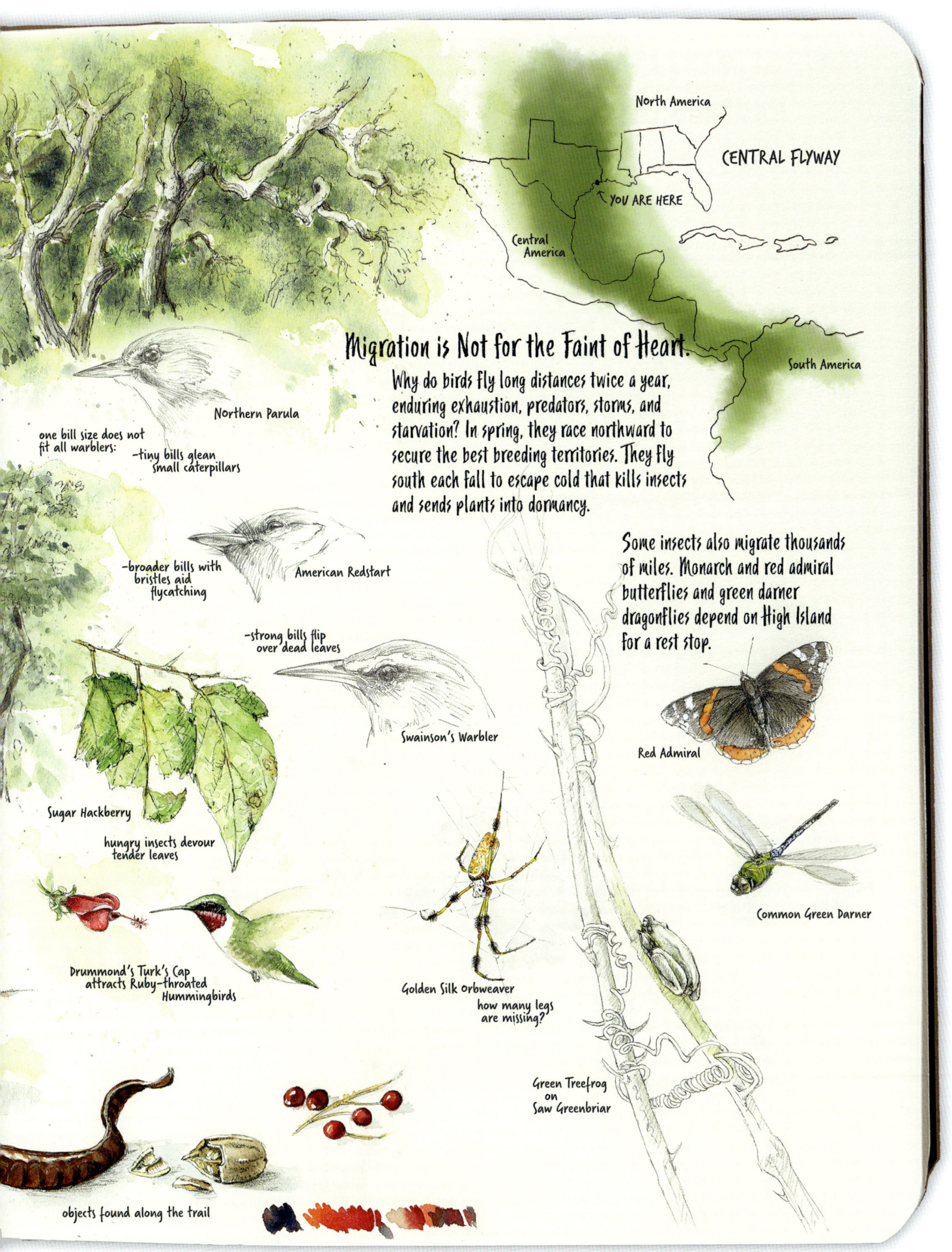

North America

CENTRAL FLYWAY

YOU ARE HERE

Central America

South America

Migration is Not for the Faint of Heart.

Why do birds fly long distances twice a year, enduring exhaustion, predators, storms, and starvation? In spring, they race northward to secure the best breeding territories. They fly south each fall to escape cold that kills insects and sends plants into dormancy.

Northern Parula

one bill size does not fit all warblers:

—tiny bills glean small caterpillars

—broader bills with bristles aid flycatching

American Redstart

—strong bills flip over dead leaves

Swainson's Warbler

Sugar Hackberry

hungry insects devour tender leaves

Some insects also migrate thousands of miles. Monarch and red admiral butterflies and green darner dragonflies depend on High Island for a rest stop.

Red Admiral

Common Green Darner

Drummond's Turk's Cap attracts Ruby-throated Hummingbirds

Golden Silk Orbweaver

how many legs are missing?

Green Treefrog on Saw Greenbriar

objects found along the trail

Raucous Bird Chorus

Listen to the cacophony of croaks, shrieks, and hisses as nesting waterbirds call to each other and voice territorial claims. Great Egrets, Snowy Egrets, Roseate Spoonbills, and Tricolored Herons migrate to these islands each spring to nest on every tree, shrub, and platform.

Watch for birds flying by with nest-building sticks in their beaks. Can you see a wading White Ibis probing the mud for crawfish with its long, curved bill? Look for a floating Neotropic Cormorant diving for a small fish. Peer down into the water. A dinner-plate-sized softshell turtle may swim just under the surface. Look up. Broad-winged Hawks and Mississippi Kites might be circling in the warm rising air.

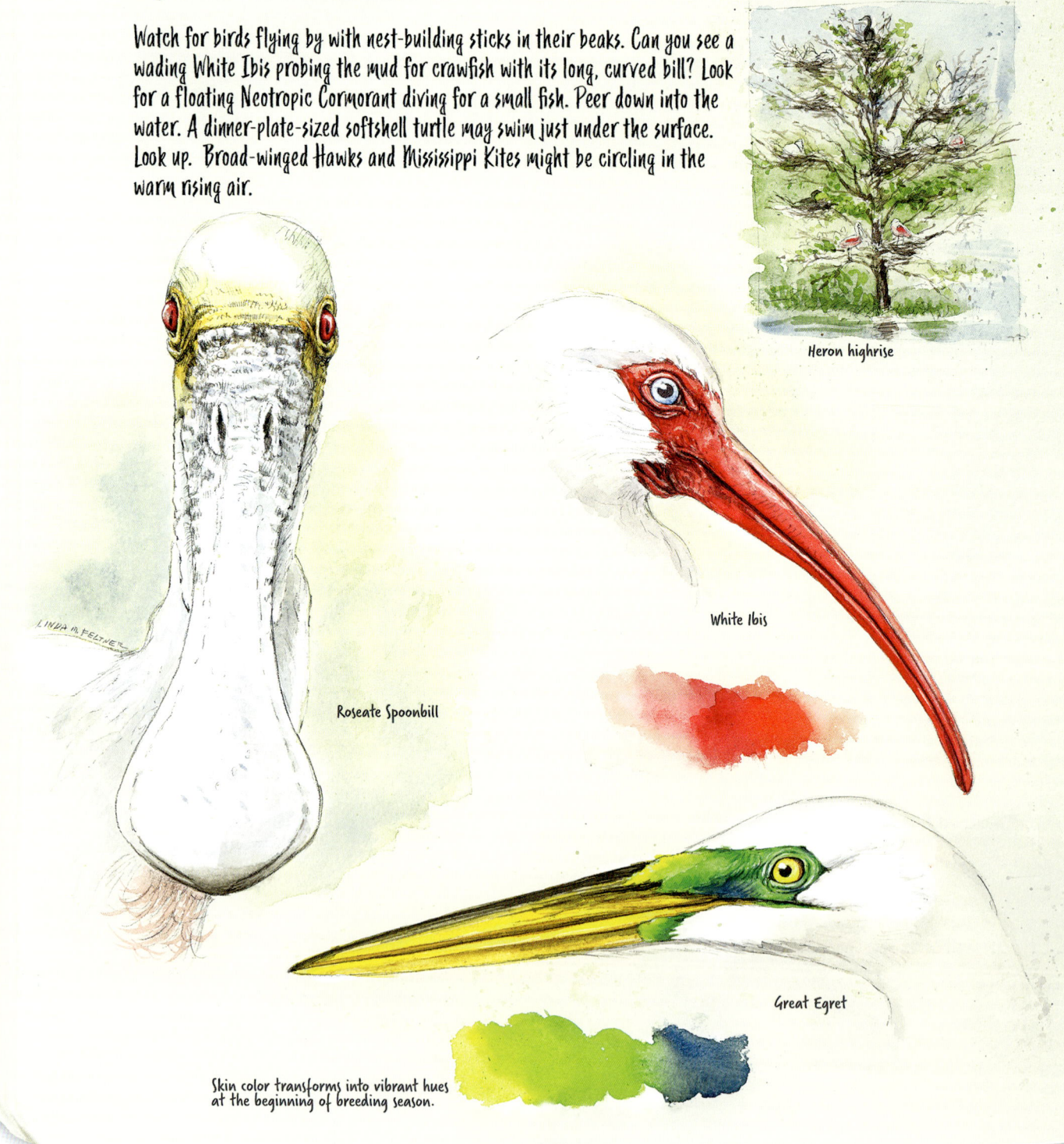

Heron highrise

Roseate Spoonbill

White Ibis

Great Egret

Skin color transforms into vibrant hues at the beginning of breeding season.

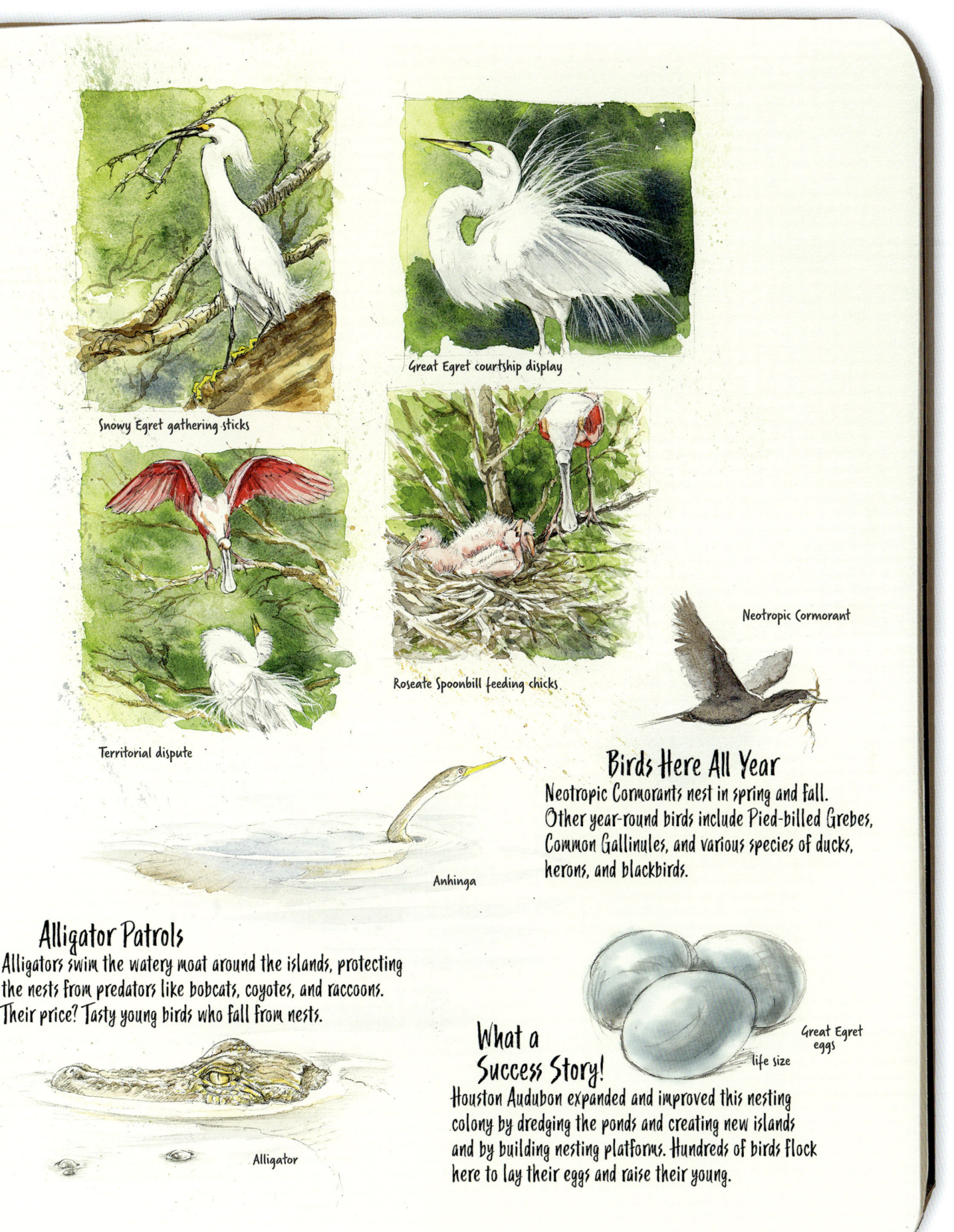

Snowy Egret gathering sticks

Great Egret courtship display

Roseate Spoonbill feeding chicks

Territorial dispute

Neotropic Cormorant

Anhinga

Birds Here All Year

Neotropic Cormorants nest in spring and fall. Other year-round birds include Pied-billed Grebes, Common Gallinules, and various species of ducks, herons, and blackbirds.

Alligator Patrols

Alligators swim the watery moat around the islands, protecting the nests from predators like bobcats, coyotes, and raccoons. Their price? Tasty young birds who fall from nests.

Alligator

Great Egret eggs

life size

What a Success Story!

Houston Audubon expanded and improved this nesting colony by dredging the ponds and creating new islands and by building nesting platforms. Hundreds of birds flock here to lay their eggs and raise their young.

High Island Smith Oaks Canopy Walk: Panel 4

Silent Skies Mural

Silent Skies Mural, an international collaborative mural mosaic, was organized by Artists for Conservation. The original installation was the centerpiece of the 27th International Ornithological Congress in Vancouver, Canada, in 2018. Each panel is 8 × 8 in (20.3 × 20.3 cm) featuring all 678 endangered species of the birds of the world.

Eskimo Curlew #2 (Numenius borealis)

I was eager to paint this bird because of its historical and personal significance to my family. In the past, it was one of the most numerous shorebirds in North America and was assumed to be extinct for many decades. My husband, Trevor Ben Feltner, in the company of D. A. Deaver, found and recognized a living bird on Galveston Island, Texas on March 22, 1959. Many birders and ornithologists were notified and able to experience this thrilling discovery. In late March 1962, two birds were observed on the island, and the last one flew north a few weeks later. It was the last confirmed record in the contiguous United States.

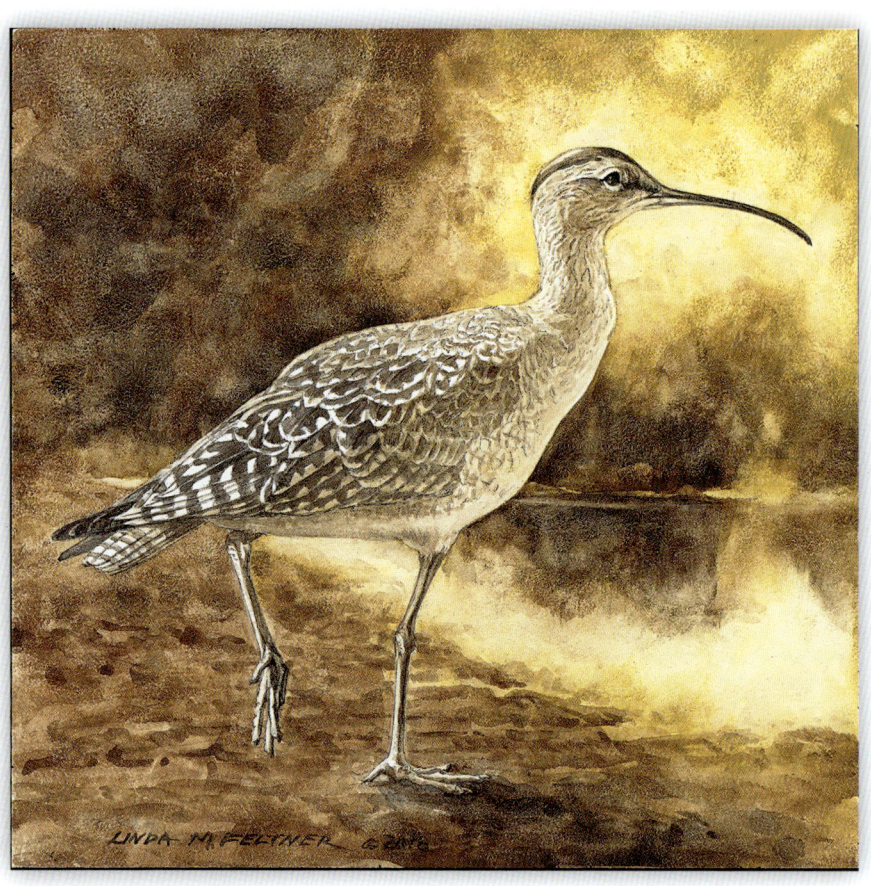

Javan Green Magpie (Cissa thalassina)

The Javan Green Magpie is critically endangered and endemic to West Java in Indonesia. They are notoriously difficult to find in their dense mountain forests. The chicks have blue feathers, and if a proper diet is maintained, they develop bright green plumage because of their food. Trapped to be kept in cages and displayed as status symbols, their market value increases the rarer they are. It is believed that there are less than one hundred individuals in the wild. There are no protections in place to decrease the rate of extinction, though several conservation programs are currently focusing on maintaining breeding programs.

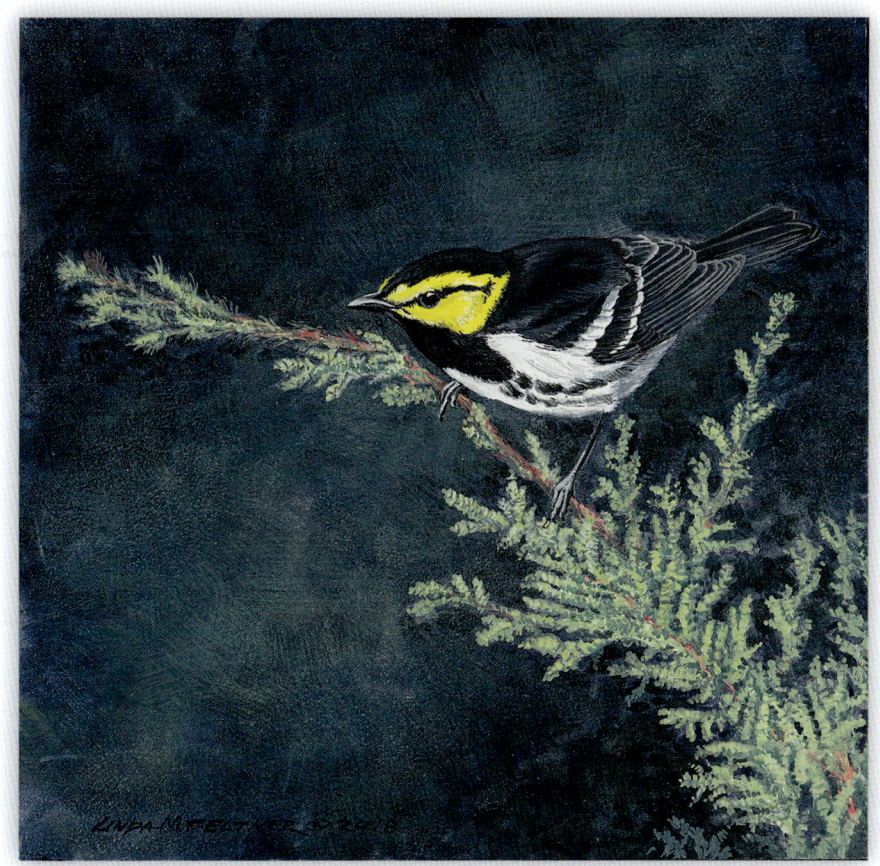

Golden-cheeked Warbler (*Setophaga chrysoparia*)

The Golden-cheeked Warbler is an iconic bird of the Texas Hill Country. They nest nowhere else in the world but in the oak-juniper woodlands, where they find older forests abundant with a diversity of insects and caterpillars. Their need for specific habitats for both breeding and wintering makes the species extremely vulnerable to deforestation for livestock, urban development, timber harvesting, and agriculture. Conservation programs have been established in Texas and Latin America to raise awareness of the need to maintain habitat.

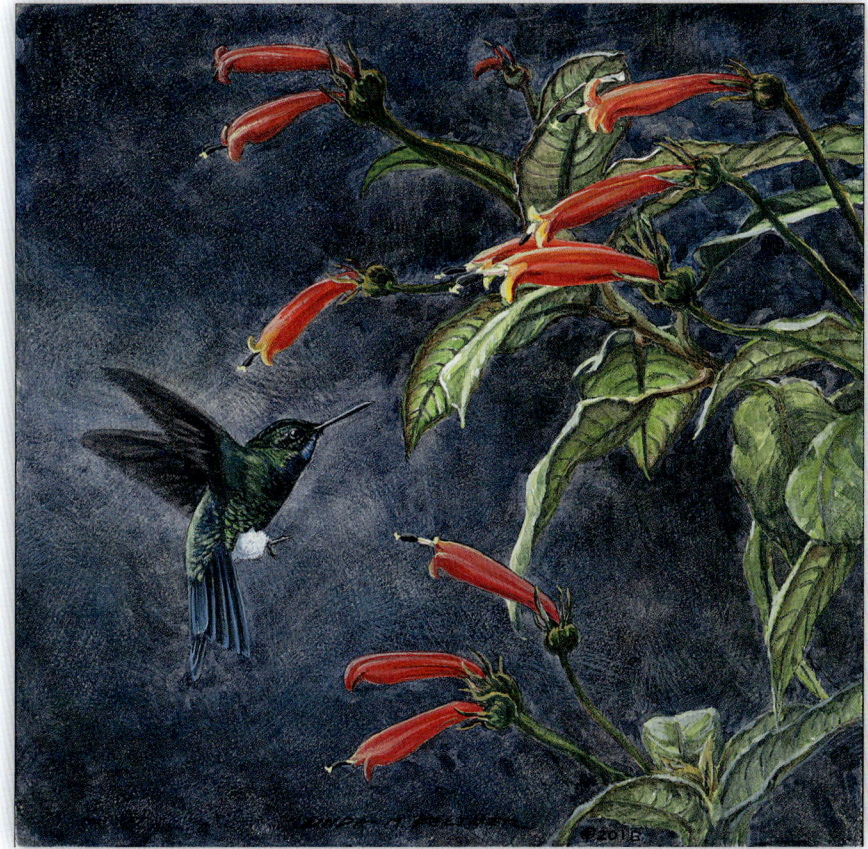

Black-breasted Puffleg (*Eriocnemis nigrivestis*)

The Black-breasted Puffleg is a critically endangered hummingbird, found only in the high mountains of Ecuador. With a population of no more than 250 individuals, it is rapidly disappearing due to human activity—specifically, charcoal burning and clearing for cattle. It is a dazzling jewel of iridescence with its bright white pantaloons. I observed several in the Yanachocha Preserve in 2004. Painting this bird brought back memories of that personal encounter.

The City of Bellevue, Washington

My long and marvelous partnership with the Parks and Community Services Department and the Utilities Department produced decades of what is called "educational interpretation," which helps introduce the public to the wonders of a city interlaced with natural wild corridors and luxuriant Pacific Northwest landscapes.

The mountainous and low hillsides bordering Lake Washington provide lush green corridors where the city has championed the extensive restoration of salmon streams, forest protection, and wetland conservation. Their interpretive programs recognize the contributions to the area made by historic townships and mines, resolute settlers, loggers, and Native Americans.

In the following pages, I represent three broad interpretive areas: wetlands, forests, and preservation. These subjects lure me to delve into the details of their interconnections and their importance to healthy ecosystems.

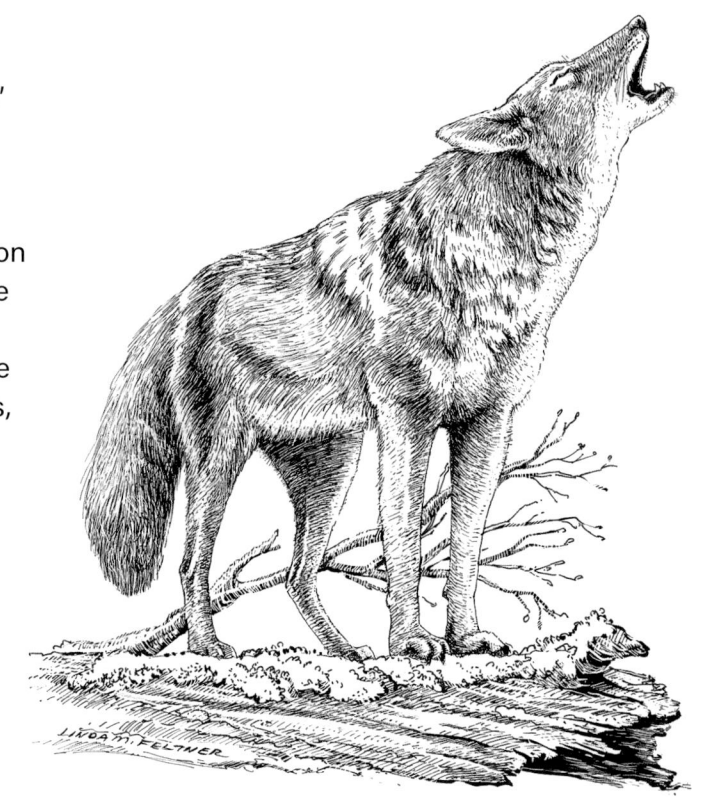

Coyote (*Canis latrans*)

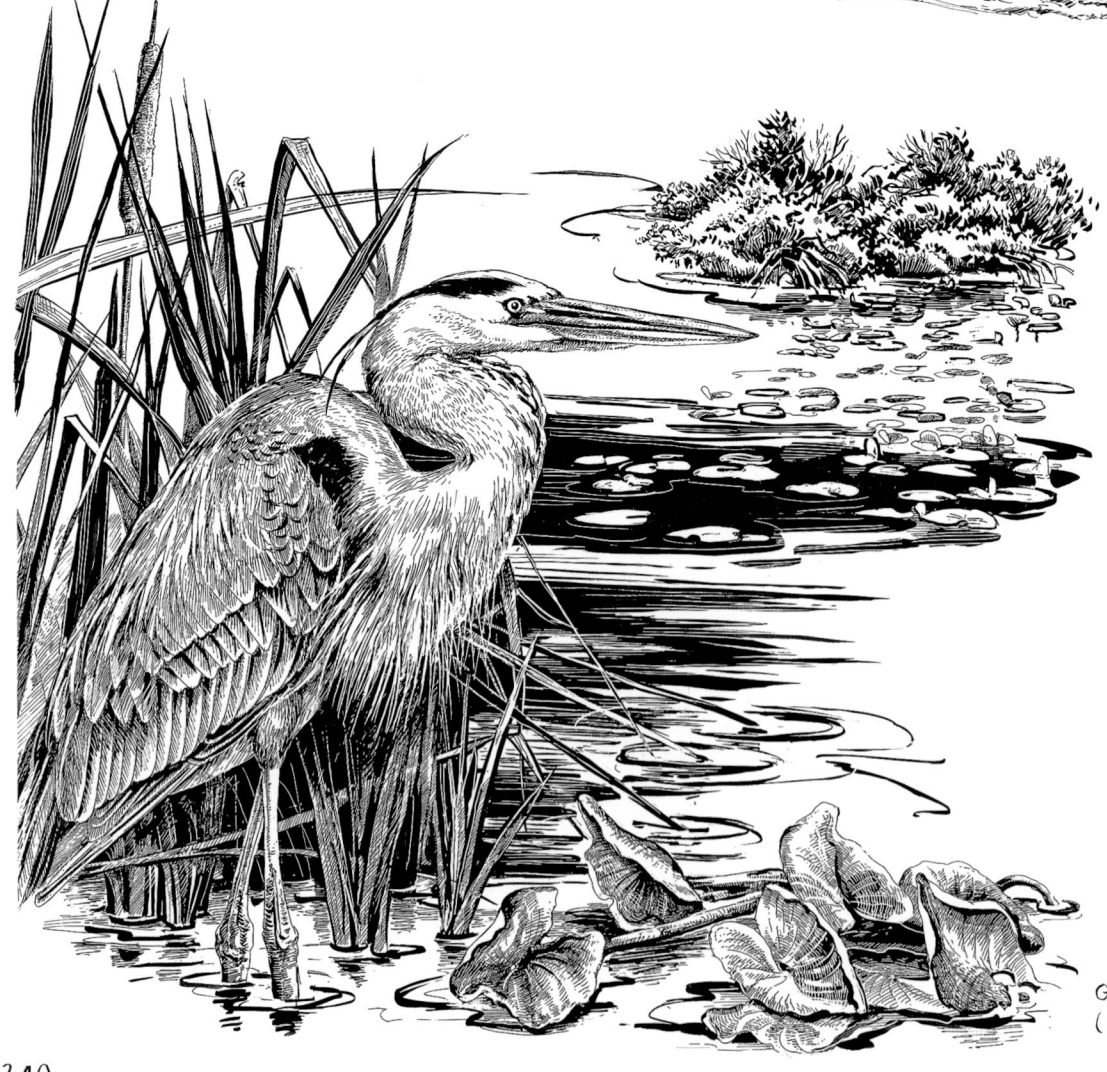

Great Blue Heron
(*Ardea herodias*)

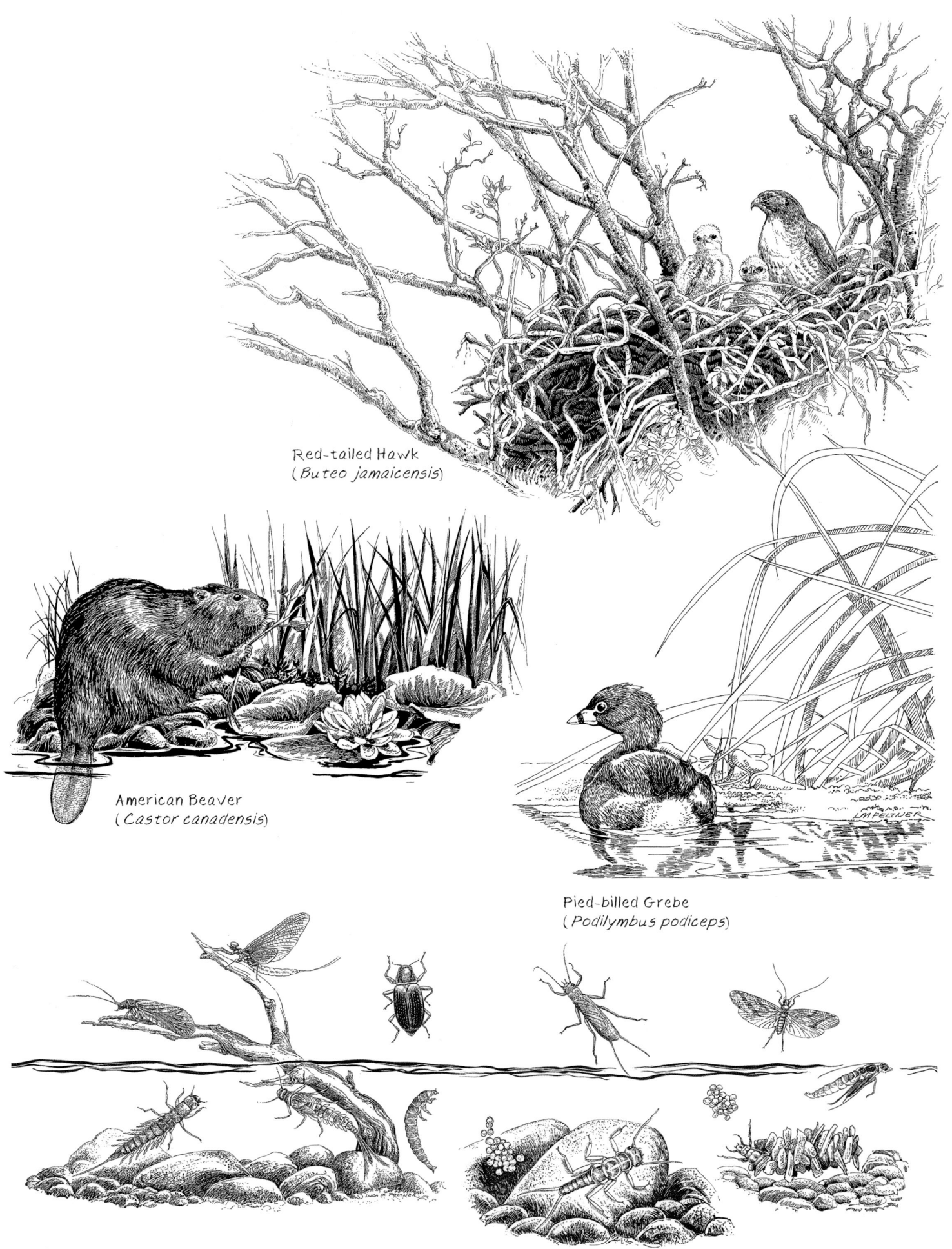

Red-tailed Hawk
(*Buteo jamaicensis*)

American Beaver
(*Castor canadensis*)

Pied-billed Grebe
(*Podilymbus podiceps*)

Alderfly (Megaloptera) (adult & larva)   Mayfly (Ephemeroptera) (adult and larva)   Riffle Beetle (Coleoptera) (adult and larva)   Stonefly (Plectoptera) (adult and larva)   Caddisfly (Trichoptera) (adult and larva and free-swiming pupa)

The City of Bellevue: Water Conservation

Bordered on one side by a large freshwater lake, the city contains numerous creeks winding down from the mountains. These waterways host a great deal of plant and animal life.

Raising awareness of the value of these waters benefits both the habitat and the sustainability of water resources for a thriving city.

Wandering forested trails along the creeks, I pondered how the physical features of both the forest and the stream sustain salmon populations. Quiet ponds that nurture the surrounding moist forests are another intriguing subject. My favorite concept involves microorganisms that create a food base for the entire ecosystem, supporting key indicator species and revealing the complexity of unseen life.

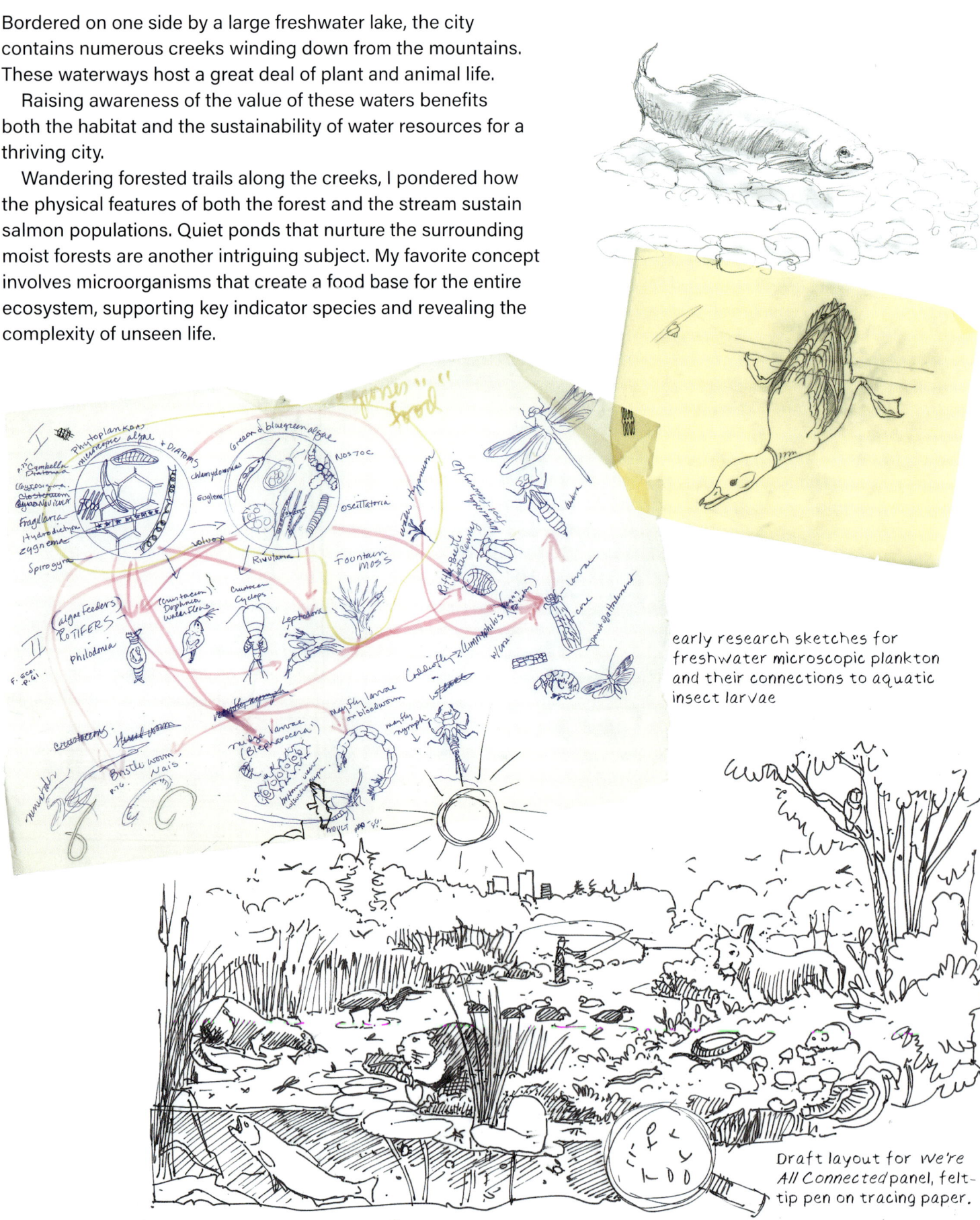

early research sketches for freshwater microscopic plankton and their connections to aquatic insect larvae

Draft layout for *we're All Connected* panel, felt-tip pen on tracing paper.

Before digital printing fabrication, I used 4x0 and 2x0 Rapidograph pens on pin-registered, frosted mylar, going through dozens of pen points due to abrasion. This aligned flat color layers for silk-screen printing on porcelain enamel panels, a popular printing method at the time. With digital printing, I fell in love with recreating a strong ink image using scratchboard.

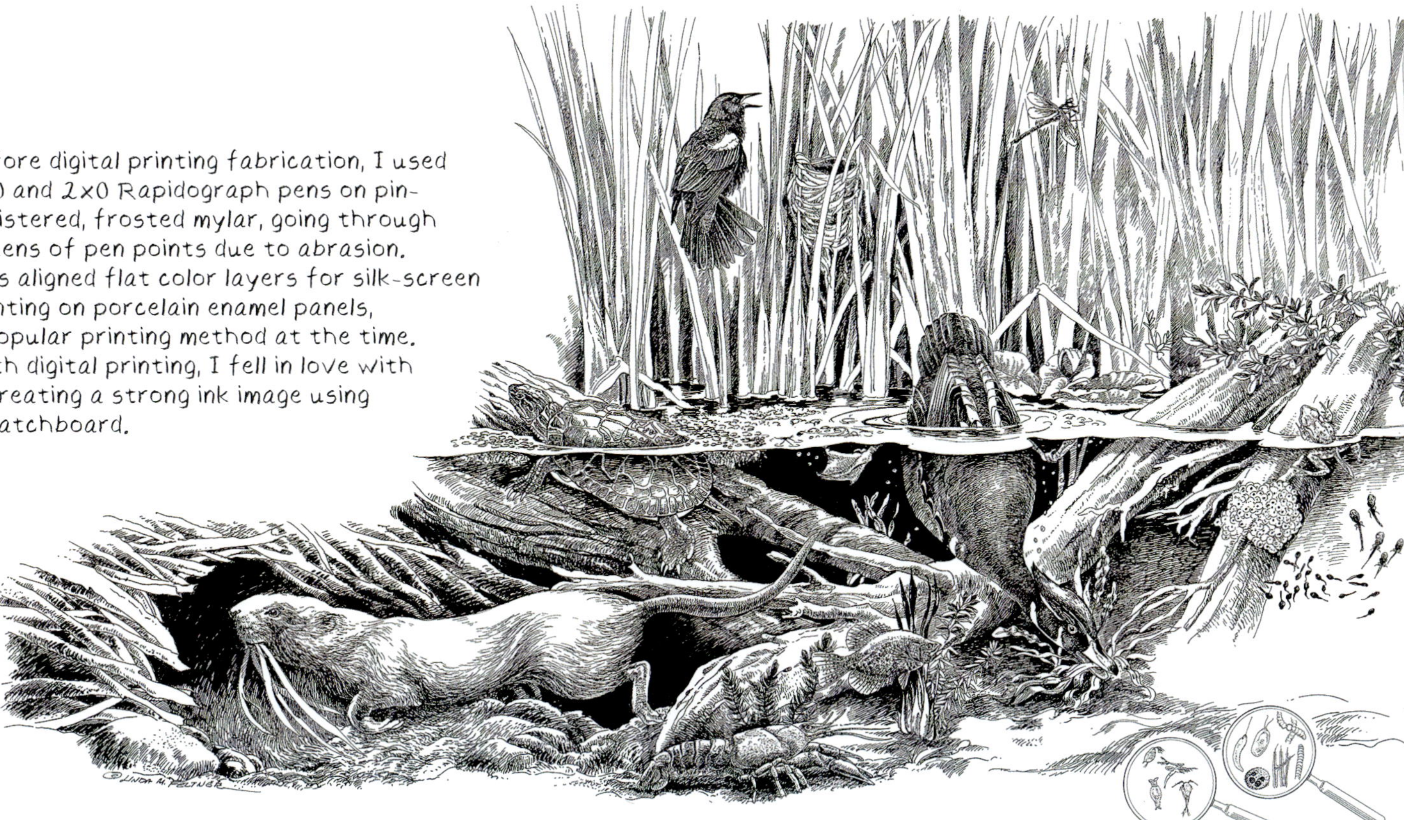

Water is Life, 24 x 36 in (60.96 x 91.44 cm), ink on frosted mylar. The image was drawn full-size for porcelain enamel fabrication with black ink printed on a tan background.

We're All Connected, 20 x 24 in (50.8 x 60.96 cm), ink on white Ampersand Claybord. Layers were created in a digital vector program for scanned art, colorized text, spider web, and the water photograph for high-pressure laminate fabrication.

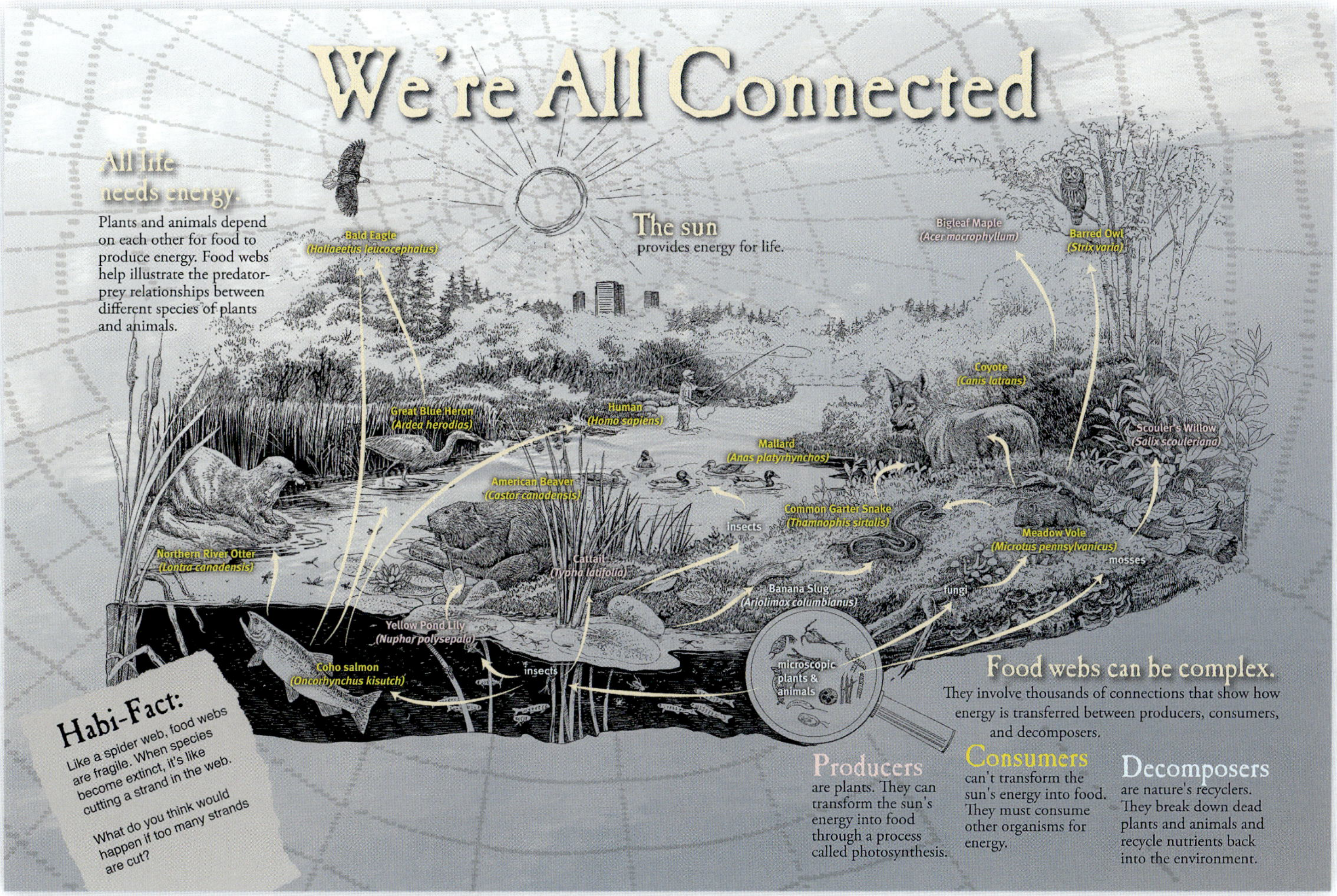

We're All Connected

All life needs energy
Plants and animals depend on each other for food to produce energy. Food webs help illustrate the predator-prey relationships between different species of plants and animals.

The sun provides energy for life.

Bald Eagle
(Haliaeetus leucocephalus)

Bigleaf Maple
(Acer macrophyllum)

Barred Owl
(Strix varia)

Great Blue Heron
(Ardea herodias)

Human
(Homo sapiens)

Coyote
(Canis latrans)

Scouler's Willow
(Salix scouleriana)

Mallard
(Anas platyrhynchos)

American Beaver
(Castor canadensis)

Common Garter Snake
(Thamnophis sirtalis)

Meadow Vole
(Microtus pennsylvanicus)

insects

mosses

Northern River Otter
(Lontra canadensis)

Cattail
(Typha latifolia)

Banana Slug
(Ariolimax columbianus)

fungi

Yellow Pond Lily
(Nuphar polysepala)

microscopic plants & animals

Coho salmon
(Oncorhynchus kisutch)

insects

Habi-Fact:
Like a spider web, food webs are fragile. When species become extinct, it's like cutting a strand in the web.

What do you think would happen if too many strands are cut?

Food webs can be complex.
They involve thousands of connections that show how energy is transferred between producers, consumers, and decomposers.

Producers are plants. They can transform the sun's energy into food through a process called photosynthesis.

Consumers can't transform the sun's energy into food. They must consume other organisms for energy.

Decomposers are nature's recyclers. They break down dead plants and animals and recycle nutrients back into the environment.

The City of Bellevue: A Forested History

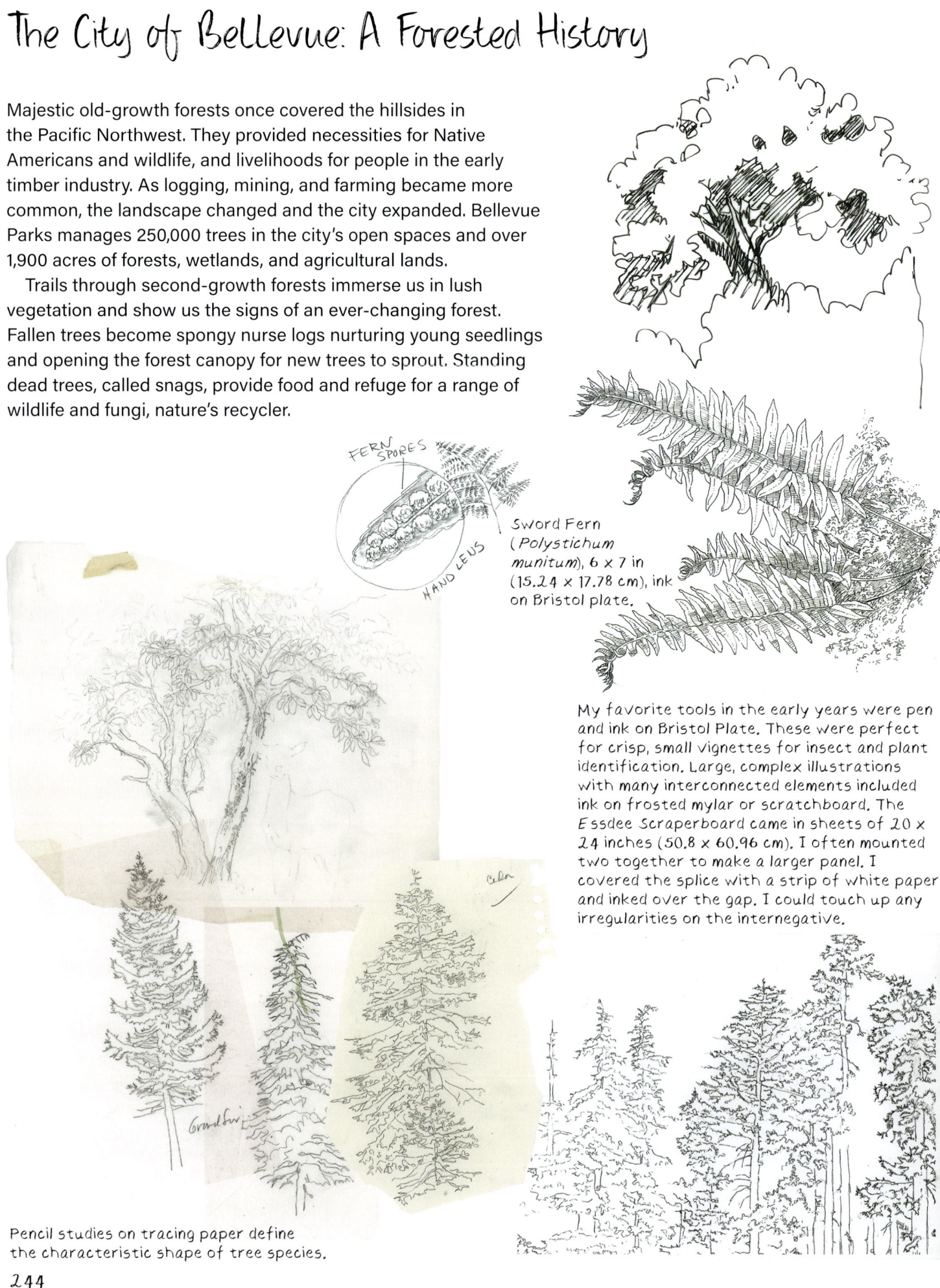

Majestic old-growth forests once covered the hillsides in the Pacific Northwest. They provided necessities for Native Americans and wildlife, and livelihoods for people in the early timber industry. As logging, mining, and farming became more common, the landscape changed and the city expanded. Bellevue Parks manages 250,000 trees in the city's open spaces and over 1,900 acres of forests, wetlands, and agricultural lands.

Trails through second-growth forests immerse us in lush vegetation and show us the signs of an ever-changing forest. Fallen trees become spongy nurse logs nurturing young seedlings and opening the forest canopy for new trees to sprout. Standing dead trees, called snags, provide food and refuge for a range of wildlife and fungi, nature's recycler.

FERN SPORES

HAND LENS

Sword Fern (*Polystichum munitum*), 6 x 7 in (15.24 x 17.78 cm), ink on Bristol plate.

My favorite tools in the early years were pen and ink on Bristol Plate. These were perfect for crisp, small vignettes for insect and plant identification. Large, complex illustrations with many interconnected elements included ink on frosted mylar or scratchboard. The Essdee Scraperboard came in sheets of 20 x 24 inches (50.8 x 60.96 cm). I often mounted two together to make a larger panel. I covered the splice with a strip of white paper and inked over the gap. I could touch up any irregularities on the internegative.

Grand Fir

Cedar

Pencil studies on tracing paper define the characteristic shape of tree species.

244

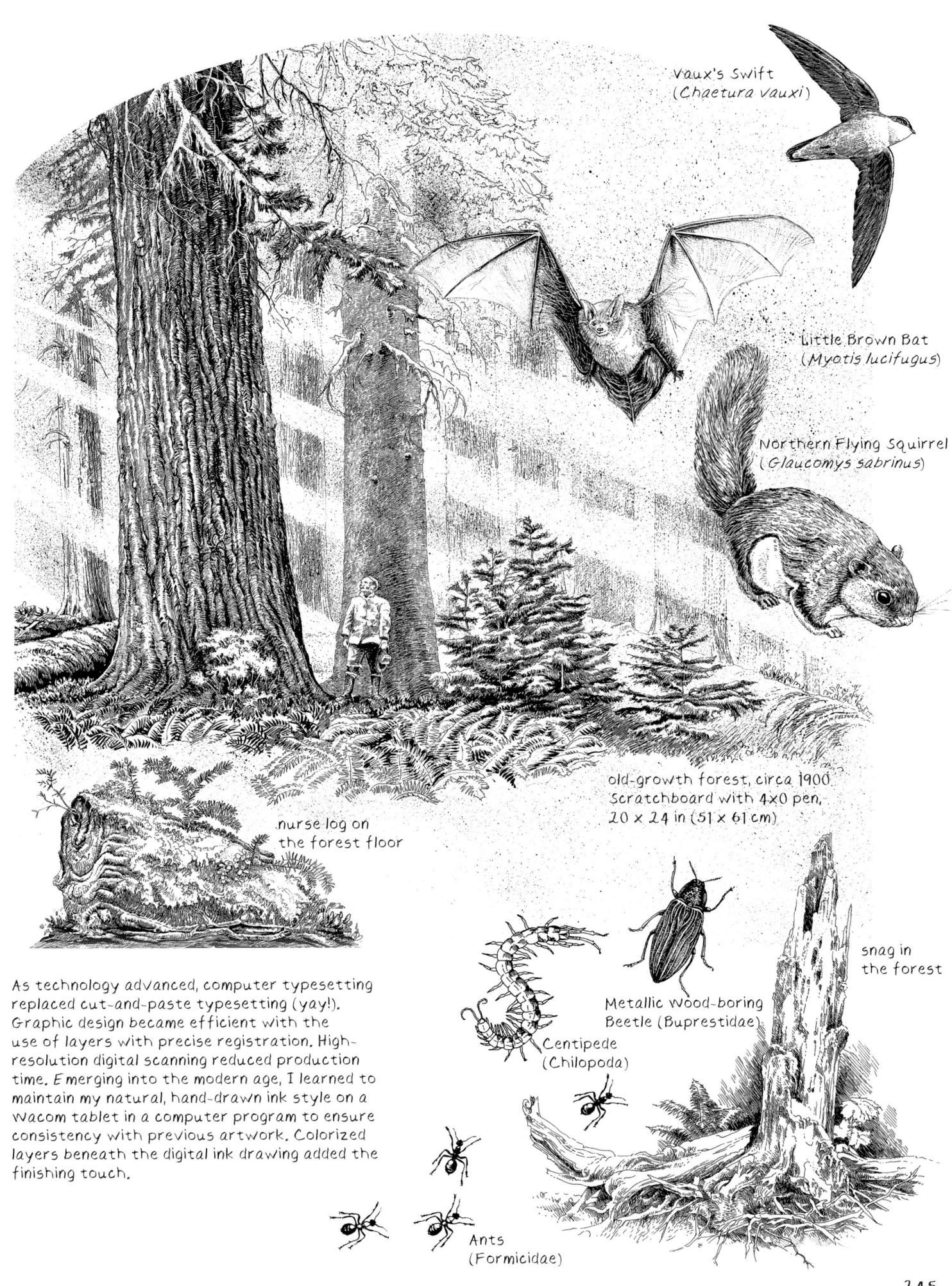

Vaux's Swift
(*Chaetura vauxi*)

Little Brown Bat
(*Myotis lucifugus*)

Northern Flying Squirrel
(*Glaucomys sabrinus*)

old-growth forest, circa 1900
Scratchboard with 4x0 pen,
20 x 24 in (51 x 61 cm)

nurse log on
the forest floor

snag in
the forest

Metallic Wood-boring
Beetle (Buprestidae)

Centipede
(Chilopoda)

As technology advanced, computer typesetting
replaced cut-and-paste typesetting (yay!).
Graphic design became efficient with the
use of layers with precise registration. High-
resolution digital scanning reduced production
time. Emerging into the modern age, I learned to
maintain my natural, hand-drawn ink style on a
wacom tablet in a computer program to ensure
consistency with previous artwork. Colorized
layers beneath the digital ink drawing added the
finishing touch.

Ants
(Formicidae)

245

Bellevue Stream Team: Kelsey Creek Trestle

The Stream Team is an outstanding environmental education and stewardship program in the Bellevue Utilities Department. Volunteers keep an eye out for salmon and aquatic wildlife. They collect crucial information about the city's streams, lakes, and wetlands. This program raises public awareness of how nearby streams nourish fish and wildlife and informs people about how small changes in their behavior at home can help keep the water clean.

Bellevue has a vast network of over eighty miles of streams. Natural waterways are part of the city's drainage system and are critical areas protected from development. By slowing down stormwater runoff, riparian areas prevent flooding and erosion and provide a thriving habitat for fish and wildlife.

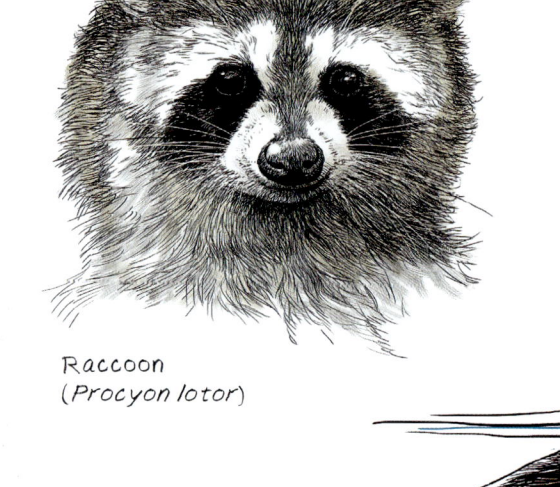

Raccoon
(*Procyon lotor*)

Sockeye Salmon
(*Oncorhynchus nerka*)
male left, female right

Slender panels installed end-to-end covered the top of the railings of the overlook observation deck.

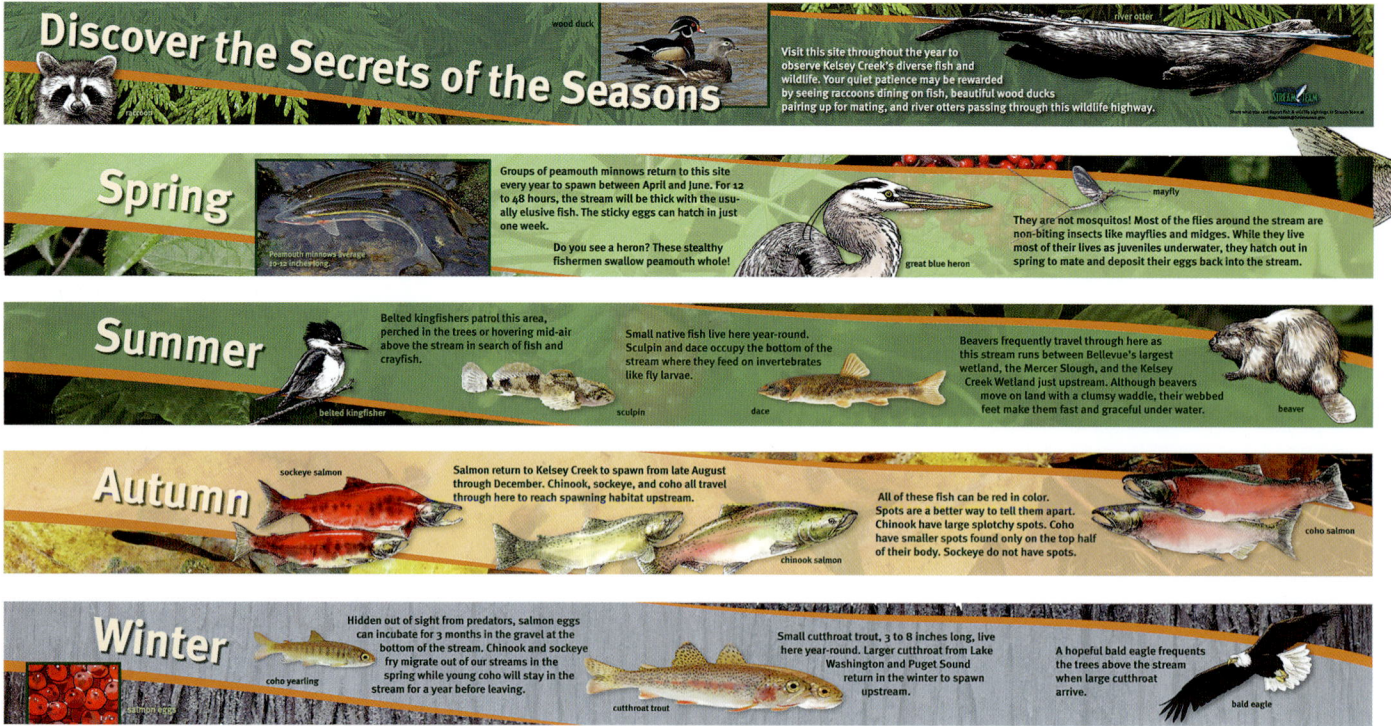

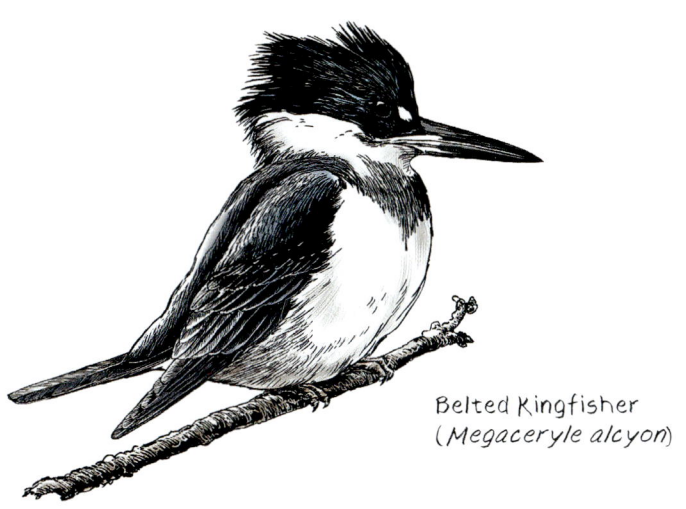

Belted Kingfisher
(*Megaceryle alcyon*)

River Otter
(*Lontra canadensis*)

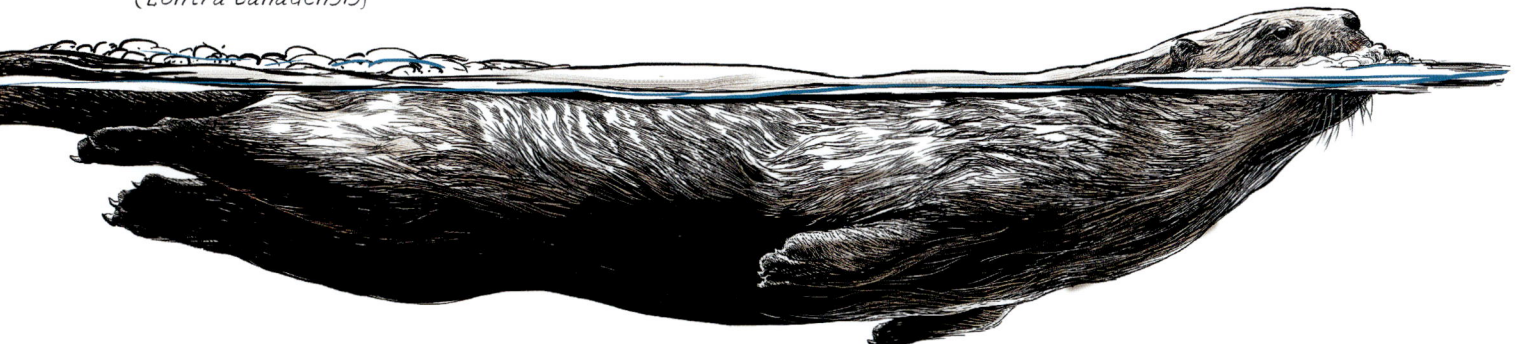

The inspiration for the interpretive panel design was twofold. First, this quiet spot sheltered by the canopy looked down upon the flowing creek beneath. Second, it needed an innovative design in order to place the panels on the wooden railing of the observation deck.

Part of the message was to encourage visitors to return with each season and experience the changes. The images showed the possibilities for discovering aquatic and land animals, along with flowering and fruiting forest plants. They combined existing colorful salmon watercolors and new digital ink drawings. The high-pressure laminate panels, 4.5 x 50 inches (11.43 x 127 cm), placed end to end, fit the space perfectly.

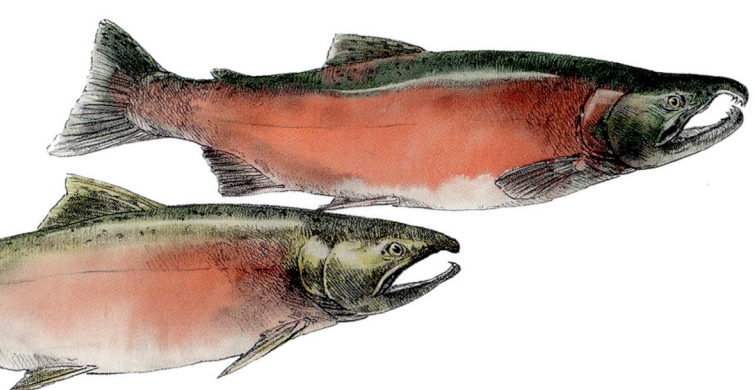

Coho Salmon
(*Oncorhynchus kisutch*)
male above, female below

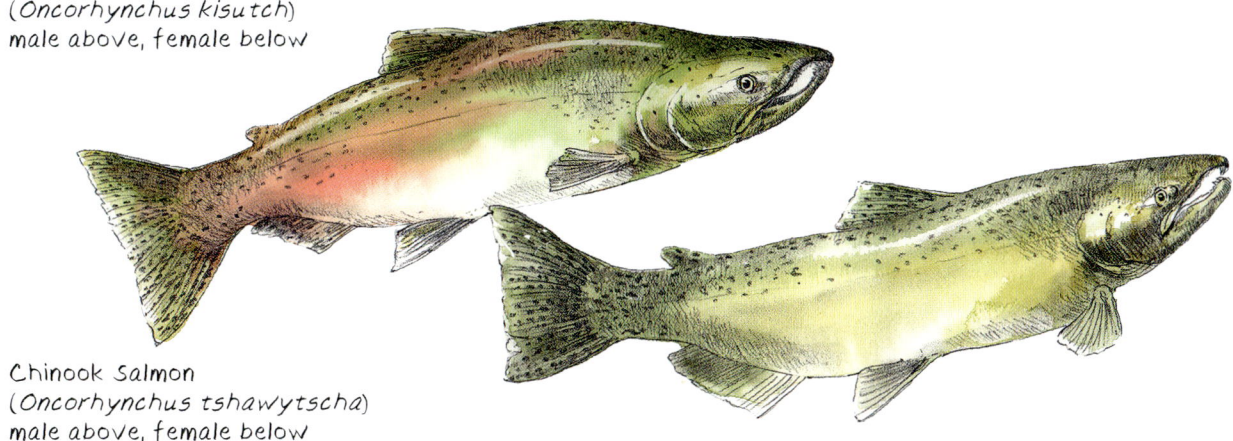

Chinook Salmon
(*Oncorhynchus tshawytscha*)
male above, female below

Bellevue Stream Team: "Prevent Pollution" Poster

The "Prevent Pollution" poster is distributed to schools to raise awareness of stormwater drainage and its direct outfall from streets to natural waterways, bypassing the city treatment facilities. The program aims to encourage people to make small changes at home that can have a positive impact on water quality.

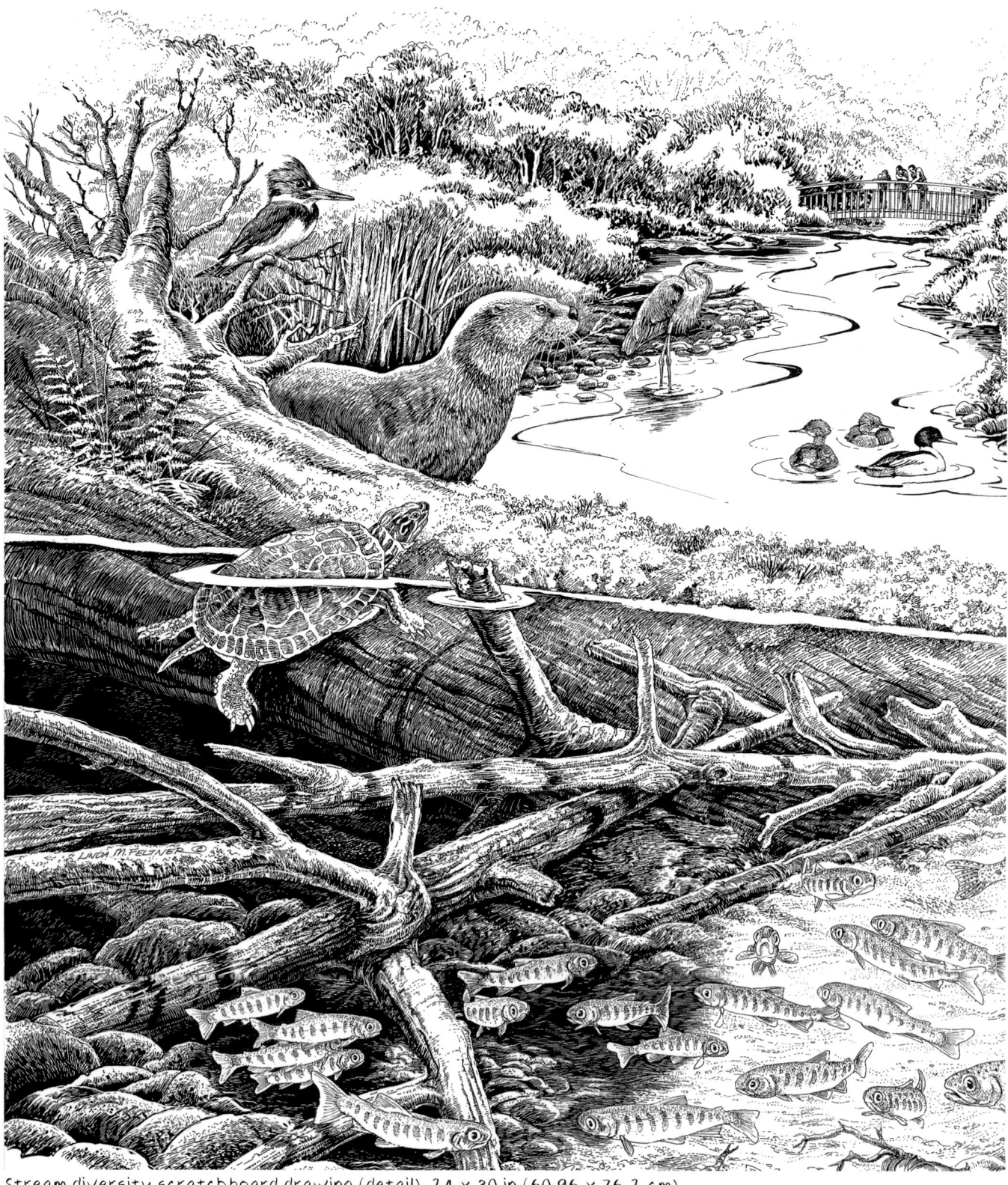

Stream diversity scratchboard drawing (detail), 24 x 30 in (60.96 x 76.2 cm).

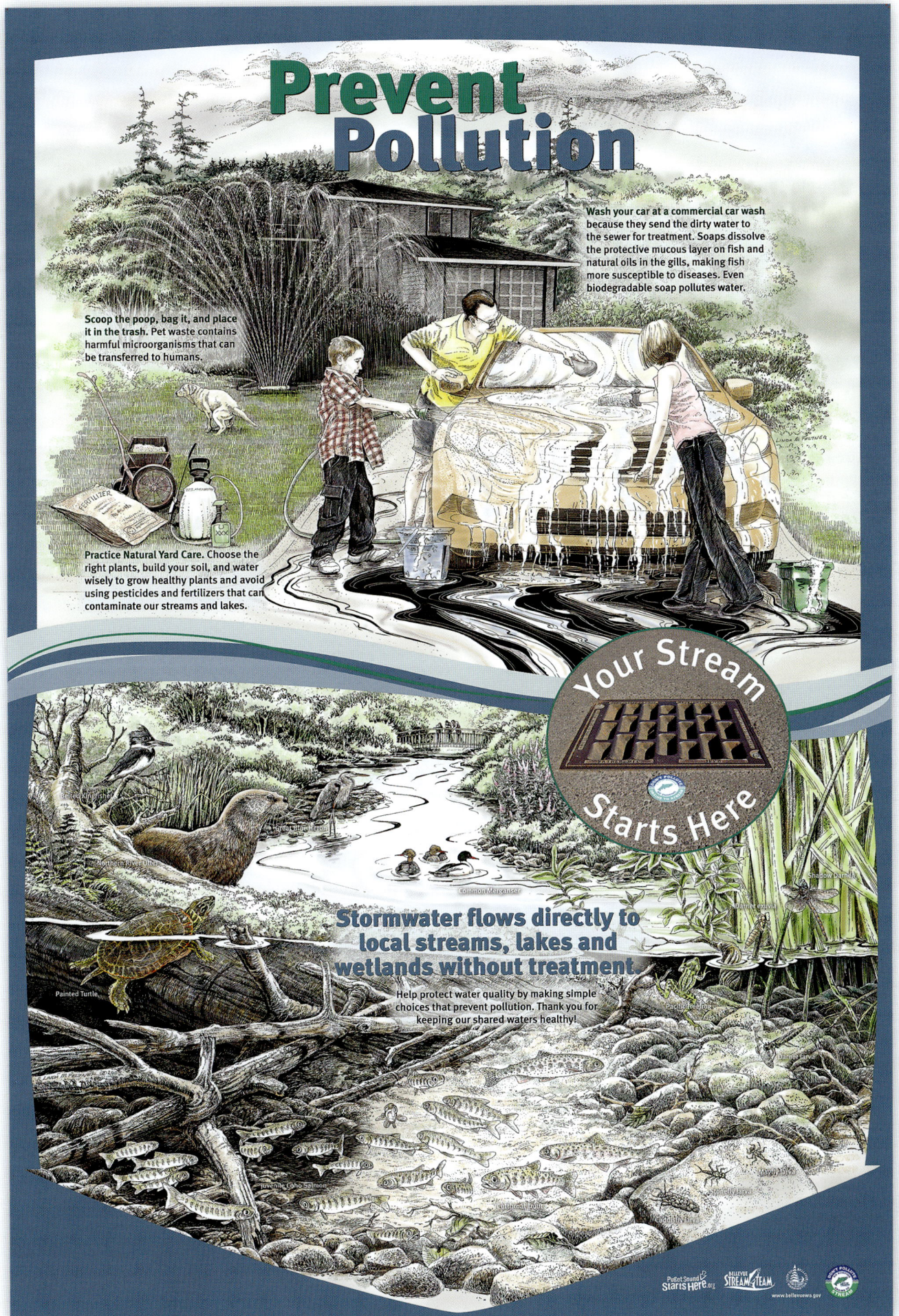

Prevent Pollution

Wash your car at a commercial car wash because they send the dirty water to the sewer for treatment. Soaps dissolve the protective mucous layer on fish and natural oils in the gills, making fish more susceptible to diseases. Even biodegradable soap pollutes water.

Scoop the poop, bag it, and place it in the trash. Pet waste contains harmful microorganisms that can be transferred to humans.

Practice Natural Yard Care. Choose the right plants, build your soil, and water wisely to grow healthy plants and avoid using pesticides and fertilizers that can contaminate our streams and lakes.

Your Stream Starts Here

Stormwater flows directly to local streams, lakes and wetlands without treatment.

Help protect water quality by making simple choices that prevent pollution. Thank you for keeping our shared waters healthy!

249

Brooker Creek Preserve

Brooker Creek Preserve and Environmental Education Center, Pinellas County, Florida.

Dense urban development surrounds the preserve. At over eight thousand acres, it's the largest natural area in Pinellas County. It is a significant conservation area for the Brooker Creek Watershed, providing wildlife habitat and protection for the drinkable water supply.

Staff ecologists and naturalists took us for an orientation hike. We anticipated getting our feet wet, which always makes us smile. We followed the undeveloped pathway of the future boardwalk through a corridor of shallow to thigh-deep water. The perspective gave us a water-level view of the habitat and the diversity of life that visitors might experience from the boardwalk.

We had fun slogging through wet cypress forests and rough boggy patches of vegetation. Wendy Walker, the project writer, stepped over a log and flushed a Pygmy Rattlesnake escaping to safety, a new reptile species for us both! Immersion in the landscape gives us a fresh insight into the natural world. I don't think the big smile ever left my face.

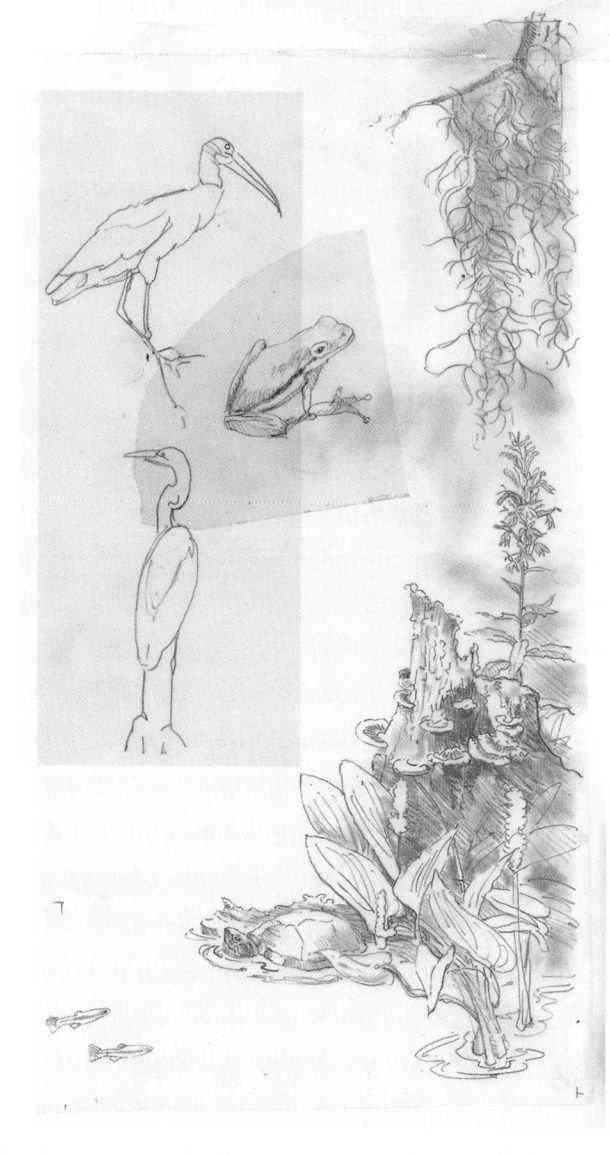

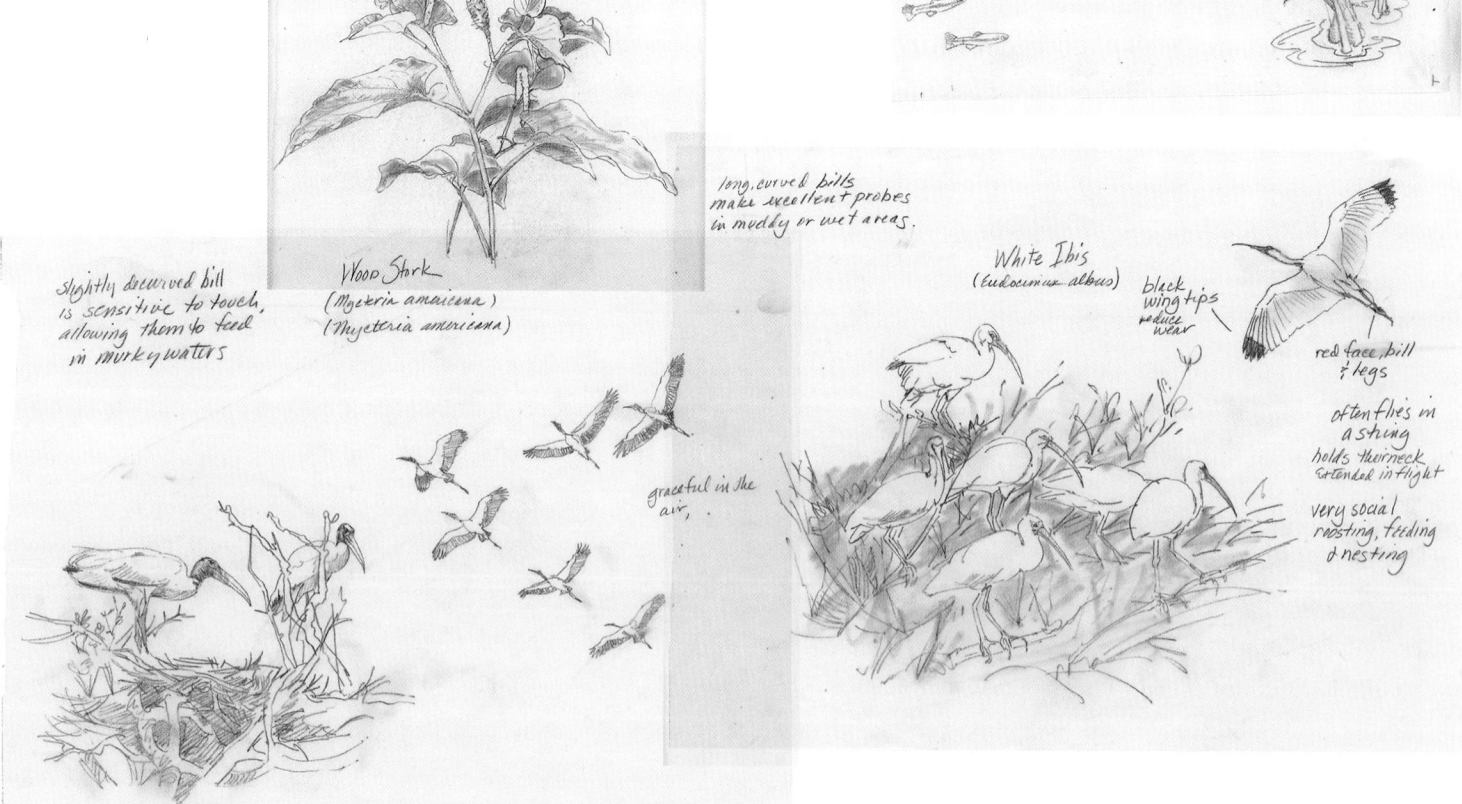

Wood Stork
(Mycteria americana)
(Mycteria americana)

slightly decurved bill is sensitive to touch, allowing them to feed in murky waters

graceful in the air,

long, curved bills make excellent probes in muddy or wet areas.

White Ibis
(Eudocimus albus)

black wing tips reduce wear

red face, bill & legs

often flies in a string
holds their neck extended in flight

very social roosting, feeding & nesting

Adapting To Change

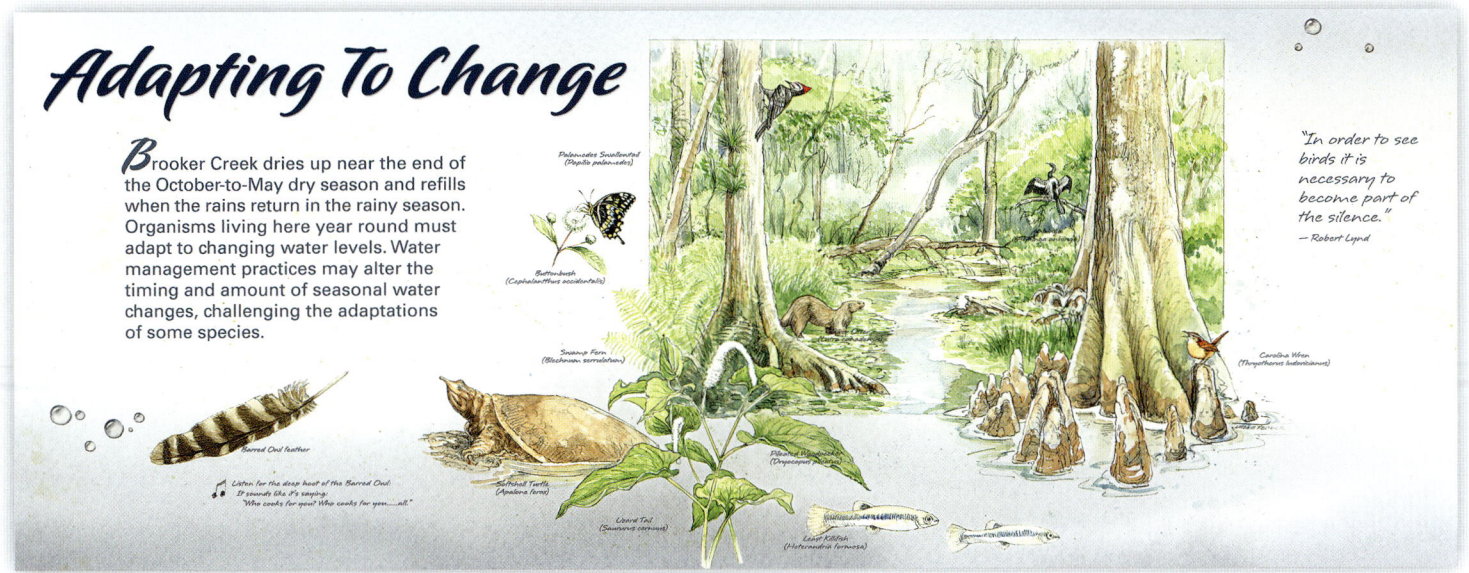

Brooker Creek dries up near the end of the October-to-May dry season and refills when the rains return in the rainy season. Organisms living here year round must adapt to changing water levels. Water management practices may alter the timing and amount of seasonal water changes, challenging the adaptations of some species.

"In order to see birds it is necessary to become part of the silence."
— Robert Lynd

36 x 14 in (91.44 x 35.56 cm), high-pressure laminate.

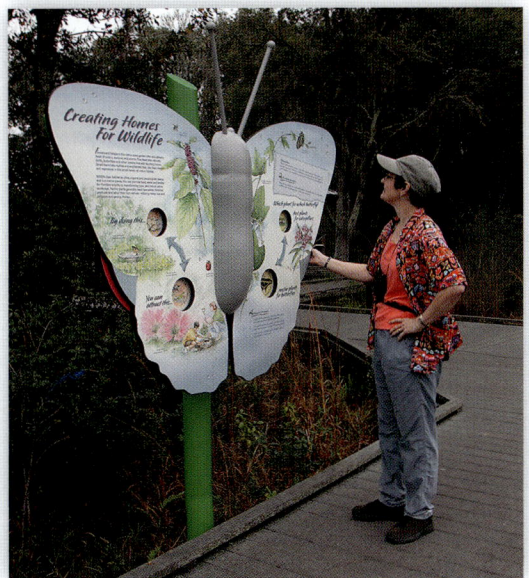

butterfly spinner interactive graphic for the Pollinator Garden

Walking through this outdoor experience kindled my inspiration to create engaging graphics. Possibilities spun through my mind. A difference of just a few feet in altitude took us to a completely different habitat. Pondering nature's connections helped me narrow down the species. I drew numerous squiggles and sketches and placed the pieces together to compose a primary landscape surrounded by species that may not be visible but still play a fascinating role.

The result is an inviting collection of interactive exhibits and panels that interpret the freshwater wetlands and different habitats such as swamps, oak hammocks, sandhills, and pine flatwoods. The visitor can pour water over a bronze watershed sculpture to watch it flowing across the area that Brooker Creek protects.

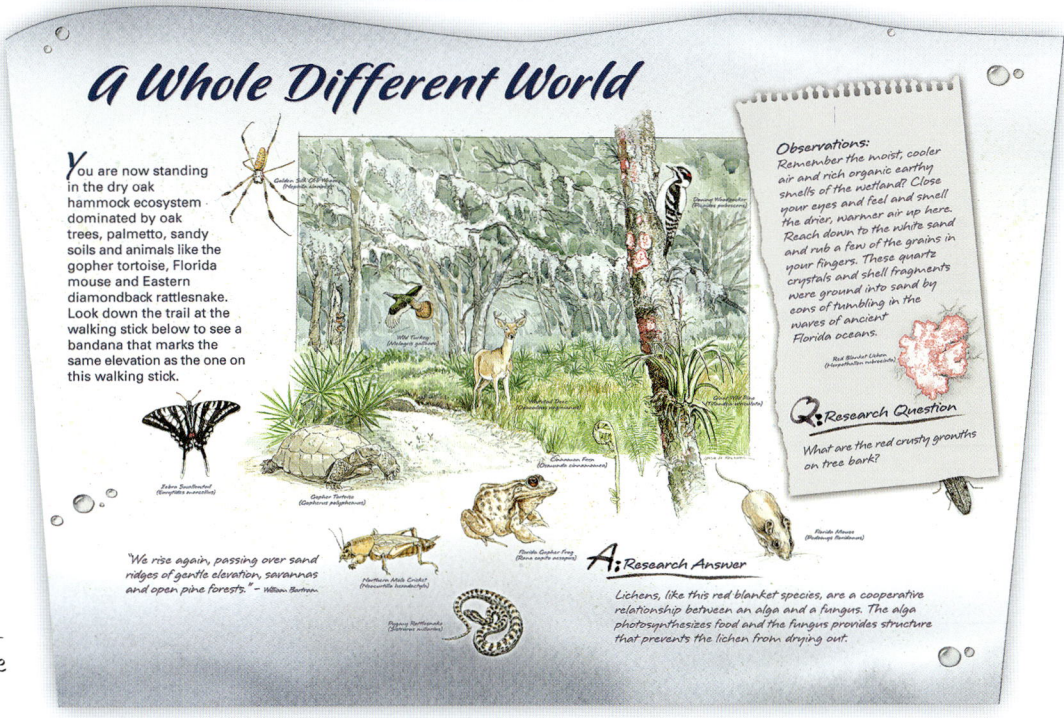

A Whole Different World

You are now standing in the dry oak hammock ecosystem dominated by oak trees, palmetto, sandy soils and animals like the gopher tortoise, Florida mouse and Eastern diamondback rattlesnake. Look down the trail at the walking stick below to see a bandana that marks the same elevation as the one on this walking stick.

Observations:
Remember the moist, cooler air and rich organic earthy smells of the wetland? Close your eyes and feel and smell the drier, warmer air up here. Reach down to the white sand and rub a few of the grains in your fingers. These quartz crystals and shell fragments were ground into sand by eons of tumbling in the waves of ancient Florida oceans.

Q: Research Question

What are the red crusty growths on tree bark?

"We rise again, passing over sand ridges of gentle elevation, savannas and open pine forests." – William Bartram

A: Research Answer

Lichens, like this red blanket species, are a cooperative relationship between an alga and a fungus. The alga photosynthesizes food and the fungus provides structure that prevents the lichen from drying out.

36 x 24 in (91.44 x 60.96 cm), high-pressure laminate

251

Visitor Center Mural

Saguaro National Park East, Tucson, Arizona.

The "Naturalist Notebook" style of drawings depicts plant
and animal life of the Sonoran Desert, including the history of
harvesting Saguaro fruit. It shows the germination and growth of
the iconic cactus with its various daytime and nighttime pollinators.
Clues appear for connections between plants and animals that
share their desert home. What happened to the lizard's tail?

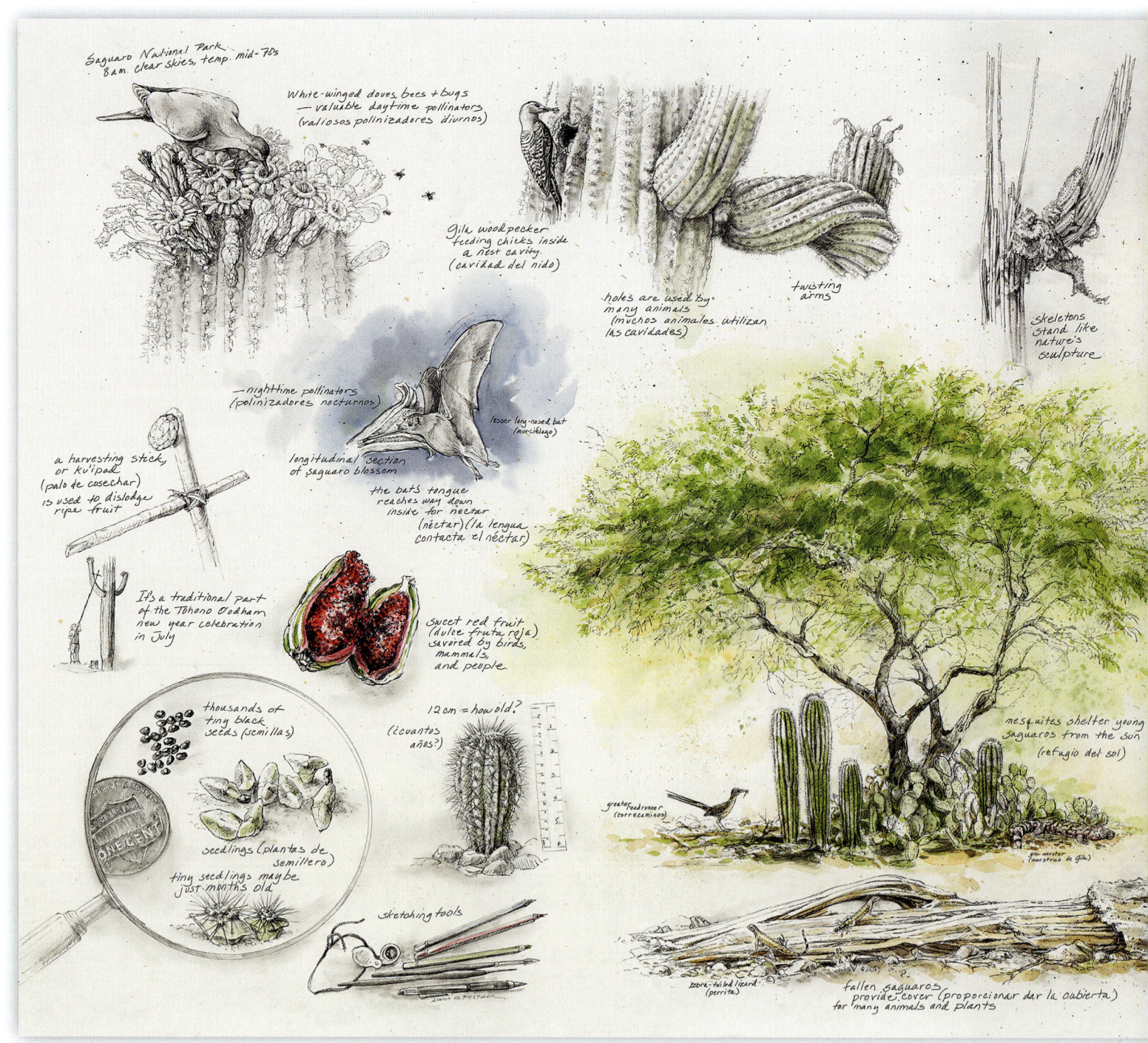

The park preferred my sketches with annotations as visitors of all ages view it as a personal subject and make connections to desert ecology. A lot happens in the desert that goes unnoticed. A presentation in this style allows me to zoom in or show an expanse of landscape. I used graphite pencil with watercolor on two Crescent extra heavy watercolor boards, 30 x 40 inches (76.2 x 101.6 cm). Each section was digitally captured at high-resolution and spliced in a graphic design program. A fabricator enlarged and printed the image. The installed mural is 9 x 24 feet (2.74 x 7.32 m).

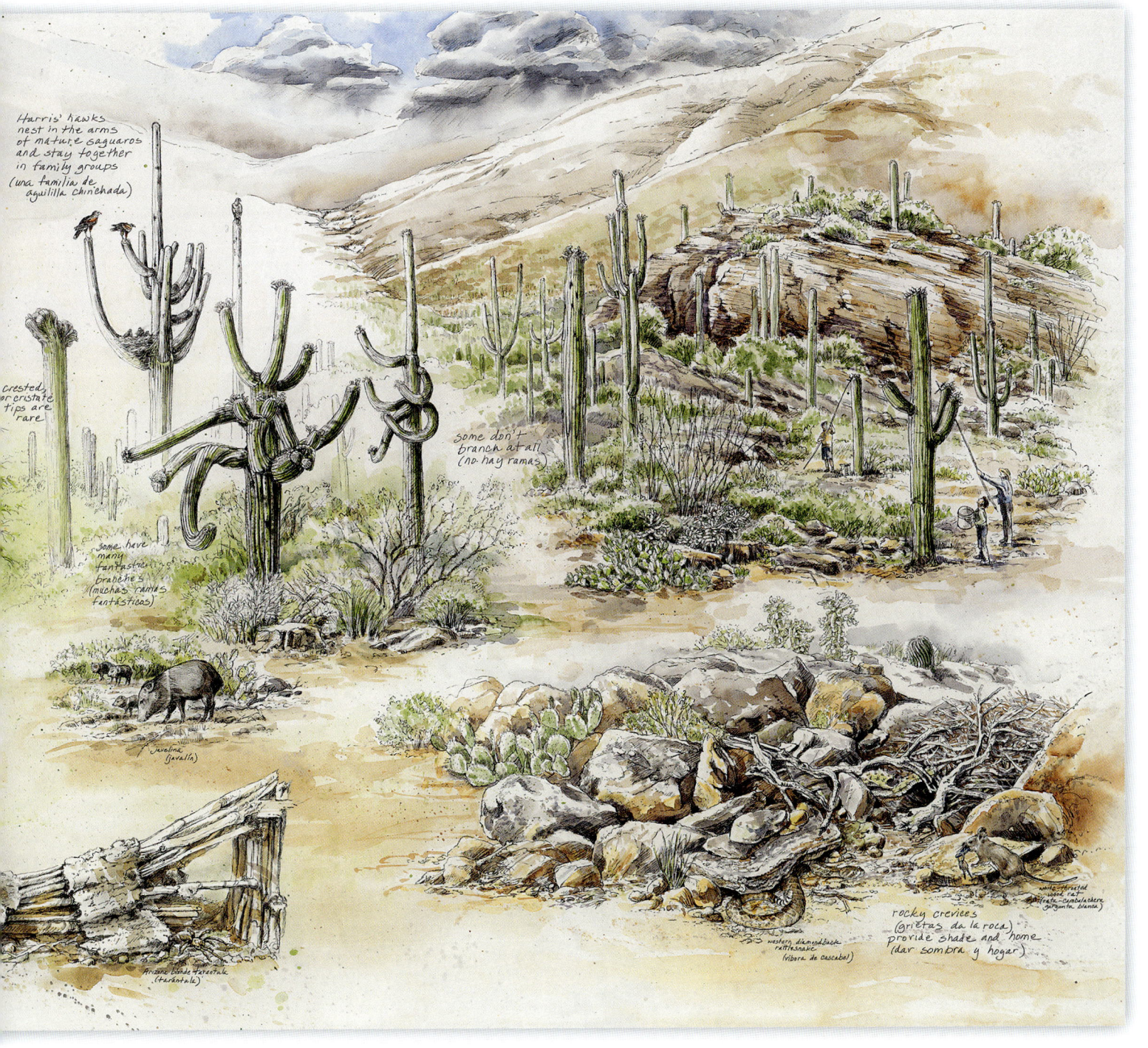

Harris' hawks nest in the arms of mature saguaros and stay together in family groups (una familia de aguililla chichada)

crested, or cristate tips are rare

some have many fantastic branches (muchas ramas fantásticas)

some don't branch at all (no hay ramas)

Javelina (javalín)

Arizona blonde tarantula (tarántula)

western diamondback rattlesnake (víbora de cascabel)

white-throated wood rat (rata-cambalachere garganta blanca)

rocky crevices (grietas de la roca) provide shade and home (dar sombra y hogar)

Arroyo Mural

Grand Staircase-Escalante National Monument Visitor Center, Bureau of Land Management, Kanab, Utah.

The "Day in the Life" mural depicts the activities of an Ancestral Puebloan community in southern Utah, occupied between the 1100–1300s.

The mural interprets activities based on the actual artifacts. The community settled in an alluvial drainage system that provided fertile soil for crops. Centuries of repeated flooding covered the site with silt. Ironically, another flash flood exposed the long-buried site discovered by Archeologist Douglas McFadden in 1993, and he spent the next decade excavating the site. The site gave essential clues to how the people spent their daily lives and constructed buildings.

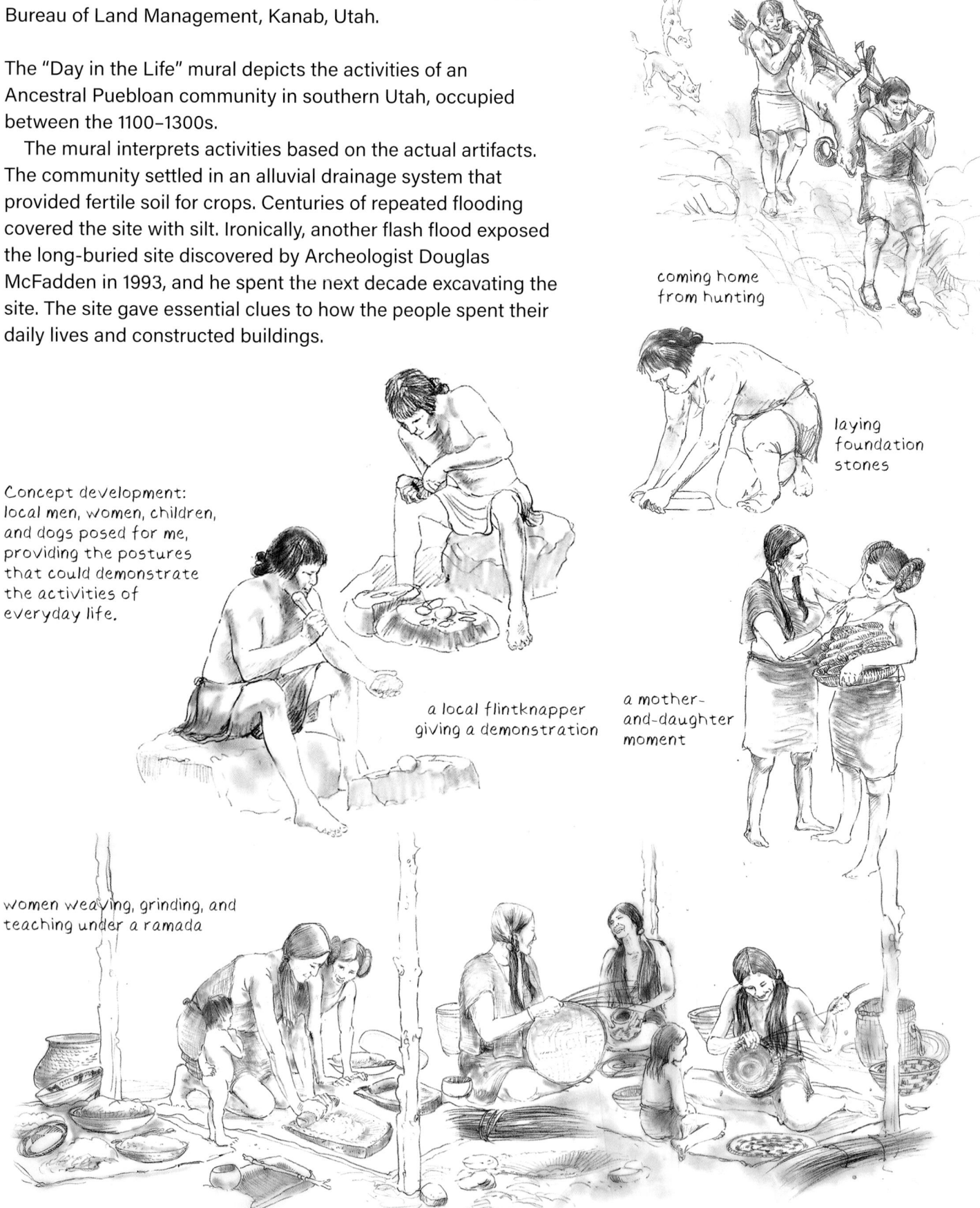

coming home from hunting

laying foundation stones

Concept development: local men, women, children, and dogs posed for me, providing the postures that could demonstrate the activities of everyday life.

a local flintknapper giving a demonstration

a mother-and-daughter moment

women weaving, grinding, and teaching under a ramada

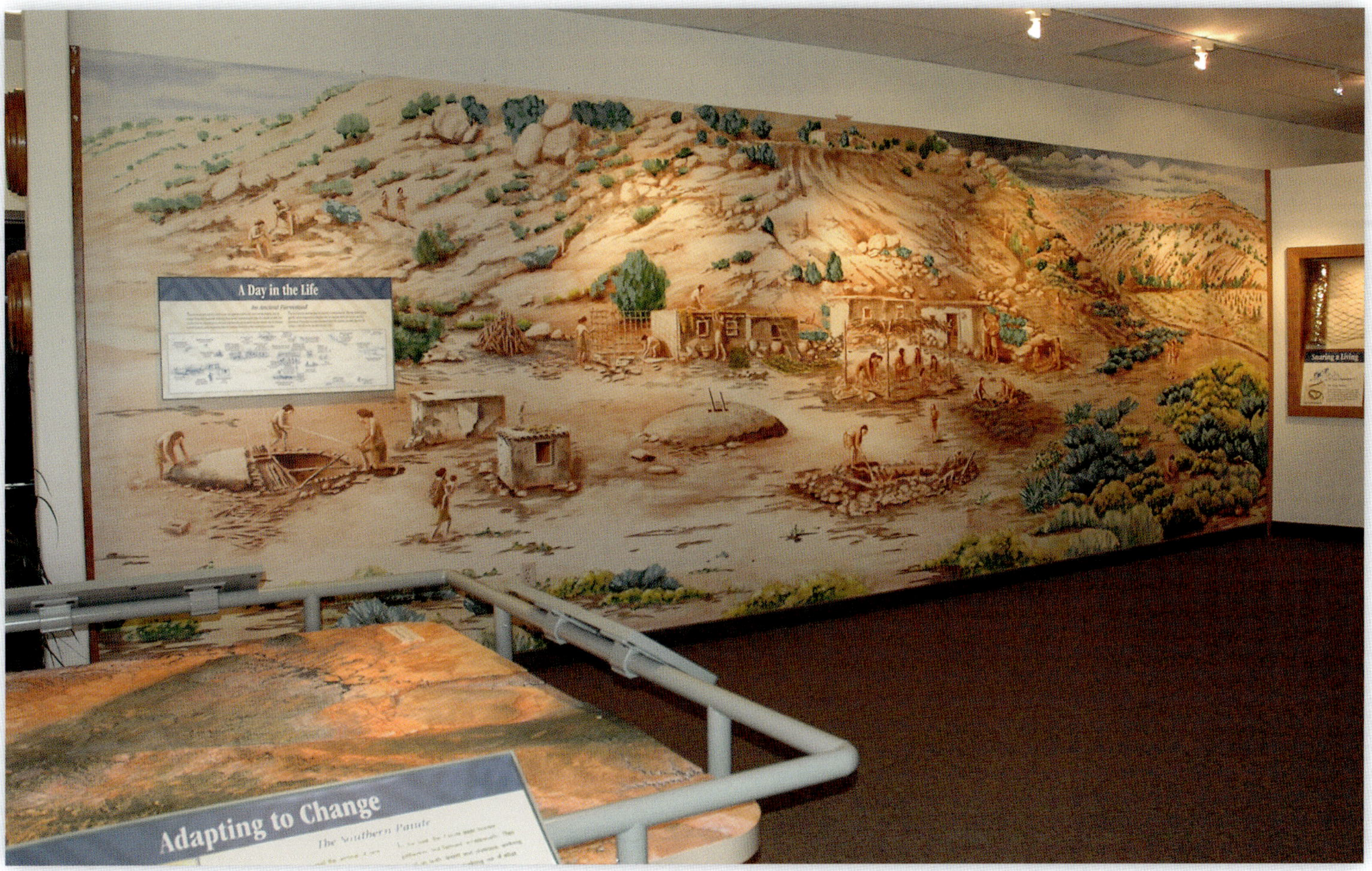

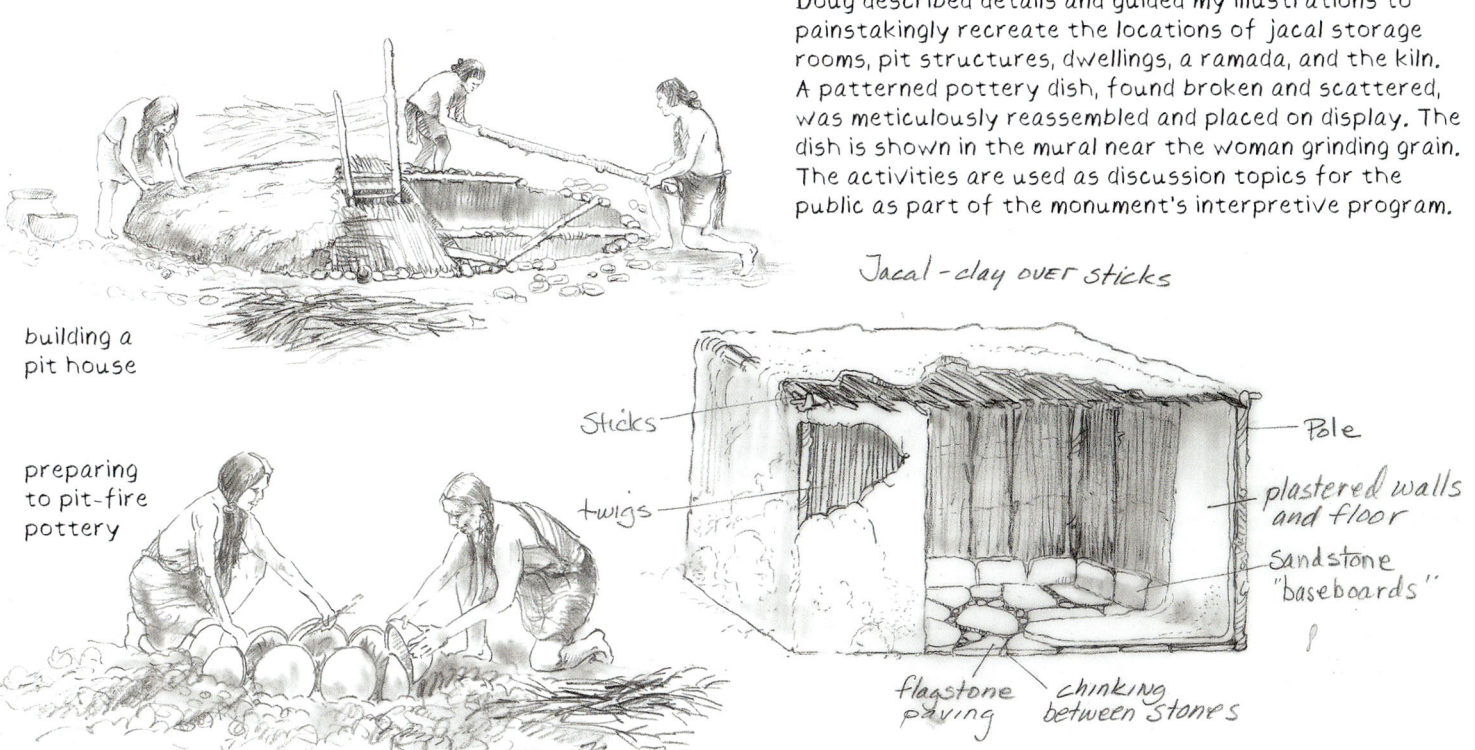

Doug described details and guided my illustrations to painstakingly recreate the locations of jacal storage rooms, pit structures, dwellings, a ramada, and the kiln. A patterned pottery dish, found broken and scattered, was meticulously reassembled and placed on display. The dish is shown in the mural near the woman grinding grain. The activities are used as discussion topics for the public as part of the monument's interpretive program.

building a pit house

preparing to pit-fire pottery

Jacal - clay over sticks

Sticks

twigs

Pole

plastered walls and floor

Sandstone "baseboards"

flagstone paving

chinking between stones

Cascade Streamwatch Trail

Cascade Streamwatch Trail, Wildwood Recreation Area, Bureau of Land Management, Oregon.

The Salmon River is a living laboratory for science education programs. Visitors here find water, forest, and fish. Wooded side channels provide quiet water where insects eat floating leaves and fish eat the insects. An underwater viewing window reveals the hidden world of young salmon and trout thriving in riffles and pools.

Each project begins with sketchbook doodles. A rhythmic graphic design reinforces the constantly moving water. Stream ecology research covers a host of ecosystems, including riparian zones, aquatic organisms, water movement, and nutrient load. The physical aspects of this section of the river provide diverse habitats, contributing to a thriving stream.

I worked alongside Lora Gale, an interpretive nature writer who created captivating stories for both students and general visitors. Each panel had an engaging theme that related to a specific trail location. My research focused on intricate details. Sketches on rolls of tracing paper helped me visualize the busy activity of spawning fish. I experimented with the best angles to show the action, whether a downward-looking angle, foreshortened, or a side view that would aid identification. As it turned out, I found occasions to use both. From golf-ball to grapefruit-sized rocks, fish are particular in their requirements for harboring their eggs. After hatching, the fry and fingerlings need quiet nurseries with nourishing riffles and pools.

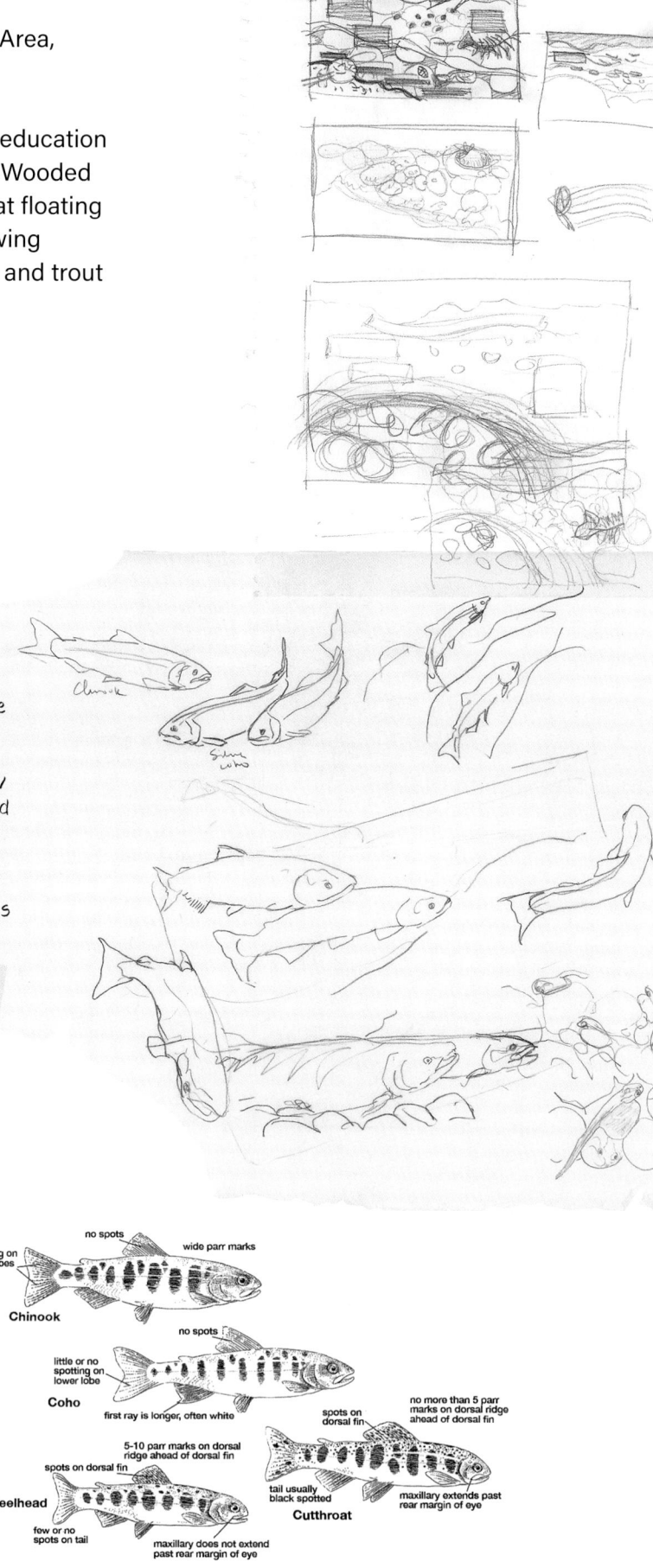

Meet the Big Fish

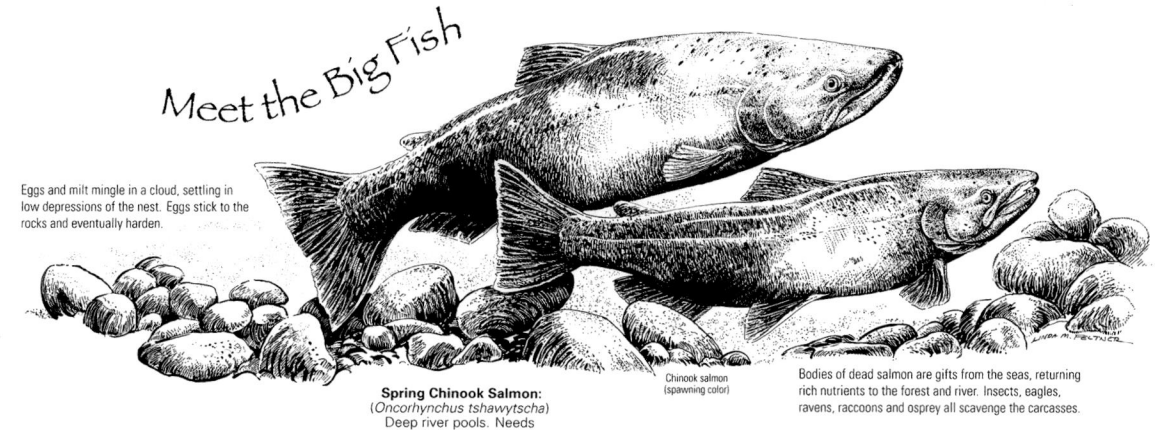

Eggs and milt mingle in a cloud, settling in low depressions of the nest. Eggs stick to the rocks and eventually harden.

Chinook salmon (spawning color)

Spring Chinook Salmon: (*Oncorhynchus tshawytscha*) Deep river pools. Needs orange- to grapefruit-sized cobble for spawning.

Bodies of dead salmon are gifts from the seas, returning rich nutrients to the forest and river. Insects, eagles, ravens, raccoons and osprey all scavenge the carcasses.

Home Sweet Home to a fish — is a Pool, a Riffle and a Log

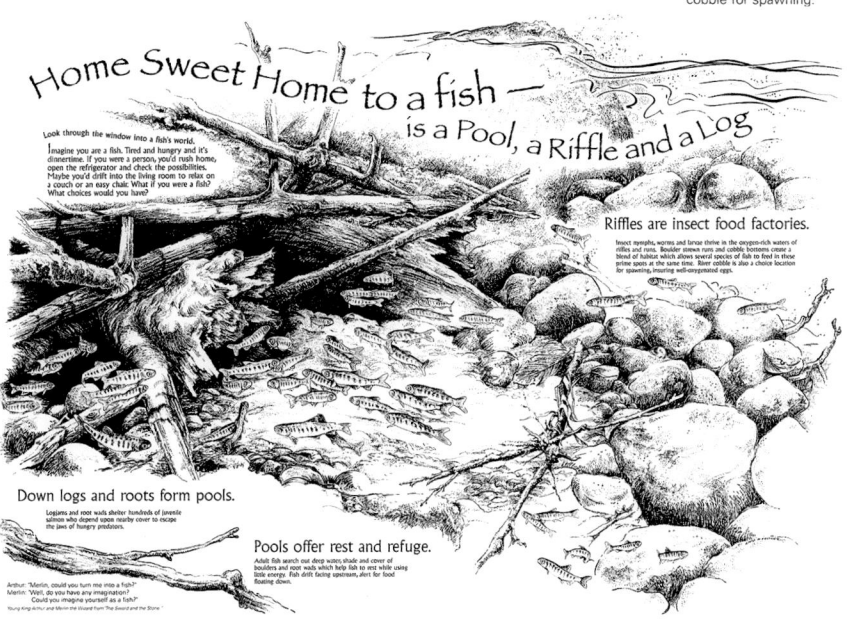

Look through the window into a fish's world.

Imagine you are a fish. Tired and hungry and it's dinnertime. If you were a person, you'd rush home, open the refrigerator and check the possibilities. Maybe you'd drift into the living room to relax on a couch or an easy chair. What if you were a fish? What choices would you have?

Riffles are insect food factories.

Insect nymphs, worms and larvae thrive in the oxygen-rich waters of riffles and runs. Boulder-strewn runs and cobble bottoms create a blend of habitat which allows several species of fish to feed in these prime spots at the same time. River cobble is also a choice location for spawning, insuring well-oxygenated eggs.

Down logs and roots form pools.

Logjams and root wads shelter hundreds of juvenile salmon who depend upon nearby cover to escape the jaws of hungry predators.

Pools offer rest and refuge.

Adult fish search out deep water, shade and cover of boulders and root wads which help fish to rest while using little energy. Fish drift facing upstream, alert for food floating down.

Arthur: "Merlin, could you turn me into a fish?"
Merlin: "Well, do you have any imagination?
Could you imagine yourself as a fish?"
Young King Arthur and Merlin the Wizard from "The Sword and the Stone."

From sketches and developmental drawings to the final surface, I relied on my favorite technique. Pen-and-ink drawings using Rapidograph pens on *Essdee Scraperboard* created a rich depth of detail. The images displayed on these pages are the black-and-white illustrations. Final fabrication was colorized porcelain enamel panels, sizes: 24 x 36 inches (60.96 x 91.44 cm) to 48 x 60 inches (121.92 x 152.4 cm).

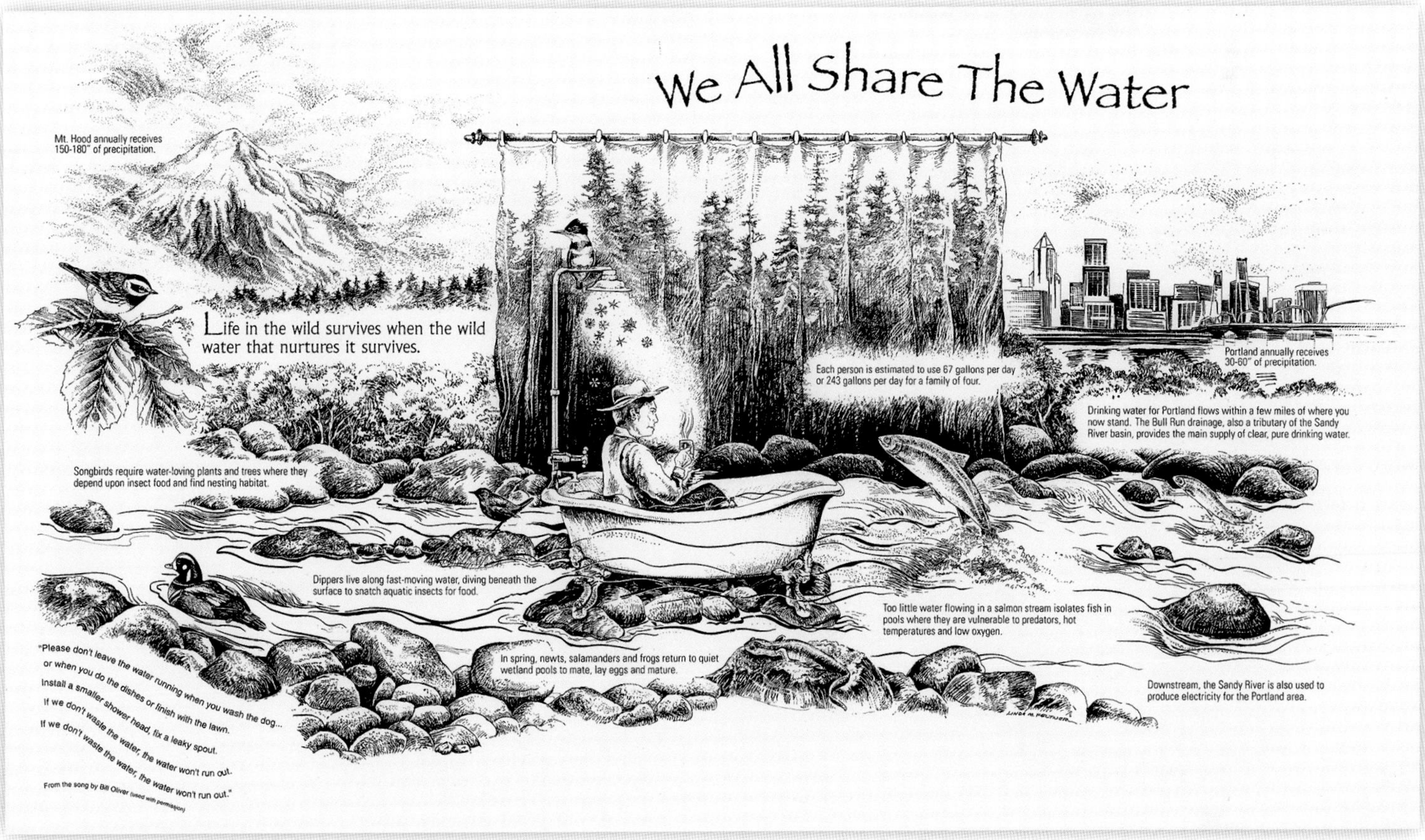

We All Share The Water

Mt. Hood annually receives 150-180" of precipitation.

Life in the wild survives when the wild water that nurtures it survives.

Songbirds require water-loving plants and trees where they depend upon insect food and find nesting habitat.

Dippers live along fast-moving water, diving beneath the surface to snatch aquatic insects for food.

Each person is estimated to use 67 gallons per day or 243 gallons per day for a family of four.

Portland annually receives 30-60" of precipitation.

Drinking water for Portland flows within a few miles of where you now stand. The Bull Run drainage, also a tributary of the Sandy River basin, provides the main supply of clear, pure drinking water.

Too little water flowing in a salmon stream isolates fish in pools where they are vulnerable to predators, hot temperatures and low oxygen.

"Please don't leave the water running when you wash the dog... or when you do the dishes or finish with the lawn.
Install a smaller shower head, fix a leaky spout.
If we don't waste the water, the water won't run out.
If we don't waste the water, the water won't run out."

From the song by Bill Oliver (used with permission)

In spring, newts, salamanders and frogs return to quiet wetland pools to mate, lay eggs and mature.

Downstream, the Sandy River is also used to produce electricity for the Portland area.

Stories from an Old Forest

Standing in a magnificent forest, I find its beauty awe-inspiring and calming. Forests have fascinating ecosystems with countless stories from mycorrhizal networks in the soil to high canopy dwellers that never reach the ground. A stroll in the forest can reveal adaptations to fire, wet and dry conditions, and a diversity of plants and animals that leave their clues. Engage the senses while in the forest to detect the intricate connections.

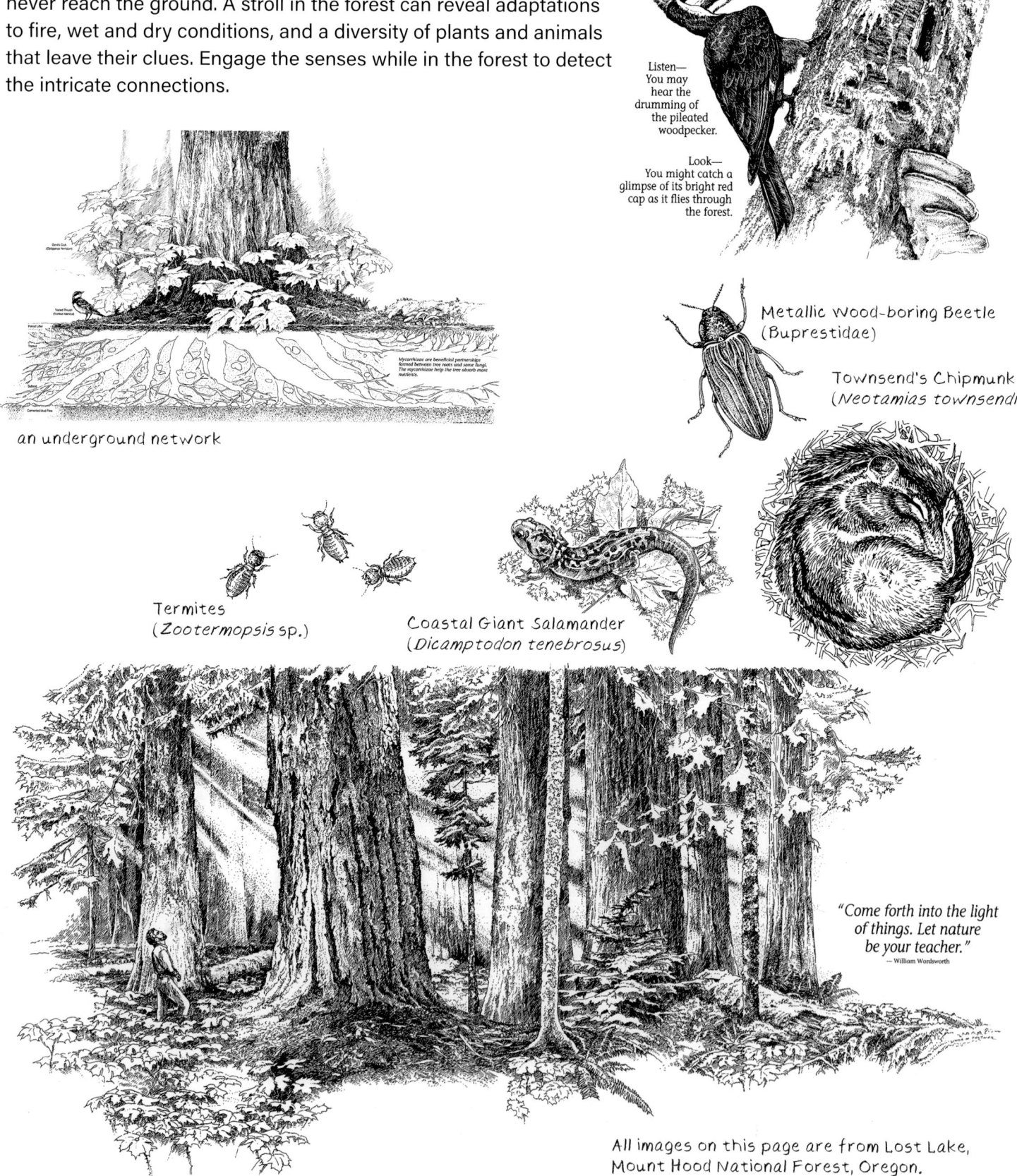

Listen—
You may hear the drumming of the pileated woodpecker.

Look—
You might catch a glimpse of its bright red cap as it flies through the forest.

an underground network

Metallic Wood-boring Beetle
(Buprestidae)

Townsend's Chipmunk
(*Neotamias townsendii*)

Termites
(*Zootermopsis* sp.)

Coastal Giant Salamander
(*Dicamptodon tenebrosus*)

*"Come forth into the light
of things. Let nature
be your teacher."*
— William Wordsworth

All images on this page are from Lost Lake,
Mount Hood National Forest, Oregon.

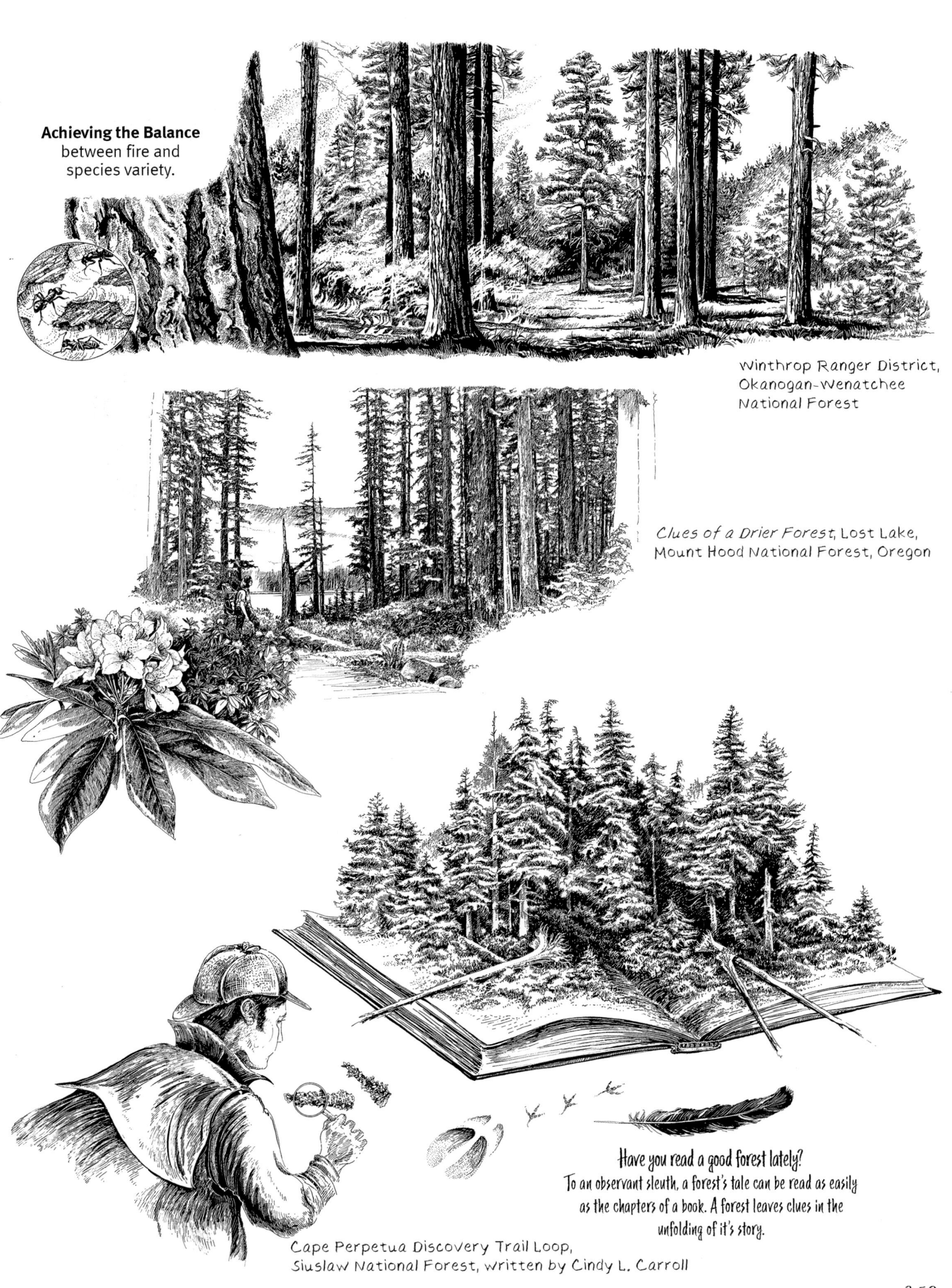

Achieving the Balance between fire and species variety.

Winthrop Ranger District, Okanogan-Wenatchee National Forest

Clues of a Drier Forest, Lost Lake, Mount Hood National Forest, Oregon

Have you read a good forest lately?
To an observant sleuth, a forest's tale can be read as easily as the chapters of a book. A forest leaves clues in the unfolding of it's story.

Cape Perpetua Discovery Trail Loop, Siuslaw National Forest, written by Cindy L. Carroll

259

Life in the High Country

Another area of fascination is the frigid high country of Washington's Cascade Mountains. I am intrigued by the small details that uncover the mysteries of survival. Delicate plants cling in the crevices of rocky outcroppings, while young conifer saplings are protected from harsh snowy winters snug between encircling parent trees. A view across rock faces exposes areas of volcanic and glacial history.

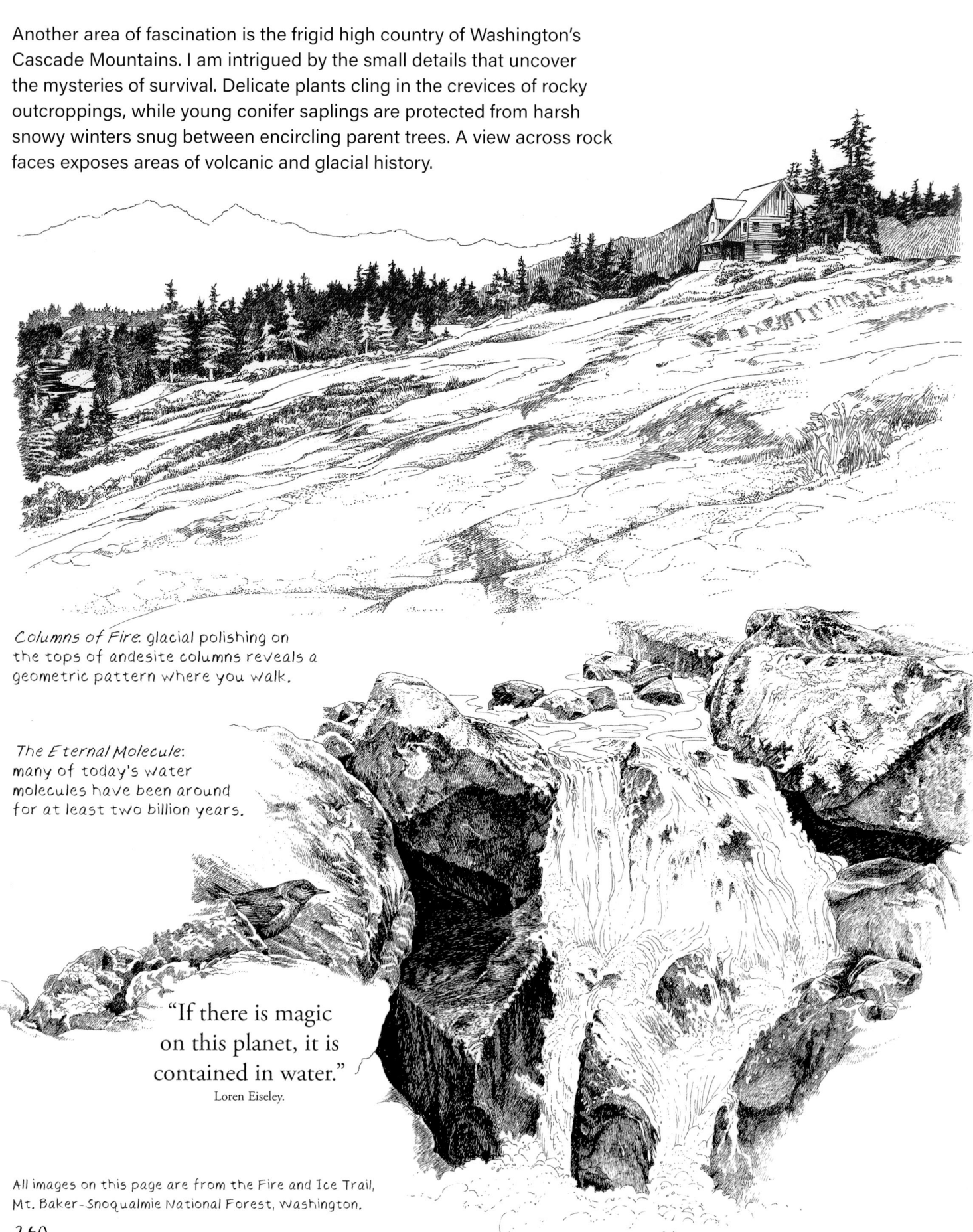

Columns of Fire: glacial polishing on the tops of andesite columns reveals a geometric pattern where you walk.

The Eternal Molecule: many of today's water molecules have been around for at least two billion years.

"If there is magic on this planet, it is contained in water."
Loren Eiseley.

All images on this page are from the Fire and Ice Trail, Mt. Baker-Snoqualmie National Forest, Washington.

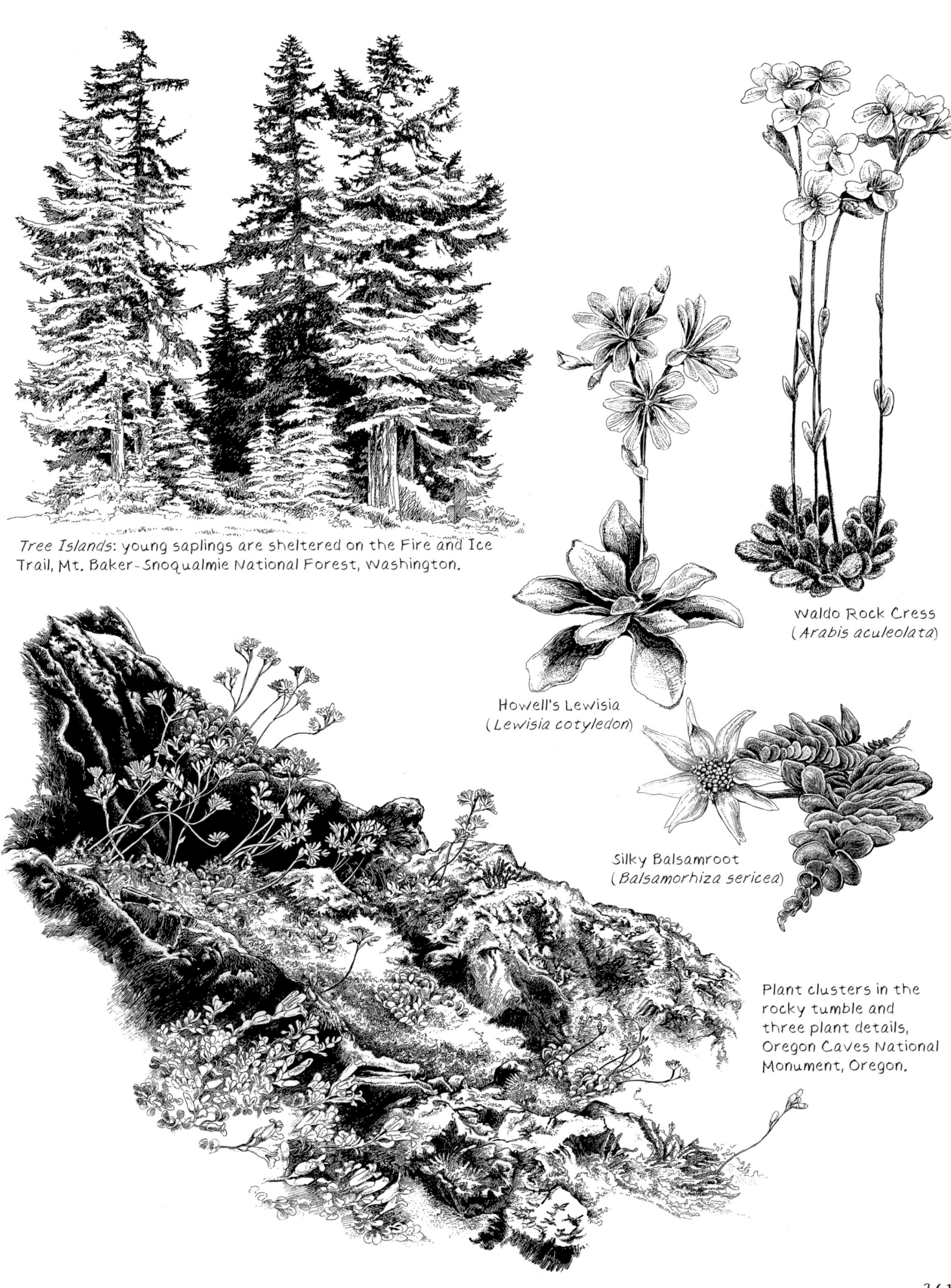

Tree Islands: young saplings are sheltered on the Fire and Ice Trail, Mt. Baker-Snoqualmie National Forest, Washington.

Waldo Rock Cress
(*Arabis aculeolata*)

Howell's Lewisia
(*Lewisia cotyledon*)

Silky Balsamroot
(*Balsamorhiza sericea*)

Plant clusters in the rocky tumble and three plant details, Oregon Caves National Monument, Oregon.

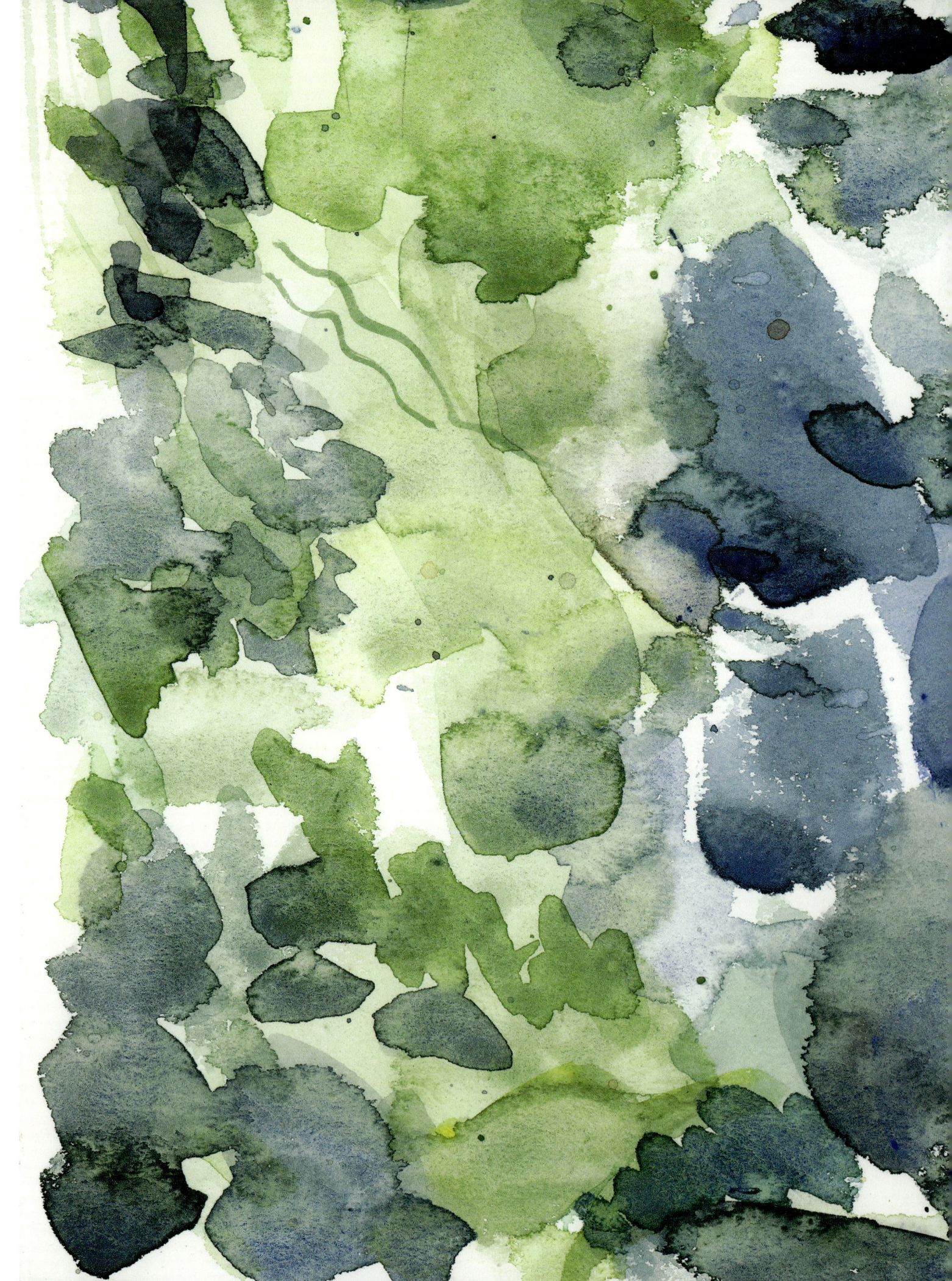

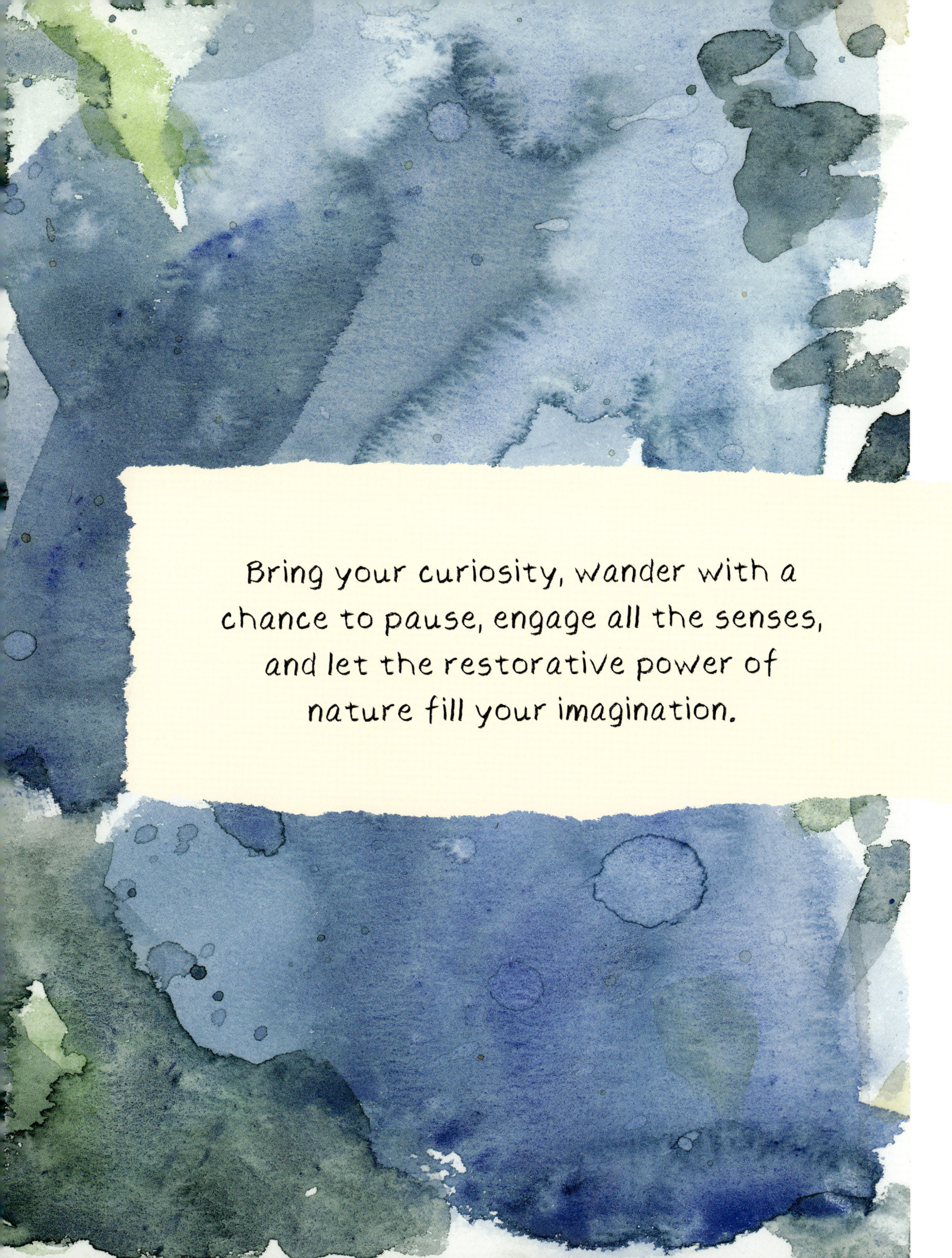

Bring your curiosity, wander with a chance to pause, engage all the senses, and let the restorative power of nature fill your imagination.

Recommended Reading for Creative Inspiration

Bateman, Robert. *The Art of Robert Bateman*. Madison Press, 1981.

Busby, John. *Drawing Birds*. The Royal Society for the Protection of Birds, 1986.

Busby, John. *The Living Birds of Eric Ennion*. Victor Gollancz, Ltd., 1982.

Brockie, Keith. *One Man's Island, A Naturalist's Year*. Harper & Row, 1984.

Brockie, Keith. *Wildlife Sketchbook*. Macmillan Publishing Co., 1981.

Coheleach, Guy, and Nancy Neff. *The Big Cats: The Paintings of Guy Coheleach*. Abrams, Inc., 1982.

Cooper, William T. *Capturing the Essence: Techniques for Bird Artists*. CSIRO Publishing, 2011.

Cooper, Willliam T., and Penny Olsen. *An Eye for Nature*. National Library of Australia, 2014.

Cusa, Noel. *Tunnicliffe's Birdlife*. Clive Holloway Books, 1985.

Ennion, Eric. *Bird Man's River*. Benton Street Books. 2011.

Ennion, Eric. *A Life of Birds*. The Wildlife Art Gallery, 2003.

Gillmor, Robert. *Cutting Away: The Linocuts of Robert Gillmor*. Langford Press, 2006.

Greenhalf, Robert. *Towards the Sea*. Pica Press, 1999.

The Guild of Scientific Illustrators. *The Guild Handbook of Scientific Illustration*. 2nd edition. Edited by Elaine R. S. Hodges. Wiley, 2003.

Hammond, Nicholas. *Artists for Nature in Extremadura*. The Wildlife Art Gallery, 1995.

Hanson, Thor. *Feathers: The Evolution of a Natural Miracle*. Basic Books, 2012.

Jaques, Florence Page. *Francis Lee Jaques: Artist of the Wilderness World*. Doubleday, 1973.

Jaques, Florence Page. *The Geese Fly High*. University of Minnesota Press, 1939.

Johnson, Cathy, *The Sierra Club Guide to Sketching in Nature*. Sierra Club Books, 1990.

Jonsson, Lars. *Bird Island: Pictures from a Shoal of Sand*. Croom Helm Ltd., 1983.

Jonsson, Lars. *Birds and Light*. Princeton University Press, 2002.

Jonsson, Lars. *Winter Birds*. Bloomsbury National History, 2018.

Kuhn, Bob. *The Animal Art of Bob Kuhn ... A Lifetime of Drawing and Painting*. North Light Publishers, 1973.

Jarvis, Frank. *A Bird Guide to the Fields of Experience: The Private Diaries of a Passionate Birdwatcher*. Vol 1. Chatterpie, 2017.

Landsdowne, James F., and John Livingston. *Birds of the Eastern Forest*. Vols. 1 and 2. McClellen & Steward, 1968–1970.

Laws, John. *The Laws Guide to Drawing Birds*. Heyday, 2015.

Leslie, Claire W., *Nature Drawing: A Tool for Learning*. Prentice Hall, 1980.

Low, Tim. *Where Song Began: Australia's Birds and How They Changed the World*. Penguin Australia, 2014.

Marcham, Fredrick G., editor. *Louis Agassiz Fuertes & the Singular Beauty of Birds*. Harper & Row, 1971.

Pearson, Bruce. *In a New Light*. The Wildlife Art Gallery, 2003.

Pearson, Bruce, and Robert Burton. *Birdscape*. HarperCollins Publishers, 1991.

Proctor & Lynch. *Manual of Ornithology: Avian Structure & Function*. Yale University Press, 1998.

Rose, Chris. *In A Natural Light: The Wildlife Art of Chris Rose*. Langford Press, 2005.

Schodde, Richard, and Richard Weatherly. *The Fairy Wrens: A Monograph of the Maluridae*. Landsdowne Editions, 1982.

Shackleton, Keith. *Wildlife and Wilderness: An Artist's World*. Salem House, 1986.

Sutton, George Miksch. *At a Bend in a Mexican River*. Paul S. Eriksson, Inc., 1972.

Tunnicliffe, C. F. *Sketches of Bird Life*. Edited with an introduction by Robert Gillmor. Watson-Guptill Publications, 1982.

Tunnicliffe, Charles F. *Bird Portraiture*. The Studio, Ltd., 1945.

Tunnicliffe, Charles F. *A Sketchbook of Birds*. Holt, Rinehart & Winston, 1979.

Tunnicliffe, Charles F. *Tunnicliffe's Birds: Measured Drawings by C. F. Tunnicliffe*. Little, Brown & Co., 1984.

Van Dusen, Barry, and Massachusetts Audubon Society. *Finding Sanctuary: An Artist Explores the Nature of Mass Audubon*. Puritan Press, 2020.

van Grouw, Katrina. *The Unfeathered Bird*. Princeton University Press, 2013

van Grouw, Katrina. *Unnatural Selection*. Princeton University Press, 2018.

Warren, Michael. *Shorelines: Birds at the Water's Edge*. Times Books, 1984.

Warren, Michael. *Taking Flight: The Birds of Langford Lowfields*. Mascot Media, 2014.

Williams, Robert. *Treasures of the Forgotten Forest*. Wildlife Art Gallery, 2004.

Wood, Phyllis. *Scientific Illustration*. 2nd edition. Van Nostrand Reinhold, 1994.

Woodcock, Martin. *Safari Sketchbook: A Bird Painter's African Odyssey*. Esker Press, 2010.

Wooton, Tim. *Drawing and Painting Birds*. The Crowood Press, 2021.